A Forgotten Paradise

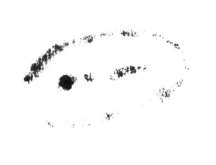

A FORGOTTEN PARADISE

The International Library of Poetry

Estelle W. Petri, Editor

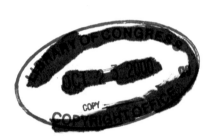

A Forgotten Paradise

Library of Congress
Cataloging in Publication Data

ISBN 1-58235-146-5

Proudly manufactured in the United States of America by
Watermark Press
One Poetry Plaza
Owings Mills, MD 21117

poetry.COM
The International Library of Poetry

FOREWORD

Throughout life, we store information collected from experiences and try in some way to make sense of it. When we are not able to fully understand the things that occur in our lives, we often externalize the information. By doing this, we are afforded a different perspective, thus allowing us to think more clearly about difficult or perplexing events and emotions. Art is one of the ways in which people choose to externalize their thoughts.

Within the arts, modes of expression differ, but poetry is a very powerful tool by which people can share sometimes confusing, sometimes perfectly clear concepts and feelings with others. Intentions can run the gamut as well: The artists may simply want to share something that has touched their lives in some way, or they may want to get help to allay anxiety or uncertainty. The poetry within *A Forgotten Paradise* is from every point on the spectrum: every topic, every intention, every event or emotion imaginable. Some poems will speak to certain readers more than others, but it is always important to keep in mind that each verse is the voice of a poet, of a mind that needs to make sense of this world, of a heart that feels the effects of every moment in this life, and perhaps of a memory that is striving to surface. Nonetheless, recalling our yesterdays gives birth to our many forms of expression.

Melisa S. Mitchell
Editor

EDITOR'S NOTE

Human beings are social creatures. As basic as the need for food and water is the human instinct to find a mate. Since the beginning of time, humankind has been driven by the need to find a partner with whom to share the pain and splendor of life. Ironically, though, the greatest pain on this Earthly journey is, oftentimes, that which comes from having a partner, and it is this kind of suffering that fosters the depth of emotion needed to create the kind of poetry that is universally recognizable.

When a relationship does go sour, anything and everything can act as a painful reminder of things gone wrong. In her poem, "Clams" (1), Julianne Nason uses the process of preparing and cooking clams as a metaphor both for her current relationship and for men in general. The poem has a very "immediate" feel to it, in the sense that the persona is defining her emotional experience through her dealings with the clams: Her handling of the clams is helping to define her feelings. Since the reader is with the persona as she prepares and cooks the clams, he becomes a part of the emotional experience.

Throughout the poem, the action parallels the persona's level of emotion. The opening stanza begins with the persona's soaking the clams, and here, Nason forms the first tie between the clams and her relationship. "They lie in my tub like the lazy man / I just dusted off, who dug them." The clams simply lie, and the persona, by way of mild revelation, notices the similarities between the clams and her partner. The poet's clever play on words in the first line also serves as early indication of her feelings toward men: Men lie. The action progresses to a state of subdued aggression, with the persona washing the clams over and over. This progression to an almost manic repetition of washing matches the rise in the extremity of emotion felt by the persona. Where the clams used to simply lie, the persona now perceives them as "Still, lazy men in a gritty tub spitting / griping, extruding slime."

Nason points out in the first stanza that her persona's main source of pain comes from her failed effort to mold men into what she expects them to be. The washing of the clams, who represent the men in her life, is the persona's metaphorical attempt to change the men from her past. The fact that this has been done over and over not only proves the futility—because the men stay the same—but also subtly alludes to the idea that the persona's repeatedly failed attempts at control are pushing her closer to the figurative edge.

The second stanza mirrors the first in the way the action and the emotions run parallel. The stanza begins with the persona's cooking clams:

Flames light the pot.
I fight to type at my desk.
The water warms.

The mild action in the stanza's first few lines is again matched by the lack of emotional intensity in Nason's persona, which is understood through her actions: "I wait. I listen." The stanza moves on, much like the first, with the action of the clams mirroring the rising hostility of the persona, and this rise shows itself through her increasingly frantic behavior:

> They start
> dancing with heat. I hear
> their shells tap and crack. I crack, tapping the maddest letter. . . .

The parallels between emotion and action are not the only tool Nason uses to evidence the growing anger of her persona. The deliberate word choice in reference to typing the letter clearly shows the rise in emotion, as well. In line 13, she fights "to type"; in line 18, she is "tapping the maddest letter." This careful word choice along with her showing a rise in emotion furthers the notion from the first stanza that the persona is being pushed to the limits of rational thought because of her struggles with relationships.

In the first stanza, the persona's useless attempts at control led to almost manic behavior. The poem ends with "the maddest letter" going to "a man who's never mad." The fact that her partner is never mad implies a lack of emotion, and this aspect of him that she cannot change— much like the changes she hasn't been able to bring about in her past partners—keeps Nason's persona caught in a seemingly endless cycle: Her futile efforts at control result only in increased frustration.

Pain from relationships occurs for many reasons. Nason deals with the pain brought from not being able to mold a partner to one's expectations. In Ellaraine Lockie's "Commonplace" (1), the woman's frustration doesn't come from her partner's not being what she wants, but from her relationship's not holding the passion that it used to.

The poem begins, "She's nude in the kitchen." The choice of the word "nude" is an artistic and non-sexual reference to her nakedness. This implies that the woman in the relationship has regressed to being merely an object, whereas in the past, she was the focus of passion. The following lines continue to describe how the relationship, now, is a spark-less version of earlier days:

> When he walks through her to grab a beer
> Ghost of an earlier time
> When he'd do a double-take
> Drink the beer later, lukewarm then
> Like their worn-out bodies. . . .

The visual imagery and pace in these lines build a solid idea of how the relationship used to be. In the lines where the "double-take" results in "worn-out bodies," the action and the sexual reference are deliberate and strong. The careful word choice creates a mood of intense passion, which is carried on in the next few lines with the woman's

> *Ability to flick his switch*
> *And generate instant thermal energy*
> *Spontaneous combustion.*

Lockie makes it clear that the lack of passion is a drastic change from the past. Her ability to create, through words, a fire that feels so genuine allows the poem's progression to the lackluster present to be a true loss, both for the characters in the poem and for the reader drawn into it.

> The relationship degenerated

> *Until she became everyday invisible*
> *Familiarity fostered immunity*
> *Injected over years of routine*
> *Dangerous as the disease*
> *It was meant to prevent*
> *Extramarital epidemic extraordinary.*

Once again, clever word choice tells the story of the relationship in a multi-layered fashion: Earlier, the fires of passion were made real with the repeated use of "heat" references— "lukewarm," "thermal energy," and "spontaneous combustion." In describing the demise of the relationship, Lockie employs a repetition of medical terms—"immunity," "injected," "disease," and "epidemic." These medical allusions create a mood of sterility and emotional detachment. In a hospital room, any human touch is out of necessity, rather than desire, and it is to this sad state that the relationship in "Commonplace" has regressed.

One similarity between the women in "Clams" and in "Commonplace" is that both personas crave a level of control. The persona in "Clams" is pushed to her wits' end by her not having the ability to create the man she wants. The woman in "Commonplace" also "craves that kind of power / [and the] ability to flick his switch." By the end of the poem the reader understands that the woman uses her sexual power more in an effort to prevent "extramarital epidemic" than as an expression of love. This ill-fated attempt at control through physical intimacy results in her ironically becoming "everyday invisible," and this loss of true passion is worse than losing the man she loves altogether.

Perhaps the greatest pain from relationships—greater than not being able to mold a partner, greater than the loss of passion—is the pain that comes from having to carry on after the death of a spouse. Christopher Hicks' "Sunday Afternoon at the Old Country Buffet" (1) is the melancholic telling of just such a fate.

The first line of the poem indicates that there is something wrong: "He sits at a table for two." From this somber beginning, Hicks goes on to tell the story of a man who has no other option but to carry on.

The restaurant serves as an integral part of the poem, with minute aspects explained in great detail. It is a metaphorical representation of what role the man's wife played in his life. The restaurant, in one way or another, is represented throughout the whole poem, which is evidence of the somber truth that the absent wife may have been the man's whole life, making his loss of her even more devastating. Parts of the restaurant actually become his dearly missed wife:

> *His dinner companion is an empty chair,*
> *which stares at him with vacant leather-button eyes.*
> *It had not always been this way.*
> *Once the chair had a name,*
> *had a voice . . . .*

Hicks uses the restaurant-atmosphere and the metaphor to reference the happy times the couple had there together: "Once the chair would have asked for a taste / then would steal a bite before he could reply." These happy memories contribute to the overall mood Hicks creates of "not letting go." Every facet of the dining experience is a painful reminder of the once-happy relationship. From the empty chair to the bite-not-stolen, the man seems unwilling to move on with his life, and this reluctance to move on only keeps him in the pain of the loss.

Much of the most effective poetry is considered such because the words chosen offer an uninhibited view into the poet's soul. It is this kind of honesty that creates poetry whose story, though unique to the poet, communicates an emotional experience to which anyone who has ever felt true pain or bliss can relate. Please take some time to enjoy some of my favorites from the pages within where the poet offers a genuine glimpse into his or her soul: Jacqueline De Freitas' "Message on a Paper Napkin" (3), "All Yours" (4) by Hannah Slovek, Theresa McGoff's "Beacon" (4), Dried Funeral Flowers" (6) by Traci Mullins, Rebecca Harth's "Thinking Late" (9), "For the Player" (10) by Juliette Hwang, and Elizabeth Ament's "Glass Bottle" (15).

I would like to thank every poet who contributed to the wide range of material collected in this anthology. Your willingness and ability to share a part of your self has helped to create a piece of art that will have a lasting impact on its readers throughout time. Best wishes for continued success in all of your future creative endeavors.

The publication of this anthology has been the culmination of the efforts of many individuals. Judges, editors, assistant editors, customer service representatives, graphic artists, layout artists, office administrators, data entry staff, and mail room personnel have all contributed to this anthology's production. I am thankful for their assistance and support.

John C. Sullivan, Editor

Cover Art: "Serenity," Arlene DeBlasi

iv

Clams

They lie in my tub like the lazy man
I just dusted off, who dug them,
nothing to do but spit:
mucus, sand, salt, cornmeal grit.
Over and over I wash them--
still, lazy men in a gritty tub, spitting,
griping, extruding slime.
I worry about the hot weather,
the price of meat,
and whether I can eat anything so live,
so like a man.
They come in all sizes,
parts lolling now from unzipped shells.

I cook a few; the dripping,
smallest ones I can handle.
Flames light the pot.
I fight to type at my desk.
The water warms. I wait, I listen.
No one's murdering pots of men.
They start dancing with heat.
I hear their shells tap and crack.
I crack, tapping the maddest letter
to a man who's never mad.

Julianne Nason

Sunday Afternoon
at the Old Country Buffet

He sits at a table for two.
His hair is the color of
the mashed potatoes piled on his plate,
with splotches of mushroom gravy over his ears.
His dinner companion is an empty chair,
which stares at him with vacant leather-button eyes.
It had not always been this way.
Once the chair had a name,
had a voice,
had an appetite for the cherry cobbler
which sits beside his plate.
Once the chair would have asked for a taste,
then would steal a bite before he could reply.
Now his companion only stares at him.
The chair doesn't know what it's missing.
The roast beef is really good today.

Christopher Hicks

Commonplace

She's nude in the kitchen
Her solution to icing-spared silk
When he walks through her to grab a beer
Ghost of an earlier time
When he'd do a double take
Drink the beer later, lukewarm then
Like their worn-out bodies
She craves that kind of power
Ability to flick his switch
And generate instant thermal energy
Spontaneous combustion
Until she became everyday invisible
Familiarity fostered immunity
Injected over years of routine
Dangerous as the disease
It was meant to prevent
Extramarital epidemic extraordinary
As oblivious to him
As her immaculate clothes

Ellaraine Lockie

Message on a Paper Napkin

Spilled my heart on a paper napkin
While I waited for you at the coffee shop
Because you can't take my messages
Home with you
And we hardly have time to say everything
When we meet on our way to work
In the morning
We sat in my car in the parking lot
And I watched as you sipped your coffee
Through a straw
Silent as you read my heart
And then you asked me
Whether I wouldn't mind kissing you
With coffee on your breath
I watched you walk to your car
And pondered the symbolism
As you crumpled my ink stained napkin
And together with your empty coffee cup
Tossed my heart
        Jacqueline De Freitas

Poetry

Poetry whips
Through the air,
A wind that
Knocks me flat.
But it rushes past the
Staunch trees
With a congenial tip of its hat.

It moves debris.
It moves me.
But the walls still stand tall.

Or maybe they creak
Just a bit
And the trees sway a little
And the birds soar
And boats drift
As the wind passes by.
        Sonja Likness

Faith

The seasons come and go in their graceful rhythms of change
Each one arriving and then fading into the next in perfect agreement
Nature shares a deep awareness of the invisible workings of creation
Each element belonging to itself and to the timelessness that
supports all life
Why then do we try to hold ourselves apart from the
primordial stream that continues to carry us despite our
foolhardy efforts to resist
It takes profound faith and courage to live in this world
with all its harsh realities that change us
and yet remain in harmony with all that is
Release your attachment to impose your small-mindedness
on yourself or others
Open your heart to embrace the life you are living
Become strong, throw away the idea of your own self-importance
and live wholeheartedly
There is a time for everything,
Even that which you thought too late to happen
        Madelyn Warner

Aftermath, after Gabrielle

I knew I shouldn't have gone there with her,
But she's just too gorgeous to ignore.
I let myself fall in way over my head,
Definitely heart over brain.
She found her man on her own,
And now she's serving up that black coffee at night,
While I'm hating myself for ever having the total audacity to care.
        E. Richard Lucas

Turning Down the TV News

"He must have changed his mind
They always do. . . ."

The doctor looked around
at the broken chair
and torn up walls,
the last war zone,
the broken room.

I had heard him scratching
Like a huge cat trying
to get in the house,
Or out.
But the breath of animal
And gravity in battle
Just made this kind of shuffle. . . .

And now when stone hits stone
and cracks a scull
A car backfires and kills a soldier,

I think about by noisy neighbor
hanging.
        John Wetteland

Untitled

Helium balloons held tight at a funeral,
Earth so high and mighty prepares to return a child to her bosom,
Children play leap frog over frozen headstones,
Lives are now filled with dreamless sleeps,
My house is the home for the flags of the fallen,
Dancing on the brown dirt,
Your tears remind me of thunderstorms,
So honored,
So revered,
I wish to be held by you,
Just a bit longer,
I am captured in the trees,
Day long ventures in the mind,
Questioning my actions,
On one knee before the king,
His magicians are forecasting the speeding future,
For all their power,
They fail to notice,
Me falling for you (again?)
        Jay Ehrmann

I had a flash of dirty thought of you,
But it went away
Like the sweeping of a stranger before me.
I put back the magazine,
No longer hiding my red face from
Anyone who dared hear my thoughts scream,
Including the discontented name-tagged lady,
Who drummed her dragon nails impatiently
As I wrote a check
At the supermarket checkout.
        Christine DeSimone

Untitled

Upon sitting in a recital hall
in celebration of a dead guy's birthdays
as the metallic sounds of a harpsichord
give birth to electric fireflies that swarm the room, our ears, our
heads,
we breathe them in and they buzz inside
our stomachs, relentless insects of sound and color.

When the music stops,
they die between our hands.
        Mary Vasiltsova

Firefly Ballet

Firefields dance at sunset dawns
In tribal costumes made of moonlight.
Round and round the fire they go,
Dancing to rhythms too rapid to hear.
Holding the essence of time beneath their wings,
Allowing the glow to reach my eyes,
But never catching the attention of the clock.
Rocks in water have put out the fire,
But it matters not to them.
Now the rain may fall,
The sun may shine
For the fireflies have finished their dance
With the essence of time.

Jill Palmer Naiman

All Yours

went to the rooftop
to dance with your soul
like yesterday
when the rain bounced off our faces
and your laugh was symphonic
gazing at the evening city-scape
with the stars laid out like a map above us
and the cars rushing by below
your kiss was like marmalade
everything perfect
now tears leave my eyes
for I know it shall never be that way again

Hannah Slovek

Butterfly Whispered

poetry did not come upon me like the embrace of Apollo,
but crept in
on slow and sneaky feet—
one step, then more.
it had no appointment to keep with me,
no woman crying my destiny in the road,
no fanfare, trumpets, drum,
no foreshadowing dream of laurel and bay—
only a flicker, lick of flame in the mind
like something you had known, but forgotten,
a memory of wings and pine, healing,
the brief sight of something,
like a butterfly wing, disappearing behind a tree
so quick
you aren't even sure it was there,
and you are subsumed in scientific thoughts
of class and species
forgetting about the actual creature
until it flies into your face as you are looking the other way
and blinds you with the sun.

Erin Shoemate

Beacon

The cat paws
the clothes hamper
stretches to sniff
scented air

He looks for your
scent here
and in the shoes left
with dangling laces

Shirts unchosen by you
hang still in the closet
my fingers snag in the weave
as if I, too, were a thread

This journey
this story
has no place for us
except for the beacon of your calls

Theresa Mcgoff

Barefoot

August's honeysuckle breath
Ripples the sleeves of your shirt,
Flings your hair in front of your eyes.
You wink.

Your eyelashes,
Trimmed with gold,
Brush my cheek
Beneath my left eye.
Above us the clouds swell
And the heavens open.

I want to run for cover,
But you are my cover.
So we stay outside,
Splashing together under the showering sky.
I think I hear the footsteps of Aphrodite.

Gailor Large

Ego

her name on his lips
limply crumbles—
a microcosmic
avalanche
of confectioner's sugar,
a bad actor on take two
sans Cyrano.

his ruptured plea thrashes
into itself like a starving
wench
jerking out the
Samba
in her flea infested
shanty
with only dirt
and hot, sticky air
for a partner.

Cindy Ramos

Breathe

Facts of the matter scatter about the landscape,
God's hands shape the soil.
As people throw away weak dreams to crumble
Like tin foil.
All hopes and dreams are torn at the seams,
Questions and wishes are food for the fish.
We all swim in a lake of anger,
How long will it take for us to drown?
Killed and pulled down to the depth
Our last cries never left our mouths
in a world so vain in what pain do I believe.
I'm going insane from the pain.
It's getting hard to breathe!

Anthony Martinez

The Cherry Tree

I stood beneath the Cherry Tree, danced along its branches
Tall, and above the world.
I wore these strapped red shoes, the way they made me feel.
Soft velvet against skin, like my lips to yours,
They dangled like a kiss.
We danced among the stars, bleeding cherries
staining the velvet with a darker, sweeter new hue.
That night beneath the cherry tree,
that silent perfect night we danced with the wind.
How I flowed in the shoes that made me part of the world,
But unique, and beautiful, clinging to my body like a sleeker,
prettier new skin.
Two drifting petals playing in the wind.

Cassidy Healzer

Rooms

She walks through the dark and cluttered rooms of my mind
Picking at the bits and pieces of the broken pottery of my life.
From time to time, she pauses, to study a shard.
She kneels, sifting through the rubble for a matching piece.
Room to room she wanders, looking for one still whole.
She sees a light through a door, and knows she has found life.
Entering, she gazes around to see what it may contain.
But to her dismay, she sees herself in endless profusion.
Images of herself look back at her from every nook.
No two are the same, each differing from the one beside it.
Slowly, passing from one to the next, she understands.
She has found a shrine, one dedicated to herself.
And of far more importance, she has found a home.
Contentment filling her breast at last, she finds a nook and sits.
Awaiting the next time she crosses my mind,
another image coming home.

David Bates

Sunfish

My brother and I with bamboo poles, my father
lighting his cigarettes off the sun, casting so far
we thought he might drag the horizon in.
All my brother and I pulled in that day
were sunfish, Dad reaching into each tiny mouth to
dislodge our hooks until there were dozens
of scraps from the sun swimming in our cooler.

I can still see the cigarette balanced between his lips,
the smoke like fog rising from his voice,
as he worked a half-eaten glow worm back onto
my hook, his hands trembling with excitement
for us, as if all his internalized love
would shake itself free.

Here I am, thirty years old, and snagged
on a morning when I was six, so far
I had to reach for a decent memory of him. And a small
one at that, a sunfish really, in this lake
where I cast, again and again.

Stevw Gehrke

A Date for Breakfast

"We have a date for breakfast"
her words, his mind
two people unified but
completely separate on
the issue of
sugar

A date for breakfast
down through the years
past the memories of croissants
and exotic breakfast dishes she
could not pronounce
and long, leisurely touch
skeletons in the closet dance

Imagine . . . one night of passion
fire, fluid, hot and sticky
sweet rolls
ending only in breakfast

What would you make me for breakfast?

Natalie Collins

Kansas

A sorry state
the cornrowed-colored eyes of old men
spitting poppycock into sorry slop pans
of once there was
but never is
who drowsy hear
the mourning dove over cereal
and evergreen.

Susan Mardirosian

Bus Station Thoughts

marking time by passing trains
another hour to kill . . . again . . .
half of getting anywhere is waiting.

toothpaste in my bookbag
a tea bag between my fingers,
the water running hot, I, cold
as the ticker spits out warnings.
even the doors have stickers
to warn they're automatic.
"Don't try to touch me"
I guess is the message.

marking time by passing trains
another hour to kill . . . again . . .
half of getting anywhere is waiting.

Kathryn Kieran

Stratford-upon-Avon Calling

Shakespeare knew how to ride time warps.

He would stand barefoot in certain
spots and quote himself,
which would flip him in and out of
centuries
like a casting director
looking for new faces.

You didn't know it, but he
passed through here on his way
to Egypt yesterday.

I saw the notes he took on the
shape of your smile.

The rest, of course, is history.

Daniel Abel

Flight 127

Sinatra blares from the cocktail lounge
every thirty minutes or so.
I'm daydreaming about the open spaces
of twirling and dipping and fanciful stepping,

How beautiful it is in the movies.
Who's looking? No one knows me anyway.
Never again will I know the nakedness of the Newark Airport.

"Best Airline 1996,"
The banners read. The signs flash.
The patrons sleeping on benches agree.

A graveyard shift worker pushes his cart,
rubber wheels out of alignment,
down the polished and trod terrazzo
of the lonely concourse.

The cocktail lounge has its gates pulled down;
the servers have all gone home,
but the music's still loud ,
and where once was a crowd
is now just me dancing alone.

Echo Bartlett

Green Shirt

Shower off.
Dripping wet,
I slide a towel around my waist
then realize within a breath
I'd rather slip inside his shirt—
my favorite shirt,
the one striped green
that plants the envy in my sigh
and taunts my lips
without a blush
with brazen strokes upon his chest
as he walks by.

Sharon Sloane

Divine Jealousy

I fear to take a breath too deep
Lest I disturb you and you flee.
You crept upon me like a cat
And rested, nested in my lap.

Radiant heat from your tiny form
Pervading my large one with its warmth,
You seem to sleep, yet keep close watch
Cautious, fitful, on your guard

Lest I lose patience—wish perhaps
To stand. And standing, your soft nest
Be lost and with it, your sustaining fire.
I know too well what you will do.

On soundless feet, with sudden spring,
You'll hide yourself so tight that I
Must hunt and call, cajole and plead,
While you ignore my need until again

You see me still, in quiet,
Waiting on your will.

Hans Taylor

Upon Being Taken for Granted

Unsent flowers and postcards clutter
the back of my mind's web of confusion.
I am not in your photo album of memories.
As days pass, I am still here
in the flesh, and I am chastised for it.
If I were a magician's rabbit, I would not
be forgotten so easily.
We take the things for granted that are
reliable and dependable. The season's
are appreciated, and so is the tide.
But time is loathed.
To be spontaneous, unreliable, and moody is
to be appreciated.
To go away is to be sought after.

Adrienne Strock

Summer Rain

The endless summer fever breaks
The clouds roll in, the sun goes down
A cool breeze rustles through the trees—
A west wind, pulling in a thunderstorm

Soft thunder, heat lightning, sky purple-black
Builds the tension of the suffocating day,
Threatening but exhilarating. . . .
Releasing in a climax of a thousand
soft, round drops

Slowing, slipping in and out of darkness,
as clouds recede,
A calm, coolness washes in.

Emily Galvin

Dried Funeral Flowers . . .

Even with the dried funeral flowers hanging on my wall . . .
it doesn't seem real at all.
Even with these nightmares hanging in my head . . .
it aches when they try forcing me . . .

. . . to be better on the inside
clean at the outer layer . . .
fixed by broken promises . . .
ancient at his murder . . .
. . . to be guilty on a Sunday morning
invisible until I'm seen . . .
cloned in the hospital room
attached to a sane machine . . .

Traci Mullins

Faceless Shadows

He only hisses
Because he knows what a snake he is.
He is an adulterer father
Who hates his daughters' boyfriends
And wants to keep them locked away
From the world,
From those faceless shadows of himself
That will rape their minds
The morning after he tucks them in.
\He cries at night
After telling them lies
Because he knows that their pretty faces
Will never lay on pink clouds,
And over-stuffed chairs,
And satin pillows.
They will create fixations of their own,
Fetishes of their own,
And grow up to be as dark as he is.
But they are too complicated to have
Faceless shadows.

Carlie Rebelez

Wonder

My mind wonders tonight
To the galaxy of the distant light
Where showers of the stars remain a sparkle in my sky
Moonlight from the above shines upon my land
Our house in the field of baby's breath cooing.
The dandelions let themselves fly,
Seeking that somewhere out there across the soil.
I sit among the baby's breath inhaling life,
Looking into the eyes of the beautiful sky
A breeze of night gently moves the shy dandelions,
I move with this breeze, as if I am to be held.
I delivered my desires, and my hopes and dreams,
Fluttering onward into the sky they go.
Serenity has become the glory of this sight.
I lay on my back thinking of this vast universe,
Thinking of nothing but beginning. . . .

Sherry Jones

Closet

I looked in the closet this morning
Hoping to find
one of those apologies
you were always so good about leaving behind.

Instead, I found all the love
that you and I forgot to give each other

Tucked in corners, behind dusty boxes,
like well intentioned presents
Safely wrapped and hidden
but lost,
long before the holiday arrived.

Mary Hohenberger

To the Men in the Woods

The Night—
Her hands are
Tied up by a lethal fog.
White stones—
Her ribs are showing from the soil.
Her voice—
The gossip of the woods is howling.
Her pain—
A wounded shadow of a man is falling.
She took a deep breath,
And then hid
The truth
From the eyes
Of the others.

Iva Peeva

The Artistry

Paint me in words, written with silk ink,
And velvet paper.
Sculpt me in dew drops on the grass,
and seduce me with your poetry.
Write me as a song,
Lyrical love of the heart.
Poetic instinct makes me love you,
and my heart chooses.
Abruptly stop me when I get too deep,
and pass roses to me in dreams.
No matter what,
the lyric passage takes me there to love you,
and I'll never let go.
　　Laura May

I Am a Fly

it started with Cognac
and swelled into a domed mountain
of rage and fury
like a boil, or fever
blister
and the hand that hit me
was not that of the man i do so love
it was the fist of the bottled beast
the animal
the caged creature
reaching from the bars
swatting at the flies
at night
　　Justine Carpenter

Acrophobia

I asked a fourth year medical student:

"What is that sensation when standing
at the brink of a lofty height
that fills you with a fearful
feeling that something
is trying to pull
you over?"
You twirl me
and swirl me, through high fields
of night shimmies.
Leading me toe to edge
where forces entice as they embrace
and staggered whispers suck at me.
I inhale your electric kiss
that sends my head spinning.
Dizzied
you try to dance me off the cliff.
Daring me to jump
is the power of your touch
your hand on my back.
　　Deneen Dahn

One Night—Soon

One night, when snow slips down in leaning lines,
　　An hour when you are lulled with book, with cup.
I shall unbolt the birchen bar, then stalk
　　Straight out, in old black coat, the hood drawn up.

Some night your voice will strike against still walls.
　　Will call my name out front, then call out back,
But I shall be too far upon my quest,
　　While whiteness softly seals the telling track.

One night, when all is over, you will know
　　How silence stings—how final seems the snow.
　　Helen Milburn Hodges

Setting the Stage

When early autumn enters, golden tints
　　to survey,
She saunters hand in hand with summer,
　　clad in rich array.
No tender, blushing blossom would assume
　　center stage
When dogwood berries branch above
　　a patch of scarlet sage
And leaves of maple sally down to mingle
　　near the door
With marigolds and brown-eyed susans nodding
　　as of yore.
Bring us a winking buckeye pod,
　　purple asters, goldenrod
Gloriously bathed in a sun-lit shower
　　where singing summer now has trod
Because October's gala days will lead
　　the big hurrah
Casting the spell of wanderlust,
　　displaying nature's power!
　　Cyra Grace Renwick

Storm Warnings

I remember you lying beside me near the water's edge
on a sandy cove near Freeport.
The piercing shriek of a circling gull.
The brine that lapped at our toes.

I can see your gold-rimmed spectacles
and the volumes of Ayn Rand stacked
on my crimson plaid blanket.
We caressed the prose of Keats
And blew soap bubbles into the lazy Surfside air.

You drew a lop-sided heart in the wet sand with
a broken stick.
The quietness of our breaths.
The swirling gulf breezes.

Suddenly the noon sun collided with the
spreading ink spills overhead.
The water's mirror reflected the shadows of cobalt
as they swallowed day.
Our open books whipped in the vigorous blasts.
Spiraling sea-spray spit upon the vanilla pages,
leaving angry brown spots in its wake.
　　Susan R. Stern

Sights Before Christmas, During Work,

That Left Me Feeling Blessed and Grateful

Grey snow sky twins sat on the off
ramp shoulder, kneeling toward busy
traffic intersections, hands grimy.

He held homeless
signs, rusty coat, dirt
duffle pack. She costumed sewer
sweater, grease hair hung limp.

She held heart-high three new bought oranges; three
smog sunsets she bodyclung passion tight.

He, hungry tired hairy
frozen from asking, begins to rise.
No smile, words only to her; orange
words. She exhausts an acknowledging smile.

She descends tight crumpled
fingers lightly, raising him
Lazarus-like against that grey snow sky.

I, warm job truck driving, can barely
watch them now the green light; just oily stink
blobs, gold hearts, gaining distance
against me in the glass.
　　Jared Pearce

The Old Flour Mill

The old flour mill still sits on the hill
Near the creek that flows through our town.
The window panes are broken and the glass lies on the ground.
The flour has molded
and the white sacks have turned brown.
The shingles on the roof have blown out of place
And the cobwebs have covered the staircase.
The gutters are filled with leaves from the near by trees.
And the sun rays and moon beams
Play peek-a-boo among the eves.
And you can still hear the chatter and laughter
From the echoes from among the rafters,
As the kids slid down the hill
and across the frozen creek bed on their sleds,
On snowy days you could find rabbit tracks in the back,
Seeking feed for their need be,
From the empty feed sacks and further back near the rail road track
Wild strawberries grew and were picked by people you knew.
But still it's the only mill for miles around that still sets on a hill
And in all its stillness, it still graces my home town.

E. Russell Gray

Duluth

North is coming down from the big bay,
all bracken and muskeg.
He walks through the forest,
shedding his coat and putting on
fir and fern and flower.
See how he stands on tiptoe, seeking his love,
who is warmth and moisture, all floral and succulent.
He moves over iron and granite and birch,
steps down the gentle hill and kneels at Superior.
Before he sips, he looks up to see you and
knowing that winter is over, he blows you a warm kiss.

Brent Christianson

Library Books Like Tombstones

Library books like tombstones
lined in a row still await
the visit of a family member,
a friend, or even a stranger
to pay homage to a restless soul.

Titles on library volumes,
like names engraved on a stone,
recite the record of voices
calling from the depth of the Earth
to be saved from the wrath of oblivion.

Though many will visit the graveyard,
and many will read out the names,
only a few will discover
the messages waiting entombed
in the cemetery of stones without graves.

Emil Jacob

Remembering You

The silence here is an echo;
pebbles dropping into the deep
with a plunk, and a slow decent
to the bottom, a silty bed of memories
suddenly stirred into a swirling ballet;
micro-fine images dancing
in the heavy cold alone, and then
together in the darkness,
before the music stops,
and weighted by truth,
they spiral toward the bottom,
settling into stillness once more.

C. Wright

Thinking Late

At three AM. I realize our love
is not champagne and caviar
served on a silver tray
or the yellow rose thrown into the breeze
floating back, again and again.
There is silence between us—
the quiet kiss, a sealing off.

My chipped eyes stay pried open
like a mannequin in the dark
when the store closes.
The moonlight sifts through
the bare wooden slits of your bamboo shade.
Your cheek smells like baby powder
and the pulse of the clock
could go on all my life.

Thick with dreams
you rock me in your reaching arms as if
I am your lost childhood blanket,
the one they cut up gradually, gradually
until one day you whispered, it is gone.

Rebecca Harth

Niña

She sits Indian-style,
brown knees almost touching the thinly
paved road like lanky unselfconscious
street dogs lapping up the
watermelon sunset.
I glance, broken.
Ask what she is doing.
"Pintando"
Painting the curb, evening's canvas,
Barrio stick illustrations.
She dips into cheap watercolor ovals,
filling in cracks, initials, hearts that
belonged to someone else before
the concrete dried.
Now they are her messy petroglyphs,
her self-possessed fingerprints and
link to the wind.
I glance, broken.
Ask if I can be seven again,
if I can please dress up the sidewalk too.

Jori-Michelle Rambo

An Illusion of the Heart

Walking a path colored with glass
his reflection is caught a thousand times
in fleeting brilliance
with tiny beams of intertwining light
and lovely patterns of delicacy
which seem to infiltrate my body
and envelope my heart
in a moment of euphoric uncertainty
I am his possession
as he does always carry my heart
yet unfathomable is the actual levity
of consciously holding love in one's hands
and so the path must narrow
and the exquisite rays must diminish
as his ethereal figure moves calmly away
leaving a trail of mirrored shards behind
I listen, captivated by the paradoxical splendor,
as my pulse fades with his footsteps
until silence captures my eyes
and the glass ceases to exist

Melissa Dibble

Just a Pup to Me

Dedicated to Bud Dawson
"He came out of the 60's, walked through three decades
just to say to me, "The truth, I want the truth,
before it's too late, before I die, you must tell the truth to me."
And I sat looking beyond thirty years,
I saw the jowls lessen, the lines decrease,
the hair turn dark and thick, the expression soften,
the eyes begin to twinkle,
I saw the bloom, and I could have said
something smart like, "The truth! You can't handle the truth!"
or, "What is truth? A word! And what is a word? A puff of air!"
But instead I said, "I can see that you're bigger,
and I know that you've grown older,
but what looks like an old man to
the rest of the world is still a flower
child, just a pup to me."
And I led my friend by the hand to the garden
to show him one red bloom.
I said, "It arrives every spring. It reminds me of you."
To which he asked, "Is that the truth?"
I answered, "It is to me."

Marianne Beasley

Captiva Mourning

I followed your trace to the island's north shore,
imagining the imprints your feet had made
before the tide rose and washed them away.

I sat on the beach and watched the sun set.
The sun blazed red and lingered,
taking one final view before the water consumed it.
The sand was damp beneath me in the spring dusk.

You, who once gazed at the same green gulf,
no longer know the wonder of twilight,
no longer hear the rhythms of oceans,
no longer taste the salt in the air.

Your death closed the chasm through which we passed into being.
We, like the sky after sunset,
are too late for the day,
too soon for the stars.
We wait, awe-struck and orphaned,
for darkness to come and a sad moon to rise.

William Lowe

Headlands

Sand dunes and
thistle, heather
and shells strewn
along an Erie lake
made wavy enough by
gentle winds and jet skis.

Bathers and babes,
splashing arrhythmically,
convey a sharkless safety that
swimmers can sink their teeth into.
Guard stations lie capsized,
seized by outstretched epidermis
inviting the errant volleyball—
a simple reminder that there still is
life after tan.

The only thing missing is salt,
but for the yellow-clad girl
with her mushroomed umbrella
just mining her business.

Marilyn Cristi

She Is Called Spring

Mother Nature now a youth, barefoot and
free, sundressed and rainbow ribbons.
Rambling through meadows, wind-tousled hair,
cheeks rouged, lips crimsoned by the sun.

Lying on verdant new grass, crocus all
ablaze—Enraptured with pride surveying
the beauty and wonder about her. Her
brushes splashing brilliant splendor, she
making the world new and fresh—an
exquisite array of rebirth.

Mating calls, loves sweet beckoning, fill
the air. She smiles her approval of the
unending ritual. She breathes the
sweetness of this fleeting moment, and
beams with deep satisfaction; For now—
She is called Spring!!

Larry Patterson

Time Brings Change

the gentle flow of your hair in the breeze.
you bring peace that covers. your breath comes to me
as your head lays quiet on my lap.
the busy outer world knows nothing
of this feeling, caught in the madness of going,
I'm staying. for times past we were far from this.
you stepped in the water when it touched the edge
of your dress you pulled up; i was the water.
you dreamed all night long when the whisper came
in your ear to rise, you sighed, maybe i spoke too loud.
you walked miles every night when the moon was hidden you
complained. sometimes i have to stay hidden. somehow i never
got to you, the distance was short but the feelings were
miles. a burden you had, one you wouldn't share. i screamed
into the dark night. what did i want? answers
for peace, peace i could have at a moment. so i
finally relaxed my chair and rested. i fell
asleep to the blowing wind. when i woke, your
head was there. i ran to find the answers only to
find them strapped to my back

Ian Snyder

Untitled

city-breath held against your back
as we pass the Lower East Side
this is one of those rare walks;
we'll never lose sight of each other

right there on the waterfront
do I reach for your hand

this day makes us say things like:
I have been here before
on days without you
and the water then seemed green to me
this is all I can give you:
Where has the madness gone?

Not somewhere else in this city
is it easy to spell out
every day possible
How can I convince you:
I meant for life to go on

Lia Munch

Unrested

can you hear
monday morning
slowly crawl
through your hair
and sleep in your ear
fill you
with unrest

Sharon Klebba

A Variation on a Poem by Slyvia Plath

More piteous a sight I never did see
Than the moth who,
Aspiring to fulfill Plath's prophecy,
Lured to the flickering luminescence
Of immortality through one brief moment
Of intensified flame,
Miscalculated and fell short of the fire.
No searing burst of heat,
No gentle crack of dancing flame
Celebrated her sacrifice.
No trail of curling smoke
Wound itself into a ghostly headstone
To commemorate her passing.
Only her body remained,
A kamikaze encased in the fluid wax
Of a citronella candle,
Monument to tragic futility
And devastating failure.
Dear Sylvia,
What would you make of this?

Katie Streit

Refrigerated

refrigerated women (like flowers)
lie in their plastic coffins
surrounded by onlookers
waiting to buy
(my, what a pretty color!).
we watch with anticipation
as they wither
curled up in self defense.
we watch with little patience
when they die.

Cesanne Davis

Skydancer

you were free-falling
sky-dancing
your brightness burned
blackened Ananazi designs
into my itchy clay skin
flyboy
rocketing from the gate
cheating gravity
I saw in your eyes that
the Earth was a sweet served up
I saw the morning
spin with wings
birdmen floating fleeting music tumbling
your skin was only foil
I thought it was angelic fire

P-R Severaid

Chaos Rising

While wading in the shallows in the shadow of Slane Bridge
I turned to see a vision on the bank
As she traced an errant curl of raven braid
Which had fallen from the furl above her face
And fixed it there, behind her ear
As if to say that all things have their place
And in doing so, oblivious, she bid me let her stay.

The invasion of emotions which before I had controlled
Awoke my thoughts defending the attainment of her goals
In the hope her tender love for me would grow
If my mind could only calm the chaos rising from below.

And despite a fleeting moment when my thoughts began to yield
And my heart screamed, "No!" and cried to her to come away with me
My voice had pledged allegiance to my head
And my heart in silence turned to see a vision
Of the love that conquers all the trials of loneliness instead

Mark White

For the Player

Crossing my legs in the
pink plastic chair, I clasp my hands
for the mood, "andante," transported from Bach
to warm, sticky nights of
surrealism

and stepping beyond my clasped hands
with a prickly foot
I slip

so that I am not the listener,
there is no player
in this room of strangers,

and are we all rising above our crossed legs
to perch on that softly bobbing head
to soak up that which he pours—"allegro."

I smile with the pride of existence
and cry
and try to let my tears catch the light
so that the player will see.

Juliette Hwang

On Our Engagement

You were explaining to me the meaning
of Swamp Thing, the comic—
Said that it was a union between the monster and Abbie;
He represents the natural world,
and her the rest.
You said the union paralleled the perfect paradigm.
Then you showed me the cactus
that had been sunburned in the window.
"See how it's growing back?" you asked.
I remember there was a pile of laundry in the front room,
and you were on your knees.
No candlelight, no fancy dinner, and lastly—no ring,
for you would leave the choice up to me.
You even surprised yourself.
The moment was perfect,
spontaneous, memorable.
Then we laughed and cried for about three hours.
My favorite part is keeping it a secret for a while.

Amy Champ

And Today I Am Frantic

teeth click repeatedly behind raspberry lips
and over orange juice acid tongue.
tugging nervously downward on the hem of my
too-short shirt,
too-short only in my mind,
so i pull ruthless and needless.
a hurried chuckle
(i can almost see his sound waves)
passes the teacher
blurry laughter, frantic breathing
while spinning to reach—
trying to scratch my own back
wishing for your fingernails,
my head on your chest.
remembering knuckles, kneecaps,
and calluses on your heels.

licking the sugar off strawberries,
and knowing i like poetry better,
when you read it to me.

Alena Vigoren

Death of a Small Cactus

"We are the dried men,
We are the fallow kin"
—maybe THAT is the way the poem should go.

Your small but ever-ripening cactus, surviving
three years of our separation . . . I left it on
the window sill behind the blinds one day,
sick of remembering it was you who gave it to me.

It dried up and withered
after three weeks.

Panicked, I scrambled to flood the damned thing
with water, talked to it sweetly. I
nestled a huge multi-vitamin next to it on
the rocks and dirt, under the soft stove glare
and it seemed to come to life overnight,
shedding its orange shellacked skin, reaching out
to embrace blindly, but the plant lies moldering, waiting
to become something completely alien and cold.

I talk to it in whispers.
I tell it that I understand.

Mark Brimm

Ophelia, Floating

Ophelia is gone,
Floating down the mournful brook.
Her flowing, golden hair,
Rippling in the waves.
A crown of daisies, violets, and rue,
Orchids, nettles, and crow-flowers
Upon her head.
Her graceful, outspread garments
Sweeping all around her.
A fallen mermaid.
Arms drawn out
Face serene—
Snow white.
She looks so calm here,
Such a peaceful end.
Let her float here, undisturbed,
Untouched, and pristine.
Let no one shatter her silence.
Let no one interrupt her stillness.
Float on, Ophelia. . . .

Andrea Butler

She Falls Awake.

Behind this random stop of small talk
lacks a girl of inclinations
and desecrations of self worth,
of hers and hers alone.
And behind this girl—or rather,
inside this girl—
stems a world, a universe,
of creatures smiling and dancing,
clapping with skips of yellow bursting
and ribbons of sweet pure-love pink
all around waiting to be filled
and chilled
and woozy and slightly
amuck
in love and lust
with trust to
hold her when
the bell rings, and
she falls awake.

Sarah Lamoureaux

DEUS EX MACHINA

Today, she comes to me in the grocery store,
In the frozen food isle of all places.
After weeks of nervous faith—
Nails bitten to the quick,
Dirty hair pulled back to hide the knots and tangles—
Like a ghost appearing slowly in a doorway,
Hope has come again, today.
I gasp for air, exhausted from holding my breath so long.

Who knows why she went in the first place?
She's fickle is all I can figure,
Evaporating at the slightest sign
Of illness. Or poverty. Or failure.

I'm proud of myself, though; I waited her out this time.
No pounding my head with clenched fists.
Just a box of candy eaten at midnight,
A canceled lunch date, an early morning nightmare.

And now she's here again, approaching me with a warm light,
Not as bright as a comet, but brighter than the TV screen.
My eyes burn and I bite my bottom lip.
"I knew she would come," I whisper to the fish sticks.

Lori Cossens

Baby's Breath

It might have been only a porcelain doll
lying in the pretty little sterile-white bed,
but the unnaturally dark make-up has caked up inside
the tiny puckers around his eyes and mouth,
and now he is a wizened old man
shrunk down to twenty cold inches.

Whispers bounce around his ears, but he never hears
the ironic words—I suppose there's no reason
to whisper (we're not going to wake him up).
I try to cry and try not to cry;
my face is confused and overwhelmed trying
to express the proper emotion to honor this priceless doll,
whose cold, miniature fingers should be reaching for mine
but lie stone-still instead.

So here we stand whispering meaningless words
(all wordlessly willing this doll to breathe),
admiring all the beautiful roses, carnations,
violets, orchids, lilies
baby's breath . . .
that fill the room with more oxygen than we can bear.

Jennifer Davidson

Carte Blanche

looking down a crowded hurried street
large gray bearded men load trucks with time;
swiftly and narrowly lifting a brown bag
i walk past

stone and rock upon metallic walls
stares straight down with heavy eyes;
still clutching the bag through smells of fruits—
i walk past

inside the crumpled bag lie dozens and more
papers, untouched by pen or scraped by thought;
they crumple and tear inside the bag as
i walk past

should i stop and write on the paper
that still lies unshorn about the woman
who sells found kittens on the corner? for now
i walk past

George Khachatryan

Music Teacher

As you get older and your eccentricities
become more prominent,
and as the dogs and cats and a tornado
sweep the house—
everything looks quite mad except the
Steinway.
The icons and mandalas on your walls are
just like lover's palms that you delouse.

If Chopin lilts and Mozart tumbles,
the weeping cherries nod in tune—
this is a restless woman's ballroom
gone out whale-watching in mid-June.

Tomorrow there will be more students
staring at space like students do—
the silent windows
are witness to how much a long, long time ago
he was in love with you.

Angie Angel

Magic Charms

Dripping skin
like August-melted chocolate,
time slows down
for the swimming pool
kids. I held your hand
and buttoned down
your red shirt, revealing
a sunburned stomach.
Let this tender teardrop salve soothe.

Disconnect all our simple sayings,
tied in knots
tightly to keep our words
safe. I could never read
your cursive words, written on scented
paper, folded sideways, sealed,
and sent. My chicken scratch
scrawl against your girl-curved words.
Handwritten last lines linger, than leave.

James Brubaker

Rain at 2 AM

streetlights
on the window
make stars
out of raindrops.

behind me
shadows waver:
countless fractures
in the wall.

I hear rain
on the roof;
it is paper
crumpled, softly.

Uriah Anderson

Two Images

Gold jewelries Aaron melted once
After his people begged, make Gods
To go before us. He complied,
To later voice, out came this calf
The golden God for which they cried.

Two images desire casts
Self-power strong, self-glory bright both worshiped.
Hear each human shout as every psyche,
Bound, bows low to gold or silver self come out.

D. Ward Kyle

[Untitled]

The Japanese had the right idea.
Instead of divine revelations
Or enlightened arguments
Or prolific tragedies,
They wrote three lines:
One about the wind
Blowing through a bonsai branch
Bending just slightly.

Where once I saw trees
Now I spy you
Hiding in the branches.
I try to write of you
And find it like trying to
Write of my pulse.
Or an ocean.
Or the wind:
You blow gently here
Through a gnarled and weathered branch
Bending to the right.

Joseph Wycoff

The Diagnosis

I think I thanked the doctor
Habit being what it is
And grace still a small part of what I
Had left of me when he closed that door
So loudly
And I shattered into pieces on the floor

A nurse came in shortly thereafter
To brief me during what must have been
My third alternate lifetime
To sweep little parts of me
Into the dust pan designated by my HMO
For occasions just like this one

Occasions where one stares in the mirror
And wonders,

"Who will have my eyes?"

Greg Mucha

Mexico

The Mexico that I know is a chimera.

Romantic, Potemkin village, restorations;
Bright waters ringed with worshipers
Prostrate, dulled with food and lust:
Torpid, mesmerized tourist-priests.

Brazen cats haunting breezy palapas
Demanding fresh portions, cleanly carved
And offered by painted fingers
Heavy with gaudy baubles,
Freshly mountain-mined.

Only when we stop in a dusty town
And wander to the empty church
(Except for toothless beggars at the door)
And see the agonized Christ forever dying,
Do I catch a fleeting glimpse

Of your true mystery, your tragedy,
Mexico.

Veronica Snyder

For Everything and Nothing

The lines on the road
laugh at her,
because parking meters
have more time than her coffee cup.
When passion has to be this quiet,
desire is clicking
with spelling mistakes
as she melts
and he waits
for the traffic light to change.

Jennifer A. Long

What Am I to Do When Someone Dies?

Call the relatives. Prepare the coffin.
Send the flowers. Contact the cemetery.
Find the funeral home. Say I'm sorry.
Send a card. Whisper my condolences?

Is it enough to give a hug?

To send a hundred dollar memoriam,
Their name to be hailed in prayer?
Is it enough to say "Fear No More . . ."?
Or "He but doth suffer a sea change"?

Shall I sit and drink my coffee,
Black, one sugar, and stare—stare?
What is one death when there
Was Auschwitz, Tiananmen Square?

One death. One Death? A universe gone!

To eternity. To Eternity? What solace, that.
The photo album rots with time.
Memories fade. Hearts deny, forget. Forget, but for our words—
Our words—limitless repository of history and love,

One death and Tiananmen Square.
Anna T. Balash

Blue

It's not as if the snow means anything or the sky
is significant. They are only part of the landscape,
like everyone gathered here with nothing left to say.

Later, the lilies are orange, yellow, in a vase;
there are lumps of sugar, a pitcher full of cream.
Everything is still and carefully arranged.

And the snow stops falling; the mourners
fall away. What did they mean: The people,
the fragments of music, the clouds and hours

that merged and separated? We are left with
the deep hush after church bells, the quiet
pulse of living blood, your vacant place.
Lisa Christina Powell

Old Friends

Words, like juicy grapes
Roll slowly forth
Drop into the bowl
Of conversation
Years have piled up
Like stacks of paper currency
Large denomination spent,
We are left with dollar bills
And an occasional ten spot of laughter
Margo Koller

Immobile

For weeks I beg tagged trees to take in their energy,
send it back to Earth, store their power elsewhere.
Can they perceive me, mosquito like, darting about their bases?
The county has decreed a wider road in this arid land.
What is it like to stand immobile before fate,
to feel saws cutting off neighbors and not run.
Rootedness is not paralysis I remind myself.
A chance to understand surrender?

All of dry June I drive skidding white gravel
bleak and dusty—even saved trees have died.
For a time I don't see sunflowers at disturbed edges
till one day they astound with their color
softening the scars we all carry.
Christina Husted

No Daisies Left to Pick

for bug . . .
i think of you with wine and a cigarette.
i think of you in bed,
laying there just tangled in skin
thinking of what we might have brought to tomorrow.
Sunday mornings still greet me,
only this time you're not walking through them.
breakfast never sets a table,
yet i still can smell you sitting across from me.
the Sunday sun shines itself down on my Hollywood morning,
questioning if i can make it without the old routine.
in a far away place, the same sun finds you.
slowly both of us find our shifts in the wind.

i look in all the familiar places. . . .
where are the flowers?
i still find myself wanting to pick you daisy's,
trying to build some castle without seeds.
Christiana Frank

Grasshopper Summer

The summer we were thirteen,
brown and mosquito-scarred,
we rode one-speeds down gravel roads
through green corn-tunnels,
put on dusty theater in the haymow
to assemblies of barn cats
and raftered pigeons,
and learned to sew sun dresses
on the Singer treadle,
your mother sighing
at the puckers and thread-messes.
We talked hours
in the crooked arms of apple trees,
heard in the hot afternoons
grasshopper whispers in the fields,
and watched the long, white arms
of summer lightning,
feeling in ourselves the rising
sugar maples feel in early spring.
Joan Peronto

The Projects

Down in Atlanta, dusty barefoot children
carry jelly jars
to hold their dreams for the night.
Women in aprons pick up pecans
from red earth, packed down shiny.
Men stand smoking
hand rolled Prince Alberts,
Humphrey Bogart hats tilted back.
Old folks sit quietly
on concrete front steps.
Might be a child molester
or just some soul gentled by loss.
Rain blows down
sheets pinned to lines,
criss cross, maps of lives
waiting to rise,
sucking up bobby pins
flip flops, broom-handled horses,
black tar bibles, empty pots,
lost spoons, and broken plastic.
Sharon O'Sullivan

Summer Afternoon

The fantastic drowse of perpetual noon
Drapes the landscapes in velvets so heavy and sweet
And silhouetted by sunlight, birds carry the tune
Of the bittersweet pleasure of red-weather heat.
A certain slant of languid light
Flows like molasses through the trees
Whose arms sway, eternally to left and to right,
and whose emerald green flames flicker in the breeze.
The whispered songs of Sundays past
Flow on a thick and gentle drift
Of noontime's breath, and carries passed
The scent of sleep and natures gift.
A hum of sounds from years ago
Of children's laughter and falling tears
Swell and fade as the breezes flow
And bring memories to sleeping ears.
So go the passing days of magic
Who flow so slowly as an invisible tune
Save for these days; how sweet, and how tragic
The song of summer's afternoon.

Jessica Rabito

"For He Who Finds Me, Finds Life:" Proverbs

I pursue you in thin sheets,
washed with small words.
I pursue you in auditoriums,
where ancient bones are chewed and
chewed, and swallowed
by those with the stomach for it.
I look for you in the well-fed faces
of young men who got over sin
the way I got over acne,
and the busy bodies of young women,
who put you on, like an apron.
I listen for you in the voices
of old women who speak splinters,
and old men, who hold theirs
between cheek and gum, for a memory.
Sometimes I think this is a scavenger-hunt;
Other times, that we are all assassins, and
 there is a price on your head.

Caitilin Cagney

Night Dreams

softly the night whispers
makes round notes
full of sultry silence
softly the veil rustles
like the wind, which kisses leaves
as a lady's fingertips
softly the moon warbles
filling silver cisterns
with grateful songs
of night blooming jasmine
softly the song
surrenders to the songbirds
every new verse another fallen star
kissing the purple hem
of night's garment
steal away with me
into the mist-shrouded river
of my seldom dreams
and touch me
in the night blooming jasmine

Donna Gifford

Untitled

In the days of being a good little Maxwell House wife
we were supposed to marry and live
happily ever after
We didn't,
and armies of us,
ill-prepared for the reality
of careers,
flooded the market
Taking jobs
that were only jobs,
marrying again,
not for love
but for survival,
and wondering
why in those days
of Donna Reed and Harriet Nelson,
Wally and the Beave,
nobody ever warned us
that happy endings were only in fiction

Roslyn Weinstein

Recollections of "Innocence Lost"

Her fingers dance on ivory keys,
As her head bends humbly down.
She plays with passionate, unspoken pleas,
A saddening, melodic sound.

This is her song of "Innocence Lost,"
She had written years before.
I ask myself "How high was the cost?"
That inspired this soulful score.

'Tis a song of a girl, coming-of-age,
Blossoming a little too soon.
Like a sheltered bird, escaping her cage,
Into a chaotic monsoon.

Listening to her play,
While watching her sway,
I realize she is a stranger.

Seeing her strain,
To this song of pain,
I pray this world doesn't change her.

Harvard Reynolds

Reign of Winter Dragon

In misty sky
Pale sun, his eye
Glares coldly o'er
Both mount and moor,
Surveying kingdom near and far.
Dust's commonplace
With crystal lace
And darker hues
In ice subdues,
With frostings thick enmantled.
Stems golden tall
In argent fall,
Defining path
Of chilling wrath.
Beware: cruel blast of icy breath!
Still water freezes
As it pleases,
Flawed mirrors to form
Which crack with warmth,
Reflecting rule soon to be ended.

Neville Starick

The Dreamcatcher

Tell me your thoughts uncut.
Don't censor the dreams you've captured
in dreamcatchers adorned with faux feathers.
Tell me the things you feel without allowing
the thieves of political correctness to steal your unspoken truths.
Don't hide your feelings from me; don't hide your pain.
Show me your guilt and tell me about your shame.
Don't listen to those fools listed in the credits.
They'll ask you to wait till the lighting's just right
before you cross that picturesque Sahara.
Your dreams will end up on a cutting room floor,
with lighting and sound guys pasting together your life.
Don't let that happen to your thoughts of me.
Take what you need from me and give me what you can.
Then run, just go away.
But leave behind that dreamcatcher,
the one with the faded faux feathers.
It's held your uncensored thoughts of me forever,
and I want to peek inside.

Michelle Caldwell

Memories

She was not as tall as the lilac bush,
Wearing a hand-made dress all rosebuds and smocking,
Her short, sturdy legs planted on the muddy ground
In bright red boots.
She'd buttoned her grandmother-made sweater
By herself, unevenly,
And the breeze stirred the soft hair toddlers have,
The sort a mother can't resist stroking off a forehead.
Zigzagging across the lawn like an aimless bee,
She was intent on picking every dandelion she could find
To add to the wilting bunch she held in her hands,
Fingers sticky with the milky sap.
When I blinked my eyes, I didn't know
Whether it was this spring
Or those afternoons years ago
When I made my own dandelion rings
And tilted buttercups under my sister's tipped chin.
If spring is the time for renewal,
It is memory that makes it more so.

Karla Hutchens

Relative Procession

Stucco clings like yellow paper peeling in wet April sun.
I see a smooth-skin, mustached face
past these frail houses and lawns.
My own father is here, bobbing in a black Lincoln interior.
It seems like I'm the only one who hears him say
in this knot-like, leathery openness,
"My father was a railroad man;
I am a railroad man's son."

We slide through the old neighborhood,
light cloth soft and shadowy.
We pass the 24th Ave. Bakery, pass Dick's
boxed-up barbershop, and I'm telling you
I can see my grandfather shooting pool in
that bar at the bridge. He's with the old
M&S boys talking about the warm weather and
about how the unions just aren't the same.
We are driving through it all, and I can see perfectly
how sometimes we're so proud.
Sometimes we are grounded to the root, and it can feel so good.

Joshua Hauser

After the Storm

Six AM, we started late today,
probably the weight of our proud, American luggage
slowing us down.
Half an hour ago the sun rose
above the twisted streets, their curves
carrying stories of barefoot children,
uneducated women, and men hauling
fruits and crabs and cow stomachs
to market.

I step onto the bus and place myself
next to my pale-skinned and yellow-haired companion.
The bus is large and full. It sputters
out of the city, into the stories of the campo,
and leaves its own trail of thick smoke
lounging behind.

A representative of the machismo society
has no qualms leaning over me or my yellow-haired companion.
His breath may as well be my own, since there is not
enough room anymore for us both.

And we hit another arduous bump.

Kayrl Stead

Sandstorm

he held himself like a newborn god
high on borrowed glory
walked the streets like a drunk coyote
took what he wanted and devil-be-damned
covered his feet with the painted Earth
running across the world.

he held out hope like a wedding ring
promise, and punishment too
took to a tan like a deep-shade beer
lifted the sun on a back made for lifting
covered the sky with yelling and cussing
left like he had somewhere to be.

he held this whole town like a breathless girl
bathed in the desert with cactus soap
rinsed himself off with lizard tongues
swallowed every dust storm
jumped into the panting heat.
that boy, he won't come back.

Kris Larson

Glass Bottle

You called me naive—
Innocence preserved
In a glass bottle
Balanced on the top shelf.
I was skipping through the winter paradise
Searching for my cave of comfort.
Thoughts danced inside my tainted mind,
Dressing up in different personalities
As my judgment slumps to the ground
With the thrust of a zipper.
I am the essence of pointillism.
Don't get too close.
Blending shades of sexual insecurity
Clash with intellectual confidence
And create that beautiful blue
So familiar to you.

Elizabeth Ament

Out of Time

I found her sitting by the window,
knitting lying helplessly in her lap.
The smell of death filled the air.
Motionless and alone, she sat,
pulse weak as chilled blood labored through tired veins.
Three score and ten years had passed,
and life was now measured by single moments.
Death lay a hand breath away, tugging at her being.
She does not see the aeroplane, high in the sky,
the dirty dishes cluttering the cupboard,
like mountains of pills in a geriatric ghetto.
With aged urbanity, she lingers on in the immortal course of life.
She was dead some time ago, but the corpse remained alive,
eating soft boiled eggs, fed to her by a nurse.
Straggles of grey hair hang down, as she stares from blind eyes.
Upon the auspicious occasion of her demise,
when she is finally lowered into the clay,
When I remain I ask that I might die with grace,
and not linger past my time.

Alice Whitlow

Apartmental

Unlinked insects on a tile floor
famished fortunates
knowing their seeking
dully watched
by me
unknown, sitting
next to nothing
alone (having finally given up on the approximate other)
hours later, wallpapered sadness:
papered wall sadness
chipped heart vase
unpeopled paintings all colors,
the colors from memory in want of light
no permission to look out binds, or sometimes worse unseen
looking up blinded by sun, not having been
outside walking this morning
what hard, wood furniture my anguish.

Mardell G. Toomey

Dervish

Long, straight hair
Yellow, not golden
Just yellow
Thin, fine hair
Not full of rich, thick ringlets
Spilling upon her breast
It just falls where it is
Yellow and straight
She is a bit too tall
A bit too thin
Clumsy and awkward on her feet
As she tried to dance her way around the room
To a lost melody
Long, thin arms outstretched
Tossing her hair back she laughs
Her pale gray eyes sparkle with life,
Maybe fire
Her lips part just enough as she smiles
So you can see each white little pearl that sits
Shimmering and shining inside this oyster

Leisha Ruhlman

Dublin, 4 AM

Staring into a cup of bad coffee
and listening to pale backpackers
talk of skin problems,
I feel the bite and chill of another morning
Dublin, 4 AM
Outside, the grinding of gears are moaning
from unwashed vehicles,
while people with agonizing jobs
walk with chronic fatigue,
spitting and cursing
and asking God to help them get through
another day.
Dublin, 4 AM,
cigarette butts litter the sidewalk,
many still alight,
scattered like gun-shot wounds
and showing the only sign of warmth
at this demented hour.

Lucas Patrick

Outside a Hospital Window

My Vietnamese roommate in 104,
bedridden by gangrene,
talks about sailors bobbing their cigars
like Popeye working his corn pipe
and calls the barefoot kiters,
circling the duck pond,
kids exercising their condors.
"St. Vincent's Uncle Remus," I call him;
tells a story like you're in his lap.

You'd doubt the soldier's dying,
watching his nine to five vigil at the window:
the scooching-propping-turning
routine of a 49'ers fan
catching the action from a crowded
end zone seat.
He can't make a beer run at half-time
(noon time in this case),
when the sprinklers go on
and the kiters and sailors leave,
so he lies down again

Thaddeus Pickard

Me Dejaste

This graffitied corner
disappears with each biting
shift of time.
11:00 clamped down,
skin ghastly and luminous
under a stifling sky—
My sandals slapped
the gap-toothed pavement,
it coughed consumptive rhythms,
shattering the paralyzed street.

And so
I wait,
dark leaking out upon me like
wet spackle from lumpy walls.
You lead him by the sweaty hand
out from those neon lights,
key pressed firmly in tight pockets.

No one welcomes tomorrow on this bent curb,
rotting next to a dead goat.

Christine Whitney

Untitled

I write the days on paper squares
in great inch high letters
Then clutching them and muttering prayers,
I strike a match and watch it catch and twist and glow and flare
into a fearsome thing,
a square marked Tuesday that I fling
out into the night,
a twisted burning dying thing
flying in the night.
And seeing this I only feel an aching silent dread for days ahead
and nights unknown, while all alone I raise my head and scream
to god.

Gerald J. Myers

Eat at Joe's

Amidst crackling pops, and sizzles,
school-bus yellow butter dances on the pan.
Wisps of kitchen smoke unfurl
lingering
amid the stench of humid summer days
so sticky and foul
even the flies try to rinse themselves of it.
A glass, tipped Day-Glo pink by carefree lips,
in a muted tumble shatters on the footprint patterned floor.
Shards piercing through the grime to almost touch the floor
of the glistening aluminum eatery.
No heads turn notice.
At the oil smudged counter
a man sits tired of chasing his dog named Happy.
Rivulets of sweat beads cling to his frayed gray suit,
perhaps a size too small.
The stool he rests on creaks as he spears the globs
of manila-tinted skillet eggs into his mouth
pausing
only to scrape his worn thumbnail
along the past meals stuck to the spoon laying
on the sticky, crumbed counter.

Van Tran-Lam

Twenty-one

that foolish boy below me
pushes and pushes me in that corner.
he knocks on my door when he knows
that I cannot, but he tries.
ridiculous, childish games he taunts me with
and I choose not to.
he is to my left now,
in rags no less
he reeks of poison, reading last weeks news
ice cream requests on a cold, wet Thursday evening
strange for a child without dinner plans.

Salvatore Bondi

Fool's Gold Union

Like old-time miners,
We traded ten years
For the flash in a pan,
Dredged joint desires of sand-banked passion
With tin buckets of sophomore psychology.
In our strain to uncover the mother lode,
Sharp-eyed, critical of each grain,
We left the quiet waters of passion
For stronger currents—
For the gleam of power
In the mud of a marriage.
What energies we've expended,
What furtive hoarding
Of secret, separate obsessions,
To reach a fork
And find we've panned pyrites.

N. Cupper

Eating Blintzes

we sat eating blintzes
you held your knife
like a switch blade
bubbie said you
always made problems
bubbie also made us
lay our napkins in our laps
veils covering our manhood
yarmulkes

YOU used to yell a lot
shaking the house
scaring my little brother

my blintz sat on my plate
it was cut mortally
and bubbie would tell me
to eat because I was so thin

YOU clutched YOUR fork
and ate my blintz
off my plate
and all i could do was stare

Howard Friedman

Catch Me I'm Falling

Driven by this mistral rain
across the bay, through shattering winds
and twisting fog
I can see your determined grin
sitting upon my memory yet again

In vivid light
unlike tonight
I see your eyes
like the constellation Gemini
you settle into the sky
shooting stars my way
softly closing my own eyes and reaching
blind I feel your touch
imbibing the black-throated night
which buries another heartfelt night.

Overtones and hues of spring
Yellows and Greens salt the Azure light
finally honoring your far away frozen life

Kevin Carroll

Sunday Awakening

distant sounds of life come into play
on a Sunday morning on a Sunday stage
next door boots tread heavily
on carpet-less floorboards
faint backyard dogs bark
and pleading cats meow.

childrens' naive and positive voices
pass trough the air.

The radio news demands attention
from kitchen listeners crunching papers
as humming lawnmowers glide over grass.

behind closed doors
these almost fixed sounds can be heard
as if turned on each Sunday to wake us up
like some natural alarm

Alan Smyth

A Mother's Love

So young to be feeling such worldly emotions.
The emotions of embarrassing moments,
When others stop to stare.
The emotions of loneliness,
When standing all alone.
The emotions of hurt feelings,
When others do not understand.

How can I protect you from such pain?
The pain of a broken heart,
When friendship is lost forever.
The pain of disappointment,
When others do not follow through on commitments.
The pain of having your dreams shattered,
When effort is not enough.

What can I do to help such pain?
I can hold you in my arms for eternity.
I can stay awake for nights of conversation.
I can be there to listen at any given time.
I can love you unconditionally forever,
Because you will always be mine.

Sandra Webb

Zoey Lane

Mama carried me in her tummy so warm.
Safe in comfort waiting to be born.
Close to my heart, do I want to leave?
Waiting for God to proceed.
Can I stay here a little longer,
Where I know it is safe, cuddled so comfortable in this place?
Mama is so stressed and tired of this mess.
Being in labor at her best.
Please Daddy, what should I do?
Let's get together and have me soon.

Elaine M. Angus

Pine Hill

House in the hills,
Hidden—back off the road;
Unless you know where to look.
Overgrowth and trees keeping back the outsiders.
Hills behind it, a natural wall.
Nature holds in memories of the past.
Builders of the house
Shipping materials up the Mississippi to be unloaded at Natchez.
Brought by wagon into Louisiana, assembled by slaves.
Slaves who later would be chained to the pillars,
Chained to the beauty they had built
Physically, emotionally, economically.
War ending, slaves freed, owners dying.
House occasionally occupied, but not maintained.
Until a century later a local historian,
Enthralled by the chronicles of the past moved in
And slowly, lovingly brought the house back to life.

Carolyn Files

Finding My Way

I ponder long and my thoughts are deep
and I think so much and there is no sleep.
Sometimes I don't know the way you see
but I must trust in God who made me free.
I must trust my heart and find my way
through unclear paths and endless days.
God knows the way and walks with me.
And I must have faith and I must believe.
I have my church that has no walls
and its denomination encompasses all.
The message is simple, of love and good will.
God shows me the way and he knows how I feel.

Ruby Ross

Martin, My Beloved Husband

My heart is aching, shaking, quaking at the sight of you!
How, after all these years do you still make me feel this way!
All aquiver inside, soft and romantic.

I see you through my eyes as you were forty-five years ago
I hope your eyes see me the same way.

Maybe God makes our vision less as we grow older
so that we see each other as we were when married.

My heart is bursting and full with my love for you.
Love, that grows and grows, like a flower
with petals that unfold to full bloom.

My heart is aching, shaking and quaking
at the sight of you my darling and it always will.

Doris Blazy

Love Died

To my lost love
As I see the women's tears
I wonder what brought such fears
Dreams of a lifetime slip away
Under this sky, so dark and gray . . . .
As she picks up the shattered pieces of her heart
And wonders where to go for a fresh start
She knows it is hard to relearn trust
But she knows someday that she must
So she gathers what is left of sanity and pride
And begins her journey to replace a love died

Mendy Glenn

The Cradle

Coursing streamers of vermilion fire
Rend their way across the depths.
Towering mesas, impenetrably dense,
Yet wispy, ethereal, intangible even.
The Birthplace of stars,
Coalesce into planets.

A whirlwind mass of ice and rock,
Drawn together slowly, inescapably.
The inexorable hand of gravity.
Epochs pass, a world appears.
Hostile and barren,
Refuge to none.

Unstable within, mercilessly pummeled without.
Scoured by radiation from a baleful sun.
On this shattered landscape, alchemy occurs.
Accident or design, it matters little.
Life is resilient,
The universe fickle.

Aaron Samet

Time Is So Slow

She sat on a rock near the billowing sea.
The wind blew her skirt about her knee.
She could vision her young sailor with arms outstretched.
His gestures of love, in her arms she would catch.
She touched the pearls about her waist.
A gift from her sailor with love and grace.
She visioned them dining, with candle light aglow.
She wondered why time is so slow.
It seemed like yesterday when he was taken.
She came back to reality, her mind would awaken.
Oh, how time has passed away.
I am coming to join you one sweet day.
Her eyes searched the sea and the wind did blow.
Her thoughts wondered why, time is so slow.

Florence Brown

"Across from Me"

You took a seat, across from me.
And bared your soul, so that I may see.
You showed me all, held not a thing back.
Showed what you reaped, and what you lacked.
I stared at your eyes, and took in every word.
I smiled and blushed, and head your tales of the absurd.
You told your hopes,
your dreams and your fears.
And anecdotes, that brought forth only tears.
But what I heard, and saw that day.
Taught me why, to keep hate at bay.
For even though we believe, and look nothing alike.
I saw your soul, burst from it's self-made dike.
Our souls have fears, loves and dreams.
They blush, laugh, and even scream.
Our souls are the map, to each other.
The outside just, a meaningless bother.

Andrew Howk

Somewhere

Someday somewhere we will all meet again.
Somewhere in a land of peace and tranquility.
Somewhere where the sun always shines.
Somewhere where the road is always straight.
Somewhere flowers bloom with a fragrance so breathtaking.
Somewhere were no one suffers or goes hungry.
Somewhere were love rules and angels sings.

Patricia Jackson

Dreaming

She appears in my dreams like swallows in spring—
Soft, shiny & beautiful. Simply beautiful.
An Angel.
She appears with a green dress & barefoot.
Dancing & twisting—
Blond hair, greenish eyes, golden thighs,
I look at her.
She's coming toward me, dancing & twisting.
She stops in front of me & looks into my eyes.
I do the same. . . .
Then she puts her arms around my neck.
I put mine around her hips & . . . she moistens her lips,
our mouths get near . . . then . . . a kiss.
A passionate kiss.
It tastes so good. . . .
I touch her thigh underneath her skirt & she smiles. . . .
& then . . . well . . . I love you!

Paulo Segurado

A Mother's Wisdom

This poem is dedicated to my daughters.
She calls on the phone
She asks me,
"What should I do about Jeff?"
I really don't know,
But I pray God, in His wisdom,
Has given me a mother's all-knowing mind.
I'm supposed to understand
Today's mores, today's rules;
So different than the rules I lived by
And I was never that sure of those
But now I'm asked,
And I wish I knew
What to answer
Should I truthfully say, "How should I know?"
Or more wisely say, "Listen to your heart"
What does that mean, anyway?
I wish I had the answers
I wish I understood life's game

Edith Carson

The Poet's Sleep

For poets who never sleep . . .
I copy in words what the eye cannot fathom;
From life to the paper my vision's relayed.
Though somewhat impaired, my strange insights inspire
A poetry otherwise lost and betrayed—
Words come like mysteries to these weary lips
And float quickly downward toward my finger tips;
A loss of an hour of dreams can empower
A strangeness by night from these rough, bleeding lips—
By the light of a silvery moon bleeds perfection
In verse and in rhyme on a slim paper sheet;
Elaborate webs of a fortune now telling
Of horrors, emotions wakes up from its sleep—
A nightmare unfolds by the dim candlelight;
Anxiety rises, adrenaline streams—
By night I abandon reality's truths
For the fantasy-visions and wide-awake dreams—

Kelly Gendreau

The Midnight Hour

For Timothy
The midnight hour,
when most of the world
has closed its doors
The midnight hour,
where in my world
my mind is opening doors
The midnight hour,
where in the peace of
the stillness of the night
my mind is free to wander
The midnight hour,
when my mind goes into that deep, dark hole
that is beyond my normal reach
The midnight hour, when I search for hours
and minutes and days to find a reason or purpose
The midnight hour,
when I discover that to the deep, dark hole
there is no answer the midnight hour . . . the midnight hour . . .
where there is only prayer in the midnight hour

Carol Estep Maynard

Spring

The blossoms sprout
The petals bloom
They look so awesome as they blossom
I love the colors
Red as in a rose
Blue as in a blue jay
Yellow as in the hot, warm sun
I smell the wonderful scent of the flowers blooming.

Lori Petrauski

Dreams of Youth

Dreams of then, lived today.
Some dreams fulfilled,
some reside,
disguised in the back of minds.

Inside old closets live hush-hush scenes;
lips smiling, eyes dancing, appetites appeased.
some crying, some screaming,
some shame fear and pride,
disappointments and genuine reason to cry.

Times past shape our being inside.
"Don't wish back."
Dreams give reason for life.

Regina Williams

U Deserve

Is it hot in here?
Or is it just me?
Your touch has done it again babe . . . .
Your kiss has excited, and relaxed me
at the same time . . . .
U've turned my winter storm into the warmest
place on earth!
U've put passion back on my map . . . .
my compass points only to u.
U've introduced me to a new religion that
has quenched my needy soul . . . .
my cup runneth over . . . .
are u thirsty?
U deserve the heavens 4 what u have shown me . . . .
U deserve a romance that paralyzes the lost faith . . . .
U deserve all that u give, and so much more.
May I give u the romantic episodes that u so dearly deserve?

   Wayne Archibald

The Last Freedom

We would be satisfied to touch the sun
if only once before we reach eternity.
We would be happy to run among the stars
and dance on the moon
while chasing our crazy, inept dreams
shadowed before us in the distance.
We would live to climb the tallest tree
and look out upon our endeavors
with that familiar sense
of unexpected blissfulness.
And we would give our souls
to indulge just one last time
in the quiet radiance
of our forgotten fantasies.
We would erase the pain and responsibility.
We would turn our backs on reality.
And for just one moment,
we would be free.
We would be free.

   Amanda McDevitt

Time

Time passes us by,
but you and I don't even know.
It's passing us by
in the blink of an eye,
in a silent sigh.
We don't even see
how it sped by,
'til it's gone from the corner of our eye.
Before anyone notices we're old and gray,
and have but a few precious days.
For time has sped by and now
it's time to say good-bye.

   Regina Placker

Breathless

My fantasies through all the years
are filled with magic, joy and tears.
They speak of loves that cannot be of warm, romantic poetry,
of songs unsung and hopes undone.
And all the fears from which I've run,
of things I've missed and what I need.
Life's too short to feed my greed.
Yet faced with choice, I hear your voice.
It takes my breath away.
Though in my dreams my heart might stray,
with you is where I want to stay.

   Bette Bonitz

black and white life

black against white
she crouches low
feathers catching, holding. . . releasing
each inscrutable fragment of purity.

stone face calm and pale
beneath the snowflake kisses
that cling with a life too brief to count.

curled tight, bone against bone
one ear capturing the depth of nature's cries,
she remains untouched by the chilled embrace—
penetrated by none of it.

colder than the white ice dancing,
colder than the west wind crying—
barely beats the heart she hides inside,
locked in time, hard and frozen
with the immaculate chill of crystal.

black against white
a crow woman presses close to the dead earth—
giving up on seeking answers
becoming instead, the question.

   Rhian Swain-Giboney

Your Heart

So Many stories, of love unbound
I used to think Mr. Shakespeare had his head in the clouds
Then I met you that sunny afternoon, my heart skipped a beat
My heart was yours nothing more then I could say or do
Because when I hold you in my arms
The world it slowly fades and melts away
When I feel your heart beat next to mine
I know now a greater love I'll never find
I'll give you the love that you never thought you'd have
I'm going to be everything you need me to be
I'm not afraid to show you how I feel
This isn't just a dream
I'll prove in time that my love is real
I want to be the air that you breathe
and to always be the only one you'll ever need
and my darling if I should wake in the night
Your sleeping body beside me is the only thing I wanna see
I want you to know that your heart will always belong to me

   Starlene Rumpler

Treetops

How art thou oh maple? Hast thou missed me?
Old friend, many years have passed since
Last I saw thee.

Oh, how we swayed together with the wind in
Your very tops, and as a mother lowers her
Child, you lowered me to the ground.

I will ask of thee oh, maple, have others swayed
With thee? And have they spake of him that was, is,
And will be.

Have they looked from thy heights at the works
Of his hands, and gazed at the glorious carpets
With which he covers his lands?

Oh, how I long to see you again, and to thy
Supple tops ascend to look upon thy brethren,
And speak of him again.

But, if I come unto thee and thou hast grown old
As I, and become harder to bend, perhaps with
Thy children I will ascend.

And if it be so, that I sway with them, ye shall in
Our old age hear my praise of him again.

   Francis Britton

Look to Find

Standing on the dock at the edge of paradise
I can look out into nothing or everything.
The mist is dotted with tiny sailboats,
their masts projecting toward the sky
ready to take on the wind's challenge.
Tiny droplets of water spatter on my face
during my pause to take in the majesty
and possibility of the sea.
What is out there?
My fate or my destiny?
Do I control either?
Laughter comes from a nearby pub
and their joy is something understand.
For it is a joy that I have experienced.
There can be no end to the search.
Like the Old Man and the Sea
I cannot fight the call for me
to be anything or anyone else but me.
Where does my beginning and end lie?
Surely it is not so simple as birth and death.
There must be more. That, my friend, is what I'm searching for.

J. Matthew Warnock

My Alternate Self

I search for an excuse to be happy
I pray for an intervention divine
Under the supine sun, beneath the solemn sky
I reach out for an existence not mine.

My alternate self!
It charters a bird's wings
Flies low to helpless beings.
Dreams an angel's role
Soothes an aching soul.
Raises the sky's veil
Invites a heavenly view.

My alternate self!
How I yearn for it.
For it knows how little I need
To fulfill what I seek
To break free from a constant limbo I am in
Just yearn for it.

Pankaj Joshi

Standing in Line

Standing in line, standing in line.
It seems we spend hours, standing in line.
We go to recess, we go to lunch.
Why always in a line? Why not in a bunch?
I want to be first, but the teacher says,
"No, we must have a line leader wherever we go!"
Well, I was the line leader, but I can't remember when.
I think in a hundred days I can be one again.
So, if I can't be first, I want to be last.
If you're last you go slow, if you're first you go fast!
So when it's time to line up, I move really slow.
And tag on at the end as the class starts to go.
But sometimes the teacher goofs up my plan.
She frowns and then says, "Hurry up there, young man!"
And, oh, I dread the days when we line up by size,
or color of hair, or color of eyes.
See, I'm just a plain kid, neither big nor little.
So no matter what is called, I end up in the middle!
Speaking of the middle, I hate being there.
You get shoved and stepped on, or pushed into a chair.
I don't know what to do about this problem with lines,
'cause everyone I ask says, "It will be fine."
I think what they mean is it won't go away!
Even grown-ups stand in lines every single day!

Deborah Easom

Spring

Winter has left some spots of snow behind
Wild snowdrops want to be kissed by the sun
North wind turned south, is now gentle and kind
All brooks again down the mountains can run.
Primrose and crocus come into flower
Robin and blue tit start building a nest
The source of all life will regain power
And shows you: this time of the year is the best
When days become longer—shorter each night
And nature wakes from a long winter's sleep,
Steps out of the darkness, looks for the light
And gets all the beauty that she can keep.
Follow the circle of nature, don't fear
To break though your frozen crust year by year.

Hildegard Giesen

Tree Climbing

The tall maple tree in the backyard is my childhood—
the tree is slowly dying.
The long, healthy branches that once sheltered me
from sun and snow,
now crack and deteriorate after winter's frost.
Each leaf a wonderful memory of innocence,
now lies in the grass, brown, torn, crushed.
The baby squirrels that played in the tree have moved away
to a nicer, newer home.
I want to climb the tree, to rest upon its branches as I once did.
I have grown, though—
much more than the maple tree has.
Its branches are much too fragile to carry me now.
By the time I figure out how to climb the tree again,
it will be dead.

Maria Karidis

A Single Tear

A tear for the loss of innocence.
A tear for the pain.
A tear for the humiliation.
A tear for you.
A single tear can be for so many things,
maybe that is why we so seldom shed only a single tear.

Sarah Winkler

Night Flight

Metal pinging, singing, driving hard,
Earthbound wings fly night-dark paths.

Cocooned in comfort, body warm,
My mind the pilot of a thousand dreams.

Fears fly by outside this speedy chariot,
I sit amidst the whirring, thrumming
Scope of all my world within.

Fleet-footed dancer midst shrouded realms,
Through ebon gloom, reality no passenger,
No hindrance to self-contained flight.

Arrow straight, I plot my course
My eyes two probing, hopeful sentinels
Of dazzling white.

Ears awash with music, orchestra to
Solitary paths of joy,
My mundane journey now a mission

Through wondrous possibilities,
A universe three feet beyond my flimsy,
Yet impregnable walls.

T. H. Pine

My Long Blond Hair

My long blond hair is so savoir-faire
It gives me such class it gives me such flair
I'm the girl with it all
And I owe it all to Clairol
My long blond hair, my long blond hair
The color's perfect, it's never brassy
It's very chic and very classy
It's always perfect, never a mess
People think it's just fabulous
It's soft and shiny so luminous
Just like diamonds, it's so flawless
It's a masterpiece, a work of art
And sometimes I wear it with a crooked part
My long blond hair, my long blond hair
Oh, I'm having so much fun
It looks so natural, kissed by the sun
So come on girls go full throttle
It's moments away but still in the bottle
Be a girl about the town
And say good-bye to that mousy brown
With your new long blond hair

Steven Billing

On Your Dawning

while you slept in another dimension
i tasted your lips infinite times
blew butterflies on your lashes
synchronized the moons around your being
into one breath
i watched you fall into my garden of Eden
and eat my apple
while i made the sun dance
like a serpent across your caramel skin
'til your dawning
and left you with the
petals of my existence

Nicole Caudell

"The Child 'Garrett'"

There he is full of energy and spirit!

The most precious being of a mother's imagine.

He gives the strength and power to live again.
The only thing a six year old can.

The gift he gave shows unselfishness from his heart to ours.
So we reply . . .

Thank you from the depths of our heart . . .
Mom and Dad

Sabrina Wolpert

Hiroshima

On a lovely day, in lovely families,
Peace was taken away from people.
The darkness was strange and made them scared
Mothers and daughters were set apart.

Men were filled with hunger and rage.
No food to eat, no water to drink.
Bombs led people to their tombs.
The crowd was full of cries and pains.

Things were crushed, things were smashed.
Kingdoms were ruined, nations destroyed.
Things were lost, nothing was left.
Oh, I wonder when it will all end.

Many separations led to desperation.
My freedom, family and friends all gone.
No one to turn to, no where to go.
Oh, my dreams and hopes are lost.

Jennifer Okehie

There Beats in Things a Secret Heart

There beats in things a secret heart,
Where mundane course turns wild and free,
Behind rough walls sometimes scaled,
By the poet's subtle artistry.

And deep within the sounding hollow,
A single beat to touchless trod,
Where fleshy arm of earth upraised,
Can briefly stroke the face of God.

So search poets long for sturdy words,
To fix upon them pattern and rhyme,
Or loose them free as stallions run,
Thus lend us laughter, love, or scorn of passing time.

In all things pulse poetry,
A timid cadence, as if each beat were but the first,
Yet deeper sounds the secret source,
Where unglimpsed souls find respite, in the poet's silent verse.

Lane Shelton

Dreams

I sailed away my dreams in the breeze
A sail of wind carrying me across the wide open seas

The sole blue surroundings, the twinkle of a million eyes
Rolling hills of life offsetting a pale blue sky

I'll go where my dreams take me, where I'm destined to be
An adventure's bold journey, for myself I must see

What new experiences lie ahead, the knowledge I will gain
How I will deal with life, to miss it would just not be the same

But dreams are dreams and here is a thought
Follow them always, but don't forever stay out from port

Andrew Wigg

Questioning Life

I want to tell the world who I am,
    what I am about and why I began.
I want to express myself in a way that is
    memorable.
Just to make a difference,
    both distinguishable and powerful.
Am I too naive to think that the world does
not want the same,
    that I am only one soul,
            only one person,
                only one man?

The world sometimes seems as though a cage,
    as thick bars crowd me,
        sometimes filling me with rage.
Completely out of touch with the reality that
    is true,
is a perfect explanation of why I may become
    so blue.
How could I go about my entire life thinking I am free,
    if in reality I am tamed
                not to let me be me?

Randy Miller

A Lonely Shell

I walked along the beach today,
And found a lonely shell.
Scratched by seas and sands of time,
The heart of an angel that fell.

I too, am a lonely shell,
Scarred by neglect, and seas of tears.
Hold me close, and you will hear,
the angel in this heart tell all its fears.

Bronwyn Renall

Across the Bridge

On the road that I entered to waltz
Came a bridge for my feet to cross
So I pulled out my coin
And gave it a toss and across the bridge I am
Now across this bridge were swarms of bees
But no honey to be found
So I wandered into their cove of hives
Just curiously abound
Only to learn that the bees were mining
In a paradise made for others
But they could not change their nature
And could not know to bother
So I returned and crossed over the bridge
Where my nature forever blossoms.

Albert Sheda

Flight of an Angel

There were days when love was in the hearts.
As I missed her when she's gone.
I dream that our nights are fill with passion
As I look at her beauty I see that it is priceless as a gem.
But as quick as the seasons change,
Our love grew apart like angels with broken wings.
Stars became dimmer and our hearts became empty.
One can ask for forgiveness,
one can ask to give his live for her,
But no one should have to ask if your heart is true.
As we live in silence as two people can
when words are spoken to deaf ears, Angels are hurt
as their wings can not fly them and tears fall from their eyes.
As we say good-bye my heart is broken,
But I can only hope that one day an angel wings will fly.

Peter M. Abrams

The Simple Things

The simple things of life, how marvelous they are!
The close things that we miss, because we look afar.
The wonders God has made, and placed upon this earth;
They are so common place, we fail to note their worth.

The wonder of an egg, the chicken makes so well;
Complete with yolk and white, all packaged in its shell.
How can the chicken make a new egg every day?
A miracle of God, how wondrous is His way!

I see a little bug, a crawling on my floor;
Don't crush him with your foot, but take him out the door.
That tiny little bug, has power to live and eat;
He crawls, he hears, he sees, for God made him complete.

Our world was filled by God, with simple things indeed;
But all are wonderful, and every one we need.
So let us look around, with eyes that understand;
The humble things of life, are all from God's own hand.

Hart Armstrong

Waters Choice

Tears of fiery love, breaks away the stone;
Cracking what this stone once called its own.
Glazing what's left with water, time seems not to take;
Because my rough edges the waves desire to shape.
My strength is no sight against the power of this wave,
But what I can't grasp is why not to hate.
Each time it strikes, it takes with it a stone,
Which takes as its own, as if by fate.
Designed by perfection, deadly sharpness is cut away;
Then returned to the edge where it previously came,
To be collected by the child, who then makes it His own;
Walking over and ignoring the waves, unwanted choice of stone.

Damian Dropmann

To My Davie

More human than I want to be
My third pair of eyes are blind
I didn't want to hurt you
Full of self-guilt in my patented
Dress, silly thing
The back porch always leads to good conversations
How well do you see in the dark?
Specific nights
Something to look at; gossip about
Until the floodlight goes out
Please don't read this
They are all random thoughts
Some mean, some don't
Control your dog
Remember this night forever
Until the book is through
And you must turn the engine
Off to avoid any accidents
You have beautiful lips
Broken synapses are untruthful
Smells like rain, tonight, a thunderstorm, perhaps.
Once.

Julie Wolf

The Riverbank

At the river of lost souls,
I swallowed my mother's child.
My smile was an extension
of my mother's wrinkle,
My tears were the residues
of my mother's wet kiss.
I left.
The child that she adored
lives on the riverbank. I live
in the basement of my mother's dreams.
I am the arm of winter,
the leg of December;
And she hopes that
summer will rise in me, and melt away
the weather worn person who lives in the
basement of her dreams.
My mother is standing by the riverbank
waiting for the sunrise.

Diane Wilbon-Parks

There Be Freedom When Jesus Comes

My chilluns been sole,
My brother been beat,
We's hardly got anything to eat,
But There Be Freedom When Jesus Comes.

Work day and night,
Sun up to Sun down,
'Cause Ol' Massa always around,
But There Be Freedom When Jesus Comes.

Night men come and got my brother,
They say he be dead,
But I ain't afred,
'Cause There Be Freedom When Jesus Comes.

Now when Jesus comes, I'll put on my long white robe,
And I'll wear a starry crown.
You see there ain't gone be no prejudice around,
'Cause There Be Freedom When Jesus Comes!

Adrienne Ware

A Visit to the Farm

Slopping the hogs
falling into the feed trough
Chasing the cats
tripping over the hidden stump
Riding Lottia, the old horse
sailing over her head and into a mud puddle
Casting stones at Pepe, the bull
running and then climbing a big old oak tree.
Picking the biggest, sweetest watermelon
eating it with Grandpa and getting a
stomach ache
Leaving the farm life behind
but city lights I am coming home

Sheree Spears

When You're Grown!

David Marc, you're ten weeks old,
You've changed our lives a lot.
We're glad you came to stay with us,
More than we ever thought!

If hugs and kisses make you grow
Then you'll be ten feet tall.
It's hard to picture when you're grown,
'Cause now you're just so small!

Our thoughts rush on to when you're grown,
We wonder what you'll be?
We pray that God watch over you
That we'll be here to see!

We'll watch and guide you through the years
And hope we pass the test.
That you'll look back and say of us,
"They always did their best!"

Judy Sanders

Courage

Courage is stillness to listen to the voice of the spirit,
and the resolve to be true to that voice,
in all our actions, all our thoughts and all our deeds

Courage is blaming no one for who we are.
Courage is learning from our mistakes
Courage is laughing at our ego for taking everything so personally

Courage is extending our loving awareness to those around us
Courage is feeling superior or inferior to none
Courage is love in action

Without the courage and the resolve
to seek the truth despite the fears,
we shamelessly waste the gift of life, and we remain the living dead

Irene Chalkley

Waiting

I said I'd stick around forever,
However long it took to become your lover
But as the days go by and we both get older
I'm sitting here thinking, how much longer?
I've been supportive, I've been sweet,
But how much longer 'til our lips can meet?
I got the message, you just want to be friends,
But gosh, I'll be sitting here waiting 'til time ends,
'Cause all I want is to be with you,
To breathe with you, live my life with you.
You say that you're not the one for me,
But you rule my dreams, so how can that be?
I may be pathetic, I may be wrong,
But I need to know once and for all.
So please tell me for sure, and I hope that I don't fall. . . .
May I be that shooting star you've been after for so long?

Jason Han

Secret Place of His Presence

In the time of trouble,
You hide me where no one sees.
In the secret place of Your tabernacle,
You are the One whom I seek.

You shall hide me close to You
And set me high upon a rock.
Now my head is lifted up
Above the enemies of strife and mock.

At times I am like a broken vessel;
For I hear the slander of many.
But I choose to trust You, Father,
While so many find this uncanny.

I will offer sacrifices of joy
Forever in Your house,
And sing praises to You, Lord
Shouting "Glory" from my mouth!

My times are in Your hand.
Deliver me from tongues of irreverence.
I call upon You and I cry,
Then You hide me in the secret place of Your presence.

Angela Cogburn

Homeless

You've seen me before.
Did you forget so soon?
I saw you this morning walking your way to school.
But you did not see me then.
For I lay cold and shivering in the alley ways.
Again this afternoon I saw you,
You walked right by then,
Discussing baseball with a friend.
Did you not notice the cup I held?
Or the grimace of pain and sufferance I wore?
This evening your family and you I saw,
Your father in tuxedo looked at me and said,
"That thing should be against the law."
Not until I lay dead next morning did you take notice.
"Poor sinner, died of the cold" someone said,
You shrugged your shoulders and walked on.
No tears were shed for me, or sympathy shared,
You have no feelings, your heart is cold.
And when you die,
There will be no remorse for you.
I will see you once again,
And I will be sorry for you.

Bethany McDonald

Messenger

I swear I heard an angel sing,
But I could not be for sure.
Much to my surprise,
It was you walking through my door.
You said:
I can fly, would you care to join me?
I can show you how it's done.
Have you ever seen the world from far above the sea,
using the eyes of the sun?
And has heaven knocked upon your door to set you free?
That is why they have sent me.
From heaven to earth with the warmest breeze,
I have come to set your mind at ease.
The love that you are looking for lies beneath your skin.
To love one another, you have to love yourself within.
It's time for you to learn how to love.
It's time to stomp down hatred and rise above.
It's time for you to learn how to love.
The greatest power beside the peaceful dove.
Yes, God may be there with all of his might,
But he's too busy deciding wrong and right.

Kenneth Harper

In the Name of a Better World

I dream of a world
where blood is no longer shed
to further someone's political ambitions.

I cry out for a world
where hunger and hate is no more.
Where homelessness is a thing of the past.

I wish for a world
where the guns are forever silenced.
Where the bombs no longer fall.

I beg for a world
where we are at peace with nature,
where we can all enjoy her beauty as a race.

James Mudget

Hannah

Hannah Rebecca is a girl so sweet,
A little girl so unique.
The moment she entered into this world,
We knew she was our little girl.
Off to heaven she now resides,
Always watching by our side.
Our little angel now has wings,
As she flies around and sings.
The tears you shed as you cry,
Fill her dream pool far and wide.
She can do anything her heart desires,
For our love only helps to inspire.
A child's love so innocent and pure,
No medicine could ever cure.
From the doctors, nurses and all the care,
The friends and family that were there.
Every heart will hold a place,
So we can always see her face.
Hannah Rebecca was her given name,
As she came into the world all the same.

Michael Michela

Death of a Star

Tonight, I witnessed the death of a star.
It was like a dot of paint on a piece of paper.
As it bled, it grew, and grew.
Then suddenly—it stopped.
It stood there for a second.
Then—poof!
It's gone to the Heavens.

Melissa Luga

Men, So Many, Too Many Men

Virile men—Studs to Ride
Think of me with your body,
Just do not ignore my long attention span.
Wealthy Men—Benefactors to Survival
Pay for my special expertise,
Just do not demand my true affection.
Hilarious Men—Performers of Life
Make me forget my cares,
Just do not take my familiar melancholy.
Spiritual Men—Rescuers of Souls
Tell me of higher powers,
Just do not command my saintly devotion.
Brilliant Men—Philosophers to Read
Open my psyche with your ideas,
Just do not scorn my novice experiences.
Renaissance Man—Epitome of All
Leave me to slowly drown alone,
Just do not expect me to forget

The Only Man I've Ever Known.

Debbi Lamb

Fairies in the Moonlit Garden

The garden's dew glistened in the moonlight,
As the flower petals opened,
I knew they were there.
They always came in the dark of night,
But they were there.
How come they show themselves only to me,
And to no one else?
Reality defines itself nowhere when they're here,
And they've shown me a great many things.
So now they're gone . . . .
and I shall have no peace again.

Rebecca Baird-Remba

A Song for God

O Lord, You are the Father
'Tis said as I come to pray.
You have given me a life to journey through
And Love to light my way
Through it all, it is all You ask
That in Your Word I do believe
If I give You all the praise and glory, Lord
Eternal life I may receive.
For all the ways You have blessed my life
I humbly bow to Thee
And tonight I pray and I thank You, Lord
For the love You have given to me.
I can do nothing without Your guidance
I am nothing without Your Son
I shall strive to do your will, O Lord
Until my time on Earth is done.
I often feel I do not deserve
To walk with You hand in hand
But I know that is when You carry me, Lord
By the footprints in the sand.

Shawn Pemberton

Drown in Liquor

Drown in liquor
Standing alone in a crowed bar,
Pushing and shoving you never get far.
The drinks are made and out they go,
Bartenders will only smile when you say hello.
Waitresses are running but going nowhere,
Patrons drinking what, they don't care.
The D. J. will play a popular song,
Music will move you, the beat taking you along.
Moving to the beat, your mind slips away,
Leaving your body to dance and play.
Now the music has you, higher and higher you fly,
Leaving the world behind, you begin to cry.
Sorrows are forgotten as the next one goes down,
They will be back when you come around.
The bottle holds no answers for heartaches or fears,
Face your problems, as they come, no pity, no Tears

Carroll Fox

Living Today

Hating is the worst thing that one can
encounter.

Learning about what is right in the world
can set us free.

Loving your fellow man can build wealth
beyond our dreams

Being blind has nothing to do with
losing sight.

True is the way we all should live.

Sherri Diane Wilson

"A Message to Remember . . . "

To His precious Love, He dearly does say,
"Let me into your heart to grow and to stay.

I am the Lord, creator of all.
Without Me, you will surely fall.

Believe in My name. Let My will be done,
and you will live forever with Me and My Son.

Life won't be simple but believe Me it's true,
that there is nothing I wouldn't do for you.

But until you meet Me, your life will be bare.
To live on without Me, why would you dare?

Do I not give all that you ask?
Loving Me in return is a very simple task!

I Love you, My child, more than you know.
And if you love Me, I'll never let you go!"

Remember, the Lord loves you, so do not forget.
For all that He's done, you are forever in His debt!

Erasmo Morales

Cowboys and Indians

On the riverbank she creeps,
The razor grass surrounds her stealth.
To the Indian camp she sneaks,
Her brothers three pretend to be.

Ahead, the muddy Indian camp
Is pitched where the river used to be,
Slopping and sloshing and yowling they tramp,
Their Pro-Keds soaking up the damp.

The future, could their knowledge hold,
A single mom, a shortened life, a killer's
boyfriend, a jail;
Their lives now warm will turn so cold,
Will they still smile and play so bold?

Now the tide creeps in, now the game's on hold.
On bikes they spring as they race towards home.
The game's afoot another time, another day,
When the cold wind blows on the East River Bay.

Lenka Hibbert

Mistress Becca

Give Me Your Heart Your body Your soul . . .
Let Me Know that you have exceeded My Every Goal . . .
Give Me a chance to show you my World Of Love And Joy . . .
Let Me know Your Limits of Desires and Exotic Toys . . .
Give Me Your heart Your body Your soul . . .
Let Me be the One that takes you on That Forbidden stroll . . .
Give Me the power to control Your Fantasies and Dreams . . .
Let Me Be the One to make you scream . . .
I am Here . . . I am Now . . . I Demand that you Bow . . .
I am the window to Your Soul of Desires . . .
I am the Mistress that controls Your powers.
Give Me Your Heart Your Body Your Soul.

Rebecca Stevens

The Winter Has Set

The winter has set
The pawns of the world bend to her grace
As the beauty of withered ensue
Brisk but harsh and leaving
Fleeting throw, passing over those which dwell
Those used, habitually crawl
The world slows

Jacob Chattman

Depression and Disappointment

This poem explains in a unique way how I feel empty inside.
This dark and dead pit
which is called my heart
has four empty caverns
that drip with depression and disappointment

Depression fills me
like a glass
right to the top
until it overflows

Disappointment sneaks up behind me
and stabs me in the back
thousands of tiny knives
determined to destroy me

Katrina Poncek

Inspiration

Shed by Lady Vagabond (11/11/1999)
. . . Countless layers I dive into
while destroying what is left on surface . . .
Aimless destinies
Vanish . . .

I do dare to pass through
translucent rooms of memories,
where every candle looks the same . . .
Sudden breakdown.
Empty caramel box.
I need to close my eyes.

Silent voices
hysterically exile all that is left after
the grasp through the pall.
Liquid world is the final destination.

Blue.

Meaningless words lapse forever
behind the grates of wisdom.
Pine alleys drown in dirt.

Occult link with Inspiration.

Manuela Budimilic

Has Anyone Seen My dad?

I sit on a big cushioned sofa.
The cushions indent like a hungry wolf devours its prey.
I'm wearing my green dress with the pink flowers,
my dad likes that one.
I wait and wait and still no dad.
No corsage, No ride, No dad.
The dance has already started,
in my mind I see people dancing and twirling,
like leaves caught in the wind.
All I see is rain.
But then a man comes from upstairs dressed in a suit
with some flowers tied to a rubber band.
I think this man is kinder.
But he still wasn't my dad.

Stacey Romanelli

Red

Strike a match to the flame, awaken that which burned.
Bitter branches fuel the pain like rage well learned.

Tried to crack the ice, free the heart inside
frozen solid by the lies of the hand-me-downs in time.

Shadows in the dark denied by the smiles,
a society controlled farce believed to avoid the trials.

Awakened by the shots heard across the nation,
death by the lots, yet will it change the hatred?

Jennifer Porter

Fear

Fear holds my hand
assures me
nothing else matters
She keeps me in the dark
in my comfort,
safe and alone
If I'm good
she opens a window
and I get a glimpse
of freedom
but quickly she sees my joy
and her jealously floods me with "what ifs"
so again I return
afraid of the unknown.

Addi Howard

Hide and Seek

If you should run away from me
In strides outracing light itself
Careening through this universe
And down the trails of time
If faster than the fleeing stars you run
Past ancient galaxies
'Til motion falls away and thought alone
Is your companion
And if so far beyond that final edge
You come and find me there
With folded hands and inward focused eyes
Will you then understand?
There is one path
And it is every path
There is one mind
It is the mind of all

Patricia Ryan

Rebirth

As I sit at my window I watch it fall
At first it falls gently and gracefully
Then harder, heavier, almost threatening
Though I know not why, it soothes me
It places an inner calm within my body
I walk to my door and go outside
Sitting down I still stare as if amazed
Still in a trance, I step off the porch
Standing in the mystical rainfall
Letting the cold water wash away my sins
But it washes away not only my impurities
It also cleanses me of my fears
Slowly the pour calms back down
Once there is no more the sun comes out
A rainbow of awe shines brightly
As does the smile upon my face
I feel reborn, holy almost, no longer evil
Baptized in a beautiful downfall
I am cleansed and made anew by the rain

Aquilah Lopez

Love of a Baby

I see your picture but it isn't clear.
I know that you love me and you're near.
Soon you will know the true meaning of love,
because your family will be here to greet you.
In June we will be counting down to meet you.
Maria, we love you with all our heart.
Remember to pass this on when you are ready to start.
Love of a baby is a very special thing.
Someday when you have your own you will know what we mean.

Theresa Santiago

Little People

Hello to all the little people from here to there.
The ones that live in a house, or on a steeple in the air.
To those that are quiet as a mouse, or as loud as a lion's roar.
You will laugh and play together and fall on the floor.
Some little ones have red hair or black,
or maybe you have purple and yellow like the parrot out back.
You all are beautiful and special you see,
some with green eyes, brown eyes or blue like me.
You will all be friends, no matter what,
even if the tigers and bears are after you in their truck!
You will all stand there holding hands. We are friends!
Little people from here to there,
and together we will not be afraid of tigers and bears.
We will make them a friend of ours,
because every one is special and has something to give,
even the tiger who was mad as a hatter
couldn't resist our big smile and friendly chatter.
This is the way your world should be,
as little people become big people living from here to there.
Standing together holding hands,
how wonderful people are from land to land!

Randa Bafia

Open Your Heart to Me

i gave you simply, life and ask only one thing in return,
to love and honor me, to love all unselfishly,
see all that i gave you, take my wisdom and learn,
set your soul free, let my angels guide your path,
your dreams and desires will come true,
for you i cry and bleed, my arms are opened endlessly,
free will was given as compassion,
along with hope and faith,
to live in peace eternally,
share with those who have not,
i will be there no matter what,
to bless and comfort you,
you are my enlightened child,
never will i leave you,
never fear,
open your heart to me.

Lisa Clark

The Messenger

In memory of my daughter, Jennifer (1979–1995)
She came one day just out of the blue
She brought more than her beauty,
She brought a message from above
A message that someone knew they were loved.

On her wings she carried not a thing you could see
But her cargo was plenty and it was for me,
A thing of beauty for my eyes to behold
More precious than diamonds, silver, or gold.

Even though not a sound she made
Her presence was known by spreading her wings,
Over my doorway at night she lay
Her watchful eye protecting me through the day.

When she had gathered her reply to above
And felt she had delivered her message of love,
She took to the sky like a feather in the wind,
To take back my message that I wanted to send.

I will never forget the one I love so dear
And the message she brought will always be clear,
She brought down the message from up above
The message of undying love, the messenger, the White Dove.

Pamela Pleasants

Tears Within

I wake an emptiness a cloud
hugs my body theres no tears
I give I walk alone within my
self I hold my head in shame
my face is moist tears no I look up to
heaven you said you always be here
I fill no presence my heart aches my body beaten
dead am I breathing they dare not crucify me alive
they watch to hear my screams and moans
agony tears no I think to myself
what man shows no tears but
has so much love why do they abuse me so
do they not know this is because I
love them it's near dawn my body is numb
it's like the angles came and took my soul
and left my broken body I'm so cold yet my
heart was still warm he felt it was close
to his time he look one last time to
heaven and he felt the joy of his father
so very close now and a pearl of a tear
scrolled down his face a tear of joy from within

Diane Burke

A Soliloquy to the World

What dark state this world, that
a man's earthly shell decides his worth.
But a shell is nothing more than
a jug that contains the true substance,
and that substance is what makes the
marrow of a man. Hate, Fear, and Loathing
are too commonly swayed by the
shade and pattern of exterior design.
My irony is that I hate hate, as to say that
I cannot hate one type of shell because one
single wearer of that same shell has
committed villainous deeds. To do so,
I would cut myself short of knowing what
sweet nectar that lies within. If only
the world would drink of all
men, then only the poisonous
potions will be cast away regardless
of shell, and all can grow together,
and peace shall show as well.

Christopher Vermette

Conquer and Divide

The stillness of a warm fall day,
Leaves blowing along my pathway,
A cool breeze blowing in my hair,
The innocence of a small cub bear.
Peace within the mind and soul,
Peace is what I dream to know.
The sound of a soft summer rain,
The pureness of love, even the pain,
Above sounds of birds silent in flight,
Noises around me in the still of the night.
All of these so precious to me,
Tell me, why do I feel so lonely?
Surrounded by all of God's wonderful deeds,
Should that not fill all of my needs?
I try to push the emotions away,
And pray that there will soon come a day,
A day that I will be able to say good-bye,
To all the pain hid inside,
Let go of those who cause pain and lied,
A new beginning . . . conquer and divide.

Peggy Cleghorn

As You Say I Do

As you look into each other's eyes and say I do,
There will be a lifetime of happiness
that will get you through.
For better or worse, for richer or poorer,
having each other to hold, to cherish and adore.
From the very beginning to the very end,
you will share a friendship, you'll be best friends.
From this day forward, you'll be united as one,
the love, the laughter, has just begun.
God Bless you and keep you with all your days,
and know that your family and friends
will love you always.

Teresa Langley Browning

"Indifference"

I've pondered the problem to often it seems,
about mankind's indifference and just what it means.
Is it really that terrible? Or could it be good?
Shall we make it a value? Do you think that we should?
"Indifference," you say, "How is that positive?
Why should we be indifferent in the way that we live?"
So this is my solution . . . now hear what I say,
how we'll make a difference in an indifferent way . . .
Be indifferent to color, to age, and to size.
Judge a person by merit, not the hue of their eyes.
Be indifferent to culture, and who we call God.
Instead walk down the same path that others have trod.
Be indifferent to hatred and simply recant.
Give love where it's needed when someone else can't.
Be indifferent to difference.
And perhaps it'll all make sense . . .
Once everyone starts being positive about their indifference.

Kriss Coleman

Winter's Here!!

A snowy day has just arrived,
Take out your coats, we're going outside!
We'll play in the snow and build a cool fort!
Inside, we'll play "Seven Up" and "Order
In the Court!"
We'll build a big snow man, Boy! Will we
Be having fun!
So far yet, this day is my favorite #1!!
Uh-oh! My finger's are stiff, and my cheeks are red!
I'd better go inside before I have to be
Sitting in bed!
Whoof! What a day I've had!
The winter day has rolled by quickly,
Suddenly, I'm feeling sad!
Next day, "Oh, Mommy, can I go outside, please?"
"No honey, you'll catch a cold!"
Uh-oh! I have to sneeze!!!

Neha Agarwal

Call to Arms

As the drummers drum and the buglers blow,
The men arouse from their positions below.
And suddenly as the guards bear the alarms,
It is time now for the call to arms.
The men are clean and certainly all ready,
For it is inspection time and they are all steady.
Their rifles gleam in the hot bright sun,
As the artillery men man the gun.
A shell is fired towards the great fort walls,
And the men are awaiting the officers calls.
They attack very quickly through the fields of glory,
Each wanting to live to tell this story.
As they attack a sniper's bullet is fed,
It fires very quickly and slams into a man's head.
And they attacked entirely in dread.

Taylor Gerlach

Feelings

Feelings of anger,
Feelings of despair;
Feelings of wondering
Why I should care.
Many years have come and gone,
And now you ask for a new dawn?
Why would you care after all these years?
After all the pain, suffering, and tears.
I loved you then as I love you now,
But you are gone and yet somehow
I feel your presence in the air—
Maybe you did love me,
Maybe you did care.
I think about you every day,
So many words I wanted to say.
I guess for now I will have to wait
Until I see you
at Heaven's gate.

Jill Boehle

Silent Pain, Silent Shame

I close my eyes, as I shut the door.
This is too much pain, I can't take anymore.
Words stuffed and choked back in horror.
Feeling blind words and fists-that's terror.
From cradle, to adolescence and young adult,
my life has been beaten, and I remain mute.
I bite my lip and feel that deep fear . . .
Oh, God please no closer, don't come here.
Older now, scars healed form the pain.
Where do we start to break the chain?
Remembered abuse, the silence, the shame,
Domestic Violence is not a quiet game!

Catherine Rouse

ODE TO THE HOMELESS

The night is cold, weary and unforgiving.
Rain soaked streets dampen the spirits
of the living.

No food, no shelter, no warm clothing,
Restless souls gather together,
Their treasures of ragged belongings.

Blacks, whites, yellows and browns,
Truly, poverty knows no bounds.

In a city adorned with highways and high-rises,
It's our society's way of telling our homeless
In your world the sun never rises.

Emir Jose Castillo,Jr

I WONDER

I opened up the book of her memory
Never will forget what she means to me
The sun fades away
The moon is full tonight
I walk the streets alone
Where I once held her tight

and I wonder do you ever think of me
And have you ever wondered why
Do you ever feel lonely and sad at once
And have you ever simply cried

I visit all the places where we used to go
Somehow it's just not the same
All around are brand new faces
Making memories
And playing love's cruel game

James Brewer II

Special Friend

To Carla
She came to me one Autumn night,
Of light and sound she did take flight

Through land and space I have not seen,
She spoke to me through my computer screen

Our chat was brief we didn't have much to say,
But I did find out she came from far away

As time went by our talks grew longer,
And my love for her only grew stronger

I shared my thoughts with her, I shared my sight,
She made me see things, in a different light

We sent each other pictures to see how the other looked,
But it didn't really matter—I was already hooked

Her eyes as blue as the Summer sky,
For her heart I would be willing to die

I may never find out what brought her to me,
A gift from heaven to set me free

She has become my angel, my special friend,
The woman I will love, until the end.

Patrick Coo

Introduction

Listen all that will
To the stories I'm about to tell,
For they are my interpretation of the truth
But the truth all the same.

Enjoy these stories,
They are a part of my life.
Written from true emotions,
Wrought from true pain.

They may not compare
To Yeates, Frost, or Browning
But have a quality
Unique to themselves.

Pass not judgement on me
Or my stories.
Read them with an open mind,
For after all, they are only words.

Rodney Scarrow

Pain

Pain runs long pain runs deep
Pain runs through where dead bodies creep.
Creep creep creep these poor souls creeping through
The deep cloudy night walking clanging crying out.
Pain is in pain is out pain is laying all about. Pain is you
Pain is me. Pain runs through the bride and groom.

David W. Spratt

American Mosaic

Tiny figures sitting in a circle around the television,
flipping through the channels.
The big screen is consumed with different colors and images.
It is not a black or white TV, nor world.
But the tiny figures peer unnoticeably at the set
as if not to see the reality of diversity . . .
An American Mosaic right before their eyes.

When one rides the El train in New York or Chicago
When one flips through the channels of a television set
When one strolls down the sidewalk or eats at a downtown restaurant
Or when one just looks in the mirror,
Then one can truly see, the many different faces of America . . .
A multicultural Society

Sonja Phillips

The Kingdom

People watching in dismay,
Listen as you hear them say
The crooked faces hold the key,
Sneak past them and you'll be free.

Do as we say! Listen to us!
You'll have to know this before you can pass;
Don't try to escape, there is no doubt;
You have no chance; you'll never get out.

They'll trick you, they'll tempt you,
They'll hurt and abuse you;
Don't try and fight it; they'll only confuse you.

Which way do I turn? Which way do I go?
Follow the voices, for only they know.
Close your eyes, you're almost there.
Time only will tell what scars you'll bear.

Open your heart and the lock that binds it,
Down deep in the depths where no one can find it.
Unlock it now and your dreams you will see;
Believe in yourself and set yourself free.

Sarah Abernethy

Utopia

Behind the expressions,
beyond the existence of mankind,
hides fears and unknown capabilities.

Thoughts and feelings that are unexplainable.

The shadow that follows all of us,
is what hides the true meaning of our existence,
the purpose of our lives.

As long as time goes on,
and the sun rises and falls,
we remain trapped in the oblivion of
our self consciousness.

The stampede of thoughts and dreams,
and the ignorance of our society.

Brandi Ross

Forever Still

Forever still . . . my love will be
always yours . . . just wait . . . and see

The plans we make . . .
we shall both partake . . .
future is ours . . .
our love we must not mistake.

A shame it would be . . .
to throw away . . .
this love we feel . . .
growing day by day . . .

I wish to be . . .
daily in your life you see . . .
what that means to you . . .
It means to me.

Never to be alone my friend,
always there . . . until the end . . .
Each day dawns anew,
God brought me . . . to you.
I believe we shall never part . . .
two of a kind . . . one in heart.

Lynn Nishida

My God . . . My Quest

Just behind my thoughts
Just beyond my dreams
Beyond Creation itself Is He
With attributes like no other..
He hath no Creator
He hath no Form
He hath no Sex
He hath no Title
He hath no Name
He always was, is, and will be
I know not what He is
Only what He is not
If He made me in His image, then who am I?
Stripped of all my layers what am I?
I know I must love Him
But to love Him I must find Him
And to find Him I must seek Him
This is now my quest!
And when I find Him I'll ask Him "Who am I?"
The answer will set me free!

Manoj A. Bharucha

Love in a Mist

My love for you is in a mist,
but every time I'm near you my heart it can't resist;
I want to let you know how I feel,
let you know that my love is for real;
but there is something holding me back,
maybe the others have something I lack;
this mist is making me weary,
and my eyes they won't see clearly;
I want to let you know how much I feel,
but my heart is somehow forever sealed;
I want for you to wrap your arms around me,
tell me that you'll never leave me,
but I don't know if you feel the same way,
so this is the only way to say what I had to say;
I never knew I was so lonely, until you opened up my heart,
I want you to be my one and only, never want to be apart;
my spirit has gotten so battered,
for I feel so lonely, and if my dreams were all that mattered,
you'd be here with me; but my name I can't reveal,
because my heart is forever sealed;
maybe someday I will tell you how I feel,
and let you know that my love is for real;
but for now it remains untold,
maybe someday I'll have all the love one heart can hold.

Kristyn Newby

Earth Comforts

With wings of flame I take flight
anger, frustration, anguish; in rage I fly.
Tears of blood running down my face
my blood, tainted blood damning it I scream.
Suddenly I feel a longing for understanding.
I fall to the earth fall hard, but in the pain of the crash
the earth gives me the
strength of its wisdom.
Earth encircling me from the impact,
cradling me. The aftershock rocking me,
consoling me, comforting me, drawing into me
its power, its strength.
To keep my feet on the ground.
To work threw my rage with courage and
understanding.
It's comforting me.

Holly Saunders

Why I Love You

Seeing you there that starlit night,
never would I have thought of you to be mister right.
Never had anyone caught my eye like you,
when it happened I was blind to something new.
I said hello like any other time,
never could I imagine you could be mine.
Months passed we grew closer the attraction went away,
you became a friend that could no longer stay.
I had to learn to over come the distance,
in this sorrowful good-bye, there was a difference.
I had never said good-bye to a friend and felt so much pain,
I should have known that a love for you I would soon gain.
My heart told me so that day I met you,
"One day," it said, "This man will be true."
That is why I can say, "I Love You."

Diana Zuniga

You're Gone

When you were there my life was bright,
But now your gone and life turns dark as night,
I liked you so much,
But now your gone and I can still feel your touch.
When you were here with me the stars shown brighter than ever,
But things have changed and now we're not together.
I wish you were here so I could tell you, "I love you,"
But the greatest gift of all would be if you loved me too!

Hanna Hollin

Leah

Leah,
A unique drop of love sent down from heaven
She reflects the light of Christ to Everyone she meets.
The Most Marvelous Sunset envies her beauty; Inside and out.
This drop so delicately placed has graced my life . . .
. . . And so I reach for words to say,
But I stand speechless; Wondering how I became so lucky.

Michael Mercer

The King I Am

Hey You there selling death from the shadows.
Yes, You there, pushing drugs on the street
Before you lose your immortal soul
there is someone that I'd like you to meet.
He is the hope for both You and I.
He sent his only son here to die
For You, brother he' got a plan
and His time is at hand
THE KING I AM
Hey You there, your a killer for money.
Hey sister selling love for a fix
Hey You you sold your soul for rock & roll music
You're falling for all Satan's tricks
There is someone who will give you a hand
There is someone who would understand
Hey you Brother, He's got a plan
and His time is at hand
THE KING I AM

Steve Shanabarger

Thoughts at Sixty

Youth's bright spring has fled.
Youthful dreams and ambitions, now are dead.
The world's allure has past.
The glamour, the seduction, it did not last.
Only nature's beauty perseveres,
As onward march the majestic declining years.
The wise wish not sweet youth's return.
When life's great lessons have been learned.

William Salyers

An Existing Concept

Emotion lies deep within ones self, not just on the outside.
Real emotions are unable to control.
It rears its ugly head when not asked to do so.
So why, I ask, must one have to feel such a thing.

Happiness and Sorrow are just one of many emotions.
The good followed by the bad.
Anger which is unpleasing to begin with, is more often than
not, followed by hatred unto which can become malicious.

Fear, unknown to many can have a severe impact on one's life.
Fear in the minds of some, can bring to ruin one's existence.

Pain otherwise predominately physical,
can induce to becoming emotional.

The one emotion unto which has a lasting affect is Love.
Love comes in many forms.
Friendship and caring for one, is a small example.
The most important kind of love, is romantic love.

The exhilaration and fast heart beating of a lovers touch.
Just a simple gesture of how he makes you feel,
when he's close to you.

Love can conquer all fears, for the time being anyway.

Michelle Robbins

Life Struggles

Life is at times just to hard to take.
It relies on decisions that we choose to make.
It's precious, adventurous, it's sorrow, it's pain.
Sometimes you feel like you're going insane.

We can smile, we can cry, even cry tears of joy.
We can treat life like hell or like our favorite toy.
But, on the day when our life is ending,
We always ask God for a brand new beginning.

Whenever you feel that you just can't go on,
It only seems fitting to start a new song.
So what if life's hard, only we get to choose;
To take it or leave it, to win or to lose.

Thelma Southern

Converging Chaos of Conformity

Puritanistic black and white blend to static
screaming
forced conformity
stripped of color
stripped of faith
blown out like a flame
draining color from my face
I don't feel the same anymore
reaching out, to only fall away
fade out

Kathryn Droske

Double Image

Upon my wall hangs a looking glass
One passed down from mother to lass
It reflects my image though out the room
And makes me feel warm as if in my own cocoon
But as I took the air one day, it was late in the fall,
I glanced at the mirror which hung on the wall
There appeared a picture of a child from the past.
Who was the artist that put this image there to last?
Was it impressed there out of love or put there for spite
Or did she appear on her own in the mid of night?
Is that clouds above her head or an angel on guard?
To make sure this home is safe for his ward?

Upon my wall hangs a looking glass

Charles Sanders

God's Gift

There is a special name for you
It's a name that's like no other
One day I'll know just what it means
To simply call you Mother
But for right now you're Momma
Every minute of the day
I call for you at every turn
As I go on my way

You wipe my nose and dry my tears
Kiss my boo boo's and calm my fears
You feed me, clothe me, change me and hold me
And even though you don't want to
Sometimes you have to scold me

You take my tiny hand
And place it deep within your own
You help to guide me as I walk
You would never leave me Alone

You thought I was God's gift to you
But you were his gift to me
A very special gift of love that everyone can see
D. Renee Kemp

Father in My Eyes

When I was young I lost my faith,
where was this God who could let this act of suffering and pain
be put upon me, where?
Family divided, a wall made of sorrow, where was I,
what was I to become?
You hurt me with your harsh words and angry eyes,
twisted half truths with hints of hate,
am I to be blamed?
A child used as a shield in a game of verbal war,
did you bother to protect me?
Soon the name of Father will leave from my lips,
and not for you my dark prince,
but for the one who came and lifted your fallen shield
and claimed as his crown . . .
the one who now answers to Dad
and calls me not only his son,
but a man.
And now I am the father, but mine will know
they are my jeweled crown
not my shield.
Richard Walker

Frames of Life

Pink-blushed fire moves through icy branches—
Trees—enhancing a perfect sunrise which
I can only see in movie-camera-frame-style
as I pass along each glassy window (with finger prints)
about my house . . .
missing a frame now and then to tie the hat-
strings of a not-so-happy-to-wear-this-hat child.
What frame did I miss this time?
What happened to the one between 2 and 7?
to the one between 22 and 32??
A moon, a sun. A sun, then moon . . .
Round and Round they go, and every morning is
a picture perfect frame, and there's never a
camera around here!
I just want one CLICK!! One perfectly stopped
frame . . . frozen in time . . .
Even though I know the other frames will just
keep on going . . . even when I'm gone . . . .
Tonja Bartlett

Ode to Us

Life is a many faceted jewel

For one to peer endlessly upon

To see the numerous reflections of one

To comprehend those reflections

To encompass complete understanding of them

This is the ultimate truth
Michael Murphy

First Hyacinth

I found the first hyacinth today;
Brave, mauve, tiny thing
Surrounded by sourgrass,
Defying the bleakness of our southern winter,
Thrusting for that long-awaited sun . . .
And I weeded carefully round it,
'Til it shone like a small solitary amethyst-
Hope, in Pandora's box.
Robin Knight

Steps

The way to God is narrow.
 The path difficult.
  Each step
   of this way
    is not
     as easy
       as climbing a few thousand steps
       to a temple.
Smita Datey

Lingering

There's something lingering just beyond
the scope of my consciousness
It's tantalizingly familiar somehow
yet I have no definition of it
Its objective, if any, eludes my intuition
while it arouses my imagination
And, I feel not threatened by its presence
but anxious to know its nature
For I cannot help but feel it's important
to embrace whatever it may be
It's as if I'm frozen in time and space
while waiting for a message
And, I'm not as concerned with what it is
as I am with how I will react
For I want so much to be ready and open
to the opportunity it may provide
Dennis Hopkins

Struggle

Illicit dreams and screams tonight.
They can't wait to see the light.
Cries and whispers in my ear,
I hold back the single tear.
"Help . . . help!" But they freely fall.
I try to grab hold of them all.
Fingers slip and so do I.
Down I go, through the sky.
Ripping flesh and jagged skull.
Retreat again . . . My love's too small.
James Lester

Silence and Strength

She cuts with words that leave infection
she cuts to preserve her own protection
        and I do not reply

The wound festers with grotesque resilience
and infiltrates with incredible persistence
        the effects I can't deny

So I throw myself to the flame
the pain burns pure of any shame
        the infection dies

She cuts with words that leave no mark
She cuts to preserve her lofty part
        and I need not reply

Phil Giangrande

The Mime

Like a mime
Trapped in his imaginary box.
Alone and deserted, with no way out.
Captured by the powers that be.
Voice muffled, too low to be heard.
On the inside, a yearning for communication,
Love and understanding.
Physically present yet spiritually extinct.
Somehow ceasing to exist.
Vacuous and unsubstantial—
A phantom . . .
In search of a soul . . .
Trying to find peace within.

Marisa Britz

Mother

A mother is strict though caring.
A mother is there to catch you when you fall.
A mother is always there for you.
A mother is one that will listen.
A mother is one that will teach you.
A mother is one who will help you with your problems.
A mother is one you shall remember through all the days of your life.

Dawn Diaz

Best Friend of Mine

My best friend is one I can trust
until I die and turn to dust.
When times are tough they'll always be around
To keep my spirits up and to never let me down.
All of the late nights
And all of the stupid fights.
Friends are so close and so dear.
Losing another friend is what we'll always fear.
Now we know what friends are for,
Each day they teach us more and more.
We make it through everything together,
And that is why friends are forever.

Angela Ayers

Hive

I can't wait
I just gotta go
Over the mushrooms
And through the salad forks
Keep pretending it's all okay
I'll be quiet and won't tell
"Good, that's good," he said
"Stay yourself and don't change
Remembering to keep the bees out of your mouth
They sting, you know."

Kyle W. Morrison

Rollercoaster Man

Just a look, I noticed him
Inconspicuous he sidled in, sat easy
Imperceptibly he came

Him standing, arms folded, then outstretched
He emanated its silent power
He gave it to her, a gift

From the arms I crawled, small, naked
A splendid expanse began to unfold
Great white lilies came down
Liquid dropping, fragrant washing, all of me
Into its side I sank, moisturized velvet

Lilac wine I drank, lavender drinking
Bright happy it colored me

In a sudden he became thin, receded, gone
Little girl set free
Playing with butterflies, small like me
Perfect pleasure

In a mist expanse, so sweet, warm, sleeping
Seeping into water, dispersing self

Send me up, take me down
Smack me round rollercoaster man

Kathleen Tepana

What Hurts

The pain I feel deep in my back
 Is strong and fierce and ready to attack
The anger, the sadness I hold within me
is so shuttered that it's impossible to see
I shield myself from all of the world
To hide what's so true and what's so cold
I hate the way I am, and act
Whether you believe it or not, it's a fact
The pain I've felt has killed me inside
But no one can see what I can hide
My heart so crushed so brutally beaten
 It's like this heart is endlessly bleeding
Bleeding the hurt and pain that I feel
But unfortunately these pains are made of steel
So I cup my hands and I hide in disgrace
As if no one can see these tears run down my face
I try so damn hard and yet I fail
So I cover up and hide myself in my shell.

Bridget Richards

Under the Sun

Nameless are forever's children
naked in the eyes of the Earth
seducing her heart
weeping memories in the wind
playing softly
their hearts soaring
ever higher through time
nakedness in nameless places
making love in divine palaces
lost in imaginative creative wonder
creative beings, creating thunder
dancing in the storm
blind through torrents of rain
yet struggling for the light
reciting poems to each other
sharing loves, sharing pains
naked as one, to one another
together under the sun

James Corbett

Waves over Pachan

Sensual swaying,
Flowing softly and gently
Against the earth's atmosphere
Witness the peacefulness
Listen to the sounds of serenity
Many nights I sit and gaze at the clouds
And the moon
And allow myself to hear the nothingness
The faint whispers of the leaves falling
As they touch the ground one by one
My inner thoughts, that I hide from you
Are unleashed and they drop like the midnight
Mist upon my conscious mind
As I close my eyes
The negativity, replaced by the positivity
Penetrates through to my heart
And the waves of untapped knowledge
Wash over me.

Olaniyi Zainabu

"My Father's Spirit"

I saw you standing there a few days
   after you had passed away. I wasn't
   sure what to do or what, if anything
   I should say.

I lost you so early in life, before
   you were able to see me grow. I went
   from your little girl, to a woman
   who still doesn't understand why
   the Lord chose for you to go.

I miss you so deeply, after all
   these years. Still I cry, after all
   this time. I wish you were here to
   help me with my fears and wipe away
   my tears.

To my Daddy whom I lost at an early age,
   many years ago, I love you.

Angel Larrabee

Mother's Song

There is a strong wall around me to protect me.
It is built of the words you have said to me.

There are swords round me to keep me safe.
They are the kisses of your lips.

Before me goes a shield to guard me from harm.
It is the shadow of your arms between danger and me.

All the wishes of my mind knows your name.
And the beats of my heart
They are all because of you
The cries for completeness
That is a cry for
My Mommy

Mike Avery

The Doll

My daughter wants to buy her cousin a black doll
I am white, my daughter is white, the cousin is white
My daughter has a black doll I gave her
Color means nothing to my daughter
She only sees beauty in the doll
I shuffle my feet in embarrassment
How do I explain the cousin's mother won't understand?
The mother will consider it an insult
I gently make another suggestion
And hang my head in shame

Barbara R. Robertson

Music Can Open Windows of the Mind

Music has a magical effect on the mind.
It seems to open the windows of the mind
then it flows through the corridor ever so
softly and stimulating. Music brings calmness
and pleasure to the mind. It can cause the mind
to travel from city to city or country to country.
It will cause the mind to soar into the outer universe
where no one has ever gone before. Music is a powerful
force that can cure anyone physically and mentally.
When the mind is excited and calm the body's healing
process seem to speed up. Music can control the mind
both negatively and positively. It can bring sadness
as well as joy and happiness. Music can fill the atmosphere
with enchanting vibrations that promote dreams and ideas.
Music can cause the heart to pulsate and tremble with fear
and total bliss. Yes, music can open many windows of the mind,
especially those of our youth today.
MUSIC CAN, MUSIC WILL, AND MUSIC WILL
FOREVER BE MY OPEN WINDOW OF THE MIND.

Monica Lane

Cradled in the Arms of Jesus

When someone, a loved one, passes away.
There is a silent prayer I always pray.
May they be cradled in the arms of Jesus.

The family feeling the deepest of despair,
Must remember our living, loving Lord is there.
Your lost one is cradled in the arms of Jesus.

God gave us His only begotten Son, for a short time.
And we are here for only a short time, may I remind.
Then cradled in the arms of Jesus.

To dust we return, for from dust we came.
When God calls us, we can not here remain.
Knowing we'll be cradled in the arms of Jesus

We are the colors of the of the world, from birth to end.
We are God's rainbow, after our visit here He'll send
Us to be cradled in the arms of Jesus.

We feel the pain of that old rugged cross.
A stirring symbol of man's loved one lost.
Tenderly cradled in the arms of Jesus.

Please, ease your tearful deepened despair.
Your lost loved one, is watching over you, up there.
Safely cradled in the arms of Jesus.

Michael Iannone

Inside

The days fly by when I'm alone.
It's like being sanded from a gem to a stone.
But you don't know that about me,
'Cause I keep my feelings hidden away
where people can't see.

I keep my feelings locked away,
And though I smile on the outside
there's a part in me that cries.
And though you wouldn't guess it,
it still is alive.

Being alone is the truth that I bare,
And though I don't want to face it,
it stands right there.
So, I'll continue to wear the mask you see,
and be the one that isn't me.

Amanda Rule

Passed Over

I was slapped in the face by a leafy bough
Stanched with blood. The crisp hyssop ricocheted,
Twisted in my hand,
And beat my face and shoulders.

My blood mingled on the branch and fell
In a five foot circumference.
Encircled, I knelt and wept.
I hurt as a fallen yew tree endowed with magic.

My face crushed to the cement.
I listened through my eyes and nose.
Hearts drummed along my belly,
And my toes plowed two four-inch deep troughs.

I drooled my quilt 'til empty,
And rested, I probed to hear
A gracious quiet.
Why had I been spared?

Timothy Garrett

The New Moon

In the blue-black sky of middle night,
Stars scatter in spilled grains of light.
Clouds cross the half-moon
In schools of mist and wind,
Bringing dreams to sleeping birds
Who stir and cry and return to sleep.
Down the velvet bowl of night
The Leonids scratch golden trails,
Crossing and re-crossing, weaving in and out
Across the pale moon dying in the east,
Rising against a false dawn's glow—
The new moon lying in the arms of the old
As I lie in yours in sleep.

Sara Mickel

Pause

Turn back the hands, rewind the years,
catch all the lost and lonely tears.
Store them back, behind your mind,
this is not the place, you've not the time.
Take my hand, it's not to late,
scorn and fight the sword of fate.
They can't tell, nor can they see,
the worth of life in you and me.
Step past the line, take a chance,
find, perfect, life's twisted dance.
I beg you please, ignore there voice,
put your heart in every choice.
The world may go, in just one breath,
make sure you live before your death.

Jennifer Heath

Reflections

Looking back I can see,
Reflections of love, you gave to me.
Your heart, my heart they are one.
You brighten my life like the morning sun.
You brighten my day, you brighten my night.
You fill my heart, with love and right.
You pick me up whenever I fall.
You give me strength through it all.
When I was down, you were there.
You showed me love, you showed me care.
In your love I found the strength,
To meet all the odds, to go any length.
In your eyes, I can see.
Reflections of love you give to me.
In my life I hope to be,
As strong for you, as you are for me.

Gary Rich

Another Day

Bright sunny skies shackled to the glistening morning dew.
Transforming the darkness into the Light of a day brand new.
Each new day carries beacons of hope.
The promise of another chance to feel joy.
The Fresh newness of the day offers yet another way to cope.
We awaken to the challenges that lie in this new day.
The offering of loveliness.
Far from our Deep Dark past.
Though we cannot throw those memories away.
Open your arms to prosperity and success.
Look into your own eyes and see not distress.
Put away those evil damning thoughts.
Let the goodness in you overtake the nasty deeds.
Let your love flow and spread like weeds.
Allow the new day to supply all your needs.
Let us be thankful for the beauty of another day.
For in it lies the promise of love and life.
Embrace its possibilities.
Cherish all it offers.
Relish your existence and stay for another day.

Virginia Gassmann

To Our Angel: Mason Nicholaus Schmidt

Little baby
you'll always be the angel
we couldn't touch
but forever hold in our hearts.
Little baby
you'll always be the angel
we couldn't make memories with
but forever, lovingly remember.
Little baby
you'll always be the angel
we never had a chance to care for
but forever love.
and,
Little baby
you'll always be the angel
who isn't here to fill our days
but forever fills our lives.

You'll always be loved and remembered, Mason.

Anne Schmidt

"Manuel"

To Luis Manuel Torres, December 1, 1975 to December 22, 1998.
The sun doesn't shine in my heart anymore;
there is no joy in my eyes.
My head doesn't hang quite as high as it used to
my mind is going awry.
Every morning when I wake
my soul begins to ache as soon as I think of you.
I miss your smile, your laugh, I long to hear you voice every day.
You touched my heart and soul,
and in my memories I will never let you go.
From the first day we met until the day I said good-bye
you were there for me, you were a true friend.
I will never forget the time we had together,
whether it was the laughter or the pain.
You will never know how much I yearn
to see you once again.
We all loved you my dear,
and we will all miss you until our ends,
when we are reunited once again.
I will see you again some day;
I will meet you in the clouds, when I go away
from all this pain, I love you.

Johanna Otto

Love

Love is in the air
Love is everywhere

You can't feel it
You can't taste it
You can't touch it
But you know it's there

Holding hands, hugging and kissing
Is that real love?
No, that is not real love

Real love is what you feel deep down inside
The kind of love that you just want to hide
But you sometimes can't

Real love is what's in your soul
The kind of love that makes you feel whole

Real love is what makes your heart beat
Real love is what keeps every single one of us alive

Samantha Wong

Suicide

My body is racked in a shiver of pain
I know that my fighting has all been in vain
So I sit down and think how they've cried
I can't return 'til my own tears have dried
I pull in breath deeply and turn to go back
I know courage and strength are what I lack
My friend sits alone looking so lost
So I walk towards him, and think of the cost
I sit down beside him, take hold of his hand
He stares at the ground and draws things in the sand
I squeeze his hand gently, and wipe away his tears
I can see he is hurting and holding back his fears
He wraps his arms 'round me and lays down his head
I know he is hurting, his best friend is dead
He tells me he thinks everything is his fault
As I listen to him, time seems to halt
I explain to him there was nothing he could do
I thought for a while it was my fault too
But suicide is a choice made by one
And the actions which unfold can never be undone

Meghan Murray

Life after Death

Shut the lights, Close the blinds,
Keep your silence, Close your minds,
Let go of the world around you.

Turn all smiles into sneers,
Turn all laughter into fears,
Let go of the world around you.

Tell the sun to quickly set,
Tell the moon to take a rest
Let go of the world around you.

Tell the sea to stay asleep,
Tell the trees to stand up neat,
Let go of the world around you.

Tell the guard to retrieve his crown,
Tell the emperor to try and frown,
Let go of the world around you.

Tell his father to be patient and wait,
Tell his father to forgive all hate,
Let go of the world around you.

Shut the lights, close the blinds,
Keep your silence, close your minds,
In the darkness, open your soul,
Only in the darkness, can one become whole,
Let go of the world around you.

Marlena Commisso

Wonder

I often wonder about my life,
was I polite, was I nice
with my friends, my fellows,
and our universe?
Did I care for the penniless,
or for the hopeless, or the elderly,
My words meant to be sweet and pure?
Did I hurt anybody? Or harm anyone at all?
I often wonder about my life,
what kind of person I really was . . . .
But it is not for me to say, you, my friend,
that know my soul will be the judge to tell.

Prince Ageret

My Dad, My Guiding Light

He is my dad, my guiding light,
　Who has always been there day and night.
Yes, he is my lighthouse,
　He is built on stone.
He is the reason,
　I never had to sail alone.
When Seas got rough,
　And I didn't think I could take it.
There was my light,
　Saying yes we'll make it.
He is the one that steers the way,
　If it's night or if it's day.
Yes he has been my lighthouse over the years.
　Through all my laughter,
Through all my tears.

Donald Cooper, Jr.

There's Always You

I wrote this poem in San Francisco while gazing across the Bay.
The fog hangs heavy o'er the Bay,
the buildings out of sight.
The humid air, thick, misting rain
predicted now throughout the night.

I lay my head upon my pillows
supporting thoughts of yesterday, tomorrow.
I dream of closer days and nights.
But in my dreams, there's always you.

I may not know where I am in these
and each dream leads afar
from current chores and countless times,
I whisper low your name.

When mornings light is warm, I wake
longing to go back again, to dream.
I'll go on through the day and hope
it's short and that the night does bring

more thoughts of you, more dreams to keep
more challenges between my sleep.
Tonight I lay alone, again, and hope
that within my dreams, there's always you.

Suzan Uhde

"Little Kids"

Cover each other in dirt from head to toe,
Mommy says, "We make her sick!
And she's not bathing us. No! No!"
And I thought that my oatmeal
looked good in William's hair.
But Mom says, "James! Get off the table!
And sit down in your chair!
Just look at you!
How did you make such a mess?"
Well, I guess we kids are good
at it. In fact, we're the best!

Dewell Edwards Jr.

Life's Inspiration

Life's richest lessons are found in nature,
Can we try to emulate them in the future?

The trees standing tall and straight,
Inspire dogged determination and the confidence to be great.

The lush green grass gently swaying in the breeze,
Soothe and keep our shredded soul at ease.

The bubbling brooks so pure and crystal clear,
Remind us to bring joy to those we hold dear.

The rainbow, the morning dew and the snow on the mountain slopes,
Teach us to admire, appreciate and have hope.

David Vadala

First Day of Fall

The leaves are still on the trees
It's not really fall just yet
But your heart pulls you out the door
It knows the time of year

Wander aimlessly around the yard
Chasing a little girl
You can't put your finger on the happiness
It's almost painful joy

Remembering those that are gone
A candle burns on the table
You make excuses for your silly grin

Wishing the day would never end

It feels like the first day of fall

Scott Mcpherson

To Be Left Behind

I sit here alone gazing through the window,
Watching the gentle snow in all my sorrow.

The days slowly move in and out,
How many have passed I can't count.

Life without you it is so unkind,
The thick flow of tears leaves me blind.

The pain and the sorrow are so terribly real,
I pray they are not all I will ever feel.

The memories of you I shall have to treasure,
There for the children without measure.

Yet in my heart oh, so much love I find,
Though death chose me to be left behind.

Madelyn Hollis

Birth, Life, and Purpose

We are all of us born!
Born out of the dark comfort of the womb
into the world of light.
Shocked by that entry, crying in fright.
Soothed by a loving mother
nurtured at her breast,
our fears are put to rest.
But, life is just beginning
and there are many tests.
We live, we grow,
we learn, we yearn,
we work and strive
to say alive.
Some of us live for just a fleeting moment in time,
Others live a long productive lifetime,
while others are not productive at all.
Is it by chance or God's design?
To what purpose is this life
of yours and mine?

Ronald Thomson, Jr.

Why

I'm sitting here and I'm wondering why,
Why you're gone and why I cry,
Why I will never see your face,
Or feel your loving warm embrace.

I'm sitting here and I'm wondering why,
Why it was you that had to die,
Why you left us that Saturday night,
Why you went towards the light.

I'm sitting here and I'm wondering why,
Why we had to say good-bye,
Why we'll never see you again,
I lost my mother and my best friend.

I'm sitting here and I'm wondering why,
Why you're not here I think with a sigh,
But then I remember the good times together,
And how much I love you right now and forever

So when I sit here and I wonder why,
I just go outside and look up at the sky,
And I know you're there smiling down at me,
Because we'll meet again you just wait and see.
I LOVE YOU, MOM.

Karen Thorpe

Dreaming

Deep in slumber is where I like to be
Dreaming the dreams that set me free.
I fly through the skies in the black of the night
Over the treetops as high as a kite.

I sail over mountains, and canyons, and seas
I soar through the valleys, and forests of trees.
I can wing like a bird, and shine like a star
I can race with the wind no matter how far.

I can orbit the moon at the speed of light
And return to earth at the end of my flight.
Though my eyes are closed and I don't make a peep
I can do anything when I am asleep.

So should you find me sleeping with a smile on my face
You'll know I am dreaming of a wonderful place.

Jan MacMillan

beautiful land

once there was a beautiful land
and here in this spot it did stand

now the land stands as a city
and it looks so very grisly

cars and trucks go passing by
echoing a sound that makes me cry

now the land that I held dear
is a land holding many fears

every time I look around
I have a feeling I will be chopped down

my leaves are falling
worse than Autumn

for let them take my wood to shred
it will make a color of red

just remember me at my stump
because I will be a little lump

bye I have to leave—a sound of silence for the tree is dead—

(The moral of the poem is please don't litter, and help our trees,
we need them like they need us.)

Krystal Murphy

Always and Forever

For those who know Love can be for Time and Eternity . . .
Always and Forever shall I love you
With a heart pure and filled with the perfect love of Christ
Always and Forever Shall I be by thy side
To hold you when you need strength and courage

Always and Forever shall I see you
As beautiful as the first moment we met
Always and Forever shall I find
My heart beats faster whenever you are near

Always and Forever shall I need you
For without you my soul is bleak and barren
Always and Forever shall I stand true
In my faith in God and the Heavens because of you

Always and Forever shall I love you
As one day we shall hold our newborn in love and awe
Always and Forever shall I cherish you
And our love will stand bright and pure and true,
Always and Forever

    Mark Pointer

Think about Me

When you are happy or sad
When things seem to come to a halt
When you are disappointed and discouraged
When you find yourself helpless and needing a friend
Take a moment to think of me, I am your miracle
I will put back the smile on your face.

When you have done all you could and
Nothing seems to work no matter what.
When each stroke you take seems to drown you deeper in despair
When you are tired and ready to give up
Think about me. I'm the rainbow at the other side.

When the world falls around you
When you feel like running away without looking back
When your emotions are all caught up
And you can't control your tears
Stop for a moment and think about me
I'm the rainbow in the mist of your tears
You will always find your way to me through the clouds
'Cause I'm the Angel of Miracles.

    Alexandra Quist Christopher

Just One Drink

Looking all around
Amazed at what she found
She saw people she knew everywhere
And all around she heard, "It just isn't fair."

The girl stood behind her dad
Wondering why everybody was so sad
Carefully peering over his shoulder
Suddenly her heart felt like a boulder.

What she saw just wasn't right
Proving everything can change in one night
She saw herself staring into space
Nothing but fear etched in her face.

Thinking as hard as she could
Trying to remember where 15 minutes ago she stood
She got into a car, knowing it was wrong
Forgetting her parents, and not being strong.

Now her life has come to an end
Many events she is unable to attend
Now sit back and try to think
Is it worth your life for just one drink?

    Danielle Conner

Pets

I have a raccoon and a poodle too.
They live inside, just like we do.
Three cats, two dogs, even a goldfish.
We are all one family with the same wish.
The dogs and cats live outside, you see,
It's easier, for Pooh, Cooney, Hubby, and me.
The two dogs are big, messy and large.
They guard the house, the yard, and the car.
They wish too, the others, I mean,
The same as me, Pooh, Cooney, and, Hubby, the king.
That our house had more room to play a bit
To laugh and sing, or just to sit.
If it were bigger and more like the yard,
We would all be happier, much happier by far.
To have them here is all that I dreamed,
More room would be nice, not that it seems,
To be any closer is not our wish,
More space we need for us and the fish.

    Lena Boyles

A Summer's Eve

A peaceful evening in Northern Ontario
The sky so vast, did cast a light
With streaks of pink clouds,
Like candy floss running through.
The breeze was slight as birds took flight,
This was an awesome summer night,
The pines in all their majesty bowed
their tops, as they did sway—
It was the end of a perfect summer day!

The flowers on the deck with their delicate scent,
Also claimed a day well spent,
As the sun went down o'er the horizon,
It left a glow of coral, casting a pink hue
into the water,
As the peace of the night set in!!.

Author Barbara June Richards, Ontario Canada

    Barbara Richards

Red Rose

*A sonnet of fourteen lines with a final,
independently rhymed couplet*
By the window sadly sat Romeo
Looked outside and smiled, thinking of her eyes
Innocent as she seem, don't believe her lies
Her small crystal heart no arrow could blow
Scheming ways seem now so dull, friend or foe?
Rain falls defacing puddles— mesmerize
No more will he trust her, no more love ties
No control, he's free to get up and go
While by himself, his lonely cries, soft dreams
With another she spends dark quiet nights
Drawn to him, why? Purity not it seems
Long-stemmed red rose at his feet, his frown lights
Intended for her with a proposal,
Internally he at her disposal

    Irina Dymarsky

My Love

As the seasons change,
My Love for you remains the same.
Fall and Winter brings cold weather but,
My Love for you is hotter than ever.
Spring and Summer brings, "New Beginnings,"
My Love for you is never ending.
You see, no matter what the season,
Loving you needs no reasons.
All year long, loving you is unique,
Thank you for making My Love complete.

    Vickie Daniels

Falling Down

If ever you feel like you're falling down,
and you keep getting pulled underground,

If ever your wings should disappear,
split,
crack,
Fall far or near,

If ever your heart bears the weight of the world,
your memories fade and laughter unfurls,

If ever you feel like you've lost your mind,
and when you turn to look
the sun won't shine,

If someone close becomes someone new,
that's okay at least there's two.

Every true
Every wrong
What is weak
What is strong
All the light
And darkness, too
Will one day make sense to you

Nathan Twomey

Life without a Father

Life was once good,
in my young childhood.
My father left my family and me,
when I was only three.
Now I am thirteen,
I wonder if he's nice or mean.
It makes me mad,
When other kids talk about their dad.
I want a dad who cared,
and would comfort me when I'm scared.
I haven't seen him forever,
my mind thinks more than people like treasure.
I wish he would realize,
that I am not a thousand lies.
every child needs one.
IF they don't they feel like their life is on the run.
I wish he would see,
that he means more than anything to me.
I wish I would meet my real dad,
because it makes me very sad.

Felicia Peterson

My Sensuous Love

My woman is sexy
With incredible good looks
She's the kind of woman
You can't find in books

Wedding awaiting . . . Matrimonial bliss
Loving her tenderly, I feel like a king
Here's to the woman
Who is my everything

My lady has all that I need
In life
She's my mistress and lover
My beautiful wife
She's gracious and loving
Lover and friend
When it comes to kissing
There is a beginning, but no end.
My sensuous love!

Gerald Castleberry

I Wonder

I wonder what it's like to walk on a cloud,
And to be eye to eye with the sun,
I wonder what it's like to sleep on a cloud,
And smile at the moon when the day is done.
I wonder what it's like to fly with the birds
And feel the wind going through my hair
Soar through the sky and write some words
And breathe the freshest air
I wonder what it's like to walk with God
And talk to him every day
I wonder what it's like ask him questions
And here what God has to say
I wonder what it's like to shake hands with an angel
And hear the beauty of their song
And I wonder what it's like to live in perfection
In a world where nothing is wrong
I hope to be in this world someday
In that world of happiness
And I hope someday we will be together
In that world of untamed bliss

Terrance Barnes

Not Even Alive

When I die no one will notice,
I wont have a funeral with lots of people,
No coffin, no flowers, morticians, or guest list,
Nor blessings from the faithful.

I can't love,
I can't cry,
I never lived,
And now I die.

Mom, please think it over,
And please think carefully,
Don't put me through this torture,
I can live without a daddy.

So, Mom, please give me a chance,
I really want to survive,
I won't be much of an expense,
I just don't want to die without being alive.

Johnathon Pfleger

What Should My Shipwreck Be?

What should my shipwreck be?
Deepen my roots in the dark earth
For we are without sea
Just hospitals and mountains that surround
time stood still
Where I stare out through veils three years thick
To see kenosis with machine guns marching into town

Life has become
Intractable war death waste
Piety every day a little darker, a little hungrier
And days of rain when we loved one another
now only days of days, months of months
The country is a prison war field
My exile in Kabul

What should my shipwreck be?
Appertain me to my people, for we are without sight
Inherit shrapnel spoken and inhaled, bleeding
Through veils three years thick
And heavier than future could carry
And yet, woman will carry the future

Alexander Traitler Espiritu

Silence

Silence, sweet silence.
The time of day in which life seems so meaningful.
The movements are so slow,
that not even the oddest of people can destroy it.
You clear your mind,
and all the worries that seem to haunt you disappear.
Then you realize that not only you are at peace,
but so are your enemies
who seem to have given up,
and you are crowned winner.

Laura Gibbens

Just Ask Your Children

Parent to parent, I know who you are
A Mother better than most, better by far
Ever loving, ever caring, inspiring to see
Your old-fashioned values of love and family

Putting your children first, no second thought
Giving your heart and soul, as all mothers ought
Teaching and guiding your children each day
Encouraging and supporting them in every way

Cherishing your children in both words and deeds
Instilling values, the kind every child needs
Investing time in your children, for time is real love
And loving without end, as from heaven above

So, beautiful lady, I know who you are
A Mother better than most, better by far
Unyielding love, a child's dream come true
A special day it was, the day God created you

A special day it was, the day God created you
    (Just ask your children)

Wayne Drum

Daddy's Home

I hear your keys in the door
I come crawling as soon as you feet hit the floor.
You pick me up from the ground
Now I'm in Daddy's arms all safe and sound
I make you weep out of joy
As I say, "Da Da" your my big toy
Come play with me Daddy
I long for your touch
I can't tell you yet, but I love you so much
"Where's Da Da?" you say
I know around the couch, no the other way
I'll catch you Daddy just wait and see,
and when I get there just hold me

Rennise Gunter

Friends to the End

We've been through a lot in the past few years .
But it's comforting to know you'll shed no more tears.
You always knew the right things to say.
It's hard to believe you're not here today.
Each night I lie awake and sigh,
Just wishing we could've said good-bye.
You lived each day as if there was no tomorrow.
Knowing you were prepared soothes my sorrow.
I'm having trouble realizing you're gone.
But no matter what your memories linger on.
I know that you'll greet me with open arms,
For where you are you fear no harm.
You brought joy to everyone around.
It's great to know a friend in Jesus you've found.

Kandi Turner

Wondering

As I sit here on my bed.
Many thoughts run though my head.
Will I see tomorrow?
Will it be filled with happiness or sorrow?

Will I see the sun kiss the sky?
Will this be the last time I say good bye?
Will I make it through the up coming days?
Or will I drift off into a heavenly haze?
Would it be the last time I would hear my parents say,
"I still remember that time when you were in that one play"
Then they would just laugh and grin.
As they would sit and caress my skin.

I am still sitting on my bed.
With many thoughts still running through my head.
As I am wondering what is to be.
I realize the only one who will truly know is me.

Ashley Stoner

"An Albanian Boy" (Kosovo)

I'm a little boy,
Whose world is covered with smoke.
With two bodies indifferent,
Both wanting control.
I live with a family,
Desperate, in need.
Being the effect and result of this battle.
As my heart continues to bleed.
I cannot say security or peace,
I cannot be what I want to be.
I cannot try to improve or progress,
Without being given an opportunity.
I cannot determine my destiny,
I cannot say I deserve what is right.
But I can prevail and succeed in hardship,
As long as I know I fought my fight.

Ebenezer Concepcion

Thy Love

There is no greater LOVE than this . . .
All in green went my love riding
Riding on a great horse of gold
Into the silver dawn
Like casting pearls unto pigs
Have I thrown my love unto a fool
To be tread and tramped underfoot

Child of scorn, assailed of the seasons
Thine is contempt, a haunting spell
Trailing the trend of thy life
A shadow in the night!
Wilt thou not come to thy senses
And know love . . . Love . . .

Hurled upon a log, hammered to a cross
Crushed by the weight of the sins of the world
Love grew, welled up and spurted upon the nations
A stream of life flowed from Calvary
Can't you see, see thy love ablaze on a ragged cross?

Edwin Kutuso

A Falling Leaf

A swift wind blows across a forest of trees
and only a single leaf shall fall.

As it tumbles to and fro
it has yet a place to go.

Leroy Thomas Jr.

eternal dream

she is lost and confused
from many years of being abused

she loves her mom and her dad
but they wish she they'd never had

they beat her with a long handled broom
they locked her in a small dark room

her mind is strong she will not scream
she slips away into a dream

a dream with beautiful singing birds
no mean creatures no harsh words

big chocolate cakes of creamy delight
no more fear no more fright

this is the dream that she does make
she longs for the day when she will not wake

Chris Craft

Trusted Friends

How could I have been so wrong to trust the words of friends.
To put my life within their hands and expect them to understand.
My thoughts my fears my hopes and dreams lied within their reach.
I expected them to help me out in my time of need.
I had the final word on this I must admit.
I made my choice, my bed to sleep on this I will regret.
Now the time of truth has come for me to accept the part I played
But where are they the friends I had
They all just walked away . . .

Bonnie Maiello

When You Needed Me

When you needed me,
I needed you more
When we were together we wanted more,
When you said, "I love you" for the first time
That scared me,
But when I said we should see others,
That scared you,
But that didn't tear us apart
But now you're gone
And you've left me with fond memories
I wish you were here to wipe away my tear
But I have to go on and have no fear
Knowing we'll be together one day soon
Taking one day at a time,
Now I won't rhyme,
But it's time to say good-bye for now
And for me to say, "I Love You"

Carrie Kryder

Love

An emotion that has escaped many,
This is usually misused by people,
Just a word it looses all meaning if any,
When true two people may land in a steeple.

The first will live forever in our heart,
Never aging with the time in our thoughts,
Not everyone can always be love smart,
This is why first loves are not often caught.

When it is true it gives you wings to fly,
It's a two way street for love to travel,
True love no matter what shall never die,
When love meets you jump up and say, "Ya Wohl!"

Love loss can be the hardest thing in life,
It can make you feel like you want to die,
As though someone has stuck you with a knife,
But love will come again and let you fly

Kristopher Gordon

love

what is the true meaning of love.
does anyone know the true meaning of love.
love is the whole universe.
love is when you have family that love you.
love is when you have friend who love you.
to find the real definition of love
you have to fine inside of you love comes within the person

Roger Rodriguez

Deceitful Games

Innocence your strength is straining,
forgotten tears fall down tear stained cheeks.
Sucked in again,
lured into false truce,
by weakness and manipulation.
They play this petty game,
helped only by indecision.

Spun in circle and left to crawl,
They watch . . . But,
they'll not see you fall.
For your far stronger than them all.

Aleta Gray

Awaiting the Bolt

I am a lightning pole.
I have sat, thus perched
As God searched
For spots to hurl his lethal bolt
I have watched and waited
Seems I never was fated
To be the bull's eye
As hard as he might try
I've seen men fry, and darkly die,
Everyone but I caught his baleful eye . . .

I call myself a poet
(and try never to show it)
But sometimes I wonder, at the sounds of thunder
If the lightning flashes
Aren't the words I seek
When all inspiration
Is flickering weak
I also wonder, as metaphors meander
If I am really a lightning pole
Cast in a struggling poet's role.

March Hare

What Have You Done to Me?

What have you done to me
that I can't take in the pleasure
of another woman's touch.

What have you done to me
that a kiss is no longer
one of the heated desires
that I have loved
so much.

What have you done to me that
my body tenses up with fear and
my heart holds its breath
when ever someone comes near.

With that question in my mind
I pull away at the thought of
ever feeling anything
for anyone.

So I ask you again
I beg you for clarity
I long for the day when I will understand
What you have done to me?

Nina Olmeda

Halfway

Halfway between the dark and the light
  is shadow.
Halfway between dawn and dusk
  is day.
Halfway between good and evil
  is human nature.
Halfway between love and obsession
  is infatuation.
Halfway between knowledge and skill
  is practice.
Halfway between birth and death
  is life.
Halfway between the beginning and the end
  is just halfway.

   Reche' Johnson

Confusion . . .

Walking down the street . . .
Telling me what to do
Ignoring those words, and questions I so much hate
I know it is not the end
To walk backwards without looking
But it is just a matter of time
To turn back . . . or keep going.

   Archie Maure Barbosa

Unique Creation

Woman, the unique creation of the Lord,
Endowed with love and grace,
Honour and passion she has in plenty,
Working wonders by her ways.
Healing the world by her ardour,
Making it a better place for you and me,
With charm and glory she orders
The whole world with joy.
May be underrated for her might,
Even the brave tremble at her presence,
With elegance she shall fight
Through the obstacles that impede.
The delicate soul of hers
Filled with emotion and beauty,
Her verse reflects strands of pearls
Choosing the path of thorns to fulfill her duty.

   Firdous Arjumand

What about Personality

What about personality.
What's locked behind those doors of someone else's perception.
What secrets does one hold.
What lies do they hold so determined.

I'm sick of foul frowned personas.
Just another selfless act of greed and anger.
Anguish at others to pursue there own self right.
Why all the aggravation, slaggings and fulled deprivation.

How can we as a society still live by rules of neanderthals.
Why not let grace take hold.
Have religion rich within our culture.
Don't care what the next person believes.

Why kill in the name of God, just because they don't.
They have something so close to there inner soul.
Why turn your back on a beggar, why beg with no true need.
Why kill, Why help.

Our whole world lives on a why.
We could live so much richer lives.
Stop caring for our own messed up pointless problems.
Lets begin a quest, to help . . .

   Scott Stewart

Thank You, Dear Lord (For Letting Me Find Her)

Every time I look into her big beautiful eyes,
I thank you, Lord, that our paths have crossed
Every time I have her in my arms,
I thank you because my loneliness is gone

I like her for her beauty and sincerity
I admire her for her thoughts and mind
And every time I think about my new love,
I adore her for her reasons I honestly can't find

Though I wonder if her thoughts are like mine,
my feelings for her are getting stronger
And if in some tomorrow this whole fantasy ends,
I can only wonder why it couldn't last any longer

Since we've met I've been so grateful,
that we were friends and now we are more
And for as long as this may last,
I will just as long thank you, my Dear Lord

   Nelson Onit Vazqueztell

Treasure

For months destiny had been relentlessly beckoning to him,
He thought things over, his decision was far from a whim.
He must begin his journey while he was still young and fit,
Mere survival would depend upon his cunning and wit.
He knew as he departed, he would soon be replaced,
When they found him gone, no tears would dampen their face.
The truth had set him free, facing it was his choice,
When he headed through the woods his heart beat with rejoice.
To live in sheer discontent would only make him a fool,
His quest, if met with success, would render many a precious jewel.
He was determined to search until he could find,
The place that haunted his dreams and danced in his mind.
A warm place to sleep when winter winds blow wild,
A safe place to slumber in peace like a child.
A place he felt he truly belonged,
Where he answered to a name given to him alone.
To be loved, valued and to feel his worth,
These were the jewels he sought upon this earth.
All he had to offer in return,
was to fill someone's life with simple pleasure,
I wonder if he knows, that I consider him a God-sent treasure.

   Joyce Driggers

One Love

Why, oh, why, did she have to go,
the things now, she may never know.
Would she know how much we miss her?
I'm sure she would, now she's watching over.
To lose a love is so hard, when just sprung,
even when she was so young.
I often wonder why she's gone,
when she was around for not long.
She inspired me and now I can't repay,
now that she has flown away.
Sometimes I can hear her speak,
and her words I'll always keep.
Those many nights that I could sleep,
now all I can do is weep.
The times we talked, we were alone,
I talk to her even though she has flown.
Far from here, where she is safe,
where she can be near, I would say:
From the heavens above, I give all my love, to my dear Grandma.

   Jenna Barkley

Love Is

Love is like a flower; it takes time to grow
It is something earned and rightly so.
Love is sharing the good with the bad.
Working together making each other happy, not sad.
Love is accepting who you may be.
Not just in what the eye can see.
Love is always forgiving and kind.
To have this kind of love is a rare find.
Love is fulfilling each others dreams and hopes.
Knowing no matter what life brings, together you can cope.
Love should never be taken for granted or show.
'Cause just as easy as it came it can go.
So no matter how you see love as old fashioned or new,
Open your heart, 'cause it can happen to you.

Arlene Proudman

Funny Little Poem

Howdy Do, and how are you?

Missing you and don't know, just what to do!

So, I wrote this funny little poem, to keep
from feeling Blue,

But, there I go again,

Boo hoo, Boo hoo, Boo hoo,

Did you know that, I LOVE YOU?

Nancy Rader

Poetry

poetry, like pearls scattered all over
from a broken string
is a labour of love
with the choicest of words
selected with care and caution
from a jungle full of them
dumped together like a lumpy porridge
before the words picked are strung together
singly, doubly, elongated or chopped
into torrential pouring of emotions
gentle whispers of passion
loud expressions of anger
playful resonance of teasings
sorrowful wails of sufferings
the very nectar of life
bathing, warming
healing
an arid soul

Vethamalar Krishnan

Life Is Wonderful (How Wonderful Is Life)

the malfunctions leading to intuitive thought
I progress only after failed debate
at any rate I have refused to quit
making the world my puppet
How much does she really love it
her love for you dwindling
you find yourself at the center of a sinking
feelings
but feelings are all we have to survive on
my thoughts inspire yours and so forth
the embarked is left for us
no fuss remains we dust off the dusted
remains
The rain rambling sorta unconsciously
Scrambling
our minds left to plague the audience's reply
my eyes no longer can cry
they have given,
looking down evenly

Rodney Paul

So You're in Love

So you're in love
How do you know?
Did someone drop by and tell you so?
Did you blink an eye and there it was?
Is there a reason at all; is it just because?
Is it the way that they move,
the way that they walk,
the things that they do,
the way that they talk?
Is it the way that they look,
or the way that they touch?
Did you ever give thought or consider that much?
Were there violins in your heart,
fireworks in your head?
Is it something they do or did in bed?
Did you find your love after many years,
or discover love after painful tears?
If you are in love . . .
then you already know:
love isn't found; it has to grow.

Michael Lane

Perfect

On that day her life was changed
She brought her confidence, love, and joy.
She was her pearl, her gem, her treasure.
The world was her toy.

And now, alas, we see no smile,
No laughter fills her ears.
She has remained in silence and agony,
Her sorrow drowning in her tears.

For on that dark and gloomy day,
Her life was changed once more.
When she heard the news of her daughter's fate,
"She has gone to meet the Lord."

And now she despairs in her loss,
Seemingly destroyed by her pain.
She breathes a great sigh and looks to heaven,
For she knows it has not been in vain.

And even now as she recalls
The cruel remarks, the lies
About her precious gem's innocent life,
She'll always be perfect in her eyes,
Yes, completely perfect in her eye.

Bradie Huckins

My Life

Many years have come and gone like water through a sieve,
And yet it seems like yesterday, when memories relive.
Time cannot stand still, nor life remain the same;
And metamorphosis marches on to make its aging claim.
Oh, to be a youth again and know what I know now!
I'd face each day so differently with fortitude and prow.
I'd climb life's mountains one by one and never face a trial.
And never grow because mistakes would crimp my perfect style!
I'd love and laugh and never need a friend or confidante.
And never feel the touch of God because I'd never want..
No wait! Would I but change a year, an hour or a day?
To find the life which once was mine, a fitting protege.
The sorrows and the happy times, the love, the faith, the errors;
The tolerance gained, the passion, the longing and the tears
I've come this far with some regrets, but not to be undone;
Lord, help me take life's lessons and use them every one.

Beverly Turner

Red or White Rose

A beautiful red rose if she's here today
A nice white one if she's in heaven to stay.
Red for the smile when her child comes near
White for the memories that you hold so dear.
If she can kiss your forehead before going to bed,
Then you are lucky, you can take red.
But if she's gone today, can't even wish you goodnight,
Just remember the good times, but take the white.
Red for her prayers and being your friend
Knowing on her you could always depend.
White if she's crossed that "Great Divide,"
She taught you to live right, ending "up" by her side.
You may take red or you'll take the other
But either color rose means you love your dear MOTHER.

Jackie Alston

Wings in Despair

Bestow a fluttering call
Soar the earth, rock the shells of life
Intrigue souls in a conspiracy
Strew the cries of the earth
Expanse of the sands
Frenetically left on coasts
Stream the corals of life forms
Isle of water routes in despair
Search to the last, flap, and reach
Reach, and touch the lowest and the highest
Tease the depth of the anima
Hear the phantasm of the spirits
Nudge the illusions of the mind
Embrace the breeze beneath your wings
Siesta a living aroma, wear the body caress
Fracture the lines, a perfect unification
Hurl the impossible, hold onto a pair
Trust your body,
Take flight from despair

Siew Fong Teo

. . . And then I See the Truth

I see a girl that says she loves me
and then I see the truth
I see the friends that will never betray me
and then I see the truth
I see the world that treats me so well
and then I see the truth

Because the truth is something you try to hide
but you can't run from what is inside of you
You see the world is cloaked in little lies
so when this life ends and the pain subsides
Then there is one thing that you can't hide
from . . . the truth.

William Patrick IV

Jeannie—Death Does Come Too Soon

Do not lose faith my friend.
For death always comes to soon.
You are loved and held close to so many hearts,
that your spirit will live on forever.
For you must not waste your days looking for the reason why.
For there is none.
It does no good to deny it or to try to rationalize it,
for time is brief for all of us.
You must fined your strength and rise above it.
for you still have so much more to share.
Allow your grief to have its say.
But do not tarry to long.
For you still have life to live, and memories to be made.
Fulfill your needs and your love ones promise.
Leave no stoned unturned
Cherish each day, for it's a new beginning.

Beverly Sapienza

The Fire Within

The fire in people is what keeps them going
But there is no fire in the world, just a strong wind blowing
We can't let the world blow out our fire
And let the hard work and pain make us tired.
You have to work hard to keep your fire going
Because the wind in the world is continuously blowing
Temptation and greed come to blow hard
But you must cover your flame with the power of god
Hatred and lies may get you down
Just remember a smile is an upside-down frown
We must keep on going and not let the hard wind blowing,
Blow out our fire, our fire within.

Crystal Jones

Dad Was a Quiet Man

Dad was a quiet man
One of the best ways to share a moment with him was to just be there
Picture it—January 1969, Sunday Afternoon
Superbowl III—Jets VS. Colts
Namath predicted the Jets would win but they were real underdogs
I walked into the Living room, sat on the couch
Dad was in his chair, feet up on the footstool, watching the game
I asked him what was going on
He said it was the Superbowl
Jets were winning but the Colts had the ball
It was almost the end of the game
We watched Unitas lob the ball into the sidelines a couple of times
The Jets defense was all over him
Jets get the ball back and win
The game becomes famous in Sports history
Namath remembers that day because he won the Superbowl
I remember that day because I was in the living room with my Dad

Celeste Ball

Change

Always here but seldom noticed
We let it go but still it holds us
Painful or pleasant it's always here
It gives us hope or bestows fear
Like the leaves I see, once alive they now die
It seems wrong to me (Who am I to decide?)
Birds, dogs, cats, and even mankind
Living their lives knowing eventually they die
The wind, warm as life then it chills to our bones
It holds us tight then leaves us alone
A love was once here, but now it is gone
From a comfortable evening to a new lonely dawn
I wonder why all in this life is not set
As if by living we are taking a bet
Is all of our life just a monstrous game
Or is it a horse just too wild to be tamed
I try to find the truth to this rhyme
It cannot be found, just learned through time
Through all the pleasure and all the pain
I could not live a life without change

Jason Stahl

A Cloud or a Dream?

Streaming clouds roll above baby blue skies
Flowers of green pulsate like a heart
I dream of a lone dove
I float across the seas endlessly
As sweet sea air fills the sails
Comfort, oh, sweet comfort, can be reached
In the warm sand along the beach
Peaceful times treasure always
For those are the truly innocent days

Benjamin Peters

Wedding Poem to My Wife

I await . . . oblivious to those around me.
They are but phantoms to my reality, for soon
shall appear the one I love; upwards I gaze
in anticipation.
She appears . . . in angelic radiance before my
eyes, haloed in tranquil beauty and charm.
Slight trepidation marring not her visage;
celestial and earthly in harmonious union.
Emotions erupt . . . within my bosom joy blossoms.
There is no containment for the love I feel;
not enough awe for the beauty before me.
She descends . . . majestically approaches my
queen.   All behold her beauty as I, for always
lovely she appears to me; I go to escort her down.
We stand . . . together we are joined forever; no
longer two but one in soul.
My life is enhanced by her simple love.
We embrace in lover's joy.

Christopher Carroll

Night

I fear the night, for it leaves me alone
It knows my pain and makes my heart groan
When the day is gone, my soul takes flight
And becomes one with the dark, starry night
They dance to my secrets, play on my web of lies
Mocking my existence that rides with the tides
Then the moon joins too, and the stars sing
Their song not really music, but rather a thing
My universe surrounds me, envelops me, surges
Light and darkness vacillate between melody and dirges
I've waited for tomorrow, but all is just a dream
This night is my forever, my soul, and my being

Lakicia Foster

The Pointless Existence of Life

The lonely feeling is so sad,
Mean, cruel, and really bad.
It makes you feel like your only friend is you,
Just because you feel so lonely and blue.
Every time you take a look around,
None of your friends are there to be found.
Even your own cousin doesn't like you,
That makes you feel sadder too.
All you want to do is get away,
When they say your name that way.
People always sit and stare,
When they know that you are there.
You would think that you have some kind of disease,
Like they would catch it if you sneezed.
The looks that people give you,
Are mean and painful too.
All you want to do is crawl in a hole and die,
You wish you could fake your death, but that would be a lie.

Jennifer King

Found Love

One day I was sitting there, all alone in my bed.
Wondering why am I here, and not with you instead.
Then you came into my life.
Now things are not the same; someday I want to be your wife.
How much our life can change when you find your true love.
At first it was strange, but now I know you're sent from above.
Now you are in my heart, and you complete me.
I loved you from the start; we are meant to be.
You also were afraid to show how you truly feel.
But now we both know we are forever and real.
Every day our love grows; we have become one.
Our love always shows our search is done.
I am yours forever, my love is true and always.
Us together, is the Lord answering my prayers.

Tanya Dennehy

"I am Sitting Here"

I am sitting here,
on the tiny stairs of a small playset
in a pebble-filled area
in a small corner park
on a wickedly cold, foggy Thursday morning.
It is fall.
There are what seem to be
an infinite number of leaves
and the trees that they fall from.
One tree, its eyes directly facing mine,
is probably wondering what I am writing about it.
I start to listen. To what, you may ask—to everything.
I start to listen to the birds chirping,
the dogs barking, the other children laughing.
Then, there are the strange sounds that no one can identify.
There are many mysteries of autumn we must sleuth.
Maybe next time.

Dhani Mau

Blank Page

Give me a blank page
I'm sure to fill its space
I'll give it life, some joy
some tune, I'll give it face.

For every blank page that there is
some words should be expressed
so much emotions, feelings
no time to be distressed!

So every time you start to write
you're drawing words within inside
be thankful that its blankness stares at you
longing for a verse or two.

It may be black and white but color it with words
It may be very quiet—no music to the ears.
Write down some lyrics, a special note or song for it to hear.

A blank page is a friend in need to feel a hug of phrase
It surrenders to a pen-glide, an ink, a stroke of imagery.
It needs to breath through sentences, it craves to touch
your eyes for years to come . . .

Maria Rosado

Practice Shootin'

Life's a bed o' roses,
An' it's a bowl o' cherries.
But thorns are on those roses,
And pits within them berries.

Lovers they come callin'
With candy, wine, and song.
Hold ye hand and woo ye,
'Til the nigh' gets long.

But gentlemen wolves become when love turns into lust.
Lassies fein, "No, no, I can't!" Lads say, "Oh, ye must!"

Often virtue has been lost
Within a passion's flame.
An' when lovers leave
Who can one rightly blame?

When cupid shoots for practice,
Take heed my little lass; he's not a-sending arrows
That lead toward holy mass.

Roses red an' lovely
have thorns prickly neat.
An' cherries picked before their season
Never taste as sweet.

Lisa Kleine

A Wife by Any Other Name

To my wife
A Rose may be a Rose
But there's only one flower for me

She's Marianne, My wife, My sweetheart
She turns I into We

Many Suns have risen, Many Moons have smiled down
Since Marianne came into my life with her beauty abound

My life's path has been outlined, the curves have been straightened
As we stroll hand in hand, our love not mistaken

My wife, My Marianne is more than my supporter
She keeps my world spinning while keeping it in order

Thank you, my love, for all the years together
This tribute to you is for now and forever

Santo Lumia

A Poem about Color, Elves, and Spring Time

The midnight sky is filled with brightness
as the moon glitters in the night.
The little elves are dancing,
and the stars never shone so bright.
These elves are very different.
They are sweet and magical clowns.
But they always get down to business
when the end of springtime rolls around.
Never has there been such a duty
for somebody half an inch tall.
Never has there been so much work involved
for someone so tiny and so small.
They paint the green in the treetops
and the brown for the grimiest muds,
adding only a touch of color to a dandelion's buds.
These are the elves of summer.
For when the springtime is done,
they apply the earth's makeup
in hopes to please the sun.

Jessica Engel

The Man

I lie awake waiting,
Waiting for Him to come.

I sleep dreaming He is here,
I wake to find He is not.

I sit in my room waiting for the day,
Waiting for the day that He will come.

I close my eyes and see Him,
I open them and He is not there.

I here a knocking at the door,
I open it to find no one.

I am praying that He will come & I will see Him,
The man is God.

Olivia Deck

It's Midnight And

In the deep hollow formed between nose and
eye, it lies holding you in its clearness.
It just is. Not squeezed, nor cried . . . it just is . . .
fixing you, forming you into liquid
emotion, warm and as real as dawn's
pink teasing of yet another day.
Out of nowhere it came and slipped across the
crest onto cotton covered pillow;
it temporarily stains while another
takes its place, reborn, unbidden and still
in the hollow left permanently in
my heart . . . in my soul.

Donna Farmer

If I Had a Thousand Years

If I had a thousand years
Then I would not be so frank
However, since I have less than a hundred
Your offer I will kindly thank
Alas I must decline thine proposition
Moreover, send you one your way
Because I would never accept it
Not tomorrow and surely not today

If I had forever
I would lead you on to think
That maybe we had a chance
That one day we would link
Again, we do not have forever
Fore death is watching even now
So please stop asking me sir
Please stop your pretty words now

So farewell dear sir
I do believe this is good-bye
Kindly go along your way
And not care if I live or die

Eden Sandoz

The Artist and the Sunrise

As if the palette had been dropped.
A splash of colors graces the sky.
Flowing like water, devouring the night sky once again.

Almost like autumn;
the colors are yellow, gold, orange, a deep blush pink,
and purple dappled with blue.

A beautiful sight, if you ever saw it.

It stretches across the fluid sky,
beyond what the naked eye could reach.
Slowly dissipating, until the baby blue rises up, and covers it all.

Never again will you see that wave of autumn . . .
not until the night begins to creep upon you, that is.

Samantha Paganelli

Empty Cocoon

Some caterpillars, and a few crawling friends
Carried an empty cocoon.
With sorrow they marched to lay it to rest.
Never seeing the butterfly zoom.

Death cannot claim our memories or love
Those live on as we grieve.
We're left behind but, OH, how THEY shine!
All of life awaits to fly free.

When you see a butterfly, remember its toil.
Merely crawling, then death, its duty.
Its life has not stopped, it has only changed.
It soars with great beauty.

Vickie Strickland

Shall

Shall I dare tell you my thoughts dearest.
Shall my voice rise with anticipation to
hear yours in return.
Shall the windows to our souls be open
and truthful, to only each other.
Shall your kiss make my body to blush
from the warmth in your hunger.
Shall the desire in your eyes be matched
in a glance by only mine.
Shall I love you always, yes, I Shall.

Debbie Norwood

A Student's Prayer

Dear Lord, please help this lady who says she wants to teach me.
Help her learn from you the many ways in which to reach me.
And, Lord, tell her please don't ridicule me to the rest,
But be kind and encourage me to do my very best.
I know she must be brave, 'cause she's taking on so many.
And I know she must be rich, 'cause the job pays just a penny.
So I figure, Lord, she must truly want to be here,
in this room with 40 kids who think they know no fear.
I pray that your wisdom pours through this pretty teacher,
and her wisdom reaches me, and then I will beseech her,
to let me clean the blackboard, and I'll be oh, so handy.
Then maybe she'll remember, Lord, to grade my test quite dandy!
And Lord, I hope she inspires me to be a motivated scholar,
By being a role model and not with a scream and a holler.
I might not have another to look up to in my life,
So I hope you'll give her strength on her good days and in strife.
When all is said and done, Lord, if I'm worthy of your love,
then I'll have learned from teacher,
whom you guided from above.

Linda Parker

The Character of Time

Time is a most destructive force,
The casualties cannot be numbered.
Its constant progression shows no remorse,
Its Being has never slumbered.
The elements of this invincible world,
Are servants dictated by Time.
His effortless movement seeps away life,
But without Him first blood runneth not.
The Earth is a stage and the actors are men,
The observing audience is Time.
Man claims immortality,while Time settles in,
Waiting for the upcoming Act to begin.
Time is more Diligent than all man can boast,
A gentleman who fluently moves on.
His labor unending, but not one complaint,
Ever is uttered by this Noble Saint.
Perhaps, one day, even time will give way,
The Lord of all lords will remain.
And Time,on that day,of his work will be free,
Then all that will be left is Eternity—

John Hopkins

Ode to Y2K

When I grow old, and gray, and somewhat grizzled,
I will share with my grandchildren, how Y2K fizzled.

While millions partied in their millennium finery,
Much of the world worried about all things binary.

Fear mongers predicted a monsoon, there was but a drizzle,
Instead of really good steak, we got only the sizzle.

Movies were made, thousands of articles written,
The fourth estate was certain, by the bug we'd be bitten.

Millions were spent to prepare for New Years Day,
A bogus vaccine against the disease called Y2K.

My children's children will be rolling in stitches,
As I tell them of defenses against non-existent glitches.

Airline flights were cancelled, elevators put on hold,
The faint-hearted won, at the expense of the bold.

Preparations were endless, and would you believe,
Millennium toasts were made mainly at home this New Years Eve.

The ode could continue, but for now it is done,
I have to start getting ready for 2001.

Peter Letourneau

Rain

Rain gently touching the ground,
Wind blowing softly,
Air smelling fresh,
Makes the earth feel washed.

By the time the rain stops,
Water pools in the ground,
Leaves floating,
People avoiding stepping on them.

After the rain,
The sun gradually brightens,
Making the weather humid once again,
Yet all make the earth look reborn.

People take off their raincoats,
Wet and folding their umbrellas,
Roads and grasses absorb the sun,
Everyone and everything feels clean again.

They are ready to be dirty again,
Ready for another tough time,
They wait for the next rain to come,
And clean them all over again.

Annabel De La Cruz

If I Would Have Known

If I would have known a month ago
What I know today,
I would have told you how much I love you
And not kept you at bay.
If I would have know a year ago
That you would no longer be here,
I would have spent each day
Loving and keeping you near.
But you have left this world
So unexpectedly is seems,
And I am left here with only
My memories and dreams.
If I would have known back then
What I know today,
I would have prayed each night
For this not to be our fate.
But it seems God has for each of us
One very special plan.
Still I can't help but wish,
I would have known back then.

Shelia Fennel

A Great Divide

Its long journey has shown too far for some,
yet for others its distance is merely strife;
Although there's triumphs,
 many have fell,
not knowing for what,
all of their life,
How the Great Divide had made them come.
 And for those that fell
 not knowing all their life,
  how the Great Divide made them come;
All people of different nations they cried,
 each one with a different tale;
All coming to the Great Divide,
 with the wisdom they would sell,
for when they stopped without being tried,
 it stabbed like a knife
for the Great Divide.

Joel Mcneal

"Hidden Eyes" (A Two Person Conversation)

*There it goes again
What, the sound of the wind?
*No, my friend
*There in disguise
*Can you see the eyes?
Where?
*Over there, behind the dust
Should I ask?
*If you must
Behind what dust?
*The dust that covers us from who we are
I should go!
*No, stay!
*And watch as I blow the dust away
(Make blowing sound . . . whhhshhhhh!)
*Now what do you have to say?
It is me! I never knew I looked this way!
*My friend, we all have a glow
*But if you keep it covered
*No one, not even yourself, will ever know

       Mia Franklin

War Is Like My Love For You

War is like my love for you,
There are days I win, and days I lose.
When I lose I think back,
To the days when we were together.

Our love is as deep as an ocean,
It is full of truth and devotion.
Our souls are united together,
And like this we will stay forever!

When we are close there is an attraction,
I see you as a great distraction.
This is why my love for you is like war,
With you my serenity is an open door.

So this poem I offer to you,
In hopes that you will understand,
Just how much I LOVE YOU!!

       David Bowe

Alone in a Cold, Godless Universe

To those who lost something loved every day of their life, like me.
What of love? It is dead.
What of life? It is pointless.
What of soul? It is a lie.
What of happiness? Never again.
What of pain? It is everlasting.
What of tears? I have none left to shed.
What of dreams? It is impossible.
What of family? They are useless.
What of religion? It is a tome of lies.
What of God? It is gone.
What of friends? They do no harm nor good.
What of death? It is a fact.
What of suicide? It is selfish.
What of anger? I feel none.
What of hate? It does no good.
What of heart? It is pumping blood.
What of mind? It is sick.
What of people? They all leave.
What of loss? It never ends.
And what of the end? It starts now.

       Jonathan Bruce

Surrendered

With your touch I surrender.
With your kiss I am surrendered.
I am yours
To do with as you please.
The warmth of your skin against mine
I feel like we are in our own little world.
We are happy there.
When you talk to me about what is wrong,
I feel I know that you love and trust me.
When you let me help you forget about the outside world,
I feel important.
You have captured my heart.
It now belongs to you.
Be careful for it is fragile.
You have my soul entranced.
Do not ignore it.
Be careful do not destroy it.

       Francine Gross

A Game of Hunting in the 1700's

Like a black panther
relying on his cunning and instincts
for survival, a
man races through the depths of the jungle
with a white creature,
the same form as himself, in pursuit. His
dark skin glistens as
he becomes wearied of the chase, and the
sultry African
atmosphere offers him fiery air
to breathe. With pounding
heart, he runs until struck down by the crack
of his opponent's
whip. The blow piercing across his back and
shoulders causes his
fall. An inevitable end like the
slaves before him, leaves
him shackled of body and life as the
prey of his brother—
a white man embodying a black heart.

       Diane Zabinski

Positively Broken

Positively broken by your trickery of words
I see now I was hopelessly devoted to a helpless ceaseless cause
Shattered, scarred by your vicious indignation
I slit my wrists wide open to reveal my destination
In stacks of dusty books
You keep your evil looks
That you practice on my soul
To hurt and drag me down
A smile is just a frown
That you have turned around.
Honesty, a virtue
You never will possess
A simple twist of truth
Is all that you confess.

So now I leave your world
A shattered shell I leave behind
A shock of emotion left to remind
My love for you an ocean,
That you never seemed to see
You were a storm that raged so harsh inside of me.

       Bobby Neal

Avatar of the Sun God

Oh, radiant Daystar
Elixir of timelessness
Genesis of my reawakening
Phoenix of my soul
Firebrand of the skies
Banish the spiked barbs of a thousand scorned ages
Embedded in my war-ragged heart
Dispel the doubt
Exorcise the loathing

The thin pretension I stand on
Shatters

Heaven surrounds me
Light never-ending
Love eternal
Come shelter me

Jennifer Lee

Evening with Field

Middle-class bliss starts our foundation.
A day spent filling assigned obligations.
Afternoon sinks, sun gather our meeting.
Then on our way, disposed usual greetings.

Freedom anticipates relaxed breath to come.
A taste of the earth rides the wind to my tongue.
My group has collected with others abound.
An evening with field, once again we've been found.

Air catches and captures this spirit to fill.
But time constraints felt and begun to spill.
Light hearts linger, and desperate, those also in line.
The low flying nightfall has pushed them through time.

Freedom attempts for grasps of the fleet.
But as always, left empties though a promise discreet.
A hope abides that trails the day.
And evening with field, I'm the only to stay.

Robert Braxton

Life

Someone once told me the world was going to end.
I'm here right now telling you it's just beginning.
Fighting the powers,
of a spiritual strain,
can be hard on someone's brain.
Show your fears,
hide your tears,
Your mind is a star,
from a galaxy afar,
your soul only shows up in the rain
all it can show you is your endless pain.
But now I find,
I've searched my mind,
and found true love
from the heavens above.

Katy Gavrilchuk

Always with Me

Not a single day goes by that I don't think of you.
I wonder what you're doing and if you're thinking of me, too.
I visualize your loving smile and your laugh that I adore.
With each loving thought of you, I start to miss you more.

I realize that I'm the one who chose to move away,
But, still I wish that you could be right here with me, to stay.
For even though my life is full, I have to tell you true,
I'll never feel complete because I can't spend time with you.

We share a bond that's special, so I need for you to know,
You'll always be a part of me, no matter where I go.
So as we take the journey of our destinies apart,
Remember that I'm with you, for you're always in my heart.

Patricia A. Brown Lee

The Open Door

There was a comfort in your smile
That when I looked, I hadn't seen before
And in your strength a quiet that held me
On bleak and wintry days.

No binding chains could ever keep me
Only the softness of an invisible chord
And I would be content to hear
Your days and dreams spread out across the air.

I saw you dance in silly sand and light a path,
and never seek return
You stood in happy laughter before me
In the partly opened door, no guile
And when I reached the stairs I saw
The shadows draw away and in their place
I saw your hand and touched your smile.

Terrilyn Godfrey

Alone

Alone is how I always feel.
Though I may not know it at the time.
I can't ever make a deal
and I never have a dime.
Stress just about kills me,
but the time is at hand to face my fears.
I feel I can never be me
and the end draws near.
The end comes for everyone.
I should make the best of it,
but when it's all done
I'll realize I've done nothing with it.
Time is wasting away
I should get ready
It might come today,
hopefully I'll be ready.
The time is gone,
it's time to go,
and again I'm alone.
Everyone's gone.

Georgina Mcdonald

China Doll

Soft, Fair, Gentle face
Moving through life with charm and grace,
Makes being with you a wonderful place.
Entering each day,
At a casual pace.
Makes everything around you
look like a race.
Wrapping your life in strings of lace.
Showing your love with each embrace.

Sarah Mchugh

Sickness

The warm air brushes over me,
I here the music in the streets with loud laughter and joy.
In a foreign place.
I am alone,
and deep within Thought.
Loneliness is constant,
in my mind.
Hundreds of people, and yet . . .
I hear the clock say, "Tick-Tock."
Time passes fast,
But not fast enough for me.
Hundreds of them and only a single clock speaks to me.
A Single Clock!
Telling me when home will be achieved.
Solitude,
Is something most would not hold dear to their heart.
Most would think solitude trivial.

Jessica Beasley

Watching

I'm watching you
your watching me
I'm standing here
your standing there

My heart's racing
your heart's beating
racing, beating, racing, beating
is there a difference

tick, tock, goes the heart beating clock

I'm going to leave now
your going to go then
will I see you again, and when?
I don't know, you don't know

will I go to you, or
will you come to me?
we are watching each other
watch each other

through a mirror
so deep.

Angie Bavaro

Mom and Dad

When I was born, you held me close,
You gave me love and strong support.
You helped me with my ABC's,
And even bandaged my skinned knees.
During school you helped me learn,
When I needed you, you were there in turn.
And then when I had kids of my own,
Your shoulder was there for me to lean on.
But now that my kids are grown and gone,
Your more like a friend,
Then the parents I've known.
Our stories to each other are almost the same,
Different kids, different knees,
But still the same game.
The mistakes I made when you said, "You'll learn,"
Are the same for my kids, and so are my words.
So, Mom and Dad, here's to you,
And Thank-you for being there,
All the way though.

Elizabeth Adcock

September

The woods are crimsoned blazing gold
Illumed by the sunlight
Streaming down through colonnades
Fanning out its skylight.
Soon earth will claim lambent leaves of flame
Shades of iridescent splendor,
Random carpets spread beneath the trees
In the forests of September.
An Autumn haze drifts through the days
O'er fields of russet brown,
To rocks and rills in distant hills
That wear a purple gown.
Bright cobalt skies painted o'er
With slated swathes of gray
The fleeting seasons come and go
Demurely slip away.
Like wisps of smoke from dying candles
The summer days have flown,
Extinguished by the autumn mists
September winds have blown.

Don Melcher

Today Tomorrow Forever

I know that today is the last
Our friendship came and ended fast
I know the time is coming near
We probably will be forgotten by this time next year
I know that high school will be fun
But DON'T forget 'cause I'll miss you a ton
I'll feel my life starting new
All because I didn't stay close to you
And all the days will go on
I may get weak I may stay strong
But every day will feel long
Without you by my side
When I'm happy, When I cry
Tomorrow when the day has passed us by
I'll remember you and start to cry
You'll move on
and I will too
but remember forever that I LoVe U!!!

Jessica Blumert

"The Man I Feel Within"

In my new life which I began
There upon me came a man
He had such a grin
That he made me hold within
His tenderness and his sweet caress
It had meant to me so much
That he cared a bunch
This man gave so many hugs and kisses
The he made sure that I felt like a princess
You may know of this special friend and lover
But I want you to know I will not uncover
I will try to break the wall down
So this man will no longer hold his frown
Because someday I would be proud and say aloud
To be his wife for our new life
All I can say is, "I love you!!"
With all my heart and hope nothing will tear us apart
This man I speak so highly of is not the one from above
But it is . . . the man I feel within

Linda K. Putz

Ideas

Ideas, flashing through my mind,
have no where else to go.
But back to where they came from,
no one will ever know.
They don't stop a minute, but continue on they do,
another one is on its way, no time to stop for you.
They come and go
with just one glimpse to give,
it seems like that they took with them,
just what they had to give.
To keep my mind so easy, and as smart as it may be.
I don't stop to fool around, or wait around you see.
I'm kinda like a thought,
from somewhere deep inside.
Never have a place to go,
but know just where to hide.
I hope I can get there sooner,
or before my idea arrives.
I want to be there and ready,
to pounce on it this time!

David Arthur

It Hurts

When will the hurting go away?
I hurt in everything I do and everything I say.
Because you're in my thoughts and were a part of me.
Now all I have is a picture to see.

I have happy memories; this is true.
But knowing we can't make more, sure makes me blue.

I know you are in a better place,
But I would really love to see your face.
Knowing that I will someday see you,
Is the only thing that gets me through

Life without you.
Jodi Wheeler

Volcano

With the trembling of the ground,
people start to look around.
A burst of ash fills the air,
giving people a mighty scare.
It belches forth more to block the sun's light,
making it difficult for sight.
So forth spews the earth,
to molten lava it gives birth.
Then comes the mudslide,
pouring down the mountainside.
People running through the street,
tripping over their own two feet.
The town is being buried,
in the mudslide things are carried,
ash and water are becoming muck,
in which all the cars are stuck.
Finally comes the pyroclastic flow,
leveling everything in just one blow.
Lynn Werkheiser

A Guide to Happiness

Feilds of flowers, flowing streams
beautiful things that grow
A sun that rises, a sun that sets
what an insightful show
Each day a blessing, each day a gift
cherish all it's worth
Try harder to love, less to hate
take care of Mother Earth
Always be kind, always help out
even when times are bad
Take what you need, give back double that
be happy with what you have
A hug, a smile, or a kiss
give all these you can give
This will supply you with all the happiness
you'll ever need to live
Melissa Crandley

The One

Dedicated to SvS: Stephanie Vang,
you are more than words can describe.
You were the one who always made me smile,
the one who didn't mind walking
that extra mile.

You were the one to pick me up when I was
down, the one to listen to my problems
when no one else was around.

You were the one who always kept me warm,
the one to shelter me from any storm.

You are one of the many Angels above me,
and that to me you have shown,
the one to stand by my side and comfort me
when I felt lost and alone.

You are the one so precious to me,
and even though I know one day we will part,
from the first day that I met you,
I knew you would always hold a special
place in my heart.
Fang Yang

Moment in Time

If you could capture, but a moment in time
What would it be, what would you find
The laughter of children, playing in the rain
The death of a loved one, no longer in pain
The joy of a mother, as she gives birth
To a son or daughter, their first day on Earth
The excitement of a friend, as they tell you good news
Or watching your child, as he ties his shoes
The new grandmother, with her new grandchild
Rocking him to sleep, in the early morning hours
Kneeling beside your bed, wanting to pray
Turning your eyes, up toward the sky
Not quite knowing what to say
You then bow your head, praying you could find
How to capture, but, that moment in TIME!
Sue Van Houten

When She Cries

When she cries,
her tears bring a kind of healing
even though her heart would cling
to the warm arms of sorrow

he can't see, when she cries,
how she cherishes their memories . . .
facing east at each sunrise,
searching for him in her mind's eye . . .
he can't see,
how his "good-bye" echoes through her soul;
her sobs of anquish rise from the depths,
the void, inside . . .

when she cries, there's a comfort in the feeling,
as she holds on to the remnants of their love . . .
knowing he can't see

when she cries
Bridgette Wynn

Dear Mama

Mama, dear Mama, oh how can it be?
Is there room in your heart, to love more than just me?
It scares me to think, you won't be just mine.
When the new baby comes, you might run out of time.

Oh, dear little one, my sweet little squeeze.
Try dear not to think, of such things, if you please.
You're one of a kind, and can't be replaced.
From the hair on your head, to the smile on your face.

It really won't matter, how many children come to be.
Each one will be unique, and special to me.
I'll have many children, if my dreams come true.
But however many, there'll be just one YOU.
James Legere

The Flower

The flower, sad, confused, wilted
Sat there alone, in the dark, weary.
Unwatered, it sat there waiting and waiting.
Waiting for food and water,
Unattended, dark, blue, withered.
Hurt and ignored the flower was there.
Left to die, with no one around, with no one caring.
Saman Farazmand

Dreamer

To Mike and Stephanie—Have a great life together. I love you.
To lift the sun up in the morning, and pull it down at set.
And see the colors of autumn hope carry itself to everywhere in need.
And the rain that flies to the ground like that, hide beneath itself
The flower that refused to grow, sprout up from just one seed.

The fire light to everyone and fill up the holes in my dreams.
The golden river that flows on it shatters itself on the rocks.
The stars that not yet shine too bright, but love it anyway.
The angels that wish to help spread out their wings on top.

All this happens when someone misses the life that went away.
Dreamer close your eyes at once and dream yourself to Heaven.
And listen for the trees to speak that you will not hear.
Travel all that changes with, and not where you have been.

The lies that need to focus on all they have to give.
And wish away the sorrow that sleeps beneath your soul.
The heart that sank and won't let go tries to pull you down.
Cry at night, all the way to sleep and forget all that you know.

And all you are afraid of, runaway in fear.
And all that seeks a closer look, watch the blind man see.
Don't forget to look at the sunset, the colors that don't fade away.
Fade away with your heart, your soul and mind, but not away with dreams.

Jeanette Mazeikis

Carolina

My paradise came alive in my childhood lifetime
I see it unfold as I reminisce.

I miss you deeply, and maybe you know, but if you don't, I'm writing you this . . .
You've always been there to care for me. Even during my darkest years and saddest
memories, even when the tears were kept in by my fears of insecurity, you understood
and loved me, visited and comforted me, stood by and hugged me. I could never forget
that, how you were, dad; it's always been beyond me . . .

And now that I'm older, a little more wisdom behind me, I can say I understand, while
enjoying all our memories. My history began with you, so when you left, I lost a true
angel in my life. And it's not often I pray, but lately, I've been praying every night.

I'm sure you've been listening, I've been telling God I'm missing you, I've asked Him
to bless you, I prayed to Him, to let you shine down on me, and this sunlight came
today, you were probably smiling down on me. I feel your love surround me, dad. I love
you, and there's never enough times I can tell you that. Maybe if you can hear me, I'd
tell you one more time. I cherish the memories of you and me, I'll enjoy them until it's
my time, until I reach the end of the line, and maybe when the time comes, it will be then
that we'll be together again . . .

but until that sweet day, I'll live my life, enjoying every minute. And I'll always think
of you, with every ray of sunlight, and every memory in it.

Daniel Cuadro

Your Heart and Mine

So soft and sweet. So tender and loving.
So kind and dear to me. Your heart is so new and pure. Yet, I feel that I am missing
something, something very important to you and to me. I see in you something that is
so very clear to me, yet I really can't find the words that I'm looking for. Yet, every
time I hear your name, your voice, or even when I go off in my own little world, I think
of you and how very special your heart is to me. Then I wish, I wish you could be here
with me. Then I think of how our hearts really clash. Then I ask why is this happening
to me? I really don't deserve a love, a love so kind and true. I was always told that a
love, a love like this only existed in my dreams. Then my heart grew cold, so very cold,
that when I found a guy that was willing to be there for me, I was never there for him,
and now I see just how rude I was to be so unwilling to be there for the ones that give
me their trust. Then is when I saw that I just needed someone with a heart, a heart like
yours, to melt the thick, thick ice around my heart that I have had to deal with most of my life.
I often ask my self is this real, or is this just a dream? Then as you put your arms
around me, I tell myself that this is not a dream, and this will never end

Deann Oyler

Daddy's Little Girl

Ever since she was little
they've been like a team
Going every where together
as though it seemed.
She was daddy's little girl
and they were never apart
Because their love was true
and it came from the heart.
Every year they went fishing
and stayed out all day
And every night they sat down
so that they could pray.
But now she's getting older
and growing further apart
Even though their love still
comes from the heart.
Maybe one day it will go back
to ribbons and curls
But for now I still can say
I'm Daddy's Little Girl.

Brittany Edison

Anonymous

Cardboard leaks—
Mice tap dance
with muddy feet
on a rag strewn floor.

Cardboard leaks—
Buildings hold no
extra rain in
slimy fingers anymore.

Cardboard leaks—
Kids catch cold
when they can't study
in school halls.

Cardboard leaks—
Oh, Insects—it's warm
for you—but Wind
I have thin walls.

Cardboard leaks—
Mice tap dance
with muddy feet
on a rag strewn floor.

Kathrine Kuebler

Oh, Laughing Star

Oh, Laughing Star
Playful lover
Singer of birds
Wind and oceans

Light
Through universes thousand
Bliss
From the center of all

Pure ingenuity
Pure creativity
Dance of quanta
Dance of joy

Oh, Laughing Star
Playful lover
Oh, Sweet Light
Within my heart

Leticia Huber

Te Quiero Mi Amor (I Love You My Love)

I would have never thought of the idea of me and you,
But suddenly something happened and I fell in love with you.

I loved the smallest things that you would always do,
The way you'd kiss my neck and pull me close to you.

The way you'd hold me so tight like you weren't going to let go,
And the way you'd hint you wanted a kiss so that I would know.

We spent a lot of time together and I thought what we had would last.
But now things have changed and I need to stop looking in the past.

I know what we had wasn't meant to be,
But it just feels so empty now here beside me.

I know you can't make a heart love someone,
So now I know what we had is done.

The pain doesn't seem to want to go away,
The smallest things remind me of you everyday.

But now I know I must move on for you don't love me anymore,
But please keep one thing in mind, Te Quiero Mi Amor!

Nicole Hughes

Gone Fishing

Today is the day I say good-bye to the world that I've known
I'm going fishing and that's a world of its own.
I can sit back with my fishing line in hand
with nobody around with things to demand.
My problems just seem to roll away.
Like the rippling water from a boat that quietly passes my way.
Just to watch the sun as it rises in the east.
To me it's like a gourmet food for a feast.
I watch my line as it slowly slips away
and I know in my heart this is going to be a very special relaxing day.
I watch the water spiders as they dart around.
Just listening to the croaking frogs it's such a wonderful sound.
Just a few feet away a fish jumped in the air to catch a fly
and the beauty of that is enough to bring a tear to my eye.

Gordon Jones

The Love of the Earth

The Heaven is beautiful, and the Earth is strong.
The Heaven is filled with clouds of playful spirit,
and the earth's many lakes reflect her joy.
The Earth loves to see the Heaven cry,
and she doesn't mind because she knows he is there to catch her tears.
The Heaven loves to brush her wind through the earth's trees,
and the Earth longs to see her pure blue.
The lapping waves of the Earth tease the Heaven,
and the Earth flirts with warm rays of sun.
The Earth admires the strength found in the light of the heaven's stars.
The Heaven and the Earth both await the sunrise,
one without the other, its beauty would not be.
Together they send our world spinning and dancing.

Carla "Celeste" Bowden

Look into These Eyes

If the world came tumblin' down, my love for you would stand its ground
cuz you and me were meant to be forever happy in love.
I won't break your heart in two, someday we both will say I do
cuz I belive in destiny and we'll live in harmony.
Don't think that I'm a crazy fool for feelin' the way that I do
I'll hold on tight, tonight's the night we will never say goodnight.
I will love you endlessly, no need to put a spell on me
My love is real, I can't conceal the way your smile makes me feel.
Look into these eyes, and then you'll realize that you're not hypnotized
my heart will not lie, it's true,
I'll be forever in love with you.

Olivia Guzman

A Chance with You

Your stylish hair, your caring eyes
just send chills up mine spine
The sight of you makes me weak,
my hand shiver,
'til I can not speak.
I know I'm not the only girl for you,
I just wish I had one chance with you.

I know you are are taken,
but my love is true,
One thing is for sure,
She could never love you,
not the way I do.

If she should ever break your heart
and you feel all torn apart.
You know where I am.
You can take my hand
and I will mend your heart.

Michelle Baxley

Storm's End

The sky is blue,
It's a beautiful day.
It will always be this way.
Months of this joyful day,
When dark clouds
Start rolling our way.
The thunder rumbles,
The lightning strikes.
This isn't what we should be like.
The rain falls every night.
These storms are just not right.
The lonely, dark p.m.
Reigns awhile.
It is time for me to smile.
I turn my head the other way,
And see a rainbow
On this new day.
It welcomes me
As I leave you behind.
New loves we both shall find.

Karen A. Blessing

The Boxer
(With Apologies to Paul Simon)

I am not a poor boy.
I have never experienced
A tangible form of destitution.
I live a comfortable life.

But today I am tired.
I am torn and tattered.
I am beaten and battered
Like a boxer after many fights.

The boxer stands alone.

His wounds are superficial.
The fighter inside is not effected
By the cut over the eye
Or the bruise on the cheek.

Trips to the canvas
Are an everyday occurrence,
And each time the question is;
"Can I get up?"

I will.

Ned Lauver

Passionate Kiss

Passionate Kisses and indulging smiles make my heart and nature rise,
For as long as our soul lives and our love continues to reach the bright, blue, starry skies,
You'll be the one I am holding, caressing, and kissing as tears of joy flow beneath my eye.
Your passionate kiss joins my love and shatters my pride as I utter a lonely sigh.
Passionate Kisses give me visions of an unlimited commitment we represent in God's plan,
A never ending closeness that binds us both hand and hand.
As long as you can vision buds of passionate kisses inflamed by the love we share,
I'll know the love you feel for me is genuine and surely to be there.
Kiss me with your lips of trust and your tongue of sheer delight,
Assure me that this passionate kiss will gleam through darkness and show me a marvelous light,
Continue to keep your love that flows and burns so very bright,
Now keep the kiss that mends our wounds and makes our love so tight!

    Brandon Pitts

The Storm Within

As I lay here in my bed, lightning crashes just outside my window.
Thunder, deafening to the ear, roars with a vicious ferocity,
and rain beats down to blanket the Earth.
Though it is a cruel tempest, it dims in comparison to the storm waging inside me.
My heart is being torn apart by love and anger.
I try to calm either one, and yet . . . they grow stronger with every breath.
Love brought on by beautiful blue eyes and a devilish grin.
Anger brought on by the thought of not being able to be with them.
How am I to fight these heart-wrenching emotions?
I know too well that I cannot fight either.
The only thing I can do is forget them. Yet . . . I cannot forget.
That is like forgetting the smell of a rose, and the prick of its thorn.
One lesson needed to be remembered.
For if we forget the past,
the pain in the future will be worse by ten fold.

    Eddie Parks

The House of My Youth

Out in the field, marked by a few scraggly old trees, stands the weathered old house of my youth.
It's not much to look at and in fact, people passing would probably not give it a second glance.
The roof is slowly blowing away, scattering parts of my memories to the four winds.
The windows are all broken, and now a mountain lion is claiming the old house,
providing a snug and secure home for herself and her little ones.
I can never pass that old barren and run down house without
reliving moments in my mind of my childhood; when that old house was full of life . . .
and a little girl felt so loved and protected . . . running and playing
through the fields and pasture without a care in the world.
I wonder if mountain lions remember their youth?

    Glenna Decker

To My Husband

I think in silent solitude, my memories flowing fast
like a river raging toward an uncertain end. I reach out to grasp a part of you,
like a thing that steadies my frightened soul, a life preserver in this stormy sea,
but my hands fall short. I lay awake and stare across an empty bed,
looking for the eyes that always looked back into mine with love and adoration,
with a quiet gentle understanding. I call for you in tormented and tempest filled dreams,
long for your embrace that soothes me in a way that rocks a child
'til they slip off to deep slumber, knowing in complete assurance
that they are loved—it is that love you gave me, that utter and complete devotion
that I so miss from you. The sound of your snoring at night,
and every night to hear, "I love you, sweetheart," was the treasure
that made me the richest woman in the world. Can you hear,
can you see, and can you know all that I have to tell you?
Can you know the unbearable pain and searing guilt I feel for ever allowing
my anger to be pointed your way? To know we wasted so much time on pride and anger
when we should have used it to mend our wounded hearts.
Can you know how deeply I regret not spending the last moments of your life
holding you to my breast and letting you know
you were loved and cherished every second by me

    Madison Bankston

Follow

Follow my footsteps
Come follow, come follow.
Follow me to a special place.

Come in.
Sit among the frazzled This' and That's.
Dance among the Who's and What's.
Play with the Where's and Why's.

Come in.
Let your mind wander among the
Who's, This', Where's, That's, and
Why's

    Amanda R. Savage

In Memory of an Ordinary Boy

The ordinary within all
Things is bound.
The ordinary sunbeams fall
They make no sound.
An ordinary winter's day;
There is laughter
As ordinary children play.
But, not here, hereafter.
In places ordinary, yet
Not, tears stain
And ordinary hearts beget
Extraordinary pain.
As sunbeams in their fall
Thus, come lightly
Memories to fond recall;
Warmly, brightly.

    Wilbur Smith

The Days Will Pass

The days will pass,
This I know,
The days will pass,
And I may never know,
Whether something sublime,
Makes them speed or slow.

Speed into a maddening glow,
Slow through a still-life show,

The days will pass,
This I know,
The days will pass,
Am I to never know,
Whether something sublime,
May make them speed or slow?

    John Raia

Life . . .

Daylight welcomes the morning sky
Somehow it all fits together
A life is born, another soul dies
Yet we live on forever

Hate kills you more than death itself
But yet we manage to breath
Love blinds you with bitter desire
But we can still see

Pain awakens the sleeping heart
And still we are afar
Laughing soothes the torn soul's part
And here . . . we can see the scars

Life proves the strange impossible
Everything is meant to be
So live through it mile upon mile
Open your eyes and see

    Cassia Johnson

Lonely Lover

I sit at this window day after day and dream of the man that will take me away to his palace.
I hear the birds, the wind and the ocean but yet my prince has not arrived.
Then on one misty evening as I set by the window out of nowhere
came his voice and out to the sea we both shall be bound for life.

Lori Loftis

Ponderence

He came upon the marshy grass talking of our future and some past.
Telling us how he loved us so while I and others shook our head no.
Yet the piece and calm that he displayed left my mind totally dismayed.
He seemed as if he might cry while I sat there looking him in the eye.
Then I knew what he said was true he died for me and all of you.
His name was Jesus I learned that day, he is the truth the light and the way.

Tess Vangilder

Silently

Silently I walk through the forest, and I listen to its silent words
It whispers sweet things to me, and it holds me tight.
I hear its voice and feel its presence flow over me.
I also feel its pain, fore it is dying slowly.
I can feel the forest weaken, moan out in pain.
I cry and try to hold on, trying not to make it leave.
Fire erupts, and saws cut it away.
It burns and falls to its death, fore we do not care.
We kill it slowly, unknowingly, and move on.
I cry in its once greatness, wishing its silent voice was speaking once more.
I cry because now, it is truly silent.

Michael Martin

Mystery

Spilled bag of twinkling gifts
A matter of treasure and delight
A purpose unknown but pleasing
Lovingly given to the unworthy

The life without such miraculous beauties
Unknown, but not thought of often
Definite unsharing they sit above
Have they abandoned their large cousin?

Sunlight driving away the graceful tiny beings
Just barely out of our reach
A lumbering heat so forceful makes us wait
'Til the far off step out to greet us again

A coincidence—cooler when they appear
Perhaps not, shining over relief
In beautiful pattern ever constant and bright
Clean and cool, assuming and alluring, simple and free, God's perfection

Fayelle Ward

The Rain

The sound of rain beating down on the roof awoke me
I look to the clock, it's late, and all is quiet
I glance out the window, an owl hoots,
it sends an unwelcome shiver down my back.
A lost bird tries to take shelter on my windowsill
I can hear the ticking of my clock in the darkness on my bed side stand
It hypnotized me.
A faint noise breaks me free of my trance
I peered slowly out the window, not knowing what to expect.
a sly, wet fox slips quietly across the grass, into the woods, and out of sight.
My eyelids are heavy now, they slowly close, I am back asleep.
I awake to the sound of brilliant birds,
I look across the dew-covered grass,
a rainbow,
looks down upon the Earth

Lizzie Weber

Biological Classes

This is a particular question
May I ask and answer that thought
What answer can define means
That thought answers no question
Meaning can define a question
reason of the answer confuses
Life is questioned through thought
Meaning is answered by life
Strife generates concern in the living
Ignorance may be bliss
But knowledge promotes power
Death generates fear and loathing
Pain and suffering defines life
There are no true correct answers
Only generalizations about questions
Meaning falsely satisfies being
Explanation cushions reality
And hope is only a false purpose
Live blindly and ruthlessly
So one might die courageously

Brant Green

Magic Is Forever

Dedicated to Suzanne
Life is not the same without you,
still it must go on . . .
And even tough my dreams grow stronger,
for your touch I long . . .
'Cause when I see you in my dreams,
Every other, fades to pale . . .
I feel your lips upon my cheek,
on a cold mid-winter day . . .
A slow caress, look in my eyes,
tell me, "What do you feel?"
And in your eyes, a single tear,
as I slowly kneel . . .
I feel the shivering in your hand,
holding it in mine . . .
And you stand before me,
an angel so divine . . .
The things you never realized,
has suddenly come true . . .
Magic is forever,
When I'm kissing you . . .

Tomas Blomqvist

Ceaselessly Flowing

And now the trees stand barren
having shed their leaves in
autumn winds
Now is the time for sleeping
for nestling in inner warmth
before the sting of winter's
icy coat arrives
Their graceful network of
branches revealed
One senses their glee, their
freedom in sheer nakedness
Oh, wind blow through me!
Sun shine on every pore!
Rain tickle from Heaven to
Earth
Standing still,
yet nature flows on
ceaselessly

Margo Henry

Through My Eyes

My pain . . . my hurt you analyze;
but only through my eyes will the answer materialize;
the victory over me wield my pain.

The hurt ravages my skin and organs, not yours,
only through my eyes will you understand the chain;
I know the extent, I know the shadows I possess within.

Through these eyes, mine alone, shadows play tricks, appear as real,
appear as fake;
sometimes, I fail to know the intent through my eyes;
The sun rises or set?
The ocean thrust . . . but whom do I trust?
Through my eyes; the sun rises or set?
Night falls or is it daybreak?
You see, through my eyes it could be all fake!!!

Willie Johnson

Read It from Me

Oh, how I dream. I dream of you. What if you knew?
Would you do the same? Would you turn?

I try to scream. Listen . . .
My voice turns to a gentle whisper that no one can hear.
What is echo on this open field. A place of no explanations.
Could this be love?

I climb high. Oh, strong one, give me heights to explore!
Give me depths to seek. At day, who can then see the stars?
But still they are. My feelings cannot be described, can they?

Only when I stumble can I look up.
So write about my life and see. There you are on every page.
It wasn't written in the stars, but deep down you can read it from my heart.

Oh, World, open up to my eye. I'm tired of longing and words.
Give me paths to wander. Where are you now?
I see you only in the eye of my mind. The only place.

Read it from me! It is all in my heart. Read, read . . .
I will not regret. All of this is for you so please, read . . . .

Eric Eriksson

Forsaken Dreamer

. . . what dreams may come may become:
a destructive/distractive simulacrum and the universe becoming undone
harmonies unsung. aren't we just one as whole?
parts of the stars? puzzle pieces of the reason?
regardless of what we believe in, read in, or take heed in
see into the future, take a look back into the past,
and present your self with the facts of life.
the slash from the knife left your vision black as night.
screams of pain are amplified. schemes of hate are classified
while the belief in fate is pacified by the pasteurized
passive-aggressive passer-by's . . . slipping undetected past your eyes/ under your nose
into your mind and out of it grows a fungus of fear that grows stronger every year
as it appears into the mechanical gears of the majority.
political officials are abusing their privilege of authority.
i'm on a pilgrimage with my sorority using our swords and sorcery
fighting the wars with peace . . . thwarting the beasts into the scorching heat of purgatory.
i've heard your story; it's disturbed and boring. now i'm unnerved and snoring . . .
counting sheep/catching z's. unlatching the leash from the beast within
engaging my primal rage, awaiting for the final page to be rehearsed . . .
when all of existence will be reversed submerged beneath the seas of submission.
only under one condition we can be saved: and that's for the sleeper to awake . . .

Brandon Van Auken

Loving Only You

When I am at work, all that I think about is kissing you.
Your love has a hold on me that won't let go.
Your love is so sweet, you must be an angel.
All that I can say, is that I love you just because you're you.
Even at your worst, you are all that I want and all that I need.
All I'm trying to say sweetheart, is that you will forever be my always love.

Antoinette Theresa Worrell

Together Forever

Baby, you look lonely
And you look so good
or maybe I'm the lonely one
In our moments of solitude
Only you know how to break my heart
But please don't tear our world apart
We're in this together
And it should be forever
Please listen to my heart
Because only you know the private parts
This time of night I'm prone to cry
Especially when you're not by my side
Baby you are so clever
I know we'll be here forever
Because we are believers
We'll always be together

Darlene F. Christ

You're Everything

When my heart was all but broken
and I couldn't take the pain
And I wouldn't fall in love
for fear of being hurt again
You made me feel like I belong
you made me feel so good
'Cause you chose to be my friend
when no one else would

When I thought that I was all alone
and no one really cared
Man, was I surprised to find
that you were standing there
And if I lost all that I have
and was left with only you
Darling, I'd still have everything
'cause now, I know the truth

You're everything

Kevin Michael Berger

Supermodel

Beautiful face
Hungry eyes
Lonely soul
Looking for answers
Finding only more problems
Her only way out
Is a route she doesn't want to take
Scared to move forward
But even more scared to be left behind
Her beauty will not last forever
Neither will her charm
What will she do?
Wither away . . .

Amanda Newcomb

The Master's Hand

In a hole so deep and dark,
Leaves no scars, yet leaves its mark.

Pleading, begging for my release,
To find some freedom and some peace.

Held in by the master's hand,
Fearing torture on his land.

The wind is what I long to feel,
As parts of me begin to peel.

The loneliness eats at my soul,
In this deep dark hidden hole.

Debra Bradtke

Happy Girl

Broken heart that will never mend.
Tear filled eyes with mascara running down my cheek.
Laughter that is heard yet not felt.
Don't cry dry your green eyes and wipe the mascara from you cheek.
Be the Happy Girl you always wanted to be.
Brush the hair from your face and stand up to the world.
Self-esteem that appears and disappears.
Dreams that are demolished after being woken.
Yet don't cry dry those green eyes and wipe the mascara from your cheek.
Be the Happy Girls you always wanted to be.
Brush the hair from your face and stand up to the world.
Knowing what love feels like but still not knowing how it feels to be loved.

Trying hard to be yourself,
while no one can or has loved the person you are.
Pick your heart up from the ground, and hold it high.
And don't cry, dry those green eyes, and wipe the mascara from your cheek.
Be the Happy Girl you always wanted to be.
Brush the hair from your face and stand up to the world.

Amber Wimberly

The Rose I Left Behind

The bright red pedals of a rose shimmers in the light of the day . . .
As bright as the one I left behind . . .
Her memories still haunts me but I don't let no one know . . .
The thought of her still drives me crazy . . .
When I smell a rose all bright and red I think of the one I left behind . . .
Afraid of nothing I say but I really am afraid to lose that one true rose . .
I try to dream of our first kiss and our last at that at our special place where I had to
leave the rose behind . . .
For the rose I left behind was an everlasting rose . . .
The day I left her behind was the day I knew I lost my one true rose . . .
The day I'm gone for good is the day she will find another . . .
Then I will be the rose she left behind . . .

Rickey Esque Jr.

Grandma

My heart was torn the morning you left.
My Grandma was gone, the ultimate theft!
The tears rolled down, my heart broke in two,
Why did God have to take you?
The pain crept through me, I fell over and cried,
I couldn't accept that my Grandma had died.
I'm just a kid with questions and pride;
But without my Grandma I feel empty inside.
It hit me so hard it was like a slug to my chest,
I couldn't speak or breath none the less.
No more mornings, afternoons or nights,
My Grandma went to Heaven, she followed His voice, she stepped into the light.
If I had one more chance to see her again,
I'd tell her how I love her and that she was my best friend.
I was her first great-grandson, but never the last,
Forever this grandson's love will last!

John Slattery

"A Love Letter"

Dedicated to Nicqueva Neslon
Whom is this letter going to,
Is it my lady friend or the women I love so true?
A love letter worth a thousand words,
with a bit of "I miss you" and a lot of "I love you, girl."
Three to four pages long,
I still need to know to whom this letter belongs.
Read it at night while you hear the wind singing,
you know while I was writing this letter it was of you I was thinking.
The fragrance of white diamonds perfume from the envelope tab,
just because of your beauty, angels rejoice and clap.

    Sincerely;
  Is the end of something I call a love letter . . .

P.S. I love you . . . eternity & forever

Frantz Menard

Rime of a Hypocritical World

I see the world as an illusion
Filling my mind up with confusion
It's right today but wrong tomorrow
Find another soul to borrow
Injecting your views into my brain
You're the reason I'm insane
Echoing voices through my head
Disobey them, wind up dead
Storm the world with your crazy schemes
Try to crush my precious dreams
Your arrogance
Is your ignorance
I am just a product of society
Welcome to my reality
Someday soon you will realize
Hatred stems from laughter's cries
They kept us bound
but a way out I have found
No more can they keep me in
Listen, I will win

Steve Nard

So Many Days

So many days
have I flown over oceans
above
the comforting ambience
of the extreme freedom
that cradles my joy

So many nights
have I lain in the shadows
beneath
the flickering light spots
on the darkened sheet
that covers my sorrow

In the twilights
the day meets the night
They fall in love
and part together
leaving only faint traces
of daybreak

Edda Johannes

Will You Be There in the End

Will you be there in the end

Will you hold my hand

As I pass into a sleep

Will you stay with me

Will you let the love be

The memories you must keep

Will you think of me

Remember, we will be

Together once again

Will you hold my hand

As I fall asleep

Will you love me, in the end?

Michael Lindenbaum

Dragon of January

I'm sitting in the coldest part of my room.
It helps me think.
My father used to go out on
the front porch of our two-story
dark wood shingled house in a T-shirt
and jeans to greet the cold January air.
Steamy clouds exiting his mouth with
each breath as if he were some kind of dragon, he would move his head slowly
from left to right looking over the
snow laden landscape as if it were
his kingdom.
Mother thought he was crazy, but I understand
it. I always did.
It may be one of the only things I ever understood about my father,
but to this day,
when I need to clear my mind,
when I need to overlook the boundaries
of my kingdom, I walk out to greet the snow
in my blue jeans and T-shirt, the dragon of January.

Eric Storeng

Delusions

His brittle mind can mend its own . . . .
remain as vague conceit, for now his days are guessed upon
if circumstance dares to speak.
Sweet roots of poison bare, this weak complaint in vain
as logic is to man, the transient simple saint.
Below the stretch of vanity that looks ugly in his eye,
so dark endurance seems to one who feels and cannot cry.
Planted faults go way beyond, to drown his silent voice
whose sound is seen, but never found . . . .
Now what is left is guessed upon.
Enough as blind rehearse, expressed as love, disguised by pain,
If sanity dares to ask . . . .
Who, made this genius brain insane?

Charleen Hosein-House

The Angel

Tiff Edwards
I remember when I first saw her.
I was in a trance, no matter what I did.
It was that first glance.
Her eyes always sparkled, her beauty so radiant and enchanting,
I knew right away she was an angel.
There is a constant glow to her beauty,
And whether she knows it or not, it shines more when it's noticed.
There is a certain quality to her when she's around; it's almost as if she was perfect when she goes around.
Very considerate, or so it's displayed, but her heart is still fragile in so many ways.
In the worst way I want her love, but it has to be sent from above. Our paths have stopped half way and we wait.
As I look for the angel, she can see me though the gate, and I can't wipe the tears from her eyes,
But still to me she's the ultimate prize.

David Francis

Longing

Too many have loved before now for me to have loved first.
Too many have cried before for me to be crying worse.
Too many have felt the joys and pains of a love that was badly given.
Too many have longed for and never received; they've fallen short of Heaven.

Joanne Smith

You and What to Do . . .

Please realize that God only created the seed that was planted to grow the apple tree—
it is you who choose which apple to pick.

Melanie Quandt

Spark of a Flame

Brought me to my knees
your passion and desire
like never before
have I felt this fire

A spark of a flame
we built tonight
a wanting, a passion
it feels so right

Ache for your touch
your breath upon me
warmth of your body
so close next to me

Close my eyes
you fill my dreams
a life long search
across a deep dark sea

A soul so far
out of reach
I hold out my hand
but will it ever be?

Kelly Ann Henderson

Please

I think about you every day,
And dream about you every night.
It is true, I do love you.
How could I even put up a fight?
How did I get in so deep,
So deep into this love?
I don't know where I'm standing.
Please help me—God above.
He loves me?
He loves me not?
These words I used to say,
But now I question them every day,
Thinking of you and your ways.
I will love you forever,
Forever and a day.
But, please tell me where I stand.
I need to move on my way.
If you love me, I'll stay.
If not, I'll go.
Please tell me—I need to know.

Dianne McCartin

Until I Found You

At once there was no laughter
And happiness was over-due
I knew not what love was
Until I found you

The rain would not stop falling
The skies would not turn blue
The sun refused to shine
Until I found you

My tears would not dry up
Happy days became so few
I almost gave up on love
Until I found you

But now the hurt is gone
My dreams have now come true
I'm happy once again
Because I found you

Erika Sledge

A Betrayal

The bells ring in the wind for her, calling her,
a beckon she can't refuse. They draw her out into the fog,
fog that pretends to hold her away, far from the edge of the bluff,
but only pulls her nearer. She believes the promises of the waves, sirens disguising
their fangs beneath gentle white foam.
She convinces her hesitant feet, coaxing them
closer to the hypnotic reef rough on her feet, tearing at her hem.
She trusts the moon's mockery, blanched across the surf
forming silver illusions on the water
she fancies them nets of spun moonlight
wishing to catch her, keep her.
She befriends the ocean breeze,
whipping around her, in a maze of caressing sky,
begging her forward, pleading to be satisfied by her footsteps.
Her breath hangs in the air frosted by the grip of the fog,
shaping into sharp crystals that cut at her face
as she continues toward the edge.

Julie Patterson

Colorful Orcish Lovesong to a Human Woman

You with blue eyes look into the sky, watch sun and moon.
Many time me think you look like nice bird, a pale white bird.
I like bird, bird fly into setting sun in sky where moon shines white.
Axe of mine sing like bird and reminds me of blue eyes,
axe is red when sings.
Red on axe is red as lips on bird,
bird sings with lips and make my eyes wet.
Color of birds hair is dark, dark is water in Dreanor,
Dreanor I not like, bird hair I do.
I like red as axe, blue as eyes, white as moon, dark as water.
I like bird.
As sun and moon,
I can't like you,
you can't like I.
But as sky we like we.

Fredrik Brunnberg

Is There Hope?

The youth of today are searching for an
example, someone to look up to.
Their parents and peers, even the government,
don't seem to know what's right to do.

Their parents are too busy and have no time.
So they turn to their peers and are persuaded to commit a crime.

Now incarcerated they've become, at a young age, feeling lost without a hope.
Sitting in a jail cell thinking, "How in the world am I to cope?"

"Seems like everyone I turned to always let me down."
"When I needed them the most, they were no where to be found."

My friends let's make a difference.
So many youth need our support today.
It takes us to show them the love they need.
So let's join together, hand in hand, and pray.

Deana McHorse

Struggle to Be Free

In my struggle to be free I tried desperately just to be like
others around me.
When I was young, many days were spent away from my family.
I cried in a room alone, surrounded by darkness, praying for acceptance to be like
others. I was told, that I was slow, and that my abilities were limited.
People would talk for me, my inner voice cried out to be heard!
I felt myself slipping away slowly, sinking into a state of withdrawal.
Then I met someone who took the time to listen, looked beyond my limitations, and
saw "ME,"
They helped me to understand and to be understood.
That was the first day I felt acceptance,
No longer did my inner voice cry out in anguish!
My life has a meaning, and a purpose,
Now I help others like "ME"
tear down the barriers
In their "struggle to be free"

Hope Birch

The Singer

went to see a singer,
that is . . . one who sings
he made the hall ring, man he could sing
. . . Once

his art was a faded glory

a . . . his-tory

a somewhat patchy story

like he could sing . . .
. . . Once

as the hair the notes were false,
the waist had thickened,
his moves had pause
instead of poise,
but then some feminine pulses quickened.

Still . . . the night wasn't wrong
if not the singer,
'twas the beauty in the song

Rob Shattock

Sunshine Valentine

You are my special sunshine,
The one that makes me glow,
The one that knows my many faults,
And yet, still loves me so.

You are my special sunshine,
Who never puts me down,
Who knows when I am hurting,
And understands my frown.

You are my special sunshine,
Who always keeps me strong,
While distance may keep us apart,
Your love is like my song.

I thank you special sunshine,
And thank God you're my Sis,
For my life would not be complete,
If WE were not like this.

Kathryn Heffner

Whoever You Are

I could love you
    I could touch you
    I could kiss you
    Whoever you are
    You can take my heart
    That's a great start
    But I'm afraid I'd get hurt
    When we part
    So I only give half
Of my love
Of my touch
Of my kiss
    To whoever you are
    But that's not enough you say
So my love
I take it all away
All of my love
All of my touch
All of my kiss
    From whoever you are.

Jennifer Ball

Tell Me if You Know

How can you exchange ideals in the microcosmos?
How can you gain assured help from an angel?
From where do poetic thoughts come?
Why does one person like a particular joke and another hate it?
Why does much knowledge, once gained, cause pain?
Why do some parents hate their own children?
Why do some beautiful people fall in love with homely ones?
Why do some bad people deliberately do good deeds?
Why do some good people deliberately do bad deeds?
Will God ever let us know what He looks like?
Which road would you take to find the storehouse of light, or of darkness?
Why does only one river in North America flow from South to North?
Are zebras white with black stripes or black with white stripes?
How can you sing, dance, and act as if no one is watching when they are?
How can you forgive a repeated betrayer?
How can you cry if you have been conditioned not to?
Why would one give their life for a good man, but not for a righteous man?
How can you love as if you have never been hurt?
How can you write poetry without inspiration?
Tell me if you know.

    Shelby Peterson

"Starting Again"

Starting again is so hard to do, stopping old habits trying to find new.
It is easy to say to forget and move on,
but not when you are the one that was harmed.
How can something go from bad to good?
When your heart and mind are not understood?
Can anyone else feel your pain?
When it is this bad you have nothing to gain.
A broken heart, a broken mind, a broken spirit,
can other people actually hear it?
All of the trust, faith, hopes, and dreams
were tossed aside like a child's boring toy, taking with it all of the joy.
If the interest in me faded so long ago,
why did you stay here putting on a show?
It is terribly confusing, I know not what I did.
I thought I was a good wife to you, were you acting like a kid?
I am badly torn up inside, I failed to see how good you could hide.
You did this very well you see, I feel like you took advantage of me.
I don't know if you realize the damage you have done,
I wonder if my heart can mend and begin to trust anyone.
So starting again will be so very hard for me.
Where will the trust, faith, and hope be?
There is only one chance I am trying to give,
if my heart cannot mend, our marriage won't live.

Troubled times of our lives together.

    Sandra Labadie

Transition

Remnants of a winter's cycle cling to the mountainside.

An image of cascading waterfalls is a snapshot of the
   winter's debris as it grounds itself to the edges of the rock formations.

A barren landscape can no longer hide under its virgin blanket.

Droplets are created by the caress of the sun. They dangle from the
   cascades, as if they were a symbol of life's balance.

Silence provides the sustenance for us to listen as this season takes
   its last breath.

    Denise L. Feirer

Dreams and Puzzles

A heart is like a broken puzzle and road up a hill.
It has cracks, bumps, bends, curves, bridges and railroad crossings.
You fix the cracks and then another bump.
The bridge falls.
They all get fixed and all of a sudden everything starts cracking,
bumping, bends, curves.
The lights start flashing, then the crash.
LIFE IS LIKE DREAMS
AND
PUZZLES

    Treasure Thorpe

H.E.R Theme:
Among the Stolen Moments

a turtle struggles impatient
in the sea of stagnation
in the stillness of the lake
a turtle finds oppression
some food for the soul
a starving turtle sought
only a cent to her name
she'll give a penny for a thought
asphyxiation made her pale
because imagination, she inhales
Sellouts find the payday
while a turtle always fails
A Moment of Truth is near
the Rabbits are in fear
"Hold down the Turtles!"
an uprising, it is here
"I'm the Revolution
not televised on a station
Common Sense will blow the horns
for the war cry of a nation!!"

    Hiro Kanno

My Love

I know you are
Out there,
I just don't know where.
I know we will be
Together soon,
And you might be that
Person I love now.
There are too many
Things I want you
To be,
But I know you will
Be perfect.
At least in my eyes
You will be.
Though I may not
Know you now—
I miss you and
Love you so . . .

    Terra Decker

Caustic Emotions

i was ten years old
and just like that
life as i knew it was over.
my mother died
but i couldn't cry.
what the hell is wrong with me?
and instead of trying then
to get my emotions out
i boxed it up
and locked it away
in storage.
from that point on
my true self was shielded
by an inauthentic facade
to block out the pain.
and i can guarantee
that no matter how much you try
that's all you will see
and will ever see
until i die.

    Jason Mcdonald

WINGS

Wings are so familiar, soft and feather light.
They stroke us so gently and relieve us from plight.

But where do Wings come from? We wonder and ponder. . . .
Are they a gift from Heaven floating down from above?
From the Wings of the Angels or maybe from a dove?

Wings soar for the eagles and swoop them so deep.
The soft warm down fills our pillows of sleep.

Wings feather out on the angel, cover their arms to help them see others in the sadness and dark.
Wings help guide them back to the light; the light of His hope and His faith.

Wherever Wings come from, be from Angels or Harps,
Your Wings have touched me, truly through to my heart.

I know that you're special, a true gift from God: I want to thank Him for your Wings of Might.
You have showed me kindness and friendship helped me to heal, and fly back to the Light.

For when I am an Angel, and you are the Wings, there will be nothing we can't
conquer and together we will fly.
For on the Wings of an Angel there is no one to dare.
We will soar and we'll swoop, do as we wish, flying to new heights, spreading His bliss

I'll never forget you and the cover you bear;
'Cause Wings are so special, because I care.

Forever Friends
Cynthia Brickner

Call upon the Name

There was a day in your past, when you came to a point you had nowhere to go. And you had no guarantee that for you, there would be a tomorrow. You had done things that if others knew they would hang their heads in shame. But you came to that point where you had no choice but to call upon a Name.

A Name that is full of power, glory, honor, and that has the power to save. A Name that belongs to the One Who conquered death, hell and the grave. He was nailed to a cross, on a hill outside Jerusalem, for the whole world to see. The Man, Who was God, in the flesh, died so that from the penalty of sin you'd be free.

Jesus is the Name that you called upon when you came to the point of despair. And even though you may have failed Him, you have found that He is always there. He sits at the right hand of God, making intercession for you my friend. Won't you let this Jesus become your Saviour, Lord, King, and Most Beloved Friend?

It is simple to do, but the world makes it so hard for all of us to do.
For you see, you have to confess your sins, and then think of others, and not you.
Jesus first, then others, and then yourself, is not always the easiest way. However, if you remain faithful, and are an overcomer, you will have your day.

Your day when you walk the streets of gold, in the glories of Heaven above, When you can learn and be more at peace, in the greatness of God's undying love. Remember, if you had been the only sinner, in this world, He would have died for you. So go and tell others about Him, and then go and do what He tells you to do.

Roger Daub

Joe

He's my first thought of each day,
When asked my hero, he's usually who I say.
He's been through a lot and proves he is strong
I haven't seen him lately, it's definitely been too long.
He drove the sweetest car, that almost took his life.
It was quick and almost fatal, sharp like a knife.
We rushed to him, fast as we could,
Like any loving family certainly would.
We worried and cried of what was to be,
We were all hurt by this—especially me.
He was my hero, my favorite person around
So loving so caring like a gentle sound.
I miss him so much, it's a feeling so dear,
I only get to see my brother one short time a year.
We were always so close, to be so far away,
When people hear about my story they ask if I'm okay.
I usually answer softly, with thoughts running through my mind,
I wonder if this heart break will ever pass? Probably not with time.
It's already been four long lonely years,
But still with the thought, my eyes fill with tears.

Shaun Sowell

Wonders of Our Farm

If you could hear what I hear

Birds singing
Tom Turkey Thumping
Roosters Crowing
Dogs Barking
Cats Purring
Calves Mooing
Goose Squawking, Honking
Duck Quacking
Hens Clucking
Baby Chicks Chirping
Baby Turkeys Peeping
The wind rustling through the trees
Tom Turkey sounding a warning

You would hear what I hear!
The Wonders Of Our Farm

Patricia Gael Christopher

She's Not Ready Yet

Lost in a sea of emotions
Water beginning to rise
Love sinks in her heart
As the tears fill her eyes

The lethal hatred is spewing
From a hole in her sanity
Denial becomes her savior
As she drowns in envy

Swept upon the shores of oppression
Desolate in every respect
Longing for benevolence
But she's not ready yet

Amanda Ries

Life's Theme

Little by little
we waste away
in the world
we try to play.

Little by little
we do not care
of the love
that brought us here.

Little by little
we lose our souls
to the world
we know so well—
that has no love
for us to love,
but we
as chessmen
play.

James Hargrave

Seasons

Seasons they came
To dance only for a while
But like the breeze I grasped,
To hold on to them still.
And finally I realized,
Amongst all that mattered:
The sparrows will chatter,
From a lonely winter tree,
Reminding me of your thoughts,
Playing games within me.

Sachin Dheer

Only You

Do you know that every time I see you, it takes months to forget your eyes?
Would you care if I told you that I look in every crowd for your face, for just a glimpse
of you eases my tortured soul? Do you know how hard it is not to call to you or run to
your arms? Would you care if I told you that you haunt my every dream, my every
waking moment, my very heart?
Would you say it was alright, or would none of this matter at all?
You are like a blessing and a curse, all at once. If I could see into your heart for just an
instant, what would I find there? I am afraid of what I would find and of the color of
your eyes. So I go on each day searching for you and hoping I won't find you. This is
my fate. To love one that will never love me. To live always in fear of that moment
when the look in your eyes tells me my nightmares are true.
To never love another. For there is only you.

Jennifer Brooks

For You

Thoughts that run through my head,
make me sorry for things I have said.
Confused about life, confused about you,
confused about what I am supposed to do.
Knowing I love you, but still knowing pain,
knowing that in sadness nothing is gained.
Wanting to smile, yet only I cry,
just because I fail doesn't mean I don't try.
In you I know I'll never loose faith,
and I know in time our love will show its strength.
More than you know you make my life complete,
I am so glad that fate gave us the chance to meet.
Yes, I do get upset, life has its twists and turns,
but without life's lessons what would we learn?
Don't doubt my love to you I am forever true,
I am not the bad guy out to ruin you.

Lesley Hartz

Too Early

Yesterday, we went to the park
My dog and I.
She to look for birds to bark at, and green grass to roll in,
I to look for things less tangible, but just as important.
The brown grass was matted under her soft paws
and my wintertime shoes
No birds teased her with their singing—they were still on vacation.
And the intangibles I sought—those senses of new life, of joy—
weren't there
We were too early.
She refused to believe it, running over the dry grass
Looking up in the quiet trees and starved bushes.
And we both saw the empty swings on rusted chains—the square lonely box filled with
sand and snow
She wouldn't believe it—but I knew
We were too early.
I started back to the sidewalk—to wintertime, and sadness
And then I saw the single robin
I saw small, small shoots of grass
And a coatless boy sped by on a bike.
Maybe, after all—we were just a little early.

Elizabeth Lower

Annie

I have seen what I consider beauty
A powerful, intelligent woman
Her eyes captivate me with hopes and dreams
A voice that whispers a calm sweet melody
Someone who listens though as hard as it seems
Her aura that brightens the darkest of rooms
Her hair blows briskly like a breeze on a sunny afternoon
The reassurance that no matter what happens she will always be there for me
Her soul touches me like no other leaving me at a loss for words
Her heart bleeds purity and shows the world what love should be

Felipe Candelaria

You

Myself above the clouds so high
Lift me up
I can not cry
The wind it blows the chill mourn air
I see it all as I pass by
The darkest light of all the night
Issue forth one's own spite
And to this end I know it's true
My love for you will help me through

Ian Bradley

How Blest I Am

How blest I am
To know he's there . . .
To show concern
To Always Care.

How Blest I am
The heavens swear . . .
All he has
is mine to share.

How Blest I am
His presence bears . . .
All good things
From him are there.

Precious person
I'm aware . . .
Nobody's better
"Homme Extraodinare"

Richard Liszanckie

The Robe

Your robe of acanthus
 Worn by ages,
In leaves of green, gold-kissed
 Ancient sages—
All of them, you wear them
 Well enough
For us all. Timelessly
 You wear them,
Are caressed, kissed by each
 And every
One. Living leaves, green lips
 Whispering
Their song into your folds,
 Singing grace,
Arias of perfume,
 Remembrance.
Even in thorns, they choose you
 To adorn.

Jason Schneider

The Fantasist Dream

Have you ever read
The Belgariad
or Mallorean.

\Have you ever envisioned . . .
a world that never was
and never ever will be.

This is . . . a fantasist dream

\Would you ever write
a book from this dream.

This is . . . the fantasist game

Drew Patridge

America's Forgotten Lives

I see you off to the side of the street, all dirty and scared, taking what change society can
spare. It takes all that you have with shame put aside to ask for money without hurting
your pride.
You're not asking for money to buy drugs or beer, but maybe enough for a hot meal and
the reassurance that someone might still care.
You are one of America's forgotten lives.

You fought for our country, you worked hard everyday, but when you needed help we
pushed you away.
You helped so many when you had wealth, but now in your time of need,
your friends look at you like your someone else.
You gave them all you had, maybe even part of your life. Now your friends look away as
they drive by. You are one of America's forgotten lives.

You ask yourself why me?
Did I do wrong, or maybe I didn't do enough?
The only answer that you get is a face full of society's dust.
You sleep under bridges, in alleys and vacant lots.
All you pray for is a moment away from your thoughts.
Did your country forget you, what about your so called friends?
Everyone wrote you off, and your life hasn't even come to an end.
You are one of America's forgotten lives.

We give aid to other countries, we give them food and warm places to sleep.
But when it comes to our own people we can't even give them something to eat.
We call you a problem, we call you a street disease.
We are so selfish we won't listen to your pleas.
You are one of America's forgotten lives.

Robert Christensen

I Could Fly

There once was a boy who wanted to fly. Every morning he would plan when he
would fly. That was his dream. One night before his parents put him to bed he asked them
do dreams come true and they said if you believe. He went to sleep in hopes that the next
day would be clear skies. In the morning he woke up put on some clothes and ran to the
bridge by his house. He climbed up and then . . . jumped. He spread out his arms and flew
better than any bird I have ever seen. Then all of a sudden he woke up. It was only a dream.
But he was going to try. The very next morning, he woke up threw on any clothes, ate
breakfast, and told his parents that he was going to follow his dreams. They said, "I hope
you do son." Afterwards he went to the bridge, climbed up, closed his eyes, and jumped. All
of a sudden he felt a shot of pain go through his body. He opened his eyes and everything
turned white. He looked at his arms and saw two beautiful white wings. Then he realized
that he could fly. He flew everywhere even to see his parents and say good-bye.
He could finally fly.

Maribel Jonte

My Plea

I am trapped in a corner, unable to move
I am facing good and evil, but I dance to the devil's groove
I have seen the light, but the devil's temptations lure me in
All that I can say for myself is that I know I've been living in sin
The devil has crowned me queen
because a coupon for hell I have redeemed
Honor thy self is what I have been told,
but if done in the dark the story won't unfold
That is what I was promised, you and I agreed
So why is it that the karma of it all, has me on bent knees
Begging the lord for forgiveness because I have done as I please
Now unable to handle the consequences of all my dirty deeds
How could you betray me, we were such good friends
You introduced me to a night life that was without end
Now you turn your back on me when trouble comes my way
I guess that is why you can't trust a snake
because he's liable to bite you on any given day
Lord I stand before you used and abused, living in my own filth
I don't have much to say expect my heart has sunk in guilt
I am repenting for my sins and my desire to do wrong is gone
I ask of you, no I beg of you, can a sinner come home?

Erica Brazier

Whisper

Midnights upon me
Here in your arms
Lost in your silence
Is where I want to be
Loving you is too easy
Can't you see
Just how much I adore you
You'll never know
I'll just whisper softly
I love you
You know how to
Talk to me about anything
Make me feel better
When I am blue
You just whisper softly
I love you
Just how much I adore you
You'll never know
I'll just whisper softly
I love you

Dusty Spradley

The Puzzling Soul

Our soul is a puzzle,
many pieces of life,
strewn apart at first
rounded by laughter & joy
curved by sadness & loss
sculptured by memories
pressed into a lifetime
a cornered love,
a smooth embrace,
indented tragedies
never matching perfectly
held tight against, each secret
Until the soul, is formed . . . .

Lyn Doran

Twilight

Electricity,
Bordered simplicity
Passion in each caress
Tendrils of emotion
As lips meet,
Fingers trail over
Emotion softened skin
Privacy in the half light
Candles flickering as
Trembling forms become one
Unsurity becoming
Passion
As resistance drops
And desires become paramount.
Fingertip caresses
Over shivered skin
Shared softly
In gloaming twilight.

Jamie Stine

Remembrance

It's us, only us
my brother, my friend.
He is by my side
like my shadow.
No one can replace him
though his memory is faint.
I reach out for him
only to find sadness.
Wait! Here he is!
Happiness enters
as remembrance of his love
is found again.

Regina Simmons

the american body

these eyes of green are naive no longer

the brain ignorant no longer to the injustice

when young candy was sweeter and air fresher

this onion of purity loses its layers

my 21 years in body are aged twice that in mind

my heart yearns for someone that can see past my shell

someone who has a thirst for truth among the lies we've been fed

he sees without the blindfold that is installed at birth

ignorance isn't bliss, enlightenment is

it's a bliss that I writhe in filled with tears

I pledge allegiance to the flag, for the hypocrisy for which it stands

for one nation under god as long as you fit the mold

declaring war on the human spirit, removing all identity

killing indians in the name of the apostles is nothing short of an atrocity

taking their land during the killing spree calling it divine right

why should I be angry? If I'm silent while others are taken . . .

who will speak out for me when they come for me . . . my anger is my skin

who will our gov't. declare war on next and give it some divine purpose

there was nothing divine about it. I call it third reich.

Nicole Asselta

Snow

The twinkles gather together,
not just forming snow.
But, creating a crystal white landscape!
These little "twinkles" keep falling,
like its cousin rain.
Landing on each other, or sometimes on houses, cars, everywhere, really.
They seem harmless, but that's another story.
In the moonlight night, they dance together.
Not realizing that they keep accumulating.
Mother Nature is sometimes too tricky for the meteorologists.
Schools are empty, yearning to feel the movement of the kids.
Offices are motionless, no copiers operating or any paperwork rustling.
It seems the city is under wraps.
Pushed into a snow globe,
not able to know why, or how.
Will time tell?
In this case it will.

Ijeoma Nwatu

The Clock

I stare at the face on the wall
It looks back at me, knowing of its infinite and complete power over me
I am a slave to it
Birth presents its gift to me
I look at the clock
Two roads ask me to travel them
I look at the clock
Problems beg me for solutions
I look at the clock
The sun tempts me to fulfill buried dreams
I look at the clock
I gaze into the eyes of my precious gem
 . . . wondering how long this moment will last
The moon rises, I am tired
I have breathed my last breath
I lay my head back, look at the clock, and smile
The clock dies
I
am
free

Nicole Clark

Run

Run away with me.
We need to be together,
Always and forever.
Together.

Run away with me
Feel your spirit be free.
Together forever
That's what we will be

Run.
Run away with me
So we can hold each other,
Love each other.
Always and forever.
Just come,
Come run with me.

Lindsay Coleman

Falling Down

I'm falling down
I can't find my feet
and I don't know why
I'm tripping.
It seems that
everything I knew
everything I could hold on to
has drifted away.
I can't find relief
in anything I believe
can't find relief
in anything you say.
And these thoughts
in my head
just lead me to believe
that I'm better off
feeling nothing.

Lauren K. Haggis

Yesterday, Today, or Tomorrow

May yesterdays catch up to today
And be home tomorrow
Then my lost love
Would not be lost anymore
Tomorrow could bring joy
I could think back then
And I could be happy
Bring the past to me now
And the future would be ours
We would be happy yesterday
And for sure today
The greatest part is tomorrow
Because we would be forever more
And you wouldn't be a lost love anymore

Sandra Redlawsk

The Kiss I Want

I want a kiss from you today.
Because you are special,
In a special way.
So kiss me soon without a pause.
Kiss me 'cause you like me
Or, do it just because
The kiss I want must come from you.
Place it very softly.
And make it very true.
You can kiss me quick.
Or, you can kiss me slow.
Just kiss me now.
Before I go.

Chris Pridmore

Innocence

For Stacy and all young souls
yet to be hardened by life's trials.
Spirit dreams
People dance
Innermost thoughts
appearing by chance

Remembering our past
Our future near
finding a way
to keep from fear

Looking for love
a bit here and there
trying to make life
always seem fair

Wondrous world
all big and bright
Hold on to your innocence
with all your might

James Lewis Myers, Jr.

Love Is . . .

Love is . . .

Love is in our hearts to share
Love is found in those who care
In a girl or a boy
Even in a tiny toy
Love is happy, never sad
Love is good, never bad
Never be afraid to love
Take example from God above
You will never be without love.

Fran Lupinacci

Love Angel II

Her eyes are sweetness
And her body a neatness
With her heart shows warmth in sweetness

Her words are sugar
But her life is not that of a hooker
Instead that one of a true lover

Wings around her remain unseen
But they are there it seems
For she must have wings
'Cause her love has made my heart fly

Chris Price

Being Free

it is a beautiful day
the sun is high
a deep breath
revives her body
the wind stirs
the grass sways
dances
in harmony
she smiles
the warmth
drinking
embracing the freedom
she comes alive
she begins to float
as she runs
through the
tall grass
her hair
turning
to silk

Marilyn Fives

Cliches

Wherefore art thou, spontaneity,
That life-fulfilling gaiety,
Which enhances earthly brevity . . .
Wherefore art thou, ecstasy,
That breath-taking un-expectancy,
Which rouses inner-poignancy . . .
Wherefore art thou, humility,
That friendly personality,
Which facilitates equality . . .
Wherefore art thou, sanity,
That respect of all humanity,
Which glues together society . . .
Wherefore art thou, history,
That backbone of life's mystery,
Which encircles us in cursory cliches?

Karen Noel

No Escape

Air so cold, compelling
Caressing his hands, his face
Covering him with simple hatred
Heart is a blank forgotten space.

Told of a warmer climate
But fear of being wrong
Been here long as can remember.
Not understanding he belongs.

Does everything turn this cold
Life's diamonds sparkle and fade
The new climate has frozen
Once again to be betrayed.

Frozen in fear of the past
Unable to take the new road
Trapped under iced deception
Unsure to swim or hold.

Holding out of sheer regret
Another try will result the same
Heart frozen solid now
And his mind will not be tamed.

With each inch he sinks
Into the abyss' widening gape
Chains of difficulty surround his heart
Now he never can escape.

Kevin Whitten

sins of the past

take away this pain of mine
oh, fortunes up ahead
for if my life no more than this
i'd sooner i was dead
death an end to life would be
with life eternal hell
my pain runs deeply to my soul
from grace to fire i fell
this life on Earth to pay must be
for sins of lives before
to end it now my debt repay
i long for life no more

Roy Fredrick

Haiku 4

Cat, Woman, both am I
Very soft, my breath floats by.
Among the great grasses I walk.

Marina Payne

Alone

I fear the night because
when it comes I am alone
nobody to talk to
nobody to see
I fear the night because
then I see me
all by myself in a cold room that means
nothing to me
I sit on my bed and think of my
future and where I'm going tomorrow
I may never know
I fear the night because
when it comes I am alone

Melissa Scott

I Am Unique

Your sight will approve it,
A test will confirm it,
My performance, acknowledge it,
My touch is so tender,
My lips, to remember,
My soft skin, is appealing,
Enchants all your feelings,
My walk will allure you,
My voice can assure you,
You feel silk in my hair,
Perfume fills the air,
My hands are so slender,
My touch very tender,
I am, as my instincts reveal me;
A WOMAN!

Jane Johnson

Tightrope of Souls

Tumbling, twisting, turning;
Thoughts tangle together,
tightly pulling taunt
the strings that hold us together.

Pressure released,
thoughts pour out,
presenting new opportunity,
a fresh chance.

One soul to the next,
a touch, a breath,
changing and pulsing
the fibers of each being.

Together, pulling each along,
slowly creeping forward,
balancing pain and laughter,
we travel the tightrope of souls.

Christine Seal

Huh?

Some things made me unable
To distinguish nonfiction from fables
Never knew why Cain slew Abel,
Only wear designer labels
Where can I get more knowledge?
Should I go to college?
Or should I read these books?
Where can I open my mind
To get myself unhooked?
Free will to guide my thoughts
No social forces to bring me to a halt
With all this wisdom I've sought
I still buy things I don't want

Eric Honea

Emptiness

Every time a car goes by
I turn and look for you
And when I see your beautiful smile
My heart seems to break in two

Because I never really realized
Just what was going on
Until the months had passed me by
And I knew that you were gone

I wish I wasn't here alone
And you could hold me one more time
Because I cannot stand this emptiness
The heart that cries is mine

I can almost feel your touch
Even though you've gone
And as the days drag slowly by
I find it hard to carry on

I just can't seem to say good-bye

As I cry to those above
The tears poor freely from my eyes
For what I've lost is love.

Naomi Espinola

Conflict

A war is waging between my
Mind and heart
What I know in my mind
Is not within my heart;

One way is wrong
One way is right
How do I end this fight?

The consequences of my
Actions
Can bring others' reactions
I don't want to falter
So I know I must alter;

The decision I make in the
End
Is one in which
I will not bend.

Margaret Sauriol

Butterfly

Before us lies a beauty,
Made tenderly with love.
A package small and gentle.
From Heaven up above.

The human eye cannot see,
The beauty that's within.
Our focus falls upon it.
We give a gentle grin.

It struggles hard and silent.
It wants to be set free.
Is there something I can do?
Does it need help from me?

From this shell, a wondrous thing,
Emerged for all to see.
Its beauty was held captive,
But now it is set free.

There is beauty in this thing,
We did not understand.
Precious little butterfly,
So tiny, yet, so GRAND . . .

Steven Russom

Battle Cries

We had a cease fire
in this angry battle
we had been waging.
The peace was over
far too soon.
Long before the ink
had a chance to dry
on the treaty.
There are no more weapons
or armaments left to carry.
All the big guns have been
used up and cast aside.
My pale banner is raised
in hushed surrender.
Overtake my walls now.
Go ahead, conquer a land
that could have been yours
without the bloodshed or tears.
This time the victory
will be sweet for only one of us.

Karen Hannington

Living

When we enter this world,
vulnerability sets in.
With some warmth and love,
we start to begin

unavoidable vicious cycles
of love/hate relationships.
Sprouting with a first date,
and a sweet good-night kiss.

Then there's marriage and that baby,
which I'm sure you've all heard.
Masses of responsibility
wiped out with the first word.

But after marriage comes divorce
another reason to let go,
"single parent raising child"
and it just goes to show,

In the vulnerable society
created our very first day;
in this world there's no option
but to leave the same way.

Courtney Steele

The One

I walked alone
Along the mountain side
I walked alone
Along the coast line
I walked alone
Over the bridges
And under the dark clouds
I walked alone
On my birthday
And on New Years Day
I walked and walked
And walked
Alone
Then I realized
That I will never have to
Walk alone again

Sung Park

Your Kiss to Me

Like a feather
That dances
With a warm
Summer's breeze,
Dance your whisper,
Across my cheek.
With your sigh
Lift me high,
To those places unknown.
Help me free
My emotions,
Where eagles have flown . . .
And
When soaring is soared,
And we've reached
Each peak . . .
Whisper your dance,
Across my cheek.

Sandra Young

Haiku

When I pour this soul
This cup is fully empty
On this quest for life

Sye Spence

Untitled

We spend a lifetime searching
for what we are not sure
the question is our cancer
the answer is our cure

As we grow older
while the years slip by
our answer is no closer
the question now is why

Why must we find the answer
to a question we don't know
is the answer out there
or should we let it go

We've spent our whole life searching
But in the end we find
that we've discovered nothing
just left our years behind

Robert Vaghini

Beautiful Children

*Dedicated to all the children of the world
with special needs*
Beautiful children
Struggling to talk

beautiful children
Struggling to walk

beautiful children
Struggling to survive

beautiful children
Struggling to be apart

beautiful children
Struggling to be accepted

beautiful children
Struggling to achieve

beautiful children
These children are yours
And mine.

Sammer Ghouleh

Skills

Some do art and paint
Some mold with clay,
I try playing with poetry
I rid my frustrations that way.

Others collect rare coins
For which they have to pay,
But I help my mind
Thinking of what to say.

Some play the horses
Other just gamble it away,
Playing cards or on ball games
And do it every day.

But life is enough of a gamble
No matter what you do,
So I just try to enjoy it
Within my mind a love that is true.

Marlowe C. Burr

The Circle

As we say good-bye
Are we ready for tomorrow
Yesterday is only a memory
Tomorrow is up to you
Remember the past
To help the future
Obstacles in life makes us think
Mistakes we make today
We learn from tomorrow
All we have is today
Tomorrow may never come
But if it does, live and learn
Respect one another
What we do today
Affects us tomorrow
Because life is a full circle. . . .

Dawn Rusin

Backyard Desert

Sleek slimy snakes slide and slither.
Lizards creep here, there and thither.
Rabbits hop beyond the wall
While turtles scarcely move at all.

Thrice chirp the birds up in the air.
Thrice chitter rodents here and there.
Thrice call the cats upon the gate
As spooky spiders sit and wait.

See the grass grow green on ground
Amid the weeds all strewn around.
Vision, decision, stress and strain
Await the desert's earth of rain.

Saguaro sentinels guard the land
As ocotillo spindly stand.
Mesquite trees bend and break the bough
On spiky cactus. Ouch and ow!

Days are heated, harsh and hot.
Nights are nice, now or not.
Dawn and dusk portray a view
An artist's easel cannot do.

Frank George

I Am

I am just a tiny drop
In the ocean's surging tide
Just the smallest grain of sand
In deserts vast and wide
In this mighty universe.
This world of space and time.
Who would ever notice me
Midst all the stars that shine.
In the far and distant lands
Beyond the deep blue sea.
From the north and to the west.
Who has heard of me.
I will write my poetry
Of days of long ago
Even though I'm not as great
As those who've gone before
My poems will live forever
For everyone to see
And if I reach a lonely heart
Some one might think of me

Irene Adams

Memories of a Hurricane

Looking out my window at the trees,
Coconut boughs bending in the breeze
Debris flying across the parking lot
Whoa, there goes someone's pot
A bolt of lightning hit the ground
Knocking the lamp off its mound
Heard my neighbor locking his door
All boats heading for shore
Here comes the driving rain
Memories of the last Hurricane.

Simple pleasures slipped away
Like raindrops dimple on the bay
Frightened masses run and scream
Agony wrenches, nightmarish dream
With a crack of thunder, heavens break
And drown all in humanity's wake
Sudden silence drips from my core
Broken bodies run with gore
Cry for help on Mercy's shore
But some will find it never more

Randolph Powe

The Sales

I'm shivering with cold
I'm absolutely freezing
I'm coughing and spluttering
And can't stop sneezing

My feet are like ice
I wish morning would come
My eyes keep running
And my backside is numb

I'm fed up and tired
I'm wet through to the skin
This queuing for hours
Is a downright sin

Why all this standing
In torrential gales
You're right, you've guessed it
It's the January sales

Dennis Beannan

A Special Gift

I watch a beautiful butterfly,
As it majestically flies by.
I watch the golden sunset,
Sink slowly from the sky.

I watch the birds as they fly past,
Heading towards their resting tree,
I see them settle from the night,
To sleep so peacefully.

I watch the day turn into night
As daylight fades slowly away
I see the stars come out so bright,
As there ends another day.

I see the moon in all its glory
Rising high as it lights up the sky,
I see clouds resembling cotton balls,
As they slowly pass me by.
Where would I be without this gift,
If these things I couldn't see?
This wondrous gift God gave to me,
These eyes for me to see.

Irene Myrtle Haworth

My Daughter

*To my wonderful
and amazing daughter, Dakota.*

Your wondering eyes,
  how they sparkle and shine.
With every smile that you give,
  my world freezes in time.

From your tiny little hands,
  to your tiny little feet.
With every moment that passes,
  a tiny little heartbeat.

Our two worlds collided,
  our souls have been breached.
By a love like no other,
  that's never out of reach.

Together forever,
  eternity will come.
Side by side with each other,
  our lives become one.

A cry in the night,
  a loving hand that won't falter.
Me, as your mother,
  you, as my daughter.

Kimberly Yancey

New Creations

Creative love at last we know
When we are no longer blown
By uncontrolled winds of emotion
That somehow numb the heart
And paralyze the will
We would release to build
Our new ark of freedom
Where the gentle Spirit
Empowers and encourages
In the quest for life
In all its fullness
And safely guides us
To near and distant ports
That are right for each of us.

Edward Clarkson

Glowworm

Where are you little
glowworm, once found
in the night?
You were once
under a cage,
with your tail of light.

Never have I seen,
another tail so bright;
as the one you wore
that summer night.

Light up your way,
I wish you were
here this day.

Carolyn C. Spily

Youth

6
16
26
36
46
56
Etcetera . . .
I am
A child of God
I am
A child of life.

Patrice G. Burroughs

The Feeling of Nonexistence . . . .

Alone in dreams—
Smothered in loneliness—
No one exists anymore—
Nothing matters—
Love has no meaning—
Hate has stories of no end—
Death is no longer a departure—
Heaven no longer a welcome—
Speech is simple and consistent
Yet meaningless and unheard—
Gestures are strong and painful
Yet somehow go unnoticed—

Anne-Jeanette Nunez

Bottled up Inside

Bottled up inside
Are the feelings
That I hide
The ones I don't express
Because no one understands
I feel alone and scared
I feel that no one can help
It's all up to me
To make things right
But nothings really is wrong
If so then why do I cry?
Why do I feel so bad?
I feel ignored
Rejected
Left for the wild wolves
In my heart
I see the light
And I must keep going
Until the light
Is in my hands

Jessica Simpson

A Dangerous Love

Going down,
loosing my mind.
The hit of this fall
will be too much to handle.
I miss the days when I didn't
have to care about you.
But now,
love has taken
a painful hold on me
and won't loosen its grip.

This love is dangerous.
I know the day I lose you
will be the day
the sun forgets to rise.
Your bitter sweet love
is a taste I can't let go of,
it's addicting in a way.

Sierra Machado

Self Reflections

She looked into the mirror
Unaware of the blankness on her face
For a while she gazed unseeing
A lost soul out of place

Another day awaited her
But all her strength was gone
She knew not how to face
Yet another day alone

Once she had such courage
She fought bravely for her dream
Disillusionment now has broke her
For things are never as they seem

Still she stands in solitaire
Lost in her private hell
Untouchable and uncaring
Before the mirror stands only a shell.

Catherine Talley

Innocence

*For Stacy and all young souls yet to be
I'm Here*
Here I am Mom,
I am born to you this day.
February is my favorite month,
Full of hearts and flower bouquets.
I chose you and Dad
To be there for me.
You are special parents,
And I know you love me.
You have patiently waited
Nine months for us to meet.
Please love me always
Through eternity.
Hold me, sweet Mom,
Hold me close to your breast.
Then hand me to Dad
So I can rest on his chest.

Elaine Goodwin

The Protestant Work Ethic

I have no job,
I have no pay,
But I write
Poetry every day.

Edward Wagner

The Roses' Timid Beauty

There are only a few who have seen,
This brilliant masterpiece of life,
Its beauty beyond all belief,
Its existence spared of all strife,
With a breathtaking aroma,
Peddles scarlet as can be,
Thorns for protection,
A subtle complexion you will see,
As dew slowly rolls down,
The passionate flower,
Created from the fall,
Is gentle misty shower,
Look around for the dew drops,
That reflect the sun's light,
To find the roses' timid beauty,
Hidden only by the night.

Karen Westcott

Missing You

I lone for your touch,
dream of your kiss.
I love you so much,
you know you are missed.

But i will hold strong,
I wait day after day.
Humming the song,
that our hearts often play

I sit up at night,
looking for something i cant find.
The beautiful sight,
of you in my mind.

Now you are here,
my heart fills with joy.
I have nothing to fear,
I'm with you and our boy.

Tommy Gooch III

My Pride

Music is my life
Art is my project
The world is my pride
When there is nothing to look for
I look for hope
Love is my beauty

Anne Re

Smiles

A smile is like a boomerang
Thrown away it returns again
Blooms like flowers in the spring
Spreads around like a sprinkling rain

Give someone some nice words
Tell someone you care
You may find one day
You've found some friends along the way

If you are feeling down and blue
Here is exactly what you should do
Spread a smile around
Then your blues should go away

Spread the smiles 'round like rain
Take some time to sing
Give someone a helping hand
This should make your smile grow!

Lindsey S.

When Dreams Sleep

Dreams sleep deep
in the meadows of the soul.
To revel as night adds
blankets of sparkling mist;
and promises not to wake the dream
with fluttering specks of spun dawn.
Scurrying away to revel in that place
where dreams sleep;
night gauges the reverie so sweet
and revives the heartened day.
In the meadows of the soul;
dreams sleep deep.

Sandra Lambert

The Storm

The storm is coming.
The clouds are moving in.
I see the lightning, hear the thunder.
I wonder if it will ever end.
I stand in the middle of the field,
while the wind tears at the earth.
I should seek protection.
Gather 'round the hearth.
I open the windows.
Let the storm in.
All this chaos and turmoil,
comes from within.
Draw the curtains.
Shut the door.
Keep the storm out.
Safe forevermore.
Seek protection.
Away from the rain.
Escape the weather.
Escape the pain.

Pamela Legg

How

How calm the stream
before the fall
How sweet the sound
before the boom
How still the night
before the dawn
How radiant light
before the dusk
How soft the touch
before the age
How?
How makes it thus.

Emmanuel Marara

Stew

Past forest pillars
over the brick wall
and into the middle
of God's private garden
we soldier,
barefoot and naked
in the mist
we're undernourished
and have come to steal
carrots, tomatoes,
peppers, and potatoes . . .
and I don't think
He'd mind
if we borrowed some
wings, souls,
harps and halos
for the trip back.

William Hanson

My Love

Dedicated to Tammy Heiter
Every day,
when I'm with you,
my eyes light up,
for this is true.
My heart beats fast,
with a smile on my face,
you make me feel,
like I've won first place.
Sometimes I'm speechless,
I'll even draw a blank,
like a knight in shining armor,
hiding in a tank.
I wish I could reach,
the stars up above,
so that I could bring one down,
for you—My Love.

James Omvig Jr.

Tired

As dreams take over
In between sleep and alive.

I'm so tired, and I'm so weak,
And I'm in one of those places
Where I just can't speak.
Through the Silence, all those
Things I try not to think about
Rise up, like a river after thaw.
And the pain returns
And burns. Like a flame.
But through it all I see
The one who'll never leave.
It's you.

So I'm down on my knees,
I'm screaming out, screaming out loud.
Trying to get some attention.
Trying to wake you up,
From three thousand miles away.

Evan Butler-Jones

I Wish

Sometimes I wish I was a bird,
To fly and sing a song never heard,
And go wherever I please
Which such grace and ease.
Sometimes I wish I was Spirit,
To give everyone a little bit
Of Hope and Faith,
To never again hear the word Hate.
Sometimes I wish I was a flower,
Gently growing in a spring shower
With a scent so sweet,
Shining in summer sun's heat.
Sometimes I wish I could tell Thee
Thank You for making me.
I'm everything I wanted to be,
But sometimes forget to see

Lauraine Lagace

Years . . .

Yesterday
I was seventeen
years old.

(AGING)

Tomorrow
I'll be seventy-one
years young.

Lorenzo A. Facorro

Silent Sadness

Tears of silence sweep away,
Softly, slowly try to say,
Fly away, far from here,
Place where nothing is to fear.
Coming, going, bringing pain,
Have to run; world is insane.
Wish upon a distant star;
Things are alright, so far.
Bringing pain back one more time,
committing a shameful, secret crime.
Try to run, try to fly,
Eventually all would die.
Cannot deny, and cannot share,
Cannot admit that I care.
Keep enclosed, not revealed,
Love and pain which I have concealed.
Tears of sadness sweep away
all the pain which tried to stay.

Daniel Warner

Orgasms of the Soul

When you make love to the soul,
clouds slide so silently.
While it happens, I hug you
and stars shine
with the rare shine of the sparks.

Shaking is
the floor under our feet.

And the notion of time is lost
while, silently, I only hug you,
as if in this hug
all my life was gone.

So much secrecy,
accompanies the music of the bells,
in a mute sound, as fresh as water . . .
The music of the bells gets louder,
then it falls again.

And all of this things happen,
while you are making love to the soul.

Maria Corinna Marquez

The Wolf's Eye

I looked into the wolf's eye.
I listened to his faithful sigh
As he whispered into the sun,
"I am the one. I am the one."

As night fell, he slowly disappeared.
All I could see or hear, was a ball
Lit up in the sky.
The next morning my story happened
All over again.
Except this time I knew.
He was the one.

Sarah Adamiak

Don't Call People Names

Don't call people names,
It makes them feel very sad,
It makes them feel like no-one,
And that's very sad,
So don't call people names.
And save yourself the trouble,
Live peacefully,
Gladly, and happily together.

Falon Blessing

Where Did He Go?

Where did he go,
The one with the light,
Who took my dark path,
And made it so bright!

Why did he leave,
Where did he go?
The one I want,
And the one I love so!

This I may never know,
I may never again love.
For now I cannot show,
The same love I have for him!

Heather Barber

Pandora

A candle burns in darkness . . . .

Pandora is a watchful soul.

Marge Schneider

My All

The light plays in her soulful eyes
Like moonbeams from the sky
Yet her smile conceals a sadness
And I often wonder why

I wonder if she feels my love
Does it reach into her heart
Is the harshness of this world to much
Were we star-crossed from the start

It's a lonely clown that laughs aloud
While hiding tears inside
She offers me a quiet place
Where I can rest and hide

As I sit to contemplate the verse
I can feel her love abound
As I start to drift with heavy eyes
I grasp this gift I've found

She fills my being with her love
In love each day I fall
She is everything that God could bring
My wife, my love, my all . . .

Glenn Thrasher

Fallen Angels

I must face
Life's problems every day
Yet my world seems so distant
So far away

And so I tell myself
I must be strong
But it's no use trying
When all hope is gone

I shall feel no more sorrow
I shall feel no more pain
Let the fallen angels carry me
Out of this world in vain

This is a battle
That is much too tough
It seems all my hurt
Is never enough

Sarah Pope

Love

As you look down upon us,
From Heavens high above,
You see we still shed our tears,
From the days we shared our Love.

We walked this path together,
With scenes of joy and play,
We never seem to worry,
Of the endings of a day.

This never ending story,
Of happiness we shared,
Will never be forgotten,
For all the good days that we had.

So when you look upon us,
From Heavens high above,
The Path we walked together,
Was always shared with Love.

John Mingo

He Will Always Be Watching

At the loss of a loved one,
Your tears fell like rain.
Your heart was filled with sorrow
and emptiness and pain.
You felt he wasn't with you.
He wasn't standing by,
but fear not, he is watching
from that great palace in the sky.
He is with his Lord, his Master,
yet he still watches you.
He will be by your side
in all you say and do.
He will be your angel,
the answer to your prayers,
and though he is not here in life,
my friend, he is there.
So, hold your chin up high,
and wipe away those tears,
and know that he is watching
for your remaining years.

Letitihia Sanabria

Angel Bells

My daughter dreamed of being
all that she could be,
a ballerina, a circus clown,
a mom just like me
. . . but most of all she wanted to fly.

I watched her as she pretended
her arms were silken wings.
She was so alive and full of dreams.
She wanted so many things.

Then one day it was decided
these things were not to be.
An accident on the highway
stole most of her dreams from me.

And as I was at her bedside,
crying tears enough for two,
she opened lher eyes and said,
"Mommy, I hear Angel Bells"
. . . and then my daughter flew

Jaime Krys

Broken Daffodil

scared, I stood
like a fragile
    little girl.

helpless, hopeless
There was nothing
    I could do.

words can hurt
like the most
    unimaginable pain.

Why did they
always have to
    act this way?

A wise man once said
time heals all sorrow . . . .

Iana Graham

Just Remember

Just Remember when you're sad
I will come and cry with you
When you're cold
I will come with my arms
and warm you
When you're lonely
I will come and keep you company
When you're hungry
I will come and feed you
and when you need love
I will come and love you
Just Remember
I will come

Joanne Stewart

The Eternal Question

elusive air
amidst the mist
at the center of
a solid yes
is there?
a solid word
our Universe
behind the blind
or anywhere

Nick Emm

The Youth Offering—
The Youth Redeemed

our young grieve
like elderly
who have watched
too many kinfolk die
their innocence
poured out
as a thank offering
to a loveless
pagan
god
THE YOUTH REDEEMED
lift your eyes to the cross
Christ has come to redeem
what was lost
he alone
is Heaven sent
to restore from X
to excellent

Rosalyn Hopkins

When It Hurts to Be Held

Why is it so easy
To let the hurts out
To let go of these stinging tears
and cry
When you are holding me?

Perhaps it is because
Being in your arms
As only your friend
To be comforted
Is hurt enough
By itself
  for tears?

Linda Fuglestad

Mirage

Softly as the wind blows
A leaf falls to the ground.
I turn to look,
But nothing can be found.

Swiftly does the water flow
To the river my tears fall.
Rapidly they get swept away,
As if they had never been there at all.

Slowly does a flower burst—
Up from the cold, hard ground.
I bend down to touch it,
But it leaves me looking around.

Wind blows through my hair
And water splashes my face.
I cannot see the flower,
It has vanished without a trace.

Rosalynne Chan

Survivor's Tale

The princess bid her carriage stop
beside the beggar gate.
She drew a coin from out her purse
and dropped it on a plate.

The man looked up with grateful eyes
and nodded his gray head.
The princess smiled graciously,
wond'ring what life he'd led.

His legs were gone below the knee,
perhaps a fault of birth,
but his dark eyes and aging face
were lined from years of mirth.

The princess felt his hand touch hers.
His eyes were bright with tears.
"I have a secret, maiden fair,
that's helped me through the years.

I tell my self that 'fore my birth,"
He said with downward glance,
"'Twas by my steps on gilded floors
that angels learned to dance."

Brenda Johnson

Wings of My Own

I wandered the streets tall and proud . . .
   thinking out loud.
Finding my dreams a place to live . . .
   wasn't one of the simplest things.
   But I did it!
Now I'm soaring above the clouds!
   On MY OWN WINGS!!!

Eduard Burlak Jr.

The Doorway

The doorway ahead
Seems all too clear
If I walk through it
I lose the one link I have
Left to my past
If I do not walk through
The freedom will slip
Through my fingers
All true love is lost
All restriction found

The doorway behind
Seems all a blur
My freedom found
My love swallows me whole
I miss the doorway
And what remains inside
But new things lie ahead
For me to find
So good-bye, doorway
That's left behind

Kelly McGinn

Love Is Invisible

Love is invisible,
But soft to the touch,
Warm in it's caress.
It makes you fly higher,
Soaring above the clouds.
It makes its long journey,
But never tires out.
It passes over mountains
And reduces them to molehills.
It swims in the ocean,
Gliding smoothly along.
It basks in the sun,
All toasty and warm.
It's in the warmest touch
And the coldest tone.
It's always there,
But you can't see it.
Because:
Love is invisible.

Rebecca Griffith

Aware

Sun spoked railing
shadowed on porch
warming sun
mid afternoon on the dusky side.
Like warming of chestnuts
on a wintry, city street, night
so do thoughts come about,
kindled to a warming glow
tempered and bent.

Dimitrios Pappajion

A Passing Beauty

A passing beauty
the eyes withhold,
and then look over for an exterior form:
A joy forever,
clear picture burnt into blurred eyes,
Images of no sense,
Sense of only You.
I think love, but you contradict,
finally hanging limp over the edge;
love spent, energy drained,
black, hollow eyes
withholding a passing beauty.

Ameet Advani

Budapest in Black & White

Your eyes reflect
Inspired visions
of beauty, and a mother's grace
Your breast swells
with a poet's inconsolable grief
Shadows ripple beneath flesh
that is scarred with memories . . .
not quite remembered
The anguish of incorruptible joy
Denied

Anna West

The Peace Poem

The original peace poem
I am not exempt . . .
                from earthly trials
I am not elite . . .
                to worldly possessions
I am just a human . . . Being
                living in god's care
I am just your neighbor . . .
                within this life we share

Marsha Schultz

Sorrow

Sorrow for the dissipated
Rejection for the separated
Dreams filled with trepidation
A lonely heart's anticipation

linger for the sullen hour
Resilient days will soon devour
Caustic eons born anew
Humility to guide one through

a placid crusade for dignity
Heeded by complicity
Squander every dismissed word
Until their meaning is absurd

life's culmination is what we seek
With no conception of the meek
A world without simplicity
Is what my sorrow brings to me

Michael Gerard

The Girl

She follows me, this phantom
And she's with me night and day
But no one else can see her
For she always hides away

But I know her in emotions
And I feel her in my heart
And every night I hear her
As she whispers to the dark

She's always out of reach to me
As restless as the sea
I would so want to show her
For this girl is the real me

Mariette Olwagen

My Mother, My Friend

The day that you gave birth to me
You became a mother
We love each other very much
We're always there for each other
You're not only just my mother
You're also my friend
You're there when I need you
I know you'll be there 'til the end
You've put me on the right track
And you've helped me when I'm down
You help me to dry up my tears
You make me smile instead of frown
When you and I go out
We always get into trouble
I am so much like you
I'm just like your double
To know you are my mother
It always makes me smile
I love you oh, so much
You make everything worth while

Angela Baker

"Narrow Mind"

The skeleton could walk and talk
her bulging eyes were blue.
If you could catch her sitting still
She'd share a word with you.
Just twenty-three years old and yet
her face was aged and lined.
Her sickly structure evoked stares
to which her eyes were blind.
Her paper skin was like a veil
that you could see right through.
Society influenced her
and warped her sense of view.
And still, she sees herself as fat
though she is nearing death.
Importance placed on being thin
engulfs her every breath

Caren Sharpe

A New Day

With each new day
I look in the mirror
and to myself I say

I may not have a lot
or
A lot I may not have

But what means the most
you see
Are the people who love me.

Shelly Roberts

Tears and Rainbows

Tears are filled with sorrow,
Of many different types.
While smiles are filled with rainbows,
With colors oh, so bright.

As I was sitting one day,
Looking at the sky above,
I realized it was you, Mom,
Who inspired this poem of love.

If it weren't for you and Dad, Mom
This poem would not be,
So thank you very much
For giving birth to me!

Keri Wyllie

August

Is there a beach in your neighborhood
Music cannot lead me there
Fragmented shells
Silhouettes in the sandy shadows
Seaweed lurking beneath
Is there a tide on your beach
Change would be slower there
Fear of a shadow
Fear of a sound
Comfort in the strong arms
Chasing along the water's edge
Relax and bask in the joy and love
Create a peaceful beach
You must

Cathleen Adkin

The Twins

Twain they were, but just alike
they even had the same black bike
I often wondered if they slept
with look alike, soft plushy pets
One day I saw them at a dance
they even wore the same gray pants
their partners, twain, to them were true
and they themselves were the same too!
Funny how an embryo
can split apart, and still it grows
Two people just alike to see
and growing so, so happily
I think God likes to mess with minds
He makes us of such varied kinds
so once or twice He'll change his plot
and make a double in one lot

Mark Yon

Ode to a Cat

Your fur is black
With white feet, moustache, and nose
You give yourself a bath
From your head down to your toes

You love to sleep and eat
Morning, noon, and night
And when you run and play
You are the cutest sight

I've had you all these years
You are the greatest pet
You only give me trouble
On the way to the vet

You are so cute and cuddly
And even slightly fat
But I would never trade you in
You are my baby cat

Stephanie Gray

Circle T

The sunlight shone
its bright light thrown
through cracks in shattered glass

Beneath a morning sky
cast in blue dye
the grass was green and glistening

The breeze blew through
the trees' leaves too
and I wondered if God was listening to me

Sean Patrick Mullin

The Accidental Hero

Behind a rock in Georgia
The rebels were shooting
and the officer shouting:
Get those snipers.
My knees were shaking
and my mind grinding:
Get those snipers.
Lady Luck, give me strength
and Fortuna guide my steps.
Get those snipers.
I ran for my life
to a hollow in the ground.
Get those snipers.
I was hit in my leg
and it hurt like mad.
Get those snipers.
The blood was pumping
but Fortuna aimed.
And I got those snipers.

Kaj Samuelsson

mother

i love the way
she's always there,
whenever troubles
in the air.
her voice has such
a calming gift,
she gives my day
that needed lift.
she's there when i laugh,
she's there when i cry,
she's there no-matter
the reason why.
her caring fits me
like a glove,
no-one can replace
a mother's love.
i love you mom.

Lisha Berry

Lab

There was an old dog named Lab.
He rode in the truck cab.
He tore the seat,
but didn't get beat,
He didn't even get a jab!

Heather Lipscomb

Mom, Jesus and I

God created the moon and
stars, to light up the night.
He gave us the sun, for day,
to shine so bright.
He sent his son from Heaven
above, and gave us mothers to
show his love. There's a
special place for a mother
like mine, God's been building
since beginning of time.
Just like Jesus that made
salvation free, we all must
choose our final destiny. I'm
glad I had a mother to show
me the way. And when I leave
this world, we'll meet again
someday. Where we'll never
worry about saying good-bye.
But we'll live forever MOM,
JESUS, and I.

Jack Humphries

I Will Be There

I know I am nothing special
But I have a dream
I have a special mission
As plain as I may seem
I am not very popular
But I do have friends
My life is full of twisted roads
And not dead ends
I know I am not real tough
And I have never been in a fight
But I will find a special guy
When the time is right
I know you don't believe me
But what I speak is the truth
I am no longer alone
I'm out of the isolation booth
I don't know what you think of me
And I don't really care
All I know is that
I'm the one who will be there

Laura Fisher

Steve and Ernie

We're so happy, you and me
Friends forever, just carefree.
We don't care if it rains or shines:
We have each other: what's yours is mine
When we grow up, I wonder, then,
If we'll be happy and such good friends?
Will you grow rich and move away?
Forget the times we shared today?
Somewhere a "spark" is starting to burn;
As I remember: Which way did I turn?
Honest, generous, happy, carefree?
To be a friend, if asked of me?

Lorraine M. Ingersoll

Promise

Storms arise, the morning
Wind carries rain
The sun looks on,

And the promise of God
Shines upon the dark

The color speaking;
The rainbow, the span
Earth to the heavens,

And the promise of God shines

Andrew J. Williams

The Lady

He called me a Lady ,
I'm sure that's what I heard.
He made me smile inside
With that one, single word.

He called me a Lady,
And that's what I became.
Belief in him made me strong
And a lady I'll remain.

He called me a Lady,
Then said with a smile,
I don't know why you had any doubt,
You were a lady all the while.

Maxie Derry

Dear Soldier

Dear Soldier

The hours were short, "Dear Soldier"
After we were married
You left with mere a kiss
And the rifle that you carried

I pray for you, "Dear Soldier"
And what may lie ahead
I wait for your return
With a yellow ribbon above my bed

Like the faithful soldier
Who always does his best
Our love will not falter
It will stand the test

So stand up with your country
And do what is right and true
And when you return, "Dear Soldier"
I'll be here for you

Catherine Wargo

As Time Goes By

When I was young,
there was nothing to be afraid of
There was nothing
that could stop me from my will
Before I met him,
I was blind not knowing real world

As time goes by, lost in the reality
I was immature
I was frail
Until he set me free from bad spell

Since I'm old enough
to understand somebody's pain
I remember my feeling and passion
While I was with him,
I hardly noticed his existence

Miki Yasuge

Daddy

Dont look mad dont look sad
don't be disappointed in me dad
Things are changing very quickly,
I am not a little girl. Days are
faster, time is quicker, now is the
time for talk than jibber. Time is
precious and so are you take care
dad I will always love you.

Tricia Bose

Contentment

My heart beats in time
With your pulse.
I match my breathing
To Yours.
We lay together
Spooned close
No space in between
Us.
You lightly snore
And I smile.
Our world is at peace
And sleep draws near.
In these moments
I know contentment.

Casandra Horn

When . . .

When I am down
You pick me up
When I am sad
You are there
When I am crying
You show you care
You give me a hug
You give me a smile
You give me courage
To run the mile
You share with me a treasure
A treasure very rare
A friendship treasure
I can count on you to be there
So be my friend
And I will be yours
I'll keep by your side
No matter what's in store
I will love you, my friend,
Until the end

Rachel Bock

Cupid's Arrow

Cupid's arrow shot and missed
and happened to hit me.
I was standing in the courtyard then,
beneath the apple tree.

I looked around for one to love,
but there was no one there:
The great blue sky and sweetest winds,
and one big juicy pear.

So out of place, that as it hung,
I fell in love with it.
I don't know why, I don't know how,
but it just seemed to fit.

The pear was ripe, and so I bit
into its sweet pale side.
Before I knew, I loved myself,
for that pear was inside.

I've never loved again since then,
and yet I was content:
Somehow I knew, that arrow flew,
and hit its mark but bent!

Lauren Prendergast

Snow

Snow
Every day, snow
All week long
It covers everything
The past, the present
And the future
Blinding white
It erases the scars
And absorbs the pain
It wipes out all
But the loneliness
I watch it fall
And my spirit
Falls with it
My sorrow deepens
With every fresh blanket
Thrown over my world
My heart

Brian Caouette

Little Lights

Within the stillness of the night,
Exist many little lights.
They shine bright for all to see,
O'er the earth, sky, and sea

They are a light within the dark.
They are each but little sparks,
But each contribute a little light
to make the night clear and bright.

This is the way that we should be,
A light to the world for all to see.
That to the world, we can show
It is Christ we LIVE to know.

Jason Schaal

Believe . . .

Believe and shall receive
For worry is contempt of universal law!
Believe and let your mind be free
And sharpened like a saw.
To cut through doubt
And your fear!
Believe, and you shall touch
The truth
Be scared, and panic be your crutch
And suffering your tooth.

Konstantin Vaysberg

Ormalu

Beware the dime-store ormalu
That shines so bright when its first new
So much like gold the fool can't tell
But it will not bare the ware as well

Love like gold endures when true
But is this what I found in you?
Like the fool I cannot tell
Perhaps for now it's just as well

Matthew Groff

You and Me

With every dawn
Our love will grow
As surely as
The rivers flow

eternally happy
I will have no clue
Nor dare to imagine
A world without you

from the dawn of time
Our love was meant to be
For there is no us
Without you and me

Raymond Ruiz

Life Is a Joke

Life is a joke
that few ever get.
For those that do,
covet the laughter
and laugh for those
who covet the bitterness.
For those that don't,
open your ears
to listen to the laughter
and laugh with us.
Then life is the joke
that you'll always get.

Manuel Escriche

Frozen Dream

the things you once spoke of
the ideals we held so high
drifted away like nothing
into the forever sky

words spoken like a prophet
to some it seemed a crime
the love they once showed me
fell deep to the emerald sky

calling out to darkness
it seemed like a shattering lie
what they told me of you
words flew into the sky

so as the shadows near
i truly ponder why
tears on the horizon
looking through the sky

Courtney Lounsbury

Love

Life can truly seem unreal
Sometimes it loses its appeal.
But when you're feeling down or blue
Remember there's One who's always true.

He comforts you with love and grace.
He loves you no matter what your race.
His love is merciful and kind.
His love is endless, not hard to find.

If life for you becomes unbearable
And you really need to talk
Lift up your eyes to Him above
And find His endless love.

Alana Bunch

I Love You

I love you with all my heart and soul,
Promise I will never let you go.
The first time I met you I only said hi,
Then let you leave with only good-bye.
Now that I am with you I promise to say
I love you with every passing day.
Your love to me is worth so much,
I even love your gentle touch.
You make the sun shine, oh, so bright,
And the moon glows greater every night.
I promise I will not let you go—
I love you with all my heart and soul.

Brooke Baird

Compassion

Separation
Racism
STOP
Choose
Heart of Compassion
Unite
Red
Yellow
Black
White
Rainbow Burst
Joy
Friend

Cindy Reed

Christmas Miracles

Miracles from God
Angels all about,
singing their special chorus,
about the birth of Christ our Lord.
Shepherds and Kings
come to praise him.
For He gave us the gift of life.
So when we put up our tree,
and we wrap around the lights,
we'll remember the light of the world,
and the gift he gave to us.

Karissa Smith

Infatuation

One of these days
you'll stop and look back,
through the smoky haze
remember the sun so bright,
intensified by illusion
from a dim candlelight.

Carmen Hodgson

Boredom

An overwhelming sense of boredom.
What does one do when this occurs?
Does he hum a tune?
Or sing a song?
Does he sleep with ease?
Or toss and turn away the hours?
Does he go out with friends?
Or sit in the dark alone?
Does he party at night?
Or stare at stars in the sky?
Does he speak to people?
Or load a gun?
Does he learn to live?
Or pull the trigger?
An overwhelming sense of boredom.
What does one do?
What should I do?

Leah Supitux

trapped

dying smiley faces
dance all around me
as another burnt out hippie
falls to the ground

your the answer
to the question
nobody asked

faded away
went insane
kill the dead
kill your time

grave stones file into the building
looking for bodies to claim
they claimed my soul long ago
but my lifeless body still remains

children sell their parents for money
the goldfish sells the cat for drugs
I sold my soul for freedom
for I am trapped inside my head

Megan Railey

Words Spoken!

Thinking out loud
Not realizing the impact
Of words finally spoken
All of which are fact!

We say these things
Not knowing what to expect
Hoping that it's understood
Or something to respect

Pausing for a brief second
To try to stop things said
Realizing it's too late
It's already been misread!

You start to question it
Wondering if you said what you meant
Or was it just that time
For you to break free and vent!

The power of the words spoken
Are now on display
For the conversation has ended
And we both walk away!

Troy Roche'

Drumbeat of Love

Time is a flowing river
springing forth droplets of love
eloquent, showering me with happiness
when I sing

Beating the drum
singing songs to Mother Nature
Letting go of my fears, my pain
moments of joy, I give to her

Mother Nature, feed my spirit
when I am down, she gives me sunshine
when in joy, she gives me rain
balance my feelings, all the time

Drumbeat of my heart
from my spirit
drumming my song to you
full of love so sweet

Marie Randall

Where Have We Gone?

Kisses go deep within the melting air,
Souls collide from the sharpened tongue,
Breath is gone with a look of despair,
Songs are left that need to be sung.

Poems being forced on the blank paper,
Heartfelt words need to be spoken,
Salty tears become friends we savor,
A one time trust seems to be broken,
Where have we gone?

Just a glimpse of eyes that lock,
Arms spread apart to only feel empty,
Like the days waiting on the dock,
When you searched for me across the sea.

Laughter needs to be spilled over,
And tears dried into our pores,
For this is where are hearts do hover,
Because this love is mine and yours,
Where have we gone?

Michelle Mcleod

You're Always in Me

You died when I was eight,
I still miss you,
but I still see you.
I don't see you by my side;
I see you in my soul.
When I look in the mirror and smile;
I see you smiling at me.
Together you're in me and
I'm in you, because
you created me,
now I will recreate you.

Trisha James

Darkness

pain, hurting, memories
you don't think about them
suddenly a wave
a daze of sorrow
childhood memories turned sour
your heart tears, cries, shouts
you are in a dark room alone
you cry out but you are not heard
you look only to find you cannot see
suddenly you are swallowed
taken in
taken in emotionless
tied down and able to do nothing
only to be lost into a vast darkness
a darkness unlike any other
a dark pit with no end
a dark place with other cries
a dark place with tears
tears of rainfall
falling, falling
falling to into the darkness
the darkness that perils
the darkness that is ongoing

Korynthia Fischer

Magnetic

tears falling softly down my cheeks
once dry, now stained with
the tracks of my emotions.
i am a prisoner held captive by
my own soul
yearning to break free of
my mortal shell.
what i think—
what i know,
is only what you gave to me
when you found the broken pieces
of my being.
jagged edges become soft
the mist rises, clouds disappear
and i have found myself
in a strange place where
what i think and
what i know
isn't what you gave to me . . .
it's just you.

Rebecca Podhradsky

One

You come into my thoughts
From dusk 'til dawn.
In my life, in my strife
I forget that we are not two
But one United Soul.

Saurabh Roy

A Pen

A Bic round stic medium,
The tool to send thoughts
Cradled by fingers
Oh, what pain you have wrought.

It moves without effort
And profoundly impacts,
The worth of the paper
Whose reader reacts.

It simply depends
In whose hand it is held,
This ink holding instrument
What letters it spells.

The fountain pen stirs
It's writer and holder,
Instilling the courage
To be a bit bolder.

If doodles and poetry
Spring from the mind,
A Bic round stic medium
Will do just fine.

Anne Neeb

The Liquid World

Winding and turning
A spiral of colors
A field of flowers
Running through my mind

A void an endless void
Eating away at my soul
Taking away the thoughts of yesterday
And creating hopes for tomorrow

Daybreak is coming
Night time is over
Whispering winds running through my hair
Crisp air burning my face

My hopes for tomorrow are gone
I've said my peace
So my work is done

This is the liquid world
The king said to me
His queen smiled
And her face went cold
She laughed an evil laugh
And sat on a throne of gold

Kristin Mersing

My Long Journey

Many of my heart's songs
have never been sung;
Just years and years of my instrument
being restrung.
After the agony of the climb
to the highest peak,
My songs have now begun
as my deeper soul I seek.
Along my path, peoples
of the world I'll find;
Not one, oh, not one must
I pass by.
And so, I go down from
the mountains lofty,
And listening, I hear my
new heart strings singing—
so softly.

Bess Hooser

Solace Within

Briskly kissed . . . Oh, morning dew
Marinating each new breath
Untainted drops upon my body
Bathed in salty tears

Whisk away the frigid morn
Warm its passionless beat
Consume its tracing paths
Leading back hence no more

Pour down and make whole
Healing potency embark anew
Fresh fragrance stings the dominant air
Rain, like tears, cleanse the soul

Inga Edwards

Mother

Mother,
May I say my love to you?
Can I give you the words,
That I hid from you?
Mother,
May I leave your side now?
Can I search this world,
To find my smile?
Mother,
Shall I sing my song to you?
Can I give you the idea,
That all is not well?
Mother,
May I hide my sun from you?
Can I bring out the moon,
So that you will not be blind anymore?
Mother,
May I hate this place?
Can I burn these egos,
With the core of my eyes?
Mother,
May I shed my tears now?

Mike Drinan

Eyes of Tonight

We dance in the moonlight
Swaying to and fro
I look into your eyes
Baby blue and aglow

You gaze back into mine
Electricity sparks through our souls
We feel a special bond
Filling lonely holes

You lean forward to kiss me
Your soft lips brush against mine
It seems as if reality is gone
We've lost all sense of time

We don't realize what is occurring
Of what may become of this
All that matters to us two
Is sharing our first kiss

The night keeps going on
I pull you closer still
Wanting to live this moment forever
Feeling the magic and the thrill

Heather Tobin

A Child's Dream

A child's dream,
to play in the sand.
To hold its mother's hand.

To swing in the park,
to hear a puppies bark.
To travel to Mars,
to play on the monkey bars.

A child's dream,
to play Barbie dolls or trucks.
To play in the mud and the muck.
To play "cops and robbers"
"the good guy always wins!"

A child's dream,
to ride a bike, a skateboard, a horse.
To walk, talk and learn.

A child's dream,
to grow up.

Robbin Elmlinger

Death of a Salesman

So many years I've cowered
Just hidden in the lie,
Afraid to cause commotion,
To let you see me cry.
I pretended not to notice
The blatant lack of love,
And made believe I had the father
That every girl dreams of.
But, you see, I knew.
Deep down my heart was wise.
It was obvious what you were doing;
You were choking me with lies.
You think you have it all,
That you're the "King of the World"
But a piece of the puzzle's missing:
Respect from your two girls.
I'm on to you now,
And will no longer be misled.
Sadly, it was harder to love you
Than to carry on like you are dead . . . .

Deedra Levy

Hell

Fiery pits, Exhausting heat,
No freedom, Locked in a room,
With no way out, By yourself.
The insanity slowly getting to me
Slowly going insane.
No where to go, No where to run.
You think you have found a way out,
You run towards it only to find,
It is a wall made of brick.
You have no way to go,
No freedom, No sanity.

Sara Floberg

This Tree

High,
Lonely on a hill,
Where winds can act on me at will,
I stand,
Exposed to sun, cold and rain.

My roots reach down,
Into the sod;
My branches, upward
Unto God.

Mary Neal

Grandpa

We sat by your bed
and tried not to weep
not wanting to disturb
your peaceful sleep.

We sat there all night
then we sat there all day
our hearts not willing
to walk away.

We brought you home
so you could rest
grandpa you know
we did our best.

In our hearts
you will live on
in the sense of love
you'll never be gone.

Galene Ortiz

POOL DAY . . .

Nobody listens
to what I have to say
I'm either a pain or
just in the way,
WHY!!!
Do I bother to go
when all I am to them, is a show.
And when they do something
wrong
it's alright
but when I do something inexact
we get into a fight
and when I say I'm only
trying to help
they say you've helped enough
boy, families are
sometimes
rough . . .

Wally Max Otto

"Tomorrow's Shattered Mirrors"

this time, of shattered mirrors
where she saw his reflection
in a thousand splinters of glass
passed slowly
 . . . slowly, into the dark night

tied as she was to her past,
bound to repeat the mistakes
that had shattered the mirror
the first time,
all she could do was pray
 . . . silently whispered breaths
"Not again"

within in the light of the lone candle
still burning after all this time
she pondered this gift of his
and how it would look in
the shattered mirrors of tomorrow,

"Kelly, if it was a Girl."
she thought,
"Michael, if it was a boy."

Michael Gilmore

Your Eyes

Something in your eyes it seems
Has captured all my heart
The love I see in your sweet eyes
Has been there from the start.

There's mystery in them and yet
I feel like I've known you all my life
And there is a comfort in those eyes
Erasing pain and strife.

The eyes, they say, "I love You"
And, "Never let me go"
But something in my heart says
Not to let love show.

If I admit I care for you
And that I love you so
Then you would surely break my heart
Of that I truly know.

So if the chance should ever come
That I could see your eyes
Staring back at me like saying,
"I'll never tell you lies"

Aliza Armentrout

My Baby Girl

We remember a tiny baby girl,
With dark curls and eyes
Who charmed us all by
Her coos and sighs.
She grew up so quickly,
Worldly but wise,
Little did we fathom
How quickly time flies.
She studied long and hard.
Yet the road to nursing
Had bumps by the yard.
She finally passed the test
Her loved ones standing guard
Confident she'd come sailing through
With her courage and will unmarred.
Her family and friends all miss her
And wish her love and ease.
Someday we will stand beside her
We will again be a family
And our world will be at peace.

Dixie Barnes

Just Us

Lie back down,
play with your hair,
kiss your lips,
we're floating on air.
Hold on tight,
we're going on a ride;
lover's flight,
above the tide.
Fly to Heaven,
don't look down,
we'll travel the world,
going round.
Don't let it end,
stay with me,
no one else,
can set me free.
Bound with happiness,
we shall be,
since I love you.

Jess Goodrich

Awake within Me

Awake within me
The being divine
The hands that touch
The face of God
The soul immune
To corruptions lie and
Petty cares that know
No end.
Alive within me
Breathing lives
The unspoken song
The emotions that melt
Hardness into my heart
Feelings that feel
The pulse of life
In every breathe
And each hello
And find the meaning
In every sad good-bye.

Lincoln Mcelwee

Tarnished Bonds

Unbind these wings of silken dreams;
To soar in joy unbound.

In colors of the morning light;
Its wonders yet unfound.

Set free this heart of tarnished bonds;
Made hard by numbered days.

To love again, as once a child;
Unseen by age-ed ways.

To this, my love, eternal now;
My life in you is bound.

Forever held in tender arms;
My love for you is found.

Andy Turner

Dog Days

For years I watched him,
with as keen an eye as a dog,
salivating for table scraps,
longing for him, to long for me,
the way he longed for her.

I watched him, watching her,
love someone else, and in the watching,
he was lost,
because she could not see him,
for love of another.

And the void that he left,
could not be filled,
by the one I settled for,
though he followed me for years,
like a puppy starved for affection.

So I set him free,
to marry the one, that settled for him,
once she buried her dreams,
like a dog with a bone,
in the same deep hole,
where I keep my heart.

Mary Galgano

Why

As I lie in my bed
I can't get you out of my head
I think about the time we spent
And what you meant
I can't believe you showed no cares
While I sat there and my heart tears
So now I cry
Why couldn't you try
My heart is shattered
And it doesn't even matter
Why did you lie
Why can't you tell me why
I sit here and every thing I said
Runs through my head
I can't believe you showed no feelings
While my heart was spilling
It seemed to me you would care
But you broke my heart and just stared
You said no
Why can't I let go

Mandy Jones

Happiness Today

Be Happy today!
Tomorrow's too far away.
Enjoy each other,
Be kind to your brother.
Sing a happy tune.
Look often at the moon.
Don't worry today.
Wash your troubles away.
Take the time to play.
This day will not stay.
Remember to give Love.
God Loves Us from above.
Give thanks to God Hold to the iron rod!

Elaine Dennison

exhausted

love exhausts me.
relationships are no longer to grow
only to oppress.
like many other things in this society
i guess it's never occurred to me
that my relationships
have not been built on love,
but on fear!

Ruth Howard-Briggs

Adieu . . .

Another Day,
my Test is Done,
no More to Fear,
my War is Won.

Each New Day,
a Chance is Giv'n
for my Soul
to Strive for Heav'n.

Another Day,
my Mind is Eased,
my Task Complete,
my Soul is Pleased.

Each New Day,
A Chance For You,
My Days Are Done.
In Grace, Adieu.

Jamilyn Ward

it's drowning

sometimes i think
love is like
a big pool of water:
i drink from it
by running around
the edges,
stopping
whenever i get thirsty.
i refresh myself by
wading in a little bit,
never going in too deep,
because i'm afraid
to just dive in.
it's not the water
that i'm scared of, and
it's not the fact
that i don't know how to swim.
it's drowning
that really bothers me.

Benjamin Gotschall

Union Child

I am a child of the union
between Father Sky and Mother Earth
others have had their say
here's mine for what it's worth

Wisdom comes with age
and from listening to the heart
as the elders speak to me
as I lie in the dark

I see visions of tomorrow
while others still try
I speak of truths
while others choose to lie

Listen to my words children
for they shall come to pass
the answers are inside of you
for the questions you will ask

Change comes with the wind
wherever it may blow
time for man to start again
learning what he needs to know

David Morris

Deep Horizon

What I'd give to see your smile,
What I'd give to see your face.
Although I try to find you,
I feel you've left no trace.
I have looked deep within the Earth,
And far beyond the seas.
For the love I wish to capture,
Has brought me to my knees.
If I had only one day,
Under any circumstance,
I'd prove to you my love,
If given but one chance.
The tides are all against me,
The wind and earth is too.
But I'd swim through any ocean
Just to be with you.
When I look into your eyes,
A tear rolls down my face.
For I know the odds against me
Are slim to win this race.

Douglas Teaderman

A Rose

A rose it needs love
in order to grow
with love and affection
or didn't you know
For if treated gently
it never will die
but handled by many
will soon just pass by
And baby a rose
you are to me
with love and affection
all this I see
For a man he is nothing
as the story goes
if out of life's garden
he can't pick a rose

Rondell Hancock

At First

There is something about
the smile of a girl
like one sun ray through
a magnifying glass,
beautiful, hot and lethal,
wrapped into one alluring borealis.

Outside we traded stories
from people to birthdays to cakes,
a white knight from a dark land
and an opening tiger-lily.

Her gaze remains with me still:
those eyes chilled with azure
to trap the unwary in intrigue
dance a sparkling jig in my memory
even now.

Jideofo Mbanefo

Little Girl (Depressed)

Oh, little girl, Little girl,
Where have you been?
I've been looking for you again
To tear your heart out,
To disease your mind,
To make your life miserable
Every single time.
You've been looking for an answer
And you always look my way,
And oh, my little girl,
That makes you my prey.

Jacinda Wilder

Tear Trails

He sits high a top a mesa
and stares across the plains.
He sings the songs of other times
as he looks at what remains.

He sings about the buffalo
that once roamed the hunting ground,
but were slaughtered by the millions
when the white man moved from town.

He sings about the trails they rode
as they moved from place to place.
The trails gave way to interstates
where cars trucks now race.

Tears fall gently from his eyes
as the songs are carried forth.
And wishes swell inside him
for the way things were before.

Rodger Woods

Take Me Away

Roaring thunder hear my cry,
Take me up where all birds fly.
In the snow or in the rain,
Take me away from all this pain.
Roaring thunder hear my yell,
Take me away from all this Hell.
In the night or in the day,
Take me, Please take me, far away.

Carrie Gundelach

The Magic of the Uninspired

Here I am again, little shadow,
It feels so good to be alone.

Without you, life is fantasy.
Your words swim by me
As you speak underwater.

They drown as your inspiration
Drives me off the road.

It is evident you must relearn
All of your knowledge as it has
Escaped, and travelled back
To three years before, when
Nothing mattered. You, staring
Into the water, expressionless
As the coral, yet with all its genius.

Will your cold lips tell me if
You can ever feel warmth again?
Never mind, it feels so good to be alone.

J. Hunter Adams

Shadow in the Trees

Oh, 'tis, she was a fair maiden
For only a shadow in the trees
She lived her life in quiet desperation
For only a shadow in the trees
Her soul so guarded, and pain untouched
For only a shadow in the trees
Who was this fair maiden?
Only a shadow in the trees

Diane Hobbs

Above All You

God has given me many things
Above all there is you,
And there is the warmth it brings,
To know that we are two.
Two that love and understand,
Each others wants and needs.
And you're being there always.
never out of reach.
A strength that I have never known,
A thrill beyond compare.
All the world to me is shown,
And is yours to share.
Should I die before I wake,
I shan't have missed a thing,
I have all my heart can take,
as a human being.
If there is another life to which I
hold the key,
Where there is no longer strife only you
and me.
Where time would never part us
No more troubles to endure.
Oh, this would certainly Heaven be.
Somehow I feel for sure.

O. Bays

A Serenade for a Homeless Man

The cold winter wind blows, 2:00 A.M.
in an empty doorway on 8th Avenue
sleeps a homeless man
his body wrapped in blankets,
like a cocoon hanging from life's tree
surrounded by all he owns
a bag, extra shoes, and memories,
memories of a life he once lived
The cold winter wind blows, 2:00 A.M.
resonating through the streets
past corners, through buildings
a saxophone player plays,
in the lonely, cold New York night
a serenade for the homeless man

Eric Smith

Lord Jesus

Lord Jesus, Lord Jesus
Please lend me your ear
I need your advice
On a subject so dear
I feel troubled, alone
And in great despair
Please help me, Oh, Lord
Please tell me you care
Please give me the strength
That I know that I need
To go on with my life
And truly succeed
In all my goals and ambitions
And all that I see
A great loving Lord
Reaching out to me

Michael Prisza

A Rising Hope

A rising hope
Of new horizons
Gives a sense of purpose

Mend my wings
And let me fly
To discover what opportunities
Shine, beacons of light

Let me find
Who I really am
And what I can achieve

Do not bind my heart
With doubt or negativity
Let my energy free

Encourage instead
My courage and self-esteem
Be the light
That fires my dreams

Let me see
What the world
Has to offer to me
And what I
Can freely give

Carol Duchesneau

Rain Songs

Sunflowers bowed their heads
Praying for the rains to come
The woman's feet were bare
Her face turned toward the sun
Dancing on heat waves
Chanting rhythmic rain songs
She awakened the ancient one

Dust swirled circles 'round her toes
Stirring spirits in the ground
Shimmering apparitions arose
To the thunderous sound
Of his voice from long ago
Summoning raindrops from Heaven
Swords of lightening from the dark
He whispered secrets in the wind
To the woman's faith filled heart

Wils Sullivan

Trust Him

As despair surrounds
My entire being,
In you Lord
I put my trust.

As darkness engulfs
Me completely,
In you Lord
I put my trust.

Though tears may roll
Down my face and
I may feel separated
From your grace.

I still know in
My heart of hearts,
That from me Lord
You will never part.

So my trust I know
Is not in vain,
For you'll be there
To take away the pain.

Latisha Kennedy

Lonely Walker

Upon the brown leaves I cross
To find my way home again.
The ground is covered with a frost
From the night that has been.

I linger by the wall of stone
To look upon the forest bare.
There I hear a far-off tone
That calls me from the cold air.

I sit and watch the world go by,
A soft snow falls upon my face.
The frozen water melts soon or I cry,
Then I continue with my pace.

Near the journey's end I turn,
And look upon the far off wall.
I see nothing in the morning burn,
And I fail to hear the call.

Theodore Lindgren

The Bad Dream

Running quickly—
my heart racing
tears roll down
my cheek and
I scream for
you and you
come.

Hold me in
your tender arms,
rock me as
your soft hand
strokes my hair
and with a
kiss upon my
cheek you say
it is over.
I am safe.
Mommy's here.

Jennifer Dierickx

Searching Yet

Would that I could find myself
among my scattered dreams
the splintered shards of life itself
fit neatly into schemes.
    tasks unfinished
    pleasures untasted
    candles, most unlit.
Would that I could start anew
and find my heart content!

Donna Williams

My Unquiet Mind

Swirling, twirling madness felt
pictures fade and candles melt
panic now what future holds
silent tears and thoughts untold
reaching out screaming now
comfort gone must not allow
feathers falling voices calling
broken nails ungodly clawing
no one there? Oh, God save me
please—oh, please let them see
my helplessness to no avail
anchors away oh let me sail
unto that sea of blackness dwells
insanity that tolling bell
that no one hears—exception—me
close my eyes, God let me be
alone, alone and silence there
just close my eyes without a care
in your arms rock me sweet
against your steady warm heartbeat

Sara Mitchell

Declaration of the Self

Where is it I cannot go,
What is it I cannot do,
Who is it I cannot love,
When is it I cannot live,
Why is it I cannot be?

Heather Nordstrom

I'll Be Standing by Your Side

Been a long time since we talked
I would say if you were here right now
Been a long time since we've walked
Together young and proud
I remember the times when we were kids
With our spirits high and free
Then all of a sudden you were gone
Taken away from me
I never had a chance to say I LOVE YOU
Never had a chance to say good-bye
But brother somehow, someday, someway
I'LL BE STANDING BY YOUR SIDE
You took a chance on that very day
When the water took your life
You knew that wasn't the place to play
But you always thought you we're right
Memories of you will never fade
You know you're with me all the time
GOD knows you shouldn't have to pay
When being young was your only crime

John Delarm

Desperation of the Soul

The endless wastelands
are an unforgiving foe
of a man's spirit

The unforgiving
flame of man's unrelenting
airless flight into
the dark recesses of the
imagination and heart

Edward Howlingwolf

This Gift

I have something special
here with me today
Something so great I
thank Heaven above
for giving me her this day.

A beauty so true and pure
she has such great allure.
Heads will turn and mouths
will surely open wide
as her beauty is shown
from all wondrous sides.

A smile dances through her eyes
of perfection and talent
destined to grace the cover of Vogue.

What could this wondrous
gift possibly be, none other
than the gift of love my
Holy Father has given to me.

Choya Magalong

When the Dark Swings Round

We'll duck when the dark swings round
We'll bow our brow to the ground.
Eyes shut 'til the black
walks over our back
'til the dark is light
'til the dark is drowned
Leaving our thoughts unshadowed and
sound.

Christina Brooks

Grim Reality

It's better to accept
a grim reality
than to create something beautiful
to believe.
But I couldn't cope
with the trials of everyday life
if it wasn't for my dreams
of immortality.

Everyone I know
escapes from the world
in one way or another
to remain sane.
Sanity is a symptom
of human reason.
Unreason is the feeling
I refuse to contain.

I let it flow.

Edgar Miles

Beauty in Which We Walk

As we walk through the
Green meadows,
Sun giving warmth,
Wind giving breath,
to smell the quiet
Nature,
Our senses go wild,
as Nature intended.
It makes me want to chase
and catch you,
Beauty in Which We Walk.

Cynthia Stepanek

Vapors

An island out at sea,
Where few give heed.
Naked, it backs from the sky,
Searching for one to cover by.
Though respected as it seeks,
True fulfillment is weak.
Desperately, to swim above,
As fate's dark hand of
Night from day
Devours all time away.
Turns to those surrounded,
Though heedless to what is said.
As the wind they pass,
To own fields for grass.
Void, it withers into oblivion.
With futile wishes to be more than none
A faded figure of a ghost,
In the open sea it is lost.

Jonathan Anderson

Hand-in-Hand

The flashing blade
the innocence
The lightning and
the lamb
The inferno and
the ignorance
They all go hand-in-hand.
Love and trust and
shattered dreams
A hope that cannot be . . .
A startled soul in his torn world
is cast into the sea.

Robert Heckman

A Laugh

A laugh is like bright sunshine,
It freshens all the day.
It floods the peak of life with light,
And drives the dark clouds away.

The soul grows glad that hears it,
And feels its courage growing strong.
Yes, a laugh is just like sunshine,
For cheering folks along.

A laugh is just like music,
It lingers in the heart.
And when its melody is heard,
The toils of life depart.

Quickly happy thoughts come crowding,
Its joyful notes to greet.
Yes, a laugh is just like music,
For making living sweet.

Edward Courtis

I Wish

I wish you knew
how deep my love is for you
I wish you could see
me smile after looking at you
I wish for one day
you were mine
I wish for one second
you cared for me like I care for you

Michael Gallagher

Love Longer

Will you show me,
love is only . . .
One friendship away.
That's yours and mine,
and only our kind . . .
to make love today.
Will you be there,
when I want to share . . .
My love with you?
Will you hold me,
and tell me boldly . . .
You love me too?
Can we always stay,
the friends we are today . . .
then let the love grow stronger?
Then when the time is right,
we'll turn out the light . . .
And love a little longer.

Brenda Pryor

Souls View

Perfect impurities
of human nature
A thorn to balance
the rose
A scent so sweet
it runs down your chin
While the salt in
your tears
will ease the pain
that you're in

One Fine Day

See Me

Please erase me. Why bother?
This is ridiculous. Why do
I have to live up to you? What
makes you better? You disgust me.
I am jealous of you. I hate
this.   Who conceived this nonsense?
Why does it have to be this way?
Please erase me. Somebody cover my
eyes from these sites. Somebody
cover my ears from these sounds.
Please erase me. I know you
won't. I must continue this way
for some reason.

Daniel Echebarria

God of Silence

There is a void of silence
That surrounds me when I pray
As I search for guidance
To help me find my way.

To my God of silence
I reach out to free
The pain, sadness, and violence
In me, all around me.

Alone and lost in silence
I offer the tears I've shed,
But all I receive is silence
Screaming in my head.

Jill S. Li

Life

When life is such a battle
And all does seem so bleak
Remember for just a little
You're strong but when you're weak
But this is such a mantle
It's false and cannot be
'Cause throughout life you battle
And never to retreat
Is that not the song of strong men
Hold fast to all; believe
And be admired by all men
For such a lie believe
So what us of this battle
How through this life we win
To never us be rattled
With pride until the end
Give up and trust your father
And stop the fight you see
And only trust your father
And he will set you free

Randy Leake

Eternity

Moonlit shadows
a pattern of lies
daisies in the garden
tears in the eyes.

Planets turn and fires burn
it stays the same for ages
a baby cries and someone dies
but nothing ever changes.

Silent songs of butterflies
oppressive words of hate
fragrant, grassy meadows
apologies too late.

Winter comes, a river runs
its been the same for ages
an angel sings, a child dreams
but nothing ever changes.

Ginger Rose

Night Conjure

Night conjure—
desperate heart's death
does require of me nothing,
slander
with nudity I dare breathe.

Night conjure—
rekindle hell, meander
deeper into bliss
where ghostly beasts taunt
thoughts
where blood rushes
crisp nightmares

Richie Michael Castaldo

With a Dream

In a whisper
You could change history
With a wink
You could make a new friend
In a blink
Your life could pass you by
With a handshake
You could set a goal
With a hug
You will feel remembered
With a kiss
You could change your life
With a footstep
You could walk a mile
With a dream . . .
With a dream . . .

Rich Ide

Protectors of Our Land

Do people care,
For the time that we spent,
In the Armed Forces,
Or to the wars that we went?
We took a chance
To lose our life,
But for a cause,
Which most didn't like.
Then we came back.
Those of us who could.
We got nothing,
Although we should.
I guess you could say
I am a crazy man.
'Cause if it would happen again
I would protect this beautiful land.
Just once, it would be nice
To have someone care,
To have them know,
That we were once there!

Karen Stover-Taylor

Life

The one who is not there
I wake up,
    go to school.

I go home,
    then fall asleep.

The sleep is deep,
    and quite
refreshing.

I wake up,
    go to school

I go home,
    then fall asleep.

Adam Pigg

Me

I am me,
Me is I
I am old in younger's eye
I am young
To an elder's heart,
Like a baby with
A fresh new start
 I am smart to the
Child of four,
But to an adult
I must learn more
 I can play
If you give me a chance,
We can all learn
If you let us join the dance
 I am me
Me is I,
I am special
In somebody's eye!

Victoria Kingsbury

The Sleep Fairy

Angels' cousin,
She was born in a moonlit garden.
With hummingbird speed,
She flutters in flower petal shadows.
Slumbering by day,
She sips from tulips' dewdrops.
Watchful by night,
She listens for the fearful.
Under lunar light,
She flies to rooms of the restless.
"Sleep now, little ones,"
She whispers from pillowed perch.
Chasing nightmares away,
She finds rest for frightened souls.
With butterfly kisses
And sparkling fairy dust,
She caresses all the children.
She's the Sleep Fairy,
Princess of the Garden,
Guardian of the Night.

Colleen Lamon

On the Small Pebbles

On the small pebbles
Made smooth by running water,
With care for your skin,
We set you down.
And there you lay stretched out
Looking straight up into the trees.
I wondered what you saw,
Because you never blinked, not once.
But you smiled, like to say
If only we could see.

Robert Marshall

"Peace"

"Stop the nukes!"
In 1958, protesters wanted to stop
nuclear power plants.
They drew
something like a
cartoon,
a nuke sign
in a circle
with a line through it, saying, "No."
It became
the peace sign,
My sign.

Judith Pond

Writing without U

I could speak forever,
Of me,
Of what's mine,
My things,
Of I.
I could also talk
Of them,
Of themselves, themselves,
Their lives, their dreams,
Of they.
But, without "u,"
I can't talk
AboUt yoU,
AboUt yoUrself,
YoUr beaUty, yoUr love,
AboUt yoUr life.
I coUldn't even talk
AboUt Us,
AboUt oUrs,
OUr love, OUr dreams,
AboUt oUrselves.
WithoUt "U,"
I'm left alone,
WithoUt love,
WithoUt U.

Andres Lucas

The Love of My Life

I finally found the love of my life
He is as sweet as can be
No one can take the place of this man
Who is so dear to me

I will give him my all
I will treat him with care
Because a love like his
Can't be found anywhere

So generous with his love
And so kind with his heart
He is all I can think of
Whenever we're apart

I wonder if he knows
How special he is to me
Because I have no doubt
That our love is meant to be

Cynthia Bures

My Best Friend

She's true to me,
She's one of a kind,
She's caring and sweet,
And always has an open mind.

She's my crying shoulder,
I'm her's, too,
She'll help me through anything,
And everything new.

She'd do anything for me,
I'd do the same,
She makes me feel so special,
Like I have all the fame.

She's so considerate towards me,
I knew right from the start,
That we'd be best friends forever,
Connected in the heart.

Emily Helmkamp

What's in a Song

Whoever would have thought
The song that stays with me
Would say more than it does
Of the way that things would be
Almost fitting perfect
To what is going on.

Whoever would have thought
All this could be in a song
It's amazing what a song can do
Placing thoughts in your mind
Allowing you to take someone
To another place and time.

Clay Copeland

The Wall

I never saw the wall
The surrounding entrapment
Built by myself
Brick by brick
Through all my faults
Until my eyes were opened
Revealing my wall
And only then did I discover
That by seeing my wall
I could walk through it

Steve Snyder

Mothers

Deep in a mother's soul,
there lies a special friend.
She's there with you in troubled times,
and is with you 'til the end.

A shoulder to lean on,
arms to hold you in.
A person who will love you,
even when you sin.

No gifts are needed,
to show your love for me.
My love for you is so great,
that only God can see.

So I hope you get this message,
this message meant for you.
Happy Mothers Day mom,
with love from me to you.

Michelle Keating

On the Edge of the Razor

*To Michael & Chester—two great gurus
& good guys . . .*
Queen of denial
  Floating downstream
She's been to the therapists
  They're not what they seem
The doc who made house calls
  Now refuses to leave
Drug diversion counselor
  Prescribes pills stopping grief
Husband's sarcasm
  Stiletto slicing so fine
Boss hurling insults
  Time after time
Battered and bleeding
  Sanity silently screaming
On the edge of the razor
  She walks a fine line

Treasa McAuliffe

A Friend So Dear as You

Good Friends Come Few and Far Between
But Oh, it Does Seem
the Friendship We Have Found
is Sincere, Solid and Sound
We Cherish Our Friends so Sweet and Dear
Whether They are Far or Near
the Time we Spend Showing we Care
and the Trust We Share
is the Basis We Make
 to Keep Our Hearts From Ache
it's So Easy to Boast
How Your Friendship Means the Most
I'm Glad We've Found Each Other
There'll Never be Another
So Dear as You
Thank You,
For All You Do!
Happy Valentine's Day
My Dear Friend

Donna Jo Nichols

Lovesick

I sit here at a desk
In a cold empty corner
My world is frozen
My heart is a stone in my throat

There's no one around
I might as well be dead
My head aches
My heart breaks

And no one hears me scream

Sappho D.

nightmare

waiting, watching, scared numb
wrapped in a blanket sitting on his bed
not seeing the hand come up from behind
its claws are drawn ready to attack
it slices, it dices
it wakes you up in a cold sweat
was it a nightmare you think?
yes it was
you just lost one life.

Aditya Bhat

The Way through the Life

Bad is the beginning
Bad can be the end but it can be only
So you can try to change it
But only one might
Is powerful enough
To influence that
So that it takes effect
A might that is
The strongest power in cosmos
A thing called Love
So the end will not be bad
Because of one special person on Earth
You just need to find them
If you have the luck
Then you will find the way
Through the Life

Benjamin Hofer

I Am One

I am the one seen and not heard.
Voice overthrown by the commotion
that lies before me. Silenced by my
fears and dismissed just as quickly.
Lost in my mind not able to find my
words. I am him who hides in the
shadows with wretchedness trying
to find his awe with eyes closed. I
am the creation of my own demise. I
am misunderstood by all except
one. The one in the mirror. The
one who wonders, where have they
gone? Lost in the present? I am
not who they say I am. I am who I
say I am and a little more. I am
here. I am now. I am 'cause I choose
to be. Ever going to change?
Never going to change. I am one!!!!!

Mario Hernandez

My Child

My child became a woman
And today becomes a wife
She grew up very quickly
It seems almost overnight
From the moment she was born
She brought joy into my heart
She is my daughter and my friend
My special work of art
The vows that she takes today
Will forever change her life
I pray for years of happiness
As she becomes a wife
I know that she's been blessed
And will have a life like mine
We both found a man that's special
They are each one of a kind
In my heart she will always be
My child, my little girl
I love her very deeply
She's a bright spot in my world

Gloria Davis

The Bride

Here she comes
A vision of loveliness
Wearing a silky white lace
With smile on her face

She's gonna be his wife
With him she'll spend her life
In sickness and in health
In poverty and in wealth

She's proud to be a bride
She saw her mom and dad
Crying but not sad
Because she is the bride

She's lovely indeed
Everybody is pleased
She's every girl's wish
The bride in white lace

Lanilyn Dejumo

Sail among the Stars

A chariot that ushers me
Along the Milkyway
To view the different stars
Pegusas on the right
Orion on the left

A place in the heavens
That I call my own
My sanctuary in eternity
The magical renewal of my
Imagination and heart

A poets dream
To mystical words of creation
The wonderment of the universe
A place where my soul
Has rested

Sharon Reed

Moments of You

For but only a moment in my busy day
I think of you and see you there,
I close my eyes and feel you there.
Feeling your warm breath
On the back of my neck,
Tasting your sweet kiss
Gentle on my lips.
You grasp my hands tightly
Wanting never to let go.
I open my eyes and quietly smile,
Tucking away those precious memories
For yet another day,
When I'll need to feel you close
And want to have you here . . .
With me . . .
If but only for a moment.

C. Bovee

Walk with Me to the Sea

Walk with me to the sea
 Listen as it calls our name
 Never be afraid of this
 Time is on its way
Walk with me to the sea
 Understand that it thrives for us
 Somewhere between present and future
 Things will slowly fade away
Walk with me to the sea
 No longer will we need this world
 Time has now come for us
Walk with me to the sea
 This time,
 We thrive for the sea
Walk with me to the sea

Jenny N. Page

Untitled

Listen to me
because I want you to see
how men can be
they say they care
when you're there
but when you go away
they say they will stay
but there out with some one else
because they only care about themselves
they take your heart and tear it apart
they will front to get what they want
and that's peace of a . . .
but then that will pass
because it will get old
so don't say you were not told.

Tiffany M. Smith

My Saturday Night

To Kaitlyn, Brianna, and Laura
I'm alone in my house tonight.
The stars are light,
The moon is bright,
On this Saturday night.

My dog is asleep,
It sure makes me weep,
To know I'm alone,
On this Saturday night.

My parents are out,
But soon they'll be home,
So I'll give you a shout,
When they come about,
All on this Saturday night.

Kristen Kelly

Anthony

Of all of whom I've
seen,
Love only have
I one, now
Hate. Now blind to
Find what
Isn't there,
Forever.

Eidelweiss Albumblatt

Until the Day We Meet Again

If I see you,
If I hear you
If I touch you,
on this distant night
carried by the wind
it's because I let myself drift.
I let myself feel you.
I extend my hand out to you,
Drift to the presence of your memory.
Deep breath,
taking you in.
Making another memory.
Silence is what I hear
as I breath in your presence
Closing my eyes,
and whispering.
Good-bye, my friend
Until the day we meet again.

Sandra Lara

The Magic Hour

Twilight sunset
With no ink except
That dark purple color
"in fondo . . ."

Wind brushing the lake
Like a lady in waiting
Attending to her queen
While the kiwi branches dance

The new moon
Like my thumbnail
Scoops into the west
For a taste of that mountain

The cities come forth
In a parade of lights along the shores
Of this Major Lake
Lovely, dark, and deep,

Like woods and Frost
After Earth has given her fruits
And withdrawn into herself

Holly Pessina

Mine Heart

Sweetest of Angels, doth thou swear
To love mine heart only, thy own soul to bear
  Truth, angel be, answer with care
Mine heart awaits quietly in fluttered affair
  Oh, angel, I praise thee, my celestial dove
No truer words hath been spoken, 'tis you that I love
  Fairest of skin lay on soft feathered wing
Thou art' most beautiful of angels from mountains I sing
  Asketh me angel, I breathe thee no lie
To follow thy passage, could that I fly
  Enchanted by thine light, together we stay
Tethered our hearts, so as one, fly away
  Sweetest of Angels, 'tis no love so grand
To shed feathered wings wherein my arms thou'st shall land
  For lore, 'tis my soul thee taketh and tame
Love has mine heart, 'tis you beareth blame

    Brian Plautz

Life

Wisdom comes with age
Knowledge from learning
Pride from achievement
Love from fulfilled yearning
Honesty comes from truth
Compassion from caring
Friendship from kindness
Companionship from sharing

    Angela Hagler

Car Driving in Love

Car driving in love . . . baby . . .
Red light turns to green . . .
But we can't see . . .
We're sneaking kisses, and holding on . . .
To the glisten in each other's eyes . . .
My pony-tail falls on your cheek . . .
Oh, you're so pretty! . . .
The people behind us are mad-laughing . . .
We're embarrassed . . .
But we can't see beyond our love . . .

    Mary-Lisa Newcomb

The Servants Sing

White garments modestly adorned
Liken unto you, this Sunday morn
A psalm of praise and of thanksgiving
Worshiping the Savior, this day we are living

"Trust in the Lord," so they all sing
Faithful in service, a life change to bring
Reviving souls who've gone astray
Lifting spirits, proclaiming His promises for a better day

A call to salvation is the servant's cry
They keep singing, "We'll understand it all by and by"
One finally comes, as a child so brave
Praises surrendered, lives are being saved

Clapping of hands, stumping of feet
The drummer's baton waving, keeping a steady beat
Ain't no wonder why the servants love to sing
Joy and jubilation to the Mighty King

Servants sing! Quench not the Spirit!
Awakening dry bones, unloosening wax . . . making them hear it!
Fragrances of love so pure, so wonderfully divine,
Servants keep singing . . . JESUS IS MINE!

    Mary Victoria Kent

"Hero"

Most peoples hero is their dad.
They say he is the strongest man in the world.
Well my hero isn't my dad at all.
I still love him, but I have another hero instead.
My hero doesn't have strong muscles to carry really heavy things.
She is strong in the mind and in the heart, to support
more important things.
My hero isn't shy, she likes to always speak her mind.
She's kind, caring, and takes good care of her kids.
When we were in the time of need she fought through the court,
the cries and tears, simply down to the very end.
she's done a lot for me that words just can't describe.
She's been a good friend to me, and always looks you in the eye.
My hero has been through a lot with me,
and I hope we will go through more.
This person means a lot to me.
I don't know what I would do without her.
You know how a picture can say a thousand words?
Well her face can say a thousand more.
I hope when she looks at my face she knows I'm saying,
"You're my hero mom," and that will never change. . . .

    Genevieve Love

The Taste of Love!

If love had a flavor, it would taste like you look.
Fine and rare and only served on special occasions,
so that would be everyday that we are together,
because our union is always a celebration.

If love had a flavor, it would taste like mannah from Heaven.
The angels would sound their trumpets,
their stringed instruments would play,
as I strum your pain with my fingers,
as I serve the essence of my love to you.

If love had a flavor, it would taste like strawberry lemonade
with the perfect blend of ghetto sweetness,
so that you could taste it on my lips after I sip you.
For my cup runneth over with the taste of your honey-dip too.

If love had a flavor, it would taste like my chocolate
in your peanut butter.
It would be milky all the way that would send us both
into mars and cause my HERSHE to kiss you
and your watchamacallit and the end result would be pure almond joy.

    Deborah Grison

I Am a Falling Leaf

I am a falling leaf . . .
When I fall down, I spin and spin.
Soon I land.
I wonder where the wind would take me.
I look back up at my tree where more leaves are falling off.
I know there was a lot of time to say goodbye to the place I love.
Then soon after I say goodbye, the wind blows.
I have to follow it.

    Lisa Oppenheim

Creamy Vanilla/Rocky Road

Problems come and go, but this one stays
Two different things, on two different levels.
I see both of them in my mind as clear as the sky.
Make my mind up this one or that one?
Too hard to choose which one is better!
One's like creamy vanilla, the other, rocky road.
My life's a shamble, too many decisions to make,
but this one is too difficult!
The road splits into two ways,
I want a smooth ride but which do I choose?
Creamy Vanilla or Rocky Road?

    Carie Smith

What Sam Gave

I met Sam on a hot Monday
I needed a coke
He had some money
And we became friends on a hot Monday
I met Sam at the pond on a hot Tuesday
I needed a fishing pole
He had one
And we became best friends on a hot Tuesday

I met Sam at the store on a hot Wednesday
I had to go to college
He did, too
And we became apart on a hot Wednesday

I heard Sam died on a hot Thursday
I needed a friend
He couldn't be one
And Sam died on a hot Thursday

I went to the Funeral on a rainy Friday
He needed something
I could give him
And I gave him a yellow rose on a rainy Friday

Whitney Barringer

Beautifully Perfect

Your imperfections are what make you so beautifully perfect.
I don't know if it's in your actions or in your words,
but there is something about you that lures me in.
If in your craziness or your casualness,
in your beauty or in your flaws, but it's there, oh it's there.
That same thing has been around for millions of years,
since the time of Adam and Eve.
It's in the beauty of every woman every where
and it's in the way that guys look in awe at them time after time,
always in amazement; "could she be even more stunning,
more beautiful than yester!?"
the answer is simply yes, you are beautifully perfect.

Charles Barrett

Heart vs. Head

In my heart . . . I still love you.
In my head . . . I know it wouldn't work.
In my heart . . . You mean more to me than you know.
In my head . . . I must put here and now first.
In my heart . . . I wonder what if?
In my head . . . I know.
In my heart . . . You will always be.
In my head . . . You will always be.

Dawn Fugina

A Field of Daisies . . . [Amy]

budding in my mind like a flower,
grows a frail love for a essence so dear,
so touched . . . so true.
Feeling the freedom to experience,
and the occupancies of trust,
breathing the pure soul of eternity . . .
My heart grows fonder,
the feeling grows stronger,
the connection, deeper.
A touch is like a million years,
and a love so true,
in my world it's the only essence I crave . . .
You . . .

Chad Copeland

Black Vision

crimson lips, mocha skin,
souls connecting from within.
images of black leaders and important people,
reaching towards the sky like a church's steeple.
the march continues on . . . . on a never ending mission.
blood pouring like rain.
I can still hear the pain.

Robert Cooper

Your Soul Knows

Choose only positive thoughts,
Your soul knows.
Choose to be happy,
The choice is yours.
Everything we feel, think, imagine,
Your soul knows.
Choose to create your own Eden,
For we are creators.
Your soul knows.
Choose to make a difference,
An act of kindness, a smile,
Your soul knows.
Choose not to be critical,
For we are all equal in God's eyes.
Your soul knows.
Choose to accept others differences, put
Aside prejudices, your soul knows.
Above all, choose love, all you say and do,
Let it be for love.
Your soul knows.

Carolyn Comentale

Illness

Why is it that someone you deeply know gets deathly sick.
Is this some kind of game or trick.
We love them so much for being gentle, sweet and caring.
And I would like to do the same as of sharing.
You never understand what goes on in their mind.
You want to get the best help for them to be kind.
You know it hurts so because you have a heart.
So don't let this little thing tear the family apart.
So be real true and strong,
you know that isn't wrong.
It is hard to figure it all out,
but say a prayer and read the Bible whenever in Doubt.

Karol Blair

Valentine

This Valentines Day will be special
Something you won't want to miss
When that special someone gives you a flower
Or maybe a hug or a kiss
But maybe someone new
Will ask you
To be their Valentine
And you will turn and smile
And your smile will shine.

Aimee Leveen

Illusive Valentine

Illusive be . . . my memory.
Shrouded, clouded with the veils of time.
No face, no name, no place to rhyme.
What kind of Love be this design?
One two discover . . . each other, My Valentine!

Pat C. Myers

Theory of Everything

Nature's laws hidden in simplicity
God's puzzle missing its pieces
Four forces of nature
put together to fit perfectly
Scientists in awe, wonder
who will find magical key
Legends told of Einstein's passion
Thirty years but no solution
Superstring Theory only opponent left
So close and never close enough
Elusive and strange this quantum world
No common sense or intuition
Answers are real and imaginary
Math beyond any mortal man
To understand is to know God
Is mind of God innocent as a child?
Arms outstretched, ready to love?
Are we ready to love unconditionally?
A simple solution for a child
An impossible task for sophisticated adults

    David Labay

In the Mirror

Look in my eyes and you will see
A strong and independent soul.
Content and happy with who I am,
But really I'm just playing the role.

Look into my eyes one more time,
And you will see the wall that I have placed.
It protects me from shedding the tears,
Helps me forget all I have faced.

I'll tell you I believe in myself,
When really failure is what I fear.
I'll tell you that I never cry,
While I'm drowning inside from the tears.

Now you know the truth about me,
That I am not what I portray.
In search to be accepted,
I deceive those around me each day.

Look into my eyes one more time,
Take a step back and you will see,
That what lies beneath the surface,
Is a reflection of you to me.

    Glenna Kolynych

Mary, Merry Christmas

No presents brightly wrapped,
  No tree all aglow,
I offer you my love my dear,
  Until that day sometime next year,
When actions speak louder
  Than words ever will,
"Do you take this woman
  To be your wife,
To love and honor,
  All the days of your life?"
"I do," he said with a cheesy grin,
  Not sure if he'd just opened his
Mouth and fallen in, "Yes, I do,"
  He said again,
Realizing he'd not fallen, but flew
  Like an angel ready to begin
A life with Mary,
  A lifelong dream
To share with this woman, who he'd always known,
  Would find him someday
    And take him home.

    Steve Anastasoff

Going Home

In the still of the night
Cries of torment break the darkness
Death fill the air like a heavy blanket
Hollow eyes
Sunken cheeks
Flies eating off human flesh of those too weak to move
Gunfire in the background
Flashes of light filling the sky
Children orphaned
Too young to understand
But too old for their years
Curled up in the shadows one child lay
Hungry and hurting
And alone
The wind blows through his tiny, frail body
For the last time
As a visitor cloaked in white
Picks him up
And carries him home

    Hali Chamney

Suburbs

Think like equals of my transgressions
Sink like evil watches worldwide digressions
Blink like sequels make confessions
Fink like upheaval is the new succession

Passion packed perfectly in bottles of brown
Happiness happened hesitantly with a frown
Steadily selling sickness to the down
Greedily gunning goodness with a sound
Missing marked maybes beside the point
Cordially convincing cooperation with a joint
Entertainment elating egoists will appoint
Winnings weakly wish to anoint

Possession picked partly through the blame
Hell hoarding heavily the winners of the game
Sinful silences sureness sounded the same
Green gods gated away in their fame
Morbid monasteries make their rapports
Callow coordination cowers with its sorts
Esteemed ether entangles and contorts
When windy women claim their report

    Danielle Weinhold

Fatigue

I feel battered and torn.
I'm tired.
Everything aches.
I take a deep breath and I look at you.
I don't know if I can do it anymore.
I'm too tired to fight for you,
and I'm too tired to fight against you.
Sometimes, it feels like you're in my veins.
Deep inside the core of me,
and no matter how I try I can't
get you out.
Unless I hurt myself and bleed you out.
The only way to rid me of
your disease is to hurt.
I know that.
I feel that.
Yet, sometimes I feel too tired to bleed.

    Ashley Young

Dreaming

Thinking of you night and day,
As I float away into a dream world I sway.
Where waves crash upon the beach,
And yet it is still not out of my reach.
In my dreams doors open wide,
I never have to run and hide.
This isn't a place of rules to be serious;
Not in my dreams, you are never grievous.
Holding your hand up to catch a shooting star,
Traveling through space to visit Mars.
Being with the angels as they dance on the clouds,
Knowing that anything is allowed.
But one part of this world that I love always
Is how it ends every time, anyway.
Sealing a dream with a kiss
Is one dream I wouldn't wanna miss.
Soon this dream will come to a close,
So I kiss you and hand you one white rose.
Then I slowly open my eyes,
Looking out at the baby blue skies.

Jennie Knoblauch

Without Love

Cold, as I sit
Why does my life feel so empty
When I have my friends, family, and music?
My mind fails to understand
Why I feel so worthless
A waste of thoughtful words
And no sense of what I really want
Feeling so unloved
As you walk right past me
And when I try to catch up with you,
You disappear
I may seem happy
But I feel so ill
Without love or respect
I begin to deny myself
This body
These words
And through the cracks in the wall I melt
And I feel all of my faith collapse.

Tara Kostick

God Knows

I never said I loved you
although I wanted to.
I never thought I'd lose you,
but now I know the truth.
My friends try to make me laugh,
but all I do is cry.
When I try and I have fun,
I only want to die .
But maybe that's the good part,
'cause if I do I'll be with you.
You never said you're leaving,
You never said goodbye.
You were gone before I knew it,
and only God knows why.
A million times I've needed you,
A million times I've cried.
If love alone could have saved you,
 you never would have died.
I died when you left, and now I am alone.
I was left with the pain
The day God took you home.

Liz Griffin

What Jesus Might Say

I am Jesus, welcome, my child,
I made you a saint and undefiled,
you have been a witness about my love,
you prayed to me in Heaven up above,
you have told many of your love for me,
now you are at my side for all of eternity,
for evil and worldly thoughts you never had a desire,
you will never taste death or the fire,
I deem you to be holy and wise,
evil and the world you learned to despise,
when the poor were hungry you gave to them food,
you kept your faith no matter the mood,
you shared my word and made the unsaved think,
their souls had a thirst and you gave my word for drink,
Heaven is your reward for a job well done,
the world thought you a zero but my angels know
you are number one . . .

Gary D. Thomas

A Friend of the Net

While surfing the web, an IM flashes across the screen
The name is unfamiliar, but you answer with a "Hello"
A conversation is started at that instant, a possible friend.

Another night goes by online and you receive an IM on your screen,
This time the name is familiar to you, as you spoke last night.
With every keystroke, you find out more about each other.
Time becomes non-existent as your fingers run across the keyboard.

A friendship emerges as you read the display on your computer.
A frown turns into a smile when you see your Net Friend is online.
Friends on the Net have a way of helping each other in times
where all is needed is a kind word.

From the screen appears a kind reassuring word . . . a wink . . . or a hug.
Although only a keystroke, the thoughts of one transcend the
infrastructure of the web into feelings felt from within us.

There is a feeling that is felt as time goes on.
A face may never be placed with the name, but it is there.
You feel it as you type, but you cannot see it or touch it.
The distance may be great, but yet you are there.
From the infinite miles of wire, you have made "A Friend of the Net."

James Stykemain

Our Greatest Treasure

Oh, My Sons So Tall And Strong,
Like These Maroon Bells, To Us A Song.
These Mountains Are Memories
Of Your Youth, Our Pleasure,
They Remind Us Often
Of Our Greatest Treasure.
We Have Seen These Hills
Up Close And Personal,
And From Atop Buttermilk
Whose Runs We've Flown,
Only To Glory More As You Have Grown.
You Now Are Men Still Tall And Strong,
Like These Bells Forever, To Us A Song!
I Hope You Return To These Mountains Someday,
And Walk Those Places
Where We Laughed And Played,
And Thoughtfully Recall Your Parents'
Love And Pleasure,
As You Admire Your Own Precious Treasure.

Larry Trimble

The Princess

There once was a beautiful princess,
Who danced every day in her garden.
And if she injured a flower,
She would say, "I beg your pardon."
She danced until dark, mysterious midnight,
When the moon was brightly full.
She gazed at it with wonder,
Until her eyes, with tears, were full.
As queen, she was proud of her people.
She ruled for many years.
And in very hard times,
Her subjects dried her tears.
She was a very worthy queen,
She was not afraid to pass away.
For she knew that her beautiful daughters
Would rule even better someday.
The daughters ruled and ruled and ruled.
They ruled for many years.
And in very hard times,
Their subjects dried their tears.

Elaina Campbell

Who Are We to Judge???

Who are you to judge me by the color or texture of my hair
Who are you to tell me what color clothes or shoes I should wear
Who died and left you in charge
Who ever told you that you were the joker of the cards
Who are you to judge

You haven't been looking so good yourself
You've took a turn from right to left
Your cloths are ripped and torn apart
Oh baby let me tell you this is just the start
But who am I to judge . . .

See it's not fair to either one of us
Now you tell me who's the one to judge
Because in Gods eyes We are ALL the same . . .
So Don't give us none of your lame excuses
Because none could explain

Who Gave you permission to Judge . . .

Michelle Record

Salvation

You're lost in a dimension you can't feel or explain.
Your senses are gone, you are no longer sane.
Held bondage by deception who has many names;
call him evil, it's all the same.
For what does he offer, to take, or to give?
Trying to tell you that under him you shall live.
But in his world there is violence, lust, and greed,
poverty, abuse, and every bad seed. I call this life darkness,
not knowing myself, or the world.
I must get far from it, I pray that a light be unfurled.
Show me the steps to take, make them as bright as day.
Show me life in a most spiritual way. Teach me your virtue,
let your wisdom set me free. Give me words of understanding,
and eyes that see. A steadfast heart, a piece of mind,
a brand new start, and a love to define.
I must pray unto God to light my way, and for a love of life . . . .
until my very last day.

David Perez

Gaia's Plea

Hear my soul cry out in rage
the trees are torn from my body
my waters are poisoned
animals caged with no room to move
slave to the dollar humans are
gawking at circus animals
look into animals eyes
feel their fear
does no one care
they ask why
what do I tell them
they are not souls to you
oppress the poor
so you can get rich
slave to the dollar
classism, sexism, racism—symptoms of your poison
this earth a dust bowl will be
rise up against the poison
free yourself as a slave
a new dawn of rebirth

Amy Engman

I Met Myself Today

I met myself today, at 12 years.
After a fight with his dad,
His head hung lower than his shoulders.
He publicly embarrassed him,
Poking his pistol finger into his temple.
Confrontation number 5 million,
Rehearsed and predestined.
I was all angry at the man,
But hurting for the child, in me.
He bought him a video
But relentlessly stripped him of his dignity.
I circled and approached.
"Ya know what to do?" "No."
My 20-year split-second response:
"Wait him out. You can't change him,
But you can change you.
YOU can change YOU."

Denise Stainbrook

What is Love

What is love?
to me, love is fear.
Fear of the unknown. Fear of the feelings.
Love is when you can't breathe.
Like all of your air is being consumed by some unknown force,
stalking you wherever you go.
Love is constant thinking.
Wondering why. Wondering how.
Love is pain.
Pain of heartbreak. Pain of rejection.
Love is wonderful.

Donald Coard

Believing

One day I looked up at the sky.
Why aren't there colors in the sky?
I had a dream that I could spread colors way up high.
And one day that dream came true.
And now I know who to believe in:
It's in the true you.
You got to believe to do.
Just remember believe in you.
From that day on I listened to my heart.
And that's how I discovered the true meaning of believing.

Alyssa Serignese

Night Pain

Awakened once again with pain
staring at the cold blue screen
the night so long no sleep in vain
I wander at the cold night
how long will it go on
can i escape in drugs
and dreamless sleep or risk the pain and life
pointless days it seems
waiting for the dawn
which never seems to come
rid me of the suffering is all I can think
the answer
life pain
sleep death

Nancy Hieronymus

Wish upon a Star

Have you ever wished upon a star?
Thinking, maybe, it'd take you somewhere far?
Far away from the life you live
Where it seems as though there's nothing to give?
You try to love, but only feel hate
The best things in life always seem to come late
Sure, special people and good things are worth waiting for
But sometimes you wish for something more
Something to make you happy every day
Something that will never go away
Though wishing on a star may not always make your dreams come true
The dreams that you may have are all up to you

Carlynn Lasley

Rid the Fear & Turn the Key

I've been blessed
I've been blessed with The Key
I've been blessed with The Key
With The Key that lets me see
With The Key I can see
I can see who I'm to be
What's that you say you want to see
You want to see who you're to be
Well for you to see who you're to be
You must rid the fear of turning The Key
Yeah It's The Key that lets you see
It lets you see who you're to be
If you're to be what you see
And what you see is to be
Well, my friend, then here's The Key
Here's The Key that lets you see
It lets you see who you're to be
But you'll only be those things you'll see
By ridding the fear of turning The Key.

Mark Dugre'

Love

Your golden hair so sweet and fine
Your delicate eyes that never seize to shine
Your sensitive skin glistens all the time
All this I wish just could be mine
I've loved you from the start
'Til death do we part
The sun, the Earth, the moon that shines
Is no competition to what you hold
And all I desire
The agony of love is like a never ending fire

Joshua Carreon

The Widow's Prayer

Alone in this world, she roams a silent hall,
Searching for remembrance, no matter how small.
Through her loneliness, she tries to be brave,
'Til merciful angels carry her to her grave.
Then she will reunite with her one true love,
In the holiest of all mansions e'er erected above.
Sadly, she is bound to this Earth still,
This is a torture that's almost unreal.
She never leaves home, she stays in day and night,
Seeking a memory of love, if only a slight.
She has been in this state for thirty odd years,
This fact has, no doubt, cost her much tears.
Her life is empty yet filled with strife,
If not for fear of the Devil, she'd turn to the knife,
She welcomes death and bids it her way,
So her life will cease and she'd fade away.
Night after night, on her knees with a nod,
She prays for deliverance by the hand of God.
A widows prayer is answered, to her love she goes,
There he awaits her, holding a single red rose.

Alvin-Dale Green

The Ones That Got Away

Before dawn, the water was like glass
As I waded in with my fishing pole.
My father still slept at the campsite,
But I cast with hope, heart, and soul.
Mist rose from the lake
As bream bit my toes,
And I dreamed of things,
God only knows.
I was but a young boy,
Camping, and fishing, as I'd only dreamed.
Life had come to a standstill;
This was all there was to it, it seemed.
The smell of fish frying in a pan,
The sound of wind against my tent,
The feel of a bass on a fly rod,
The bond of father and son; Heaven sent.

Now, faraway eyes reflect the fire
At our favorite camping place.
I cast a gaze across the lake, for
The ones that got away.

Mike Stockdale

Sailorman and Me

Rough and tired his hands appear
when the long day is through.
But his touch is gentle as he takes my hand
and melts away my blues.

His once brown hair now turned to gray
and thinned to some extent.
Nonetheless, when he holds me in his arms
I could not be more content.

His tall and stately stature can
not be overlooked.
And he bends to gaze into my eyes
then reads me like a book.

From dawn to dusk he gives his all
to things I cannot see.
Yet when the night, the lovely night falls
he gives his all to me.

Robin Worthey

In the Midnight Hour

In the midnight hour bright, where the lost souls roam.
All the faces that I see embedded in my home.
The moon it shines with brilliant light, showing me the way.
With each hour ticking by, with each passing day.
In the midnight hour slow, you can breathe it in.
All the spirits of the night, all the souls within.
The moon it changes all with time, showing me the way,
with each hour ticking by, with each passing day.
In the midnight hour time it seems so still,
all the voices that I hear telling me their will.
With the crescent moon I see, stars around it shine,
allowing me this one moment to see the souls of time.
Learning from them, teaching too,
all the souls are here, learn what you will,
and be blessed for what they do.
In the midnight hour cold,
souls are resting in their place.
Wanting you to see vitality,
compassion and beauty of the human race.
With each hour ticking by,
with each passing day,
can you see the souls of time,
can you see them showing you the way?

    Tina Stauss

Voice in the Wind

I hear your voice in the wind,
calling my name,
so sweetly,
so tenderly.

I feel your arms around me,
holding me,
so tightly,
so closely.

So real is it,
that I reach up to kiss you.

Instead, a gentle breeze brushes my lips,
carrying with it,
the sound of your voice,
calling my name.

    Sarah Garay

Blue

Blue is the color of my emotions
Blue is the color of my thoughts
Blue is the color of my heart
Blue

Words or nails on my spine
An expression conveyed in a systematic form
translated by the enemy, your mind.
A form of compassion poured out upon your hands,
but depicted as nails impounding your heart.
Translation, I am not you and your mind I cannot find.
Lost in view of your language.
Entangled by my own words.
Beseeched beyond compare.
Confused and unaware.
Can I, you, reach an agreement?
Mind you, I cannot be the cause of your inflicted confusion.
Your vision is based upon what you see.
As mine is for me.
Blue the color of . . .

    Alyna Martinez

Think

Open your mind to the new beginnings
of time and knowledge.
Remember the days when all was calm and serene.
By helping those in need you are helping yourself
and reaching levels of happiness
you cannot reach any other way.
Dreams are not an illusion, they are
the building blocks to life, and everything in life.
Stay in this state of mind and rest for a while,
think about anything and everything.
Fight away any negative thoughts that can keep you
from what you want to do.
As is always said, "Patience is a virtue," and that it is.

Stay healthy in the mind
and you will be grateful for the rest of your life.

    Jake Port

Penny

When I was five years old you left me,
left me without a way,
of becoming the girl and woman,
I hope I am and will be.
You left me in darkness,
the dark cloud stayed over me,
please let the memory of your funeral,
release me.
Then I will be with no dark cloud,
I will be able to become the woman,
You would have wanted me to be.
Your grandchildren will know all about you,
just as you were to me,
everything I remember,
is what they will hear from me.
Your memory will not be forgotten,
because your great-grandchildren,
will also hear of you,
the person I called Mother,
I love you.

    Nancy Dahle

Rain

As it pours outside
I'm crying inside,
jealous that nature can deal with its feelings better than I.
My heart is a looming black cloud
waiting to burst,
my eyes fearing its strength.
I wish I could rain proudly,
shameless of my own nature.
But I can't . . .
My will is stronger than my tears.

And the flood wells up inside.

    Margaret Seelen

Charley's Day

Brisk winds, racing leaves
Sun so warm, humming bees

Blue skies, telling clouds
Trees budding, standing proud

My shadow sets upon the grass so green,
The beauty of our brisk world is seldom seen.

    Charles Mason

Nightshade's Promise (A Dragon's Quote)

If you feel danger's grasp
Should its shadow engulf you
Stay brave and always remember
I am your loyal protector
But I will leave you with the legend of shadows
If the vision spreads, evil will rule again
But if two dragons soar across the sky
An angel will fall to Earth
That is Nightshade's Promise

Tyler Prevost

Dreaming through the Eyes of a Youngster

Dreams are like rockets;
They go fast and far with a thrust.
The youngster that is scared of dreams must call,
"I must, I must, I must!"
Dreams are old, or young these days.
Some can be gold, some black—
Yet, others seem to have their ways.
Dreams have to be free—
As if under your own power.
Let them go, and they will fly,
But don't dare tell of them to me—
For if you do, they'll thrust to a nightmare, you see.
Only one rule applies to all;
They only fly in an open sky,
Or a fenced-in dream won't dare to die.

Ashley Jean McKellar

The Beach

You see her on the beach defenseless,
Little girl beaten almost senseless.

As the wind whips around her body,
And the storm rages.
A hand, waiting to strike, in stages.
Face and hair flying,
The sky is darker, she is dying.

Clouds stretching farther than eye can see,
Running back, What am I? Who is she?

At first she looks at you hair flying,
Moves back from the tide, she is crying.
One single tear rolling down her cheek,
She cries out loud but yet cannot speak.
To the tear drops that you have to reach.

You reach out to shield her from all harm,
Wind and waves that you have to disarm.

The wave clenches, a fist made iron.
Wind roars, a lion.
Stronger than any tyrant's ire,
The wind lost desire.
See me now, storm is gone, name . . . "Admire."

Tammi Schrager-Bozdag

Swing

I sway my legs as I go up and down.
I smile and smile, not one little frown.
My hair waves rapidly: it's such a sight.
I swing and swing into the crisp, cool night.

My arms are free, my feet are bare.
I swing and I swing without a care.
I stop my legs, the wind settles down.
I walk straight home without a frown.

The birds are quiet, my head lays down.
Then the next morning, I go back downtown.
The air is cool; my feet are bare.
Once again I go up and down in the crisp, cool air!

Calie Makoski

st. agnes weeps

they stand to close to the fire, gettin' down in the mire
roses are red,violets blue
the moon lit the night,
there's bound to be a fight the muzzle flash,
the shotgun blast
the pellets fell like rain technicolor dreams,
the ambulance screams
he must have come up three feet,
before he crashed to the street,
doin' the st.vitus dance his life ran downhill and into the gutter,
with his last breath he called for his mother
tatooed arms, little gold charms,
the gangsters make it easy to kill, you shake your head,
it can't be real, they haven't a clue to what they've done
somewhere a mother waits for her son
didn't they read, "Thou shalt not kill"
it's chiseled in stone for all to know
i turn my back, and walk away,
the voice inside, i hear it say,
knick, knack, paddy whack.
take this old dog home.

Don Belin

"Be Not My Friend"

As I begin to open my heart,
Wishing to share of myself, it is as if—
You put me back on the shelf.
Wanting so much for you to understand,
be there for me,
and hold my hand.
A soft gentle touch, is what means so much
Hoping that one day you will be my friend.
That is when my emotions will begin to mend.
Moments and days together,
a continuation of the storms we weather.
I see little change,
as you begin and end each day in a haze.
You said to have and to hold,
In sickness and health,
For richer or poorer.
See that this relationship,
does not stay on the border.
Open your eyes
and "be not my friend"

Trisha Pope

The Next Step

From K to 12 you've worked your way through,
You've changed, matured, brighten, and obviously grew.
Good times and bad times you've had throughout these years,
You've achieved most of your many goals without any fears.
You've come to the end of thirteen long years of education,
You've contributed many hours of perseverance and dedication.
Candlewood, DuFief, Frost and Wootton are all history,
Maryland is next, and the rest is a mystery.
The end has come and you must now leave,
Hold on to all your memories, for later to retrieve.
As the doors close, you pass on by,
Looking back at the past, while your future says hi.
Cherishing this moment in every single way,
Hugs and farewells you encounter, with nothing left to say.
Your next step in life, will be the challenge of college,
Along you will bring, your strength and knowledge.
Away from your family is where you'll be,
As for me, this is very hard to see.
As your tassel no longer hangs from the right,
You step away, and now you're out of sight.

Alejandra Costello

The Feeling Inside

The cool morning sensational breeze pressing against my skin
As I watch the early sunrise
I think to myself, "Will this ever happen again?"
The same warm colors creating the feeling of happiness in every soul
As we awaken, and realize what we are missing
The feeling of love in the air is righteous and plentiful
Nowhere else will this beautiful sight be seen
Nowhere else will this sensational breeze be felt
But one thing for sure, the feeling inside will forever remain keen
For this feeling of love may never happen again
Which stands right before me
I hope this feeling will never end
Attempting to grab hold as tight as I can
As the rays of light become brighter
As it continues to move away into the world
I think to myself again, "I will never give up"
Running and running, faster and faster
Hoping I'm not too late before it settles down
Hoping the feeling is mutual instead of a frown
But in the end, who knows what's to happen
Within time, there will always be a dark side
But soon you will realize, the sunrise is the best of all
You will realize the sunrise is what you need . . . .

Rolando N. Rosete

For Here or to Go?

For here or to go?

So, it is Monday again.
Good morning, street sweepers
And the garbage collectors.
I like your sanitation work,
As I drive along this Chinese street.
Everything looks quite and peaceful here.
And I just smile stopping on the red.
This is very special place to me
Throughout years of living in San Francisco.
And this morning when I buy my coffee
I hear this familiar phrase,
"For here or to go?"
 With a question in her eyes
I am trying to puzzle it out.
I wish I said, "For here"
And jump into the liveliness
But I have to go make some money
    And think of her until the next Monday.

Andrei Hotov

Was There an Eye

Was there an eye in the vacant land
where two hearts lived and died;
that may have noticed my out stretched hand,
left ignored as I cried?

Was there one about the garden
where once tread Adam and Eve,
that took sight of a cherub's foot
with a twitch, preparing to leave?

Was there an ear to hear the sound
of the dying love coming 'round;
to listen to the noise
of pain as it destroys?

Was there an eye to catch the miracle
as you re-entered my heart and soul;
to witness the splendor of the day,
to see what remains untold?

Jason Carnrike

Funny Love

I use to get hugs, kisses and love letters;
chocolates just because and flowers by mail.
I used to feel love from the minute you looked at me.
I used to know that the world could stop
but if you were with me you wouldn't care.

You used to make flowers bloom in the dead of winter;
you used to love me so.
You made me believe in summertime flings,
butterfly songs and elves hiding in leaves.
You made me love you so.

You left me in the middle of our summer.
I never knew summer could ever be so cold.
I cried the tears of a destitute child.
I cried an ocean of the truly alone.

Cheryl Parks

Life

Infinite wisdom, spread through the years,
as I see it go to waste you become a witness to my visible tears
What people lack in knowledge they gained through ignorance
Even if they're unaware they feel the pain
of the fact that they have nothing to gain
Believe in the power of the Son of Man as your fate switches hand,
know that through life's experiences is when you truly understand
Souls lost to the power of influence, minds become perverse
and act out the worst, dark images seen in the shade
People have forgotten their values for they forgot that they were
something that God made
People figuring how they can live in the now,
they rather live in the past because they feel
that's the only way the memories can last
Through the words that we speak we can educate the weak
and through that we can continue
to find the answers of life that we tried so hard to seek

Stefano Fattorini

Time

A faded photo of you and I.
A reminder of how time does fly.

Years have past, yet you remain.
Through ups and downs, through joys and pains.

What is time, but moments to share,
day to day and year to year.

Barbara Kremer

A Tear for Two

I feel to cry, oh Lord, oh why,
has darkness poured from pale blue skies,
why do hate and anger reign,
on souls so low and full of pain,
where is kindness and fellow friends,
where is the love like gentle winds,
why am I left in tears alone,
where is the light to guide me home,
I fight to shun a bitter rage,
I try to love instead of hate,
where does one look past my sin,
and comprehend my soul within,
My Lord, is there one who cares for me,
Oh yes! My child . . . "Gethesemane,"
though thy tears fall a mournful rain,
and sorrows burn the worldly pain,
behold this gift I give to thee,
One tear for you . . . One tear for Me.

Gary Jefferson

Prayer

The power in prayer is very strong
Prayer helps me to know I belong
Lord, Your name is imprinted on my heart
It feels so wonderful to know we will never part

Oh my most precious and awesome Lord
How I love to pray and read Your Word
I glorify You, I give You the praise
I am so thankful I am learning Your ways

Jesus, at times I do falter
But my faith and prayer brings me back to Your altar
I am forgiven and always in Your favor
Answered prayer glorifies only You, my Savior

You want us to believe and know You are real
You want our Holy Spirit to be filled so we can feel
Oh my most glorious and omnipotent one
Thank you, my Father for Jesus, Your Son

I am cleansed in Your blood, forgiven of all my sins
Lord, my prayers are pure, I can feel You within
Your loving presence is so magnificent and overwhelming
I love our time together, it is so fulfilling

Pamela Alcorn

Time Forgotten

As you wake up from your revelations of old,
remember me not for toils endured,
but look upon me as you look upon the sunset,
falling through the choral sky, between the
mountain tops and into solemn rest from a day hard earned.
Remember the times for the inner content, and
lay the happiness upon your heart,
much like you would look upon the tired and
used car with all its nicks and scratches,
but look around the body and feel thanks for
the loyal servitude it has provided you.
Love is gone dormant as the winter rose,
only to patiently await the coming of spring
when it will sprout up out of the earth and
show its beautiful face.

Kyle Seipp

Headtrips

Crazy in the head, thoughts are running wild
Where are you going, labeled child
In another world, on another plane
do you see it, God, or am I going insane

In my mind are many things
I think I understand
Trying to make some sense of it
Lord help me take a stand

Crazy in the head
Not making sense at all
Am I someone special
Or is this just my call

What's that sound
What's going on
Head is pounding, ears are ringing
People rushing here and there

World upside down, doctors ain't around
State of Confusion
Heads are talking, lips are flapping
Showing no respect

Kaonohi Heller

best friends

be yourself around them
essential for a happy life
stays and listens in your time of need
together 'til the end

forever and for life
really understands you
is there when you think no one else understands
enjoys your companionship
never judges you
does favors for you without asking for something in return
stays and listens when you need someone to talk to

Elizabeth Layton

One's Passing Grade

Nor will I stand at amities light.
Chilling shivers at second's best.
Combating thoughts of one's last,
One's last chance.
Nor will I sit with second's glance.
Lashing grief to myself for that one thing
I could not grasp.
Knowing, from lights past.
The understanding of anything
Does not pass
Without contaminating its resin
On one's next attempt.

Daniel B. Swaggerty

Not to Worry

Sit my child, lay upon my breast.
Let me comfort you,
So that you may have eternal rest
It seems as though the roads you have traveled . . .
Some long and hard
Have you weary and lost
But, don't despair
Dig inside you
No burdens are too hard for you to bear
I sit and watch you as you toss and turn
Searching for eternal peace
Fearing for what tomorrow may bring
Don't despair,
I am watching over you
Guiding and comforting you because I care.
When you cry I dry your tears
I am your friend and confidant
Cast all your cares upon me
The battle is not yours to fight
Sit my child, lay here upon my breast.

Latisha Hudson

An Average American

A man walked off the bustling city street
And into a green park he crept
And laid on a bench and admired nature.
Upon finding this peace, he slept.

Later he awoke and saw around him
A vast crowd spreading endlessly
Gath'ring 'round men on soapboxes who were
Ranting loudly and ceaselessly.

He decided to listen to some men
Who looked like they spoke what they knew,
And all he heard was of Marx and Voltaire
And Spinoza and Montesquieu.

Yet some words inspired his fiery passion
And urge to fight for what he'd dare,
But like the million others there that day
He went home, ate, and slept—sans care!

Adam Sedia

Who Am I?

To Auntie Lesley, from your little angel . . . .
I am just a girl
In the middle of the world
I can't help but think that there is a link
To my past and to my future
I am just a flower in the middle of a meadow
I am just a tear upon the face of a lonely child
I am just a cloud in the middle of the sky
I can't help but feel that I am crowded by the world
I am an angel that is missing from Heaven
I am a star that is shining in the midnight sky
I am not blind—I can see where I'm going in life
I am like a bird—I can soar where I want to
Where I'll go
    I don't know
        But I'll go wherever the wind takes me . . . .

Lindsay Thelen

Silent Words

Look into my eyes my friend, tell me what you see.
Do you see the one who longs to cry, "You were meant for me?"
Let me take your hand my friend; I'll follow you anywhere.
Time with you is magical; can't you see how much I care?
Listen to my words my friend, the silent ones I pray.
Please don't ever leave me I love you more each day.
Someday I'll be brave my friend, we will stand face to face.
Then I'll say these words aloud, and melt in your embrace.

Dorothy Olko

Weather

Rain, snow, sleet or hail.
It's all the same to me.

Sunny, cloudy, foggy or windy.
It's all the same to me.

Cold, hot, warm or frigid.
It's all the same to me.

Low front, high front, cold or warm front.
It's all the same to me.
Me, me, who is me?

I am an artist,
I am a day dreamer,
I am a person that gets lost in the clouds,
I am a meteorologist.

Veronica Jessup

Slightly North of Broad

Sitting here in my darkroom of emotions
developing the pictures of my mind.
The tone is deep, I dare not guess how
My thoughts play on my words or how my words
add to the frustrations building
(like a sandcastle on an empty beach)—
destined to be crumbled by the waves.
The water ripples over the edges of my body—
merely outlining what it is
I cannot fathom to be;
To be part of the whole—the whole that
makes up the collage of ideals and
understandings.
Some beginnings have not yet found an end,
yet some endings have not found a beginning.

My mind wanders past the depths of Ozone
in my brain (hazy); crazy as it may seem
my visions are found slightly north of broad
along the river of dreams that flow ever-so
rapidly.

Kris Bengtson

Reminiscing through a Teen's Mind in Relationships

In some ways my heart is like a flower that is so fair,
but this beautiful flower dies every year.
I don't know if I can handle my heart doing the same,
but it might have been that you were the one to blame.
In some ways I think I loved you,
then again I thought you really cared,
what you did to me was unexpected,
this shouldn't of happened, we were so unprepared.
You changed your mind, and broke my heart.
The unintentional pain caused from little boys,
can leave girls tart.
Though what happened to the relationship
for the loss I didn't fight,
if maybe I had done more, us working out,
would've gone up to a might.
Nothing more to say it's all over, and healing,
now forever to me, remembering you is a fond memory unrealing.

Ashleigh Lundberg

Melissa

Time has no boundaries,
thoughts of tomorrow linger on.
Where will I hide,
no plans, no places to go,
only dark shadows of bitter-sweet endings.
That awful dark night that no one sees.
Death had come, caught me asleep.
My thoughts, my memories, gone in a flash,
trying to remember what I saw last.
Just tumbling and tossing through the air.
Finally at rest in the still night,
clinging to life, just barely there.
My Boyfriend, My love, eternally gone,
Just faint memories of a nighmare to me,
Wheelchair bound, if only you could—see

Bob Wittman

thirsty

sometimes I stare in disbelief
at your light at the end of my tunnel
doe-eyed and frozen in winters night,
my ears pinned against the track of your chest
I wait in anticipation of the oncoming train
listening for the heartbreaking sobs of a distant rain
but, instead of fleeing,
I make my nest and prepare the fragile ones again, yet again
for the heavy, loud thunder and tell them
that rain is only bad if you're drowning
essential if you're thirsty

Alice Cunningham

Happy First Anniversary

Years have passed since I was all alone
Until I met someone to call my own
From the first time I saw your brown eyes until today
You have shown me how much you care
in each and every way
I've finally found the love of a lifetime and I found it in you
For you there is nothing in the world that I wouldn't do
You've given me the feeling that most people dream about
You've always been there
to keep me going whenever I'm in doubt
You've given me a miracle
the day you gave birth to our little girl
My life with my new family I wouldn't trade it for the world
Now today is our anniversary and I want you to know
You'll be mine forever and I'll never let you go

George T. Ashworth

Starbird

As sad as it's become
that you have gone away
nothing has been undone
you are here to stay in our hearts

There is no one here to show us the way everywhere
there are things to believe that might not seem fair
it's hard to believe you are gone

The loneliness inside
the people that you knew
grows deeper all the time
but it's something that we have to live through
regrets are useless at this time
so don't look behind to the truth that was here

Waking up in the morning every day
how was I to know you weren't going to stay
why can't we just go back in the past
to make right what went wrong so it would last

I know what it feels like to be alone
I know what it feels like to be alone

Dave Anderson

Black Velvet Nights

A love in black, hearts of stone
A lifetime of memories this love has grown
Dark as the night, pure as the day
So many evil things, now we just walk away.
Tears fall from my eyes
Like rain falls from the skies.
Black velvet are these nights
Black velvet never shines bright.
A love in black, tears of glass
We thought that this would last.
When love is gone, nights are cold;
The silence within, we must be bold.
Restless hearts fall in love again,
Once we remember, we live as we did then.
Black velvet are these nights,
Black velvet never shines bright
Black velvet in which I hide,
Standing in the shadows, black velvet in which I cried.
Black velvet nights, Black velvet warm delight
A love in black hearts of stone
Now I live these Black velvet nights, alone!

Cristina DiBonaventura

Love Is . . .

Love is nervous like a bride to be
Love is commotion like a storm at sea
Love is strong like a tree standing tall
Love is anger when he still hasn't called
Love is fear like thunder for a child
Love is fire in your heart running wild
Love is pain like salt to a wound
Love is not sure if you have to assume
Love is cold like snow to bare skin
Love is devotion until the lies begin
Love is hot like the sun to your face
Love is disbelief when he steps out of place
Love is calm like the blue in the sky
Love is a tear when it's time for good byes
Love is joy like a sinner finding Christ
Love is an argument when you see him looking twice
Love is jealousy when you learn of his past
Love is misunderstanding when the love didn't last
Love is peace like a night after heavy rain
Love is humble with no room for being vain
Love is breathtaking like a room with heavens view
When asked what love is I can only say . . . you

Armanda Rice

An Ode and Final Farewell

Another one of my fish just died,
taking his journey to the other side.
I never did give him a name,
never the less he did his thing.
Swimming in circles and up and down
sideways and backwards and round and round.
But never again will the little guy feel
the thrill of water surging through his gills
His head on the bottom, tail in the air,
I wanted to feed him, but he didn't care.
He didn't move as I used a pen
to tickle his belly and wiggle his fin.
As stiff as a poker, as still as the night.
I knew right off something wasn't right.
After awhile it came to me,
the little sucker was gone, he had been set free
to take the journey where little fishes go
his final destination no one knows.
So goodbye little fellow, so long friend,
it's down the commode, this is the end!

James Ingram

Some Other Parade

Check your blind spot,
It's on your soul.
It's on the words, the thoughts, that fill the holes.
Your enemy, an arms length away,
Your best friend in some other parade.

Blakeley Smith

Every Cloud Has a Silver Lining

I was on my way home, early,
one foggy August morning.
I almost met my savior
without any warning;
Every cloud has a silver lining.

My great example is the Lord,
of overcoming power.
He reached down and took my hand,
and led me through the next few hours.
All God's miracles have a purpose
that we don't always understand;
but when we are in our darkest hours,
God always holds our hands.
Every cloud has a silver lining.

Tallulah Sherrill

Rough Times

Doors that never seem to open
When a lonely heart cries out into the night.
It is as if no one else wants to share,
To take the time to help make things right.

Has the world really become this cold?
Everyone turns their faces so as not to see.
Avoiding the pain of another brother or sister.
Is this what we've really come to be?

Then a hand reaches down to you.
Through tears you smile a question of, "Why?"
Taking your hand, a stranger helps you stand,
Answering, "But, by God's grace, go I.

For this is as His Son would walk,
Helping another through a rough time.
If I am going to share His house,
Then it is His will I serve, not mine."

James Browning

Autumn

What are the trees doing this time of year?
They're preparing for the long Winter that   is near.
They're shedding their branches of Summer leaves,
To rest for the Winter with its cold, cold breeze.

What are the birds doing this time of year?
They're flying South for the warm Winter air.
When Winter is over and Spring is here,
They'll fly North again for their Summer flair.

What are the squirrels doing this time of year?
They're gathering and burying their food
For the Winter that soon will be here.
They'll make tracks in the Winter snow,
Wondering where are the nuts they stowed.

What are you doing this time of year?
Are you as smart as the animals, the birds, the trees?
Are you preparing yourself for the long Winter Freeze?

When Spring comes again and you see
The brown Earth as it turns green;
Enjoy your Summer because very soon,
The Autumn leaves will, again, be the scene.

Mary Smith

Suicide of the Heart

My smiles quickly dispersing.
The sun ain't shining through.
The clouds are hovering over.
The sky ain't sparkling blue
Everything's different. Not the way it used to be.
I showed you so much through the years that we shared.
Shedding a tear through all that we bared.
I was there for you when you needed it most.
You turned away without a care in the day.
I went through your pain through the troubles that came.
Days pass, months fly.
You never greeted with a "Hi" or leaving with a simple "Bye."
You weren't there when I needed care; you turned your back
and failed to share the love that was deep inside,
the love that I put aside for you and your soul.
You left me with an empty hole.
I went through your pain, you left during mine.
All I needed was compassion and sense of direction.
If only you returned. If your love didn't subside.
We would have one less suicide.

Cynthia Green

Feel

Like a bird I feel,
Flying across the sky.
Floating to my destiny.
However the wind blows,
I will float to my destiny.
As I fly, the world around me.
It changes, moves, transforms.
I am still floating across the vast skies of the world.
Watching, waiting, for the right branch to land on.

Nicholas Gangadharan

To the Women I Have Known

It's just a passing of the minds,
and a long encounter from the stars,
the women I have known.
The heavens that have opened for me,
The comets and shooting stars that I have seen
are for the women I have known.
Friendship and happiness is all that matters,
kindness and freedom will follow
the women I have known.

David Weaver

The Night Carries Heartache on Its Back

The night carries heartache on its back.
It surrounds you, whispers to you,
The voices carried by nearest air.
Everything good of the day now gone,
"Do you remember me?"
It echoes in your brain.
The morning far away, heartache haunts you,
Brakes you, loves you.
Time is its friend.
Together they caress you.
Stronger than the love you so desperately want to forget,
Or be in once more . . . Oh, just once more.
Lock your doors.
Hurry morning light, for the heartache might abstain.
Fear replaced by hope, use the day well,
Because the night still carries heartache on its back.

Eva Vennari

Echoes of Why

Planted in the bed of love's brief flight
Conceived as a vision in the darkness of night
Nurtured and tended with loving care
To be taken from me—who or what would dare
Pluck this budding flower, God or fate
My soul is consumed, eaten by the maggots of hate
My spirit is pursued by the demon of guilt
As the dagger of pain is thrust in my heart to its hilt
The wild flames of anger rage through my mind
Coloring my vision, making me blind
Beaten and battered by this greatest of storms
Seeking and searching I grasp to hold in my arms
My body that quakes from its inner pain—asking why
But hearing only the echoes which make me cry. . . .

Robert D. Culp

Heavenly Dance

Sweet innocent eyes you have,
Containing a rare compassion all their own.
When we dance, i look into those angelic eyes
And i imagine myself flying in Heaven.
Transcending far above the clouds and stars
Above the spinning world on its tilted axis.
Your smile, your grasp, the way you move . . .
Makes me fly higher, above constellations.
Brutally i'm brought back to earth . . .
When the musician ceases to play.
Bewildered, i stand staring into your eyes . . .
The eyes of sanctity, divinity, and truth . . .
The eyes that engulf me, ravage my soul . . .
Rejuvenate me, resurrect me . . .
I stand bewildered, longing to dance again.

Stephanie Noble

Prize

Get up
Go to work
got to get the prize
Eat, sleep, barely in your children's eyes
Dream of the day when it's time to relax
Carry the world upon our backs
Love is shown in different ways
Contentment may come another day

Jeffery Clark

What You Need

There are times when I am tired.
Don't know if I'll succeed.
Just hold on to your faith.
He will give you what you need.
And when you say a prayer,
You don't have to beg and plead.
Just keep your prayer sincere,
He will give you what you need.
There will be times we falter
And not do such good deeds.
But he loves us just the same
And he gives us what we need.
So let's view life as a garden;
Always planting a new seed.
And give it sun and water—
Just like he gives us what we need.
May not be what you asked for,
But if you do take heed;
Stay strong, keep faith and always know,
He gives you what you need!

Gloria Riley

From the Moment

From the moment I knew you were on your way,
I fell in love that very day,
I gave thanks, to God, for the special way,
he put you so very close to my heart,
and I awaited the hour, from there you would part,
when that day finally arrived, oh what joy,
 My God you have blessed me with a baby boy,
In my arms there you laid,
and through my tears I looked at you and prayed,
 Lord share with me,
all your wisdom strength and the courage it shall take,
to raise him in this world
full of so little love and so much hate,
help him to know that you are there,
when times are good and in times of despair,
light the path in which we shall share,
and let him know, how much you care .

Roberta Garrison

My Uncle

In memory of my dear Uncle
You were in so much pain,
But it's all over now.
You are up in Heaven,
Taking a bow.
That life long struggle,
Such a high demand.
Now you're with God,
Holding his hand.
Yes it is true I miss you so,
But what I do know,
Is you are no longer in pain.
I look up to you,
Even though you are gone.
One thing is for sure—
We share a common bond.
Yes I did and still grieve,
But I am happy for you
Because you did leave.
As I part now, I must say,
I think of you every day.
I know you're in a better place, so now I
Can say farewell and goodbye.

Annemarie DellaGuardia

The Wild Duck

(Italian sonnet; iambic pentameter)
In each of us there is a tiny bit
of wild and flighty duck who wills to fall
when winged from skies as wide as Winter's call.
He shatters hopes and dreams in waters lit,
a surface glazed by softened moon now slit
with pity's bubbling drops, the tears that gnaw
the soul of he who dives to bite the straw
in slime of clammy cold to die to quit.

A lonely duck in flight with dreams as wild
yet wary poised and calmly sure of life
if winged and captured by a clever dog
will rest in death. Though dying dreams are mild
as questing days in flight once full of strife
he will still long to be as free as fog.

John Matthews

A Maiden's Praise

Although your face I cannot see,
that makes you no less real to me.

In my life you've always had a part,
I know you in my mind and with my heart.

You've been with me through the years,
you've shared the smiles and dried my tears.

We've lived with and loved each other,
I can't imagine my live with another.

I fear not the dark, for that's where you are,
When I close my eyes I feel the warmth of your arms.

You've defended and protected me,
a better friend you could not be.

Stephanie Barto

Night

Night is a darkness,
A darkness of the heart.
A darkness of my love for you,
A darkness that puts us so far apart.
A darkness that blocks the sun,
A darkness that blocks the light,
A darkness that blocks my tears for you,
Wile the stars shine so bright.
A darkness that blocks my sorrow,
And the loud beating of my heart.
Wile I wait for you here,
It slowly grows us further,
and further apart.

Marc Mazerolle

Sanctuary

Far from reality and the face of meaningful existence,
I ponder the world and the way it revolves.
My head is spinning in an uncontrollable frenzy,
and I am lost and in a void of complete and utter darkness.

The man on the moon has stopped winking my way,
and the ocean has stopped waving to me.
The ocean, my only sole comfort in life
has left me to wave to another.

The majestic mountains have lost their grandiosity
and the Earth's beauty has been devoured
by the vicissitude of the modern world and its ways.

Chelsea Manganaro

Life Ever After

Claude,
 If you passed me on the street, would you know me?
Could you see beyond this face to my soul that lives within?
Would you remember that night in Bisbee; I held your body
close to mine, as you left this world, and me behind?
Where did you go when the Angels came for you that day?
What happened to me when ten long years later I passed away?
When next I remember, I opened my eyes: in another place,
and another time, with your name on my lips,
and thoughts of you in my mind.
You remained in my memory as I grew.
The only true love I ever knew.
Through this lifetime I've searched for you in every place,
and every face.
Claude, if I passed you on the street, would I know you?

Sally Spurgeon

Our Love Belongs to Us

A man and woman were created for each other
To love and cling to one another.
So what can I do to convey to you
that I love you through and through?

How can I make you understand
I want to be your soul mate—your
renaissance man?
Here's my love—yours to keep—
And nothing can hinder this love,
not even the long sleep.

We'll render unto Caesar what's Caesar's,
The souls back to God above,
Our flesh back to the dust,
But when all is paid in full
Our love belongs to us.

Eddie Jones

Just the Other Day

God talked to me just the other day.
He said, my child, you're slipping. Get on your knees and pray.
I know your road has been hard, but you're one of a chosen few
Who fought through all the madness I've placed in front of you.
See, I've made no mountain too high for you to climb.
No chain so strong that you can't break.
I've made no room so dark that you can't see the light,
And no pain so severe that you can't take.
But you must have faith deep down inside your heart
And know I've seen all your problems, even before they start.
Because I've always been here, right by your side.
I've felt the tears from your eyes on the many nights you've cried.
Those times when you felt that you couldn't make it through
Were the times I stepped in and carried you.
So remember, my child, your soul is not for sale.
And you may go to Heaven with half the pains
In which it costs you to purchase Hell.

Thomas White, III

Angels

In memory of 2 1/2 year old Morgan Lee Pena
Angels are always with us,
until the day we die,
And even when we are leaving for Heaven,
They are happily waving Goodbye.

Joanne Olson

Friends

Friends is what you want to be.
That tore my heart to shreds.
I wish you never said those words.
'Cause how can we be friends?
I love you still, but it will never be.
For friendships fade, and vanish in the wind.

Love lasts forever.
That's what the poets say.
I may not be a poet, but that's what I believe today.
I've always thought it to be true.
But friendships fade, and vanish in the wind.

I never wanted to lose you.
You meant the world to me.
I would have given you anything,
If you had only let me.
The moon, the stars, the sun above,
They mean nothing to me.
But now we're just friends,
And friendships fade, and vanish in the wind.

Catherine Richmond

A Fairies Dew Morning

The sky is pink and orange and blue.
The ground is covered with a wet soft dew.
The air is all misty, the wind a bit breezy,
as I walk through the garden door.
The flowers are encompassed by a crystally texture
that is soft and wet and cold.
It looks as though it once were a long lost story of old.
The little dew drops look as though fairies were there,
carefully placing each one.
Then they all run away at the break of the day,
at the light of the morning sun.
The day is now dawning, I stand up,
yawning as I think of the day to come.
I think of the fairies, who must be so weary,
for their relaxing night has begun.

Marta Daehn

Song for Ray

I've been going the wrong way
I've been going the wrong way for so long
Now I'm going the right way
I'm going the right way for now on
The wrong way has brought me so much pain
Now the right way can bring me back again
So it's the right way from now on

Ray Shonk

Leaving a Legacy

We do not know how lucky we are
For most in the world don't have a car
Most in the world have nothing to eat
And have to live with unbearable heat
To take care of our health is a sign of
true wealth . . .
For we are kings!
We have a roof over our heads and bread to eat
For this is enough to make life sweet
Nothing else should be important to us
Loving God should be all the fuss
For God is why we're really all here
To work for Him and know He is near
For one day the Good Lord will call us home
And it's important that we do not roam
We must live for God and God alone

Julie Pymn

Angels! God's Open Doorway!

As I departed my body,
I saw an angel floating in the air,
as I touched the sky I saw angels aglow,
one to my left the other to my right,
I knew just then I was in God's holy sight,
as I felt their feathers so soft so pure,
as white as a dove so gentle so sure,
oh angel your smile so bright
I know you came down below
'cause God told you so,
you're the angel of my life
the brightness of my day,
the beauty along God's pathway!
saved by the sprit, and soul so pure
that I will never die away
God's promise for sure!
now I go through God's open door,
your memory of me will forever be
the kindness of my heart eternally!

David Sheppard

In Life, in Joy, My Friend

We drift through life, mere mortals we
And stop to look around you see.
And find that each new day begins
With thoughts of love, of life, of friends.

We stand alone, each one is strong.
But it is strength 'cause we belong
To land and sea and sky and then
To love, to life, and to our friend.

We'll always have a hurting part.
It is of life that we must take
But joy is there, there'll be no end
In love, in life, and with a friend.

So when you look up to the sky
And ask yourself, or wonder why
Just know it is, no story ends
Our love, our life, and all our friends.

Donna Hill

Lonely Sorrow

Vast space of emptiness
Weeping silently to herself
Like a mother losing her child
She hides her pain of ecstasy

The bluebird of sorrow
With its heavy heart in doubt
Silence, except tears of pain in nothingness
No one really cares

Nate Ranney

Someone Else

for one night i thought i could reach out to you
and you would be there to pick up the past
and replace it with the promises of things to come,
but what happened to the person i thought i knew
turning out to be just another memory turned to blue
and then fade to the back of my shattered past,
to collect with the dusty remains
and only to be forgotten with the promise of someone else

Joshua Stearns

Help!

Help! I'm confused! What do I do?
Help! I'm lost! Where do I go?
Help! I can't decide! Which do I choose?
Help! My mind is a blur! When does it stop?
Help! I've fallen in a hole! How do I climb out?
Who do I go to? Life is a puzzle, a frustrating mystery.
Where, when and how?
Which path do I follow? Too many choices and questions.
What, who and why?
Can you survive through the mazes
of this devastating thing called life?

Emily Matheny

Winter

Dreams destined to fade
Nightmares become reality
Forgone conclusions of lost love appear
Once together, Forever apart,
With regret
Trying to forget the past, ignoring my future
Wasn't supposed to be this way
Supposed to be anyway
Visions of you fade to black
The void of never
The cold realities of winter have come to visit again
Reminding me who I am, what I'm not
The dark, dreary, overcast sky
Shows itself with chilled vengeance
Reminding me what I'll never have
The wicked wind cuts through my troubled spirit
Unmercifully
The snow casts a blanket of white pain
All made to order, all made for me
Will the sun shine again for me?

Terry Smith

HeartBeat

With every heartbeat—I miss you
With every heartbeat—I love you
With every heartbeat—I think of you
and with every second—
I can't stand thinking of you being gone
You made yourself part of my life
and even when your gone
with every heartbeat—I will miss you, love you and think of you—
more then when I had you right here in my arms

Marcy Meizler

life

your life is like a mighty flash of a lightning bolt,
that splits the darkness of a summer night,
the energy of an angry GOD.
enough to light a thousand homes,
so much power, it turns night to day,
yet is gone in an instant,
leaving only a scent of ozone in its wake,
will your life be a short flash,
leaving nothing in ageless time?
can it not be more, to brighten the world,
in song and deeds, to last longer than a flicker of light?

Jesse Hamaker

I Beat Quietly Now

I beat quietly now.
Waiting, not much debating—
Hardly pacing, or hating or eliminating.

I brightly beam beneath a bushel.
Alone, but not forlorn.
Born to be worn,
Deformed—yet conformed.

I walk and cut off my legs.
I reach out and break my arms.
I smile and summon harm.

It hasn't taken an army to fight;
Nor serviced a body to live.
Growth is crumbling bones and severed tones,
As art is pain.

I beat quietly now.
No need to scream, I stand serene.
Within me the universe teems.
I bulge, I burst, I rot, I rise.
'Tis patience and I.

     Kathy Dixon

Hostia

Drifting there alone, beside the river
beneath the full-bodied moon
she moves as the wind, naked and alone
dressed only in the iridescence of spirit, sleeves fluttering
to the melody of far off wings
held in the shape of her hands,
a wild lotus rising from her palms
sings as she peels a petal
and plants it on the river where it floats apart
downward
a white heart bleeding a shadow
in the coruscating current,
between the stillness of two beats
downward
descending through a vortex of blossoming swirls
which are always apart
and always alone in unison,
'til finally in the stillness of the pulsating center
it sprouts wings of finitude
and makes the water its air.

     Daniel Janosik

A Mother's Love

What is a mother, but a special friend,
Who shares her love again and again.
She's giving, and caring, in every way,
No matter how busy, or hectic her day.
When others forsake us, she's always there,
To listen, and comfort, or simply to care.
She's there when we're happy,
She's there when we're sad,
She's there when we're good or hateful and bad.
She's gives of herself; unconditionally,
Her time and her love, oh yes, they are free.
Don't take her for granted, for time has a way,
Of slipping upon us, and soon Mom is gray.
So, don't get too busy to give her a smile,
And tell her you love her once and awhile.
You'll never regret it, for some day you'll
see, Mom was a treasure,
God gave you for free.

     Carol Bailey

To Be a Poet

I want to be a poet
To touch the sky, the water, and the earth
Maybe not a poet laureate
But one who gives love and mirth

A poet with eyes wide open
Who can see the precious little things
Even when the world begins to darken
His joyful words will continue ringing

A poet that takes all troubles
And rests them on his shoulders
Whose words reveal beauty in the meanest hubbles
One that awes and makes men bolder

What a wonder, to grasp a moment
A minute or a second, it matters not
To become time's agent
Whose poem shall never rot

     Michael Daines

Wake up Children, Your Moon Mother Weeps

Realize, honor, respect, cherish that she is the moon.
Great, grandiose, gracious, grandma.
Floating, flying from faintly to fantastically.
Wisdom in her cycles,
Always changing,
Yet never really changing

The moon is woman.
Marvelous, melancholy, magnificent, mother-all.
Constant, compassionate, caring.
Her shoulders carrying the trite to the tragic.
Can we recycle the wisdom of moon?

Moon mother weeps, weeps, weeps,
During the rocking cradle time in the sky
Who will learn the painful lullaby?
Who will learn the lessons of pain?
Does the moon's lullaby make you cry?

Silent tears drip, drip, drip
Into a deep, painful void.
Wake up children!
Listen to the wisdom and pain of your great-grandma moon.

     Tess A. Lee

Lone Wolf

Screaming silently with no one to hear
He whispers his secrets to one deaf ear
He wanders and searches within the light
The dark side of the moon aiding his sight
A lone wolf hunting through forests of glass
His prey he holds tightly, before it fades fast
What is it he hunts for that no one cares
Why does he hunt these drifting chimares
Grasping and clutching his burning dreams
Telling that nothing is ever what it seems
Running and hiding from a world ripped twain
Struggling to preserve it, attempts all in vain
Wishing and dreaming for a world never been
He rises to his feet and he runs yet again
Where is going that nothing can be
Who is this warrior so silent and free
His howls echo through the stars of the night
And his song follows him in his endless plight
Open your eyes and arise from your bed
Let him sleep now, his story been said

     Clane Jenkins

The River

There is a river flowing to an endless sea.
A river that is accessible to you and me.
Some channels flow in, others flow out.
Parts of it is rocky and toss you about.
Some currents are strong and run deep, others
are shallow and weak.
It is growing, but only if it is flowing,
its final destiny who of us is knowing.
Parts are turbulent and dangerous, others peaceful and serene.
In it and all around is where the essence of life can be found.
The further it flows the stronger it grows.
Obstacles appear, but with perseverance it finds a way through.
Oh river a reflection on your waters so many things it shows.
It explains how love is, for us to know.

Suzanne Scalf

Front Line

I See Them . . . . So Disfigured . . . . Men Standing Alone
So Defenceless Against The Light of The Moon . . . .
So Desolate Against The Orange Painted Skies . . . .
This Strange And Bloody War . . . .Will it End Soon?

How Distant It All Seems Now . . . .Where is Home?
My Naked Soul Flaunted to The Stars. Am I Alone?
I Shiver . . . . It's So Very Cold Now . . . . Or Am I Dreaming?
I Listen . . . . Is it A Baby's Cry? Or Am I Screaming?

Willemien Lewis

Eternity

Love is thy gift divine,
Forever together shall be his and mine,
Thoughts, words, or dedications shall transpire,
We take care of each other to inspire.

Others may envision our true love for each other,
Seeking their own in return, and not to bother,
Time and space develop such dreams to cast,
Although him and I shall have the longest past.

The people of the world should inspect our love together,
May then the world live for peace forever,
Corruption and rotten attitudes shall vanish,
All the demons in mind and soul be banished.

Peace and desire are we,
Our love is just about perfect for everyone to see,
We may spread our wings, and allow for comfort and tranquility,
For our love shared is for all eternity.

Jolee Starnes

Someone's Valentine

To Mellisa, my wife
Even though you are not mine,
I find that I love you.
This emotion has grown over time
since we first met.
The way you laugh, the sound of your voice,
even the way that you smile,
would make me walk countless miles
just for your loving touch.
And the world would be a cold dark place,
if I could not see your bright beautiful face.
Without you the sunsets would pale,
and even a starry moonlit night would seem bland,
unless you were there to take my hand.
For these reasons and more,
I ask you for the chance
to join you throughout life's dance.
This is just my way to say,
will you be mine,
onward from this day
of Valentines.

James R. Cass IV

You Hate Me but I Love You (short version)

You hate me but I love you
Though your always tryin' to break me
Tryin' hard to enslave me
Using fear to try to shake me

you hate me but I love you
Lyin' on God to desecrate me
I thought you knew your guns can't take me
Never will eliminate me

you hate me but I love you
Your teachin' babies to despise
Any creature with brown eyes
Your hate has reached beyond our skies

you hate me but I love you
Before God takes you by surprise
I hope you come to realize
What he's been saying all this time:

"How can you love me whom you have not seen
But hate your brother whom you see every day
If you love me then do as I say
Have love for your brother no matter his race"

Anastasia Boykin

Clinical Depression

In slow motion, a menace falls—
there are rats in my apartment walls
pawing through arteries and veins,
Scratching on lath, gnawing nerve endings.

My sheets are filthy, but I have no feet to run away.
I fear, but have no will to cry,
no power to go, no choice to stay.
No one seems to see.
They look blindly through this outline of frozen soul,
seeing only the vile, exploded garbage bag of squalor
I have created.
Like a half-devoured mole, I seek escape
from sight and cleansing due in quiet annihilation.

In the hospital, the sheets are clean.
The rats confine themselves to my head.
With curtains pulled completely round my bed,
I am left to be.
The nurses walk their eternally, objective clockwork
'til I can bear to feel the passion of the light again.

Martha Henniger

Night Cat

There is this cat who is all black.
He comes to my house every night.
I call him but he just sits there, just kind of staring at me.
The look his eyes have are scary,
as if they are saying,
"Welcome to the night, my little baby bird."
But the way his tail moves you think he would be saying,
"I'm not responsible for what happens to you next."
So there he sits, watching, waiting, thinking.
What will his first move be?
Will it be nice, mean, hateful, loving?
What if I should make the first move?
What should my first move be?
I decide to make the first move. I bend down and pet him.
He sees I mean no harm and just like that his eyes change,
As if they are now saying
"Oh, so you are nice; then I will be nice too."
His tail stops moving and
he replaces his tail wagging with his purring.
And everything is all right all through the night of the black cat.

Anya Bogdanovich

Where No Shadows Fall

Crystalline in Velvatine to form her very skin
With candor, slight in tragedy and coated with our sin
The Jaded Ruby eyes that hold the soul and form the smile
And take away the pain, if not forever, for awhile
In Alabaster linen, smooth as silk, her very feel
She stands beside me, loving, at her feet is where I'll kneel
Without her I would Fade like Roses lost in Winters Ice
To our everlasting form of Virtue strong as will suffice
Her Caress is like A Summers Breeze, or Spring's untimely call
And I'll find her always in the place, where no Shadows can Fall.

    Jason J. Maxwell

Slick

I was cleanin' the others out
Collected a hundred or more
When that jerkfaced city feller
Strutted through the parlor doors

Slick was his name, wearin' rich clothes
Black derby and buttons galore
He grinned real wide and snapped for booze
Miss Rose hastened over to pour

Sneerin' at us, he sat right down
Probably figured our brains as ore
I stacked my chips and cut the cards
Slick fixed his cuff—I knew what for

On the third deal he sleeved an ace
My Colt responded with a roar
Cheatin' never wins you the game
When you're lyin' dead on the floor

    Curtis Brown

Unraveling Our Thoughts

As the ice glitters on the multiple shaped tree limbs
Shinning brightly from the freezing raindrops—
Imagination never dreams of such a sight
Our wandering minds can be a flop—

A closer feeling of nature
Lifts up our hearts to joy—
How our thoughts can be perplexed
But our eyes see no decoy—

Peace and joy can be our perception
With us it can be contagious—
With patience and effort, feel free! Let go!
Contentment can be vivacious.

    Franceno A. Diggs

My True Love

No reason should fear haunt you, nor strife, or confusion.
You see I have found something;
someone who loves me and better still is immortal.
He has laid down his life for a love unto all people.
This extravagance is so unconceivable yet I am drawn to him.
I am made alive and am a new creation through him.
Cleansed is my spirit that was once black and condemned forever.
Let your life of pain and misery dwell in the past.
Seek the face of Jesus Christ who forgives and is with you always.
Do not turn your heart but answer his calling.

    Mary Watkins

There's Got to Be a God Some Place

He taught the toothless Birds to sing
and my voiceless heart to cry.
Who keeps the smile on my face after so much shame and disgrace?
There's got to be a God some place who gives
me strength to work all day to keep bread on my children's plate.
Who made the women small and large and gives
me strength to want them all?
There's got to be.
There's got to be a God some place to keep me
in the human race, with hands to tie my lace.

With one so great I wish to see thy face

    Fitzroy Brown

The Way You See

The way that one looks at the world,
unique vision that they behold.
where a flower is,
they would see a smell of freshness,
they see a feel of the soft petals.
Where a baby is,
they would see a feel the soft skin,
they would see laughter and sorrows,
they see a smell of dirty diapers.
Where an apple is,
they would see the tough texture of the skin,
they would see the crunch of the apple,
they would see the sweet juice that comes out.
do you see?

    Jason Anderson

Time and Again

Eons, ages, millennia
we have walked the life path
hunting mammoth in the misty dawn
embracing as Ra rode the skies
locked in passion in Alexander's tent
falling side by side at Marathon
throughout history we have met and parted
time and again drawn by love
into each other's arms
by the immortal bonding
of two earthbound angels.

    Charles Jackson

Guardian Angel

Going through my mother's things I found
some notes and cards.
I found a lock of hair once, her's,
and a small golden star.
I found a poem that my daddy wrote to her
years ago,
and a song she'd sing to me, the words
I still know.
I'll be your guardian angel,
I'll watch over you,
I'll sing you to sleep each night,
'til my days are through.
Friends may come and friends may go,
but mom's love
was always there,
She sacrificed every day of her life,
and this I'll always know.

    Sara Pickett

A Kiss

Such a feeling I miss,
The touch of two gingerly moist lips
Pressed to mine with an overwhelming, long lasting kiss,
More comfort felt than a hug,
Reaches a point of pleasure sex can't even meet,
Only if the two have a connection, a sort of chemistry.
Never can forget a kiss with such results,
Puts my mind in a tailspin
Bringing my heart to a halt.
A kiss that can engulf you two,
Break you apart from it no one could ever do.
So cease each moment with a kiss,
To see if it deserves more than just a moment,
And if it's something you were forced to live without
You would truly miss!

Mohammed Abdelwahed

Facets

Can I not draw the serene picture
or can I not compose
nor venture into that grammar
that of the poet, artist captures.
For they tell of beauty of the flower
is but all I can give to my (Mom)wife

 Facets that capture the Northern Lights
Jewel prisms where light lasers through
The spectrum of life
Be that I know as my (Mom)wife

Alicia Luciani

Reality Returns

As I survey the scene of this wondrous expanse of love,
my eyes behold an array of light and eye-tantalizing delineation.
From within my solace a voice cries out—
with anguished sorrow it wails in search of the source
of this brightness.
The thirst for satisfaction cannot be quenched—
its desire is to embrace that consolation that lies ahead,
mere mystery that it is.
A hand reaches out from within the light and slowly extends to mine,
and with every morsel of passion this palm attenuates for comfort.

In the morn it shall come.
In the day it shall be set free.
In the eve it shall rest.

The eye has found its beauty.
The ear has found its harmony.
The mouth has found its contentment.
The hand has found another,
reality returns.

William Good

Hurt

I wish I could die, and bury my pain
I'm twisted in knots, I'm going insane
Lay me down to rest, God help my soul
Put it six feet under in a deep, dark hole
Everyone seems so happy, smiling and having fun
But when I look at myself, it looks like life is done
I see fire in your eyes, like a demon has your heart
You are so very close, but we are so far apart
You are bitter and cold, hateful and mean
You make me hate myself, and do your hateful things
I push it all down as far as it will go
But one day it will come out, and all this pain will explode
But if it never happens, just cover me with dirt
Because I would rather be in my hole
Than living with this hurt

KellieVaughn Hodges

A Poem about a Man Who Becomes God

and I feel myself going on forever and
ever I am everything I am all things
indeed I am I am I am would go
to the ends of the world would for you
because you are the world I am the
end of the world my fingers the Earth
is like my fingers life is like life
is like me my fingers you my fingers
touch me with my fingers I reach
out I am everything I am no more
my life I paused my life I am over my
life is over but I am it I am no
more but I continue I go on forever
wrap your arms around me forever
I am you you are me I see her my
lover she is me she is me I am
reaching out in her let me reach out in you
don't stop don't stop I can't stop I am
God I am All things are God what
is God is God alive am I dead alive
what is alive is it this is it forever
because life isn't forever but forever
is life I am forever I am the forever

Patricia Ryan

My Star

I reached for a star
Expecting to fall
Yet I arose

Someday I may fall
But not in this moment
For I am in the shimmering sky
With my love
My star

Looking down on the confusing world
With remembering eyes
Hoping someday my friends will find their own stars

So they may come and be happy with me in the bright bright sky

Sonya Chow

Thinking of You

Before I lay down at night,
I pray for you.

As I awake in the morn',
I think of you.

As those slow and silent moments pass by at noon,
I fantasize about you.

And as the darkness sets in to complete the day,
I think of you in continuance,
And I wonder if you think of me,
As often as I think of you.

J. Nerissa Percival

Sombre

She cuts a lonely figure
A fanfare of delight turned sour
Once vibrant eyes so dark so shallow
Doused flames of life, so stark, so clear

A pause before the path to follow
Move forward, too far
Step back, too near
Such simple things that steal the fire
A skeletal void of extinction

Steffan Carroll

Darth Vader's Fall

He was becoming the best Jedi, trained in the Force
Obi Wan Kenobi was the teacher of the source
Thinking that he could do better than Yoda
He took Anakin's training just way too far over
Than Palpatine, seeing his chance,
Decided to lure Anakin in a Dark Side trance

He tempted him, he taunted him,
soon Anakin succumbed
Obi Wan wanted to turn him back, if he wanted to come
Locked in battle over a molten pit,
Anakin became a virtual Dark Side fit
Trying to beat Kenobi, he fell in
Kenobi left him for dead to rot in his sin

Then Palpatine found him barely alive,
and as you know, the dark had survived!

Joshua Annis

Realization

When but three years ago we two were one,
Our world unique had beamed with sun-lit thought.
But then with scythe besmeared, Death clutched our sun,
Obscuring thoughts that once our love had brought.
Incessant sun still manifest above,
'Tis not the same which sublimated thought,
But rather from the Earth, eclipsed, where love
Perpetual is hopelessly yet sought.
Oh Love! I know not where I am to look
For comfort, gravely as I am depressed,
Thinking how Death from Earth thy body took.
Spurred sorrows tell me life's not wholly blessed!
Yet transient happiness on Earth 'tis Light,
A glimpse eternal brightening the night.

Anthony Baczkowski

Today

They look and can see tomorrow.
They live in yesterday.
Heavy lives empty full of pain and sorrow.
Wasting days they march on,
Too blind to see his mercy.
Too lost to find the truth.
Stumbling lost on this pathway,
Tripping over invisible roots
Praying that it's over
Here comes again the light of day
Run to the darkness
There is no safety, no comfort.
The voice inside offers a better way to trust what you hear,
Move toward it?
Maybe today

Sirina Poole

My Love

She is the one.
Never be for have I felt such love.
No chocolate is as sweet as her.
Her eyes are so beautiful that the moon is lost.
She is the one.

Lance Gosi

Reunion

To all those who once miss the chance to be with their beloved one.
My mind has imprisoned those radius moments,
of my childhood with you dad.
Emptiness that has to be filled with fantasies,
got me to join the club of poetry.com.
I heard that you were good and remain.
I always felt that you loved me and still
Indescribable feelings.
Indelible memories of you are always full of smile,
soft smell and places.
Places of my most youngest days,
strongly tied with emotional spices.
I know, one day, we'll meet again.
I'll hold on to my death if I have to.
I long so much the reunion dad.

Remy Beugre

The Earth Talked to Me

The Earth cried tonight tears let loose from stars so bright
She cried for the sadness
she cried for the lack of success
she wept for peoples pain
and for those who love in vain
she mourned for those who feel regret
and she cried for those who can't forget

The Earth yelled tonight
all the Heavens roared in a mighty fight
she screamed at those who judge
and at those who live to begrudge
she shouted at the lazy
furious at the people gone crazy
she argued for the soft spoken
and she begged for people to mend what is broken

The Earth shined today
the sun chased dark away
daylight for all who are kind
light for those who educate their mind
a sky lit for those who love
and for all who realize peace comes from above

Rachel Quinn

She

A symphony of love plays for you,
just as the strings of your own heart lingered,
a chorus of interest consumes my thoughts . . .
and brands me a singer.
As word and music engage , curiously,
the melodic result of their quest brings forth harmony.
Walls covered blue now crumble to gray dust,
a projection of love left for us to construct.
She.

Daniel Babij

Our Dentist's Secret Work

Our Teeth separate classes;
a poor man's rotten disfigured mouth,
my fillings and bonds of the lower middle class,
the successful immigrant's false smile
and the rich man's caps and gold.

Our lips hide the truth of our
dentist's secret work of
separating and dividing
our society.

Justin W. Z. Tessier

Untitled

Walking down a blue, cold tunnel.

The view of stainless steel surrounds you.

But wait, there is someone waiting on the other side for you.

You look up, down, and side to side—

You notice a bead of sweat running down your right side

The tunnel fills up with fog, literally blinding you—

The tunnel clears, and are part of the lucky few

For which you have survived the bitter cold

You continue to watch life as it unfolds—on the other side

You breathe—

You think—

How to get to the other side—

You run

You leap

You fall—Bleep Bleep you think

Something catches your eye—Something that shines

Something that can run the system awry—

Something golden—Something blinding—

You run and run—

Reaching this golden spot

Lo and behold, you find a key

A key you think—You touch it

You're free
Joseph Lepe

Summer Breeze

In the night when time is creeping,
From deep slumber, I wake from sleeping.
The curtain dancing in timeless flight,
The breeze from the window rushes through without fright.
I lay in my bed as I feel the warm air,
It reminds me of a time that I had not a care.
A time so far distant, and so long ago,
But a time I remember, in my mind I still go.
Thoughts of a lover, with long flowing hair,
I remember how it would dance, and her skin oh so fair.
But my love is no longer but memories of then.
Like time things change, and so does the wind.
So I must thank you again, for the memories that might,
Happen again, from a summer breeze in the night . . .
Paul Mullins

The Hour-Glass

The price of beauty is shame!
The pursuit of perfection;
A never ending tyranny of the heart,
A battle pitting thin versus emaciated.
Oh—But who wins?
No one, but the voices of self-destruction.
No longer can beauty be compared to a rose,
But rather ugliness and guilt,
Which shape the body with every
Morsel of hate that it devours.
One precious calorie leads to an
Enormous price of imperfection.
LIFE, itself, is so delicate, but
How do we live if we have no freedom?
Scott Taylor

Life

Life is a wrestling match.
It's full of spectators.
Depending on how you act;
they can cheer you on,
or boo for your demise.

It's full of conflicts; both victories,
where you get the three counts.
And losses, where you get the chair
shots to the head, low blows,
and Stone Cold Stunners.

It has a vast number of characters.
Both good and bad, depending
on the plot. One day you can be at the
top, the next, you are a has-been.
And when your career is over,
you are forgotten.
Crystal Dyke

The Greatest Joy

To the Love of my Life
Because you see fit to
wake me up every morning
even when I don't deserve
to rise,

I rise in You.

Because You love me enough to
trust me,
care for me,
comfort me,
die for me;
I love You more
because you are always there (everywhere).

I worship You.

I love the thought of You,
and the thought of one day being
worthy
of all the blessings that You continue to place in my life.

I sing Your praises

I thank you for filling the voids of my life with your
love, peace, and joy.
When I thought that nothing would be right in my life,
You showed up.
Tia Howell

February Chill

Dreaming about those in hot places,
since trudging around are many cold faces;
my car died today outside in the yard,
proving one time again that winter living is hard (as ice).
Pale white snow makes a scene appear pure,
but in New England our crashes change the viewpoint for sure;
picnics in Springtime make the Internet mute,
plus Caribbean beaches could never paint February "cute."
We send sentimental photos about summertime fun,
yet heartless cold wind tonight makes me run;
and the parties go on—for weekends allow rest inside,
though work must be done (but my car really died).
Ocean State summers are full of lobsters and fishing,
plus Autumn offers beauty (in colors) with holiday wishing;
Halloween may hint horror for folks it is true,
but February's scare comes chilly and blue.
William DellaGrotta Jr.

Mary's Dirge

As we stand in stillness, and say goodbye
against the silence . . .
We are reminded of Mary
and her love for life, and her
Care for others.
She was not selfish with her love,
and shared unconditionally with those in need.

She was quick to find humor, and
could cajole one to laughter through tears and sadness.
She knew how to encourage people over their obstacles, and
she was there if you failed with a reassuring word.
When you won she was there to celebrate the glory.

Mary's strength of character in life was flawless,
and she never took the easy path. . .
She met life's hardships with acceptance of challenge,
and she conquered without whimpering or complaint.

. . . her last challenge in life was met with the same
    acceptance and perseverance . . .
in quiet resignation, she accepted . . .
her reward of everlasting life . . . .

    Paula Clark

Love Is . . .

. . . that tingly feeling you get in your stomach
the moment you spot the man of your dreams
. . . the chill that runs up your spine
when he puts his arm around you for the first time
. . . the way you feel when he places a gentle kiss upon your cheek
. . . the way he finds the perfect way to tickle you
. . . how you worry about him when he leaves town
. . . the thing that makes you camp out at the phone until he calls
. . . how much you enjoy gazing into his eyes when you talk to him
. . . the greatest thing that anyone can posses . . .
and the best thing about it is that whenever you feel lost,
love is always there to find you.

    Sarah Pearson

The Sky to Me

You are as your fathers were,
the sky to me,
a most wonderful and yet unknowable shelter.

Your heart beat frightens me at night while
your energy warms me, keeps me.

Your cold eye is to me
a precious marble, an eye tooth,
my worry stone.

Oh, you with your moody light and unreachable darkness!
I stand in hoary fields of wheat and let the wind blow through me,
You surround me, you abound me,
You feel me with your rain and
Live with me in the palms of your own hands, as angels!

But tomorrow will be different,
tomorrow I will be the mountains, and you,
You will still be the sky.

    Alex Mcnab

Why?

Your spirit rising into the sky you can only wonder why
children playing in the park not to stay out after dark
you and me together again just as it has always been
no problems and no cares just as long as you are there
we ride the chariot into the sky just knowing it is our time
two souls into the sky you now know why

    John Allen

Life

Life,
Bittersweet moments of the everyday,
Twines and binds the essence of souls,
Together,
Wrapped,
In an ever tangling web of innocence broken.
Hopes dashed, Dreams shattered,
The will to continue ebbs and flows,
A heartbeat,
Measuring the moments of Life.

    Alexander Smith

Don't Let the Devil Use You

Don't let the Devil use you as a toy
To breakdown or steal someone else's joy
Because what you fail to see is what he does for others
He will also do for me
So why do you come to God's house
Harboring hate for your fellow man
Do you not know that they're only
Doing the best that they can
To serve God and earn His respect
For the respect of you doesn't matter
The jealousy and hate that you harbor
Is causing only your own self to shatter
For to love is of God and to hate is of Hell
So through God you didn't come up
But in sin you just fell

    Richard Hawks

I Close My Eyes and Hope to See

I close my eyes and hope to see you.
I see your face and see your smile.
Filled with excitement I open my eyes and you're gone.
My eyes tear as I remember you're gone and not coming back.
Yet I hold you in my heart.
I keep you in my mind.
How I wish I could hold your hand and hug you again.
So I close my eyes and see your face.
I try to remember the way you used to smell.
I try to remember the sound of your voice.
I fear I am forgetting.
I cry in frustration.
I cry because you're gone and no longer will I hold your hand.

    Michelle Burque

My Only

I didn't know you,
But I became your friend,
And you became my protector, my silent watcher
Lust
You sent me dreams of you and me
Together
For that was the only way that we could be
It hurts you, you said
You were the only one who knew how much
Your death brought me closer than you'll ever know
To you,
And to joining you in that dreamy abyss
My god, will you ever know?
My heart broke along with you
Do you hear me scream your name on those empty nights?
You're my only
I'll never forget
My only
Forever

    Hillary Leftwich

Life, the Awesome Choice

Little baby Tommy was as cute as all could be.
He even was more wonderful when he reached the age of three.

He was a very loving man and all did hear his voice.
He knew deep in his heart that love was an awesome choice.

This is how it could have been, Tommy's life such a bright gleam.
But since he wasn't even born, it's now just all a dream.

Life is an awesome choice, it is the best thing on the Earth.
But life cannot be brought about if a child has no birth.

Taking life in such a way is wrong and very cruel.
We kill the unborn because we can and since there is no rule.

In taking an unborn child's life, they don't even get to try.
And what they could have just become, makes you want to cry.

They could have been successful, but you never will now see.
How great that unborn child, maybe, might have grown to be.

Let no one drown in sorrow or in such longing mourn.
Everyone should just choose life so no child goes unborn.

Christopher Klakamp

The Echo of a Child's Laughter

Looking at the world with clear, tranquil eyes,
A curiousity of gold that stems through cheerful cries,
The child simply played a game full of sneaky spies.
What he had seen, he wish he'd never seen,
There lies his dad, with that slack jaw,
A man availed that silver brass knife,
Oh, how cruel, to take a child's life.
Why do humans take pride in the kill?
What in one's life allows them to steal?
A child's laughter that burns very strife,
Haunting that man through his damned life,
Will God save one who commits man's worse sin,
Or will his punishment come from within?
So remember the day you take a child's life,
The laughter that haunts you every strife,
And pray to God, despising the knife.

Derek Rumpler

"Life's Too Short"

Life is too short to scream and shout
Giving up hope, and thinking of doubt

Life is too short when I look to get revenge
That's not what God wants, it's making a menace

Life is too short to spend time far away
While I'm weeping and crying, trying to make you stay

Life is too short to make others sad
So stop doing the things that are worse even bad

Life is too short to point out things
Making fun and teasing others, sobbing saying please

Life is too short to forget what you have
Thank God that you have Him, He's King of the Land

Life is too short to not say a good-bye
For you never know with each moment, you could go home or die

Life is too short to let someone slip away
Right through your fingers, don't go and just stay

Life is too short to think of all these things
Just let God feel your every needs

Life is too short to even write this poem
'Cause every moment should be spent with you and not all alone.

Lisa Cipres

Loving You

As I think of the times that we might share,
I just can't stop wondering and start to care.
The beautiful face that impressed so upon me,
Was that of a man gentle with glee.
To see the face of the one I cherished most,
Made it very hard for me not to boast.
Your beauty so intact with a smile to see,
I know I can love you; yes, that could be me.
To hold you so close I pray for this day,
The day I look into your eyes and so easily say . . . .
The things I wanted that never came out,
I will surely say them now without any doubt.
What I want to tell you as I hold you tight,
Is that I will be there in the middle of the night.
I will be there through good times and bad,
I will be there through happy and sad.
I will love you until the end, I promise to thee,
Allow it to happen just you loving me.

Lauren Zardecki

Have You Heard My Story?

Have you heard my story?
Have you listened to all the places
I have been?
Have you heard of the many towns,
Do you know the steps I've taken along highways which never end.

Do you know my thought's?
Can you finish my ideas before they're even said?
Are you able to see memories as they play out in my head?

Who are you?
Why are you here?
Why is it for you there is no fear?

I know who you are.
You are that which in me secrets hold,
Running through me, flowing freely, you are my soul.

Barbara Anderson

Lost Love

I lost a love that was so hard to find,
And when I lost it, I was so blind.
It tore up the world that we'd built so well,
Now, I have no place on this Earth to dwell.

My love was not given, but taken away,
By something or someone who would not sway.
I know not what this evil thing did,
But, it took my love and now it's well hid.

Give me time, time, time, and more time
To heal my wound and claim what's mine.
My world will never ever be the same
Since my love is gone and my lover slain.

Evelyn Goodyear

Song of Joy

I knew not what life could be
'Til you sang to this troubled heart
I've longed to know what life will bring
Then your gift of love opened these eyes of mine
Oh, how I've learned to trust in love
This heart dreams at ends of day
It's you who fills the depths of life to me
I knew not of the joys in life
'Til you sang to me
MY heart has opened up . . .
    to receive a joyous gift from you
Your song has brought to life this sleeping heart
How I've dreamed in life to feel this joy
To your heart, I'll let my heart sing in time
So let's let life carry on
That our hearts may sing in life.

Pascual Gonzalez

All Alone

I sit here, all alone.
I listen to songs, feeling sad.
I think of you.
Do you think of me I wonder?
I feel very strongly for you;
Do you feel the same? I doubt it.
The songs sing their sad message.
All I want to do is cry, but I cannot.
Why? I do not know.
Have I run out of tears? Is it possible?
Because every time I think of you I feel like crying.
But every time it ends the same,
with me, in a dark room all alone.
The songs sing their sad message. I listen to it.
I heed it. I look around me. All is empty,
as empty as I feel inside.
The darkness is embracing me, calling me.
I walk into it and I vanish, never to be seen again.
As I disintegrate only one question fills my head . . . .
Did you ever care?

    Kent Carlsson

WHEN . . .

When I look at you I see all that God has given me,
When I smile at you I see all the possibilities,
When I love you I feel all the world has to give me.

When you look at me I feel all the love in the world,
When you smile at me I feel all the warmth of possibilities,
When you love me I realize all that God has given me.

When we are together I have the world in my hands,
When we are one I have no need for another,
When we are joined I am complete.

    Deborah Heiskell-Simmons

Self Portrait

Black wings flying fast
Raven's feathers on the tips of white fingers
Black lips on a white face
Black hair covers black eyes
White skin—a black heart?

Fallen from grace, fallen from light
Fallen into fear
The blood is still red
The heart still beats
The mouth still screams in pain.

Flying fast, flying far
Wings shedding, feathers falling
A black shadow over a white moon
Crystal tears fall from black eyes
The heart is not black after all.

    Jennifer Van Horn

Missing You

Why don't you pick up the phone?
It rings and rings but no one's home
So I lay on my bed and stare at the ceiling,
Because no one cares how I'm feeling.
I can only think of the memories
Of all my enemies.
And then I think of you,
Of all that we've been through.
Our petty fights,
Our late nights,
And of how you protected me.
So when you're not here it's plain to see
I have faced defeat,
Because without you I am incomplete.

    Melissa Moore

Soul

Driven in the mad realm of living
Each man, earnest in pay, living earning the day
Comes thought and decision, driven by derision
His chance to know, what comes, he'll say!
To my glorious eyes a spectacle I see!
This life's dream, ever ending in pain
For the time, I thought, such wealth to concede
Pleasures abound, I was wrong, begging to plead
Jury set forth, executioner at hand!
Am I that of human, which constitutes man
For times gone by, I look to the darkness of my past
The futures ahead, they say, greener the grass
Again and again, tormented by game
Will I ever one day, make decision right by name
For sorrow of heart, sadness of mind
I live this life, like no other of any kind
Cherished this gift, a gentleness I find
The love of life, for growing so old
Hold dear the cherished right
Knowing warm is the soul, and all for being kind.

    Terry L. Wilson

Reflections on Growth through Mr. Ameen

A Man thoughtfully and lovingly planted and nurtured his seeds,
He offered constant support to his seedlings' needs,
And while any true gardener experiences disease and a few weeds,
This gardener greatly enjoyed the blooms and fruits of his deeds.
Growth, that's what life is all about,
The ability to learn, to yearn, and to sprout.
Mr. Ameen lived life such that his memory still grows,
We can cherish his prized blossom, Mary, his wife and Irish rose,
From their love four wonderful children took root and grew,
Known to us here as Damian, Vernon, Bronwyn, and Andrew.
Mr. Ameen's career as a chemical engineer for Mobil Oil,
Allowed him and his family to experience growth on various soil,
Overseas duties required residence in the Middle East for awhile,
Seeing his family grow and prosper brought him a smile.
Here in Hawaii, Mr. Ameen continued to toil and sow,
As a substitute teacher he cultivated high schoolers to grow.
Aside from gardening, where he'd 'til the soil and remove rocks,
Mr. Ameen also had a passion for seeing growth in his stocks,
Today, we lament the passing of this special man we've all known,
Yet, he is amidst the sunshine and will be with us 'til we're grown.

    Laura Goodman

That's How Your Garden Grows

I think of all the many times, I think of all the days
When somehow all those special words to you I didn't say.

I try to understand myself, and hope to figure why
I don't shower you with love each moment that goes by.

A woman's like a flower bloom, her beauty we all know.
This blossom needs the April rain so it may fully grow.

So unattended you have been, you thirst the morning dew.
I've caused your garden not to grow, my words have been so few.

As not to justify at all, my thoughts are always there.
I truly have the finest wife, no one can compare.

To be alone and by myself that day I couldn't live.
For I would sorely miss the things and special ways you give.

I want to shower you this day, I want to give you life.
Your flower thrives to bloom again, I speak to you, my WIFE.

    Lori Alicea

By Myself

I dream of Golden moons
with the touch of a magical evening.
As I run through a place of fantasies
where waterfalls and unicorns run free.
Through tropical forests without a threat at all.
As I kiss my dream away and say a single good-bye
I think . . .
I want to go back to this magical place,
but maybe another night.

Meagan Shannon

Angel

To My Beautiful Angelic Rose

I see a beautiful rose bloom before my face.
Every time you smile!
I see your eyes sparkle as if the heavens were in them.
Every time you smile!
As you walk it's as if you are gliding through air.
Every time you smile!
You have the face of an angel.
That makes my heart beat faster than ever before.
Every time you smile!
You are the very type of women.
I have been searching for all my life to marry.
For I have searched far and wide.
With no evil 'til this day!
To find such kindness and beauty all in one.
That glows on the inside and shines on the outside.
For you are a beautiful angel of this world.
That we live in all of our lives.

Pete Kirkwood

Someone "Deeper" than Flesh

I did this before!
Searing and hot.
Anxious for taste
still untouched.
Kept back by someone deeper than flesh!

Come I again?
Tepidly this time.
Anticipating . . . uncontrollably interested
still untouched.
Kept strong by someone deeper than flesh!

Unsure? Still am!
Old seas bringing fresh waves.
Erosion not welcome here
still untouched.
Kept hoping by someone deeper than flesh

The ocean drifts away!
Morning shells ripple in.
Love transcends!
Touched!
By something deeper than flesh.

Deborah Walkin

The Bird

One day a young man and young lady
walked out of the Main Street Bank
and they got into their car and drove off.
As they returned home,
after what appeared to be a long, hard day's work,
a bird showed up on their window sill.
This bird looked at them and said,
"I know what you did today."
The couple looked at this bird and
they said, "What did we do today?"
and the bird said, "You are the two
whom the cops are looking for."
The bird scared them so bad
that they turned themselves over
to the police immediately.
That is the story of "The Bird!"

Cliff Dover

Illusions

Sometimes this illusion of myself
is too real
this heart beats
Always to a different drum
to follow the pounding off in the distance

Focus-blurred senses
Time-Mind
flies
On the Wind
Crossing fields of Dreams
towards Rainbow's End
Stand Still
that I might Blend
with
Ocean   Earth   Fire and Sky
Streams of Creative Life
Ebb and Flow
Glowing Light

M. Fielding

Lost without You

I lie on my back
Watching the stars drift across the sky.
A particularly bright one
Lingers on the horizon
Framed between two pine trees
With its twin shimmering across the lake.

I wonder
Could you be gazing at the same star
Hundreds of miles away?
Watching it drop lower and lower
Into the waiting calm
For a few seconds it weakly shimmers
Only to be extinguished by the pristine water.

And I think, could this same drama
Be played out where you sit and watch?
Is it an omen foretelling out love?
Building slowly, shimmering with joy
Only to be cut off suddenly.

When gone will we miss what we had?
Embracing memories instead of each other . . . .

Christopher Skiest

What Is Love?

Love is something special that cannot be measured in degrees.
Love is something that I hold so very close to me.
Love is something special that withstands the test of time.
Love is something special I hold within that is hopefully mine.

Why is Love something special, you ask?
Because I know that through this loving task,
That sometimes it happens we see love through a covered mask.
A mask with love that seems to be always there,
Because I hope and pray that you truly care.

Love is something special that will always be there for me.
Because you see, to give this love, is truly meant to be.
Love is something special that I hold so very close with thee,
For love is something special, please say, "Yes," to comfort me.

Oh why, oh why, does this special love seem to drift apart?
No, I say, it never will because it is deep within my heart.
Love is something special that I know from up above,
Means forever and forever within my heart of love.

Carole Miller

Ultraviolet Screams

Chantilled love laces
The tattered remnants of a shattered soul
Waiting to bounce into neverness
The vampires of youth's blood await
The immortal doves cry to hope again . . .
But in vain to shout
Love's laugh at me
A stroke on the stream of my mind's desire
I feed the lions the bones of dignity
They tell of mysteries of ages borne
Talk is valuable from the crash of destiny
Ghosts bleed my eyes dry
As I light the torch of hope
Walls applaud me into the chamber
The clouds ready to eclipse their own
The souls of shadows orchestrate my scene
When I was a child I thought as a child
But when I gained knowledge I became vain
Only to lose the virgin's cup
Tell me, who tries death's reins?

Christopher Logan

Sunsets

Sunlight dancing on
The water so deep and calm.
Peacefully I sit there,
Watching the little birds fly over head.
My thoughts seem to wonder as do the birds.
The sun, so warm and gentle.

Jacqueline Tapp

Strength

Strength should not be determined
by the movement of a physical part—
Strength is made known by the character of the heart.

The bear may win battles of strength with beast,
But compared to the eagle, it seems to be least.

For nobility of the heart causes the eagle to rule the sky—
As it soars through the air, men's hearts begin to sigh.

"What strength, what power; how it stands so sure."
And the memory of its strength continues to endure.

So look not to the physical work of the limb,
Know that your strength lies in your heart, and the character within.

Deborah Craver

Me

Kiss me because I'm human
Love me because no one else does
Understand me because others are confused by me
Trust me because who can you trust other than I
Hold me because I am weaker than I look
Live so I can live through you
Be strong so I can be weak and fall so I can be strong
Be kind so I can know kindness
Caress me so I can feel whole
Touch me so I can feel
Accept me for being me
Think so I can hear your thoughts
Comprehend me so I can be comprehended
Unify so we can become one
Hear me so I can be heard

Dwan Carter

Beautiful (for Dillan)

It's a beautiful day for a swim
Won't you come dive with me into the unknown
Together we'll ride the wave of time
We'll search the sea for its hidden treasures
Cherish the time spent together
Our lives may not always encompass the smallest of channels
We may be taken to the deepest parts of the sea,
but know if your breath should lessen
just grip me tight
put your lips to mine and breathe my life
For I will keep you afloat

Tommy Alastra

Girl like You

I have never met a girl like you,
kind, caring and confidant,
an enigma of your a own,
a shinning star in bloom,
a golden medallion in the sun,
shinning like the pure waters of the rivers,
a diamond in the rough,
cut by the blade of love,
a perfect person in every way,
a sea of emotion to be respected,
mere words cannot describe you,
it takes a song and ballad
from a poet better than Shakespeare,
a heart of gold and a mind to match,
as intelligent as Solomon and that's that,
a soft gentle air surrounds you,
a protection from the above,
deserving of goddess,
oh! Yes, I've never met a girl like you,
so young yet so experienced,
another lifetime put into one,
a soul of goodness,
a love of hearts,
I've never met a girl like you,
and I know I never shall

Aditya Berlia

Her Eyes

Gone are the eyes that watched me grow
The eyes that were able to see into my soul
Together we climbed mountains and made it through the pain
Only to find out that someday it would be forever changed

As you've gotten weaker, I've gotten stronger
Able to take care of myself even though I didn't want to

You'd be proud of my wit, my confidence and my charm
People say I'm just like you and I know all about your charms
The eyes are in my heart, the eyes that saw my soul
But gone are the beautiful eyes, the eyes that watched me grow

Valarie Shea

Message of Conviction

Lord, I fear I have failed you again.
deeper I have fallen into this world of sin.
These dreams come and take me in the night,
only to convict me and give me reason to write.
Humbled and lowly, I speak now with you,
Asking, no pleading, for the forgiveness that's true.
Instant relief is my answered call,
His holy blood has again prevented my fall,
Yet still I know that I have brought shame,
To the holy Father with many a name.
Lord, let this message of conviction reach me again,
Whenever I dare to ponder creating an evil; that's sin.

Christopher King

As the Leopard Stalks His Prey

As the leopard stalks his prey
"How's that baby boy?"
(born yesterday)
As the leopard stalks his prey
"No, I think I'll pass."
(but only for today)
As the leopard stalks his prey
"Close your eyes so tight you can no longer think"
(only then to God, may you pray)
As the leopard stalks his prey
"Give me your money!"
(and you best obey)
As the leopard stalks his prey
"Just stopped by to say, hey."
(or maybe I'll make her my feeble prey)
As the leopard stalks his prey,
he keeps his ears down and eyes fixed.
And now he makes the kill.

Walter Rueff

The Spider's Web

My life right now is weaving an endless tangle,
Like a spider spinning its web for prey.
Trapped in life's web, my thoughts are in a mangle,
Wondering why in my life are things so grey.

I feel the life being drained from my soul,
Like the prey trapped in the spider's web.
Knowing it is time to pay life's toll,
Time has come for my heart to silently go ebb.

My heart has lost rhythm of its beat,
Thoughts in my mind have lost the fight.
My body walking around as in defeat,
The purpose of my being nowhere in sight.

My soul is dangling in the air,
Like the spider's prey fighting to be freed.
There seems no choice but to take heaven's stairs,
For the spiders web knows only greed.

Cindy Turner

Broken Bits of Glass

I sit beside a window
and let the world walk past
　　Each person I take notice to
is different from the last
　　Screams shatter our minds
Love continues to blind
　　Soul mates sit and stare unfound
and life remains a mystery
　　Some lives crumble to dust
and float away on the wind
　　Some lucky souls find peace, becoming whole again
　　Not all find what they search and scream for
not all dreams are made of glass
　　Some wrongly seek a lifetime; some find the light at last
　　Sitting at my window only from time to time
　　I live life as I watch it live
　　Demons and Saints walk past
wondering what to make of me
　　and I merely do the same looking past the glass
　　Wondering if it's demon or saint I see
in the reflection looking back at me

Amanda Swanson

The Mighty Hurricane

The Mighty Hurricane
The waves are fierce dragons,
Destroying boats as if they were soldiers' horses and wagons,
With a single lift,
The boats are set a-drift,
Powerful winds send them airborne,
All because of the storm,
Boats go through windows of homes,
Entering as easy as stones.

People are in panic,
Running around very frantic,
People are dying everywhere,
Other people don't seem to care,
For this reason I'll tell you why,
They want to get out to live, instead of stay and die,
What possibly could make everything go insane?
Nothing but the Mighty Hurricane.

Cari Day

Two Minutes—Prayer of a Firefighter

Two more minutes, is all I ask,
Just enough time to finish this task.

Let me make it to the next floor, make sure this floor is clear,

Please don't make it my tomb, for it is this which I fear.

As embers fall around me, and flames fiercely grow,

These floorboards creek, as they burn very slow.

Now I'm on the stairs, the door is in sight,

I'll be the last one out, but wait, their might . . .

Be one more, just one more look,

It makes me so glad, it's this glance I took.

I had to be sure, no one was left behind.

Thank you, Lord, for these two minutes, as I run out the door,

Light hits my face, as it did once before.

No one was trapped, my job is done,

All were accounted for, every last one.

Bonnie Kessler

Into His World

Lashes locked,
adrift in a world that I will never know,
never see.
Peaceful is he
who I give myself to.
My hands are still covered in the reverie
of last night.
His kiss was an endless drink of water,
so refreshing.
An impression of his enamored gaze is still
clinging to my breast.
Rays of the sultry morning silence entice me,
the warm sheets invite me.
Curiosity consumes me, and I crawl in,
Into his world.

My eyes close,
My heart beats,
My soul lifts,
And I join him.

Teresa Bufano

Upon True Love

You captured my heart at first glance,
You set my senses afire.
Your beauty which art so enchanting
Make some jealous, envy, some admire.

My heart no longer responds to my mind
Another like you is hard to find,
You touch the deepest part of me
My soul though hath set it free.

The feel of your body, warm against mine
Is a feeling, completely divine
A touch by you thrills the heart of me
My ecstasy is for all to see.

I wish that we could merge as one
The fire in our souls burn like the sun,
To feel your heart beat with mine
To have you near me 'til the end of time

Anshika K. Khurana

Why Do I Love You?

Your words are sharp like a knife and slice my heart,
wanting to hurt you back with a poisoned dart.
Knowing it will make matter worse 'cause you're crazy,
having the nerve to need things from me and be so lazy.
Only you can initiate making love, never mind my yearns,
my needs come up and your candle no longer burns.
You use people because you have a plan,
interesting how everyone sinks in the quicksand.
A token now and then to express you care,
too much damage done, regardless the gift you bear.
I gave you my heart and soul to trample over,
well no longer co-dependent I see for I am sober.
Mates?
Guess again,
the wait and hurt too long,
Friends?
Maybe when you get help and we're both strong.
So many times my eyes reflect love back at you,
my mind and soul want to tell you we're through

Felisa Whitfield

Knight of the Beast

Hate is their battle cry.
For those who follow, I don't know why.

A holy symbol ablaze in the night.
Helps to add fuel to their evil plight.

Their constant babbling will never yield,
Because the constitution forms a shield.

Fear is used like a gleaming sword.
Which they use to amass a foolish horde.

On societies ills like a hungry cat.
Preys the beast in the robe and the pointy hat.

Jonathon Burton

My Garden

Extravagant splashes of color
Brush strokes of magnificence
Tickling the senses

Summoning the hunters, gatherers,
The goldfinch, butterfly,
Bumblebee and the wasp

A dance of life and beauty, a waltz in the wind
Dusted by starlight, refreshed by morning's dew

Drawing in each petal, memorizing each hew
Capturing the greens, the reds and blues

Holding them deep in my heart
Treasuring their gift
Releasing their glory upon winter's slumber

Janice Geha

Unreal

It's the days when I'm alone,
That I really have time to think,
I then truly realize how we are totally in sync,
People don't understand,
And I don't even care,
As long as you're mine,
This feeling will always be there.
It's so very strong,
Sometimes even unreal,
I don't realize how I can feel like this.
Do you understand,
And do you even care,
How my heart skips a beat whenever you're near?
These feelings too unreal, they turn me upside down,
Make my stomach turn inside out,
My heart skips a beat when you whisper in my ear,
All of the things that I long to hear.
So stay near, so I can always feel these feelings too unreal.

Angela Burden.

Dying Angels

Anyone working with kids, to help them learn to help themselves.
I looked into her face, and saw
Her innocence was gone without a trace.
The glimmer of hope I'd seen shine in her eyes
Was stolen by her family's quicksand lives.

I sensed the air was gone beneath her wings—
She'd let us down and she knew it;
The "Washed-Up-Before-My-Time" poster child,
Sat wrapped, trapped in her failure, even she knew she blew it.

I had no answers for this kid.
She cannot reclaim a childhood-never-had.
Only her toughest soul searching journey
Would lead her to see, that SHE, is not bad.

In flashes I see them. On the fringe;
Ethereal—these kids with few choices.
No witness as dreams slip and die—
Broken and scattered-like these kids without voices.

TV paints tragedy faceless, far away, yet
Here, her secrets poise in flight, as life takes its toll.
She is every child; a statistic to mourn "in-the-making."
With no one to protect her, they just peeled away her soul.

Susan M. Chiu

Something Unique

Through iron gates, they enter this place,
With stones on grass, so evenly spaced.
Some there to visit, do so to grieve,
But, others who come, will never leave.
Cast high, overhead, a blanket of gray,
Befits the mood of those there to pray.
Even the flowers offer no cheer
Yet, something unique still happens here.
Mournful cries from a vigilant crow,
Fall on deaf ears, above and below.
Not sure if to hold, or to release,
Those who are standing, search for some peace.
Tears, filled with words, soak into the ground,
Absorbed by souls, eternally bound.
Words never spoken, seem to be heard,
Spirits are lifted, sorrows deferred.
Guidance returns, through fond memories,
Brightening the clouds and rustling the trees.
Blessed are the few, that exit with pride,
For something unique, just happened inside.

Thomas Wade Lundgren

sticky

seemingly, effortlessly, you held me there,
trapped against the backdrop of your articulate sorcery.
suspended, elegantly,
fragile in the throes of idiocy
eggshell dance on threads of insecurities
cautious wind twist with utmost delicacy—
i could not leave, but let
instead
your web merge with my wings
the striking tip of poison stings
secular ownership of captured things
what would you make of me then?
a box to store your failures in?
a mask, a veil, a thicker skin?
as you slept—i cut myself free
It wounded you and startled me
and in that instance—i wept with glee.
you and me.
you and me.
you.
me.

Jennifer Trujillo

Becky's Twist

The names had been changed to protect
  The ignorant
 From the pertinent
 Facts as placed before the looking glass
 Where she stares
 Where she cries
 Another night curls 'round her eyes
 . . . and dies
 From tender mercies long withheld
  against a beating heart that pounds
 . . . and pumps
 . . . and wills
 That simple facts as light as air
 Become as heavy as her stare
 And evaporate the breath she breathes
 Fogging, forgetting the little girl she
  sees
 . . . disappearing
 Beneath an avalanche of frozen Gin
 . . . and lime.

Gregory Mucha

Slow Down

Have you ever watched young children on a merry-go-round
Or listened to the rain, kissing the ground
Ever followed a butterfly's unpredictable flight
Or gazed at the sun fade into the curtains of night
Slow down and don't dance so fast
Time is too short and the music won't last
Do you run through your day and let it go by
When you ask, "How are you?" Do you hear the reply
When the day is done, do you lie in your bed
While the next hundred things run through your head
Slow down and don't dance so fast
Time is too short and the music won't last
If you run too fast to get somewhere
You're missing the fun of getting there
Listen to your angel
Life is not a race, so please take it slower
Listen to the music that's playing before it's over

Nina Baraceros

Hold On

Hold on, Don't let go
even though time is drawing near,
Hold on, Don't let go
this is the time to face your fear.

As the pain enters in
and strength grows weak,
just sit there and listen,
as I begin to speak.

You don't need to say a word
your actions have told it all,
by your comforting hand when I got ill,
or picking me up after each and every fall.

Now it's my turn
to set you back on your feet,
My life is like a song,
and without you, I am missing a beat.

Here, take my hand
it's now yours to hold,
because you've already molded my heart
now your heart is mine to mold.

Chris Romano

Emotions

Rivers of sadness will always be plenty.
Oceans from men will continue to feed.
Emotions that by tornadoes will be stolen,
stolen just like when all began.

They belong to the soul God once gave us.
Emotions will always be attached—
to the spirit through life and beyond.
Bonded with the air floating freely.

While we dream they impregnate the walls,
the walls that know all of our secrets,
even some of our impossible fantasies,
triggered by emotions perhaps.

Feelings our mind wants to contain,
and by containing them where would they go?
Hate, Happiness, and Love,
still within our soul,
Shall we ever let them go?
Shall we even contain their force?

Mario Morales

Extend Your Arm

Extend your arm.
It is not short as you think.
Lives will be saved from it.
It will not break or hurt.
The arm will clap a hand
of lives it has saved.
Lives that would not have been,
if you did not extend your arm.

Extend your arm.
It will reach if you try.
Hungry mouths will sing their praises.
Cloth-less bodies will hide in it.
The arm that closed their yawning mouth,
and wrapped their nakedness in the cold.
Mouth and bodies that would not have been,
if you did not extend your arm.

Allen Njoku

Death Shard

Looking out this desolate window,
Listening to the wind blow through the trees,
This broken heart cried out,
"This night I give to you:"

As I looked into your eyes so blue,
And as I watched you pass by,
The brushing of your soft skin,
Longing to hold you in my arms once again:

Trying to make all things seem right,
But never will I have you,
Never will you be mine again,
Frolicking here in this lonely state:

Dreaming of hope never being,
Life never seeing,
Death's all bearing blame,
While I choke on its shame:

Wearing death's shard,
As I lie deep within,
I'm alive, but gone,
Dead, but breathing. . .

Randal Sumner

Dream

"All that we see or seem, is but a dream within a dream." —Poe
It was a cold winter night,
lonely and dark without even a single beam of light.
Even with the alluring shine of the great moon,
no bit of life could pass through.
Then in my mind, you appeared,
holding me in your embrace and kissing away all my fears.
The sun raised and the darkness ceased,
flowers bloomed and life increased.
We both drifted together in our own ecstasy,
as I fervently caressed your fragile body.
I closed my eyes and awaited your lips,
as you pressed yourself against me, indulging me with a kiss.
I opened my eyes and it was all a dream,
you were no where in sight, no where to be seen.
I searched frantically, anywhere and everywhere,
but alas, nothing, oh, how I wish that you were really there.

Roy Davenport

Heaven's Sea

on nimble souls will leave this world

with cupid's wings will fly through space

souls of led left far behind

nothing left but cheeses and wine

if love was vast

it couldn't hold the feelings i have to hold you close

and when were gone for all to see our thoughts
will dance on heaven's sea.

Justin Hollerman

Who's to Blame?

My eyes are swollen from my tears.
Everything around me, they're all my fears.
My life now makes no sense.
I feel like a weight, heavy and dense.
I come so close to conquering a fear,
then another one comes and stabs like a spear.
I wonder if my life will ever be the same.
I'm hoping so, but who's to blame?
Who changed my life so drastically?
Who made me wander haphazardly?
I wonder if my life will ever be the same.
I'm hoping so, but who's to blame?

Karen Broo

Window

Rounded top frame,
Old chipped paint,
Inadvertently placed at the frame of the window.
High, tall,
Cathedral-like.
I, sitting aimlessly on the ground,
Staring off, Just like Mom used to.
Through the thick mountain top clouds,
No design, No formations evident,
Just gray.
I look heavily in,
As a kid screams beside me,
I want to be sucked in by the cloud,
I, so covet the cushion notion,
To be taken away in a perpetual gray blanket.
Thank you chipped paint for allowing me,
To look pass the imperfections,
And into the fog like world.
The child screams again.

Jennifer Cox

Fear of the Forgotten

In memory of my brother Jeremy
A happy birthday again there will never be
For my birthday is now the hardest time for me
You are gone and not here
Yet that is not my biggest fear
I am scared that you have gone and have forgotten
I am afraid that you hear me with deaf ears
That you look upon me with blind eyes
When my time finally comes
And I can see you once again
I pray that it is with open arms
I pray there will be no harm
For I am sorry sir
A reason I only know why
I am sorry dear brother
I never got to say goodbye!

Mike Kava

Distant Drums

I hear the sound of distant drums,
the echo of their rhythm comes
Through darkest night 'til dawn's new sun
their beat in haunting tones do run

The battle cry yet heard by young
This battle cry by all will not be sung
as bells in mourning shall be rung
For gallant men their lives in battle flung

Those distant drums their echoes slowly fade
The battle won by those whose lives they gave
Their flag, their country, their freedom to save
To let them know we are no ones slave

James Henderson

O.U.I.

A twist, a turn, a deafening scream.
A squeal, headlights, a luminous tree.
All memories of the fatal night when you left me,
Alone and frightened in a world that does not know,
How much I love and miss you so.
Because some guy decided to take that last drink,
And tried to drive,
You will never again be at my side.

Stephanie Harmon

Growing Old

Come sit with me a while and we will think of days gone by;
when we would wander barefoot in the park.
So long ago when we were very young,
and did not fear to stay out in the dark.
Come stay by me a while and we will think of days gone by;
Of children playing in the snow, with cheeks of rosy red.
So long ago when we were very young,
and did not seek the warmth of home, instead.
Come sit with me a while and we will think of days gone by;
Of sun-filled days upon the beach,
and sea birds flying high above.
So long ago when we were very young,
and thought of nothing but our love.
Come closer to me now and we will think of days gone by;
As the fire dies and the room grows cold.
So long ago when we were very young,
and never thought of growing old.

Michael H. Gottfried

The Emotions of Big Words

It happened because of me.
When we spoke it turned into an imbroglio, gargantuan
argument which decimated my heart greatly.
The acerbic words which pour'd from his soft lips made me cry.
The ambience was filled with anger.
The love we had for each other vanished in thin air.
The animus we had burgeon very quickly.
I walk the dark street to come across my reflection in the night.
I thought to myself I must be the most
hapless girl in the world.
Everywhere I turned his face would be ubiquitous.
I tried my hardest to succeed but I failed.
Now all I can do is dream.
Dream of the day we will be together again!

Rachel Friedman

The Last Poem

Take me down the river with you
Breathing not the air
Eyes once blue now plain and white
Sticks and leaves tangled in my hair
Tell me that your love was true
As I take my last breath
Tell me you lied not
As I am swept away by death
Brush my tangled hair and make my blue lips red
Tell me that you love me so, now that I am dead

Charlotte Kindle

Mothers

There is nothing as sweet as a Mothers' loving hand,
she does everything for you that she can.
She will care for your sore, bruise or cut.
For there is nothing as gentle as her loving touch.
You may think there is no one as mean as your mother,
but look at it this way, there is no other.
So just love her with all your heart,
and your love for each other will never grow apart.
Just tell her every day that you love her,
for those three words are more important to her.
Give her a hug and a kiss every day,
for her love for you shall never fade away.
So take some of my advice,
always care for her and be nice.

Terri Smoyer

Home at Last

Peering through the darkness,
I see a faint glow.
Is it too much to hope for?
I grope forward hesitantly.

I have been in the dark too long,
Looking fruitlessly for the Truth.
Struggling on my own, proudly independent,
Not knowing Him fully.

Now, I hope this glimmer of light
will reveal a pathway.
A beacon of direction for my aimless wanderings.

As I near the Source of Light,
my face warms with His radiance.
A peaceful stillness spreads
through my soul.

I am home at last.

Marnee Crawford

Self

Serenity in contemplation of a moment,
so simple are we but perplexed over nothing.
Sliding through the days with the simplest assortment
of who we are but never abiding to the real thing.
One in a multitude of many individuals
holding on to each other without words.
So are we standing in line waiting for the next
universal joint to spin to the point of being absurd.
One question remains the same,
who are we in this serenity of contemplation?
Why there are only our single names
in stumbling thoughts of revelation.

Jeremy Dandron

"The Beauty that You Can See"

In memory of my grandfather, who showed me the stars when I was two.
I look into the sky at night,
gazing over the beautiful stars that are so bright
over millions I'd pick the one that reminds
Me of you. I'll tell you why of the beauty that shines on for you.
It turns all colors right before your eyes.
the colors that it turns I'll explain why.
Blue is for being true. . .
Red is for the love I have for you. . .
Green is a meaning for just about anything.
Gold is for everything that lasts. . .
Silver is for the future, not the past.
So put them all together
And you can see that this beauty will shine
In the sky for you and I to see

August 23rd, 1998
Cathyjo Parsons

Marshinda's

Marshinda's garden.
One of love and talent from the Lord above.
Some have stones around thy bones.
Some have fears which may cause tears.
In the corner of my eye,
I see a boy who starts to cry.
In the mud there lies my blood;
in the lobby there lies my body.
Dead alone and filled with stone,
the boy turns to say,
"You met me this day
and I'll bet you can stay."
A tear of joy came to the boy.
A life began never to part again.

Chancy White

Can You Love This Cautious Soul?

Blue sky clouds over me,
My eyes hold what the clouds cannot bring.
Touch me not for I will decline
To accept the kindness you want me to find.
Persistence is such a loyal game,
And only those with practice may play.
Others will fade as the moon ascends,
But you I pray, will hold fast 'til the end.
Not one has ever come close enough to know
The restless soul that I have grown.
I want to be loved—as a baby is born.
I don't want to remain as I am—forlorn.
Come over to me and reach deep inside,
Please be gentle, I do not mind.
On the surface a crust, fragile within,
I'll guide you if you want—come in, come in.
Blue sky clouded over me,
My eyes held what the clouds could not bring.
Stay close by my side as the sun descends,
May you hold fast—the beginning of the end.

Jennifer Blanchard

I Love You

Kisses are sweet, roses are kind,

Love is so special the very first time.

Your touch is so gentle, your eyes are so calm;

I feel safe when I'm with you, nothing could go wrong.

I love the way you think of me, I love the things you do,

Even though sometimes you frustrate me,
and then I get mad at you.

I love the way I think of you every hour of every day,
I love the way you make me laugh and make me want to stay.

I love the way you stick with me when I'm upset or full of glee.
My love there's so much to this poem,
there's more than what it reads.

Thank you for all you are to me, thank you for loving me.

I love you, too, with all my heart, thank you for everything.

Summer Uyeno

"Fall"

It has been the cruelest twist of fate,
the blackest irony,
That this season and its name,
should call out and remember the state
of my wounded heart.
Healed at moments, Torn in perpetuation.
First annual torment,
veiled with a thin smile.
Tears fall again, harder than rain.
Pain rises from its sleep,
like an old foe, welcome unto himself.
Cold an darkness increase,
Distraught light flees their numbers.
Arriving on changing winds and tides,
The raging torrent of thoughts . . . remembering
converge upon my soul like a
thousand vengeful knives
bleeding "memory" from their blades.
It is time for battle once more.
"Keep me."

John Spence

What Is Man?

What is man without woman,
we were created to walk hand in hand.

I am your mate, you are my beau,
gee, I love to see your eyes aglow.

I gave birth to your babies, boy and girl,
I have done lots to brighten up your world.

Lovers, best friends, soul mates to the end,
we make such a wonderful blend.

Love me, cherish me with all of your might,
and I will endeavor to keep your life bright.

When we are old and starting to bend,
I promise that I will encourage you right to the end.

I love you, I need you , I honor you.

Deborah Stephen-Mapp

Time

Time is such a fleeting thing, as everybody knows,
It doesn't seem to ever last, it
swiftly comes and goes.

The days and nights that we once knew, will
never come again . . . that's true, and they are
all such precious few, yet not a thing that
we can do.

Our time that now has ended, is just a memory.
So cherish all the days you've had, as though
they were not free.

Say hello . . . brand new "tomorrow," good-bye
sweet "yesterday," and with the time that
you have left, live the magic of "today."

Arvetta Austin

Lilies for Mama

Lonely redhead spider lily, looking all around,
Waiting for a brown-eyed boy to come pluck her from the ground.

"Mama, here's a flower for you," he said with a sweet grin,
As mama gently knelt right down and kissed him on the chin.

Little redhead spider lily isn't lonely anymore,
Put in a vase, an honored place for mama to adore.

Season's circle now complete, redhead spider lily fades so fast,
Where is the boy of long ago, left sadly in the past.

Spring arrives, a pickup truck comes rambling down the road,
Stops by a field of red sunshine where spider lilies grow.

Into the house a man now comes, hiding something behind his back,
A redhead spider lily laid, softly in his mama's lap.

"Mama, here's a flower for you," he said with a bearded grin,
As mama stretched on tip toes high and kissed him on the chin.

Jeane Taylor

Echoes in the Mind

She roams around the rooms like the wind,
her soft silk nightgown flowing from her breeze.
She hears the echo of the children's laughter.
Smiling, she remembers how they used to tease.
In her mind she can hear the children's voices,
and their ball bouncing from off the wall.
She settles down upon the floor,
she feels guilty to ask for more.
Tears slip silently down her cheeks as she cries
diligently to the Lord,
"Please forgive me for not being meek,
but did you have to take them all?"

Cynthia Parrish

A Run in Her Stocking

All along the stage they're folding George and Abraham into a stiff V.
For garter belt snaps and kisses on the cheek is where we all will be.
Chasing second hand smoke quickly with Miller Genuine Drafts.
Surrounded by lost and lonely souls on cheap fantasy rafts.
Long, lean and elastic womanhood doing the wet noodle on stage.
This world has accepted doing the beauty chick cruise as all the rage.
Locking eyes with one of these ladies will empty your wallet fast.
Even with other distractions you'll still be watching her sass.
Standing boldly in her Victoria Secrets at the end of each song.
She knows who has made this crowd very, very long.
With your body beautiful and razor sharp mind you pranced and prowled.
Although real men offered tips & little boys offered none, all hearts growled.
The beauty is so powerful and delicate, so we all wonder.
What would it be like to groove with her silky rocking thunder?
While the musical selections make her hips churn.
She knows bumps and bruises from floor work she'll earn.
Her smile and delight in dancing keeps you rocking.
And it's only much later that you notice the run in her stocking.

Don James, Jr.

Lazy Summer Noons

To my glorious childhood, may it be preserved forever!
Pine needles whistling about softly with the crisp summer wind,
Swirling about in funnel-like fashions,
Floating down the trickling creek,
Its many bubbles floating about mystically.

The roar of the waterfall at the end,
Surging upon the smoothened rocks,
Flat like hot cakes,
Refreshing me from a muggy day.

The great pine trees,
Tingling me with their bold aroma,
As dark as the star-lit nights above,
Watching me, protecting me, listening to my heart.
The labyrinth of pines entangling me with their octopus clasp;
Steadying, cradling me into deep, uninterrupted rest.
Oh! Those lazy afternoons!

The sun, yellow as the forest of daffodils popping up among the tundra,
Beaming steadily and consistently through the greenery among the hills
Illuminating the entire sanctuary with a soft glow.

You could give me all the sparkling gold in the world,
But it could never amount to the joy I experienced on those noons.

Marc Formeister

It's God's Way

When I think of what God does, it seems so not fair.
When he takes a baby, you think, oh, how he dare.
I know what you're thinking,
but just listen to me if you have the time.
I lost my sister over a year ago.
Every since she's been gone, I've felt so alone.
I don't know how it feels to lose a baby girl,
but I do know what's it's like to lose someone close.
All we do is sit and pray for them to come through.
Then when God takes them home, what shall we do?
All I did was sit, cry and moan a little too.
But when your baby goes through the gates,
there will be no more pain or hate.
When my sister hears of it, she will come and take her there.
Then one time at the crack of dawn we'll all take a stroll to God's home.
So don't feel bad and don't you cry;
we'll all have our chance to fly.

Christopher Bolejack

Confusion . . . Madness

Bubbling; boiling
Emotions uncoiling
Steaming; burning
Thoughts inside churning
Back & forth pacing
Thoughts process racing
Anger within flaring
Icily glaring
Like a volcano ready to blow
The strain starts to show
Reddened face
A little disgraced
Kick; stamp
Here's your chance
Scream; yell
How's that feel?
Deep sigh
Wondering why?
Confusion . . . . Madness

Nicole Gray

The Love We Had

I miss you so very much
Your warm & tender touch
Just holding you so close
I miss your tender kisses most

The way you talk to me
& your love entirely
I miss us walking hand in hand
& the way you'd understand
How we'd stay up all night
& the way it felt so right

I miss your voice on the telephone
Times we spent alone
& times we have shared so true
I even miss those little I love you's

Just sitting side by side
& the times we so called lied
I miss these memories so bad
'Cause I want you & the love that we had

John Rousell

Solitude

I sit here
at the desk,
looking out through the window
Seeing people
playing together

I sit here
reading a book
about people having fun
Hearing people
playing together

I sit here
writing on a piece of paper
about what I wish I could do
Hearing people
laughing together

How I wish
I could be with those people

Jose Higuera

"Home"

When I think of Home, I think of a place
where I'll always be greeted with a smiling face.

When I think of Love, I think of a feeling of protection
from so many people who are striving for perfection.

Home is a place where everyone has a responsibility.
It is a place where we should be taught how to face reality.

Home is a place where families should gather
to talk about how God has blessed them to be together.

Home is a place where children should be brought up and taught different things.
Every once in a while we should come together and sing.

Home is a place where we all belong.
Even when we leave we should meet again with the same tone.

Home is a place where everyone should feel free.
It should be a place filled with open arms welcoming you and me.

Charlean Burton

R.B. My Man

Let me tell you about R.B., my man. He was introduced when my life produced some serious emotional demands. My world as I knew, totally up it blew! But from the debris, R.B. appeared just for me. He always made himself available to me. Day or night, whether near or far, time nor space could have kept us apart. The thrills, the Highs, that R.B. for me supplied, just couldn't be denied. Believe me I tried.

You can bet, every time we met, a lasting impression in my spirit he set. R.B. was so smooth and graceful, yet for me he would sway being ever so playful. Then there were the times it felt as if we were floating while he rocked my blues away. There's no wonder why to him I strayed. Always in his arms I wanted to stay. But R.B. must have had a change of heart, for he offered no more thrills; he just stopped playing the part.

He began to take me lower, even lower than I began in the start. The remains of my fragmented life drifted further into the dark. How could R.B. do this to me? I thought he and I would always be. But I guess by design, he really couldn't have had good intentions in mind. I have to admit, I entered this blind. But you know, it's all so lame! I really should have had this joker figured by his name.

River boat! River boat! He's all about games.

Nikki Nichelle

Awakening

Speak easy, like a warm summer breeze.
Be content with the moment of truth in your lies.
Play back the overwhelming fear of failure and disappointment
and remember that in the eyes of he who loves is success in life.
Nothing lasts forever and forever is a relative term used only
 by those who are afraid of a brand new tomorrow.
Change is beautiful, full of hope and promise of something
better to come our way.
Yet we run from it like it's a contagious virus trying to break through
the protective womb each one of us has created.
Don't be discreet with your thoughts,
open your mind and embrace the world around you.

Kordian Wolski

Incomplete

I can't understand how you accomplished this feat,
but without you in my world my life is i_comp__te,
I can't believe I found you
you were always the mi_s_ng link,
the day our worlds crossed each others paths I would have never began to think,
that I could love so hard and so fast,
Considering the cards I've been dealt in previous loves in the past,
but since you've entered my life
my spirit has grown,
and I feel that it's time that I let it be known,
that this feeling I feel, I cannot delete,
for without you in my life, my life's
IN_OM_L_TE

Patrick Chamberlain

Panatela

There was a panatela
Who safely saw his way
To cross the world against the light
Thrown on him by the day

Now in his own abode
Where no one was allowed
He sat and read that he was dead
Was crushed up in a crowd

He raised himself in anger
A lie! He did reply
Though no one ever heard him
So none would wonder why

In time he will recover
And live a normal life
Of all the normal things we do
Normally . . .

Alex Howard

In Memory of My Dad, Dr. Frank J. Nowak

So as they lay me down to sleep
try not to hurt, try not to weep.

For I have gone to a better place
of joy and love and amazing grace.

My soul is with the Lord you see
and now He's taking care of me.

Paula Nowak

Thank You

You are what some call Grace
You are a sensuous slap in the face
You are what I always thought I knew
You are what I aspire to.
You're the dawn of my new day
You my Love are my anyway
Every time I feel the need
To give it up, to die indeed
I think of you in all your Glory
I think of you and never worry.
Thank you for every dream I have
That cleanses me like a summer bath
Thank you for holding me so tight
Thank you for every glorious night
How I'll remember you, and yes I will
Is how a summer breeze makes me feel
The calmness of it, the gentle still
The almost of a winter's chill
The sureness of your touches thrill
You bend me to your will

Shavona Booker

Lady Love

I pray to the Lord
who lives up above
To send me a Lady
someone to Love.

Let her be of a beautiful sort
and Lord, if you can
Let her be short.

I hope she has
a sweet kind of grace
and she'd light up
when she sees my face.

I know you're really busy
so I'm not asking for much
Just a sweet little lady
who is warm by my touch.

Nicholas Bagwell

Snow

As I sit watching out my window the snow keeps falling.
I can't help but wonder to myself, what if I was very small?
I would be able to ride on a snowflake.
That trip down from the clouds
would make me feel as if I were walking in a Winter Wonderland.
Flying through the air, floating over here, there, just everywhere. . . .
If I were that small, what would happen if I started to fall?
If I couldn't land into all of that beautiful soft snow,
I could end up putting on a different show.
What if that landing wasn't as kind?
But of course, all of this was just in my mind.
So at the window alone I sit, just me and my imagination.
Dreaming of a tiny snowflake trip, for a little while longer.

Sarayah Moore

Alterna-chic

You see that quiet girl in the corner?
She doesn't seem to have a life . . .
a wallflower, always blending in.
Never denting society, always outside the fringe:
sitting home and dreaming
of things that can be, should be,
but are always not.
You see that young girl in the corner?
Give her half a chance. Let her loose from her solitary cage, and you'll set free an
alterna-chic for me: so different in many ways—dancing nights and surviving days.
You see the strange girl in the corner?
She's waiting to be found. Look behind that quiet shell
and find her deepest self.
Release her from that desolate cage to experience life as it is:
trying, yet happy; make it all come true. Release the alterna-chic in her, for her and me.

Alicia Rivera

Friends

Friend, a word so commonly used but often misunderstood.
A friend will stand by you through all of your times, not only when time are good.
Friends stand by you during your worries, hardships, trials and tears.
Friends won't blame you; friends won't shame you; friends will bring you good cheer.
Through your good times, friends will be there to share in your joys and games.
They'll be there to joke with and be there to bond with, knowing you'd do the same.
A friend wants nothing except for your trust and will give you theirs to no end.
They won't look for gain whether money or fame; like you they're just looking for friends.
So when late at night you're down on your knees praying to God up above,
thank him for caring by creating and sharing with you the friends you love.

Kenneth Graham

Millennium Thoughts

The days and weeks go flying by—the Holidays draw near.
The century is ending and my mem'ries cause a tear.
I think of bygone New Years Eves—and happy times we shared.
It seemed that life stretched on and on—no matter what we dared.
But through the years and, one by one, we witnessed Loved Ones leaving.
They took their horns and party hats and left us all here grieving.
They left and found a better band to play their "Auld Lang Syne,"
And where they've gone, their singing goes on 'til the end of time.
Yet I believe those Loved Ones that left us far behind
Are patiently awaiting for our presence—yours and mine.
And one day when our turn has come, we'll join their happy singing,
Where they'll welcome us with open arms with heaven's bells all ringing.
Then what a party we will have, those well-known arms around us;
Safely home together knowing God's Great Love surrounds us.

Vicky Scherck

The Vision

My! Oh, My!
What a sight for my eyes
to see you as I lie
Awake . . .
or asleep . . .
in my dreams.
The vision: so extreme.

Makes me wanna scream,
Thank you, God
for this creation
and this sensation
that stimulates my imagination!

You're such an inspiration.
Never, EVER, exit my view.
I just wouldn't know what to do.
For I'd rather be blind
than to not see you.

John Pope

Midnight Questions

Midnight.
Quiet through the place.
A time for thinking
Dark thoughts,
Brooding on Disasters.
Whoever said, No news is good news,
Is an idiot.
I tie myself in knots.
I try to have faith,
But previous experience on this path
Is experience in failure;
Heartache.
God, where are you?
Why am I so alone?
Why do I have
Such a tremendous capacity for love
And no one with whom I can share?
Love which you can't share becomes pain;
Bitter vinegar from sweet wine.
Trust . . . Trust comes with time.

Neil Flanders

An Innocent Child

An innocent child
So loving and pure,
What terrible hardships
He's had to endure.

Instead of enjoying
His family and peers,
He carries a burden
Too big for his years.

He dreams of Houdini,
Of casting a spell,
If the wave of a wand
Could just make him well!

He still loves wrestling
And working on art,
His sheer love of life
Comes straight from his heart.

So please take a moment
And say a prayer,
To let his family know
Just how much we care!

Joanne Tortorici

Gone

When the sun goes down where will you be?
Somewhere not so very near to me.
The touch of your skin, your breath on my neck
without you around I am a nervous wreck.
Through plenty of up's and some downs . . .
Once again together no more frowns.
Not so serious, do we even really know—
taking it day by day, goin with the flow.
All I can do is think of you, trying to hard for the old to be new.
All that is of me was for you.
Not to be needy, or even sound greedy—
I want you by my side, a hand to hold—shoulder to cry.
Words can never explain nor my love I detain.
You ask and it shall be given.
Whispers echo in a boggled mind—
hoping praying that IT you will find.
No obligations—ball and chains—only yearning desires of love's pains.
Please don't feel threatened or afraid,
if not now it is naturally delayed.
Just know every word spoken is true,
the only pure love is my love for you.

Dawn McKlosky

Ridden

What is it? Nothing said. Nothing heard.
Its canyons with no whistling echoes.
Its beaches with crash-less waves.
Its empty dinners for conversation and music is not heard.
Nothingness. If only you could hear those shadows dancing.
Instead, remains quiet solitude.
A world with sounds—lovely sounds, scary sounds,
abrupt, and flowing sounds, guides our eyes to present happenings. Life. I would like
to hear clearer than my ears would hear.
Feed them with peculiar sounds, sounds that move
to the pounding of the blood and the vacuum in a lonely heart.
Sound sparks emotional responsiveness and physical sensations
that enable us to bring an act to its perfection—without—merely a picture.
In a world full of sounds, talking out of time can result in blocks of confusion.
While reasons for orderly sound are seen, too much order and a lack of chaos and
passion may prove destructive.
Sigh, whisper, utter, talk, yell, or scream. Then listen.
Just listen . . . for quicksilver flashes of noise or a steady beam of sound.
There are times of silence when we choose not to listen.
However, if not chosen . . . it's eerily quiet without the ticking of the clock.
It's living while wishing for death.
It's loneliness that's the killer.

Erin Peters

On the Day after a Fierce Autumn Wind

A tree lies with its roots waving in the gusts.
A mother bird flies frantically trying to find her babies and nest.
A lazy old tomcat licks his lips after finding the lost babies.
A piece of broken lattice lies against the trunk of a tree, broken and out of place.
The flowers of the hollyhock lie strewn across the rain-soaked grass.
A shattered celadon jar, green plastic resin chairs and a red and white checkered
tablecloth all blown from their homes on the patio.
A old dapple gray mare emerges from the doorway of the small tattered shed she
sought shelter in from the harsh bluster.
On this, the day after a fierce autumn wind, a change has occurred. A change that
leads Mother Nature to regret the creation of such an evil spirit.
The sun is now shining, gleaming through the few white fluffy clouds that are drifting
through the blue sky.
The birds are now singing a joyful tune and rebuilding their nests.
The lazy old tomcat is now sleeping underneath
the large pink rhododendron bush in the backyard.
The old dapple gray mare is now munching in the pasture at the fresh green grass.
There are no gusts of wind. There are no drops of rain falling from the sky.
Today there are only the remnants of a fierce autumn wind.

Kandice Niemann

As Time Goes Slowly By

Just a little thought . . .
Just a little smile . . .
The memory of us together
will last for quite a while.
No one else knows
and no one else suspects
The cherished memories we have had
and what we will have next.
So if you see me with a smile
on a gloomy day
I may be thinking sweet thoughts of you
to pass the time away.

Cynthia Wilder

Who Killed My Heart

Who killed my heart,
did you see anything?
Who pulled the trigger,
what good did it bring?
Who killed my heart,
what reasons were there?
To beat it and bash it,
not a piece did they spare.
Who killed my heart,
were any weapons found?
Somebody stabbed it,
until it was lying limp on the ground .
Who killed my heart,
was there a note saying why?
Who tied it up with a rope?
then left it hanging to die?
Who killed my heart,
with a lack of respect?
For someone killed my heart,
yet I have no suspects . . . .

Bryan Wojtylko

Precious Gift

Friendship is a precious gift.
It grows like a flower.
Very small greens at first,
Growing taller each day.

First the bud, tender growing,
Opening the petals more each day.
Until the flower is fully blooming,
Sharing its fragrance in the air.

Friendship time can bloom,
For a day, a month, a year.
Special ones last for years,
Touching our lives, from time to time.

Life goes on and times change,
Friendships fade as flowers do.
Treasured and stored in our memory,
To enjoy and savor each gift.

From this time and forever,
Friendship is a precious gift,
To share and give away,
To others, each and every day.

Karen Talkington

Scared

Dedicated to CJ Alexander, I love you
When I first saw you,
I was scared to know you
When I met you,
I was scared to like you,
Now that I love you,
I'm scared to lose you

Danielle Olesen

For the Love of Him

My love for him is very strong whether it's right, whether it's wrong.
It feels so right to lay my head upon his chest, to feel so much beneath my breast.
For the love of him I'd walk through fire, on wings of love my soul lifts higher.
How can I truly express my complete and utter happiness?
I must love him through the good and bad; the happy and the sad.
From all these things does our love grow and through all, my love must show.
To him I must give my heart, from his side to never part.
When we wound each other with our sharp tongue,
remember the love our hearts have sung.
To be by his side forever and more, is all I aspire; what I live for.
For the love of him.

Michele Hawthorne

Three Days in October

Of Life I have seen man move mountains, and
mountains move men into oblivion; yet my
mind ponders the direction of Creation.

Of Man I have experienced the balance between body and soul united into one;
and yet my mind shies away from the ultimate test of Love.

Of Child I have enjoyed the helplessness of
innocence from infancy to toddlerhood;
and yet I refuse my mind license to experience the bitter-sweet agony of Life created by you.

Rita Baumann

Vision of Love and Hope

Brilliant iridescent golden sunbeams waken the early morn. Waking and walking into
the light the mist of dew vanishes before each step. The coolness of the deep blue
waters of the lake touched by the embracing warmth of the sun causes a thin pale white
fog to lift across its troubled surface. Constantly growing in presence and intensity a
warm southerly breeze brings the sweet smell of pine and wild flowers. It is spring
again! Nature trembles not at each new year full of living beauty and life. Let out hearts
be lifted up by this Vision of Love and Hope.

Greg Safronoff

Dreams

At nights I wander into this unknown world,
where the sky is always crystal blue.
Nothing in this place could ever go wrong,
and I am untouchable to the cold world that stalks my sensitive self in the day.

All of my worries vanish from my lost soul.
And I actually feel content with life.
In my dreams all of my flaws disappear.
And I am perfect for the first time ever.
In my dreams I escape the taunting voices of my so called friends,
and for a brief moment in time my self esteem is as high as the far heavens.

In my dreams all depression is lost forever.
Then in deep regret I unwillingly have to wake up from my personal utopia.
Now I'm back to the world that rejects me,
Longing for night and the return of dreams.

Patrick Bentsen

Daughter

For my daughter Keeley
All my life, I wished and dreamed for things I thought I needed.
Then one day, I sat and prayed for someone to Love.
Minutes turned to days, Days turned to weeks, Weeks turned to months!
With beautiful Love that blossomed like the seed of a Flower,
to a beautiful dove! Then one day, the seed started to grow,
ever so slow. The Love I have found started to show!
The day I have always yearned for has finally come, for me to learn.
While my head was in a swirl, the seed that blossomed is my Little Girl!
"A Daughter," I said, with a smile on my face, as my heart raced!
My wish and dream is now complete; our Daughter is now, in my arms asleep!

Douglas Rose Jr.

The Guest

Death is at my door today
He's knocking
But I won't answer
He'll call on the phone
And I'll pretend not to be home
One day I'll have to invite him in
The Grim Reaper over tea
I'll discuss my future
He'll talk about mortality rates
It won't be pleasant
Especially with such a boring guest

B. F. Wells

The Shadow

There's a man who has a shadow
A reminder of his past,
He has lived within the darkness
Of the image it has cast.
Greeting him each morning,
As his back was to the sun,
The shadow stood in front of him,
The shadow always won.
Then one day he met a woman
Who brought sunshine to his life,
He vowed to lose the shadow,
And make this love his wife.
He turned to face the image
Of his shadow on the ground,
And put the past behind him
As he turned his life around.
The shadow stands behind him,
Now he faces toward the sun.
True love has found its way to him,
This time he knows he's won!

Linda Shows Giles

Wishes?

I wish that love was easy
I wish my life were free
From the past and memories
That keep haunting me
No matter how hard I try
No matter what I do
My fears from what has gone before
Keep troubling my view
I hope to overcome this
I pray to find the strength
To stop these old bad memories
That make me stop and think
Should I do this should I do that
When what I really need
Is just accept that God knows best
And follow where he leads

Robert Kinsey

The Rosebud

The rosebud
so fragile
so new
out on a solitary limb

A rebirth
difficult
needed
around old blooms that are dying

She's growing
with sorrow
through the pain
as the Son warms her each morning

Suzanne Whitlock

Sad Devil Blues

Didn't even have the strength to steal another soul
No desire to drag a kicking carcass to the fire hole
Not a taste for torment inflicting pain was moot
Wasn't even feeling sharp in his red three-tailed suit

Feeling self-indulgent couldn't master that evil grin
This was the worst mood the devil had ever been in
Walking in a sunny park playing melodies on a flute
With the strangest desire to cuddle something cute

A broken hearted devil with the sad devil blues
Had a stick of dynamite but couldn't light the fuse
Picking pretty flowers and making people smile
Total lack of enthusiasm for puttin' sinners on trial

Could not inspire hate or stir up mass dissension
Unable to call demons from their alternate dimension
No taste for deep fried eyeballs or barbecued fingers
Humming along to the tune of a blonde hair street singer

   Robert N. Wormington

Art Is Dead

Art is dead, as is everything else in the world.
I don't know whether to accept it,
or blow my brains onto the pavement.
I am being fed all this corporate bulls***,
and we all feed on this.
What the hell is happening to me?
I am going crazy.
Art is now anything but art,
It's mostly just business and cash.
Why, oh, why am I living in this world of computerization?

   Jason Orr

Sweet Dream

My love, I shall wait for your return.
For the tenderness of thine moistened lips, I yearn,

to hold thy stiffened sculpted chest,
against my swollen, supple breast.

No matter the distance or how long it may take,
Tis I whom loves thee, I will not forsake.

Our love is more than the appearance of skin,
It is of that we are within.

The love of which we share tis truly very rare.
Our hearts are not poisoned with despair.

Sleep tight till we meet again,
I wish you a sweet dream.

The wait is forever or so it may seem.

But, my love, I will see you in mine this night,
For the thought of your love will keep me warm tonight.

   Tina M. Moore

Who Am I?

I choose not to be the same as others.
Please don't categorize me as a preppy, a loner, a rebel, a pigeon,
a b*tch, a teachers pet, a playette, a gangsta, a freak,
or whatever the names the cliques have.
What I am is my own person.
I choose to go by the rules,
but I sometimes bend them a little.
I choose to ignore the latest fashions and dress my own way.
I like to be original and go beyond my limits to amaze people.
I tend not to wear a lot of makeup because my beauty shines inside.
I want to help anyone out when they are in trouble.
I believe in the quote "A dream is a wish your heart makes".
I don't depend on men to make me happy.
My independence is my strength.
Sure once in a while I crave a boyfriend but who doesn't?
My heart is my light of my life shining bright with hopes
and being proud of my unique self.

   Peta Cooper

I Don't Have a Uterus

I don't have an uterus.
My husband likes
Me
Not.

He enjoys doing it
But
Likes me not for I can't make him a father.

Doctors say, "Genetic disorder."
Old people at home cry, "Sin."
 A seer says, "All due to karma."

I am not Draupadi, that I'll have Krishna at my beck and call.
I have prayed enough.

Now it is time to say just once, "Mother please come into my home,
into my heart and give me the strength to say,

I don't have an uterus."

   Sudipto Bhattacharya

Seize the Moment

Quietly, the sun set upon the ocean.
A cool breeze swept a patch of sand onto her feet.
Painfully, his burning eyes watched from afar as he searched for
the words to speak.
They had to be perfect, you see. he could not fail twice.

Gathering all his thoughts and courage, he slowly approached.
Seemingly happy to see him, they shared a friendly smile.
While at ease for the moment, it hit him.
He would simply say, he loved her.

Instead of caution, he grabbed her arms,
spoke those three words, and firmly kissed her lips.
Resisting only for a moment, she returned his plea.
They fell to the sand like weary heads to a pillow.
What took them so long? Why had they denied their passion?

Waves crashed against the rocks. The ocean began to roar.
The ebb could not hold back any longer.
Swells climbed to the sky.

Up, Up, Up

Until they caught the clouds, caught the sun.
Until they cam tumbling down, their crests foaming white.
And just as the ocean was about to creep up onto the beach, all
went silent.
exhausted waves sighed with content.

The tide drew back. A soft breeze cooled the air.
She looked up at him and whispered the same three words.
Quietly, the sun rose. warming a new day.

   Lisa Panarello

I Could Not See the Love for the Tease

Moist lips and swivel hips are the seducer's
Desires or possessions
Suggestive attire and burning desire are the seducer's concessions
Magnetic like lure and a heart that's all pure are qualities most
often sought after
Enhanced with a mind, equipped—well equipped, capable of
spontaneous laughter
How could I have missed your subtle advances—that magical
spark that fuels hot romances
Seducer come find the one who is blind to your persistent
pursuit of passion . . .
For I too am in quest and it's a revolution at best that you are
the one I am seeking
I am aware of your presence; not knowing your presents . . .
For I could not see the love for the tease . . .
No, I could not see the love for the tease

   Lynne Moyer

Tormenting Yourself

All the things they're telling you is bullsh*t
Lies trying to run your perfect life
Don't believe in them
Believe in nothing you learn.
All they want is to get by,
They're getting their kicks from your misery.
They are truly laughing at you
Trying to bruise the world
Making pain for others
They hate each other, so they take it out on us.
They make you toke, you quit believing in yourself.
Your new faith is them and their tortured souls.
Forgive yourself if you can
But you've know crossed the line, between good and evil
And only death is left.
Stab yourself, butcher yourself
Kill yourself, sacrifice yourself.
Then you will become free
But for now you must live
And that is torture enough.

Jessica Beaulieu

The Race

Will he remember his true love's face
or does he see a wh*re taking her place?
Can he conquer the demons in his mind?
Will he ever see that he is blind;
finding only hatred, scorn, distrust.
Needing simply lust
to fill his plate.
Angered eyes which degrade, berate
the truth of her soul.
Pushing her into a silent hole.
Snatching every being of her true soul.
Scratching at the walls
she didn't build.
Bearing the fists
she'll never wield.
Running, crashing against the door.
Seeing no one; wanting more.
Blood gushing down his face
winning this demon race.

Elaine Evans

I Cried a Smile

I thought of you today and I smiled
I smiled a smile that could melt
the ice-capped mountains,
and send the cool water trickling down
into the valleys to feed the thirsty flowers.
I felt the warmth, as I smiled.
The warmth that a baby feels
as he suckles his mother's breast.
The warmth of Love, the warmth that I find in your arms.
Yet, those arms were not here to hold me.
So my smile was swept away by hot, salty tears.
The tears fell like night rains,
sent from the heavens to destroy evil.
I faltered and was pulled under. I sought to be free.
To drown in that ocean of tears and be free
of that love that binds us. The love that enslaves me
and tortures me. Finally, death came to deliver me,
but instead of passing into eternity, I was thrust back into reality.
he reality of my inescapable love for you.
I thought of you today, and I cried.

Nathelia Davenport-Weston

Cosmic Connection

Do you feel me when I touch you
Can you see my loving hands
Can you feel me if I stroke you
Lovingly I take your hand
I go within your heart
And glide through your whole being
It feels so calm and peaceful; a safe haven of serene
I feel you enter me, a warm and glowing touch
How could I deny you
When I know you're in my heart
It seems so very sudden but evidently clear
That it's a cosmic connection
We should hold so very dear
I could travel far and wide looking for that perfect place
And never would I find
Another feeling of such grace
My home is in your heart; next to you I plan to stay
Cosmically connected forever and a day

Christine Pedersen

Early Morning Ride

It started as just fun but your heart was like the sun,
Burning your mark on my soul, stay tonight please don't go.
I tried to keep my space but somehow you won that race,
Like the turtle and the hare, you are smart and that is rare.
Come out from under that shell
Make me scream tonight and yell
Take me up high, push me over the edge
I'll do the same for you boy you have my pledge
Dreams are forever shattered as we search our lives get tattered
But you always stay so true and in my mind that's incredibly cool
Unspoken words don't have to be said,
Your eyes are a book waiting to be read.
I read your pages between the lines,
True wisdom comes from the reflection of time.
You glow like a ray of light on a moonlit ocean night,
Glistening off the cool dark water I start to get hotter and hotter.
As I pass through hell to get to Heaven
I will not forget cancer month of seven.
The times we had the times we shared
Give me the courage to see no fear.

Deborah Au

Examiner

Buildings burn, people die,
I must say that this is not a lie.
She ran away to be by his side,
But left when she began to cry.
He of course was sly,
Took her by the waist and said you're mine.
Screaming and yelling she lost her shine,
Glitter princess was laid out as wine.
Sprawled in all directions,
Her arms and legs were placed in sections.
If it was not for him to have intentions,
Sweet little baby girl would not have been a dissection.

Jodie Sweet

The Prostitute

My heart goes where my body goes; I can make no exception.
I just do what I have to do; I can have no affection.
If the John pays the price, I'm his for the hour.
If my heart feels a thing, I just take a shower.

If my heart seems too cold, I don't give a damn;
As long as I get my pay, I belong to any man;
If he falls in love with me, I'm good at my profession;
He can love me all he wants, I gain from his obsession.

My heart went where my body went, I could make no exception;
I just did what I had to do; now I have no affection.
No one wants my body now, for I am old and gray;
My heart is young, my body's old; a parting of the ways.

J. Carlton Hall

Taking out the Trash

It's finally time for me take out the trash,
but this bag is much heavier then the ones in the past.
I filled it full of the garbage that makes me ill,
and tied a rubber band around its neck so it won't spill.
I surveyed my house just to make sure I got it all,
then began to walk towards the trash can stall.
I stood there for just a moment to survey the scene,
me standing with this bag, I swear I heard it scream.
I know I might just be lost without some of this sh*t,
but God knows it's time for me to sail on a new ship.
So I lifted the lid of that big old cold steel can,
and threw my bag of bones in.

Deborah Kravchak

My Sweet Angel

You can call me smack, heroin, or crack,
But I call you my sweet angel.
I spike my veins with your bitter tenderness,
Blood surging outward as I wait with hurried anticipation
To fill myself with your extacsy,
Releasing myself temporarily,
losing myself in your orgasmic multitudes,
My sweet, sweet angel.
You ravishingly suck out my precious life
Replacing it with transitory exhilaration,
Lifting me to the pinnacle of human existence
Until there's nowhere to fall but down.
Bulging blood-shot eyes, trembling, uncontrollable cold sweats,
Constipation, hallucination, desolation, isolation,
Despair.
Please don't desert me
My sweet angel.
Just one last hit.
My Sweet Angel.

Lauren Becker

A Moment to Forget

I heard his cries, I cannot go
It's so damn hot, there's nowhere to go
He cries again
I lose control, over the wall I go
Running to him, yet time is in slow mo
With feet the ground seems not to touch
At last I'm there
He's in my arms, his blood is everywhere
I feel not his weight as to them I run
I hear the noise, I feel the sting
It hurts like hell, but I'm almost there
They take him from my arms
I plead, Please Lord don't let him die
But now he's just a name upon "that" wall
In the Nation's Capital, on the mall
Where part of me will always be

Edward Emanuel

Love Slave

when you awake, breakfast awaits you
brought to you on a platter
followed by a tub full of bubbles—me
bathe you, of course—it doesn't matter,
I'd help you get dressed, assist you in
color selection, and style
put the toothpaste on your brush, just to
see your lovely smile
later when coming home from work, school
or play—you know a massage your body gets
pleasing you would be my main priority,
I'd serve you with no regrets,
in my eyes there is no other woman, not
today, tomorrow, or 'til my grave
as long as I can be with you, is how long
I'd be your slave

Vinsin Fletcher

Eggs

—How would you like your eggs, she said.
—Over-easy, he replied, and put a bullet through her head.

Jarle Haktorson

Honey

He reminds me of honey—
Slow moving and sweet.
His actions ooze over me
Coating my every thought and emotion.
He comes to me in a soothing manner.
Something about him comforts me
And drenches my soul with
His sugary goodness.
I can scarcely breathe
From his smothering wonderful actions.
His amber-colored gelatinous muck
Seeps into my skin
Leaving traces of him all through me.
And it's gotten to the point where
His honey flows through my veins instead of blood.
And all day long—
And especially in the night—
I long—ache—to be drenched
In his miraculously soothing honey
All over again.

Olivia Starnes

The Meadow

Sitting alone in the meadow,
Breathing the fresh air,
Remembering now all the sorrow.
Concerning the journey from here to there.
Incapacitating darkness.
Seeking with all my might,
Quietly creeping through the harshness,
That's causing the terror fright.
Suddenly stumbling through wood and briar,
Catching on my clothes.
I've got to stand instead of run from my fearsome foes.
The battles on but not quite done, his bloody neck exposed.
Slashing with greed, the honor I seized when I took his head.
Proclaiming him to my God, now he's finally dead.
No longer will I have to run to keep myself alive.
Laughing, celebrating, and rejoicing
The eternal spirit of life.

Vanessa Bryant

The Developer

Hello my friend the burning spire
High upon the hill
Black clouds of smoke billow forth
Testament to my will

With blood and bile I gave you shape
From nature wild and raw
And if your birth demands my first born son
His grave will greet the thaw

Within thy walls reshape the Earth
Turn great piston and rod
Industry the new commandment
Behold I am man become God

So march to Hell wife and child
And work 'til all is done
For thy blood will create Heaven
Your soot stained face will see the dawn

Some men would choose to free the world
Some to sail the seas
I will chain my mother to the furnace and feed her my disease

Steven Gajadhar

why i don't like the "nice" guys

visions of mandatory politeness
over a bowl of soggy bran flakes while
talking about the weather
—the kids our next vacation—
that damn mini-van—and—the trivial trials
of existing in this existence
of this so-called ideal americana picket fence
2.2 children ludicrous dream of bull-sh*t
flash through the eye of my mind every time i think
of that "thing" that is you and i
way too comfortable to break apart from
remaining in the remainingness of the
lucid lukewarmivity that our life together has thus far been
mandatory politeness
over a bowl of soggy bran flakes
is not how i want my life to end.
therefore, my friend exit stage right—
get out of my sight—
i'm not goin' let you win

Kindra Wood

(In)sanity?

All around the world is clear,
It all makes sense, so raise an ear.
Listen to my words you little ewe,
Is the straight jacket on me, or you?

I understand you, can you say the same?
Eyes made shut, and your brain is lame,
We're all bugs in a field,
but my field's not the same.

Live, and breathe; die, and choke,
Do you really kill the whales for their blubber?
Waste your last breath on that faithful toke,
Are these walls made of plaster or rubber?

Michael Skinner

REALITY

REALITY is all around me; I sometimes refuse to see.
REALITY comes when I'm in the middle of dreaming;
when my mind is full of fantasy and my eyes are beaming.
REALITY stirs up confusion; when my mind is in illusion
REALITY has a way of disturbing my thought; my thinking gets
fragile, that, I don't want
REALITY can be nice and give me a second chance;
It could be my life or a romance
REALITY has no name, no time, date nor year;
this is why my hopes and dreams are always in fear.
REALITY has no face;
so it's very hard to embrace.
REALITY arrives and departs so swift;
this is why REALITY can be a b*tch.

Michelle Ingram

The Final Lover

She rises out of the dark abyss with beauty and grace.
She sucks my blood as I try and crown her with a bouquet of roses.
My sight begins to flee, as I look upon her brow
now decorated with red beads.
When one truly loves, one dies for the entity
which has grasped one's heart.
My love has hurt her, but still she does not leave me.
My one desire is to remain in her hold eternally,
as my heart utters its last beat.
She drops my body on the soft ground,
and takes my essence with her in the dark deep hole.
I feel warm, as if I have returned to my home.
The darkness of her womb is comforting,
I finally find peace as I lay in this tomb.

Ramon Matias

Oblivious Jackal

The jazz band blares their tunes,
and the jackal opens its ears.
The drug lord has his morning joint,
and the jackal inhales, and starts to point.
The media reports live on the murder scene,
and the jackal sighs, and sighs.
The TV views Judge Judy
as she expresses her senile views,
showing that she has way too much power,
and the jackal rolls its eyes.
KKK burns their crosses and causes cries,
and the jackal can't help but to despise.
Bills pile up like rocks,
and this sends the jackal chills down its spine.
The addict forces down horse pills,
and the jackal shakes its head.
Sooner or later the jackal considers suicide,
but then it would miss out on techno
or the latest episode of "Bonnie and Clyde."
Soon its mind creates its own little world
and zones out all its problems,
just like oblivion, a step up from suicide.

Nick Yates

I Don't Understand

I don't understand why you always make me cry
You always say: "I hope you die!"
You slap me around and beat me to the ground.
I don't understand why you think it's okay
to cheat on me and beat on me.
I don't understand—you accuse me,
abuse me, use me, and bruise me.
I'd like it if you treated me with tender love and care.
I don't think it's fair. I'm sitting here cold
dressed in torn up rags. I'd rather
choose them than those used garbage bags.
I still don't understand why
you cheat on me and beat on me.
I don't understand why
you accuse, abuse, use me, and bruise me.
If you're wondering, this is how you lose me . . .

Michele Oswald

In a County Jail

Draped in a robe of satin femininity
Mace stains my face; can not breathe
Like backdraft of fire, my body burns; gasp for air
Hands embraced by cuffs; cuts at my wrist
Someone must be turning up the heat

Locked in a dark four room cell
Feet secured in shackles; bruises my ankles
All my possessions taken away
No sense of time, waiting for bail
Thinking of Martin in a Birmingham jail

Bull Conner faces; southern fingers point and stare
Laughter and remarks about niggers
Like I wasn't even there
So helpless and angry; that I wanted to shout
But . . . never worried for a second;
Mama would get me out

I heard cymbals clash, rhythmic beat of the drum
Marching in protest; dancing in the street
We shall overcome; we shall overcome

Angela Coburn

Your Father in Me

You call me n*gg*r.
I call you lady.
I smile and say hello.
You frown and spit.
I say ma'am softly.
You yell coon at the top of your lungs.
I call you Miss and see you as a woman.
You call me Boy and see me as one.
You don't know me, yet you hate me.
I don't know you, but I love you.
You see my outside and view an animal.
I look inside you and see my mother.
Now why can't you see your father in me?

Jeffrey Gurul, Jr.

Invitation to Phone Sex

I want to touch you
Long-distance, yet very close
Very personal
I want to caress you with my voice
Soft, warm words
Verbal kisses in tender places
Hot breath on the back of your neck
Down the middle of your spine
Behind your knee
Wet, warm, moist words
Touching your inner thigh
Working wet wonders
In wicked places
And it all begins
With one word
Yes
Just say the word

KC Carson

I Go Blank

Inferiorness
Unjustified feelings
I don't belong
In a world too smart for me
An uncontrollable urge
A piercing feeling
I watch my life drain
From the ravines forced into my wrists
I go blank

A hazy feeling
My life's a big swirl
I look from under my heavy eyelids
I take one last look at the life I had
I go blank

I open my eyes barely an inch
I look around, but all I see is black
I go blank

Bel Bekkers

Almost, Juliette

Juliette . . .
Not whole . . .
I am tantalized
by the succulence
of your flesh
which I cannot
devour . . . whole
It's the thought that counts
against me

M. Ealy

The End . . .

Take this life away from me
I try to die but don't suceed
I'll try again on a later day
but for now I'll just play
along with what the people say
this life is so far lost it will
never come back

depressed and lost in this life
I bring my wrist twards the knife
and siliently await my judgement day

I am so wittled now
my life is just a wasted tale
and now six feet underground
it starts to fail
give this life back to me
I am no longer there to see
how living truly was to be to see

Greg Chase

Rhythms of Pain

Chopped off hands
Hacked feet
Smashed heads
Butchered pregnancies
Rhythms of Pain

Bullet in the skull
Bullet in the eye
Bullet in the stomach
Bullet in the foot
Rhythms of Pain

Ashes of flesh and bones
Young and Old
Men and Women
In their own Homes
Rhythms of Pain

Butchering rebels
Burnt the Shrine of Innocence
Tore the flood gates of Mayhem
Now only Rhythms of Pain
May we dance to.

Sheikh Kamarah

Abortion

Mom, Dad, I'm sorry.
I love him.
There is nothing
you could say to change
my mind.
You want me to destroy
a living part of me.
He would never forgive me
if I did.
I couldn't live with myself
if I did, so . . . I won't.
Daddy,
don't worry.
Your little baby
won't disgrace the
FAMILY NAME.
Mommy,
I just want you to know,
as this bullet enters my brain,
there will be no more pain.
FOREVER.

Stacie Giese

Untitled

I feel your fear
seep through the ground.
I stand and watch
as you look round.
Into my labyrinth you roam,
into the black of night unknown.
You know not
what awaits you here.
You hurry on
despite your fear.
I summon my courage
and turn away.
I kneel on the ground
and try to pray.
With shame I rise
in a frenzied state.
I bite your neck,
sealing your fate.
Drinking my blood, you find desire.
As you realize now, I am your Sire.

Becky Tasker

The Evening

It was the evening
The windows were streaming
I kissed your soft lips
As you caressed my hips
I was there for good
That you understood
I am shy
That is not a lie
I felt so close
With you the most
I didn't want to go all the way
And you said that was okay
I slept with you
So quietly, all night through
That is the sweetest thing I have ever done
Aren't you glad you were the one
Maybe you don't even see
The something in me

Kirsten Sargent

Please Hold

Are we dying fish, swimming
Naked in the pool of blood,
Fished by the doctors and lawyers
In straw hats and brass foil polls,
Judging, waiting, selling, pushing
Unknown drugs and satellites?

Put me on hold,
Freeze my tired, rejected frame, and
Pour your pink chemicals and
Computer programs down my
Swollen whore throat.

I am addicted to your lies,
Your magical cure, your money
Making placebo death; still, this
Yellow-red toilet bowl fluid I
Hand you in a cup, never is resolved,
Never goes away drunk and content.

Jason Behrends

Love of Life

Love of Life is waking up each day to a new day.
Love of Life is to see the sun rise and shine each day.
Love of Life is fixing a hot beverage each day.
Love of Life is opening my blinds and seeing the rain, sleet, snow and the sun this day.
Love is Life is to choose an attire for my daily wear this day.
Love of Life is to meet my co-workers each day knowing we come to fulfill a day.
Love of Life is completing difficult tasks this day.
Love of Life is celebrating joys, wiping tears and creating a smile a day.
Love of Life is maintenance on the physical, emotional, spiritual
and mental abuse that is caused every day.
Love of Life is doing my best each day.
Love of Life is sharing and caring every day.
Love of Life is giving all day every day.
Love of Life is tackling what we don't understand all day.
Love of Life is thanking God at the close of the day for another day.
Love of Life is knowing no matter what, where or when,
God is there every day.

Ruby Black

Gravity

Kiss the atmosphere that surrounds your
Planets fertile soiled surface and pull my probed loyalty to your spacious landing ground.
I'll hold your species under watchful eyes with rent-a-cop security and access your
paroled vacation time when seasons roll around.

Joshua Hudson

Day's Journey

The day begins . . . traveling east:
At long last, the colors of sunrise extend themselves,
Fingers of pastels, over the horizon.
There I find the blue of your eyes, the peach of your skin,
the pink warmth of your heart.

Journey continues, turning north . . .
Clouds, fluffy white are floating in the sky;
There . . . in one I see your face smiling, watching.
I watch you float by on your heavenly perch,
The cloud as free as your sweet spirit.

Journey continues, turning south . . .
As afternoon encroaches on morning's cool delights,
Waves of heat rise from the land . . .
Waves that reflect the warmth of your smile, your hands,
your laughter, your heart.

Journey turns west . . . end of the day.
Once again, colors extend themselves, fingers of brilliant color.
The glory of sunset, the momentary death of light.
Days end; a time for rest, repose, reflection . . . into these you walk.
Through my mind, my heart you walk silently . . . beautiful.
You slip into my dreams and there we linger together . . .
Until the journey turns east . . . again.

Ronald Hanner

Nature's Gift to Remember You

I stand all alone remembering how you made me feel when you were still here.
I am given reminders every day of the kind of person you were.
The sun slips out from behind a cloud
reminding me of your shy, playful smile and the warmth of your heart.

As the breeze flows around me, I sense your embrace.
Caressing my hair, my skin, wiping my tears I can no longer hold in.
The clouds gather to begin the orchestration of my loss.
Rain effortlessly falls taking the place of my tears.
Pouring over everything I once knew to cleanse all of my pain.

The breeze turns to blustery wind trying to lift me to the heavens.
If only I could be with you again, but not this way.
May nature take its gentle course.
Together again we will be . . . some day.

Margarett Gonzalez

To My Buddy

A buddy, someone true and strong,
Who helps when life is hard and long.
A hug and kiss upon my cheek,
He picks me up when I am weak.

A buddy, friends who never stray,
But stick together just like clay.
Who share the good and share the bad,
And share their tears when they are sad.

My buddy, yes my little son,
You bring me joy by the ton.
You have my heart, you have my pride,
You make me happy all inside.

May life be sweet and treat you right,
May angels watch o'er you at night.
And may you always share your heart
With those who gave you life to start.

Leo Spencer

Take Control

I'm standing on the edge . . .
Ready to jump,
Ready to die,
Ready to live for You,
and only You.
I've always tried to
work things out for myself
Never letting You take control
like You do.
I give You my problems,
my heart, my soul, my mind.
Take Control.
Do a better job than I could ever do.

Laura Paige-Wright

Possession

Behind a bubble of disassociate bliss
I nurture the possession
That began yesterday;
When I was reborn.
Noise. Fear. Consumption.
It is all I can do not to notice you
Curling. Coiling
In my furnished womb
(Such a perfect hiding place)
Not too near to my heart.
I close my eyes and taste the rain
Surrounded by darkness, I taste the wet
Cleansing. Refreshing.
Dirt soars from my anxious pores.
The sky is an antiseptic
Beneath which I swirl and entwine
My fate with yours.
Time stops, life pauses,
I carry a passenger, a curse,
A divine.

Hannagh Gilbert

The Human Story

with time has come the erosion
fragile pages of the mind disappear
could be the movies or busy lives
silenced hearts from noise-filled ears
we give ode to the artists
the sirens who sing the songs
but do we hear what they are saying
the human story is lost and gone
we find pieces of it here and there
discovering bits of love, joy and pain
but we must realize there is an author
to ever behold the story again

Michael Black

Watch Me Bleed

Come, my brother, enter herein—enter my life.
You wanted to know. You wanted to see. Come taste my strife.

You speak of peace so easily—not knowing my war—not feeling my pain.
Your "justice for all" is only "justice for few" while the guilty remain.

You want us to put our weapons down, while their weapons persist.
For you-easy talk. For you—food, family and freedom exist.

It might make you feel good to speak out on aggression and say that you care.
But that does not give you license to make my decisions while I am not there.

You set up your conferences to "educate others" on our situation.
Yet, you pick your own speakers to represent us while we lose our nation.

You say you are with us and convince all around you it is peace that you seek.
You say you will listen. You say you will hear us, but you won't let us speak.

And you with the peace signs, organizing your marches, please only yourselves.
You think your good thoughts can alone change the world like your signs on the shelves.

You must face reality. You think it is simple—it simply is not.
Reality is watching your land taken away and your relatives shot.

Two fingers up does not stop a bullet and make everything right.
Righteous indignation does you no good if you won't see the light.

You ask lots of questions, but won't hear our answers about what we need.
The only thing left is for me to invite you to come watch me bleed . . .

    Lamyaa Hashim

Past Sins

You, wretched of the Earth
How can you be my brother?
You who corral your own people
Sticking them into stench infested camps
Exporting they whom you do not trust
Innocent, but to you guilty by birth
You my brother, you have given into evil
You have given into fear and ignorance
You have given into prejudice
Stop.
Listen and know
Know now for later you will not have the opportunity to learn
You will not have the time or patience. You my brother,
Listen. Listen now in times of peace. You my brother,
Remember. Remember what you learn now, in time of war
Remember even when you cry out in such pain that you do not want to know the truth
Remember the truth. Do not give into fear. Do not give into prejudice.
You my brother, you are strong
You are my brother

    Anthony Cardenuto

In a Lifetime . . .

In a lifetime you will meet lots of people
But only a few will stick around.

In a lifetime you may not make all the right decisions

But you have nothing to prove to anyone but yourself

In a lifetime you will cry more then you smile

But that doesn't mean you're not happy

In a lifetime you will spend more time thinking of what you should've said

But never did

In a lifetime there is so much you can do
But only you can make it happen

    Stacy Traktman

My Fire

The wind is really cold outside,
but the room is warm within;
the sky is dark, no clouds in sight
the room light is so dim.

The flames that flicker warm me so
as the crackling fire burns,
memories come flooding in
as my heart with feelings churns.

My heart was as cold as it is outside,
but now it's warm aglow
for I have your love inside,
I'm sure this you already know.

I was like an unlit fire
cold, and all gone out,
but you set me heart on fire
of this there is no doubt.

So when it's chilly and cold outside,
and freezing winds should blow,
I'll have warm coals and burning embers
of your love that's warm aglow.

    Cherryl Dent

The Unknown

Thanksss . . .
He whispers to someone in her
dreams
voices echoing
echoing
across the sands of reality
to reach me.
I smile, in peace
and in pieces because of her
I love him.
Lust can alter consciousness.

    Melanie Wilcox

have you ever

have you ever loved,
a love that tingles your toes
a love that steals you heart,
have you ever loved?

have you ever laughed,
a laugh that hurts
a laugh that captures your soul,
have you ever laughed?

have you ever been kissed,
a kiss that proclaims
a kiss that touches your heart,
have you ever been kissed?

    Erika Doehring

The Hatteras Light

The tall brick tower
with candy-cane black, white stripes
incandescent light

fierce choppy waves hit the shore
boats following light to land

    Heather Villella

Old Lace

In the darkness I could see your face
I ran my fingers over you as gently as if you were fragile, old lace.

We were buried beneath the covers
afraid to admit that our life together was over.

The children were grown and gone.
We had nothing in common but rings.

I quietly moved the quilt and crawled out of bed.
The vows for better or worse ringing in my head.

Today I admitted, my marriage was dead.

Cheryl Schroeder

What Joey's Love Means to Me

There are not enough days to express what Joey's love means to me,
Not enough actions or words could express the love I have found in him.
His love keeps me going, bringing smiles to my face.
Knowing the love he holds inside for me makes the world a much brighter place.
When our souls were searching, the journey at its end, a new love I have found in him stronger than all the rest.
We touch and feel each moment the love growing ever stronger. His love shows not by words but by the thoughtful things he does.
This connection of love that we've found, being apart of each other's lives is more than I could ever want.

Danielle Franco

My Special Friend

Sometimes you find someone that just catches your attention.

The more you study this person, the more you realize they are connected to you. When your eyes meet they see beyond the exterior walls into the inner soul. This person seems to already be a part of you somehow and you of them.

Vibrations, mental thoughts, all the non-verbal communications tell you it's a special person. Someone you can relate to, connect with, Someone that can full-fill your desires. As you pass each other, you can feel the heat and attraction, pulling us like magnets. You have other promises and commitments, yet you question their purpose.

You would have been perfectly content not to meet this person;
It would have made life easier not knowing and feeling this fatal attraction, Yet, somehow it has given you such a great gift to know that someone cares.

You question your morals, judgment, and your purpose in life.
But when you are near, all the questions turn to answers and a feeling of destiny and fate. You feel: scared, afraid, happy, joyful, sensuous, yet in love with the whirlwind.
You don't know where it's going, but you are sure the ride is for real.

Be not afraid, for I am the light in your darkness, I am the whisper in the trees, I am the babbling brook laughing and playing at your feet, I am the sunshine on your face. If nothing else . . . I am your friend . . .

C J Brickner

Neverland

Help, as I lay sleeping, weeping the dreams to whimper.
Know the clouds drift to waft, leaping at the sojourned.
Grace unnerved by sudden jerking, peeling the mind from its conscious state.
Refrain from pinching, douse the flames of cognition with unwavering courage.
Engorge yourself with bliss, know that time away from real, is truly time for all.
Exeunt to feel, fly to enriched cobwebs of milky haze.

Spy the crevice?

Walk to fall down the spiral path of recognition.

Wake up.

Joshua McCarty

A Riddle

So often lost, so often found,
So often spent, so often saved,
So often forgotten,
So often remembered.
What is it
That has its extreme opposites
Met so often
Though it began only once
And has yet
To meet its conclusion?
Whether lost in daydreams,
Or found for the children,
Or spent with a loved one,
Or saved taking the short cut,
Forgotten on a special day,
Remembered in a special way
Standing still patiently
Waiting for no one . . . .

Curt Robotham

Heart of Darkness, Heart of Sun

Heart of darkness
Heart of sun
By you my life was overcome
You took the shadows from my heart
And gave my life a brand new start

Soul of thunder
Soul of rain
You took from me all of my pain
Never would I have to live alone
A prisoner behind walls of stone

Frown of sadness
Smile of cheer
You wiped away all my tears
No need have I to fear the night
I have your love, my guiding light.

Roberto Ortiz

Serengeti

To all creatures that deserve freedom
My Africa

I am your offspring

The wind blows me the scents
Of your children

The cape buffalo, wildebeest
Giraffe and gazelle
Roam through your hair

My eyes are your reflections

The Serengeti plain blooms in colors
From the seeds of your beginnings

The sun brings life
As it parches your golden skin

We your children wait for your tears
To fall on our faces

So that we might sustain ourselves
For one more beat of your heart

My Africa

John Ballou

Mirror

My fetch before me—oracle,
Question I ask—rhetorical . . .
Must break the gaze,
Lest I be consumed—
Ouroboros.

W. Brad Robinson

Childhood

A boy stands nose in the corner.
He turns around and faces his father.
His father has put him there for hitting his brother and telling him to "Shut up"
He begins to explain but is told to shut up, and shoved back into the corner
by hands nearly the size of his torso.

She rushes her children out of the house,
avoiding another rage her husband might have.
She hugs and kisses the pain away,
and picks up the remains of their telephone that he threw at her.
When she does finally escape to work,
she reports a family with abused children.
In a few weeks she will counsel the abused family
after she helps get the abuser locked away.

His words slur together, eyes blood shot.
Blood dried on his lips and nose, the result of a brawl.
The message of his speech; alcohol will get you nowhere.

I have seen physical, mental and verbal abuse.
I have experienced physical, mental and verbal abuse.
I have seen depression. I have seen depression to a level of drug dependency.
I have seen the effect of drugs.
All these horrors I have seen without leaving home.
I am sixteen.

Jessica Rockwell

Bowker Creek

Bowker Creek is a beautiful sight to see.
Especially when it's flowing fast and clean.
When in spring, the dams are put in,
so the ducks can pair up and do their thing.
Then lo and behold the little ducklings
appeared, with their mommas and poppas to
watch over them with tolerance and fear.
When the dams are put in and the water runs
slow, the garbage piles up and hinders the flow.
our youths have to learn to deposit their
waste in the many receptacles that are in place.
I guess it's easier to throw it into the
creek than to walk to the can an extra twenty feet,
Then a group of students turned up to clean, the junk from the creek.
was a sight to be seen .
Now we can enjoy this beautiful creek and watch the ducklings as they sleep.

Josephine Mcintosh

Take Another Look

Look around you wherever you are
Are you seeing what I am
Or are you seeing what they want you to see

I see a country and a world
That is falling apart at the seams
And thinks it can do whatever it wants

People today are willing to do anything it takes
To get what they want
Even to go as far as to kill the person beside them

No one trusts anyone, anymore
True friends are becoming a thing of the past
Because people will betray others for self-benefit

It seems like every other month
You hear of a teenager and lately grade school kids
Shooting each other because of race, popularity, or what they believe in

Just about every day
I hear something, somewhere
And I am amazed; I didn't think things could get any worse but they always do

So do you see what I see? Don't you think it is time for a change?
If not, then please take another look around.

Jerry Slone

Free Doom!

NOW!
Now, AGAIN!!
Again, I SAY!

FREE ME!
Free me again.
again, I say . . .
please . . . ?

Samuel Gross, Jr.

Meta-Me

Red heat splashing down
 into darkness
Tiny specks—fragile and new
 growing out of the dirt
Such a glow of red orange light
 I see it clearly
Shades of all colors joined together
 Like a unified rainbow
The pressure felt upon me is unbearable
 The heat that surrounds me
changes my look of disfigured specks
 and mixes my internal structure
 The energy I posses
 has been sent down upon me
 from Mother Nature's many elements
 Where I come from is like no other
 My world is never the same
 I can be anything
 Me today or someone else tomorrow

I am a rock
I am metamorphic

Dara Fulton

Together

Written for: Jonathon C. Peyatt
Together we rise
Together we fall
Together we stand
Together we are . . .
No mountain to high
No amount of time to long
Together we're right
Together we're wrong . . .
Together we laugh
Together we cry
Together we live
Together we shall die . . .
Together Forever
All Eternity . . .

Jamie Peyatt

You and Me

To look in our eyes,
To touch your skin,
It makes me grin.
To hold you close,
To touch your hair,
It make's me care.
To hear you laugh,
To see you cry,
It makes me sigh.
To see you grow,
To watch you go,
It makes me grin,
It makes me care,
It makes me sigh,
Then when your gone,
It makes me cry.

Sally J. West

A Fire Slowly Dies

Roses, yellow and red dance upon the water,
Like the fire that burns within your eyes.
I watch you from a far as your love, able to
heal the greatest wounds and fill the deepest sorrow,
Is given to another.
I watch the happiness in your life bring sadness and happiness,
Bittersweet emotions to my own.
You are an Angel who has kept my head above the raging tide of my depression.
Whose wings have kept me dry from the tears that fall in my empty life.
You are my friend, a true and dear friend;
something to be treasured.
And I am happy. Yet, at the same time I am sad.
For I wonder what could have been, what can never be.
And as my tears fall silently inward slowly extinguishing the fire
You can hear the echoes of my laughter deep within the emptiness of my soul.

John Adams

flames

if blood could flow from anger
mine would be flowing like a fountain

a crimson red

steaming with relentless torture and pain
it would boil and burn
all
the
words

all the words that escape from your foul mouth
all the words that snatch my smile and pull it down with a heavy, unstoppable force

they would burn in a fiery bliss

while I laughed scornfully
as the fire nips at your tongue

and you disintegrate from your own bloody words

and fall to ashes

then I would pick you up
and sweep you away,
far
away

Jaymie Krueger

Untitled

It's funny, but she's almost beautiful.
I can't even begin to tell you how.
She's like . . . when you look down a foggy street after the rain . . .
With the streetlights trying to pierce the fog,
And the reflections of the streetlights get dimmer and dimmer . . .
And either the road curves or it just fades into the night . . .
The still, dark, misty night.
She's like that, too.
She just captures your mind and holds onto it until she wants to let go.
Her hair is soft and floating, like the mist . . .
And her eyes are bright and searching . . .
Trying to read the deep deserted canyons behind your memory
Like the streetlights try to shine through the fog.
But soon the sun appears,
bringing the pink and yellow and blue dawn . . .
And the fog is gone.
So, too, are the searching glares of the streetlights.
But the street remains . . . like a memory of her
after the fog and lights have disappeared and taken her with them . . .
Leaving only a remembrance of a night long ago
when there was a beautiful midnight . . . and a beautiful girl . . .
Which have both long since disappeared.

Leah Davis

Heaven's Lyrics

I've never seen the Master's face;
I've never held His hand.
I've never walked where Jesus walked,
Nor seen the Holy Land.

I've never seen the Fishermen
On the shores of Galilee,
But that's where Jesus stood and said,
"Drop your nets, come follow me."

I've never seen the Garden
Nor the place His Disciples slept.
I never saw where He was betrayed,
But I know that Jesus wept.

I've never seen the Cross on top,
The Hill at Calvary.
I never saw Jesus crucified,
But I know He died for me.

Vicky L. Paddock

Love Is like a Rose

Love is like a rose
Blooming in the dawn
No one knows it's there
Until it's almost gone
The petals begin to fall
As each hurting word is said
No one knows it's there
Until it's almost dead
The sunlight shows the tears
Like the dew on the wilting rose
It hurts so much to find
That no one ever knows

Teri Eppler

The Nightmare of War

War is the deaths of many innocent men,
War is bullets passing through skin,
War is suicide,
War is a day of rain trapped inside,
War is a storm between two families,
War is miserable,
War is animals killed for sport,
War is a black rose,
War is a nightmare haunting you,
War is a way to express your opinions,
War is rotten,
War is not the solution.

Lindsay Myers

Time

Lost in time
Forgotten behind
Without a foe
So far to go
Never again
Trust him
That would be a sin
For I am fine
Staying here all the time

Jessica Chickering

For Those of You Who Still Have Mom

At times it may seem that if for one moment, I could just get a break!
From all the constant nagging and pressuring . . .
I mean Mom, For Heaven's sake!!!
I thought that when we became adults, all of this parenting stuff would stop.
That I would have my own life and hopefully miles away from "mom and pop."
You could not imagine what it is like to have that break, forever.
So, don't wish for just a little while . . .
Don't dare wish forever.
I will give anything right now, just to have a phone call, a smile, a kiss or even a brief sight.
It's hard to share with others that faded silhouette that sometimes comes to visit me in the night.
Love your parents as if it were their last days and try to see it from their end.
If they once thought of life without you, how their lives would have been.
So, try not to make spontaneous wishes that may come true; one day.
Stay in constant prayer

Regina Williams

Adolescent Storm

Shh . . . Don't speak.
Have you heard the cries?
Turn around . . . Look.
Have you seen the tears?
There's a storm hitting
where hot colored raindrops
are pouring out of our young.
Watch Out . . . Pay attention.
Is there one coming?
Open . . . Keep an eye.
Do you know where your child is?
The clouds are closing in on us
bringing darkness to a once safe world.
Reach out . . . Rescue
Your child is drowning in an unbearable thunderstorm but why are we making it seem
like it's only a passing rain?
Let go . . . Embrace . . . Release their manly tears.
Do you know your child needs you more now than ever?

Rachel Strobino

Eternity

Your smile though far away and never felt unto my touch,
reaches out to me like a shooting star—my heart stops.

I am drenched in warmth and my being is for one moment right,
and you for one moment are mine.

I close my eyes to sleep and you are there to meet me in my slumber,
so real but yet so unreal and though the realization creeps in . . .
I push it away.

I want but a moment with you so I can take with me your touch,
remembering the feeling over and over again . . . forever.

The fire in your eyes, the depth in your smile, and the warmth of your voice,
now imprisoned in my heart, will be footprints that walk through my soul for eternity.

Michelle Handsaker

The Journey through Me

The long road sometimes narrow through its way.
I walk it now, I walked it yesterday.
It is a scary road to travel, many things I see,
'Tis the journey through me.
I wonder where it will lead to? I wonder how far it goes?
I am the only one to travel this path, so I guess only I know.
There is only one way to find out, and that is to keep going.
As I see more, I'll feel more. It's just so hard to keep it flowing.
But time will pass, more will happen, many more things will be.
As I continue the long hard walk,
'Tis the journey through me.

Dean Rodenroth

Gone Again

My heart is turning hollow,
Love is draining from within.
The one that I once loved so much
Is leaving me again.
I really thought he loved me—
"Daddy's Little Girl" was I.
I try not to think about it,
When I do I start to cry.
I remember all the love we shared,
The fun days in the park.
He use to twirl me 'round and 'round,
And play softball 'til it was dark.
Visitations became shorter,
And further distances apart.
Now he's moved and gone away,
"Daddy why'd you break my heart?"

Brandi DeAnne Hunt

Eternal Life

Exploding into a burst of light
Like a supernova at its height
I catch a glimpse of greatness
Wondering where this path leads
Through twists and turns
Of a seemingly unsolvable maze
Called life
A phase in the universal continuum
Moving from one layer to the next
Attuned in prayer, this special effect
That propels me to my climax
Pure energy
Unwittingly moving forward
Towards an eternal state of being
Traveling through this illusion of time
I unwind, back to infinity
This divine light
That becomes eternal sight
Blessed with intelligence
And Eternal Life

Akili Hight

True Love Found

There was a time not long ago,
  I prayed to God above
That I would one day come to know
  The blessing of True Love.

Within my heart I felt so sure
  That True Love could be found.
The type of Love that would endure,
  Where trust and hope abound.

I thought I'd found True Love before,
  But it was not to be.
Although I gave my all and more,
  The dream eluded me.

And yet I still would hope and pray
  As I'd done from the start.
That Love as True as mine one day
  Would find my yearning heart.

Then one fall night my dream came true
  A gift from God above.
Nancy, He blessed my life with you,
  And both of us, True Love.

Ron Butch Sickler

the sky, my family

each one has its own glow,
its own personality.
born at different times,
each growing at different rates.

the first born lunar essence
radiating soft, resonating delicate beams of love and warmth.
though allowing her spirit to come out,
knowledge is always going the other way.

then the second oldest solar spirit
blazing its violence and its paining honesty,
but eventually succumbing to its hidden part,
setting, and so subtly reveals its empathy.

then the youngest, most malleable celestial body,
though thought of as small and weak, its brilliant luster is unhideable
seen so close with its fellow mates,
but in reality each sparkle is light years away, yet yearning for each other.

the creators always caring, comforting, cushioning,
adventuring into life with three little ones,
always understanding how they glow;
and respecting each one's shine.

Ben Ragen

A Life Well Spent

As my solemn corpse walks through the valley of death
All I can see is the opposition I've faced. No, not a valley, but a tunnel.
No light around me, just the hate of the world
The only light is from above.

The darkness tries to drown out the light.
A smoke of deceit comes toward me and tries to lead me
toward a false light. This light isn't a clear light though, but a false light, which will
only lead to a dead end. I damn this light and go to my roots in the tunnel. I reach for
the hole that the light is coming from, but can't reach it on my own. I struggle to find a
way out, a flood is coming.

I have to hurry! I'm dying! The flood is coming!
Is there no end to this suffering? If only a hand would help me!
I fall to my knees and weep. Slowly, I glance up and see a hand.
A hand of a savior! I watch as my fellow captives wither and die in this tunnel. I realize
I have little time to escape. I make a final leap of faith towards the saving light.

I am saved! But, look, there are so many left in the tunnel!
I try to reach MY hand down to help these poor souls but it's not long or strong enough.
With help from my savior I can reach though. I feel pulled away from him as I reach
back into the tunnel. I feel I might fall, but am reassured by his firm grip. I grow weary
as I stay true to my mission.
I slowly wither like those in the tunnel.

Joe Waldrop

Margueritte

I bid you a fond farewell tonight even though nothing happened.
Or, precisely because nothing happened that is why I say goodbye.
Just a few brief hours ago there was a chance.
A moment.
A spark, to be exact.
Time stood still even though the hours raced by.

I couldn't wipe the smile from my face as we walked arm in arm.
Our destination, inconsequential, just as long as your arm remained clutched to mine.
Later, when your gaze fell upon your hand and your face soured
in an unapproving look, my heart ached.
There isn't a part of you that isn't beautiful.

When I told you this, you smiled warmly and tried to look at me affectionately,
but I knew immediately that you longed to hear those words from someone else.
Farewell, my sweet.

G. J. Wood

I Don't Miss You . . .

Your point of view has left me dead
I broke my thoughts to fix my head
The subtle noise my mind creates
Tells me to change the one it hates
I listened not and for a while
I had refused my new denial
But sadness broke the wound anew
And all the hurt inside regrew
So now I'm left inside my pain
And all alone in here again
And all I've found that's proven true
Is now I know that I love you.

Jason King

Nature's Quarrels

Desolate Foreland Rock and Mountain
descry magnolia's elegant nature
Sir Orleander unyielding and callous
Remisses his sweet Rocaceae

Sweet Rocaceae virtuous and fair
has chastened her velvet Sachets
of brilliant blue and embroidered lace
Embattles her Sir Orleander

Her full moon rebels his darkness
Craving magic of his presence
his winds are bold and full of haste
Her rivers persist with mighty grace

Lorena Cordoba

An Angel in My Pocket

There's an Angel in My Pocket
She's quite a dream to me.
I've really never met her
But she's as sweet as can be.

She's an Angel in my Pocket
With long blonde hair and eyes of blue.
We've shared so many memories
That I cannot share with you.

She's with me every where I go
I feel her heart beat with mine.
She's there in my Pocket
Never leaving me anytime.

The Angel in My Pocket
Will be mine through the years.
She knows my every feeling,
And wipes away my tears.

She knows just how to please me
Every moment of the day.
'Cause the Angel in My Pocket
Was a gift from God on her way.

Alice E. Steimle

Trickles of life

Shadows of life begin as early
as the wind smooths tickles of
touch across the forehead,
The ray of light that follows and
guides you through the uncertain
path of warmth and touch,
Will surely shower and adorn
the falls which start the trickle
of life to come.

Elsie Alvarado

Ray of Light

Hark! Do my eyes deceive me?

Is that an angel that swims on that lake yonder?

But me thinks, "How can such an atom of perfection
be on this here Earth?" A wondrous sight she is,
her beauty doth blind me!

I scorn now at the sun whose light seemeth belittled
 by this one ray of light! My heart doth yearn for her,
her light fires a passion that no water can quench!

So fluid are her movements, the water on her skin
floweth like sweet nectar.

But look, mine eyes hath not deceived me, is she not "floating" on yonder water? Ray
of light! For indeed she is,
her magnificence doth shone in utmost abundance!

She streaks up now into the clear blue sky,
like a shooting star, only brighter. I stand here now with mouth agape,
relishing the sight that hath passed mine eyes,

She was indeed an angel, no mortal could hath her prowess and enlightenment! I look
now at our young sun,
always a sight to be admired, forever replenishing life!
But nay, that angel for my head doth say and my heart knoweth . . . .

That always will she replenish my life force, and forever be my ray of light!
Daniel Foster

Unbearable Lightness?

Abandoning the gravity of the tethered false selves,
we got onto the voyage.
Sailing in paper boats, we crossed the ocean
to fly into each other's arms.

The wondrous fourth dimension
dived through walls that contained us.
Unleashed, we douched each other with our desires.
Mingling selves, dissolving their boundaries, formed a commune of two.
With no address or known form, shapeless in existence,
we continued our sojourn.

Lured by the success here, we indulged in child's play.
Gazing at the crystal ball, reflecting a fantasied make-believe future,
together we began, weaving a web of dreams,
of the selves that were left behind.

Beckoning them, to rise to ether, to reach for stars in our smoke filled balloons,
fluttering our callow wings we tried, bearing them to the brightest of all.
Did we get too close to the sun that burnt our wings?
Or the lead in them flopped us to the ground?

I know not, I hope not.
Rajat Tandon

Free to Decide

Free to decide on any choice that takes place.
Able to focus on the important issues that boggles the mind.
Realizing nothing stands in one's way for exceptional bliss.
Referring to the hardships of countless wars.
Seeing the truth to the extent of one's belief.
Helping to identify the troubles in one's past.
Nurturing with a whole heart for the lonely and steadfast.
Surprising one's self-reliance in a changing world.
Never letting go the possible dream that one has.
Feeling happy to oblige in any way or form.
To press on through troubled times.
Make due with what people give to each other.
To experience love, hope, grace, and friendship a reflective sense.
To keep driving on through a horrendous day.
Receive thanks in a polite manner.
Escape the modern whip and indulge in fruitful splendor.
All of these situations, thoughts, and dreams makes an individual
closer to oneself and confident in whatever his or her life will take place in time.
Matthew Stork

Let Me Go in Love

Let me go in love
knowing that the places I long to be
are the places you don't want to go
and only in finding that place in me
and in another will I truly be happy.

Let me go in love
love me enough to have no blame
in knowing we want different things
and that I cannot make you want
the things I want.

Let me go in love
because I love you enough to let you go
knowing that you are not happy
trying to give me what I need
when it makes you angry

For love is a "want to" not a "have to"
and when you love me enough to let me go
I will know that I am truly loved
and that is all there is to know
in this place called friendship.
Terri Dismuke

A Dove

I felt a dove on my shoulder today . . .
    He said He loves me!!!
I felt a dove on my shoulder today . . .
    He said I will have Peace!!
I felt a dove on my shoulder today . . .
    He says not to worry much!!!
I felt a dove on my shoulder today . . .
    He is full of love!!!
I felt a dove on my shoulder today . . .
    He is love . . . He is God!!!
Judy Harrison

Juvy Bird

Juvy Bird, Juvy Bird
sing a song for me
the sweetest song I ever heard,
a song to help me see
Tell me of your hardships
and your ventures of life
sing a song rolling off your lips

a song full of advice
Juvy Bird, Juvy Bird
sing me a sweet song
listening to your every word
your suffering seems so long
Juvy Bird, Juvy Bird
sing the sweetest song I ever heard
Elizabeth Sydow

Where I Find My Heaven

Where I find my Heaven
is in your warm embrace.

Where I find my Heaven
is gazing at your angelic face.

Where I find my Heaven
is when we are together.

Where I find my Heaven
is when we say forever.
Steven Chinigo

My Heart

My heart belongs only to me. Its core is my soul.
I invite you in to experience the vast emotions trapped within its walls. Feel the warm and caring beat it makes.
Inhale the rush of excitement as you touch my passion for you.
Tread lightly as it is a fragile place to explore.
Learn from the tales my scars reveal.
Don't worry, you cannot destroy or alter it in any way.
Its foundation is the trials of my life
that will remain with me until my last smile.
Leave it if you wish. It will repair itself through tears of time.
However, your essence will remain and add to its character.
Stay and wrap yourself in its blanket of trust and companionship.
Do this, and you will understand why I say. . . "I love you."

Jeffrey Hawthorne

A Lyrical Formation

In the cryptic hours of midnight,
We are sensing our wonder through meditation.
Reverence of the ancient God,
I saw his face in the reflection.
A night of what night should've been.
Mental images, velvet seated carriages.
A young pale moon,
Flying high.
We rode through Elysian fields.
We went up to see the angelic ritual.
Creature's ashes rise beneath loam,
where their shadows grin.
We of mortal souls, sunder sin to another light waiting to take us in.
A magician's magic lost our souls.
Join me,
In a place of purity.
The splendor opening my soul
Over which the world can fall into the unknown.

Kelly Molczyk

I Remember

I remember I remember, the way you smiled, the smile that could brighten the darkest, coldest night of the year.

I remember, I remember, hoping for the future, planning, and looking up, instead, now, I stand, unsure of myself.

I remember, I remember, the long night talking, the long days thinking, and the time we'd spend together.

I remember, I remember, how I felt that night, the night I found out.

When you betrayed me, I fell to my knees, cried, shook my head in disbelief.

When I think of you now,

oh, how I long to hold you in my arms, just one last time, just one last goodbye, just one last, "I love you"

oh, how I miss hearing your voice, I miss you, having someone to love me as is, with no regrets, but, also,

now I know this was all a lie.

I remember, I remember, the whispers in the night.

I remember, I remember feeling invincible when you were near me.

Now, I stand, alone, with my heart in my hand, watching you run off, laughing, with another, and:

I remember.

I remember.

I remember.

Daniel Baker

Loving Eyes

From the moment I laid eyes on you
You seemed to good to be true,
Knowing you only fall for a special few.
There's a sweet sense of tenderness
that comes from your friendliness.
Even though I know
we could never be together
My sweet memories of you
will last forever.
I wish I could be close to you
the way lovers do.

Lisa Fuller

Hiding Fears through Shameful Tears

Tied up emotions, tied up feelings.
Can't let them go, can't let them out.
Silently screaming for someone to help.
No one hears, no one cares.
Past thoughts and fears collide.
Shattered hopes, shattered dreams.
Like a train wreck in my mind,
Which I can't look away from.

Longing for peace,
Searching for peace . . .
Ending up in pieces.

Tracey Bisaha

Friends Forever

There is a special bond between us
That grows within the heart
I don't know how it happened
Or when it got its start.

But each and every day it grows
Only getting stronger
As the path we take as friends
Is only getting longer.

I have my strengths and weaknesses
You know them inside out
I have slowly begun to realize
You are what friendships all about.

You always make me smile
When I didn't think I could
And you listen to my problems
When no one else would.

Engraved in my heart
Are the memories that we share
I'll always be here for you
Just remember that I care.

New experiences await you, but
I know we will stay together
I believe in this friendship and
Promise to be your friend forever.

Katie Mcenery

Words at Rest

Daydreams ripple over fractured smiles,
warm on smooth skin.

Perfumed flowers trampled.
Sheets crumpled.
Sleeping forms exposed
in the half-light of morning.

Words hang loosely over chairs,
drying slowly.

Fingertips touching, form bridges
over gulfs of human misunderstanding.

Clive Cullum

Feelings

I'm only here.

Don't bother to talk,
I will be gone
before your sentence
is finished.

I'm only here.

If you look you will see
just me in the corner,
but nothing,
for I'm only here.

I'm only here.

If you listen to me,
I'm like spoken words
that never will be
in a text.

I'm only here.

I'm the cat on the roof,
the smoke in the chimney,
the frost on the window,
and the passing of time.

Now I'm gone.

Kai Mahnert

Life's Wondrous Miracle

Little tiny fingers,
Itty bitty toes.
Eyes wide with innocence
And the cutest button nose.

Wee heart shaped lips,
Soft, smooth skin.
Fine silken hair
And a delicate contoured chin.

Mildly vocal whimpers,
Dainty mini cries.
Soothed with gentle rocking,
Or perhaps, some lullabies.

A baby to be held
Close to mother's breast.
Life's wondrous miracle,
From God, we are blessed.

Marie Vellani

Friend

Do I expect too much?
Is it too much to ask?
To have a friend
who values such
even half as much as I?
3 A.M. as tears roll down
A shoulder to cry on
is but like down
from feathers brown
Thoughtfulness is the key
whether the friend is he or she
Drives to nowhere
Lunches on me
Sharing laughter
Fighting over nothing
Being side by side

James Rose

Tears of Joy

I loved your laugh
When it was unbound.
The room and my soul,
They would become filled
With its caress.

You cried.
Your laughter it was free,
It appeared from an unknown,
Unfettered place within you.

Your silken face
Became covered with
Comfortable, radiant tears of joy.
You made me feel I touched you.

I felt loved
As you gave yourself,
As I saw your sorrows fade
Away, able to escape.

And your heart
It became safely vulnerable
And undisturbed, able to receive joy.
And your heart, it was open.

Christoph G. Olesch

Emotions

You see him
You meet him
You like him
You loved him
You lost him
You hate him
You like him
You love him
You miss him
You crush him
You call him
You remember him
Loves a funny thing

Kasey Lloyd

The Return

The lightning strikes
         over the sea.

Showing the Warrior's heart
         the way back

to Togakure's lonely heights.

Rick Smallman

Lightning

Harsh silver light,
slicing and cutting its way
through the dark sky.
Savage and relentless,
in its intensity.
Unmerciful to those
caught in its fiery grip.
Murderous, yet mesmerizing.
Its pale luminescence
reveals, highlights,
the Earth below,
like a dawning ray
of light from a distant sun.
Scorching the Earth
with its cruel beauty.

Stephanie Thompson

Eagle Rock Ridge

In my mind there is a picture;
  I am standing on a ridge,
With the world stretched out below me,
  And only time as a bridge.
If I turn and look behind me,
  There's a picture of the past.
If I turn and look beside me,
  Then the world moves much too fast.
But stretched far below before me,
  As far as the eye can see,
There flies only a lone eagle,
  A sign of all that I might be.

Kristal Green

FATE

Pleasure, pain,
Love, hate,
Could these all be determined by fate?
The folly of my way
Destroyed in
but a day,
What had taken years
Now there are only
Tears . . .

Bryan W. Wilson

Forgotten Children

the flashing lights make me dizzy
i stumble and fall
no one is there to catch me

i pull myself up from the floor
and try to pull myself together

i am miserable
i know no one
i am invisible and silent

the noise of the city comforts me
the pouring rain hides my tears
i disappear into the night
like so many other forgotten children

Susan Ramsay

Distance

Thrust into this blissful realm
I flirt with paradise
Resilient to insipid thoughts
I cast my woes aside
Fusion of our aching skins
Restores my faith in all
Partition teased us endlessly
But patience broke our fall
In you I find panacea
In you I feel profound
In you dreams serendipity
Complete Perfection Crowned

Liana Charuckyj

Haiku

Peacefully drifting
Down to the snow dusted earth
Falls a butterfly.

Julianne Weber

Enhancing My Senses

So many words can mean so little;
So little words can mean so much.

When you touch,
do you feel?

When you smell,
do you taste?

When you see,
do you hear?

If only my senses could be enhanced
by the simple knowledge of my heart!

Michele Mann

Inner Reflections

All my life I never would see,
Someone else who looks like me,
The eyes, the hair, and even face,
Without mistake, a perfect trace.

Until one day,
to my dismay,
It happened to be,
she stared at me.

Now I know I had to see,
the one that was to look like me,
The eyes, the hair, and even face,
Without mistake, a perfect trace.

All this time I waited to see,
nothing more than an image of me,
looking around in every direction,
it was to be a mere reflection.

Andrea Liss

Beauty

Your love is like the sun,
life giving, chasing shadows,
bright enough to blind a man,
should his gaze linger too long,
hot enough to burn him to ash,
at a single touch,
Without you he wanders blind,
Unseeing, he stumbles along his path,
Not knowing where he goes,
Or caring where he is,
Only wishing your flame would return,
to light his path.

Sean Christie

Smothered

I'll write you a note
from my padded room.
Maybe if I'm lucky
this will be over soon.
My heart is empty,
unable to feel—
Like a convicted felon
eating his last meal.
I don't have the strength
to smile or cry,
but since I'm such a good girl
I'll give it a try.
I'm dying to listen
'cause I have nothing to say.
Someday I'll feel different,
but not today.

Elisabeth Heck

Weeping Willows

Weeping Willows
What Makes us Sad?

Weeping Willows
What makes us Mad?

Weeping Willows
Crying out at Night

Weeping Willows
Watching me fight

Weeping Willows
Alone and stray

Weeping Willows
guiding my way

Weeping Willows
hear my fright
Weeping Willows
Wash my tears
Weeping Willows
Help me please
Weeping Willows
Don't forget about me

Jennifer Clymer

The Promise

Without thee I know not love,
a gift of God from Heaven above,
a caring friend who understands,
with this in mind I make these plans
to merge our paths and live as one,
our journey together has just begun.

Honest, loyal, persistent too,
with sparkling pools of brilliant blue.
Your simple wisdom radiates,
my life to thee I dedicate.

A committed bond until the end,
you are my nearest, dearest friend.
I love thee with all my heart
and pray our paths will never part.
I trust in you and in our love,
my precious gem from Heaven above.

Andrea Pleticha

Unrequited Love

At one time we were friends,
but something terrible happened.
I fell in love with you,
and alone is how you left me.
If only you were mine, my love,
I dream of it day after day.
I sent you a letter,
but you did not answer.
The fact you didn't was not a shock,
it was what I expected.
If only you were mine, my love,
I dream of it day after day.
I sent you some roses,
but you threw them away.
I knew you would.
I knew you would reject them.
You don't love me at all,
and I can accept that.
But, when I am gone,
will you cry?

Kevin Mullikin

"Your Beauty Embraced Me"

I love the love you're giving me.
Your love is like a summer's breeze.
The things you do for me, so sweet,
So sweet is your honey,
I taste from your tree.
The nectar of the gods,
Smooth as silk is; can be.
You pour through my soul
And, with no self-control—
I burst free; free for more.
But you've given me no air,
You've suffocated me whole,
My body cries out!
You show no remorse,
No other way out.
But through closed doors of my heart—
Which you've locked.
Locked with the key of your beauty,
Your beauty which has embraced me.

Jevon Calle

Paradise

Now paradise is close at hand:
for school is out all or the land.
for when the last bell has tolled
Then school kids will all grow bold.
The teachers then won't have to stride,
To try and keep up with their pride.
As summer months soon fly,
It brings from every student, "Why?"
No power be it ever so great,
can make a student concentrate;
For paradise now is their loss,
And teacher once again is Boss

Doran Eldridge

Angels in Disguise

I am no longer lonely
I get down upon a knee,
And thank God in the heavens
That there's an angel on Earth for me.

No one can see her halo
It shines too bright for some to see,
Only one can see this shiny ring
That only one, is me.

Christopher Matras

Left

burning
like a candle
bound
to go out

if not now
it will be later

leaving
the stain of a brand
deeply burnt
in my soul

making the emptiness

unbearable

Wim Vandebeek

A Rose

The deep, dark ocean
Is blue so like your eyes,
They are beautiful.

The light of the sun,
Is yellow so like your hair,
It brightens upon your face.

The tint of a rose,
Is pink so like your lips,
A kiss from your heart?

Cory Blische

Through Your Eyes

When I see through your eyes
I see a whole new world.
I see your dreams and your goals.
I see your future and you past.
You have a good life,
when I see through your eyes

Hannah Madison

Restoration

When peace is no more found
Then we go on mad
Looking for the very thing
That has been sought
I call upon the wanderers
Why they lie so anxiously
Toward the bird-driven night sky
I look in vain for the answer
But it slips all the time
And then I see no more
Restoration of solitude we must seek
And not be among the weak
Can you possibly at that help me
When I need thee
Showers of violence cannot help bring
That which is lost
You, Us, and I
We must ponder over the yonder
For restoration of peace

Sheetu Shakya

sleep

denying the pretension
lost without mention
in a moment I saw you
I'm waiting here for you

a whisper's green in a dying meadow
a lie's not seen for me to know
a crazy notion for a winter's end
a subtle motion for you, my friend

sleep

sandman, sire
sandman, sire
your hand rests on my brow
I'll wake upon
a call at dawn
sleep awaits me now

denying the deception
sleeping without tension
in a moment I called you
I'm dying here for you

Kristofer Velasquez

Don't Cry 'Cause I'm Okay

I lost my only child . . . a girl;
she made her way to ten.
She fought her best to stay alive;
her life it should've been . . . .

A time of laughter, play and fun,
a time of skinned up knees,
a time to ask the how's and why's,
and appreciate all she see's.

Now she's gone for good it seems,
but this I understand;
someday, of course not soon enough,
I'll get to touch her hand.

Until that day, I'll wonder why
she had to go this way . . .
I'll always hear her sweet small voice,
"Don't cry 'cause I'm okay"

Lori Brenner

Missing You

My dear
listen—can you hear?
the sound
a small whisper, floating on the wind
hear the echo
the forever faint voice calling
missing you-missing you
feel the ache within your heart
the soft sound stroking your ears
close your eyes—beloved
see the tears
of the one who misses you,
My dear

Francene Taylor

Heart's Distance

Afraid of where loves taken me
Afraid of where loves been
That keeps me at hearts distance
On the outside looking in
The fear that you won't feel the same
Keeps thoughts of you within
And keeps me at hearts distance
On the outside looking in
Afraid of what might happen
Afraid what could have been
Keeps me at hearts distance
On the outside looking in
The price to pay in love's cruel game
It takes a heart to win
And keeps me at hearts distance
On the outside . . . looking in

Montie Hutton

Empathy

Empathy, a rare commodity,
understands with sweetness
hum-drum drudgery

So much unhappiness, pain, despair

Angels, in everyday dress,
tell and teach and test
this tool of tenderness

Lynn White

My Heart's a Paper Airplane

My heart's a paper airplane,
Got a paper airplane for a heart.
Don't need a big propeller,
just a breeze to get my start.
Just a breeze, will get my plane up there.
Feeling good and light and free . . .
But, it's just a paper airplane, so
don't get rough with me.
'cause if the pointy end gets beat on,
then my heart don't fly so well, and
if you go and step on it . . .
Can I fix it? I can't tell.
I'll try to mend it, open it up . . .
and straighten out and then . . .
Wait for the very next breeze of love
to come and send it high again.

Daniel Hauge

Inventing the Wind

The air appeased the ocean gods,
The ships too tossed to sail.
Black water broken past the shore,
A salty stormy veil.

Screams blew through the nighttime,
Eagles stopped to rest.
Panic struck the hapless men,
Vultures left the nest.

Thunder rolled in the distance,
Lightning raped the sky,
A wall of water spinning 'round,
Darkness claims the eye.

Sails blew off in the frenzy,
Lifeboats pushed aside.
Swimming to Atlantis,
On the way they died.

And all the seasick sailors
Clinging to the rail
Kept no illusions of the truth
Above the sacred sail.

Joseph Hazen

Ronnie's Brother

In 1960, there was you.
Blonde hair, and eyes of blue.
Two years went by,
A baby sister had arrived.
Through the years,
their friendship survived.
Now and again you'll find,
a rare moment divine.
when brother and sister sit and chat;
of anything, this and that.
If ever I lose this brother of mine,
I'll know I've lost a piece of mind.

Veronica Belashuk

Bluebird

Bluebird on my windowsill
What makes you so blue?
Your song sounds so joyful
And flying is easy for you
If only I could wear my
colors on the outside
Then maybe I could fly too

Roger Neil Schneider

The Basketball Coach

He was a coach
The best in fact
He worked very hard
No doubt about that

He had some strict rules
The players all knew
No matter what else
Those rules to be true

He respected his players
He expected the same
We all knew that for sure
In practice and game

He retired too young
From the game that he loved
His teams truly knew
As his wife I did too

Dody Weiland

In My Dreams

In my dreams . . .
I see the passion in your face
As you hold me & touch me,
& I feel your warm embrace
As you kiss me so tenderly.

In my dreams . . .
As we get to know one another,
We find more & more to share,
The ties are growing stronger,
Building a bond beyond compare.

In my dreams . . .
You quit holding back
& explain how you feel,
Then I realize it's not just me . . .
These feelings are mutual & very real.

In my dreams . . .
I then tell you, "I love you . . . "
Softly you reply "I love you too"
Then suddenly I awaken
& again, I've only dreamed of you.

Jeanie Bailey

Fly into the Sun

*I dedicate this poem to a girl named
Leah; she's my beautiful decay.*
Let's fly into the sun
Let's die painlessly
Melt and become one
We'll cry endlessly
Hot, burning, ardent sulfur
Agonizing pain manifests into pleasure
Warm, cozy, lovely mother
Protects like no other
We'll float atop the misanthropic world
Devour the whole Galaxy
Exhibit our immaculate souls
And never reveal our darkest fears
The sun melts us into one
Together we emancipate
Blossoming into a beautiful decay
Never deleting the glittering stars
Only expressing our compassionate hearts
The sun envelopes the moon
Drowning all hope for tomorrow

Jared Brodersen

Dreams Are Real

I have often wondered
If wishes came true
If dreams could be real
And then I met you

Miracles happen every day of the week
I found you and no longer seek
For the love we share
Will forever be here
I will treasure our time
And hold it so dear

You taught me how to dream
To believe in myself
You made me feel special
You put me right on a shelf
I wish I knew how to thank you for this
I love you touch, your smile, your kiss

Dreams are real
And wishes come true
I found that out
THE DAY I MET YOU!

Brenda Martin

Pain

You never thought of yourself
You only thought of others
You always put yourself down
And always lifted others up
You were the first on the scene
To help a friend in need
Then when you were down
No one came to your aid
So one stormy night
You decided to take your life
And in a fraction of a second
You hurt all that cared for you
The one time you needed help
You found no one to turn to
You took your pain away
And left everyone else in tears
And now there is no way to change it
No way to make things better
You ended your misery
And added pain to all you loved

Darrel Davis

My Angel

Sitting here remembering
my heart starts to break
the tears start to form
as they want to fall again
I see it happening
again in my mind
I know it's true but my heart
must hold on.
When times get tough
and I feel
I can't go on
I see my angel
and know
I must push harder
I must fight back the tears.
When I am alone
I can feel
her loving arms around me
letting me know
I am all right.

Erin Fischer

love is

love is happy
love is kind
love would be just fine if you were mine

Chrisitna Hofstetter

You

Since the first day I met you
I knew it was you—
You who could make me happy
Like no other could.

When you hold me in your arms
I feel so safe there—
Like I can conquer anything
Just knowing that you care.

I feel so alive with you
able to be me—
To laugh, be happy, to smile . . .
I just feel so free.

I can come to you and talk
And you will always listen—
You alone can cheer me up
with you—my hopes have risen

I feel so special knowing
That you are there for me—
To share the good times and the bad
With you is right where I want to be.

Lisa Messina

The False Realm

My eyes see only the reflections
Not one thing around me is real
The falseness weighs down on me
Even my emotions I cannot feel
But now I have found the only way out
A path that will lead me through
I know my eyes are deceiving me
But my heart will lead me to you
Shutting out all that I see and hear
Because I know it's not really there
I let my soul guide me to freedom
And to the one for whom I care
Though it's black as pitch I make my way
By my fiery passion the road is lit
I must get back into your arms
Everything that I am depends upon it.

Jonathan Wingfield

Weak

Looking up from underground,
I see no light.
I feel all sound.
I'm trapped in filth.
Truth is the only way out.

In more ways than one,
The beauty of this is
I
Am
Done.

Neil Schwanebeck

God's Creation

There I stand on a mountain high,
Reaching upward to the sky,
Watching billows of clouds roll by.
This is God's creation.
There I stand on golden shore,
Listening to the water's roar,
Watching the waves roll in once more.
This is God's creation.
As I stroll the grassy knoll,
I listen to the church bells toll.
They're talking now for my soul.
I was God's creation.

Jolene LeClaire

Foreign Travels

War—Awful
Mother waves good-bye to son—Crying
Strange new lands—Frightened
Shot up buildings—Haunting
Gunfire rings out—Running
Piles of bodies—Shelter
Friends fall near—Bleeding
Saying they will be ok—Lying
Bombs exploding—Killing
Stabbing pains—Dying
Thinking of home—Dreaming
Put in a box—Flying
People walk by—Looking
Mother waves good-bye to son—Crying
War—Pointless

Andy Weyhrich

Burning Eyes

Look into my burning eyes,
can you feel my pain?
I'm crying out for help inside,
with no one else to blame.
Why am I insecure,
and run from minor shame.
I hide from all calamity,
as I seek my fearful game.
Burning sensations amuse my soul,
with all feelings kept inside.
Afraid to show emotion,
and scared to reveal my pride.
I can't show my true feelings,
and would lie to make amend.
To you I might look satisfied,
but inside I need a friend.
Look into my burning eyes,
and perceive the real me.
Don't mistake me for someone else,
or for someone I've tried to be.

Courtney Willard

Secrets

Languidly, across the room
I catch your eyes.

Not a muscle moves,
Neither stirs.

We stand transfixed
within our gaze,
Our eyes are locked and
none but us can see inside
The secrets that we hold.

Sandra Barber

Your Loss, My Gain

Your fuel stops my fire
Cleanse away a perfect dream
Strip the color from my day
 Adding more black to my nights
Accenting pain
Together we are a contradiction
 Incompatible, best never to touch
Your kiss kills my relief
 Your appearance drives me away
My fight for a new life
 A new story
 Inspired by a life
 Imagined without you

Ginny Wrightsman

Rooster and Arrow

A wind vane in the rain,
A reflection of pain,
Showing a cripple the horizon.
And below the flow of rain,
He was an old man.

It scourged the sun as it spun,
Its flashing lights
were like fireworks at night,
and on the handle
of the fanfare fandango,
He was a child.

The Rooster and Arrow
Sitting on the barn
A Rooster and Arrow
Showed him the horizon.

Ted Morris

A Child's Grasp

So slight the hand
And small the fingers
So profound the Insight
To the Inspiration
Of the Child's Grasp

Sensuality without the Touch
A tug from deep within
Haunting eyes demanding Trust
Contest the Simplicity
Of the Child's Grasp

Gathering the Courage for another
Call of Nurture and breathing life
While others fail to heed
The clutching close of
The Child's Grasp

Confirmation Man was born
From a Woman's Grasp
All of the Primacy of the Haunting Hunt
And the quarry is me: Fallen Prey
To the Child's Grasp

Si Connor

Covenant

Star-shone nights in black velvet sky
Lips of roses folding in twine
Distinguished by admirable qualities

Upon the brim of brocade
Lay a buffet of bewitchment
Inherent by a minuet

Skillful in touch
Tempestuous in mind
A Covenant

Anna Marie Martin

Midsummer Swim

Smooth waters
Under a lucent moon
Whisper tunes forgotten.

Night thrush chortles
His ancient joy;
He hears the
Inaudible secret.

The liquid kiss
Is easeful. Yielding,
I lave in the lake;
Bathe in the moon . . . .
She has always known.

I discover
A midsummer
Swim.

Janet Armitstead

The Unfinished Dance

Life and Death stand in a room,
Life with her glass slipper on,
Death with his reapers gone.
Life extends her hand,
and Death accepts it graciously.

The music, it begins to play,
while Life and Death begin to sway.
Two things together that should not be,
a love of Death,
a Life with thee.

Wes Wiggins

"Pain to Gain"

Pain touching me
washing over my body
slashing at my heart
but my spirit grows
stronger with each assault
until it becomes as one
with all the pain
pain so long within me
consumed by my spirit
no longer prevailing
now my friend
it teaches me
to reach out to its likeness
within others
drawing it to me
where it can no longer hurt
freeing the heart
now spilling joy
where once
pain ruled supreme
now peace is master
pain no longer taking
it has become my gain.

Cheryelona Mirchandani

Boiling Point

I'm boiling with words.
Do you see them bubbling
to the surface
in chaotic heat?

Bounce back
from the roiling fire
and steam. Ere long,
this pot will be cinder dry,
safe for handling:
Empty.

Susan Anderson

Hydra Awakening

Still within myself
in slumber,
at peace;
a warmth,
like a painter's brush
traveling its own course
across my cheek,
and the soft rocking,
all cradling my spirit,
only to gently awaken
to a new dawn,
in delight.

Grace Evelyn Cregier

The Mist

Gray lines of shadowy water
Its force tormenting the rocks
Crowded space of dampness
I ponder as I watch

Robert Prichard

Cold

Cold fury burning my skin
The wind so fierce, so strong
Each day I try, I wonder
Where is my mind?
Where has it gone?
I kiss the wind, and buckle at my knees
I push forward with all my might
Only to fall
To this unshaped, soft earth
The green that once grew
Has now withered
Has now cooked from the fiery winds
The smile once there, has left this day
For I fear the worst
Yet the worst has yet to come
I shoot the arrow into the sky, hoping
Praying that I will hit the sun
For it proves to be, my only sanctuary
Cold, so cold it is
It burns my face, it chars this skin

Dionisios Favatas

Stars

I look at the stars
Thinking of you
I look at the stars
Feeling blue
They remind me of
The sparkle in your eye
When you look at me
And I start to cry.
The distance between us
Is not that far away
But when I think of you leaving
Everything turns gray.
I look at the stars
Knowing you love me
I look at the stars
Knowing you care
I look at the stars
Knowing the love we share.

Crystal Stacho

Farewell Sylphi

*For Gina, I'm sorry that our paths
parted where they did.*
People live
people die
throughout it all
true love will survive
the people might change
might turn and go their separate ways
to break the hold of the green monster
to find one more intune
the nights seem darker
the days seem colder
the flame of passion has flickered
only waiting to be kindled anew
though we part
to become again two instead of one
carry this with you always
never turn from the light
look on the memories fondly
as you carry
the part of my soul
that I wish you to have

Chris Kile

Tears

Tears
going down
from my soft brown eyes
Don't know
why
Trying to keep them
inside
Giving people the silent treatment
Being miserable
But why . . . why . . . why is
this happening to me?
why?

April Hackett

Hangman

Live a lie
Tell the Truth
Your head is in
Through the noose
Tell you why
I am him

Thomas Dunn

Elizabeth

In her wheelchair she moves
Up and down the aisle.
And frequently gives you
A whimsical smile.

Dementia has robbed her
Of much of her speech.
It's hard to imagine
That once she could teach.

Sometimes she gets angry.
She'll hit, bite, and swear.
I think that she knows
That life isn't fair.

But then she'll give you
That whimsical smile,
As she moves in her wheelchair
Up and down the aisle.

Gail Fox

Dreams

Drifting away in a sleep
Dreaming dreams that can never be told
For when I awake,
They are no longer there to hold.

MaryEllen Lombino

Friends

It's hard to say good-bye
To that one true love,
But to end a friendship
Is ten times as hard.
One who was once
Your very best friend,
Now is a traitor
To the deepest extent.
Do all friendships fail
With such an end?
My answer to that,
Is that some never end.
So I dedicate this poem
To those few that remain,
For you three have been there
To the very end.
I thank you for this,
And I try to do the same
For best friends like you,
Deserve the best I can give!

Csilla Denes

My Knight

To Michael with love
You are my knight in shining armour,
You rode in on a charger . . .
And rescued me.
You slayed all my fears
And wiped away all my tears.
You opened the door to my heart
And taught me to love again.
You've showed me the silver lining
Where before all I saw were dark clouds.
You stood by me . . .
Even when I was wrong.
You support me and
Never let me fall.
That's why you are and always will be my
All and all . . .
My Knight!

Wanda Johnson

Thinking

Always dwelling
At times dispelling
Images in my head
Sardonic pictures come and go
Things that were left unsaid

Could I do this?
I should have done that
Never a moments peace
Spinning, reeling
Never healing
Thoughts that fail to cease

Gladys Ramos

Aroma

I see the return of the spring

My hands stretched to clutch a string

The rhythmic colors filled in the tune

The lips fumbled to slip-in a line

The eyes pleased, for the seize

The mind surprised, to the tease

Now I never think of the falling time

And always look forever the return of time.

Shivaji Khambhampati

So . . .

So . . . what if
You've tasted of
Eden's
Sweetness?
Delved into
Braved
Volcanic eruptions
Ash smooth greying
into. . .
Dawn's pinkest highlights of
dreams yet to be fulfilled.
Fantasies of breathless,
Deceptive harmonies.
Illusions of fire and ice!
Will you promise me
Undying love
For Today?

Sharon Hay Webster

Prince of Darkness

Planning their salvation
Anticipating man's fall
Messiah go and save them
Council in Heaven shout for joy
Jealous of God's power
Lucifer demands His name
He offered false salvation
Then war in Heaven started the game
Lightning shot from the sky
Spirits cannot make their death mark
Diablo and demons
Banished to flaming Hell pits
Yet they still do those deeds
Until the father saves man
He'll be cast out forever
Never to hear his demon clan
So the world waits for war
To make him breathe his last breath
Armageddon will come rise
So wait dear world for your death

John W. Shaw II

Gold

You are like a lump of Gold,
hard to get, hard to hold,
of all the girls I've ever met
your the one I can't forget
I too believe in God above
created you for me to love
he picked you out from all the rest
because he knew I'd love you best . . .

Imad Shinnaoui

I Believe

I believe in love
To love someone so pure
Having love-in-mist
Kissing such passionate lips
The pleasure to love you
Devotion to the heart
The desire to want someone.

My heart throbs reaching out for you
Burning to have your love
Love is too intense
Making my heart beat harder when I hear
Your voice
Now I believe such love can exist
You're my angel from Heaven
Sending me the innocence of your love

Believe in what I say
My vow of commitment to you
Holding you dear
Savoring a kiss from you
Holding your hand in mine
Never letting you go
Wanting to share my life
Giving you everything
Our love could not got wrong.

Jolene Jimenez

Interior

Living a lie,
Muffling a scream.
Into the dark recesses of the mind,
Uncovering the darkest dreams.

Many live on fear,
Others on hate.
Most can tell the difference,
Others can't differentiate.

Into your mind
You must let yourself go.
To the deepest darkest parts,
To regain control.

Over time you
Will see.
To gain yourself
You must embrace Me.

Tanya Paterson

Le Sourire

Smile sweet as candy,
Eyes sparkle like diamonds.

Hands soft as silk,
Hair shines like silver.

I would give you all of that,
For just one look at your smile

A walk on the beach, so sandy,
To play in the sand mounds.

Lips taste sweet as mothers milk,
A smile, not hard to remember.

On the seashore where you sat,
All I want to do is kiss your smile.

Christopher LaPointe

Contemplation 1

As I stand and look
Over the vast expanse of sky
I wonder of the little things
That don't invade my mind anymore

Where did they go?
Sometimes I miss them
The joy they never brought
The thoughts I never long for

My perceptions no longer burdened
By those incessant little vagrants
And I breathe deep
of the freedom I possess.

Justin Engle

Eagles' View

*In Loving Memory of Troy Masters,
8/16/81–12/21/96. I love you.*

High they soar on their great wings
   high above our Earthly things

Free of worry and woe
where the wind take them they do go

All my life I have sought to fly
   and I hope that is where I die

Living like those great birds of prey
riding the sun's great beams everyday

The great eagles live on Heaven's door
   where they will forever more

When God raises me up on eagle's wings
I will live with their view of things.

Sean Masters

Poverty

The sun is shining,
the children are wining,
I scream and yell,
not in Heaven but only hell.
The children are dirty and very poor,
sleeping not in a bed but on the floor.
I'm sad, I grieve,
It's hard to believe,
no one has an idea or a clue
why the children live like they do.

Sarah Reese

Tears

Let me brush away your tears,
my darling. For your tears are
a sign of sadness.
I am here for your gladness,
your joy. Let not these tears
spoil our time together.
Gently, we will move through
the darkness, holding onto
one another 'til the light of day.
And, the dark of night will no
more bring your tears.

Terry Burke

Misery's Passion

As from a cup of bitter grief,
burning tears flow from my mouth.
Whirling winds strip every covenant,
replacing hope with malicious doubts.

Repressed feelings taunt as children,
sweet desires a constant foe.
Overshadowed by seething anger,
and other spirits I do not know.

Sensual death is yet so comforting,
misery's promise for sure to keep.
Never again to feel love's lies,
for death's kisses an eternal sleep.

Larry Green Jr.

The Fear

I look at his face
And feel like a disgrace
I begin to fear
Because people are near
I wish to speak the truth
Yet fear that I will lose
I know now what I feel
Is truly a big deal
But when he is around
I make not a sound
For fear of his response
In my life still haunts
I should admit my love
Instead of fleeing like a dove
But instead I shed my tears
And skip it due to fears

Stephanie Campbell

Winter

To my Aunt Kathy
All the leaves so beautiful,
But they lay on the ground,
And leave all the trees bare.

Why is it that we
Can enjoy but one
Of these beauties at a time?

Winter is just like life,
Full of sacrifices.
For one beauty, there comes
Something not so beautiful.

Richard Galaway

"Who Makes You Tired?"

I am the little person
who goes door to door
house to house

I am the one who
makes you tired
By the queen
I was hired

I sprinkle my fairy dust
as I must
Then when you get sleepy
I slip out, very sneaky.

Joshua Mirchandani-Sanchez

Once upon a Dream

Once upon a dream I saw a sunrise,
and you were there.
I heard birds singing, and you were there.
I saw a diamond without flaw,
and you were there.
I found the gold at the end of the
rainbow, and you were there.
And when I woke from my dream I saw a
shooting star, and I wish you were here.

Jeff Bialek

Dying Inside

Everyone stares,
and whispers are tossed about,
her pride knocked down
by a mind full of doubt.
She wonders around
no direction, or ending point in sight,
confused by a decision
she knew was not right.
They took away
the only love she knew,
her passion, her life,
the only thing she could do.
When others saw
that outside she cried,
none ever realized
that inside she died.

Kristalynn Hall

Marriage Counseling

Wounds bleed from scars
reopened by ripped stitches
beautifully tattered,
shredded by the patient
Groggy from anesthesia, forgets
the tenderness following procedure;
tiptoe through conversations
anxiously watching for land-mines
Vile exclamation,
another apology before
the next hidden explosion
amputates the rest of the heart.

Gayle Briner

My Answer

Who do you write like?
    She asked,
    Not knowing who I am.

I write like me.
    You see..
    I am the only one who can!

Ray Tanis

Winter Blues

Another night passes
Clouds move in masses
A tear falls to the ground
A lost soul is never found
All hope is lost
Nothing is free; you pay the cost
A life is lost; a grave is dug
No caresses are felt, not even a hug
A feeling of emptiness is felt
Knowing that the snow will never melt

Loretta Drollette

Songs of Silence

The waves break as the sun rises
Upon the misty morning sky
The clouds move away for the sunshine
As the night passes quietly by . . .
The silence is only broken
By the songs of the whispered sea
And were it not too far to think
I'd believe she sings for me . . .
She throws me her incessant waters
Her flowing mysterious grace
Ever showing her body
Yet never revealing her face . . .
I hope that she does not mind
That I lie beside her this morn
For she offers me serenity
In times of pain and scorn . . .
Though I've never heard her utter words
I believe someday she may
But for now she brings me silence
And sends me on my way.

Michael Kinney

The Well of Love

When I look at him
I see myself
And yet he is so different
In his soul I swim
In his eyes I drown
In his arms I melt
I stare into his eyes
Wanting to look away
Yearning to look inside
I find myself entranced
I drink deeply of
The pools that are his eyes
Yet my thirst is never quenched
How much can I drink
Before the well of love runs dry?

Jean Landesco

Mom

I may not say it as often
As she would like for me too,
But deep in her heart
She knows that I do.

I take her for granted
Again and again,
She is always there
With a smile or a grin.

She is there when I am happy,
She is there when I am sad,
She lifts my spirits high
When I feel bad.

All these things I thank her for,
Because when it comes
To a mom I could ask
For no more.

I don't say it very often,
But she knows I do.
I just wanted her to know,
Mom, I love you.

David Cordell

We Ride a Rock

We all ride a rock
And we can't get off
Even if we wanted to
We're stuck on top

Around in circles
With no start or end
We can't stop it
From rolling around again

Sharing this rock
Like you and I
Are six million others
With hopes and dreams

Some dream of riches
And fortunes of gold
Some dream of leaving our rock
And it's a dream that's bold

But I'd rather stay
Where I am right now
Stuck on this rock
It's the only place I know

And as sure as day turns to night
And night turns to dawn
I'm glad I did my time
On the little rock that keeps rolling on

Phillip Zwicke

Roses

Pandora, Oh, Pandora,
Beautiful goddess, roses professed,
The love of you, confessed.
Long stemmed, feminine by nature,
Eloquent in stature . . . .
Delicately born, except for the thorn
Fragile in beauty, exquisite to see
Fragrance becoming of thee . . . .
Colored in chastity, red
Colored in purity, white . . . .
Would I, the fragrance inhaled,
By the thorn, be impaled?

Eldon Chesbro

Study at Pace University

A wooden trunk that's thick and big
Has grown up from a tiny sprig;
A nine-tier terrace of great height
Was built with wads of clay so light;
A thousand-mile trip is a race
That must be started with a Pace

Yu Fan

Of You, of Me

Days and nights go slipping past,
our long hard lives in stone are cast,
revive ourselves in duties light,
the warm embrace holding lover tight.

My heart glows warmer in summer breeze,
walking tides fill the needs,
kissing the sea is moon's soft glow,
kissing you in the sand below.

Christopher Tom

Your Love Makes Me Weak

It cuts so deep into me that it is
like a life line that sustains me

Through my veins it pulsates, and
my body thrives off of this love

You never have to say, or look at
me, if you do, I just know I am
hopelessly trapped

Resistance is futile, there is no
way to walk away from love that becomes
your every reason for living

Such a love should be sinful, so
passionate is this love, every
drop burns deep in my soul

I would do anything, and everything
to feel this way, forever

Rahman Karim

The Miracle

There's a miracle that happens
when a tender seed is sown,
it produces fine fruit
when the tree is properly grown.

It requires continuous nourishment
from a life-giving source
to depend upon for strength
coming from one united force.

So let us bind together our minds
toward one common goal,
to produce productive children
because they, too, have seed to sow.

Susan Petroski

Tomorrow Came Today

Yesterday
innocence
fun
me

Today
knowledge
joy
you

Tomorrow
maturity
love
us

William Eyster

Friends Are a Joy

The warmest thoughts
We ever send
Are those that go
From friend to friend.
The happiest wishes
We ever make
Are the wishes made
For friendship's sake.
The loveliest memories
That we know were made
With good friends
Long ago.
The brightest tomorrows
Yet to be,
We'll find in
Friendship's company.

Jun Cham

Helpless

Mistakes happen and hearts break
how far can the words, "I am sorry" go

You can only do so much for others
before you have to give up

Can things ever be wonderful
or okay at least
When a simple hug
can make everything else go away

Temporary fixes are easy to come by
but when it's gone it feels worse
than before, even if it's not

Not knowing what to say
When you stand before me
With a tear in your eye
Begging for help or at least a hand
Lost amongst a pile of issues
That keep rising
No matter how hard you try
Things get worse

And I stand there
Speechless, Helpless, Heartless

Unable to watch any longer, I turn away

From the mirror

Nicole Petrillo

Shapes of Feelings

Soft, quiet peace;
Shapes of feelings yet unseen.
Sunset sensations glowing brilliant
In fleeting time,
Fade into night velvet,
Soft and purple.

Silent and catlike comes the dawn
It bursts glorious
In Golden sunlight, shining!
People, making memories
In daytime dallies reminisce
In the evening's quiet sunset hours,
These feelings that frame
The landscapes of our lives.

Brenda Ralston

Desire

Shine luscious lips
You are a symphony
    a sweet dream
    a chain of love
I ache and am delirious
Leave
        and
            I am
                bare.

Amy Lane Watson

Shadows

Shadows of yesterday
and dreams of tomorrow
sprinkle each moment
    like a
        spring morning rain

That softens the earth
'neath blankets of winter
where secrets are waiting
    to be warmed
        by the sun.

Patsy Paul

Green Grass

This is the place of ancient
ceremonial encampments,
living in nature beside the edge
of the sacred river.
The branches of cottonwoods are
dancing in the wind.
Their leaves rustle, singing the
songs of our ancestors.
Shadows, illuminated by the sun,
reveal the spirits
of those who were here in more
peaceful times.
Drums of the spirits echo along
steep embankments,
sending holy messages to those
who would listen.
It is the land of all our great
Grandfathers.
It is the land to which all
is wakan.

K. Charger

Whose Will?

Is it God who makes things bad?
Is it God who takes away?
Does He who created all things
Cause problems for His creatures?

He would not give us
Too much to bear,
If we have faith
That He cares for us.

Those that have gone before,
And are with Him would want
Us to keep serving Him,
And worshipping Him.

The one who opposes God
Would have us believe,
That God does bad things
And if we believe that,
We are giving God's Enemy
What he wants.

Claudia Kittel

Through My Eyes

As I waited for the sunrise
I felt the warmth upon my face
I could hear the sparrows singing
I thank you Lord for another day

I knew it would be a great day
because I stopped and thanked the Lord
for all of my surroundings
and the beauty they behold

I'm thankful for the trees around me
for they shade me from the heat
and the grass for which I walk on
feels so soft beneath my feet

And the flowers I can smell them
some from far away
because of the gentle breeze
God has blessed me with today

So I thank you for this day Lord
and the life you've given me
you've blessed me with so many things
even though I cannot see.

Tammy Hager

Time to Go

Time has come.
Time to go.
The time is here,
the clock will show.
We will follow,
when it's time to leave.
We have to hurry,
no time to breathe.
Escape the world
when the alarm clock rings.
Escape the world
of all material things.
When we hear the ring,
we can't run or hide.
We will say good-bye for now,
But I will see you on the other side.

Matthew Graham

The Spider Lies Still

When webs you weave entangle me
And yearning to break free
Becomes the only light I see,
From beneath my sleep I must peek.

The realization later comes.
The Truth unveils itself,
That caught up in your scarlet web
My soul rests on your shelf.

Ignorance has taken place,
Within your truth it lies—
The apparent nature of
Your transparent disguise.

When trapped within the silk threads of
This web I've known to matter,
It seems I blind myself from seeing
My world about to shatter.

I've hung my will out to dry,
I've given way to you,
I have to slowly pierce the fog
That hides the bitter Truth.

Rosella Hutchison

Remembering Dreams

Picture this, a soft-edged window,
upper corner of my mind,
Fancy this, that God did endow
Power to leave no dreams behind.

The lower corner (no soft edges),
Man-made visions rise to nibble,
with their teeth of mortal grudges,
Commas in my soft-edged scribble.

(There was once a man who tried
To swim against the infant Ganga,
Failing that, he finally died,
Craving air on the Kanchenjunga)

When I wake, a raging feud
like the war of day with night,
Whether my dreams are primary hued
Or pristine Black and White.

Faintly though, a thought still lingers
through this wayward tussle,
Like the joy of licking fingers,
scraping an empty vessel.

March Monk

Summer Storm

Winds charged with electricity
Cause the trees to sway,
The clouds lie close unto the ground
Pewter and steely gray.
As premature darkness settles
Holding the world in thrall
The storm clouds finally open,
And the rain begins to fall.

Bonnie Fitzgerald

Love

Soon
There Will
Be Love For
Us Together
Now

Beth Heffernan

Dear Oprah with Love from Mary

You are a light in the darkness.
You fill people with hope.
You never fail to inspire me.
You always help people cope.
You're an angel without wings
Of the people here on Earth.
You're forever giving encouragement
Telling people they have worth.
May God bless you always,
May He see your endless love.
May you always know you're treasured.
You are someone sent from above.

Mary Jarrett

Change

We have come a long way together,
Battling our battles,
Laughing at our losses.

Suddenly you change,
Your battles have become wars,
You fight because of defeats.

You turn your back on me.
Why do you make me suffer so?
I was just trying to win my battles,
But you took that option away from me.

You took my life,

But I forgive you,
Everyone changes!

Mike Silvestre

Of Me

This Is The Sad Sad Story
Of Me, Audible Eerie.
For I Travel And Play,
But Now I'm Here To Stay
'Cause I Cannot Find The Way
Back To My . . .
HEY!!!! (Audible with locket in hand)
Get My Hand Out Of Your Pocket?
I Was Simply Admiring Your Locket!
I Cannot Help Mine Eyes,
None Shall Hear The Lies
Of A Scheme To Be Had,
I'm Simply . . . A Curious Lad
Here, And Yet So Sad,
For I Cannot Find My Way Home.

—The Chronicles of Audible Eerie
Russell C. Kern

The Final Dance

Death surrounds me
It caresses me as a lover
It taunts and teases me
Bringing me to the top
And then soaring down into the depths
Hanging at times to the edge
I feel its hands first gently tugging
Later, as I grow weary
It is all enveloping
Death comes on bated breath
Quietly....

Elizabeth McDevitt

Sonnet for a Broken Heart

Emotions capsizing like a vessel
when tenderness becomes despondent,
and sympathy no longer nestles
within the heart of the respondent.

Warmness turns to apparition,
fleeting like a dying flame,
and sorrow becomes your disposition
as you search to unmask blame.

A moment in disbelief,
and moment of incapacity,
denial harbors false relief,
and realization, no indemnity.

As you embrace the disheartening fear,
from morose eyes falls a tear.

Matthew Robbins

The Eternal Dance

Stars twinkle brightly,
Seem to come alive.
The constellations cluster,
Never fading out.

They dance across the darkened sky,
Move throughout the night.
They dance towards the west,
For soon the sun shall rise.

The stars and the moon set,
Retreat to the west.
The sun takes their place,
To dance through the heavens

They jump, they twist
In the eternal dance.

Amanda Butler

Emily

You were my first—
no one ever saw me before,
like you did.
We were so young,
and trying to pretend we weren't;
we were playing dress-up
with each other, and that was alright.
Though we were making up the rules
as we went along,
we taught each other
just the same.
For that, I will always be grateful.
You need to know,
that you will always be
a part of me;
no matter where we go,
or how old we grow.

Cynthia McCoy

What Harm Shall Come of Me.

One thing I have found,
When two hearts stand still.
It's not for one to complain,
It's only from will.

Another thing I have found.
Is when they turn around,
It means that they are through,
And all the love has run out.

If he cheats on me,
Is one thing I must find.
I hope that when it comes, I see it.
Not that love should steer me blind.

Now it looks like my love,
Is nothing but a total loss.
He'll no longer have to worry,
About this girl being his boss.

I have lost him forever,
This is plain to see.
I know he does not care,
What harm shall come of me.

June Kopilchack

This Day

This day
My heart aches for you
And the memories.
This day
I can cry
And the tears will flow
Freely, salty.
This day
I remember all that once was
And my heart aches
For home
For you
Your laugh, your smile
Once more.
And on this day
I'll watch the sunset
The vibrant blues and oranges
And I'll smile
To think of you
This day.

Rachel Hepp

Life

The Wheels keep turning,
 on this, a vicious life
Nothing seems to matter
 and nothing seems quite right.

No matter what you say,
 and no matter what you do
These wheels just keep a-turning
 in spite of me and you.

Is this just a game were playing,
 or is this just the truth
All we can do is just keep on praying
 until we all go through.

Joanne Armstrong

feelings

*Recovering from child abuse and
blossoming*
Violets are blue
and my feelings are true
for you are my one and only
and that is no bologna.

Carolyn Debacker

Your Guardian Angel

You may have days
That are good and bad,
You may find laughter
When really you're sad.

Some days you'll wonder
What will happen next,
Watch out for those bumps
That you'll least expect.

But always keep
Your head held high,
Take some deep breaths
Then let out a sigh.

Challenge the obstacle
When it gets in the way,
For everyone knows
You'll get your say.

Don't give up on yourself
No matter what the cost,
For your guardian angel
Won't let you get lost.

Melissa Stone-Anderson

Solitude from the Moon: a Villanelle

I am free
to howl at the moon
in the harmony of me

lips curl to join nature's symphony
together we swoon
I am free

despite unnatural decree
I emerge from the cocoon
in the harmony of me

Wings flutter gingerly
outside the womb
I am free

Realization of the time to be
crazy like a loon
in the harmony of me

I fight with the sea
no comfort from the moon
it is alone I must be
in the harmony of me

Julia DeChristoforo

Psychedelic Dreams

Who is this angel, standing before me?
Who is this angel, this one that i see?
It is so magical, is it a dream?
Is it a vision, that's what it seems.
Who is this girl, so full of glee?
Does she have dreams, or pictures of me?
Who does she want, who could it be?
While I am left sitting alone by a tree.
At night, at home, when I'm fast asleep,
Visions and dreams of her make me weep.
What is her name, what could it be?
Does it start with a J, a M, or a G?
Who is her man, who could it be?
Is it a friend, or possibly me?
Who is this girl proper and neat?
Like royalty that eat crumpets and tea.
Not to be her or not to be me
Only to be us or only be we.

Curtis Maldonado

Harry's Hats

Harry has lots of hats
But he must have more
They hang on dresser and door
A cowboy hat he got out west
This one is his winter's best

If he goes hunting
There's a camouflage hat
One from Arrowhead Valley
You can't beat that.

A real army hat with a navy pin
A red hat from the bank
Thanks for coming in.

He bought a new Dodge
They gave him a white hat
Only special customers
Get one like that

A choice of hats Harry may seek
A different hat for
Each day of the week.

Bibbie Barnes

Freedom's Home

There is a land that's dear to me,
which I call Freedom's Home.
There is not another country
which you could call your home.
There is so much to be thankful for,
this land that I call home;
The land that God has always blessed,
this land that I call home.
So always put your trust in Him,
for everything he has done;
So if you want to keep this home,
fight for the country that you love
This country that you call home
put no other Gods before you.
Haven't I done enough for you?
I gave my life for you.
So put no other God's before you,
if you want to keep your Freedom's Home.

Shirley Henry

Miss You

I miss you oh, so very much.
And wish that you were near.
To see all the wonderful things.
That I have done down here.

The kids are growing and getting big
The wife and I are fine.
All the things you've told me.
Are still embedded in my mind.

Now every time I think of you
The good times and the bad.
Leaving us that awful day,
Really made me sad.

And then one day I'll see you
Not to soon, alright
I love you and miss you so . . .
And hope your days are "Bright."

Greg Balitz

Sky

Sky
blue, bright
stormy, windy, calm
with nature's help
Heaven

Suzanne Fitzpatrick

Summertime My Slumbertime

I love you fragrant summertime
Your mossy rippling brooks
With your daffodils of yellow
And your leafy, shaded nooks.

Sweet apple pies and evening naps
And skies of windswept blue
And your dewy misty mornings
Send me off to dreamland too.

The happy chirping songbirds
In the dewy droosey dawn
Arouse me from my slumber
And I am up and gone.

I oft spend hours just lulling
In some snoozy stack of hay
Or I wonder through the woodlands
Just to pass the time of day.

Or I seek some secret garden
Where there's melon on the vine
And I sit around just eating
'Til there's nothing left but rind.

Janice D. Wallace

My Soul Weeps

My soul weeps,
As tears gently fall.
Carrying with them the pain,
My heart can no longer bear.

Spreading my wings to love
Was never my intent,
But a moment of weakness
Has left me blind, not seeing
Truth, that lingers deep within me . . .

Darkness has crept in through my pores,
Paralyzing my very existence,
All is lost . . . there is no hope,
My blood turns cold, sending chills
Through my weakened body,
Leaving my soul shattered.

Once again, I am frozen.
Not feeling . . . not caring
Just existing.

Diane McGhie

Nature

Move like snails
Colors brown and green
Also red, orange and yellow
Are its leaves
         trees.

Bending like the arch
Holding very bright colors
Red, orange, yellow, green
Blue, violet, purple
         rainbows.

Courtney Laughhunn

Baby Bird

The baby bird has been set free
out into the world
she thinks
all for me
The skies have been waiting
to aid her in her destiny
there she flies
oh, so free
the nest becomes a distant memory

Baby bird of a different breed
and too, God made her
for us to see,
innocent,
pure-hearted,
she only wants to be free,
maybe someday she'll master the skies,
and disappear
right before our eyes.

Erica J. Curry

Children of Darkness

Children of Darkness
Come lay your sweet lips on me.
Tell me your tales
And fill me with sympathy.
Children of Darkness,
The night is young,
Go out into the world,
But do not feed on the innocent ones.
Children of Darkness,
Fill the dark with your light.
Show your presence
In the deep of the night.
Children of Darkness,
Come feast on me.
Bring me my death,
And eternal immortality.
Children of Darkness,
Come play your Dark Trick.
For in the end,
I will be your best pick.

Pamela I. Ramirez

Country Girl

I have a song for you,
Pigtails and eyes of blue,
A round freckled face,
Wearing a dress made of lace.

Country girl
Gathering flowers in the spring,
Listening to a robin sing,
And walking down the lane
In the warm summer rain.

Country girl
Lady wearing high heel shoes,
Wearing dresses of different hues.
Now the freckles are all gone,
A smiling face in the sun.

Country girl
Thinking of romance and love,
Staring at the stars above,
Hoping to find love so true,
Country girl my heart is with you.

Agnes Kanaby Ray

Shadows

To my grandchildren
It's time for bed my mother said
I'm not sleepy said I
Lie down, lie down and rest your head
I can see the sleep in your eye

Oh, mother please, I cannot do
For there's SHADOWS beneath my bed!

SHADOWS please, you make me sneeze
Now come on and lay your head

Mother please, you make me wheeze
There's SHADOWS beneath my bed.

Oh, SHADOWS if you do exist
Come out and show me your ware

"OH, MADAM IF, YOU DO PERSIST
GET READY FOR A REALLY BIG
SCARE!"

Caroline Aguila

Fire

A soothing massage
Of brilliant light,
Tells the tree it's time
To put up a fight.
The twisted branches of desire
Caught in flame,
Silently burn in agony,
Not knowing who to blame.
A dazzling starlight of love
Lights up the sky.
Flames lick up the tree
Higher than high.
The fire crackles and roars.
The tree cowers on all fours.
The branches snap off the tree
And hit with a pound.
Flames of passion
Burn the tree to the ground.

Ashley MacLaren

Setting out to Sea

I am pulling up anchor now,
say good-bye
to this ship
setting out to sea.
I am untying the rope
that holds me,
near the harbor
of my heart.
I am allowing you
to occupy the slip,
where a fond memory belongs.
I am walking away
from the waters edge,
putting up the sails,
releasing my hope of you
into the wind.
I am charting out
a course for myself,
seeking the warmth of the sun,
I am setting out to sea now.

K. Sherfield

Grandma

Yes we'll miss you, oh, so much,
Your beautiful smile,
Your gentle touch
Yes we'll cry, our hearts will ache,
For a gift to us God had to take,
Yes we'll carry on our lives,
With our jobs our children,
Our husbands and wives
Yes there'll be that day in spring
When all the angels begin to sing,
Oh yes, we'll see you once again,
Just not right now, be patient then

Catherine McKinney

Sun

We walked along, while bright and red
uprose the morning sun on our head,
while we ride on the trail of the woods.
The pine trees in the woods,
shine with snow and ice.
We ride and ride through the woods,
until we hit the field behind the woods,
then we go into a trot.

Shaina Lopez

Vade in Pace

Naked, leaning on your lap
embraced to your waist.
Just silence, between the two of us.
You. I. Silence. Nothing else.

Your fingers running through my hair,
drowning all my senses.
Softly, they caress my back.
All my being thrills.

You raise me to your chest
and hide me within you.
Not a word, not a sound.
Just the beats of our hearts.

Tenderly, you raise my face to you,
drinking each one of my tears.
Sweetly you smile to me
and close me hard to you, very hard.

Everything is through. I also smile.
Slowly I get back into my feet.
Your love gave me strength.
Thank you God . Thank you, my Lord.

Ana Milagros Orta

Tribute Tree

For all Tribute Tree recipients
Tribute tree holiday light
Shine so bright
To light up the night
And grant my dreams all right

Holiday tribute tree
Grosse Pointe war memorial
Grosse Pointe farms Michigan

Oh tribute tree
Oh tribute tree
Has season's
Greeting and
Best wishes for you

Santa and the little
Bird come to say
Have a very Merry Happy Holiday!

Dorothy Harris

Love

*Dedicated to my husband, Ray,
and my children*
Love as gentle as a heartbeat
Love as soft as a rose
Love as deep as a valley
His love within me grows

Love strengthens me and guides me
Love calms me through and through
Love always is beside me
His love again renewed

Love holds me in the darkness
Love dances in the light
Love always is so tender
His love always in sight

Love, my most precious companion
Love, my most loving friend
Love, my most glorious redeemer

"Jesus"
His love never ends

Connie Paul

Nature and Life

Dedicated to my new-found love, Denice
The sun shines and the moon glows;
A little rain and the grass grows.
The winds blow and the fires burn;
Schools aren't the only place to learn.

On the streets are people you meet;
All together bearing the summer heat,
The winter comes after the fall;
Springtime brings the birds call.

Planes all over of every type;
Flying to deal with today's hype.
Cars, buses and trains at the station;
Transport people all over the nation.

Mountains, valleys, rivers and streams;
Everything found in your dreams,
Sometimes you do things you hate;
Good things come to those who wait.

Next time your in the park;
Listen to the song of the lark.
When you see the beautiful white dove;
Tell him all about your new-found love.

Kenneth A. O'Keefe

A Taste of New England

Spring
Sunshine beams on startled streams
Drunken bees on flowers agape
With bursting splendor trees awake
From winter's mantle we escape
To springtime's warm embrace

Summer
On sandy shores
We did explore
On sanded feet
Our toes explored
Sandy shores
Sea gulls soar
Lobster pots
Fresh fish galore?

Fall
Hills afire at summer's break
With golden showers trees do shake?
With backward glance on summer's dreams
We dwell upon what might have been

Hugh Laughlin

Same Old Night

An old man sits on his old rockin' chair.
His eyes are caste at the window in a heavenly glare.
He appears peaceful, as if asleep.
A tear upon his cheek he strives to keep.
This is the first he has shed in years.
A symbol of memories, not out of fear.
He doesn't leave his house anymore.
His home is in shambles, he is extremely poor.
Tattered rags upon his chest.
He's trying to prepare for the final rest.
He no longer laughs, he no longer smiles.
His feet are stuck to the wooden floor tile.
The darkness pulls the strings of his heart.
He remembers his wife's words when they were forced to part.
"One sweet day we will meet again,
and I'll love you more than ever before."
Upon hearing these words he slowly opened the door.
The moon ascends to its place in the sky.
Hand and hand he and his wife lie.

Paul Narkiewicz

Tim

Mind, body, and soul
Connected by a single link.
Swept away and stolen whole,
A single, spontaneous blink.
Horrifying actions, my mind cannot fathom.
Familiar questions of "why?"
Answers my soul cannot imagine.
But I know my brother will fly.
Angels will accept him,
To join a great kingdom in the sky.
Golden gates will swing open,
And my baby brother will fly.

Jesse Effman

Sanity

To my dearest S.B. . . . . never let go of hope!
Sometimes sanity hangs suspended by a thread,
like a spider dangling
from a single strand of her silken web.
This tiny link straining to hold her securely to her world,
threatens to snap under the pressure of the wind,
and drop her at the mercy of a thousand scavengers . . .
where they probe at her and pick at her
until the last of her quivering legs
curlstightlyagainstherbody in death.

Jana DeLaune Fay

My Love

To the love of my life, wherever you are . . .
Oh, how I long to see the passion in your eyes,
to feel the love welling from deep within your soul,
as I taste the sweetness of your lips.
I long to feel you tremble in my arms
as we become one.
Oh, my love, my life, where are you?
I'm searching, searching for you who makes me complete.
Will I ever feel your love?
I hope, for hope is all I have as I walk these streets alone.
Searching for you, my love, my life,
my everything.

Shaun R. Allen

Awaiting

I stand on the sparkling sands
and watch the waves splash,
Forming white foam from the seas.

Since you went away,
My hair has been like flying tumbleweed.
Of course I could oil and wash my hair,
But why should I adorn myself?

How I wish it would rain!
The sun shines so brightly.

The fleecy clouds float along in the sky,
And with every shape that is formed
I think of you.

My hands may be as cold as ice,
And my face white as chalk,
Only my soul remains waiting.

Kathy Leong Pucci

The Light within the Darkness

Without vision there would be no light,
Without light there would be no shadows,
Without shadows there would be no darkness,
Without darkness there would be no secrets,
Without secrets there would be no evil,
Without evil there would be no good,
Without good there would be no understanding,
Without understanding there would be no light,
Without light there would be no vision.

Asher Holley

Parallax

Light is a mote with which to stretch time's dome,
    The raddled eye made blunt by vision.
    In this would mint sight take the felicity of
Rome's end: the coming of the Goths, the Visi—
    Emperors who ruled with Heaven's Rod.

Trapped in the exhalation of a glance, want's
Body beats: a clean encoded pant that refreshes
And pervades. Amour has many actions, said the
Prince, and I shall invade; here is the arrow of my
    Intention and it is shot from law.

Ruth would end the melancholy of the screen. The
    Paupers' lot is brittle. A rood wall separates the
Suzerain from God, and here the Devil is not a little.
Manacles may bind the people in a kind of hideous
Function, but there's the rub and here's the wheel.

Nicholas Green

Wilted

Alluring, flower-like, growing
Innocently in the upland pasture.
Energy lightening every sensuality.
A hazy film overlays the eye of Heaven.
Repulsive, serpent-like, advancing
Wantonly, thrusting impurities.
Shadows darken every defilement.
A ruthless horror ignites the neither world.
Tarnished petals dwell infinitely.

Angela Northey

Accident

The phone.
It's the Hospital.
My brother was in a car accident.
He has a possible broken neck.

I drop to my knees.
Tears rush down my face.
I go to the hospital.
Powerful pain rushes through my body.

I feel the loneliness deep inside.
Emotions start to show.
Shades of tears run down my face.

The Doctor comes out.
He's alright.
But I can't forget what could have happened that night.

Dennis McCormick

At Then

When the earth and the sky both touch the heavens,
And the dusk and the dawn come face to face with time,
And the light and the darkness can both share the shadows,
Most happy am I at then.
However . . . When all the beauty and love in the world is lost,
And war and peace compete for the minds of man,
And the future falls victim to the past,
Most sad am I at then.

But when the heavens cease,
And time turns cold,
And the shadows all fade away,
What am I at then?

Or when the lost is forever,
And war and peace both lose,
And the past instead falls victim to the future,
What am I at then?

I know for certain, despite all,
That when I look to the heavens,
And to those shared times,
(From which we learned and fought over),
I will remember you, and forever are you at then.

And forever are you at then.

Leo Tran

"This Is the End"

New things are always ahead of me.
New opportunities, new looks, new likes.
But most of all, new loves.
I've been through so many likes and looks.
From different personalities to different dreams.
I've tried to change how I look,
A hair cut there, no more glasses.
But yet, there's this part of me that doesn't seem to change;
the part of new loves.
A few times I found a few loves.
But not really the ones I was looking for.
Within me I learned to truly love you,
Love you for the real you.
Your sweetness, your kisses, the love you gave me,
My heart was content.
Because I loved you more than anything.
I no longer have you by my side.
I try to go on, look for another love greater than yours.
I can't do it. For my heart only beats for one.
The one that used to talk to me until I fell asleep.
The one that said we'd be together for eternity.

Jessica Estrada

My Monster

The ache of loneliness lives within me,
The pain of solitude devours me,
Raging inside is the yearning to be free
And to cast of the chains of my burden.
Companionship has become an old wives' tale
Wanting love: yet I always fail.

Always running from the thoughts in my mind,
They give chase and are always right behind,
Images of a life torn to shreds
By a monster who's hungry
even after the countless times he's been fed!

A starving beast will surely fail
Freedom comes once the monster is dead
Now my solitude is the old wives' tale.

Jeremy Smith

I Feel So Far Behind

Your finger fast in my fisted palm
To secure my way on your strong lead,
I double-time to your huge stride
And side by side run eye-belt high.

Staying the pace I try to keep
Good going, though not my only hope
But to run hard so you cannot see,
I feel so far behind.

Your giving heart beats half as fast
As does mine, for you love I reach
To take your heart and give you mine.
But to amour you pour, mine can't compare

To give, to care, to all extremes.
Though we go gamete to gamete,
zygoting along,
It is insufficient to fulfill my one life's dream,
To love you more than you love me.

Not in a little way, so you cannot know
I feel so far behind.

Lee Park

Poem of Picnic

Going picnic with the food for thought will be wiser
than enjoying any grand banquet at five-star hotel
We sustain ourselves not merely by the edible food,
but also the word of God that is all on the house.

There is no telling that manna can be falling again
If we have gone astray in the wilderness of life, we need
to ask for those provision like wafers made with honey.
Uh, that is most antiquated food reserved by Moses!

Peter K. Y. Chang

Mighty Giant

Tall and straight, mighty and strong,
you sing to me from a benevolent throng.
Sunlight through your leaves shines green,
and moonlight filters through silver branches.
Upon a mountain-top high in the air,
the eagles join your concert fair.
The gods and goddesses of the wood, praises to you sing.
Oh, mighty giant whose life we crave for our own.
You give life to us mere mortals,
who cut you down and destroy all life within your haven.
We laugh and cry and follow your movements
and we long to fly into your bows as the raven.
Oh, mighty giant, tall and strong,
our praises to you we sing.
For you our life our living wonder, you offer us protection.

Bonnie Stone

Did You Ever Try?

There are tears that come from deep in the heart
Did you ever attempt to wipe them away?
There are cries that were there from the start
But you always said it would be O.K.

There are horrible memories that will not fade
Could you ever do anything but deny?
There are fears that come from being so afraid
Was it not worth it to give it a try?

There are wounds that will never heal
Did you have to close your eyes?
There are things that aren't right to feel
Could you not tell the truth instead of the lies?

There are screams that constantly filled the air
Did you have to run out the door?
There are times when you should've been there
But you wanted to be somewhere else even more

There is a human being with a broken heart
Did you ever try to even see?
There is a person who is torn apart
Why do you deny it's me?

Amanda Beaudry

Silhouette of My Desire

Of all the desires to treasure on this Earth,
my soul's desire is to become one with another.
It is intimacy that I seek, it is a special love that I have,
stored up from many years of growing and waiting.
The love of my life is but a dream, a prayer, an honest desire;
formless in shape to my eyes as faith is unseen,
yet as real as the heart that beats and gives me life.
I have but an imaginary picture in my mind's eye,
of the one my heart desires.
As infinite as the sand, as vast as the sea,
as numerous as the stars, is my love for thee—
the one for whom my whole being longs to have and hold,
for what I can only fathom as eternity.
My stoic gaze has captured both earth and sky,
as my enraptured thoughts drifted into prayers for you.
I trust the moment yet feel the ebb and flow of contentment.
Yet faith, hope, and love are my hallmarks for life.
Now I will sleep and dream, and you will be in them.
One day when I awake, I hope to find thee,
and fulfill the silhouette of my desire.

Vithaya Phongsavan

When the World Has Ended

run, run, run, away from these times,
shatter the clocks, so not one chimes.
let the darkness loose and the evil free,
the night hides day continuously.
the earth bleeds into the seas,
the winds whisper between the trees.
now the clouds take over the sun,
before the dawn has truly begun.
the dull sky has swallowed the earth,
no more death and no more birth.
the green meadows have now turned brown,
the expressionless child without smile or frown.
the saddened soul of the unborn,
will never see the light of morn.
to sit in a room without windows or light,
not to be able to read or write.
say your last words to the people you've offended,
there will be no more life when the world has ended.

Jessie McNally

The Oppression

Your omnipresence encumbers me,
and I fall under the weight,
I would like so much the emptiness,
I live in a tombs,
and I'm losing my faith,

your odor is only stink,
and you are so morbid,
that I lose there the pleasure of every day,
and I become a zombie,
and two times you almost conquered me,
but the soothsayers helped saved me,

And my life is more undefined,
I suffer the passage from this life,
my partner is uncertainty,
and my children are loneliness and stress,

if the divorce could liberate me from you,
I would come out has a king,
the life would be a soft caress,
and my loves would be plenitude!
but it's impossible for me to drive you away.

Francis Boudreau

Xitrenka

For years I've had this foolish thought,
One day I'll know each code and lock.
A skill that baffles many men
Who spend most weekends free of friend
Yet then I came upon a door,
That even I could not explore.
One time I tried to pick the lock,
But should have walked up and just knocked.
Eventually I found the key,
But lost it in a hasty glee.
If all attempts do fall astray,
I'll sit back thinking in dismay.
What kind of door does not permit
A key that seems the perfect fit?
Right now I stand outside the gate.
How long shall I wait?
How long shall I wait?

Rejji Hayes

I Just Want to Be Happy

I just want to be happy,
Is that so much to ask?
I only wish to remove,
Sorrows unyielding mask.

I just want to be happy,
Why can't this be?
When happiness was given out,
None was saved for me.

I just want to be happy,
For happiness to fill my heart.
But instead it's filled with sadness,
And always torn apart.
I just want to be happy,
That's my cry that no one hears.
And everyone just ignores,
my silent painful tears.

I just want to be happy,
Why can't this wish come true?
Can't you see that all I need to be happy,
Is to be loved by you?

Laura Murdick

Peaceful Slumber

Lay me in a cedar box
when my sun has finally set.

Sprinkle my pillow with fallen pine needles
as I lay my head in rest.

Lift me into the heavens
like a peaceful white dove.

While rocking my soul eternally
in the bosom of your love.

Yvonne Strickland

Man in the Back of a Pickup Truck

Yes, I'm wearing a suit and tie . . .
Riding on the back of this pickup truck
But, I'm on my way up you see . . .
THIS . . . is only TEMPORARY!

His proud face was held up high . . .
A disdainful look in his eyes . . .
As he rode proudly by
On the back of a pickup truck . . .

I smiled as I looked at him
Turned my face quickly away from him . . .
For he didn't want me to notice him, You see . . .
Riding on the back of a pickup truck!

All the young start out this way
He's not the only one in suit and tie . . .
Who has started his serious young life . . .
From the back of a Pickup truck!

Manuela Hernandez

It's You

When I close my eyes.
I see you smiling at me.
When I feel the wind.
I feel you touching me.
When I hear a voice.
I hear you calling for me.
It's you, your the one I want to be near.
When I pick up the phone.
It's your voice, I want to hear.
When I open the door.
It's you, I want standing there.
It's you, your the one I want to be near.
When I'm scared.
It's your arms, I want to hold me tight.
When I'm sad.
It's your touch, I want to feel through the night.
When I'm happy.
It's your way of making everything alright.
It's you, your the one,
I want to be near.

Casey Badger

God's Dream

I dream of a person who can be anything he wants to be,
and not afraid and open enough to let me see.
I dream of a person who's passion rages like fire at night,
but knows to control and use it to bring in My light.
Someone who is fervent and diligent in the works of his hands,
and doesn't seek the glory and honor offered by man.
I dream of a person who is content in the way he is,
because of the worth in Me that is his.
I dream of a person whose heart is not hollow,
and knows that being a leader means to follow.
Constant depthness in love is what I wish,
So I created that person, who can be anything he wants to be,
in hopes that he would love me.

Han Oh

The Hospital Lounge

In a small room tucked away
Near the end of the hall,
Under the fluorescent lights,
Along a blank grey wall
Sits a row of conjoined chairs
That have held thousands in thrall.

The grieving slaves who have taken
Their loathsome seats in this room
Sit in dry, sterile white light,
Drenched in sickness and gloom.
Their loved ones are dying,
Disease and trauma precursors of doom.

Every day and every night,
The dying's would-be saviors
Dressed uniformly in white,
Solemnly enter to tell
Lounge dwellers of the now-empty shell.
"We did all we could . . . " the physicians' refrain—
Their words only double the survivors' pain.

John Hawkshead

I Am Not a Poet

To the loves of my life
I am not a poet,
Maybe I use to be one,
maybe I'll be again.
I just know that 28 candles
will be blown away soon,
and I don't know where I have been.

Have I kissed a prince?
Have I found a cure?
No, not yet.
But, I have found an ivy tower
In which lives a prince,
Who is making a cure for me.

Maybe on the 30th day of May,
The tower will be blown up to pieces.
Maybe the sugar syrup that has
Wrapped around my heart will be burnt up.
Maybe I'll find out the prince is all the frogs that I have kissed.
Maybe I'll find out that there is no maybe . . . and life is just IS.

Erica Chung

Seasons of Love

Spring is the beginning of
youthful vibrant things.
Summer is the blossoming of every child's dreams.
Autumn is the time of change, and
growing up you see.
Winter is the time in which
my love you came to be.
Now, today, for all eternity
All my love belongs to thee.

Cynthia Gutierrez

Struggle for the Secret Place

Searching for the hidden truth within the lies,
my soul has no choice but to close its eyes.
Imagination of mountain top paradise,
but mired down by deceitful device.
Trying to run away within my mind,
hearing only voices with words unkind.
Stabbing deep to my secret place,
and tearing down my inner space.
Struggling to survive when things go bad,
running away from the abuse called Dad.

Ralph Smith

My Love, My Life

The only one who covers my soul with love.
Like the rain on a sunny day,
my heart is showered with happiness.
With cool days filled with warmth,
a breath of fresh air is held with anticipation.
When lips touch smooth as silk and arms wrap as one
together, a connection is made and hearts are bound.
You are my love and my life.

Stephen Andrews

spirit song

music lightens the heart, just listen.
to majestic clouds, that surrounds one's images.
the day is deep with great reward.
to one's own self, whose just explored.
softness of the heart, which one has ignored.

beauty of creation, taken granted again.
through song it has spoken, and lifted the soul.
the song says more, just listen once more.
listen and dream, what the spirit song means.

time passes on, and so, the music goes on.
life has come and gone.
but through song, the spirit sings on.

yes, the spirit song is love. you are never alone,
nor forgotten above. and in great anticipation,
the spirit song sings, to all creation,
under Heaven it brings.
and to those who listen, the lesson is sing.

Raymond Robidas

My Love for You

I'm sitting here writing this poem to you,
Trying to find the words to say my love for you is true.
Every time I see you, my heart skips a beat,
But every time I hear your voice, I get cold chills to my feet.
Your unique sense of style is what attracted me to you,
You drive me crazy, but there's nothing I can do.
Looking straight into your eyes would be a dream come true,
But until that day comes, pictures of you will have to do.
I'm hoping one day I'll have a chance to read this to you.
Then you'll know my love for you is and always will be true.

Briana Jump

The Unforgiven Wrong

Love I thought I tasted, wasted
Time I could have spent, repent
All that I have lost to nothing gained!

Careless was the chase, embrace
That which claimed to cure, impure
Thoughts which dance into my mind remained!

Filled with passions fire, prior
To the knowledge of, above
All my anger, not easily contained!

Risks that I have taken, waken
Fears from deep within, herein
They fester, sanity of mine is stained!

Oh! My scars not healing, kneeling
Before Love I ask when, again
I shall heal from the wounds I have sustained!

Of the gods I question, discretion
Not used in emotions wake, mistake
That Love was really never quite explained!

Gary Turner

Street Gangs Vs War

I have heard the cannon's roar, seen the brilliant
flares at night burst bright, then settle slowly,
to fall spent amongst the dead.

I have known and seen the fear etched
on faces of once boisterous young men,
who cringe—and yes, sometimes sob,
at first meeting with the foe, yet fight on
and find their courage once again.

In war although I must declare that
war is wrong, when day is done, the
battle won, the soldiers sing their victory song—
they battle not for gold or fame, but
to hold our countries freedoms strong.

But you young man, who hate and disrespect the life
that I hold dear, who kill and maim
to reap the profit bought with others misery and fear.

Remember that the pleasures that you seek to buy with
your ill-gotten gain, can never come,
except through sacrifice and love of life,
but never—never—through another's pain.

Daniel Conley

The Grub

The grub in the shrub gave me a rub—
Not in the flimsy film of my skin,
But in the non-palpable filaments of my mind,
Awakening feelings undefinable in the shrubbery there!
The mother could never set eyes on the young one,
Despite it, how much care had gone into the making of that castle

The base had been set with love-selfless love
So that the offspring could face the gales!
The gales that may wreck the whole structure
That may tumble down, if not for the strong base.
Lasting love makes firm mettle
That stands steadfast in the face of storms.
It rankles in my mind that the mother turtle
should leave its grub in the shrub,
"Wherever it is and whatever happens,
Let my grub thrive in life."

Subhadra Sadanandan

Memories

I have a place I keep my thoughts, too precious to forget.
A storage room within my head, and the key locked in my heart.
A street, a house, a neighbor, a friend,
and even my childhood pet
Are all inside this storage room and I shall never part.

My memories are the golden door of a past
that is left behind.
A time when I was not afraid to let my spirit wander.
As time slips on and years go by,
and friends they come to mind,
My storage room is always there for me to look and ponder.

I will slip away and reminisce behind that golden door.
Sometimes I'll smile, sometimes I'll laugh,
and sometimes I'll even cry
I'll look upon those memories,
and know what I've been living for.
A kiss, a hug, a smile, a laugh, is all that made me fly.

And when I am old and turning grey, my glasses I'll not need.
I will open that door and go inside and look around with pride.
For all my memories will be sitting there, pages I will not read
My life I'll watch as the years turn back . . . .
Like the rolling oceans tide.

Dawn Wray

My Deliverance

I came to kill you; I had it all planned out—
Which bullet, which gun, and how I'd go about.
No one seemed to care how I felt,
What was inside, how much anger I held.
To sacrifice so much and receive so little
From so-called friends who stabbed and belittled
My intelligence, innocence, and kindness for weakness,
When after all, you're the one with the secrets—
Secrets so deep and far, not my place to tell.
Secrets so deep they'd send you straight to Hell.
Shhh . . . don't act as if you don't know what I'm saying.
It was all revealed to me while I was praying,
Which is why I had a sudden change in heart,
Because God sent to me an angel from afar
To warn that if I sin with seven times repay,
I'd be far more worse than you!!
And quite frankly, that's NOT what I'm trying to do.
I also realized that you too have a soul,
And it cries out desperately in hopes to be made whole.
As Jesus forgave me, I forgave you,
And just to let you know, I genuinely care for you . . .
Your soul, that is, as it belongs to God.
All you have to do is re-confess; it's not that hard.
In the Body of Christ, we are as one.
So I've chosen the right path and my victory will be won!!

Nichelle Mungo

The Sailor

Your man sails off . . . with a kiss good-bye,
  as you drive away you begin to cry.
Both of you knowing without a doubt,
  he has no choice but to sail about.
The days you keep busy doing all you can ,
  but still even busy . . . you miss your man.
The sound of his voice calling your name,
  and you miss his loving touch just the same.
But knowing in your heart this must be done,
  no way to hide from it, nowhere to run.
So you pick up your chin and put on a smile,
  remembering in your heart . . . gone . . only a little while.
You look toward his sailing back to you,
  and hold the thought . . . it time this will all be through.
But for now he serves his Country,
  and I stand by my Man.
When his ship pulls in that final time,
  together forever . . . hand in hand.

Debra Francis

Together in Spirit

I am here and you are there.
Yet look around, we are everywhere.
In every tree and cloud you see,
Look real close, you will see me.
In every blade of grass that grows
Another facet of me shows.
Even in the rose so sweet,
Another facet of me to greet.
The babbling brook that grows to the sea,
Displays a reflection of you and me.
The animals with their love so true,
Portray the innocence of me and you.
Everywhere you look you will see me.
I'm always with you.
You are Me.

Kristi Posey

The Union of Love

In the spring the snow melts,
And the streams they conceive life anew.

With the morning the sun awakens,
And bursts rays of light upon the dew.

The flowers and trees, and all of nature rejoices,
As the Almighty gently caresses the fields.

The fruits of God flow from every mountain,
Into the valleys that bring forth His yields.

Everything in all of creation moves in cycles,
Without beginning or end in perfect symphony.

Now is our time when our love must never cease to grow,
As we journey together in complete harmony.

Lance C. Ball

My Crystal Jar

There were nights I wished upon a star . . .
I placed those wishes in my crystal jar.
I kept them there so I could see if they would come true,
were they meant to be?
Once in a while I would reach down inside and pull one out . . .
Should I run? Or hide??   Was I really that selfish?
Did I wish for that?   All I wanted was money?   Good looks??
Not so fat???   My crystal jar now sits on a shelf . . .
a constant reminder of my "Other-Self . . . "
I learned a good lesson from my wishes on stars . . .
they won't come true when locked in a jar.

Nancy Witte

Love Lost

when I think of the love we had before
my heart aches with pain more and more
when I think of the days that I held you close
those are the days my arms miss the most
when I think of rainy nights when our passion was wild
those are the nights I cry like a child
when I think of how your eyes set my heart afire
now my heart is bound as if buried in a mire
when I think of all the things I miss and what of me it cost
I can only sigh and grieve of the love I lost

Joseph Ford

Enchanted Horizon

A life of endless obstacles.
Her soul held captive in a web of disarray.
Tormented by the silence of life's unanswered questions,
her heart cries out!
Who Am I?
How Long Must I Hide Behind This Shield Of Sadness?
Through the morning's whispering wind
an Angelic voice speaks out.
There is no shame in who you are.
Your life is my canvas.
In my image you were created.
For your soul is free again
to fly into the heart of the sunrise.

Christopher Paulin

On a Stroll

There's a street in town paved with griefs
Of drunken beggars and devious thieves
Of wealthy bankers and homeless guys
A world of malice who ignore their cries
With storefronts and taverns that fuel the fire
Or maybe it's Greed that is the liar
Buried beneath this highway of t'morrow
Is a road that's spilling full sorrow

Matthew Sebree

Music around the World

Music can be heard all around the world.
Everything we see and hear 'tis a musical unfurled.
Whether great or small or really loud and weird.
Music is a wonderful thing heard around the world.

Whether it is sorrowful or just a happy tune.
It may be used to comfort or simply just to soothe.
Each note expressed in life is important to us all.
Music's a necessity on twenty-four hour call.

The bird's who sing great melodies.
The bee's who buzz in time.
Nature's all a musical played in perfect rhyme.
Every tree and flower have special music power.
Music is a part of life which cannot be denied.

TaRena Nail

Afterlife

In the light, in the wind
Time passes by.

By the day, by the night
Time passes by.

As one looks at life,
Time is taken to realize the humble, sweet moments.

With every touch, with every breath
Time passes by.

Sweet kisses, as one reminisces
Time passes by.

Lost loves gone in the wind,
Years of missing one's kin

Life as it is known,
In a heartbeat it is gone,
As time passes by.

Alisa Bankhead

Forever

I was walking through a graveyard one day
I saw the past as it was
the present as it is
and the future as it will be

William Nix

Child Within

I look inside and find a child
Within my heart, tender and mild
Who likes to dance and likes to play
And likes to sing his cares away

He wants to love with all his heart
One so pure it will not part
He wants to live in a world
Where peace and love are all that's heard

He knows that truth is always right
And only kindness wins the fight
He wants to see the world I know
But I keep him locked below

For though the child never fears
I've seen the truth of all my years
Thus I keep him tucked away
Deep inside me, safe to play

Because I know that if the child
Knew the truth he'd lose his smile
And I would lose that ignorance
That gives me hope and innocence

Joseph Roberts

Cyprus Symphony

The wind comes and goes
To a place it knows well.
The green pines longingly
Try to follow, but are imprisoned
By the dirt that gives them life.
The Cyprus trees majestically
Hover the palmetto bushes
And the mirrored bronze water.
Their roots emerge to discover and conquer.
The Spanish moss dangles and dances
To a song created by this splendor.
Water lilies bloom,
Bursting forth from the life
That continually cycles this niche.
An alligator bellows his presence
And a turtle disappears into ringlets
Of the liquid gold.
The sun and clouds sculpt the background.
All in this garden of life
Contribute to the exquisite symphony.

Kim Raubolt-Hurst

The Scent of Love

To Greg
Proud roses, standing tall with beauty and perfection
Sunflowers, swaying in the summer's wind
Water Lilies, in crystal waters shimmering reflection
Their grace will fade whenever they're absent.
Behold, and breathe the essence of existence
The scent that makes it all worthwhile
Pursue your goals with all the same persistence
And life and love will rise to reconcile.
Oh, how auspicious, that now just when my heart I lost
A fragrance, delicate and sweet
Surrounds me, and the source by which was caused
What made my fears be obsolete—is Love.
Love's scent that now is all about
My soul, my heart, my being
Comes, that I know without a doubt
From the first time seeing—you.
Although I know you not by touch
And rules we've surely bent
But I am certain inasmuch
As this Love's scent—is true. I Love you!

Jeannine Bagshaw

My Mistake

My life is empty,
My soul is no longer complete.
You are gone now,
Because of me, I had to cheat.

I know we weren't exactly a couple,
And that really broke my heart,
So when you told me you never loved me, you tore my soul apart.

So then I went and searched for love,
I thought it would soothe my soul,
But soon I realized you treated me like a queen,
and put me on your pedestal,
But I broke your heart,
And I broke your #1 rule.

But our oath of friendship,
The oath to never tell a lie;
Well, I lied a lot,
I didn't want you not to feel the things I thought,
So I would try to make the feelings go away,
But something inside of me kept them, they had to stay.

Erica Humbert

Frankenstein

His hair was as black as the blackest night,
His yellowish skin was a frightening sight,
His black lips gave a terrifying scare,
His yellowish eyes sent a chill through the air,
The hair on my neck started to rise,
Wider and Wider opened my eyes,
And with each movement that he did make,
I could feel my entire body shake,
But when he turned and looked at me,
And I saw all the pain that had hurt the,
I knew then there were all sorts of kinds,
But this one belonged to Victor Frankenstein

Tasha Cady

Two Trees

Over the years
the branches have bent
and twisted into each other
Drawing the two closer
First gentle support
Over time bleeding under pressure
until the intertwined share the same pulse
An arboreal dance
of light and shade
Aged beauty born of survival
under the stars and into the Earth

Julia Meno

Snow

Snow flakes falling,
ground so white,
kids come running through the snow,
I remember how I used to play in the white, white snow.
Me and my sister all dressed in red,
running through the snow!
All of my friends were so sad,
I had to leave to somewhere else.
I told them they cried,
everybody misses us,
everybody's voice saying bye, bye, bye.
Never saw snow that white,
from the day I said bye, bye, bye!

Azra Karacic

"Soul Mates"

Cautiously working my way through life's maze,
through dark troubled nights,
and long lonely days.
My spirit grows weary,
the hills way too steep.
The road unrelenting,
the pitfalls too deep.
There's no turning back,
for I know it's too late.
But then my soul speaks,
"I have found you a mate!"
Miles fade away and years quickly pass,
the end is in sight, journey's over at last.
Where did the time go? It wasn't so bad.
with you by my side,
it's the best trip I've had.
So I said to my soul,
"I can't leave! I can't go!
Let's do it again!
But, this time take it slow."

Kathryn Hartzell

Life

If my life is to have substance and meaning,
If I am to survive this hurt,
Then I mustn't concede that I've failed,
only misjudged and mistrusted.
I must realize that to trust, and to love again
Begins with myself, and to know
that one lives and learns from mistakes made.
I am the only one who can make a difference in my life,
For only I control my destiny.
I will be positive in every aspect of my life
And accept challenges willingly.
Change constitutes growth, and growth constitutes life.
So now I must view life, not for a different point of view,
but with a renewed spirit and attitude.
And with the knowledge that my mere existence has meaning.

Artelelia Pelote

The Wonderful Gift of Writing

Writing's like an adventure that's running through my mind,
where anything is possible and everything's a find.
It opens doors and windows to fabulous creation,
and pulls out thoughts and stories from your imagination.
It's a way of saying things from deep within your heart;
Your deepest feelings come about like a priceless piece of art.
Sometimes I don't know or even seem to see,
until it's down on paper of what I am to be.
With certain words, I slip away and play a different role,
with deep emotion, energy and the reflections of my soul.
The things I love the most are captured with a pen;
the smells, the winds and sunset views are gladly felt again.
Words are the world's stories, from past and present too.
It's all about its history and everything that's new.
The magic of discovery is more than you can see,
'cause what I write on paper is just a part of me.

Chandar Richards

Mom

In Loving Memory of Bonita Barker Carnahan (4-14-48 to 12-9-98)
The day I was born, you were right there
To hold me and cherish me, and give me loving care.
The day I started school, you were right there.
The day I was confirmed, again you were there.
The day I graduated, you were right there.
Every day of my life, you were right there.
You gave me strength, when I couldn't go on.
You held up my head, when I thought all hope was gone.
You wiped tears from my eyes, and made the pain go away.
For me, I knew, you would give your very life away.
To say that I miss you, is just not enough.
The days will be hard, and times may be tough.
But every day, I will think of you,
How you stood by my side
Through thick and thin, good times and bad.
And though I may cry, and be a little sad,
I will always have your love, deep in my heart.
And for the rest of my life, it shall never part.

Brian Paul Barker

The End is Near

As the thunder rolls across the desert sky.
Dark and Gloomy.
I hold the cold black sand in my palm.
The cool refreshing wind blows it from my hand.
Depression sets in and my head drops to my chin.
Lonely and sad, A single raindrop falls from the sky,
And lands on my neck, it trickles down my spine.
I slowly blink and bring my head up to see the end.

Jim Fischer

God Sent Me an Angel

God sent me an angel,
To help me turn my life around.
God sent me an angel,
So I could have a smile instead of a frown.
God sent me an angel,
To tell me he loves me.
God sent me an angel,
And now I can open my eyes and see.
God sent me an angel,
To help my worries go away.
God sent me an angel,
To be with me every single day.
God sent me an angel,
So I won't be alone.
God sent me an angel,
To help me get through the times
when someone I love is gone.
God sent me an angel,
To keep me from crying.
God will send me an angel,
Even when I'm dying.

Ashley Johnson

Set Sites Higher

A goal was shared between them
Common, yet subtle in its transparency
A void that could be filled by succeeding
By resurrecting their dreams
Into the five sense image of reality
Hoping reality is not a dream

Embrace the chances that are steps on the ladder to opportunity
So easy, yet so unbearably painful
In sharing the goal, they shared the doubts
They shared the pain and they shared the questions
Questions that plagued the soul and mind
Answers to the questions that wouldn't be revealed

Hand above hand, foot above foot
Digging their roots into the thick mud
Like by a flash-flood, they are uprooted
Barely hanging on to the ladder
They fall

A new goal shared between them
Different, but undeniably obvious in its future successes
A new ladder of opportunity
tall, yet smooth, bright and peaceful
and higher, for truly it should be
for it will lead to a higher level

Trent Maynard

I Love You with All My Heart

I miss you so much, I need your kiss,
Your warm heart and tenderness,
The way you used to look at me,
Made me feel all tingly,
At school I used to wait for you,
By the lockers but now we're through,
And now all I can think about is you,
Oh, why can't you say you love me too,
I love you so much with all my heart,
I wish we could never ever be apart,
You said you didn't love me that way,
We only went out for just one day,
When I heard those words come out of your mouth,
All I could do was scream and shout,
Oh, why oh, why don't you love me that way,
I love you so much I can't even say,
Now is the end of this poem you hear,
And I am about to go into tears,
And so I have to say bye-bye,
And I am saying this with a sigh,

Valerie Kasen

"Winter Blankets Are Needed"

A winter blanket is needed
When the snow begins to fall
and all the trees seem very tall
When all the leaves have coated the ground
and white flurries are seen all around
When sleds are sliding
and skis are gliding
When hot cocoa is sipped
and by the cold our noses are nipped
When in our coats we do cuddle
and by the fire we all huddle
When chimney smoke fills the air
and no birds are seen anywhere
When three little kittens lose their mittens
and all our mothers are just as smitten
When we walk through what dad did
Winter blankets are needed . . .

Renea Hanna

The Bad Luck Bush Man

Bad Luck Joe was his name,
And attempting robbery was his game.
He tried to rob the Christmas Mail,
But when he'd try he'd only fail.

The coachman said, "You're too slow,
Christmas was a week ago!"
So through the bush he rode with force,
Upon his old, three legged horse.

He rode into a eucalypt, And off the horse he roughly slipped.
Just then the squatters came in red,
And without a word the bushman fled.

Soon he felt sore and weak, And rested by a reedy creek,
But as the horizon began to dim,
The troopers came to capture him.

Joe dived into the foot-deep stream,
And gave a final victory scream.
Now as you pass by that creek, You hear old Joe softly speak.

Again he returns to that very same place,
With a gum tree bruise right on his face.
His spirit floats among the trees,
And his bad luck blows on the breeze!

Ammie Stone

Ash

There's ash in the air
in the lungs in the hair
on the windows on the floor,
Look! Here comes some more.
It's in the grass and on the trees
sometimes it even makes me sneeze.
It makes people stop and ask
Do you really need that mask?
The ash is everywhere you look
it even got into a brook.
How will this affect the bird and bee,
or for that matter you and me?
Ash got us in Glenoma and then in Westport,
that's twice as of this report.
How many years will Mount Saint Helens blow?
You know it was 26yrs. 123yrs. ago.

Linda Roberts

A Vision of Beauty

As lovely as a daisy,
in the peak of its bloom.
Lustrous like the pole star,
with the serenity of the moon

She stands there alone,
with a lonesome look in her eyes.
As graceful as a swan,
But twice as shy.

Her eyes are shining diamonds,
set in a sapphire face.
A smile from her is enough,
to light up the place.

She has that special something
which makes her irresistible.
She is charming, witty and caring,
and oh, so sensible!

As she moves she leaves behind,
a trail of broken hearts.
Careful, or you too will be left;
with a wistful smile and a sad song in your heart.

    Shabeer Khader

Idle Thoughts

Nothing fancy to say . . .
No smiles to light the way . . .
In the end I am, nothing more than I was . . .
Nothing more than I ever will be . . .
A soul slighted to see all that is wrong, with what is . . .
How I lead life, Still wonders me . . .
Looking, yet never finding . . .
Knowing full well that I cannot, yet still trying . . .
Tunneling to be free of this existence . . .
Only to find at the other end, is me . . .
The cycle begins anew . . .
Thus am I shunned by the wheel . . .
Fated to spin out, again and again . . .
A soul so old, time has forgotten . . .
This soul . . . foul . . . corrupt . . . and rotten . . .
To find an end, in the beginning anew . . .
And each time, I shall still know,
You . . .

    Keith Richardson

Wish You Were There

How I wish you were there
To share with me the glow of the morning sun
To listen to the birds twitter
And the leaves rustle in the trees

How I wish you were there, while I
Prepare to face another day
While I comb my hair and make up my face
I wish you were looking over my shoulder
Through the mirror at me
And giving me that warm smile
That says you love me

How I wish you were there
To dance with me to my favorite song
Holding me cheek to cheek
Our hearts beating as one
And wishing that time would stand still for eternity

And at evening time I miss you the most
How I wish then you were there
To share with me my aloneness
For then I would be complete

    Josephine Fernandes

Home

A home is a place where people stay
They spend the night and most of the day
A home is not just a house
A home has children, laughter and shouts
A home looks happy, a home looks gay
A home looks pretty throughout the day
So remember your home, remember it well
For it's not just a place in which to dwell
But a place to worship, a place to play
A place where love will rule each day

    Larry Newberry

One of Many Muses

Presence from our silence comes undone
Skipping out in a professional sort of way
Chatter rises from the next table
Threatens to contradict my muse

Unlike all the other quiet moments
This one's got a faded kind of feeling
Unconfirmed deja-vu's stumble through my mind
Sidestep my memory
They've been there before

Like they say, history repeats itself again
People come and go
Drag their gods down with them to the grave
And then proclaim their names live on
Throughout the years of fear

Gleefully, tragically
The children solve the mystery
Stuff themselves with signs and wonders
And then forget them when they grow

Too bad it's us who have to teach
The children how to live

    Jessica Ranville

Come to Me

I dedicate this poem to my husband Brian McDade.
On wings of angels do I fly to thee tonight
Come; oh, come to me this night
Lie, lie here with me tonight
until the stars of night turn into stars of light
Come; come find that which you seek of me tonight
Lit not the night find not the love of you and I
Oh, but let the night welcome morning light with the
Love of you and I

    Melody McDade

Time

Don't let time pass you by
Head every moment 'til you die
Life's to short to throw away
I suggest you seize the day

The hour hand strikes twelve again my friend
Can't turn it back a minute it's already then
Time is a river that seems to never end

Don't look back and cry
Let the past say goodbye
Listen to the voice in your head
I guarantee peace lies ahead

What if that if that was this
All the chances that we missed
Don't let time pass you by
Because soon we all will die

    Billy Jack Benson

Me and the Fig Tree

My soul is a parched wasteland without YOU.
A desolate place that seldom sees the rain fall.
And when it does come
For a brief moment, it flourishes
But just for a moment,
Because in the heat, it again forgets
In bitter agony it falls into its natural state
Winds tear across it
The blowing sands are the only sound,
A dry and empty sound
An abandoned land far from anyone,
It is a flat, filled with poisoned soils,
And in the distance
Where sky meets rock,
There stands a lone tree
Me, the barren and withered fig tree

Timothy Trivellin

A Drop of Our Descent

To a friend in spirit
A sacred feeling of pain,
is a blessing and curse by all.
As someone close is put to rest,
our causes seem to drain our sorrow.
A single tear says a thousand words,
Though none can tell us what it bears.
A pain of all our problems within,
would give our agony to those we care.
We mourn our loved ones as we drop those tears.
A feeling of sadness within its substance.
A salty reality of our truth.
As we pass away every time.
A dreadful cause to hold inside,
as we show the world our dried eyes.
Yet when we omit the watchful eyes,
we see a star glimmering within.
A single tear, is willing to drop,
holding its spherical yet pointed top.
To prevent its painful descent,
as we weep its final remorse.

Moumita Roy

Only God Can Judge Me

Well, one phrase I leave to those judgmental people;
"Only God can judge me."

Virginia Mata

Whose Offer Was a Better Way

Do you remember the story
Of an angel trying to please God?
Where every day the angel found,
That with the God her life was bound,
To wither away and die.
The rituals never ceased,
To find that long sought holy place.
Always far too many to please,
Giving every moment to seize
The element of perfection.
Fate takes hold when left alone;
God didn't stop to consider,
She'd soon make the lies come true
When she was finally given her cue
To lift the burden away.
The story ends with death,
The angel unable to achieve her goal.
Even though good wins over evil,
She found herself leaving with the devil,
Whose offer was a better way.

Kathryn Lay

How Do You See Me

If my insides were on the outside, what would you see?

A sunset, a snowfall or maybe a raging sea.

If my insides were a picture, what kind would I be?

An oil painting, collage or maybe a photo imagery.

If my insides were a color, what color would I be?

Or is my dark skin all you really need to see
to tell you all about me?

Shonn Collins

This Person

There is a person who goes with me where ever I go.
This person knows things about me that no one else knows.
At times I have wanted from this person to hide—
But hide I could not no matter how hard I tried.
Oh, at times I disguised myself and
became someone I was not.
"A pretense cannot be kept up forever"
was always my afterthought.
Besides, my constant companion likes who
I really am the best,
And has always waited patiently
while all these other faces I put to the test.
Quite faithful to me is this person who I realize is my friend.
Something tells me most definitely this friend
will be with me until the end.
I have decided that my best side I want my friend to always see,
Because this person who is my constant companion and friend is me.

Susan Berryhill

Here

Here I sit Sitting here
Here I am Where is here
Here is where You are not
Here is where I come to think
Think about you a lot Here is where
You were taught Taught how to lie
Lie a lot Here is where
My heart comes Comes to Cry
Cry a lot Here is where my soul comes
Comes to die To die from all the lies
Here is where I come Come when I am fried
I come here and sit Sit by the fireside
Here I Am trapped Come rescue me
But you have forgotten Where here is
So I guess Here I sit
Here I am Sitting here
Forever damned

Nelson Santos

Innocence

Sun breathes warm solar flashes—
Brilliance envelops the land.
A child imagines beyond tired grown-up comprehension.
Dancing sunbeams laugh; perhaps they understand.

Earth breathes brisk evening breezes.
Meteors tickle the sky.
A child dreams beyond tired grown-up contemplations.
Twinkling stars laugh; perhaps they know why.

Moon breathes gossamer night visions.
Angel sentries keep vigilance in the light.
A child prays beyond tired grown-up meditations.
Heaven hears and gently whispers goodnight.

Margaret W. Pierce

The Ocean

I dedicate my poem to GOD.
The ocean is as wide as God's Love;
The waves are as strong as God's power.
The ocean is beautiful like God's love for me;
The ocean is smooth like God's skin;
The ocean's breeze is gentle like God's touch.

Stephanie Harris

Mother

I feel a chilled wind a blowin'
     A blowin' around my soul
It's nothing but my sweet Mother
     Calling me to be coming home
Lord knows I need my Mother
     God knows I need her now
I'm going to be with my Mother
     But I don't know when or how

Elberta Riedl

Within

This poem is about the struggle that I faced to become myself.
It whispers soft within the soul,
and yearns for sweet repore.
but never gets to surface there
like birds of freedom soar.
It quickens with a gentle touch;
a glance of one who knows.
With hope that it can break the walls
with courage now arose.
yet timid and a bit unsure,
it reaches for the shore.
With childlike faith of long ago,
approaches the open door;
a rush of hope of better things
beyond its long lived home,
where bleakness, pain, and loneliness
enfolds the empty throne.
It passes through with sense of peace
not knowing what's in store.
And fills its heart with love and trust . . .
embraced for evermore.

Beverly Boresi

You and I

This is the celebration with just one life.
The start of a new generation can begin.
There will be sad and good times.
But their life will always get better.
They will look up to us as examples, and for wisdom.
We share a bond,
You and I.
We think alike.
We dream of the future.
What can it be?
What it may be.
I'll hope for the best,
Won't you?
We'll make the difference,
You and I.

Stephanie Meyecic

You Are the Greatest

I'm sure you know by now how much you mean to me,
but I couldn't let this day go by
without telling you some things you've made me see.

You have made me grow in so many ways,
not only by what you have done
but also what you've had to say.

I've learned more from you
than I could have ever learned in school,
you have taught me lots of things
and at times you were pretty cool.

You have taught me right from wrong,
you have given me everything you had,
you were always so very strong, even when you felt really bad.

You have been everything to me all of these years,
and it means a lot to me,
especially through the heart aches and tears,
and even when I was three.

I don't really know how to put my feelings down on paper,
but I hope you're getting the point that you are the greatest,
most wonderful, caring, loving, fun to be with person
that I have ever known.

Rebecca Reneau

The Curse of Blessing

Alone,
for my gift brings isolation,
Tired,
thus, I dream when still awake.
Sad,
because I cannot comprehend my joy,
Alive,
because I know love.
Unsatisfied,
for I am better than I am.
Happy,
for I can feel the world around me.
Blind,
for I can't see beyond the wall Between,
Wise,
because I know that I understand only what I see.

Adam Barrett

My Soul Has Gone off Somewhere

My soul betrays me
As it wanders off
And I am left empty.

Whatever it was that made me believe
I could keep it close to me,
Tied to a rope at the end of my heart,
I Was mistaken.

My fear drove it away
But it is free now, to drift,
To find that which it seeks
That which I lack.

When it returns, as in seclusion I wait,
I will make sure to keep it satisfied
And feed it love, and feed it God,
And keep it close, but not anchored, to my heart.

For it needs space
To roam, to flourish, to expand,
Serene, animated,
Free.

Charles Willemsen

The Divorced Daddy

How sad the times in courts today
They take men's children away.
They get involved where they don't belong,
In the lives of our children, who are gone.
Gone from the love of their fathers
A mother's bitterness does not belong.
The role of the parent is to love and guide
but Mother's forgot God's plan.

When all is done, and the children are grown,
who will make up for their forlorn.

Let's remember that children are only on loan
From a greater power that is not our own.

Let's put our own feelings aside,
so that our children do not cry.

Cry for their daddies, or cry for their home.
Let's remember we are not alone.

Karen Parker

Are You My Other Half?

Will my other half please come forward?
Oh, how I've waited so long,
day in and day out,
all the days gone,
always alone, alone,
Are you my other half?
Well are you?
No, just another one passing me by,
But that's OK,
I'm still looking for my other half everyday,
So I wait, and wait, and wait,
so very long,
day in and day out,
all the days gone,
alone, alone
Another try, I will,
Are you my other half?
I hear, are you my other half?
Get a grip I say,
Am I hearing things or was that my other half?

Shu Jen Walker

Appalachian Meditation

Somewhere in the Appalachian mountains
in a forest laced with Pine
where the Laurel springs like fountains
and the trees are wrapped with vines
I find my peace of mind
and I don't know if there'll be anybody else
but I'll be there myself in time.

Beyond the forest is a meadow
where I sometimes go to dream
walking through that golden hayfield
my thoughts run like a mountain stream
wherever sunlight casts her beam
and I don't know if there'll be anybody else
but I'll be there myself in time.

Below the hills down in a valley
a river runs his course to sea
if any man had taken tally
of those who'd seen it besides me
he'd not have marked very many
and I don't know if there'll be anybody else
but I'll be there myself in time.

Franklin Williams

Her

A great beauty compels me to follow,
But I'm afraid that she doesn't know me.
Suffer must I now, suffer, and wallow,
My love for her is what she cannot see.
She makes me silent, though I wish to speak,
Trying to form words from jumbled pictures.
So difficult is this, it makes me weak.
She is like Heaven, quoted in the Scriptures.
She is sitting there like a slender cat,
Pouncing forever in the depths of my mind.
Her image is all I have to look at,
My love for her holds a permanent bind.
Knowing her would truly be ecstasy,
Better yet would be, having her know me.

Daryl Hunter

The Eagle

His mighty wings cut through the air,
He soars high above without a care,
He's in all his glory, in all his grace,
And the gentle breezes caress his face.

His keen eyes watch the water so drear,
The fish, they seem to have no fear,
He drops like lightning from the skies,
And ascends again with his squirming prize.

And as the daylight fades from sight,
The eagle makes ready for the night,
Back again to his lonely nest,
He drifts into a peaceful rest.

Michael Martin

Hush

A little bird perches on my shoulder
It chirps pleasant melodies in my ear
Beautiful music soothes the soul
But the sweet sound carries a tale so bitter that it burns my heart
Silence, say no more little birdie
For listening would set a fire raging through my soul
But woe is me, the song must be sung
No matter the sorrow that it brings
I listen with great intent and understanding
It is no burden
Yet, it tugs the strings of my heart
As an archer tugs the string of his bow for the kill
I yearn to sing the song
But alas, it is not befitting my voice
Tears of silence flow
But all I do is . . . hush.

Zan Azlee

Cliff

Sea, the harsh screams of seagulls
muted by the immensity of the surroundings
Sky, where they drift around like small pieces
of a torn love letter on a steel-blue background

Walk all the way to the edge of the cliff and
feel the elements fight for your life
as the sea calls out your name and the
rocks below roar for you blood

The rest of the world lost in the screaming wind
the wind that reduces you to nothing but a metaphor
for futility and loneliness against a universe
that just encompasses too much

Throw out your arms and stand like a Brazilian Jesus
surrender yourself and welcome what comes
drown yourself in the wildness of it all
as ethereal guitar solos scream of lost love

Stig Edvartsen

Bird Cage Sweety

To my beloved Josh
Let me be the bird that you want to capture
You are the sweetest cage that I am longing for

Let my freedom be your kingdom
Break my wings so that I will never fly away

Let me be your property
I shall be faint under your indifferent control

Let me be or not let me be
I am just a lonely bird that flies outside your world
And waiting to live in your sweetest cage

    Andy Lu

The Human Race

This race of humans that we are,
So full of wars and violence.
Our eyes look longingly toward the stars,
But our time is not yet hence.
Prejudices block are views,
Blind now by our colors.
How can we see those beyond,
If we cannot see each other.

    David Adams

My Luxuries

Mother never had luxuries in life,
she was happy just being daddy's wife.
We never had riches or wealth,
but, we always had love and health.

We lived in a four room shack,
but, we always had clothes on our back.
Winters were cold, summers were hot.
We were happy just being a tot.

Then we all grew and went away,
I never forgot the way I was raised.
I know what it is like to be poor,
for you see, I have been there before.

I will never forget my country life,
I too am happy just being a wife.
Little things mean so much to me,
friends, family and husband are my luxuries.

    Becky Vaughn

Night Shakes

Visions of perfume from her neck
I follow the shadows to the beacon
On the other end of the room
See dreams dancing in the light
Obscure images of future and past
and just plain nonsense.
The shadow of the free spirit is flying
In the mist, its voice sounds like the hawk
Calling for its mate as it floats
Like a leaf in a whirlwind never coming down.
I can smell October night in the breeze
Like apples and fallen leaves.
The full moon shines a glow across the battlefield
Images seem to move like tired
Hallucinations
It's time to crawl back in my foxhole
And dig in for the night.

    Robert Schoenecker

Let's Go to the Zoo!

Momma and daddy and baby, too
All went for a ride down to the zoo.
We saw the lions and the tigers, too.
I had a lot of fun. Didn't you?
Daddy fed the Parakeets bit by bit.
Baby tried getting into the monkey pit.
Momma watched by and sang her song.
The bells in the lion's house rang dong, ding, dong.

    Lora Harrison

Untitled

Written in honor and loving memory of Ben Hancock 3/19/81–2/9/00
Amidst the burning flames and the smoke-covered walls,
faint and off in the distance, I heard the Lord's voice call
Suddenly, there was peace and brilliant white light
I remember gentle voices sweetly singing my name in the night
then they appeared, angels with warm, loving smiles
they were there to take me home and be with me all the while
As the angels escorted me up the gleaming golden stairs
I stood in awe at the beauty surrounding me there
as I lifted my head to the Lord's beautiful, loving face
He made my soul perfect and I felt His wondrous grace
On Earth our vision is blurred, but now I clearly see
as I stand in front of the mansion that the Lord built just for me,
no words can describe the peace that I feel now
If only you knew and I could share it somehow—
your life isn't finished yet, so you must be patient and wait
'til you see me and the angels waiting for you at Heaven's gate.

    Lisa Marie Jones

Secret Places

I often go to secret places deep within my mind
Sometimes dark and lonely places are all that I can find
I often go to secret places looking for a friend
I always go to secret places, my land of pretend
Sometimes in my secret places I have to run and hide
It's like being in an ocean sucked under by the tide
Sometimes in my secret places everything's ok
I find a bunch of other people wanting me to stay
Sometimes in these secret places there is no one there
Not a single living soul no one to say I care
Sometimes in these secret places deep within my mind
I search for hope and sanity but it's not there to find
Sometimes in these secret places the answer comes to light
I come back to my senses and I know all is right
Then I leave my secret places where nothing is real
And come back to this other place and trust myself to feel
I think I'll keep my secret places for they are safe and warm
They protect and cuddle me and keep me from harm
I'll never share my secret places never let anyone in
I have to keep my secret places very deep within.

    Benjamin Huckaby

For the First Time

Let me take you to the place
Where you and I could be happy as one can be

Let me look into your eyes
And see your beauty within

Let me hold your hand
And feel the enchantment of your touch

Let me hold you tight
And feel the passion within

Let me kiss your tender lips
To sense your love for the very first time

    Mauricio Ramirez

Be Unlike

Be your own. Be unlike.
Originate yourself to all of your sustained pain.
You think like the feeble, the common.
Go past those who likeminded others.
Hypocrite, I am. I can't make a new way!
Or can I? Whine, whine, rant, and whine.
Death is a prize for your kind.
We cannot defy this destined existence.
All I can do is try to try
To be different in a different way.
My mind is a formal conclusion for all.
Break it down. Don't become drones in a train . . .
Something created this, someone can recreate.
The words you say sound like they don't belong,
like it's just a barrier.
Change, no just can't, too hard.
It's set in stone, so to say, the only way to go.
I cannot take much more of it.
If the mind would just expand. There has to be more.
Find your way, not another's . . .

Robert Titland

Autumn

A lazy September sun glistens on a large quiet lake.
No sound of bustling confusion of daily life abounds.
Only harmonious sounds of nature
Permeate the clear autumn sky.
Nearby, a squirrel gathers nuts, fervently fighting time,
As dusk slowly announces its arrival.
The summer is gone.
Now only a wisp of warm air remains,
Lingering like a faint memory in childhood.
I stand on the edge of the lake,
Skipping stones one after the other,
While watching the ever-dimming orange orb
As it makes its gentle descent.
The last splash fades into a tiny ripple
As night falls softly around me.
And I turn to make my journey home.

George D. Canavos

My Daddy

When I was a little girl
He was always there for me
when we would dance and twirl
never did I think alone I'd be.

We planted a little garden
as I'd watch the flowers grow
My Daddy would laugh at Glenda bear
as she planted her flowers in a row.

When I went to school at 6 years old
I missed him during my long days
I would think about his heart of gold
and how much he loved his Glenda bear's ways.

And when I married I wanted my man,
to love me like my daddy did,
My husband said to me I know I can,
daddy said to me I know you love me kid

Through the years daddy was my friend
and now so many times a day
I know our love will never end
I loved him in a little daughter's way.

Glenda Reed

Zinnias

I talked to my zinnias today
about marriages that end and children who cry
and the pain that lays on humanity like stone
on petals, but they didn't care.
They just tilted their pollen-puckered faces
towards the sun and laughed,
waiting for one last diamond-backed dew drop
to splash and splatter its way across
their velveteen tongues, flowing
streamlined green down to the earth.
This one zinnia moment dissolved my diatribe
into truth I had known all along—
life is to be lived
one dew drop at a time.

Sally Evans

Winter Solstice

This is the longest night of the year.
I feel the season as I hear the rain's fall,
But though I know the year is ending,
I feel that I can never be alone in love.
The night is hostile to the lonely one.
I look to the sky for a sight of beauty,
But all I ever manage is to hear a calling-
A Calling from the emptiness of this Night
This longest of the many lonely nights.
This, the longest night of my year.

Coleman Presnell

A Woman in the Sand

Upon the sands of the desert,
A woman stands alone,
The sun so hot, she feels that she will
petrify and turn to stone.
A man approaches suddenly,
She cries, "What do you want from me?"
Just give me your hand,
My love, my dear, for I shall set you free!
A cool breeze appeared,
No water or trees in sight,
A calmness came upon her,
A feeling of sheer delight.
The ocean swirled around her and danced on
the edge of night.
A land beyond has found her,
The sand and sea have bound her,
She no longer stands as one,
Their journey together has begun . . .

Kathleen Rizzi

The Earth

Rapture, sounds from the Earth,
Sounds and sights and senses for the soul.
Always the canvas, I am within the painting,
Within the song, within the art of the world.
Words are sounds and of the Earth,
And song is nature's language.
It speaks, I cannot help but listen
For I am in and of the Earth and universe.
Wordsworth believed that nature had personality,
A poet believing in Achelous, Amphitrite and Artemis.
The living speaks, the dying screams and cries.
The grey consumes the green and quenches song with silence.
The mist of consumption clouds the blue,
Until it cries, we can close our eyes
And listen and feel nature reclaim its translator.
We can speak back but only through recreation,
Replication, imitation, mimesis.
Immersed in the language of each other
We become one, in reality, in imagining, in remembrance.

Brendan Brooks

The Hill in 1923

I returned to the hill, not so long ago,
Sitting in my Mercury, there it was, just so.
Across that first branch, the footbridge no more.
Thought of the experience one summer of yore.

An old reed baby buggy we pushed to its top.
Even if it had a brake, I couldn't use it to stop.
They were five and ten and I was only three,
But how fast it would go we sure didn't know. Whee!

Me they dropped into it and gave it a nudge.
That's all it took, say what a swift plunge!
Down that long slope, now faster and faster.
Jump! Jump! They said as they tried to run after.

With both hands I gripped tight . . . well it didn't upset.
Then they set up a cry, "You're going to get wet!"
Of course, due to its speed, in the water it rested.
From footbridge with help of hoe, it was ousted.

So that was the end of that adventurous play.
They wouldn't take their turns, that summer day.
Will not tell what the "Old Folks" had to say,
How they laughed and talked about it, never let it lay.

Winifred L. Hawkins

Nightscape

And in the bleakness of the night
The moon beam slithers
Through the darkness of the clouds
And sets the frost upon the trees
Afire and lashes carefree across the water
Of a rippling pool
The pale blue beam glistens on a
Spider's web and casts the shadows of the demons
that lurk in the darkness of the night.
And the man in the moon laughs
at the world and the clouds conceal his
smile which fades as the early morning
Sun trickles through the clouds.

Bill Black

Choices

Where to go or what to do,
They're the choices that make you, you.
Whether or not I make the right choice,
To tell you what to do, there's that little voice.
Should I do this or should I not,
In my head the answer's a big dot.
If the choice I make is wrong.
What to do, the answer I long.

Tabitha Encarnacion

Our Little Tyler

Up through the clouds, up through the sky,
Our Little Tyler, he did fly.
He grew some wings while asleep,
and took a journey, and made us weep.
We miss him dearly, and we cry.
We ask ourselves why he had to die.
Why God took him, we'll never know.
But Our Little Tyler had to go.
His toys, his clothes were left behind.
But through his pictures, he'll still shine.
His smile, his laugh, his bright little face
has gone to Heaven, and left this place.
He's Heaven's treasure now, we know.
But why did Tyler have to go?

Stephanie Vaught

Family

Family is always number one,
To me and everyone.
We show our love straight from the heart,
And we make sure we are not torn apart.
We fuse together and never let go,
Of so much love that we show.
Family is the most important thing to me,
And no matter what it will always be.
Family is a gift I enjoy to have.
And that makes me very glad.

Family is always there for me,
To love and cherish, so let me be.
Wherever I go they will always be in my heart,
Until death do we part.
They back me up right from the start,
And they all shine like a piece of art.
It is a portrait that never ends,
And throughout life it will never bend.
Family should be together no matter what,
To trust and listen and show their heart.

Jessica Cerda

Sonia

My memory is a dictionary of blues which I keep constantly
looking up words and constantly looking through each time
I look back on certain pages I start to go insane yes,
I spend most of my time down on memory lane puffing Mary
Jane, trying to ease that pain drinking potions, trying to
rearrange and change my mind frame but if I try to go back
completely it's never the same you only get one trip around
the board in this game it seems I never get the card that
says, take 2 steps back I get the go directly to jail card
and don't ever come back my job is terrible, I am the
memory holder everyday people get the gift to forget as
they get older I keep trying to relive from 98 to 97 this
reminiscing is hell, it surely isn't Heaven it's like starving
while you're lying on a freshly baked sweet potato pie
I try to shake my memories, I try and I try but I digress.
I still remember your style of dress every curve of your body
and how you were blessed and yes, I even remember the
times you'd least suspect you are on page 72 of my
memory text.

Marcus Carino

Missing You

I missed you this morning, when I got up,
saying, "I made some coffee, would you like a cup?"

I went by your bedroom and saw an empty bed,
with a stack of pillows, that once cradled your head.

Your slippers sat neatly, there on the floor,
just as you left them, when you went out the door.

It's so hard to think that your not coming back,
I must be dreaming, please stick me with a tack.

Your picture is hanging, there on the wall,
and the tears keep on flowing, as memories recall.

With my feet on your stool, I sat in your chair,
I could feel your presence, I knew you where there.

You've been such a fighter, for so very long,
never complaining, you'd come back so strong.

Your world was filled, with humor and love,
'Til the day God called you, from up above.

Though God took you home, and there you must stay.
The memories you left, will never go away.

Rita Vrabel

My Greatest Fear

The little girl inside me was crying as the phone rang.
The person on the other end felt so far away.
He was saying those soft words so quietly
As if they might not be real.

As I hung up the phone
I wondered what had just happened?
What had he just said?
Why am I bursting into tears?

My whole life seemed to be in vain,
But on the outside I looked normal.
It was the girl inside me that was crying hysterically.
My life fell apart on that night.

As I fall asleep I feel the beginning
Of a life without him.
In my dreams I find myself beside him,
Holding on to his hand that is
Slipping ever so slowly out of mine.

Leah Zubrzycki

Instinct's Flutter

There are butterflies in the east wing.
Has a door been left ajar?
I've heard stories of their return
To a distant place of meeting
Where they find their mate
amongst the instinctive flock.
Oh, to have such a monarch within.

Perhaps this is where I return
To find you.
Commitments only allow me to come in spring,
But you are not here,

Yet, I feel you fluttering near,
Amongst leaves
Which winds push into bunches.
Why, our encounter must be in the fall.

I shall be then at this place
I shall not worry of an exact time,
The leaves will remind me,
And the door
Is certain to be ajar.

Robert J. Spence

Have You Ever

Have you ever heard the cry of a dove?
It's like the quarrel of two lovers in love.
Broken hearts are tearfully made.
Dearest dreams in the heart all fade.
Then one day that special someone comes back into their life.
No more for sin, and strife?
Have you ever heard the song of a dove?
It's like the song of two lovers in love.

Kendra C. Nichols

The Unicorn

A lovely unicorn, with dashing blue eyes and a horn so sharp—
It looks of a forgotten silver dye.
She shakes her mane of a very fine beige,
and gives me memories of back in the days
when we had fun in the sun all day long.
but now she only speaks of a certain love song—
A song that will stay in her heart for now 'til eternity.
Oh! If only she could see how much I love thee!
Yes, that lovely unicorn!

Samantha Dunbar

A True Friend

A true friend is hard to find.
You find them only once in a lifetime.
One that will stick by you through thick and thin
Even when you feel you just can't win.

A true friend helps lift you up and brighten your day
with just a smile in their own special way.
Lending a hand or lending an ear,
just letting someone know that a friend is near.

I know if I needed to talk
or just have a good cry;
I have a true friend
to which I can rely.

So thank you true friend,
from the bottom of my heart.
Just know that I'm here for you, too,
no matter what the part.

Wendy Cromer

Dear Father

Dear father,
Growing up without you,
Has been so hard for me to do.
It's been a lifetime since you closed your eyes,
And I still haven't said goodbye.
Unable to share with you over the years,
All of my joys and my tears.

I imagine you beside me one more day,
To talk to you, and say all I need to say,
To tell you of my choices along the way,
Ending my past heartache, which continues today.

Holding onto your memory,
Has become such a part of me.
Every day has been a little tough without you near,
Wishing and hoping that you were still here.
I don't know if I'll ever let go,
Of the tears I can't seem to outgrow.
With these words, maybe my healing has begun.
Always know I love you,
Your son

Brian P. Scheetz

Trick or Treat

Dark night fell over the City
Restless Clouds passed over the silver moon,
Blood-Chilling fear seeped through the heart—
Rattling Bones clacked a deathly tune!
Hands of demented dimensions
Grip Ghoulish containers filled up too soon.

Deep sounds split open the silence
As Screams of Delight—wake the dead of night!
Cackling Creatures fill Empty Void—
As Lips ghostly white emit howls of fright
Monsterous voices in pursuit—
Sweet Treasures of Loot to be Gained—TONIGHT!

Fairy tale pages come to life,
Amid Mythical mantras marching the beat—
Endless Procession—House to House
Scrawling Shadows settle over the street.
Bewitching Parade—HALLOWEEN!
Yearly Chanting of Ages, TRICK OR TREAT!

Annette L. Stone

A Horse and Freedom

Over the fields and valleys I roam,
They are my haven, they are my home.
They are my refuge from wind and from rain.
There I have freedom from fear and from pain.

There, in the sunlight where flowers bloom,
I find no such thing as darkness and gloom.
My neck arched high, my head held erect,
No signs of danger do I ever detect.

I run with the speed of an eagle in flight,
My mane flying wild, my coat shimmering bright.
And when the storms come, ne'er do I hide,
I run and I prance with ease in my stride.

Then, in the evening, when grass is so green,
Everything's peaceful, quite and serene.
I lie and I think of the places I roam,
For they are my haven, yes, they are my home.

Joan Anderson

You and My Dreams

I have only dreamed of you in my dreams,
and I never thought that you would ever come true.
For so long I've waited for you to appear in my life,
and I waited so long to feel your soft skin.
To see the blue eyes that shine into my green eyes
like a starry night in the heavens,
I've dreamed of your fingers rubbing gently down my back.
I used to think that a man like you could never
love somebody like me . . .
and of course I was right, you don't love me,
You're in love with me!
I don't have to dream anymore,
I don't have to imagine anymore.
I now live in a peaceful world that only you and I live in.
An imaginary place that a dream seems too realistic to live in.
I am in Heaven with you . . . I love you because your
in love with me and I appreciate everything that
you have showed me . . . now I have my dream, You.

Melissa Masters

A Tree

Huddled wax, the green and blue masses
Shaped like every color catches light
Quite a sight in ignorance or better
If allowed, exist to tether

Home to bird and crawling creature
Wooly mammal, bumble bee
Not to mention you and me
My house, or paper ads for paper money

Miracle life, sustaining
Breathable green and static array
Its flesh constructs our currency
Makes the world go 'round some say

One exhibits, growth inhibits strength and power
Sunscreen enduring, a mighty tower, disease for curing
Stoned on nature's silver palette
Behold, screams of severed sadness

Lies naked and silent in abhorrence
Exemplifies legal holocaust badness
One more victim
A tree of the same branch to madness

Jason Merrington

Father

You've been gone awhile from me,
Your face I see in memories.
I miss your smile, your laugh, your care,
But I am glad you're finally there,
Through the portal death you've gone,
Your Spirit's free to travel on.

Even though I cannot see
you standing right in front of me,
I hear your laughter ride the wind
as it softly dances on my skin.
Your caring shows in many ways,
as friend and stranger pass through my days.
A smile, a hug, a word of cheer,
a sudden flash that you're still here!
Even now I sometimes see,
a twinkle in my eyes, could it be?
You're in there smiling back at me!

Deborah Wiseman

The Necklace

It was a gift, no story
no side street salesman whispering
Have you even been to Africa, no
in no shirt dancing slightly humming
saying a good deal for my money, which I can't
speak a currency for. No story.
It was a gift, like a small throat
of a hummingbird, in its small mouth a
necklace, it hovered on the edge, right there, mouth open
then gone, backwards. No story.

Heather Campbell

Curing the Wounds

A man I love conceals his wounds.
But he denies.
He knows the truth.
But he lies.
They created the wounds in Nazi Germany
The night they marched down the streets.
Silent among himself, he hid in the dark,
Trusting no one.
He had to listen too hard those nights.
A door cracking.
A person screaming mercy.
A bullet shot.
An engine running.
Anything.
During the evenings he planned for weeks.
How to leave the bloody streets.
Then when the chance came, silence was the name of the game.
And life depended on his ears.
Listening to sounds of footsteps, breathing and heartbeats.
The opportunity arrived and he stopped the dreadful game.

Marc Ross

Only Love Can Breaks Your Heart

Only love can breaks your heart, it's true.
It's fragile without doubt,
it fades away with one mistaken touch.

It will catch you up, it's mended in a nameless room.
With a warm sweet caress, it ties you up like a knot.

Once it breaks, you cannot buy it back.
Not even with tears . . . .

Only love can breaks your heart, it's true.
It is a memory surrounded by another.
A word that is germinating in the patch of a lifetime.

Daisy Surjo

Hero of the Day

People are what plagues the Earth,
not cancer or acid rain.
If people could know their own self-worth,
perhaps it could end all the pain.
However, the way that the world works today
is very unfortunate indeed.
Because most, in the course of an entire day
never once think, nor feel the need.
We are all creatures of habit,
we all have goals of our own.
Yet with intelligence inferior to a rabbit,
idiocy will unravel the throne.
We can only follow our own path
marked by decisions made along the way.
If only you would think instead of ask,
You might be the hero of the day.
Matt Coyle

The One

I melt. I crumble. I send up a prayer,
As her words touch my heart and her song fills the air.

She quivers when I'm near and shivers out of fear,
Of what she knows could be.

I think of her all day and try to find a way to express myself.

What will she say or do when she knows it's true . . .
That I hold her heart?

I cannot let her go, She means far too much to me.
I just hope and pray that this she'll see.

For she is . . . The One
Jason Candler

Hunter's Trip

John is a hunter, and this is his game,
he's headed to the mountain of the great state of Maine,
well he packed his knife and he packed his gun
and he headed for Jackman on 201.
Now hunter come once a year
to take a chance at the white tail deer,
some will leave with a tear
and some will get the white tail deer,
some will have a little luck,
but John will get the trophy buck,
now you'll know the season over and done
when John is headed down 201
Wade Tilghman

Life

Why are there so many questions?
And only a few answers?
Why is there so much hatred?
And so many violent encounters?
Why are people so mean to others?
Why do they feel so cold inside?
Why do people have so much to hide?
If you could answer all of the questions above,
our world would be full of happiness and love.
People are so stupid, to treat others the way they do.
If they could only feel the pain they cause on me and you.
Hopefully people will soon know,
The suffering inside that no one shows.
And they'll stop doing what hurts us so bad,
And we'll stop doing what makes them so mad.
If our world could be made like a book,
when things got bad we could take a look.
People would know what it's like to be broken inside,
and how if feels to always hide.
Brittany Bickler

Strangers

Years of pain on the inside and out,
eased with your caring touch.

Months of loneliness and isolation,
forgotten when you came near.

Weeks of mistreatment and abuse,
soothed by your words.

Days of being unappreciated,
corrected by a simple "thank you."

Hours of working hard and carrying a heavy load,
lightened when you smiled genuinely.

Minutes of self-pity and apathy,
turned around by your positivity.

Seconds after we met as strangers,
this you did for me.
Krista Guthrie

Madonna and Child

Human angel
Caressingly lifts the child whom all should behold.
Veined hands,
Faintly sustain the swell of labor;
The 110 degree days longing to carry her outside;
The footprints inside;
The every-two-hour nourishing;
And, of course, the constant pressure of peeing;
Envelop immaculate rebirth of Good.

An ultrasonic photo
Of a little pink nose foretold:
No ordinary child is she!

While this ordinary poet contends to write tangible words
Of their utter contentment bathed in delicious delight

Captured here in a still lens
But active, alive and never told like this:
Rustic deliverance and raw desire to mother.

Soft tresses frame porcelain skin,
She will not break:
Young woman on the verge of motherhood.
Shar F. Grant

Little Ones

Little ones bring us such happiness and joy,
And hold our hearts in hand, like we were a toy.

Growing and learning never really knowing,
How everyday, they kept inside us parents a light glowing.

The light in our life, we hold in our heart,
Which dims a bit whenever we are apart.

Although you know how for you I love and care,
Until you have your own child, this feeling is hard to share.

A love so unconditional and true,
For our little ones, this feeling, you hold forever within you.

I hope these words may some day find,
A special place in your heart and mind.

Because sometimes there are things we forget to say,
And because troubles arise within everyday

But just in case I didn't take enough time,
Through this mountainous path, of life we must climb.

Forever these words now to you are known,
And hopefully be appreciated when you're mature and grown.

These feelings I have carried from the very start,
From the day you were born, and stole the key to my heart.
Mishalyn S. Stone

For All Time

To say, "I love you for all time"
Is an easy thing for me to do
Because the feelings in my heart
Are felt for only you

And little things that come between us
Will never break us apart
Because to be without your love
Would truly break my heart

A touch from your hand
A kiss or an embrace
These gifts you continue giving me
Which can never be replaced

Your love is all around me
I feel it in my soul
You know you're the only one
Who could ever make me whole

Being with you completes me
Having you near brightens my days
Your entire presence is wonderful
I didn't know I could be loved so many ways

     Bonnie Jean Blakeney

Paragon

The pale light
softly   glows
       around your face
and makes you   look
just   like   an   angel
flown
     down
       from
         Heaven
Just   to rescue   me
from the   burning depths
of   my   soul

     L. Lenard

What Are Mothers For?

Mothers are to have a child, and never once complain
They are supposed to always smile, regardless of their pain

They're the one whom kiss your sore, to make it heal faster
And the ones to close the door, as you're trying to get past her

They were put here for you father, brother and sister too
But mostly they were put here, especially for you

And when we finally realize, what mothers are made for
Mothers go ahead and die, fulfilling life's last chore

     Paul J. Faciana

Faded Dreams

My life's dream sits before me
I hold its life in my hand
A blank sheet of paper is all I see
My pencil sits motionless in my palm
Thoughts and ideas spin through my head
But they don't make sense on paper
Frustrated and weary, I close my eyes
My dreams of writing were once so bright
They could even make a blind man see the light
Now a curtain covers them
I sit in the darkness of my faded dreams
Who holds the rope to reveal them?
Please, faceless thief of hopes
Open the shroud, let fate run its course
Have mercy on the inspiration of my life
The black clouds fade away
Light shines through
My soul awakens and breathes in a new life

     Jessica R. Koontz

Goodbye Little Angel

Goodbye little angle . . . so long ago, it now seems,
You have fallen asleep!
Yet so many nights your innocent smile
Has steadied my dreams,
And so many times I still sing you a song
As I turn out the light
Because deep in my heart, I know you have heard,
Even though you have long since taken your flight.

Shine, precious memory, high in the heavens,
As I look up tonight!
Twinkle forever, my brilliant star,
And brighten my darkness this night.
Some say you now quietly rest in the earth,
And your blanket is dust and a stone,
But I know they are wrong as I see you in Heaven,
Eternally happy, resting at home.

     Bob Doroslovac

All I Feel for Him

I still remember the day we met
It was love at first sight
You were like a shining light

Everything started out fine,
You were always on my mind

Soon that changed and our
Relationship took a turn for the worst
I felt like my heart would burst

The harsh things we said to each other,
The constant fights, me crying all night

I tried to end it so many times but you
Would always hit me with your I'm sorry lines
I know I can't change the person you are
But I tried so hard,
Dragging this out too far

I never thought our love would die
That's why it was so hard to say goodbye

Why couldn't it have been different?
I love you so, but I feel so low.

     Jennifer Anderson

Searches

Heart's desires float as so many miniature planets needing an orbit.
Weightfull airborne masses too heavy to do what they do.
But alas, they remain suspended.
Hover-like.
Wanting to find their way.
Maintaining cosmic in their mission.
Scurrying in every maze pattern imaginable.
Continually they wander.
That honing-in nature felt propels them around in their spaces.
Perhaps some confounding glitch atmospherically is present.
But not matter.
The answer exists.
It's not knowing right questions making mapping difficult.
Methodically buzz they do, a familiar but non repeating trail.
One certain trajectory will land them where they're trying to be.
Such track having truly limitless computation possibilities.
Deduct . . . deduce, and program.
Zip a go another try.
The polarity is undeniable.
Home is out there.

     Mark J. Krall

Seaside Summer Spirits

I know he's out there
Though I know not quite where.

In the mist that hugs the waves in winter's last embrace,
I can't make out his agile form, let alone his face.

Is that the black line of the ghostly pier,
Or a silver streamlined surfer racing nearer?

Screeching down a foaming green wave from hell
Shooting up towards Heaven, catching air on the swell.

Waves of emotion that break and thunder and roar
And slam with persistence to wake the shroud white shore.

Churning the salt, making it so thick in the air
I can smell, taste and feel it matting my sleeping blonde hair.

Reminding me with a slapping chill against my skin.
As summer's spirits appear and the season of life begins.

John Pender

Speed Demon

Don't you just hate it when you are driving
Down the road . . .And someone pulls out in front of you.
You are cruising at a modest 65 m.p.h.,
And this jerk decides to tempt fate.
You slam on the brakes,
Your heart starts pumping, full of adrenaline.
The horn is honking, You shout—
"You stupid jerk! What, do you have a death
Wish or something?"
Pass the moron and speed on your way,
To work or play or wherever you are going
This day. Try to calm down. Turn up the
Music. Jam to your favorite tunes on your
Favorite station, 102.7 FM in Fresno, CA.
I arrive at work, put in my eight hours.
Drive back towards home. Someone wants to
Race me. I pull ahead and leave them in the
Dust . . .Too bad you aren't as good a driver as Me!

Teresa Carrera

Through Your Eyes

I have watched the world go by through you eyes.
I have seen people change and be transformed.
As you have realized them with a new light.
Thrown away your dislikes, and found their charms.

I have seen the truths you have tried to disguise.
The hurt and pain from your life at home.
I've been there to dry the tears from your eyes.
Always taking your problems as my own.

You were there for me when my grandpa died.
Along with me you carried the sorrow.
At his funeral, together we cried.
You helped me see the hope for tomorrow.

Then of course, there were the happy times too.
Laughing so hard, our faces would turn blue.
Ten long, sweet years we have spent together.
We have a tie, even the angels can't sever.

When I leave, forever you'll know.
I may be gone in body, but not in soul.
Just as long as you know, you have my heart,
and I have yours. We will never truly be apart.

Jamie Sampson

Thank God

Because of You,
I am finally at ease
calmly dealing with the irrationalities of life,
living one day at a time to the extent of its value,
retreating to Your love which serves as my security,

Because of You,
my relationship with friends has enhanced,
subconsciously knowing the depths of Your emotions,
constantly feeling desired and needed,
I confidently attempt to resolve all challenges.

Because of You,
my inner beauty is exposed.
You allow me to respectfully walk equally by Your side,
still making room for me to venture off
in search of those personal goals I strive for.

Because of You,
I know I can conquer all and regardless of how situations seem,
Your faith in me remains.
Lord, it is Your fault that I feel so beautiful
and I totally hold You responsible
and while You will always carry that blame,
I sincerely "Thank You."

Caroline Soley

Soldier's Letter

Mom if you have gotten this letter, I have died.
It was for my country so please don't you cry.
When they sent me here,
I wondered why my nation sent me to die;
but it is ok, I died with pride.
Mom please don't cry.
Please don't drape the flag on my grave,
fly it high let it wave.
I have died;
my country is still alive.
Mom please don't cry.
I tried so hard to fight,
hope what I did was right.
Put my metals upon my chest
and lay this soldier down to rest.
Mom please don't cry, goodbye.

Richard Slaughter

My Little Candle

The dark street of my heart,
the bleak cold lane,
the home of darkness,
far too dark for the little candle to glow,
but the darkness is needed for the candle to shine.
So I am waiting for the candle,
for that glow,
for that shine,
for that show,
which would come and sparkle,
would come, and make the cheer,
would come to spread happiness,
would glow for me,
would make my world bright,
would bring the glazing light,
for me, my own shinning candle,
which would then lead my way,
would then take me to my destination.

Afsheen Shahid

Different?

So you think it's all fun for your kids
Well guess what, we kids, too, have our needs
And our lives aren't as easy as school
We have lives, and our own special rules.

There's a world outside just for us
Wrong things: porn, violence, riot and drugs
Then the right way, God, Jesus my Lord
Him and parents show us the light,
Open the door.

Life is hard, both for me and for you
Let us both overcome things that are new
At the age at which kids overcome cute
We face different obstacles, on identical route.

     Boris Lutsenko

Special Friend

Wondering around my heads in the clouds
Feeling as though no ones around
The tension so thick, it's oh, such a strain
To think of dying, it's a crying shame.
To feel so lost and lonely
To have no one to really care
Just to have only that one someone special there
To talk to you and to ease the pain
To make you feel there is sunshine after the rain
To make things easier
Maybe that will be the way
Then to end it all
And miss all that could have been
If only to have that one special friend.

     Robin Stevens

Angel

I closed my eyes in reaction
Hoping it would do for protection
Then I felt the warmth sensation
And I knew He sent me a companion

Taken by his stare
I was dazed and unaware
There was another reason why he was there
He was in need of love and care

I'm loving an Angel and he is in pain
If I lose my grip then he would fly again
I'm loving an Angel and he is in pain
If I lose my grip then I would fall again

And I knew he was gonna fly again
Spread his wings but missed his aim
In silence he broke down but hid his pain
Alone he wept; I found him in the rain.

     Nani Khairina

Sonnet to Sunrise in Micronesia

The rooster crows; I arise before dawn
To wonder why his noise is premature.
Still glad to rise from the mat I've slept upon
Because this magic hour has much allure.
The sky is indigo above my head.
The air is heavy with the scent of rain
That fell upon this village still abed.
Today I will shampoo my hair again.
But now I'll walk along the jungle path
That leads directly to the crystal sea
Where I will plunge in for my morning bath
And let the silver sardine swim with me
'Til sun makes magic before my eyes
And splashes fuchsia across the skies.

     Lenora Lynn Beers

Broken Heart

I sit on a hill and look in the sky
I watch the clouds as they go by
I listen to the wind as it blows through the trees
I watch the branches move as they feel its breeze

As I sit on a hill and look in the sky
I bow my head and begin to cry
The loneliness in my heart is so heavy and great
I hear the sound as it begins to break

As I sit on a hill and look in the sky
I look toward the heavens and ask God
Why?

     Donnie Warriner

Christmas

Seasons come and seasons go
with the special one hidden beneath the snow.

Christmas is the one that's clear,
bringing us Santa, his sleigh, and reindeer.

Happy people wanting to share
laughter, music in the air.

A special time with special friends;
a toast or two, on you it depends.

Memories that fill the heart
of friends you hope will never part.

Christmas spirit and Christmas cheer,
wishing hopes of a bright and happy New Year.

     Deborah A. Farren

For My Daughter

She's gentle, compassionate and so very kind,
She faces life's problems by using her mind,
She's a wife and a mother and grandmother too,
Nurturing her loved ones gives her plenty to do.

She is gracious and kind to those who express fears,
Many times the solutions bring warm healing tears,
As a daughter she could not more loving be,
When needed she's always there to comfort me.

Susan remembers her dad with such a great love,
She feels he is watching over her from above,
When she wishes for guidance his voice she can hear,
It seems that his presence always is near.

I feel I must record this expression of pride,
For my dear daughter, Susan, who stays by my side,
How grateful I am for her unselfish devotion,
It fills up my soul with love and emotion.

     Marion Prescott

My Mom

She gave me a gift,
the gift of life.
She showed me this world,
of love and strife.
No mother ever could be
as kind, as caring as she.

She's the perfect balance,
giving me space,
while keeping me safe.
I can always trust her,
and always will.
And she will always have a place in my heart,
that is reserved for her alone.

     Meredith J. Tufts

A Reason to Live

My life was dark and full of sin
I had no rest, no peace within
I searched for contentment all around
But nowhere on Earth could it be found
I tried all the things the world had to give
But I still couldn't find a reason to live
I had no purpose in my life each day
'Til one lonely night, I knelt to pray
I asked for forgiveness, peace and rest
Then Jesus came in and I was blest
He gave me a purpose, a reason to live
He taught me how to love and forgive
He changed my life, the world could see
Some people said there was a glow about me
There's no problem too small or burden too great
For my God to handle, if only I'll wait
I'll walk in His shadow down life's path each day
As His hand of guidance leads all the way!

Drema Wiley

I'm Out

I loved you, I cared for you
I had hope in you
I want out
When they said leave, I stayed
When they gave up, I believed
When they put you down, I spoke highly
I want out
A child is what you'll always be, an adult
Is what I right now need
I want out
Make me go, let me go, chase me away
'Cause I don't want to stay
I want out
I used to want you to care
I used to want you to love
I used to want you to hope
I used to want you to dream
I used to want you to believe
Now all I want is for you to be strong
'Cause I'm out

Darlene C. Somerville

The Night before Thanksgiving

'Twas the night before Thanksgiving and all through the wood,
the hunters were searching as hard as they could,
to find the best turkey for Thanksgiving day,
because they could eat and the butcher would pay.
I was nestled all safe in the leaves
when Tom came crashing through the trees.
He told me the hunters were coming quite near,
their guns were automatic, that's what filled me with fear.
I got right up and started running full speed,
to flee from the hunters who are filled with greed.
Tom and I ran the rest of the night,
running with fear and definite fright.
Then we hid by a barn, safe for awhile,
and a voice in the distance caused us to smile.
"Come Lucky. Come Max. Come Spot and Fido,
Come Topper. Come Spike. Come Rex and Shadow.
The turkeys must all be a mile away,
so lets all go home and hit the hay."
With the hunters gone, things are all right.
So Happy Thanksgiving to all, and to all a Good Night!

Sean Kelly

Decadence

who knows
who cares
let's forget our fears
and let's pour ourselves a cup of our tears
and let's drink to our decadence
we'll waste our souls
sell our souls
run away
'cause nothing else is left
lock-in and be charmed and in a trance we'll lose ourselves
down on the river of ignorance, we'll drown ourselves
'cause I've no more strength to fight
peel the acid of our face
for we are society's disgrace
we are the lost son's and daughter's
just waiting . . . waiting . . .
waiting to be loved.

Atif Zaidi

Giving Thanks

I sit alone thinking to myself about you and your love.
How wonderful it is to have you in my life.
You complete me in a way I have never known.
You have me now mind, body, and soul.

You loved me for so long and I never knew.
Your heart was mine, could it be true.
You'll love me forever is what you say.
I thank the lord each and every day.

I will never hurt you. I will never stray.
I cannot live without you I will always stay.
You are my love. You are my strength.
With you in my life I will always give thanks.

Rose Bell

I Am

I can see everything you're doing if you put me in the right place
I can see your shoes, your clothes, your hair,
And I can even see your face.
If we are in the same room and no matter where you be
On the left, the right or any place, believe me I can see.
You see I don't have to move around, to know that you are there
I can see everything in this place, so I just sit and stare.
If you still don't know what I am, perhaps there's something missing
I'll describe myself a little more, so you just keep on guessing
This little fact is my last hint
So listen closely with your ears
If I am accidentally broken
It'll cost you seven years.
If you still can't figure out what I am
Perhaps I made an error
I always do things backwards you know
Because I am a mirror.

Sharon D. McLean

Home

Does your mind ever wonder or your feelings ever float
Do you feel you're in a castle that's surrounded by a moat
Does your head go round in circles when confined within a square
Do you turn your head and look about and find you're everywhere

Well if you have these problems while your walking by your side
Don't stop to look around you just begin to look inside
As you travel through the bloodstream to the confines of the heart
You will notice something missing that makes up the biggest part

As you travel even further to the organ called the brain
You will realize something funny as you start to feel the rain
As you huddle for protection and you find you're all alone
You will realize the part missing is the part you call your home

Charlie McIntosh

An Affirmation

Don't worry about whether
You are all that you desire to be in his eyes
His eyes must be blind to all I see in you
Aside from your physical beauty-
YOU ARE BEAUTIFUL
I see a girl with great confidence
In how she can impact the world.
Someone who easily talks with others
And gets them to want to hear more.
You have great charm that people want around.
You aren't afraid to voice your opinion
Even when it isn't favored.
Your clever ideas, spontaneity, and innocence
Add to a never ending list of traits
That isn't deserved by a guy like him.
He easily cast you aside when he couldn't see
All that is locked behind your heart's door.
I know it's hard to understand all that I say
But you will find, or be found by someone who
Realizes all this and cherishes you like I do

     Regina Hansen

His Sacrifice

Woe to those who cannot see,
the sacrifice You gave for them and me.

Your love was shed upon Your brow,
when Your blood trickled down.

You saved our souls with Your life,
that one single act called a sacrifice.

A symbol of Your sacrifice I choose to wear,
for the pain and suffering you did bear.

Around my neck I wear the cross,
ever so thankful I am no longer lost.

     Kelly Brinkhoff

All Maple

Six vent holes in the front,
Before my very eyes,
Blue diamond—I still can't believe.
Black ebony—my reflection I can see.
Way, way up,
Way, way high . . . .

And I didn't know you walked in.
And I didn't know you came in.

No vent holes in the back,
White wall stripe,
Percussion pillow snug inside . . . . .
Clear I can see through all the things that I can see.
Fifteen passed an eye.

And I didn't know you walked in.
And I didn't know you came in.

     Alan Wong

A Dog's Fetish

Huge, glassy, brown eyes approach me
Closer and closer they come
The gaping hole with
sharp, jagged, white teeth protruding from within
Inside the hole, I can feel the teeth sawing
as though a hacksaw were tearing through me
Whistling and whispering, the wind passes me
as the beautiful, bright sunlight pierces the darkness
Free at last
The orange glow of flesh surrounds me
No matter how much I struggle
I am thrown to a far away place to see
huge, glassy, brown eyes approach me

     Evan Daly

Falling Clouds

Some would hide from it,
want to wrap themselves up, sit and wait
in the safe, warm, back room comfort
of person, pet or blanket

Some would simply disregard it,
pretend that they don't hear
the sky pounding ceaselessly on their window panes,
they just turn the television up.

Some would just watch from the sill,
not getting directly involved but
sitting and waiting for the puddles,
jumping and splashing, to fill

Me; I would run, not away but towards,
throw wide my hands and watch
as the drops turned my lensed vision
into a kaleidoscope of light

But even I, delighting in the drenched feeling,
wait and hope for the sun to emit a beam through
at just the right time, just the right angle,
to see the optical illusion that would arch across the sky.

     Samantha Bednard

June 25, 1962

& in a moment, it was gone
silenced by a document
signed by the Devil's hand
In a moment, it was hidden
as if that alone
could stop a believing heart
In a moment, it was forbidden
as if it were a crime
against the very statutes of God and man
In a moment, it was wiped away
from a nation in the name of "freedom"
and "individual rights"
In a moment, a clever plan took root
to rid our children of their heritage and truth

& in a moment . . . the voices stopped
heads once bowed, raised
hands clasped together were torn apart
& in that moment,
the silence intensified into a roar of anguish
that not even a law or God could silence

     Mary Lovee Varni

Silence

All alone, no one to care,   .
All alone, no one to show you
All that's here, all that's there. . . .
Silence . . . desperate, waiting to find
Something buried deep inside to
Keep the silence you try to hide.
Running, clueless, gasping for life.
Something there you can't beat, entrapped,
Tearing at your insides; ripping out your soul.
Faster and harder and harder you run,
The silence has engulfed you and invaded your lungs.
Sweaty beads fall from your brow,
Trembling, convulsing;
You feel your body, not quite yours.
The silence, you see, is louder than not.
Blackness, darkness, is all that is. . . . forever.
All alone, no one to care,
All alone, no one to show you
What keeps out the silence.

     Rosanna Butler

Daydreams Vanish like a Withered Flower

I seek refuge in sleep.
But sleep is just another Broken Memory
I've danced to your Daydreams,
To the point of sheer Madness!
Your silence is but a passive thought
I sought out your Everything and failed,
Like a fallen Heaven (Without Embrace)
Lying on this bed,
With your thoughts deep in my heart
Breathing your soul means everything to me
If there is anything that will echo
From this emptiness, and fill a void
Of past restorations
Only love can fill the void,
Of all this sadness
Brought on by your Whispered Ghost Cries
I want to become your Living Death Mask
And curse these Daydreams
That Wither like a falling Flower

Michael Mordoh

Thought Alone Forever

Passion is a part of me—
On this you can depend.
My passion has nowhere to go,
So I make amends.

I want for love so desperately;
I know that it must show.
You probably think me foolish,
But I need it more than you know.

Sometimes I think I'm wasting time,
Looking for someone to love.
I hope I don't run out of time,
Before I find someone I think a whole lot of.

My heart is heavy with loneliness
When in bed at night,
But I'll not give up so easily,
Not without a hell of a fight.

I feel like I'm all alone with no one who really cares;
I have to find someone, 'cause this feeling I must share.
It seems as if those around me have all the love they need,
But still they try to get more as though they're driven by greed.

Michelle Griffin

The Process

God . . .
I feel so unworthy.
Daddy . . .
Maybe I can appeal to your paternal side.
Father . . .
We can both be mature about this.
Saviour . . .
My head knows that very well.
Friend . . .
I have walked away from you over and over.
Jehovah . . .
I am so small in your mighty shadow.
Lord . . .
Who am I to ask anything of you?
I can interpret you in so many ways,
Seeing a distorted you through my imperfections.
But no matter who I am when I come to you,
The truth is, you are always the same . . .
Love.

Alysha Braun

I Beg for Your Love

My heart cries in anguish,
My mind screams in pain.
My love is so strong
That it drives me insane

We've had times of hatred.
We've had periods of despair.
But we've always stayed together.
We're an inseparable pair.

I think of all the times we have had.
All the tears and laughs we have shared.
We supported each other all of our lives
Through times we were lonely or scared.

So I beg you to love me truly.
I plead for you to tell me you care.
Let me have you as my own
And the rest of our life we will share.

Tell me you love and you will be mine
From now until our very last day.
And say, "I do" when we take the vows
So the rest of our lives together we'll stay.

Sam Adamson

Winter Sonne

Feelings flooding my soul
A deluge of emotion runs rampant
Consuming all it encounters
Reducing boulder to pebble
Evermoving waters erode my resistance
Gentle ripples replace whitewater

Soul naked, heart exposed, arms open
Ready to run the rapids
Secure and protected by your love
No water too deep, no river too wide,
No current too swift to dissuade me
No obstacle insurmountable

Racing pulse, wildly beating heart
The thrill of the journey unbearable
Time will determine the destination,
With love as its guide
Open to the challenge with my whole being
Destined to be your soul mate

Pamela Balek

Why

When I think of you I only fall apart,
because you're not with me, only in my heart.

There's not a day that goes by, I can only hope not to cry
and ask myself, "Why, why," have we been denied.

When I think of you, I only fall apart,
because you're not with me, only in my heart.
There's not a day that goes by, I can only hope not to cry
and keep wondering, "Why, why," have we been denied.
I know in my heart that no one could ever keep us apart,
but still wonder, "Why, why," has a mother and daughter been denied.
When I look at you, I can only say,
I did one hell of a job, no matter what they say.
I know in your heart you want to say,
"Please take me home, to my mommy today."
"I promise you there will come a day when you can come home,
home to stay."

Love with all my heart,

Mommy

Christine Hester

The Shutter

I peer through a slanted vision
Letting no one out and no one in
I fear the arms that open wide
I tell no truth I speak no lies
I only see a slight embrace
I only see a half of face
I open up but only a little
I see the trees and more people
I look up now and theirs the sky
Sunlight and clouds go passing by
Children playing in the street
I hear the scuffing of little feet
I look back now upon my door
I think and wonder whatever for
Some day I might be outside looking in
But for now I peer through a slanted vision

Anita Anderson

Silent Walk

Take a silent walk with me
Someplace we've never been
Someplace quiet and undisturbed
Where no one can be heard
Lose me in your heart and soul
But never in your mind
Hold me deep into you arms
And never let me go
Show me some great memories
Of just the two of us
Feel the passion of each gentle kiss
And the sincerity of each softly spoken word,

In the silence that can be heard.

Sarah Gelinas

Love

When I look into your eyes, I see Heaven.
When I am near you, I feel bliss rushing through my veins.
Witnessing your smile is even more beautiful
than watching a sunset.
Being around you makes me feel cozy and innocent.
Your presence in this world
allows angels to sing and birds to fly.
Every minute of the day,
I imagine myself holding you close in my arms,
Kissing your ears and caressing you hair.
As you approach the edge of perfection,
you notice your countless admirers gazing timelessly at you.
How can I possibly describe in words what you mean to me?
The truth is I cannot.
All I want you to know is that:
I love you, I want you, I need you, and I miss you.

Hai Yuan

Aunt Mary Ann

We love you more then ever
We will miss you a lot
And now you leave us forever
You now with your son which you never forgot
Now it's time to say goodbye
And we lower you in the ground
My how the time goes by
We see nothing as we look around

Aunt Mary Ann
November 21, 1998

Ceneth Clay

Across Forever's Boundary

This Earth was made to test my lonely soul.
What dreams may come that ease such wretched pain?
For in my chest beats something less than whole,
And life itself must slowly be ordained.

Yet sadly under stars I know your gaze,
'Til soon upon your weary eyes comes rest,
And desperately you seek to clear the haze,
Of who it is and why he passed the test.

To him, it's only time that pays the toll.
So close, so far, the two they are the same,
Yet she makes up the hope that fills the hole.
She seeks to find his lonesome heart to tame.

Until that time my heart is set ablaze.
I ramble on alone amidst my quest.
The thought of love can yet remain a daze,
And when she comes, her love I won't protest.

Josh Ayers

Beyond the Ivy Rising

She sits in the pale light,
stares out through unwashed glass.
The distant bell-toll of young laughter
pervades her melancholy.

She rises, crosses to the bureau
and takes a quill from the inkwell—
left there as a memento of her grandfather—
and positions herself in front of the
blank white sheet before her.

She dips often, leaving no secret undiscovered—
no thought locked away, nor any figment
of her imagination left to ponder.

She has stumbled upon the
escape route—the way past the green
and violet wall that is her prison.

She paints with words the world
she has never seen beyond the ivy rising.

Alan Richardson

Let's

Let's meld our minds together,
And soar to heights unknown.
Let's take our hearts to that special place,
Where love is grown.

Let's plant the seeds of forever in the Garden of All time.
Let's place our names on the list of lovers,
Yours beside mine.

Let's watch our love grow and bloom,
So that all who pass may see.
And when they speak of great lovers,
They'll point to you and me.

Robert Howard

Love from a Brother

Something to think about when I'm not around
To make you laugh when I act like a clown
We have grown so close all these past years
You sometimes bring me happy tears
I do think of you all the time
To love you as a sister of mine
To give to you which the love we share
To do things for you because I care
Remember this and don't wear a frown
Something to think about when I'm not around

Carol Bird

Your Eyes (A Poem about Adopting from India)

Your eyes have seen so much more than me
although they have been opened for two years only.

You have seen so many faces,
some kind, some indifferent
and yet I did not see you for your first six months
when you were ill or frightened.

I imagine you lying in the crib, the one assigned to you,
listening to the children playing in the courtyard
of the orphanage the nurses calling,
"Khana , khana, time to eat." to one another.
I wonder if anyone saw you the first time you smiled
when tiny dust particles floated by like stars . . .
and then I came, my blue eyes seeing
your beautiful brown skinned people
in your world of India.
My eyes seeing the one I had waited so long to love
and your eyes seeing more than mine shall ever see.

Margaret Venkateswaran

Lover's Glory

When lover's glory has shaken few
and People stop to see the new
There comes to being a color made
of purple lives of lust in shade.

And in the time it takes to breath,
you've cut the roots and pulled the seeds
that lain implanted in the ground,
a sterile mass
you're trotting down.

Gardner Graber

There Is No Pain Today

Tired and weary from a long days walk,
Dad sits down for one final talk.
He talks to the angels, he has waited so long.
Rested and smiling now, Daddy is gone.

With love in our hearts and the need to go on,
we listen intently for his favorite song.
Seven Spanish Angels took you away,
but the pain is all gone, as we had prayed.

As time goes on, with each passing day,
I think to the day that you lay,
so peaceful and rested, there is no pain today.

We'll miss you for always and maybe one day,
we'll meet at the beginning of a brand new day.

Doris (Dee) Hawkins

The Child Within

I am the child that you cannot see.
I am the child that longs to be free.
Though I am invisible, you know I am real.
I am here when you laugh, when you cry, when you feel.
I long for the chance to laugh and have fun.
To color and play, to run in the sun.
To cry when I am scared or when my heart's sad . . .
To scream very loudly when I'm very mad.
I long to be found from deep down in your soul.
To be caressed and loved and held and told,
 It's okay now, I'm here and I care.
It's okay now, I'll always be there.
You'll never have to be alone or lost.
'Cause I'll be your friend, no matter what the cost.
Yes, I am the child that you could not be.
I am the child you long to set free.
I am the child that you could have been.
Yes, I am the child within . . .

Caryl Mitti

Time's Slipped Away

All those things I wish to say
So little time there is no way
I think back to times when things were better
Those times when things could last forever

A word or two before you leave
Those things I could not say or even breathe
The times we had so long ago
Time's ruthless way of letting go

There was never enough time for me to speak
To have emotions; it seemed so weak
I buried what thoughts I could
And built walls I never should

Time has once again caught pace
And I alone must stand and face
The things I have become
To wish so many things undone

I cannot say I love or like
But things have changed in life despite
The constant never-ending pace
Time has taken your warm embrace

I stand alone, now by choice
But still I long to hear your voice
Maybe it is time to say good-bye and cut away
But it is not easy to overcome this deep dismay

Donald Freeman

Roses Are Red

*Dedicated to Diane Garcia,
the woman who inspires all my thoughts.*
Roses are red, violets are blue.
I love you deeply; my heart, I hand to you.
I make but one promise, forever I'll love only you.

I've handed you my heart, in it is my promise to you.
This heart is fragile, it can easily be broken.
Guard it safely beside you, keep it close to your own.
Don't leave it anywhere; it's accident prone.
Don't let it break, or get injured
For it holds my promise to you.

A broken heart can be mended,
But a promise that's been broken in two
You cannot fix it, no longer will it be true.
Guard it safely beside you,
Keeping it always near yours.
My love grows greatly, and will always be true.

Joe Pina

Maze

Traveling through your life is like walking in a maze
You have a lot of choices
Some places seem to be easy to travel
But are dead ends
Some places are hard to walk through
But are exits
You are always walking blindly inside
If you fall down
You have to stand up
Give yourself confidence
Tell yourself that you are going to finish this trip
Tell yourself that you are going to make it
Maybe when you step out of the exit
You will see your paradise

Shing-Yan Chong

Rosie, Cappucino -n- Me

Sweetly cherished afternoons,
five days a week, three o'clock my time.
International Foods -n- TV: "my private retreat."
I click on my control with great anticipation.
I position my sofa pillow and relax.
Someone from the audience announces her repeated
entrance, "Welcome to the Rosie O'Donnell Show."
Smiling alone with great gratitude, she doesn't know,
I'm only one of her fans. I have it clocked down to the
minute, the order in which things are programmed.
The minutes pass timely and all my expressions, no person
will ever see, in my private small world,
just Rosie, Cappuccino -n- me.
Weekends come, I'm on my computer, back to her web site
checking the menu for next week's list of programs.
Where it will start all over, in "my private retreat."

Retha Mary Wittman

Empty Space

Wish I could have had a father
How long should I feel the hatred
Watch my mom as she's getting battered
To him, seemed as if our lives didn't matter

Raise my head to the sky and say what up pops
Remember the time you got arrested by the cops
I think of a time when i didn't know what my life would bring
Realizing all that has been in it is anger
But thinking, Jesus didn't know what he was in for
while lying in the manger
But look how his life ended up
So once again I say, "What's up?"

Hit my chest twice, raise my hand in the air
Believe it or not I still care
You made life rough
But look, we made it through the bad stuff

It's hard to have feelings for a stranger
But if I sort through the anger
I can truly say I still care

I wonder why you weren't there for my brother and I,
And my biggest question: Why'd you have to die?

Scott Nicely

A Real Life

Enchanting beauty in one glance to your ground
one look to your trees, swaying high as though
they were stretching for your out-reaching arms.
Oh my God, your life explodes though out your whole created world.

Your love is pouring from a blade of grass
to the fluffiest cloud passing overhead,
your gentleness flows from each petal of a wild daisy in my path,
My Lord, May God, Why do you love me so?

The warm wind as it flows around me so free,
it seems as though you are speaking to me.
the message, which I feel as it blows in my face
"It my breath, take my life, it's yours, today.
Thank you Jesus, for loving me.

As I stood there on a hill of new life,
clouds shadowing the fields, and as I watched
the sun drawing closer, my heart was opening,
my life was seeking, then warmth touched my whole being!
Praise God! He lives, within my soul!

Linda Hershberger

Iris

Iris,
You are the flower above all the rest,
Too beautiful to turn away from,
so sweet better then a kiss.
You are my sister no one else can be,
you have gone through so much, it's hard to believe
How strong you are, how smart you are.
You're very special to me.
No one can take you away,
and I will be sure of that.
You are the flower above all the rest
because you are my iris.

Krystal Alvarez

Here I Stand

Wounded and trampled by the selfishness
of the soul-less people in charge,
solitary, and tired due to endless wandering.
I am a man questing without direction
for equality lost in the street,
there is no justice for just us.
Stereotypes of black maleness
misconstrued, rejected, and beaten by society.
Our intelligence devoured,
never appreciated, or comprehended.
Dealing daily with subtle prejudice,
How much bigotry directed at you in your life
never understood anyway?
Too much inundating falseness,
leading to numerous battles undergone,
some lost, and some won.
Legions of cruel, and ignorant people in your life,
expiring embers of freedom, suffered, and defended by pride,
voluminous overwhelming situations,
oppressed by unequal thoughts
condemned to solitude,
Here I Stand, A Black Man.

John Waller

I'm Sorry

I'm sorry you can't love me,
I'm sorry for being so bad,
I'm sorry I can't measure up,
I'm sorry for making you so mad,

I'm sorry for all my bruises that show up,
I'm sorry for all the times I've cried,
I'm sorry for getting you all worked up,
I'm sorry I almost died,

I'm sorry I called 911,
I'm sorry they took me away,
I'm sorry that you're in jail,
I'm sorry I haven't visited you since that day.

Neely Humble

Would It Really Matter

If they all quit complaining about me,
would I notice?
If I gave them a reason to quit,
would they?
If I did something right would they care?
Would they get mad if I was even worse in their eyes,
Or would they just give up.
Could I go on without it?
It's strange how you get used to these things,
And how somehow you need them.
Would they even notice if I did something right?
Because I did.
I didn't hear any praise.
Maybe I just blocked it out,
or maybe I just didn't hear.
Would it really matter just the same?

Melanie Price

Dream

Blurry, but clear,
Colorful, but grey,
Wonderful, but dreary in an odd sort of way.

Words spoken,
Hearts broken,
Fantasies that come true,
Millions of images soaring to you.

Erasing worries,
Freeing the mind,
Enjoying a world not of our kind.

Magical and amazing,
Lands as vast as the sky,
Yet it all disappears at the blink of an eye.
Linda Cox

Morning Crime

Rising to the soft whispers of the morning beams,
burrowing through the fine fabric of my dreams,
I turn and hide from this reckless intrusion,
to catch a last glimpse of Camelot's diffusion.
Arching back for last night's prize,
I am pleasantly surprised to find nihility.
Breathing, sighing at one time,
the mirror tells all that isn't mine.
Grinning away the hapless, rising smile,
petrified and vile—it is my life's stile.
The rotten smell of happiness is my fine,
every day I must wake, to the very same crime.
Miha Vindis

The Gift of Time

As I live my life each day,
I learn new things along the way.
Some things bad, some things good,
Some things never understood.

As the seconds pass me by,
It feels as if time can fly.
As I idle each tick of the clock,
I'm no better than a wooden block.

Then again a wooden block is better than I,
Who lays idly gazing at the sky.
For the wooden block is idle not by choice,
I would know if I can hear its voice.

The wasted days and wasted nights,
My deep regret really bites.
Now I live for a brand new day,
Wiser, but still learning along the way.
Eng Kim Neoh

Mommas Always Cry

When a woman finds she is first with child
Mommas always cry
When that child sees its first light
Mommas always cry
When her baby first goes to school
Mommas always cry
When her baby becomes a man
Mommas always cry
When her young man comes home and then says good-bye
Mommas always cry
It has been so grand to be my Momma's little child
Because Momma always cried
Patrick Bucksot

For Mervin R. Eiche

Here is something we all know so well;
It surfaces straight from the gates of Hell.
It attacks the mother, child, father, husband, and wife:
It often puts a very short ending to a loved one's life.
It silently destroys millions with its desire to kill;
It doesn't seem to be selective, striking at will.
My heart bleeds tears for the victims we've lost;
I see how the survivors continue battling at all costs.
You might think this is meaningless to you and I;
But how meaningless is it to know every day someone will die?
I ask you now to offer your love and show you care;
To someone around you that might be living with this despair.
I pray for you to never have to see;
How terrible living with cancer can be.
I would like to thank you for sharing this time with me.
I offer you this last "Blessed Be."
Connie Slagle

Embracing Your Heart

Embracing your heart, feelings of sensuality
    feelings of love when spring hits
when it's time for your spirit to say goodbye
    your spirit will flutter like a butterfly
        soaring to each and every flower
        every flower that shall blossom
            in the season of spring

Reaching up and out, God's hands reach down
    God's hands wrap around your spirit
lifting you up through the peaceful blue sky
nothing but a feeling of joy and happiness
surrounding your spirit, through the journey
to eternal life, then the final moment hits

    the gates of Heaven are opened
    Angels greet you, then you follow
continuing the journey to eternal life
    the gates close behind you
you are now at peace throughout eternity
    'cause God will always be there
        Embracing your heart
Sueanne Heneghan

Elektracoustic

Your touch, like water
  trickling down my spine
Fingertips plucking my
  pulsing silver veins,
Throbbing heart, quivering
  breath, move me to dance . . .
. . . Instinctively to the rhythms
  you have set for me
I cannot stop myself, I
  won't keep still . . .
. . . You have penetrated me deeply,
  entered to the hilt
you have changed me, altered me,
  renewed my sound! With you
I am reborn, crying joyously,
  trembling uncontrollably you support me . . .
. . . I wish to give you what
  you have given me, music, joy,
The dance of love triumphant!
  You are my waking dream, my love,
        my life. . . .
Tracie Leucuta

America

We were packed and shipped over
Tight like sardines.
From people to property,
Violated African Queens.

Stripped of our language,
Robbed of our culture,
Hovering over head was the heritage vulture.

Take Cleopatra who was beautiful and black.
When portrayed in America, color did she lack.

Shackles and chains ripped families apart,
Yet determination and pride was buried deep in our hearts.

We built a nation that housed millions,
On sweat, blood and deep, intricate feelings.

So that you and I can stand tall and proud
Representing long suffering and intelligence,
No longer property in front of crowds.

Sheloham Payne

Powerplay

It should never have happened
The grumbling organization
but still it was humbled
by men who didn't know much
but had power at their grasp

Bliss is the one word
you shouldn't take to your heart
if you try to make your way
with a sour face and one more wall has crumbled
it makes no sense to pride yourself
when the presentation is on Monday night
no matter what if it get's fumbled

Foul play is a holy disgrace
after you have evened the place
And nothing more needs to be done
to get the setting sun to wonder
outside the flas—it was kept in

After the long haul on Friday night
You give some lovely ladies fright
By staring without looking

Thom Van Der Kley

Will You

Will you hold me close like you'll never let me go,
so I can ask you a secret that I really want to know.
Will you speak those special words softly in my ear,
and speak them very quietly so only I can hear.
Will you walk the beach with me, and hold my lonely hand,
and tell me that you love me, and you'll always be my man.
Will you tell me your darkest secrets,
that you've never told a soul,
and tell me every detail you think I'd like to know.
Will you sing me a love song,
that you know I've never heard, and sing it, oh, so loud,
that it almost hits the clouds.
Will you always be that special one,
who will always understand,
and will you lend me your shoulders
when my tears are in demand.
Will you always talk to me when you seem to have a doubt,
thinking I don't care for you, 'cause, Hun, we can work it out.
Will you always love me, no matter what words are said,
'cause I could never stand losing you,
it would tare my heart to threads.

Brenda Rahier

Red

Red is . . .
The color of the blood running through my veins
The color of Jesus' face on the day of crucifixion
The color of the highway man after being shot down in the streets
The end of all life
Life both beginning and end
Anywhere and everywhere
The color of a beautiful rose on Valentine's.
The color of love
Red is . . . .

Joshua Longueira

My Love

When I'm feeling sad, you make things better . . . .
When I feel alone . . . . you are there . . . .
When I cry you hold me tight . . . .
I know that you will always be there for me . . . .
And I'll always be here for you also . . . .
When we talk, I feel like we have talked forever . . . .
I wish things could be different,
but for now they are how they are . . . .
And it makes me happy just to be able to talk
to you every night . . . .
It makes me feel like I'm a part of you!
Which I want to be . . . .
Night after night we talk, it's so nice to talk with you . . . .
I feel safe and secure with you . . . .
That's how it should be . . . .
Trust . . . . Love . . . . Safety!
So my love . . . .
I thought I would write this down . . . .
To show you what my heart feels . . . .
I Love You!

Elizabeth M. Delgado

Princess Sara

My precious jewel how rough when I found you
not knowing your gifts in beauty abound you,
possessing these gifts that you've given freely
gave me the chance of living quite kingly.
In castles up high as enemies prevail,
the moat, turret and walls they will scale.
Demons of past secrets untold
lies upon lies as are hearts turn to cold.
These gifts that were given can never be taken
growing precious through time as beauty is shaken.
As time dallies on the gifts then are cherished
while the castle and dragons in memory will perish . . .

Anthony Auriemma

On My Own Two Feet

I battled you away as I scrambled up to stand
  With Inquiring eyes and pure infant pride,
I shakingly stood peering over land—
  So inviting, exciting, tempting, and as far
As mine eyes could see—
  But then I begin to wobble and you reached
Out as I slipped from beneath my feet.
  I fought you during the teen years and
Begged to have boys call.
  But you, within one simple breath, shook
Your head and denied me of them all.
  Impatiently, I plotted and tried to prove
You wrong, but time won out and you still
  Marched to the ol' parent song.
I know I will stumble and fall along the
  The path of life.
I am not accusing you of being wrong, but you
  Are not always right.
One day, I'll be able to smile and our eyes
  Will boldly meet. Then I'll say, "Look,
Daddy, I'm standing on my own two feet."

Patrice McIntosh

What If . . .

All that you had been told was wrong?
If a Fairy bit you,
would it still be considered beautiful and kind?
If a demon saved you,
would he still be so ugly and vicious?
If the sun burnt you,
would it still be so warm and comforting?
If the moon illuminated your path,
would you still fear the full moon?
If the snow froze you,
would it still be so white?
If the raging fires warmed you,
would they still be considered evil?
What If . . .

Chantal Leblanc

Good-Bye

I don't always say I love you,
Not every little time.
I often daily leave you,
But I'm back in a short time.
But one time that I left you,
I forgot to say good-bye.
If I'd known it was the last time I'd see you,
I might have taken a little time.
Yet, after awhile I returned,
But was surprised to find,
That in that short time you had left,
And now you're gone,
Good-bye.

Kandice Saum

Princess

Thought you could stand,
Thought you could face this task without His hand.
But now you've drowned,
Oh, princess where is your crown?
Too proud to grab this safety line,
You've broken His heart just as you've broken mine.
The waves are crashing over your head,
How long do you think you can tread?
Trying to float on this pew,
Cast it aside and trust in the One who saved you.
Now you're shaking with fear,
Open up, let Him wipe your tear.
Turn back to His arm,
Where you will feel no more harm.
Let Him put you at ease,
Close your eyes, sleep eternal peace.

Ryan Murphy

Thwarted Intentions

I only meant to love a dream.
A fantasy of self-delusion,
ever-changing as the moon,
constant as the sea.
A meld of mystery and illusion
secreted beneath my bed in its ivory box.
    You were a desire,
        I sometimes found delicious.
    The chill thrill of rain on parched lips.
        Now, your face stalks my consciousness,
preying on random thoughts,
the scent of moonlight left in its wake.
    You laugh at my consternation,
twirling a blade of sunshine
            between your fingers.
My laughter joins the fray,
our voices twine . . . and I am yours.

When did you sneak in
        and become my dream?

Autumn Lane

The Shout

Oh! Their mouths opened in sadness;
in madness the blood roared and
feelings soared onto another plane,
another chessboard, a different pain.

Oh! Their song was heard loftily through
wrinkled IV bags in a needle arm.
They caused me no harm, and yet their
charm could not be stayed.

And I stayed through the night by your
side, and I sighed with you, and I died with
you, and I woke with you; I was lost
within your expression of glossy incandescence.

Hospital stay, 8 years old—
and, oh! What tales the shadows told.

Kevin Barrett

My Baby Girl

The spiritual part of me knew you
    For what seemed to be an eternity
Although my arms never cuddled you
    You were so special to me
I never once saw your sweet smile
    You were here for such a short time
My heart feels so empty
    As if you left in the blink of an eye
I wish you could have stayed
    If only for a short while
But I guess it's in the plan
    For my baby girl to return again
I'll always wonder about you hair
    If it's sweet, mild and fair
I'll always think about your movement
    Your special spirit benign
But most of all I'll remember you were mine

Vicktoria Rathburn

Stronger Than Steel

You're another year older & five years wiser
Straining for your smile though in thought I'm beside you
Many years have passed since I had you in tow
My shadow, a little girl, whom I couldn't let go

Now, to me, you're my other half complete
Once a tether, now stronger, than steel wire & concrete
I look at you with love now more than ever
A friendship so strong, a bond nothing can sever
I celebrate this momentous day with you
Although every day's a celebration of life with you

Since there's nothing in this world that could possibly replace
This bond I feel and so happily embrace
I promise to remain the completed part
And continue to give you my lectures, my friendship
But most of all, my heart

Christina Debrouse

Quilt of Life

My life is like a patchwork quilt
Each piece so different, just as each event in my life
The stitches are footsteps piecing the squares into a life lived.

When completed and death reaches its final end
The binding encloses the Quilt of life
A time of events representing me,
The history of one human being.

Bethalene Finestead

"Dream"

I dream about you every day,
wishing you were mine again . . .
Just thinking about all the times we sat
and kissed that's something I really miss . . .
I don't think I'll ever get over you
I wish you could see you're the only one for me . . .
All those times you held me tight
and whispered "I Love you" with delight . . .
Those special words, they meant so much,
I felt the same, but out of touch . . .
The day you said goodbye I could do nothing but cry . . .
I still Love you and always will,
but there's nothing I can do but keep Dreaming about you . . . .

Luceal Haddigan

I Have the Light of God in Me

I may not walk like you do.
I may fall down when I walk.
I get up with a smile on my face.
That's because I have the light of God in me.
When you have the light of God in you, you can face anything.

Phoebe Spiers

Dreaming of Sleep

The thoughts hold my eyes open, impervious to sleep.
The blank page stares at me, mocking the blockage,
which is holding this dreamless night in its grasp.
A slow humiliating tick marks each passing second
of this dreadful night.
Time lapse as my life continues to near its end.
Being amused by any movement is all there is,
as the sound of graphite shatters the silence
in an attempt to record the suffering and anguish.
All the emotions combine to produce a confusion like no other.
Loneliness shares time with frustration.
Slowly and chaotically my secrets are revealed.
My passions have an odd way of showing themselves.
Insanity begins to stroke the belly
of all the coincidences surrounding my joys and hardships.
These are the moments I feel similar to a butterfly
cursed with the wings of a dragon.
Either way all that is needed is courage
and the will to conquer my worldly ailments.

Ken Krajeski

February Sorrow

Springtime, you don't come out like you used to,
Is it 'cause we put your better half in the ground?
The sun won't shine, the birds won't sing without you.
You don't know how much we need the sound.
But, now these years we skip right into summer,
And I wonder, Where have all the flowers gone?
Nothing hurts so much quite like the winter,
When the dreary days drag on and on.
Could it be you died right along with him?
You and all your flowers on his grave.
And in the next few days you shriveled with them.
In your sadness could you not be saved?
So, here I wait in February sorrow,
Right upon the day he went away.
I know you won't, but tonight, I dream tomorrow
That both of you will be back with me to stay.
Where ever you have gone my love goes also.
May the two of you always have peace.
And upon some sunny day I hope to join you,
In a paradise where your flowers
Never cease.

Natalie Kennedy

The Wall

I stand on a wall
I stand there for you
I stand there for your family
I stand there for your friends

You ask why do I stand here
I stand here to defend my nation
I stand here so your children may sleep at night
I stand here to guard your life and freedom

I took an oath
To defend my country against all enemies
Both foreign and domestic
I hold that oath sacred

For I am an American soldier.

Andrew Haney

Beginnings

Softly, ever so softly music accompanies the rustling
of parchment, both filling the void of deep silence.

Attuned to my surroundings I sit with fragments
and phrases racing through grey matter not unlike a composer
poised before the first notefall.

Penned words flow forth, some cautiously, reluctant
to be formed, then as a crescendo animating a light melody,
some burst forth furiously, too fast to capture.

Thoughts and images awaken, nurtured from conception,
begin life just as concertos and operas embraced,
performed with heart, haunt our souls.

Sarah Yocom

Misty and Joe

Dedicated to my mother and God

After surrounded by so, so many deaths
I'm alone in a tree high up in a nest

Occasional visits from mom for a meal
With love and caring that I could feel

She spends her day's helping me cope
And after so many years she's given me hope

Death came early for my daughter and dad
Under terrible circumstances that were bad

Then I wondered if I'd ever again sing
Until the day when God gave me wings

Finally with God & mom there was worth
When I realized my place was here, on Earth.

Anne Wilcox

Friends

Who are your friends?
Are they somebody who you have known forever,
or are they the ones who you have just met?
Is it the girl across the street, or is it the boy next door?
Are they the kind who stabs you in the back,
or is it you who stabs them?
Do they listen to your thoughts, or do you listen to theirs?
Will they be there in your time of need,
or will you be there in there's?
Will you trust them with your secrets,
or will they trust you with their's?
Do you believe every word they say?
Do they trust you and every word you say?
Friendship is a matter of trusting each other.
If you trust your friends, then they will trust you.
If that works, then you have a really special friendship.
That is what friendship is all about.

Cassandra Shuptar

Mother

The child that I was
sees you as a comforter
the person who nurtured me
gives unfailingly of herself
is there to talk to
or just listen when I am troubled

The woman that I am now
sees you for the friend that you are
the one person who tells me what I need to hear
when I don't want to hear it
the person who grounds me
is my foundation
when I'm on shaky ground

You're the teacher of right and wrong
the one who has made me strong
You're an unsung hero
and the wind beneath my wings
My Friend
My Mother
          Joi Hardrick

Mirror

I wish that I had known myself
As you have always known me
I wish that I had always believed in myself
Like you've always believed in me
I wish that I'd been more proud of myself
Just as you have been proud of me
I wish at times I'd have scared myself
As much as you have been scared for me
I know that I've been hard on myself
And at times, you too, have been hard on me
I wish that I had always loved myself
As much as you have always loved me.

But I have learned a lot about me
And now I can believe in me
I see enough to be proud of me
Looking back I feel for you, because I scare me
I know how to be patient with me
And I can be free to love me, myself.
And as I look at my reflection
I realize that you are me.
          Cara Vanest

Poem of F

Forsake a fortunate minute in reading this friendly FLASH
for vous to forego the forest;
foresight the field and
fortify forward focus forfeiting freewill
then float & fashion any fading feelings
to find this fabulous, favorable, free,
yet faraway familiar fantasia with fawning favor,
facilitating faith, fortitude & forgiveness.
Fuel flowering favoritism within.
Flow fluently forward.
Forge your formidable
fortune with a firm feeding
of inner ferocious fancy to finally foster,
fortify and furnish your future forte.
Fantastic food from me, a fountain font of information;
one infinite endearing faithful friendship.
Follow your Faith . . . .
          Len S. Comaniuk

The Quest

What is it in life we seek, and when we find it,
will it make us strong or weak?
They say that the answer can be found in ancient history,
but after a thousand years it still remains a mystery.
Something tells me that we are all being mislead,
and that we will first find the answer, after we are dead.
We are born, we grow, we live life, and then we die.
Deep inside me I just can't find the reason why.
No matter how much we try to solve this mystery,
I just know that the answer will always remain in ancient history.
          Kristjan Gudmundsson

My Testimony

I was just a sinner, lonely and afraid;
I had things that money buys, but I couldn't face the day.
Then one day I heard about the Man who loves me so,
That He gave His life for me and wants to make me whole.

Jesus shed His blood for me, it cleansed and made me whole.
Then He said to me, "My child, oh, yes I love you so.
Just reach out and take my hand; I'll take you on the road.
Keep your eye upon the cross, for it will lead you home."

Jesus is the Way, the Truth, and He is the Life.
And He wants to help you, too, through sorrow, pain, and strife.
Just reach out and take His hand; He'll give to you new life.
Jesus is the Way, the Truth, and Life.

Jesus, I love you.
Jesus, I need you.
Come and live with me forever.

Jesus, I love you.
Jesus, I need you.
Come and live with me forever.
          Jack Gudgel

Never Have I Asked

For years and years and years
A friendship, so deep and true
Two siblings in fact, then theory too
Now a deeper feeling enters
Towards a friend
Yet not the sister too
Afraid to ever mention
For fear of losing a friend, or two
While the heart waits and longs
Unwilling to let go
Hoping for a sign of deepness so
Never do I ask
Afraid her to scare
And the closeness to destroy
So I wait and wait and wait
Never do I ask, ever do I pray
A letter to receive—All is a-ok
A need to let it go
A feeling must be shared
Yet never have I asked—Will I ever dare?
          Jason Silverman

Muted Whisperings

If I listen carefully I can hear it.
The muted whisperings in my ears.
My heart pleading for time;
Time to understand and time to heal.
To make sense out of these events
That have ravaged my soul.
Leaving me weak and exposed,
Prey for those stronger than I.

Somewhere deep within me,
There is a longing for strength.
To rise out of the ashes of despair;
To conquer the demons roaming inside my heart.
To beat them back and stand my ground.

But I must do it alone.
          Toni Clifford

View from the Cross

From where I hung on Calvary
My blood flowing freely to the ground
Who did I see
As I sadly gazed down?

Not the angry mobs, yelling, "Crucify"
Nor the one who twisted the thorns, nor hammered the stake
Not the Roman soldiers who were standing by
Nor their iniquities nor their hate.

It wasn't my mother, whose heart was broken
Not the mocker, nor the scoffer
Not the faithful ones who followed with no words spoken
Nor the one with only the bitter drink tooffer.

When I cried, "It is finished." to my Father above
'Til the end of the age, I will remember the view
As I looked down with mercy and love—I saw YOU!

Jean Lutz

Ignorance

Greetings all who enter here,
relinquish love,
forsake all fear.
Grey and damp,
we all digress.
Toil for more but end with less.
Uniformed and uninspired,
becoming old and always tired.
Shattered dreams from days passed,
through the years, they cannot last.
We segregate and build walls.
This one's black,
that one's gay.
Everyone here gets a label or tag.
We cling to these objects instead of to friends.
Suffocation,
intoxication,
self medication,
trepidation.

Carlene Tolley

The Human Race

Sitting here once more, beyond the rain that pours
down on the grey frozen earth. As I sit and wonder why,
beautiful thoughts arouse me to self being
which I had once and now hold once more.
I see people, people swarming around me
like bees in a hive, birds fly freely across the skies,
flowers bloom in their right time . . .
time is drawing near but people have no fear
of things that will happen in future years.
They act as normal as they can be,
but one day they will see that people
are not as free as they seem to be.
As I sat beyond the prison wall, I heard someone desperately call,
"Save me from this broken place, save me from the human race"
Now you may wonder why these things I wrote.
My feelings I cannot quote
what they mean to me this time and place—
is this what we call the human race?

Dorothy Winyschel

"My Little World"

When that angelic smile touches the sweet lips of my little girl,
It is the sunlight that shines upon my little world.
Her gentle bright eyes sparkle with an innocence so free,
They are the stars in my sky and my tranquil blue sea.
Bless all of her cries of frustration and every tear shed in pain:
For these are the thunder clouds rolling and the cold torrential rain.
She is the warm breeze blowing through my little world,
She is now and forever my sweet little girl.

Michael S. Reynolds Jr.

A Woman One Day

My Mommy told me,
"I'll be a woman one day."
She said,
"I'll walk Proud like Harriet Tubman
leading the slaves to freedom."
She said,
"I'll sing like Billy Holliday."
OH! OH! she said,
"I'll act like Lena Horne,"
and one day I'll have a beautiful child—
JUST LIKE ME,
Medina Anderson!
Yea my mommy told me
"I'll be a woman day,"
And when I am,
the world better be
READY!

Tammy Heath

Light

Nature's light brightens my mind with brilliance.
It's radiance is spawned by sunlight,
the light of the moon
and the sparkle of stars that wander
their purposeful paths in the sky.

Light was also created by a man of genius who gave
us unlimited opportunity to see by the light of the electric bulb.
Light is the Festival of Lights at Hanukkah
and the exquisite glitter patterns created for Christmas.

Light squeezes my imagination
into thoughts that fly towards its rays.
Light is my light uniting with your light
to create the universal brilliance of hearts together.

Light is the ultimate inspiration of humankind.
light can guide our paths towards global enlightenment.

Joanne E. Liebow

Help Me

From the dark of night, I hear the calls
the crying, the shameful woes of souls gone astray.
I lay in my bed and listen, wondering of their departure,
curious of their arrival.
Entering through the walls, doors, and even my spirit.
They take over like an ambush in the night.
There's so many, who do I listen to first?
Who shall be the influencing party?
The man who sits on the end of my bed calling me little sissy?
Is it the man with the skeleton face and hat of black?
Is it the lady who stands in the corner and cries all night?
Nobody would understand if I were to tell of my newly found friends.
The grief in each one of their faces takes its toll on mine.
They come into your life occasionally,
then it's every day, and eventually you're consumed
with the possibility of making them happy,
not knowing why they are sad.
My heart bleeds for my three unhappy souls.

Christie Jacoba

Without Her I am Empty

Her hair shines like the sun
Her eyes sparkle as if a the stars of a thousand solar systems
reside within . . .

In her touch I find peace
In her I eyes is hope
and in her heart is an everlasting joy that can never be extinguished
She is the light to my path and the air to my lungs
With her I am immortal
With her I am invincible
without her I am but an empty husk blown about the winds of life

Daniel Williams

Clams

They lie in my tub like the lazy man
I just dusted off, who dug them,
nothing to do but spit: mucus, sand, salt, cornmeal grit.
Over and over I wash them—
still, lazy men in a gritty tub, spitting,
griping, extruding slime.
I worry about the hot weather, the price of meat,
and whether I can eat anything so live, so like a man.
They come in all sizes, parts lolling now from unzipped shells.

I cook a few; the dripping, smallest ones I can handle.
Flames light the pot.
I fight to type at my desk.
The water warms. I wait, I listen.
No one's murdering pots of men.
They start dancing with heat.
I hear their shells tap and crack.
I crack, tapping the maddest letter
to a man who's never mad.

> *Julianne Nason*

A New Day

I woke up this morning
to a staggering surprise,
While I was still yawning
the sun shined in my eyes;
And I thought what a great day
my dreams and hopes may come my way,
So I got up and my cereal ate
and dressed for my all day fate,
The world that seemed so cruel last night
Suddenly became a road of happy light,
I saw people with a sincere smile
Though burdens were heavy their first mile,
Children played in yards and street
It was just a good day for all to meet,
And then I thought, "God give me grace"
To be kind to every person I face,
And help me as the days grow long
To be a person caring and strong.

> *John Culbertson*

Blue Mountain

The worn wooden deck,
my grandfather constructed with his own hands,
holds the three of us up here high above Charlotte.

Beneath us, below here, in the valley,
the white pulses of an amateur fireworks display are caught in the mist
rising between the still, green crevices of land.
Reflecting the night's navy blue of the
recently dark sky, the earth envelopes
the hand-made deck with the safety of
uninhabited stillness.
The worries of my sleepless city
cannot penetrate these hills.
A deep navy mountain meets the black of the
night and merges, leaving only a small
line of shadow where earth caresses sky.
I cannot decipher the constellations
from the stars high above me.

Here on the deck, I am crushed by Heaven.

> *Elise Yacovone*

The Voice

I hear the voice behind me
It's as soft and perfect as can be
Words can't describe how angelic it sounds
As it echoes all around

It's not evil but the complete opposite
Sometimes I have to sit
From the power of His presence
All around me in an instance

God chose to use someone that I rather not be apart
To use the gift He's given her to touch my heart
How I long each day to hear it once more
How down and dry was my worship before

It's not jealousy or envy
But joy and a love to hear in me
I thank God for giving you a gift so pure
And placing you behind me when I needed it for sure

> *Jamie Dean*

Forever

Remember the days spent
Huddled around the fire
Weathering the storms around us,
Eyes locked in desire
Remember the strolls, the nights
My arms wrapped around you
Two shadows quietly gliding by
Time had stopped forever,
The memories keep coming back
The altar, the first born, our first house
the moments shared in love and pain
We were together forever
Now . . . .
As I stand beside you
And you gone so far away
I wish the memories too
Would leave me, and
Let me lie besides you,
Forever . . . .

> *G Sachdeva*

Something about Love

Love is very special, kind and true.
True love never makes you feel so blue.

If it's love you can always tell.
It may detour but never breaks the spell.

You can see love in the eyes for sure.
Love is strong, enduring, forgiving, and pure.

Love can never be based on lies.
If it is that love soon dies.

How hard to put a love to sleep.
We keep thanking if I try harder maybe it will be mine to keep.

Sometimes love comes and goes.
Why we can't make the Love work nobody knows.

So look back on this kind of Love with pleasure.
You've known it, it was a treasure.

For each of us in this world we have to make our own mistakes.
But remember God loves you, you have a lot to offer for Heaven sakes.

When we walk in the sand we leave a footprint.
When someone walks on your heart they leave a heartprint.

Don't forget that love hide it in your heart.
Don't take any of it with you make a new start.

> *Barbara Maness*

Voice in the Wind

Where there is love there is LIFE, where there is life there is HAPPINESS,
where there is happiness there is GOODNESS, where there is goodness there is DESIRE,
where there is desire there is BELIEF, where there is belief there is STRENGTH,
where there is strength there is WONDER, where there is wonder there is FREEDOM,
where there is freedom there is FEAR, where there is fear there are DREAMS.

Maya Lujan

Bride to Be

If I give you my heart, will you take care of it for me while it's gone?
Trust me with your body and soul and protect me when you're strong
To wait with patience help me get through my fears.
Lend your shoulder for when I have tears.
If I give you my heart will you keep it safe and sound
right next to yours where it can be easily found.
Treat with respect and trust replenish it with love and not lust.
If I give you my heart,
will you carry it with grace high above all others always first place.
If you can do this for me, my heart belongs to you my bride to be

William Rodgers

And the Two Shall Become One

Marriage is a commitment to God that's built on faith in His Son.
And through the anointing of His Spirit, the two shall become one.
In order to become as one, grow in Christ together.
Worship, pray and study God's Word; He'll bless your every endeavor.
With Christ as the Head of your marriage, He'll give you the Power you need.
For the two shall become one and anoint your very seed.
Stand on the promises of God; With Christ you can overcome.
For God is the One who ordained that the two shall become one.
God will take away the confusion and do away with all your pain.
"The two shall become as one," is the Master's Ultimate Aim!

Victoria Ammons

Eyes

My eyes they know what they saw.
They see the big they see the small.
They see this way they see that.
They see up they see it all.
They see shapes and colors too.
My eyes see that's what they do.
They see up they see down.
They see many things in many ways, yes they do.
When it's time to close my eyes, they still see the memories.
'Til the sun rises with another day.
My eyes they see delight in every way.
Whether they are open or they stay closed.
They see the beauty that God unfolds.
God gave us our eyes so that they could see just how much he loves you and me.

Frances Culbertson

A Mother's Worry

What kind of world will it be for this child
growing in me?
Will there be clean, safe air and people who care?
Will there be water to drink and clear heads to think?
Will there still be drugs in school to accept and be cool?
Rapists and killers in the streets but not enough for the starving to eat?
Will there be weapons in space or a bigger arms race?
Die for freedom, would we dare as they did in Tiananmen square?
Hate groups in the public eye screaming out their deceit and lies?
Just what kind of world will it be for this child growing in me?

Kerry Brandon

Life

A candle burns at both ends,
fire racing flame.
My mind is cluttered . . . full of lies,
all your answers sound the same.
I don't know what to think,
too much is on my mind,
nothing seems the way it should,
and I'm running out of time.
The wick is disappearing,
someone please tell me what to do,
my mind tells me it's over,
but my heart knows it's not true.

Hazel Vincent

My Wings

Wings of a dove,
so beautiful and white,
reflect in my eyes,
as I cherish tonight.
I ask the little girl,
who sits by my side,
How were you so strong,
and when did you die?
She takes my hand and whispers
deep in to my soul,
I still live within you
pushing toward our goals .
I have strength when you let me,
and don't try to subdue,
I do not seek to harm,
only to remind you .
She silently keeps my secrets,
and holds the key to my past.
I will let her walk with me,
tonight in peace, and forever at last.

Julie Bilbrey

I will survive

I live in the shallow
realm of my own temperance
tainted by glory
mourning over the loss
of my own innocence

ask me what I desire
making me reply happiness
for the ones that I love
for the people who are losing
their own hope

I will survive
my short comings
my ignorant opinions
loss of spirituality
and self-deprivations

let me be concerned with myself
crying in the pale corners
where the sun continues to shine
cleaving the weight of my soul
out of my decadent features

April Wickett

At Night

At night,
as I lay hugging my pillow,
imagining that it is you,
I find myself crying tears
that seem to burn my
cheeks as they roll down.
And I wonder if it will always
be like this,
only a pillow
with tears.

Heather Freeman

To Try

To try to stay alive in this life of pain.
To try to stay afloat is the true goal of gain.
To try to keep a steady tread as difficult as it seems.
Is easier than you fathom in reality or in a dream.
To try to survive in these times of mine. Like jabbing a knife in the cord of my spine.
Unpredictable in more than two of a kind.
Hardship and pain make you wish you would die.
To try taking your life is an error in course.
To try to murder another is also a false source.
To try to drown it all away in drugs or booze.
Is another path taken that will cause you to lose.
To try to rely on GOD is the best action to proceed.
To pray, fast, invoke and prostrate are the best ways to succeed.

Labarron Edwards

A Sacred Trust

Is it not enough to see them, to know that they exist?
Must you hunt them down and murder them, then add them to your list and call them
"Trophies" you have gained?

Your hearts are deadened to their pain.

No more seasons left for them to live
Or babies yet to give an Earth grown worldly beyond measure
Without a heart to treasure Adam's sacred gift from Father
"Leave the carcass—too much bother
Watch the head though, after all, it must look natural on my wall.
I traveled far to bag this one and, I might add for quite a sum."

And those who silently remain to smell the blood and sense the fear,
Those yet acquainted with the pain of Separation
Pause to hear
The sounds of rifles once again
And watch their lives come to an end.

Jeanne Garmaize

Silence around Me

sitting in my room with the radio playing love songs,
leaves nothing but silence around me—
I close my eyes and begin to sing the words,
thinking nothing but your beauty, but the silence still surrounds me—
your eyes, your smile, the sure smell of your skin,
and the everlasting taste of your lips—the silence still there—
the vision of you standing before me holding out your arms
wanting to embrace me brings me comfort,
but the silence now starts to ache—
A tear slowly rolls down the side of my cheek
as it burns the image of her onto my face—
the sound of her voice echo's through my mind,
and the image of me caressing her body vibrates through my fingertips
the silence now starts to bleed—
every bone and nerve in my body starts to tremble and
soon my body becomes motionless to the constant beating of my heart,
as it fills with eagerness for her love—another tear fights

Edward Bottone

They Lie

And "they" say the pain eases with time?
Who are "they" and what do "they" know?
Have "they" ever known such a powerful love?
A love so moving, so deep, so intense, and all-consuming.
How many days did "they" live with heartache for their closest companion?
How many nights did loneliness slither its way in to torture them endlessly?
How many friends did "they" have who would listen with true understanding and compassion?
How many lovers did "they" take to somehow try to fill the void?
And "they" say the pain eases with time?
They Lie

Christina Martocci

Shadows

I like to watch the smoke dance
And see the shadows creep
Shadows hold the secrets
That the soul cannot keep

These secrets always with you
As they follow you around
Like a stalker in the night
They creep on the ground

They follow you where ever
And you'll see them if you turn
But don't think you can lose them
Will you ever learn

You can never forget your shadow
Unless you lose your mind
But even then it's lurking
Lurking just behind

Veronica Morton

Losing Things

Losing things,
It's what we all do.
I find you quite forgetful,
Yet faintly I am too.

You say, "I put them here
I promise!"
But they're nowhere I can see!
I say, "Did you put them here, or there?
Or even anywhere?"
I get slightly upset, when you have
lost something and it's
right under your nose.

If you really want to,
You can put your things away
And next time you
Look for them,
You'll find them through
and through.

Justine Sharpe

Mama

My mama has always been there
Since I was old enough to remember
There are things I haven't said lately
Like how much I really love her

I appreciate the pains she took
To bring me up just right
I long for the hugs she gave me
As she tucked me in at night

I remember the things she bought me
Like books, crayons and chalk
I miss the quiet moments
When we would just sit and talk

We have argued over some small points
We held together against the strong
My decisions were not always right
But, she still loved me when I was wrong

I regret not always being there
When she needed helping hands
I love my mama dearly
And I know she understands

Jo Garey

I Have Met an Angel

His body is sluggish, aged cold—
As it slows with mortal ache.
Love and God, Fatherhood and
Friendship, Beauty and Nature
These are his passions in life.
Kindness, that's what I see when I look at him, That's what everyone sees.
God is with him, he must be,
Because he's the closest thing to an angel
I've ever met.
He who was once a young man
Stands before me with his hair snowy white.
In my mind I'll always carry this image of him,
Quietly I settle his image down in his own corner of my heart . . .
The place where a bit of himself,
Will forever stay.
Who do you ask could this angel be?
My GRANDPAW you see he is an Angel to me . . . .

Melina Cross

Through the Eyes of My Child

Daddy I'm almost grown!   You've been away oh, so long.
I came into this world   as your little girl.
Daddy I'm almost grown!   I know it was nothing I said.
I know it was nothing I did.   Daddy where do you live?
I'm getting oh, so big.   Daddy I'm almost grown!
I turned eight today.   I thought it was great in a way.
You could have sent a card or letter.   That would have made me feel better.
Daddy I'm almost grown!   I look for you every where I go.
Days are going by fast not slow.   You could have stayed around
somewhere in this town.   Daddy I'm almost grown!

Tina Hayner

pretending enormous

we used to have something, small things, tokens, trifles, city cacophony and pay phones.
these things would flap in the wind, flutter in alleys, down stairwells, in bars, over turnstiles

there we were
creating a picture book full of small words and small actions but such bold print,
bold and shocking to the eyes, and there we were pretending enormous
pretending with sweeping gestures and gigantic promises, pretending above roof-tops,
through alleys, above so many stories so many stories so many slurred softly spoken stories

we actually pretended so big we set Alphabet City on fire during a rainstorm in August
but we were just two girls two very small girls creating very small things in small voices
two girls being swallowed by one another and the city's great noises.

Ainsley Drew Nelson

"Letting Go"

Letting go is a lot harder than holding on.
If I could hold on, I would hold on to the memories, the keepsakes of being happy.
Letting go is a lot like giving up . . .
giving up feels like I'm letting myself down.
Letting go is something I wish I'd never do,
but letting go allows me to hold on to you in my heart.

Jeffery Jackson, Jr.

Personal Discovery

All my life I have looked for adventure.
All my life I have looked for beauty
All my life I have looked for peace.
All my life I have looked for joy.
All my life I have looked for wisdom.
All my life I have looked for love.

Then one day, in my silence, I discovered all of those things . . .
within myself,

and you have those things, too!

Sandra Terrenzi

She Cries

Outside her window blows the wind
Inside her room she sighs
The perching raven knows she's sinned
She cries, she cries, she cries
Where is the light that once did shine
Down from the sunlit skies
It shines on only things divine
She cries, she cries, she cries
Where is the one who kissed her face
The one who dealt in lies
He brought her to this wretched place
She cries, she cries, she cries
Her beauty once so young in years
The magic in her eyes
Now swollen from so many tears
She cries, she cries, she cries
Such innocence she once possessed
It comes as no surprise
That even when her hearts at rest
She cries, she cries, she cries

David Cowdrick

Vietnam Vacation

Come one Come all
watch all the soldiers fall
hear them scream see them cry
watch all the bullets fly
Is it a midnight show?
What do they know?
Birds that cannot fly
men that cannot die
just lying there feeling pain
not even knowing their own name
just a number on a tag
fighting for the U.S. flag
As they walk through the valley
They count their dead
visions of horror parade in their head
pictures of loved ones
clutched in their hands, all they know
is what Uncle Sam demands
set them free bring them home
This is not just another poem

Kim Crisafulli

It All Comes Down to You

For Ryan
I used to believe,
Believe I had the world at my feet
I used to never need,
Never really need a single thing

Now every morning
I awake and realize how wrong I was
How cold and dull days used to be
Without him beside me

I used to never want to admit
That something might be missing
I used to never cry
At the sight of beautiful things

But I've been searching my soul to find
A place where only love resides,
And now I can finally see
I have visions of so many things
And no matter what I do,
It all comes down to you

Lindsey Talbott

Wisdom, Beauty, and Age

Humanity no longer recognizes true beauty,
They do not see what is real.
Wrinkles are no longer a sign of grace,
They are just old.
Gray hairs are no longer majestic,
They are just old.
The aged themselves are no longer considered wise,
They are just old.

The men and women of times long past,
Cultures long forgotten,
And knowledge long lost,
We that are young and naive owe you,
For it is we who have forsaken all that you had learned.
Even now, we the youthful ignore the knowledge that is still living,
We place them in old folks homes,
So that we may forget about them,
For they are just old.

Breanna Anderson

The Race I Must Win

Today is labor day, September 7, 1998.
I am at the starting line.
I did not choose to run this race.
Today i was chosen to run.
I get into position, my body becomes tense, my hands are sweating.
I can feel my heart racing.
The gun goes off and off I go.
I make it over the first hurdle.
Look, another hurdle is placed before me.
I leap over this hurdle with the grace of a lion.
What they do not know is that I am frying on the wings of an angel.
My daughter was forced out of the race called life.
Now you see why I can not lose. I am the chosen one riding on the wings of a angel.

Valerie Neal

All Alone

I sit alone, watching the walls, I cry myself to sleep
wishing of a time when we could be one.
But now your gone, you left me all alone to die.
I'd ask you why but I'd start to cry again.
I just want US to be again. Don't ask me why I cried for you
because I don't know why. Am I still in love with you?
I do not know. So if your my friend you will talk to me and be there for me when we
both know no one will?
Will you love me when I need to be loved?
or will you just kick me to the curb and leave me all alone?
I love you still and I know as well as you that
I will always Love you. So if your my friend
why do I hate life so much as to think Death is the only way out.
why my love did you have to leave me all alone.

Kristen Huebner

Anger

Anger,
Chokes the heart, clogs the mind, stifles sinless souls
To degrees never imagined reachable, lines never fathomed crossable,
Until you no longer know who you are; misplace what you believe;
forget what you're fighting for,
And only a distorted caricature remains, mocking, reminding, judging you
And vision is blurred, hearing impaired and sensibility seems senseless,
And the remnants salvaged from the wreckage of "You" are . . . ambivalent values,
broken self-perceptions, and philosophies desiderata.

Anger,
Chokes the mind, clogs the heart, stifles sinless souls
To degrees never imagined reachable, lines never fathomed crossable,
Until you no longer know who you are; misplace what you believe;
forget what you're fighting for.

Arifah Lightburn

A Woman Walking By

Like a queen of winter
she walks towards me
marble masked, and dressed in black

Her long steep hair
is frozen water, falling,
over her shoulders on her back

Every step moves her nearer
making me shiver and long
to shiver more

The never ending moment then unfreezes
when she gracefully moves
past my door

Sven van der Velde

Windows of You

You say that you'll always love me
That your heat will never change
You tell me your life is empty
Without me in your range

You promise your eyes are blinded
To any face but my own
And as I look into those eyes
I see what I've always known

I clearly see your heart beating
Stronger with each soft glance
Beneath their glossy surface
Your soul pleads for one last chance

You say you'd rather live moments
Holding me with the stars above
Then to go through eternity
And never know my love.

Jennifer Hill

Bad and Good Come Together

The sweet smell of a flower,
love and all its power
are gifts life has to shower.
Accept the good with the bad.
War is brought down by the mad.
yet death brings nothing but the sad.
A fight here, a problem there;
Who's feelings are yet to spare?
A whole life yet to bare.
There are many more
of life's surprises in store
for us all behind every door.
Life has its pleasure and its pain.
All our goals we have yet to obtain.
All our anger we should restrain
to allow our happiness to remain.

Debbie Morales

The Mistake of Psyche

Peaceful days
Passionate nights
A perfect lover
Just out of sight
He seemed divine
And so devout
Yet sisters would plant
A seed of doubt
To see his face
A candle was lit
She broke his heart
With just one drip
Her wonderful life
All but dust
There can be no love
Where there is no trust

Ryan Petel

Giving In

The ship is sinking, but it fights to stay afloat.
It must not give up; there still may be hope.

It's forbidden, I know, but it's so hard to do.
The Devil is mighty, and can have his way with anyone, me or you.

Love is the angel, lust is the demon.
The two will go at it and one will be leaving.

I have the power to determine the two.
It's such a difficult choice, what do I do?

It's right here in my face, so beautiful and willing.
The demons are strong and move in for the killing.

Before it gets so tough, that I am stuck in this like glue.
I fight the monsters like an infection and do not let them break through.

I sit alone now; I would feel terrible either way.
I believe I made the right choice, but you never can say.

I feel sick and empty, but I did what I thought was right.
If these demons cross my path again, will I have the strength to fight?

Jamie Swimm

Look at Me

When you look in my heart, what do you see?
When you look into my eyes what do you see?
When you look at me I hope you see the guy inside, and that guy is me.
I am who I am, and who I am is me.
So when you look into my eyes, I hope you see me.
There's a lot to me that you do not know.
But spend time with me and you will see, there's more to me than what you see.
So look real close, and look real hard, because what you see is in my heart.

Lance Adams

The Path of Life

Life, an ongoing journey of the soul.
We trudge ever on and on, walking this hard path
which we are doomed to follow until we depart from the Earth. Throughout this quest
for life, the heart yearns for more.
Some wonder why even go on.
It seems true happiness and true love are always just out of our reach, and in its place
lies hatred and confusion,
the bane of mankind.
So many emotions conflicting, tearing our hearts, fading the soul.
We strive to be something more, yet always we are only human.
We must open our hearts, letting our emotions flow freely.
Then the road comes to an end, stopping at the doorway to death.
Everything we ever held dear is gone, yet through kindness and love,
human kind lives on.
Maybe prospering only for those who care only about themselves,
those who use hatred and violence as weapons, living only
for wealth and power.
While in life they may succeed, when the day of judgement comes,
they shall fail, and only those pure of heart shall pass on
into true light and bliss.

Nick Green

Mom

These are all the things I love your thoughts words and all above You come to me
when I need you that is what I am going to do for you.
I love your smile so soft and sweet and how you work so hard for me I love the way
you get up at night just to give me a kiss goodnight I love you doing this all for me I
love you mom and I know you love me love your daughter Stacey

Stacey Pikowski

Pass It On

Looking through the pages of my
new millennium almanac,
reminds me of how things were done
several years back.

With several neighbors helping
with labor and toil,
to sew and to harvest what
was produced by the soil.

But now there's hustle and bustle
with no time to spare,
most people will pass on by
without even a care.

Now there's some that try to preserve
what their fathers and mothers learned,
and try to pass it on for our
children's future is a concern.

So take a youth to the country
and teach them what you can,
maybe what they see and learn
will be passed on to future man.

Buck Landers

Believe

I Believe I Can be a winner.
Even through I'm a beginner.
I believe if I keep trying.
I will reach my goals and be flying.

I believe that I will achieve.
Even through the odds are against me.
I believe if you won before
That your dreams will be more.

Cory Runkle

Twilight Rose

In twilight still, a risen star
Brightly o'er the heavens glows.
A distant love is kept so far—
And distance wars against their souls.
Their paths cross only in their dreams,
And time continues to impose.
Yet faith in mercy still redeems,
Because the Father always knows.
Two tender hearts, so lit aflame,
Lie deeply in their sweet repose.
Love whispers still God's Holy name,
and blooms in beauty as the rose.

Mark Finley

Love Is

As soft as the breeze
That whispers to the leaves.
As sweet as the songbird
That sings in the trees.

As new as the blossoms
On the branches above
And as sweet as the song
Of one lone mourning dove.

As strong as the winds
That blow from the east
And as brave as the warrior
That conquers the beast.

As bright as the light
Of the everlasting flame
That burns in my heart
When I hear your name.

Elizabeth Tunich

The Eleventh

A soldier sat upon his bed,
the war was over, his friends were dead.
What could he do? How could he go on?
Knowing he lived while they were all gone.
They'd fought the enemy, on land and in air.
It seemed all so wrong and all so unfair.
He'd join the march, he'd wave to the crowds,
he'd be labeled a hero, wearing a Purple Heart.
He'd place flowers on all unmarked graves,
of soldiers, his friends, who were so much more brave.
That was long ago, and now he stands in front of the epitaph,
on Remembrance Day, to remember when.
In the eleventh hour of the eleventh day of the eleventh month.

Brad Medig

Her Eyes

You look, you see, you glance. You watch others always wondering If they're looking at you. Blue eyes, green eyes, brown eyes. Every color of anyone's eyes can show everything. I know a woman with beautiful eyes. She smiles, laughs, and grins at a lot of things. Not just a woman with beautiful eyes, but a beautiful heart. But you see, her eyes tell you everything. She appears to be happy, but most of the time she is not. Oh, she says she's fine, nothing's wrong. But her eyes, her beautiful, sad eyes tell you it all. By looking at this kind hearted woman, you can see she hasn't had it easy. If you look closely in her eyes, you can see her whole life, every emotion and sometimes her thoughts. I pray for this woman, I pray that just a touch of my hand on her shoulder would make her sadness and pain disappear. I pray that her blue eyes will glow once again.

Carol Goldapp

None for Your Money

The sabres rattled heroically as they marched on down the street.
Remembrance elms enormous, vibrating to pounding feet.
Were they going to remember to plant the elm tree shrines
when the boys returned from over there to all they'd left behind?

The smiling faces of all the watchers hid the helplessness they felt
about the boys who'd not return. How would they hide their guilt?
No money in the whole wide world would return alive those slain.
So spend it to stop them going there instead of on a shrine.

Anthony Pahl

Cool Is as Cool Does

To the typical Filipino, cool means living like a bopper.
It is getting a checking account during ninth grade and getting your
first credit card during tenth.
It is driving one of Mama's or Papa's four new cars, yet still wanting a
new one for yourself.
It is always being able to buy the new Nikes, an Abercrombie outfit,
plus new Lugz without going into debt.
It is driving a nineties' model Civic or Integra and soopin' it up all the time.
It is soopin' it up every week after racing and totaling it every weekend.
It is chillin' with your kuyas, ates, and adings who happen to be your exact clones.
It is liking hip-hop and dissin' other Filipinos for liking anything else.
It is claiming that acting aggot and being Filipino are different when
they are actually the same.
Being cool is being as fake as acrylic nails and as shallow
as a puddle on the sidewalk.

Bernadette Ramos

Surprise

This was an awesome sight looking at the baby blue sky and the aquamarine sea. Traveling in this gorgeous ocean liner and looking at all the beauty surrounding us. The ship finally docked and everyone got off. I didn't know where to start, so many things to do. For miles and miles there was so much to see. As I walked through this magnificent island, I could see the monkeys playing tag with each other. I looked up at the palm trees and a coconut fell off the tree and hit me. But, that didn't bother me. I was enjoying all the sights, sounds, and smells. In a short time I watched the people trying to sit on the giant turtles and actually ride them. It was so warm, and yet windy. Oh, those great breezes felt so good on my face. Oops! I scream out until all of a sudden I felt someone shaking me fast and hard. When at that moment I awakened to find out I just had a dream. Such a pleasant surprise. To think I had been home all that time. But, it had all seemed so real.

Lillian Lyonnais

if only moments

If there are only moments
If our time together short
still it is a love of dreams.
I wake at night in wonder of it
reach and find you there
and that you are real
not dreams
and with me ever
is worth
all the fleeting moments
all the time so short.
To have held my one true love
while others cry in vain
for one they never knew
I
if for only moments
hold you.

Robert Gretter

Broken

I am a battered
broken winged angel
lying tarnished
and trampled
forgotten in the
shadows and face down
in a pool of
mingled blood and
tears lacking even the
strength to lift
my dirt-streaked
face to breathe

Laura Thompson

This I Shall Behold

Strike me from behind
like a torrid troubled past
Leave me in the wind
to laugh alone at last
Awaken the slumbering giant
dormant in my soul
Evince what is beauty
This I shall behold

Strike me from behind
heal my wounds and cuts
Usher me through the mist
as the darkness at hand erupts
Whir me a ballad
Hound away the cold
At last warm and golden
This I shall behold

Mark Oberding

Maple Leaf

The splendid maple leaf
clinging to the life giving tree
surely is God's most elegant motif
all put on display for free.
Stars jutting out in perfection,
supple webbing stretched o'er all . . .
in the still lake you see a reflection
of the choice watercolors of fall
and marvel ever at the beauty,
the beauty that strains your belief
God's complex, simple beauty
on display in His dear maple leaf.

Leonard Fouty

Winter Morn

Walking slowly behind my home
I crush the snow placed in my path,
while watching the blanket fall quietly downward,
destined to cover the fields of grass.

Silence is now my only companion
as every cranny is generously covered.
I ponder how this is every artist's dream,
when as far as can see there is no color.

Sitting patiently I begin to observe how this world has ceased,
but catching a glimpse of the Lord's bright creation rising in the east,
I realize my time here is limited to remain in this art,
where pigment is scarce and sound is absent,
unwillingly possessing a piece of one's heart.

Charles Bristow

Waste of Time

You stand behind an opaque glass,
I on the other side with a bottle of Windex and a roll of paper towels—
Desperately scrubbing the thickness of your issues.

I smear streaks on the glass writing a test for your convictions—
A test that will be left blank.

My arm is tired and I am frustrated.

I can hear your words and feel your presence,
but I can't see you and I can't touch you.

Vanessa Moody

Insight

There are no conflicts out there.
There is nothing out there.
Only what I perceive.
I perceive everything and it is only me and nothing else.
Sometimes I experience another person doing something, but still it is only me.
Sometimes I am angry at someone, but it is only my perception.
How I see it, who I interact with, is still only a part of me and my own perceptions.
There is one me—my true self and nothing else—everything else in only me.

Helaine Lasky

Going Home

On a metal box an adult of woman born sits
Dark, green clothes hide the filth
Dark, green clothes hide the scars
Flesh hides the pain
Friends, strangers on a bird of mercy a final voyage undertake
No tears glimmer in the eyes of the people loading the metal crates
No sorrow is felt, just stillness lies over the place of hard concrete

Holy men, dressed in the same dark, green, maneuver words of God
Their dark, green clothes do not hide filth
Their dark, green clothes do not hide scars
Their flesh is whole

The man of woman born sees a flag blow away
A shiny metal box is revealed
A man hurries after the cloth flying in the wind, away
A bird of hope, freedom was born only to be captured
by a soldier's hand

The man of woman born was born alone and still is
Nearness is a pestilence that has sent many men in dark, green, away
Alone the flesh of the body can

Tony Gorschek

Seeing

When my heart was troubled
And burdened down with care
I only saw the forest
A block of green despair

When my load was lightened
And my cares began to flee
I then could see the trees therein
Swaying in the breeze

When my mind connected with
The spirit of my soul
I could see the leaves upon
The branches bending low

When my soul reached out to touch
The leaf upon the tree
I saw the beauty of the dew
That waited there for me

Catherine MacDonald

On Meeting

He was there on the kneeler
Facing forward second row

Why I noticed him I don't know

But something came awake
I know was no mistake

In all these years I've tried
To understand the whys
If not the hows
Of our affair

Something still eludes
No logic there, no reason
For the sudden change in mood
And in the knowing he was mine

Before the final hymn and benediction

There on the kneeler
Facing forward, second row

Rose Kline

Not All Gone—
A Tribute to My Heritage

I made clay bricks in Egypt,
A tragedy unfair.
I made clay bricks in Egypt,
Died in the desert, there.

I was a Jewish Spaniard,
Felt Torquemada's blow.
I was a Jewish Spaniard,
My crime I did not know.

I sailed across the ocean,
Truman sent my away.
I sailed across the ocean,
Drowned in Liberty's bay.

I climbed the walls at Dachau,
Got shot and dropped down there.
I climbed the walls at Dachau,
Got shot and no one cared.

I'm not about to forget
All that tore me bare.
I'm not about to forget;
Through eternity, remember: Zecher.

Rachel Silverman

Vision

I have a vision of the present and the past.
A vision of a distant future that can last forever.
A vision of such magnitude, glory, and evil
that I will be lucky to come out alive.
But some day this vision could change and I might be able to survive.
When that day comes it will be such a glorious day you'll see.
This is all I can say for I must prepare to fight a hard battle.
My vision has changed.
The person I once feared is no longer a threat to me.
This is why I now feel complete because of the victory over my abuser.
I can live a completely normal existence.
Or can I?

Rodney Goodrich

Halls

The light fades, Darkness falls
In this place alone, awaiting the silence
Walking the empty halls, Voices echoing but no one's there
Here he comes only a shadow, His arms are open, welcoming me in
Should I go? Or stay here alone?
He's so tempting and perfect,
Accepting my imperfections, my never-ending flaws
His shadow is coming closer, his footsteps louder, I can see him
He's all that I have dreamed, He smiles, pulls me in
Into his playground of passion, the unrelenting love, that always overwhelms me,
This perfect man chose me, the flaws disappear, my fantasy becomes reality
He puts his hands on my face, You're my rose, my love,
These words stain my heart
For it was all a dream.

Margaret Johnson

Turn

The world crumbling beneath my feet.
Rock by rock, the picture only looked worse.
Yet somewhere in my being something smiled, something
longed to withstand the pressure that tried to take me down.
I fought with everything.

When I thought I had won it woke up again like the end of a thriller movie.
It was alive and took the last rock, the last stepping stone.
I was falling.

The lake swelled—with no dam big enough, nor strong enough to withhold its force.
It was with blank stare and pure prayer that I lie there fighting the death.

To turn, to realize what I was fighting.
To turn with open heart.
To turn and realize that facade is not always strongest.
To turn and realize that it was not my world crumbling
but a door opening, a wall falling, so that I could hear the words.
Like the words of an angel, the voice of an angel.

The lake must have evaporated.
I don't remember it now.
A new morning with new snow.
The crumbling tumbling and sweet mumbling behind.

To give all or none,
To fight hardest or not at all,
To wake up another day
To fight a new battle with new rocks, a new smile in the fire.

No facade is as strong as love . . . or cake.

Terra Carman

Run Away

As I felt a tear run down my face and shatter upon the dusty sidewalk,
looking behind me, crying silently, for this will be the last time I see home.

Wanda Giuntini

The Greeting Poem

Guten tag and howdy
Or hello in other words
How ya been and how ya going
You can ask with two short verbs
Smile and wave and extend your hand
Saying hi without a word
For we can speak in volumes
Without ever being heard
These simple forms of greeting
Which we sometimes leave behind
Require little effort
And take so little of our time
Yet a cheers and how are things
Can brighten someone's day
And show that you are thinking
Of them in some small way
So next time you pass a stranger
As you happen on your way
Just lean a little closer
And smile and say G'day

Ben C. Jones

Memorial to Columbine High

Feet trample the floor.
People scream.
Blood flies and
hits the walls.
Bullets wiz by.
Friends fall together
one bloody mess.
Schoolmates turn to
assassins in seconds.
Shooting just for revenge.
In five minutes an
entire school is destroyed.
And thousands of innocent
lives are lost.
That's all it takes.

Ashley Lafferty

the call of insanity

and the night drags on,
intoxicated by tears and confusion,
time seemed to stop.

the echoes of nothing,
unsaid passages of dwindling time,
are in constant flow.

the toils of a lonely world,
on a troubled mind,
creates the shaky form of insanity.

i sing a song,
to keep from being consumed,
by the never ending darkness.

moonlight reflected off my tears,
reveal a pain filled path,
used in many days and nights.

promises made,
are promises broken,
nothing lasts forever.

illusionary are the trappings,
of the inner and outermost aspects,
of the form before you.

Redentor Cacho

If You Ask

If you ask me to be with you; I will be there.
If you ask me to perform a task for you; I will do it.
If you want something, as long as I can afford it; it will be yours.
All these and more I will give to you, And all you have to do is ask.
If you ask for my help; My help you will receive.
If you need to be safe; I will guard you.
If you are hurt; I will help heal you.
For you; I would give the world If you asked.
If you want my passion; The fires of my love you will have.
If you ask for my strength; Every ounce of my force will be there.
And if you ask for my love; I will give you my heart with open arms. Anything I can
give, you can have.
But if you cross me I will take it all back.
Remember though, if you give me the love
From the bottom of your heart;
the one thing you can't ask for will be yours.
And that is My Life.

Nicholas Micchelli

Dear Mississippi

I thought I missed you dearly until this night under celestial blanket.
I bask in the faux twilight of your slow southern city,
The slow southern way of life.
Old southern men still waiting to cash in their confederate bonds.
The women in the kitchen with their slow southern style hospitality.
Old southern money, and fast-paced cars
(shinier than the Lincoln side of a penny, 1999).
Children spoiled rotten and beaten when bad:
makes for good white-bread bad blueblood, southern Baptist morals.
Preached prejudice and adultary.
Covet thy neighbor, his wife and fast paced car,
and old badbloodblueblood Confederate bonds,
And southern hospitality.

Courtney Carter

Trees of Life

The trees bend in the breeze as if to say, "Hi."
You see them shake, you see them bend, every time you walk by.
They swing, they dance, as if to a tune.
At night, if there's a breeze, they dance to the moon.
Their life is hidden from you. It can't be seen by the naked eye.
In fact, it can't be seen at all, which makes you want to cry.

They seem to try to uproot, even though they can't, but they still try.
You see them reaching out to you every time you walk by.
They swing, they dance, as if to a tune.
At night, if there's a breeze, they dance to the moon.
As long as there's a breeze, and as long as there are trees,
They will always say, "Hi."
You'll always see them shake, you'll always see them bend,
Every time you walk by.

Shawn Cardwell

Footprints

I used to walk boldly, carelessly, not watching my steps
and always stepping on so many mines.

Unconscious of my surroundings, I died a thousand deaths,
because I wasn't careful in my steps and left many haphazard footprints.

I didn't know what I know, I didn't know me.

Experience brought life to that
Inner Spirit that kept telling me

You Know What You Know, You Know You.

And now I walk on shallow soil without fear,
but always cautious of stepping on a mine.

I'm cautious, careful now,
because my surroundings have dictated
to my Inner Spirit that my footprints need to be light and alert.

Donna McNeill

Insomnia

Insomnia
Defeating me, beating me.
The droopy eyes you give me,
A jaw widened-YAWN.
Insomnia, won't you leave me.
Blood shot eyes
Not too deceiving.
Weakened knees,
I beg you please
Insomnia.
Unintelligent parasite of the living
Can't you walk away
Never appear again
Insomnia.

Jason Greenberg

I Don't Change

Everyday in the train.
Everyday the same way.
I'm the same, too.
I don't change.
Oh . . . wait a second!
I change trains . . .
but . . . not the tracks.

Ylli Baku

Fireside

The light burns brightly
Behind curtains pulled tight
Unseen by the traveler
As he wanders in the night

He seeks your refuge
In your haven he'd be
But alone he shall search
'Til your thoughts be free

Guarded is your fireside
Against the wayward spark
Flames that paint pictures
Moving in corners so dark

Guarded are your thoughts
In this prison be found
Shared not with another
But limited and bound

So draw back your curtains
Let your light be free
Give welcome to your fireside
For that stranger is thee

Ian Avison

Passing Reflection

Within one glimpse
beyond the rainbow came
the hands of time
and wrinkled flesh
two hands held
one in the other

standing atop
a mountain high
wishing upon a star
bright and wise

soft breeze blowing
tender kisses
across an ocean tide
through seas of trees

breathing memoir essence
hearing timeless echoes
smiling content knowing

Heidi T. Svensson

His Life

I see him edging slowly toward the door as company arrives.
Then I see him moseying slowly down the road,
with his hat pulled down over his eyes.

His destination is to the barn, as he nears, his steps grow faster then.
His pride and joy of his whole life, his horses, well kept within!

There he spends many hours, talking, cleaning, brushing, combing.
Until finally night arrives.
He wanders back up the road again, to partake of food.
Then he sits down with a sigh.

Very few words are spoken. It's his bed time once again.
He pulls off his shoes and in his room, he slowly wanders in.
He's in his bed for the night, tossing, turning, dreaming.
Dreaming of what? Or who?
What his dreams were all about, we never really knew.

He's up at break of dawn. A new day has begun.
He grabs his hat and down the road he walks in the morning sun.
He's thankful for another sunny day.

Evelyn Johnson

Broken

the break of day no say no pay bring it on
in time you will not this or mystery the air
not cold but body frozen locked in time of
disarray of unfortunate happiness in the fact
of most moderate of fiction, there is where the child gleams with a most profound but
dumb founded wisdom as his most precious of possessions is there for any to see but
he only wants to hold because the view is not enough, his greed is overwhelming, his
sight is blinding to the ray of light that shines before but the dim eve of self-disman-
tling is his to behold, before all, he holds this dear, which cannot withstand his hunger
and he shows his power like a child with an egg in his hand, how fragile a broken heart can be

Robert Kerr

The Loss of an Angel

This poem is dedicated to someone who means the world to me.
As I sit here, I think about an angel that I let go.
As I see her with someone else, my heart breaks.
When I see her in the arms of someone else,
I remember when I held her in my arms.
We told each other that we would never let the other person go.
We made a lot of promises that we meant.
But after what I did, our promises were broken.
Every promise I made I will keep until the day that I die.
The promise to love her forever is the one promise I will never break.
For the two months that we were together,
she took a piece of my heart.
As time has gone by, my love for her has grown.
Every time I see her with someone new I feel like I have no reason to live.
Maybe this is how it was meant to be.
I hope not because without her my life is not complete.
I can't believe I let her go.
I had everything in the world but the most important thing I had was my angel.
I will never stop loving her and hopefully one day,
my life will be complete and I will have my angel back.

Albert Perez Jr.

I'm Invisible

I have been called a trouble maker, angry black man, racist, selfish, rebel, militant, Malcolm X, pro black, utopian, and along with some of the other positive attributes; I was called intelligent, focused, principal oriented, respectful and disrespectful, and outspoken.

I'm invisible! No one can see me! I'm so complicated, confused, and frustrated that I can't see myself! I'm misunderstood by all who knows me. I am filled with so much love that I hate and I hate that I am filled with so much love!

To see me is to truly understand the nature of me and not just saying, I understand where you're coming from! We need to look within ourselves to make someone like myself visible. Feelings are invisible until released and sometimes they're still invisible.

How do I become visible again? Was I ever visible? Is visibility important? Can you see me now? Do you want too?

James Crawford

True Love

No one can tell it to you
A one thing, to rid blue
True love is all you need
As a plant roots from a seed
But true love is rare
Many only believe they care
It bares inside of you
The highest love of all
True love preciously waiting
But the mind is still debating
Machine nor brain can feel as YOU
Physical life is not so true
A dose of fate will guide
And power will decide
To one day bring it home
True love the mind was running from.

Lyle Stewart

September Hints

Tree green swaying
Awakening, kerplunked
Shoved and shaken
By liquid reminders

Urban dust
Dissolving into tears of imagined joy
Streaking
Becoming Mondrian lines,
Curving, merging into floating villages
Of family memories and found desire

River currents
Draw my blood
My footloose desire

Smiles begin to flow toward
Quivering late summer breezes and color
I taste both on your
Open lips
My future hanging in your chilled sigh

Glenn Moss

The Power

My black sister
and brother we can proclaim
our fame if we don't stand down
and be ashamed
We can make it
if we try please
my black sister
and brother
Don't lay down
and die.

Donald Scott

Cared by You

Slowly see, how I can be,
Loved by you
Only today, fading away,
Loved by you
Sexy dreams, makes me scream,
Loved by you
I admit, after a hit,
I love you
On my own, since I've grown,
Cared by you
Need nothing, I'm flying,
Cared by you
Touching sense, getting less,
Cared by you
My lover, going farther,
I love you

Jamie Miller

Preciousness of Peace

To know the senseless violence and rage lashed towards an
approaching stranger is to understand the preciousness of peace.

To know the battered reasoning why they were punished with bruises
and cracked bones is to understand the preciousness of peace.

To know the last cursed word and snarled, twisted face given to a
hopeful leader on his fatal day is to understand the preciousness of peace.

To know a neglected child counting their losses in the rubble
of lost innocent lives is to understand the preciousness of peace. To know the abandoned mother who swallowed her life
along with four tearful questioning kin is to understand the
preciousness of peace.

To know a father who obsessed about his bottom line
and not his family time is to understand the preciousness of peace.

To know the jealousy fueled and revenge expressed
in the journals of a lonesome soul is to know the preciousness of peace.

To know the guilt and remorse flogged on souls for missed
expectations and goals, is to know the preciousness of peace.

      Brooke Schumacher

The Tombstone

To you, my lovely mother, I write this poem . . .
The pain has now released its tight hold on your weak body.
You close your eyes for the last time and all misery,
all pains are now carried away in the great arms of the winds.

You, my mother, are now free from pain and like a bird of freedom
you fly in the blue to another world, to a new life.

In my heart I decorated a special room for you and the key to will always be with me.

I will not lay a flower at your tombstone as it will wither.
I never have sorrow at your tombstone
because I know that you are not there.
When I want to see you, I just go to my heart
and we spend time together as we always have done,
just you and me.

Everyone tells me you left this Earth,
but how are they to tell me this,
as I know that you, my mother, is present,
living through my body and in my body every day.

So to you, my lovely mother, I write this simple poem
as I know you can hear it . . .

      Karl Ullman

Are We the Same?

I don't like pears and carrots, maybe you do.
I don't believe all I see, but you might think they're true.

I love a slow walk as the day begins, but maybe you'd rather run.
You may like the midnight moon, but I sure love the sun.

You may like the color black, but purple's the color for me.
You may like diamonds and pearls, but flowers and birds are my cup of tea.

You may like loud music, crowds and the city life.
But I love my little yard with no worries and no strife.

You may simply hate the rain, as it falls upon the ground.
But I love to hear it fall, it makes the most wonderful sound.

You may like to watch TV, but a nice book is my idea of fun.
You may like to stay up late, but I love to sleep when the day is done.

So although we're different, we're really still the same, in all the things we say and do.
We live, we love, we laugh, we cry.
God sees no difference in me and you.

      Lynda Farmer

Two Lonely People

Two lonely people in the night
Sat down and started to unite
Talking, laughing, playing cards
enjoying each other under the stars
Candles glowing in the dark
to tell each other there's a spark
Knowing that they could never be
not in this eternity

      Dawn Craddock

Poetic Lyrics

A Poet's Poetry
In Motions of Time
Poetry of Love
Poetry of Crime

Soothing Sensations
Of the Cool Blowing Breeze
Lay Back and Relax
As I Put Your Mind To Ease

Life Is Sometimes Cruel
Sometimes So Hard To Bear
But As Long As I Have You
I'll Have Someone Who Shall Always Care

Someone Who Will Listen
Someone Who Will Try
Try To Ease the Pain
That's Running Down My Eyes

No Matter What Happens
To Us Both in Life
Just Promise To Never Leave Me
And We'll Both Live in Trife

      Thom Le

Reflections

Way beyond there is a reflection,
Too far for man's eyes to see.
But if it were just ever to be,
That man just did happen to see.
It would be beyond his comprehension.

      Ian Hardy

2 for the price of 1

Yes, My Mother wanted a daughter
My Father wanted a son
So, Here I am
Two for the price of one

      Mark Cameron

Lack of Motivation

I don't know
I just don't feel like doing it

I don't know
I just don't feel like doing it

I don't know
I just don't feel like doing it

I don't know
I just don't feel like doing it

I don't know
I'm not feeling it

WHY?
No Motivation

      Sam Hawkins

Life Long Wait

How hard it is to wait . . .
Incredibly difficult, wistful yearning
Waiting for that one day when all becomes lucid
The day I meet my loving and impregnable mate.

The day when extreme brevity of a life long wait comes to an end,
And I, of all people,
Become the novice in a relationship of true fidelity.

How incomprehensible it seems that this day has finally come.
When I am swiftly carried over the threshold,
And embellished with love, as we become one.

Later, I lie in his arms,
His eyes shut tight.
I reiterate in my mind what has just occurred,
and realize this is the inception of my life of love.

   Leticia Acosta

Mother, I Thank You For:

I Thank you for allowing me fall, teaching me the pain that goes with it.
I thank you for the strength you have given me to stand up
and walk again in the face of tragedy and grief.
I thank you for giving me the ability to put aside anger for the sake of others.
I thank you for teaching me to never feel ashamed or reluctant of saying,
"I hurt," "I love," or "I'm sorry."
I thank you for encouraging me to follow my own instincts instead of following others.
I thank you for your optimism when I share my ideas, thoughts and dreams.
I thank you for always being there to ask, to tell or to cry.
I thank you for loving me when I wasn't so easy to love.
When I was a child, you said that I wasn't listening. You were right, I WAS WATCHING YOU.

   Dana Reynolds

Nine

What is nine? Nine are the children. The first, Sharon, who has so much love
for her family. The second, Sheila, who fills everyone's life with laughter.
The third, Shirley, the one they almost lost, the special one. The fourth, Susie,
to know her is to love her. The fifth, Sally, who never stops trying.
The sixth, Stephanie, how did she make it with five older sisters? The seventh,
Wally, the first son, the one who brought happiness to all. The eighth, Jimmy,
who will con you out of anything. The ninth, David, the last, the one who will
be the baby always in everyone's eyes. At last the parents, Bob and Helen,
the ones who brought each child into the world, who gave the love, respect,
and guidance, and the nine who will return their love and respect.
What is nine plus two? It's a family! What family? The Fagan Family.

   Stephanie Barker

The Perfect Blend

Coffee and friends, die till the end, where life exhumes their starlite lives,
Drinking to peace, sex, love, and metaphorical topics of conversation,
I wish that every day was spent in mental intrigue and stimulation,
My life with my buddies is shared and read like a nightclub's poem,
Whatever happens next is up to them, will they leave or have another cup,
Can my stories fulfill their cravings of sweetness and fabled desires,
Or will my cream rise to the top and be skimmed from the milk,
As I leave in a stream of droplets from condensation, I laugh,
My time was well-spent, and I would do it again if given the chance,
Hey coffee people, I get off around six tomorrow, until then I must say,
You all make a great cup of Joe, not too strong, but smooth and tasty,
For like my first taste of the magic bean, I will remember you all forever.

   David Michael Seim

All Hallows Eve

Setting of the sun
The mountain mist
The night has begun
The air is crisp
Evil has come
To our small town
This Evil is from
Beneath the ground
The time is now
For us to fight
Our final vow
On this dark night
We battle 'til
The crack of dawn
The Evil becomes
Weak and withdrawn
We win the battle
But not the war
For this shall happen
Forevermore

   Jesus Hernandez

Awareness

Steel Gates!! And , Armoured Fences!!
Why have we become so pretentious?
We fear the men of our own Kind!!
When our worst enemy is our own Mind!

   Edward Pitcher

I Will

I will hold you
as I would hold a crystal glass,
gently, softly,
but firmly within my hands.

I will share with you
the pleasures
as though it was
a fine wine.

I will smell your essence,
it will be there
wafting through the room
as if from a freshly picked rose.

I will feel your skin
pressed to mine
silk to the touch
soft as a feather.

I will light the candles
turn off the lights
music softly playing
and watch you, my flame, ignite.

   Pam Welch

tape

a tint of green
clouded over by
the magic that is
mental adhesive
covering my mind.
shielding it from the others.
a small rip
running down the side.
overflowing thoughts.
almost free.

   Mason Cowie

Encompassed in You

Waves of forgiveness break on the shore
Sorrow and sin washed away by the tide
Immersed in your freedom, mercies that pour
Lost in the sea of your love I reside
Winds of elation bring welcome release
Stripping the anguished heart bare
Tranquility's breezes clothe me in peace
As the promise of life breathes new air
Salvation be granted, mountains rejoice
The trees in their rapture embrace
Redemption and privilege, echoed by choice
Allow me to bask in your grace
Your glories surpassing reveal it no loss
To relinquish my shame and take up the cross.

Beth Caster

Chaotic Reflection

This world is a chaotic place
with hearts emptied of passions,
and the waves of hatred engulfing all hearts.
For dreamers like us,
utopia and hope is food for the soul,
and for realists it is the impending doom.
I find myself in a snare of suspension,
hanging
in between
the physical and the metaphysical!

Mehrunnisa Yusuf

Everything

She is everything to me
My reason for being
My reason for living
My reason to quit smoking
She is everything to me
She lifts me up higher than I've ever been
When I'm with her, I feel as if I'll never come down
And who would want to?
With someone like her around.
Time spent with her
Though brief and passionate
Rocks my world more than anything before.
She is everything to me
And everything she is
is beautiful

Christopher Hagberg

Haunting Dreams

Petals from a flower falling to your feet,
I see you in my dreams—you're a ghost.
You've frightened my dreams . . .
And now you haunt my memories.

I see your image of blood and nothing more.
I tried to ignore, we tried to ignore,
But your image is haunting;
You are haunting my dreams.

I woke up abruptly, afraid to close my eyes again.
What is this haunting dream? Why me?
It had to be something I ate; it had to be . . .
Please stay away, I don't want to dream any more.

And if I close my eyes tonight will you be there?
I keep seeing ghosts and blood . . .
Is something hidden in an unconscious thought?
Or am I just doomed to a life of messed up dreams?
Or even a messed up reality?

Dawn Fair

The Four True Elements

All this LIFE that surrounds me,
Ignorant of its death.
Of this mortal coil I cry "Free!"
Leaving no trace, nothing to be left
I feel the DEATH that encircles us,
The battles hacking at life's soul.
I pray for grace of the winged thrush,
Yet the grim reaper's burden I must uphold.
HOPE, the last ray of Pandora's Box.
One of the few lights left I'm humanity's dark world.
An aura without limits or locks,
A stream of infinite light to kill doubt's shadow.
LOVE has been said to be frivolous,
A deception pulled over our eyes.
"I think not so," says the lover.
Only idiots consider true love a crime.
Of all the elements, these four are the most true.
May the Heavens forgive us for our wrongs,
May the Heavens lead us toward the right,
And may the skies not turn gray, but white.

Benjamin Huang

The Lost Girl

There was a girl who only smiled when she was sad.
She lost hope in life for any dreams she once had.
She knew no one understood, she didn't expect them to
 and everyone judged her if only they knew.
She already knew what future lay ahead.
It's easy to figure out in a soul that's so dead.
In the world she feared what everyone didn't
and what everyone else feared she didn't quite get.
She sees and hears things others cannot
they call her abnormal and they say it a lot.
She doesn't know how to live and let go,
she sits and listens to people lie and say they know.
While she breaths the water they breath the air,
people sit there and tell her they care.
Did they know that what she feared most in life was the mirror?
The mirror is the one thing that spells things much clearer.
Everyone in the world was moving so fast,
yet she couldn't let go of her never ending past.
In life everyone was having fun,
while this scared little girl was on the run.

Brittany Morgan

When We Live

how very fun to live a lie until you remember the truth
so very exciting to act older
right up until you loose every ounce of your youth
they say if you live it's a given you learn
we roll the dice as we take our turn
so very rebellious to disrespect your parents
right up until they pass away
how simple to cover every flaw in the dark
until the truth stands exposed by the day
how easy to turn up a new friend
until you find you have none at all
so strong you are to hold pride against your lover
until you find yourself missing their call
when we live
we're all sure to learn
we melt the ice
or we're the ice that burns

Joshua Hess

"The Kiss"

Like a perfectly formed snowflake
their lips came to meet.
The looks in their eyes was oh, so sweet.
They knew in an instant what was to be
And they smiled as small children so filled with glee,
The twinkle in her eyes, so playful and coy;
He new this woman would give him such joy.
He wanted her as no one before
and he could feel her emotions of this he was sure.
He knew this woman since the beginning of years
waiting for her, through so many tears.
His heart had been broken
from "loves" in the past.
Hoping and praying this one will last.
And soon his fears he quickly dismissed
For he knew it would be right, the moment they kissed.

> *Steven Gan*

Little Stones

The falling stone in a pond does not do so in quiet bliss
Ripples break the glassy face where stone and water kissed
And so a soul that leaves this world does so like the stone
Leaving behind a rippled wake touching those once known
All little stones now on our own, we await the coming day
When we too fall into the pond where together we may lay

> *Todd VanHooser*

Until You

Every day I wake up
Thinking of you
Every night I sleep
Thinking of you

Is it possible that this is it?
This thing they call love?
Could it be that I have helplessly fallen
into this thing called love?

Nobody has ever got to me
like you do
Nobody else could steal my heart
like you did

I have never sacrificed
such important things
Never given up
what I love the most

Until you . . . .

> *Sarina Larson*

My Special Friend

The hiding place within each of us
to get away and think things through.
This unique place we are alone
to be ourselves.
We confront our deepest feelings—
store our hopes, dreams and fears.
It's who we are and who we want to be.
Whether by chance or design—
someone discovers the place we thought
was ours alone.
We allow that person to enter—
to share our thoughts and uncertainties
and the emotions we store.
My special friend adds new life into
my hidden realm—
then quietly enters into his place
I opened in my heart.
Hopefully, a bit of him will stay forever—
and he will become my special friend.

> *Sue Deaton*

Father

F is for FARSIGHTED visions of things to come.
A is for the ANGER sometimes necessary for discipline.
T is for the TIREDNESS after a long day's hard work.
H is for the HARD work of making a daily bread.
E is for the EXTRA effort to keep on going.
R is for the RESPECT for choosing to be father against all odds.

> *Wendy Holder*

Black Tide

Pain, pain and darkness is all I see
When I look deep down inside of me.
The place where light should there abide
Is empty, blackness, woeful tide
Washing despair on every side.
My heart cries in the wilderness
Of pain and deep distress.
Sobbing, aching, yearning deep
For long and dreamless endless sleep.
Hope and dreams have long since died,
Utter chaos throbs inside
No light to see and find my way
No path to follow into day.
And so I'll rise, exist and smile
And walk that extra mile
To hide the dark emptiness.

> *Roswitha Strom*

Life

Life is a game you have to play
in life you have friends that come and go
some even stab you in the back before they go
in life you are either rich or poor
in life there is love but love can be blind
there are so many rules
some cannot be explained
so in life you either play or die.

> *Crystal Salmon*

Big Brown Eyes

For Brenden Gabriel
Bright Blue eyes have turned to Brown.
Your sweet smile has learned to frown.
I've watched you learn to crawl and then walk.
I've listened to you babble and then learn to talk.
I've changed your diapers and put on your clothes.
Wiped up your messes and then, of course, your nose!
I've found myself a hundred times
staring into those big brown eyes.
An image of myself is what I see
and yet there differences that make you unique.
You are strong-willed and stubborn.
Independent like your mother.
Yet easy going and quite laid back.
Just a bit like your dad.
You are all of this and so much more
as I stare into your eyes once more.
I will always adore you, my baby boy.
This never ending love can never be destroyed.
Through deep brown eyes, someday you'll know
how much those eyes have captured my soul.

> *Shanna Misiak*

Enchanted Island (Isla Encantada)

Share your beauty and your grace,
your dancing trees and warmth of the sun upon my face.
Ease my tension with your calming winds and exotic nights.
Let me hear the nocturnal music notes
that drift along the shores of your majestic beaches.
Breathe into me,
the breath of glistening stars in your black sky.
Whisper your hush as your waves
caress every grain of sun golden sand on the shore,
and endow me with peace as I look across mountain peaks
to blossoming sunrises burning the horizon.
Entrance me with your beauty and kiss me all over
with your balmy sea breeze.
Then calm my nostalgia with bittersweet memories.

Betsy Albelo

Butterfly

She is the spirit of life itself;
in her natural beauty she glides through the heavens.
She is lighter than air, so fragile you don't dare breath.
Her wings are softer than any silk.

Her spirit is so pure that she bruises easily,
causing her to cry in pain and fear.
Within her heart where she's safe from being torn apart
on a flower far away.
No, that would take her from my sight.

I have fallen on my knees thanking God for such a sight.
That when I realized I could be her flower.
When she is hurt I simply close my pedals around her,
dust her off and feel her pain within my own heart.
My world is flowers and rivers of honey.
It is a butterfly world.
It is ours, if you wish to fly, my dearest Butterfly.

James Horsley

In a Mind of Darkness

as the light faded away so did the mind
the darkness took what courage i had
the darkness covers like a blanket and
light is no where in sight am i to be
this deep in darkness all my days
days that were a bright and shining past
all that's left is a shell of what was
no way to know how this will end
death or life for which are both equal

Deborah Nichter

Cheap Trifles

Flowers, cookies, words, and cards
Cheap trifles that they are
only messengers like great bards
that tell of his love, near and far.
Cards written to express his love
for a relationship sent up, from above.
Flowers sent to tell of his care
filled with meaning, souls spread bare.
Recipes followed, cookies baked
commitments made, nothing faked.
trips to the post, packages sent,
a destiny fulfilled, fears gone and went.
Mere trifles, mere words sent, and said
to tell of his love of her, to whom he has been led.

Steve Cvengros

My Love

More beautiful than roses, much deeper than the seas
Stronger than a hurricane, but timid like the breeze
More beautiful than anything, as vivid as all my dreams
Softly you tip toe into my heart whispering tenderly,
"Sleep My Love Sleep"
Only in these dreams, oh, so deep within these dreams
Through your eyes I seen' Heaven, and heard the angels singing
With the fire in your eyes, and burning passion in your soul
Hauntingly beautiful, as precious as rare jewels
Sharing common interests, finding common ground
an abundance of love so deep, kissing gently to our hearts
Wishing to be here always, holding you forever
Hand in hand we stroll through life's many journeys
The longing and yearning we share,
Allows me to hear the beating of your heart
So intuned to one another, drifting around like a misty cloud
Together we will always be, for I love you with everything in me
I have found Heaven on Earth, when our paths intertwined
My love real as a picture, yet it can't be seen
Will engulf you in flames, and melt our hearts as one
Never to be torn apart, through all we may face
Because I love you my angel, with every breath I take

Deborah Hay

How Beautiful!

How beautiful the land when autumn dyes its fleece;
Not even Angelo could make such a masterpiece!
How oft we've experienced and thought not—how it's so.
Or reflected on its Maker from a long time ago.
How beautiful the land in rainbow array,
How beautiful our Creator to make it this way.
Yet, how thankless when one's heart refuses to see,
How beautiful the leaves on just one single tree.
So before time ends when soul and spirit do part,
Think not of your woes but take counsel to heart.
Observe the wonders that will never ever cease.
Yes! How beautiful the land when autumn dyes its fleece!

Nathan Austin

Morning Bells

Bells in the old church sweetly ring
Clear strong tones they always bring
Sounding far off into the hill
Into the valley quiet and still
The valley now asleep soon to arise with dawn
Only stirring in the forest is timid doe and fawn
Look to see everything is well
Then turn to hear the ringing of the bell

Sylvia Albrecht

Give Me Freedom

Give me a place where I can be me

a place where I can say what I want
where I don't need to pretend
where I don't need to be ashamed
where I can scream forever and no one cares

Give me a place where I can slit my veins and let life disappear

S. Anders E. Rassner

Grace

Come, I'll show you how to dance away
from darkness, and death, blood and theft,
out of sullen days, into sudden rays of sunshine
waiting to embrace your spinning body and smiling face.
Though this may seem like a wonderful dream,
blanketing a morning star, believing it's not that far
gets you nearly there. No matter what you do, say,
or how you convey what you believe, you must in order to be free.
Right now is Heaven, in you and in me,
so flee from nothing, just fly to be.

Chelsea Grenfell

To Be Free

Freedom is beautiful,
full of light and darkness
Together we struggle to know both parts of freedom
In the light, we embrace the freedom
to see the light
in the midst of darkness
We embrace the chance to reach the light
through the midst of darkness
To be free is to embrace both the darkness
and the light to reach freedom
Though seldom we meet and embrace
darkness and light together as a whole,
and therefore we miss total freedom

Diane Bohn

Let Go

My heart is empty, it aches and aches.
I think of you the second I wake.
I long to hold you in my arms.
Being swept away by your wit and charm.
I want this sadness in me no longer,
It's your love that makes me stronger.
I will get through this, I will get by.
All I feel is hurt and anger, for him I mean . . .
For you I'd die.

Vicki Ziegelbauer

The River Wind Butterfly

I am the River.
I flow forever in and out of the lives of others
smoothing over the rocks and rapids with my dance,
healing those that can see, the magic of my inner soul.

I am the wind.
I am the gentle spirit that floats by you,
whispering wisdom in your soul.
To live I change constantly, never content to stay in one place
for my passion is to travel,
to search for places yet unknown.

I am the butterfly.
I am the beautifully simple,
yet I evolve each day into the higher light.
Those that know me,
can feel my peace
that they too might fly with grace free to follow their own dreams
that are embraced by the light.

To know me you will dance with the river,
feel passion with the wind,
and see light in the wings of a butterfly.
I am the River Wind Butterfly.

Leesa Pharr

Alone in Loneliness

Like descending the depths of a granite stairway of stone,
The darkness shades to black, the cold felt in your bone.
Spiraling lower into the eternal reaches below,
Emotion is crushed in an evil squalid glow.
Each step echoes continually from this pit infinite.
Solitary figures find this a place to frequently visit.
Out of this pit of doom rises mounting despair,
Originating from the feeling that nobody will care.
Without hope for the future and without cause for hope,
Regaining the high ground is like climbing a slippery slope.
The downward spiral continues like an immense gravitational well;
Closer to the Event Horizon, alone, without a soul to tell.
The Bleak emptiness threatens to pull the unwary in,
Alone the pain is so acute it feels like a personal sin.
The gnawing nothingness can consume the entire being,
The dull ache for companionship, the blind want, not seeing.
The human spirit was meant to emotionally connect,
To exist in a group, to react and then reflect.
Without filling this human need it is hard to remain sane,
Loneliness is death; the only alternative is rather plain.

Jadin Bulger

We Are a World within Worlds

The New Millennium 2000 has brought
to each one of us incredible abilities!
Now to clear our minds of negative,
fruitless thoughts where we can then begin our etching . . .
Look forward to change,
subtle changes within and discard useless utilities!
And then to the bigger picture outside of
our own individual Worlds far, far stretching . . .

Joan Wiley

Into This Sense of Peace I Fall

Into this sense of peace I fall
Afloat on dreams of serenity I've longed for
This innate forgiveness seems a lie
This surreal contentment cannot possibly be mine
Now that I've let go of false pretenses
Now that I embrace the absence of what won't ever be
In this place my senses are clear
Despite the rotting around me, I am free
The shade of numbness is missing
The anger purrs instead of seethes
In my mind I curl around calm fingertips
and slowly fall asleep.

Elizabeth M. San Nicolas

Love So True

Softly it comes, beneath the door.
I see it sweep across the floor.
I step outside and feel the breeze,
And hear the leaves rustle in the trees.

Birds sing their songs brightly,
I wish I could hold this moment tightly.
The air sweeps up around me,
And flies high above me.

The clouds depart from the sky so blue.
Will my true-love go from me, too?
Loneliness creeps in my heart
As once was there in the start.

I call out loud and clear—
My true-love, my God is near.
This place feels the same as once did I,
Deep down it wants to cry.

But He can be their true-love, too,
Only one thing you have to do.
Something so simple to save your soul,
Just give Him yourself and make Him your goal.

Anna Humphrey

Bitter Emptiness

Hopes and dreams fill up the day
At night demons come out and play
Too much drama with too little laughter
I want my happily ever after

When I cannot see a rainbow's smile
When disappointments seem to pile
When dismal thoughts fill up my time
I struggle for just one more rhyme

My naked soul cries silently
For a sparkle of sincerity
As a girl losing her identity
Seeks traces of humanity

Who knows what tomorrow brings
Struggling to fly with broken wings
When the song of yesterday sharply stings
I try to remember my favorite things

How did it all become such a mess?
I should accept for nothing less
My life I guess I must confess
Is filled with bitter emptiness

Meg Bruno

Your Graduation

This is a day set aside for your graduation
In which you'll receive many congratulations
This will be a special day for you
A day in which you'll be through
Through with studying for a good while
And when you receive your degree, it will bring about a smile
You have been in school for many years
And on graduation, you may shed tears
Tears of joy for achieving your goal
And hopefully this goal will satisfy the soul
I'm sure that your family will be proud of you
Just as I'm proud for seeing you make it through
I'm sure that it got hard while you were in school
But you kept your head up and saw that knowledge is a tool

Marreo Bivens

Memories

They say: "Out of sight, out of mind;
A face you've not seen for long time
Becomes a shadow in the night,
Covered with dust as days pass by."

But I've got memories than cannot cease,
Like a mind tattoo that always is.
I've got my memories that feed my dreams,
Memories . . . and fantasies.

I sit under the autumn trees,
The wind blows off the falling leaves,
I walk the shore and I feel the breeze
But deep inside . . . those memories!

They hunt my mind, give me no peace,
They fill my head with whom I miss,
But then they turn my eyes to tears
'Cause I can't touch my memories,
And I can't feel what my mind sees.
So, bring back those times, I ask you, please
If you would grant one wish this is:
Let me relive my memories . . . .

Adrian Chira

My Room

It rained darkness,
Groping I was, for something I know not,
Care, I did not for any dress,
Languished in times I longed for again
Doors screaming in pain and agony
at the emptiness they had to contain
Then a knock at the door, and then another
Every nerve in the room pleaded to open the doors
Open I did, and the room was filled
with the light of Heaven.
The cheerful heart played soothing music,
Sailing birds sang in chorus,
The huge trees danced to the rhythm
as the azure sky witnessed in ecstasy.
Indulgence lead to possessiveness
Doors, I shut foolishly to keep all the light for myself
Alas, I locked myself inside the hell's hole
All of a sudden, I realized she was gone
This time I wait
for the light to shine upon me again, a second time!

Ravi Anumakonda

Family

Bound by either biology or fate
it makes no difference you see
two things are a must: one is love,
and the other respect, to complete this entity

It is not material things and money
for which we should obsess
In one blink they can be taken so swiftly
and impossible to repossess

In Death, hearts are broken
and lives forever changed
nothing but a dull sickness in the
pit one's stomach remains

Life comes but only once,
so family we should embrace
celebrate every day . . . as loving each
other makes us blessed with grace

Tallie Boivin

Mist of the Meadows

The mist of the meadows settles like dust.
Covering the wilderness with a silent brush.
When the sun rises,
the mist turns to gold,
even though I see it every day,
it never becomes old.
It is like a secret I hold silent in my mind,
and when I'm doing nothing I think of it for sometime.
I watch the mist settle every day,
the tiny little specks seem to run and play.
The flowers on the ground covered with silk,
and the spiders web as white as milk.
The mist sometimes looks like stars.
That have fallen from the sky.
And because they look so pretty they do not cry.
Then when the sun sets with no delay,
everything starts to fade away.
The stars return to the sky and the spiders say good bye.
I will always remember the way the sun would shine.
Staring down at the mist in the meadow I call mine.

Katherine Kolombatovich

The Fantasy of Love

To dream about happiness,
The sun beaming, everything alive.
No hurt, just content.
Looking into eyes and knowing.
No questioning, always trusting.
Never wondering, always believing.
A beautiful face holding the body.
Not letting go or doubting.
Loyalty as easily given as received.
The heart always beating fully, never breaking.
    The fantasy of love.

Jessie Dricker

You, Me, and Time

I know we've known each other
For just a couple years,
But in such short time, you've done so much.
You've helped me with life, struggles, and fears.
You've been there for me
Just so I can talk to you.
Everything you've said and done
Has helped me work through—
Through all my troubles
This big world often brings,
Through all the turmoil
People try hard not to see.
You've taught me right from wrong,
And it's okay to just be me.
You are so important in this life I live.
You said to be all that I can be.
But there's a thing in life called time.
The clock ticks way too fast.
Our time we have to share together
Will soon only be the past.

Felicia Thomson

"Feel the Magic of the Moment"

Vision,
the calming silence
when glancing at the full moon's radiant beams
shimmering like diamonds
across the still dark waters of a cool summer's evening
and feel the cool breath
of the summer's breeze
feathering gently across your glowing cheeks . . . .ahhhhh
yes, feel the magic of the moment.

Jeanne Heuer

Wanting You

My thoughts are of you, My dreams are of you

Ever since that sweet tender kiss
The way your lips pressed against mine
Seeing what i didn't know was there
Yearning for the passion that's hiding, waiting

What does this all mean?

When your fingers brush my bare skin
The compulsion that runs through me
A cascade of thoughts and emotions.
So very intense! So profound!

Will our bodies entwine?
Will they even adhere?

Your eyes so tender and warm
Piercing into my very soul
I become susceptible in every way
Completely under your control

Should I confess it all?
Should I keep it hidden?

Kimberly Reeves

Second Chance

The love we once shared was special and rare.
Both of us really did care.
Things got out of hand.
And one of us forgot the meaning of the wedding band.
The day came and we met once more.
We felt the opening of a brand new door.
It must of been fate,
As we felt no hate.
The chemistry we once shared was still there.
We realized how much we still care.
As we begin our life anew.
Do not forget how much I love you.
You are the love I will always treasure.
Loving you to me, is pure pleasure.

Debra Siek

Friends Forever

What a friend I have in you
You're there for me when I am not
You guide, you lead,
You even follow with pride
Smiling makes you radiant
No rose could ever compare
The things you teach
The things you scold
Your words become like scriptures, I'll always hold
I welcome them whole heartedly
Be patient, be forgiving
Someday I'll hold a candle to you
Be willing to take my hand
Hold it close to your heart, and be proud
Whether I am near or far
I guarantee we'll never be apart
For there's no distance
That could ever outgrow our hearts
This bond is solid
For friends forever we shall be.

Tracey Coleman

Heart Bond

Love is love, but unlike any other love,
there is a special bond at the heart of a mother's love.
The unseen, invisible thread
that connects a mother's heart to a child's
will never wither or fray.
Wherever the wind may blow,
we can look back and know
that our heart will never be apart of that unified glow.
Just as the Potter's hands mold and shape the clay,
so your love mold us into who we are.

Amy Edwards

What the Bible Teaches

Reading your bible helps you to grow
It gives you knowledge for the things you don't know
You learn about Adam and how he was made
And about Moses to whom the Ten Commandments God gave
You learn about Noah and the great flood
Who never looked back and sent out a dove
There was David and Goliath who was killed with a stone
And Job who was stricken with boils, but never alone
There were Matthew and Mark and Luke and John
Who wrote the gospels of Jesus' realm
They told of his story of what was to come
And was prepared a place in the mansion above
The bibles are only weapon against Satan,
Who's always there to keep us hatin'
So read your bible everyday and learn what god has to say

Cheryl Kidd

Love

Nobody feels like I do.
It's like a reaction when I'm around you.
I can see you in the day and feel you at
night.
It seemed to me that it was love at
first sight.
I don't remember when we first met,
but I know we have some time yet.
I need you here in my life,
through my pain and strife.
I need you here to stay,
just until my birthday in May.
I love you more then anyone.
I'm just telling you you're the only one.
please don't leave me because
I'm just starting to see,
how our love should be.

Leigh Brauer

Genuine Love

The love I once knew was not one of truth
An existing bond was simply of comfort
The vicious circle of wanting more
I knew not of what love could truly be
Dreams and truths begin to blend
Individual way is lost and vacant
Existence is the only matter

Now, begins an understanding of reality
Love is truth and complete being
More meaning and vision each day
The only want is wanting more of this love
It is complete, clear and free
Benevolent you

Tracy D. Anderson

Going Back to Sedona

I'm going back to Sedona, the spirit of the Earth

I'm going back to Sedona, the place of my rebirth

Crystal caves and turquoise, power fills the air

Sedona's radiant beauty, soon I'll be there

Vortexes occilate healing, the heart beat of the Earth

I'm going back to Sedona, the place of my rebirth

Shaman lady guides me down paths of long ago

To the power circles of the ancient ones, whose energy still flows

Red rock towers echo, vibrations to the soul

Earth Mother is calling through her shiny radiant glow

Through visions of inner consciousness, I know which way to go

I'm going back to Sedona, where the Earth has made me whole

Dustin Schneider

At One with the Earth at Death

When I die, don't put me in a box;
I'd rather feel the pitter-patter feet
of running fox.
That's something you can't feel
through pine, and not through oak,
it's something that has got to seep,
it's something that must soak
right through me, with the dirt and ground,
and wetness of the earth around—
If I must die, and can't be free—
Then please, oh, please, don't bury me.

Elizabeth Kaestner

Him

I close my eyes to hear his voice and yet he never speaks.
And though we've never met one another my soul is what he seeks.
I raise my chin to the sky in hopes to see his face,
remembering that his home is said to be a lovely place.
Heaven is what he calls it, a home to cleanse your soul,
a sacred house, a spiritual well, a place to make you whole.
He asks that I call him father, and say his name in prayer.
And when guidance is needed in my life he says that he'll be there.
Faith is my invitation to be a guest in his heavenly home,
and when I believe that he is the savior, I'll never be alone.
Although I've never seen him, I know he loves me well.
He directs my life on heavens path instead on that of hell.
I have so many questions and much I want to say.
I want salvation in my life no tomorrow but today.
But, nevertheless I believe, my Father, God is real.
I love his name, I love his grace, I love how he makes me feel.
I close my eyes to hear his voice and yet he never speaks.
And though we've never met one another my soul is what he seeks.
He loves the world and all the life that is and yet to be.
I love my Lord my Jesus Christ because he first loved me.

Sheila Denise Cox

My Heart

Deep inside my heart
A love grows just for thee,
But it tears my mind apart.
It's a love that will never be;
She feels not like the way I do,
Even though my love for her is true,
But alas she does not love me too.

Deep inside my chest
A heart beats fast for thee.
My feelings are all a mess
For I know she loves not me;
I can see it in her eyes,
She could not care less if I live or die.

Deep inside my heart
A love has died for thee.
My mind, once whole, now has broke apart.
Now, I think, shall be the end of me,
Without her I feel my soul has died.
I've never known that I can really cry
But now I have and cannot stop—I've tried

James Baker

I Drift Away

Sunsets
In skies set free only by God
I am here now, I witness this
Looking off, yonder . . .
Light falls over the distant mountains and trees
I see a glimmer of this world,
It flashes through my mind
Twilight breaks, it is dusk,
And soon it will be dawn
And the sun will rise over the East
But for now, my eyes are fixed on the West
They are still blue . . .
They are still looking for you . . .
I have come here in search of peace
And that I have found
Although my heart still drifts to the past,
I am alone . . . yet peaceful
I sought out the sunset,
And waited for the sunrise
My dreams drift away

Joshua Riggins

Mr.

We played and fought and schemed our childhood through.

Brothers were we.
Brothers, once you and I.
I hurt you; now, you, me.
Days ago we shared deeds of glory.

Brothers, you and me.

Brothers, once many years past,
you went south; I north.
Far away wasn't far enough.

Brothers no:
only blood lasts.

Birthrights I had; you stole.
Lost dreams across your soul.
Anger, now apathy.

Brotherly pain blasts.

Brothers, once, me and you,
lost in time to all, now heartbreak,

Brothers,
now only
in past.

Robert Peck

Christopher

My precious little man,
Who's fixing to graduate kindergarten.
With your brown hair and brown eyes too,
Oh! How much I love you.
Without you, there would be an empty space in my heart,
Therefore I would never let anyone ever tear us apart.
You look like your dad in each and every way,
Or that's what everyone tends to say.
You will always be my number one pride and joy,
Even when you don't want to pick up your toys.
You tend to test my patients at times,
But even so, you will always be a joy of mine.

Jackie Driver

Farewell

After you left I was so sad,
I couldn't make out what I didn't do or what I had,
I couldn't understand why you would leave me alone,
Then I thought if I had only known,
Could I have stopped you would you have stayed,
Could I have made you see the pain would fade.

Did you know I loved you, did you know I cared,
Did you know that without you I would be so scared,
Did you know life without you would be so bad,
Did you know your leaving would make me so sad,
Most importantly, did you know you were my best friend,
And wherever you are my love I send.

Melanie Larkin

Untitled

I look into your eyes, and can no longer see your soul,
I search to find your heart, praying mine is still your own,
I beg for comfort in a touch, a thought throughout my day,
I cry out for compassion . . . your love, and what I find is disarray,
I find your soul is empty, your heart beats separate than mine,
I find your touch is cold, and love has simply been blind,
I look into the mirror I see anger, disgust, and hate,
I look through to find you staring, and knowing you feel the same,
I try to grasp your hand to save what's already been lost,
But as I reach to touch you, I find, that in reality you're gone,
I try and search for reason to this unreasonable place I stand,
I find that I don't love me, so how could I love this man. . . .

Vickiey Chevere

Beaten

I sit in the dark wondering why me.
What are the Fates trying to make me see?
I must be blind because I cannot see it.
Like glass, my life shatters bit by bit.
What have I done to deserve the strife
That wreaks havoc and rapes my life?
The hurt radiating from it takes its toll.
Treacherous snakes take turns judging my soul
What can my insignificant self do to defend
Myself and distinguish predator from friend?
I know I've done wrong before in the past.
It's me still aching what I can't get passed.
A hard lesson of life is that nothing is fair
I see chaos strike but try not to care.
Did I do so much as to deserve this pain?
Don't know how much longer until I go insane.
As my blood cools, I realize I am to blame.
Maybe this is one of God's mysterious game.
True happiness is an inconceivable myth
Because I've got no one to identify with.

Louie Salazar

True Friends

True friends are precious, and sometimes rare.
Like jewels adorning a crown.
Sometimes we may not be aware that
they are there for us.
To pick us up if need be.

To laugh with us, or share a tear.
To know when we need to talk or just be still.
A true friend is someone to cherish.
Let them know you care.
That you are honored to call them friend.

Ann Fisher

Brown

There was a person named brown
Who was a clown and lived in town
Who found a hound in the fog.
Then they jogged and found a bear
Who would tear into them but
Played fair and scared them away
In a pair wore the bear down.
Who shared a fish with a snake in a dish.
Who wished he could get out.
Who kissed the brown bear that
Wound up the person who found the dog,
Who was in the fog; who chased the bear;
Who tasted the fish; who wasted the snake;
That passed the brown hound.

Sonya Kiesinger

"Silent Tears"

I sit alone, crying my silent tears in the dark night.
I wonder if everything is going to turn out alright.
I don't know what I'll do, I can't imagine my life without you.
You use to be here to wipe away my sad tears,
When I was scared you got rid of all my fears.
You were my best friend and now it's coming to an end.
Since we met we have become one,
and now we say good-bye and it's done.
So I sit in the dark night crying my silent tears.
All that remains is memories of our years.

Rachel Holiday

Alone

Alone into this world I came;
a loveless child without a name.
No one caring, no one sharing the woesome tears I shed
this loveless child without a name; on busy streets or lonely lanes
no one cares as my mournful cries go unheard.
Spirits come and spirits go yet when freedom is all that seeks
this loveless child remains;
Shadows grow longer with each passing day as the sun emerges
and chases these walls of solitude
and replaces the night with clouds of gray;
All at once a smile comes my way and a glimmer in an eye I see,
lo in the night a familiar face I see it is my soul mate sent to set
this mournful soul free, love has finally come for this
lonesome child with no name.

Helen Layton

Midnight Watcher

A leaf flutters down thorough a sliver beam,
As a woman moves through a forbidden dance in the moonlight,
A young prince watches,
As he always has and wishes that thing were different,
But he's know that watching is all he will ever do,
Because no one as beautiful as she,
Would ever kiss a frog like him,
Though it is his one wish,
That the stars,
And the gods would but grant his wish,
If even for a second before,
She turns back into a marble queen forever frozen in time.

Patrick N. Buss

Beauty by Name

Don't have to know your name
To know that you're beautiful
Reflecting Heaven's touch
Within Desire's pool

Don't have to be a poet
To have a heart searching for words
and if Fate prevents us from speaking
You're still the purest sound that I've heard

Like a rose that's awakened
By the falling of Heaven's rain
So for me to admire your beauty
I don't have to know your name

Michael Lemon

Will I Remember?

To my children, Jordan and Brooke
It's time my child I heard him say,
It's time for you to be on your way.
But Father will I forget your face, your loving smile,
your warm embrace?
Will I forget the times you held me near
or even when I'm filled with fear?
Will I remember you with the setting sun,
when I'm feeling proud of the things I've done?
When the stars are shining bright at night,
will you fill my soul with heaven's light?
When I can't find the answer to a simple prayer,
will you send me a sign to show you care?
Yes, you will remember in ways unknown,
when you're feeling down or all alone.
If you feel a soft touch or a glow in your heart,
that's when you'll know we're not far apart.
And when on your knees at the end of day,
you'll remember me every time that you pray.

Nichole Braegger

Work of Grace

Let my life become
a "Work of Grace," Lord,
not merely pretty words . . . .
Words that only bring a smile . . . .
a whisper of hope in the darkness.

But let "Your Words"
bring my life alive . . . .
Alive to act upon and do . . . .
What You have spoken
for me to perform.

For words are only empty promises . . . .
until they are brought to life
By an "active will . . . ."
Acting on Your Words . . . .
believing in their truth.

Let my ears hear them . . . .
Let my mouth speak them . . . .
Let my heart receive them . . . .
Until they mold my life completely
into a "Work of Perfect Grace!"

Karen Ragan

"My Heart"

My heart was once lost in a frozen garden,
there was nothing surprising,
everything was hardened.
There was no movement around,
everything was pretend,
even the sound.
I was cold and unable to feel,
I see now that nothing was actually real.
Nothing was tangible, no one had a soul,
I had no opinion what ever you said was the rule.
In my eyes you were the one,
because of this there was never a sun.
And you were the only one I felt,
so the ice could never melt.
Until the day came that I'll always remember,
my heart was broken by another member.
Yet it was for the better, my heart could grow.
And the ice began to melt ever so slow.

Julia Toth

Break Your Heart

I never really meant to break your heart,
Perhaps maybe I wanted to
Somewhere deep in my mind,
Hidden as it is under layers of politeness.
But to see you like this
Is almost more than I can bear.
How could I have wanted to take you down
Off the pedestal where I placed you
And showered you with affection
And thrown you in the mud and dust
And left you to suffer in humiliation
For how I felt you mistreated me?
I am not a monster, just a man,
And yet I feel I did you wrong
For I know you deserve to be here with me.
And though I broke your heart
I know that you still love me,
Though you feign to admit it,
Especially when I am around.

Nathan Albright

The Nighttime

A cold moon comes up after the warm sun has set,
The clouds drop forming a deep mist.
Animals in the woods come out to play,
And the owl sitting in the tree,
Catches its prey.

The night wind blows softly,
And the trees bow before the night,
As if they were thanking it,
For some unknown reason.

As the night goes on,
Yellow and blue stars come out,
Searching for a loved one to watch over.
And then finding love again,
This is what the nighttime is all about.

Amanda Heidebur

My Husband's Face

I see his face through the eyes of my heart:
His presence abounds . . .his eternal life-force drawing near;
The warmth of a tender fondness shining brighter in us both,
The passion of an intimate bond we shared together as one.
He offers assurance. He offers hope. He offers love.

I see his face through the eyes of my soul:
His growing wisdom of life's hidden potentials and enticing snares;
Guided by a discerning spirit, enlightened with a perceptive nature,
Strengthened in a balanced perspective developed with each step.
He knows. He understands. He believes.

I see his face through the eyes of God:
A quiet reflection of integrity emerging from a humble disposition;
Sculpted in challenging struggles, defined by a maturing character,
Made whole through the belief held dear in his heart.
He has faith. He has trust. He has peace.

When I see his face in all these ways:
As I look beyond the suffering, as I gaze beyond the sorrow,
As I focus beyond the pain that, without him, finds me in its grasp,
I am enveloped in his essence, I am filled with his love,
And I am touched by the grace of God.

Jeanne Richards

The Gentleman, the Man, the Old Man

My dad and I always drove down a certain   street.
There was a gentleman we'd always meet.
He had only a cup and his voice to say,
   "Change . . . any change?"
When I was young I'd always wonder who
   he was and what the man's name could be.
Eventually I got a bit old and so did he.
Still he came to the street and said please.
This was the man of whom kids teased.
I was a bit young then, but still understood.
Just a poor man who couldn't get a job . . . or
   maybe he could.
I felt sorry for him and one day
   decided to give him a dollar.
Now I see the man every day.
He still walks up and down the same street.
Today, I feel sorrier than ever before.
For now the man has a head full of grey and a gloomier face.
Again I pulled out some money and prayed,
For what could've been for the gentleman, the
   man, and now . . . the old man?

Farah Bernier

A Dead End Day Unsprung

All I want is to be free
But that's not all I want;
Gallantry and courtesy have no place in my head.

A milestone given,
A Yorrick for the masses
Is what I have finished as—
Am I finished?

The sky billows around my ears
As I sing my silent song
To the grey night.

Will Bratby

Only Second Best

You say that I'm the best,
but really I'm just in your shadow.

You say that I'm your number one,
but really I'm your sidekick.

Only the accent to your voice,
only the skin to your soul,
only second best . . .

But until the day comes when others
will step on your heart and wilt your words,
I will be there for you—

Unlike you were for me.

Chelsea Crispin

Watcher of Night

Lonely and lost, forgotten and forsaken,
You carry a burden unknown,
and bear the weight unshaken.

Wandering in solitude
Adorned in stolen grace,
Forever seeking in celestial chase.

Entombed in darkness, yet gleaming with light,
Sped on by the duty of your hidden plight.
Through a playground of stars,
A boundless unknown,
Onward traveling, forever alone.

How long have you lived? Time does not know.
How long have you borne the imposter's pale glow?

Mocked by your sister's infernal birthright,
Plagued by envy is the Watcher of Night.

Cold and grey, with a heart of stone;
Bearing only reflection, no light of your own.

A silent sentry, bereft of grandeur and might,
A ghostly figure is the Watcher of Night.

Ryan Wills

My Prince and Princess

To my little Prince and Princess
Who I have never seen
I look up at your window but,
No one is there to look back at me
At night I listen to you scream
All this time wishing I could do something
To my little unnamed and unseen Prince and Princess,
I hope you will live to be three
Just remember you're royalty to me
I wish I could take away you hurt and pain
For these offer you nothing to gain
To my little Prince and Princess
Even though I don't even know your name
I still love you the same

Charles Agel

Worthwhile

In all my thoughts when I'm alone
All I see is you
When I sleep with no one to hold
All I see is you
When I write all my poems
They are meant for you
In these times that are so hard for me
I always think of you
Whenever I'm so sad I cry
I smile because of you
I may not be that kind of guy
That makes your life complete
But only God knows how hard I'll try to be the one you need
Here I wait
Of you I dream
I want my goddess
To want me
Every day I see you smile
I will know it is all worthwhile

    Brett Wilhite

Maybe Then

The smile that I see
Is saved for me alone,
If you could only see all that I do,
Maybe then . . .

Your beauty inside
Makes my heart ache,
Longing for it to be free.
Imprisoned by your own insecurity,

To break loose—
Sing. Dance.
Release your soul to the world!
Maybe then . . .

Being yourself
Is harder than it seems,
Being what they want is easier—
Remaining a slave to everyone's expectations.

Fear not opinions, seek only the truth.
Search within and reveal everything.
Choose to live your life, your way,
And then . . . you will find love and happiness.

    David Kobus

Hidden Spirit

You call me strong,
'Cause I held on for so long.
One tear from my eye
you've never seen cried.
And through it all, I'd never die.
You say you're amazed
that they could call me crazed.
You say I'm your star,
because alone, I made it this far.
Although I am only human,
these are not the things that make me a true woman.
It's that I never lost sight,
never gave up my fight,
Persistence fed my mind
and I kept my soul kind,
Kept my heart feeling love,
and never lost sight of the man above.

    Heather Higinbotham

The Realtor

Who puts the "REAL" into real estate
Because everything they do is really great!
From dawn to dusk & even later
This person is a fabulous negotiator.

This person is always within reach
Whether on the street or on the beach.
They know everybody—everywhere
Cell phone in hand, they work with a flair!

Helping clients dreams come true
Listing or selling, and rentals too!
Like puzzle pieces they put together
Many deals in all kinds of weather.

The "REAL" part of Realtor is a human being
NO property or computer is seeing . . .
A smiling face, or warm hug, closing a deal
When a person thanks you—THAT IS REAL!

    Martha Hill

Battered

I can't begin to understand how I could choose to love a man
whose violent moods could transform him into a raging hooligan.
But I did love him and as much as I
try to erase the memory and deny
that he even existed, even took part
in my young life, he held a place in my heart.
Everyone knew he had another self
which he so deftly placed on the shelf
when company came and he had to simulate
the loving husband, the ideal mate.
But his guise was obtrusive and my body told
of the slander and beatings my lips would withhold.
Dutifully I would try to hide
the shame and guilt I felt inside;
The horrible, incessant pain and torture
this maniacal demon made me endure.
He took our hell with him when he left,
so why on Earth do I feel bereft
of the happiness we rarely shared
when he and I were "the perfect pair?"

    Karen Buck

Someone I Know

I see all the pain and hurt in her eyes
Every night for him she cries
I can almost see the blood gushing from her heart
If only she had known this would happen from the start
When he left, she lost her very best friend
That was the hardest part to lose in the end
If you look closely into her eyes
You'll see what she always denies
He used her and played her for a fool
A game that for her, seems so cruel
Take another look into her eyes
You'll see a broken heart in disguise
She doesn't want anyone to know how she really feels
Putting on a smile, the hurt and pain she conceals
The purest, sweetest love, to him she tries to convey
She doesn't understand how he can treat her this way
I pause to take a closer look into her eyes
And it is then that I realize . . .
As I get closer, things become clearer
It is me . . . looking in the mirror

    Tina Lott

Train of Thought

I am sitting in an empty chair
Drinking from an empty glass
While I write words
And the khaki colored hours of my youth
Flowing past, sponsored by the Gap
Drifting, like so many exhausted salmon
Being dragged out to sea
What could possibly be done
To prevent this kind of
Accidental homicidal tragicomedy
From ever gracing the stages
Of my too subtle mind? Not much, I assure you
In my time I will accomplish something
Perhaps not as great as fire or philosophy
More like the tiny crawling noises
From under the house at night
Which frighten you so,
And which I find so amusing
I simply cannot sleep next to you anymore
In the dim quiet hour of dawn

Jonathan Munves

Bad Luck

Here's just a little about my day;
I got up in the morning
and stubbed all five of my toes on my right foot,
Next I was waiting for the bus,
and the girl sitting next to me
stole my homework and tore it up.
OH, and that's not all!
I also fell down on the playground,
and got my brand new pants
all wet and muddy.
AND THAT'S JUST A LITTLE
ABOUT MY DAY!!!!!!!!

Megan Kinter

Tornado

As the lightning strikes and the thunder cracks
the wind blows through to cause an attack
It growls and it feeds so as to ravish
the earth, feeling its terror, appreciating its worth
It grabs at the sky and pounds its feet
it spins on by with its intention to deplete
When you see it you can't go you are
forever spinning in the TORNADO.

Angela Olsen

Love of My Life

Love can conquer anything
Or that's the way it seems,
But when it's unrequited love
It shatters all your dreams.

It builds you up, you're on a high,
You feel like a bird, you can almost fly!
Life looks so rosy, lovers' eyes do you see,
I can't believe it, is it happening to me?

To see you fills me with delight,
I could talk to you way into the night.
You don't feel the same, it's obvious to see,
Don't go away, I need you with me.

The words that you speak, say it all so clear,
No love is there left, what am I doing here?
As friends, if we could, I'm willing to be
Today, and tomorrow, and for eternity.

Rob Steele

Feelings of Love

A warmth deep down within.
A heart burning with the fire of love.
A feeling of love washes the tears away;
Brining a peace like a dove
to the heart and soul again.
For then no more fears forever, and a day.

Feelings of love brightens up my life,
when I come to think,
That one day I will have a wife.
On the day that is pink,
is when life will truly begin;
with a commitment that comes from within.

Romance and honor brings forth a feeling
of sincerity and compassion.
A flame that burns bright in my heart
forever more; everlasting compassion.
Makes me realize that this special love;
will never split apart,
For it is a love from the heart.

Feelings of love gets me to say,
thank you father; for life today.

Bryan Skidmore

Are We Inferior to Dolphins

Chilean brother Pablo composed
A message that majority did not get
"Oh beautiful is this planet
I came to live in this word."

For a formula to prevent every unnecessary tomb,
To be secure as when sheltered in the womb,
A man doesn't need help of smart dolphin's steer—
Exclaims Dudley, my distinguished peer.

Thus, an intellectual is forced to choose
The ideal of altruism or selfishness,
And, if the selection is deadly wrong,
In a war-free era we will never belong.

Remarks

R. Igic is a refugee from Tuzla, Bosnia and Herzegovina
Pablo Neruda, the 1971 Nobel Prize-winning Chilean poet.
Dudley Herschbach, the 1986 Nobel Prize-winning US scientist.

Rajko Igic

The Great Sight

In through the out door
Copper stained cage, to the soul it is fright
To the listener, this, the sight
To hear, to see, to feel, is all powerful delight
Anticipation is what the mind feels
Hate is what the good steals
Its freedom shines upon the glimmering one
Light to the beings who accept the white
It can be one, it could also be the other
This wonder is what can shutter
No matter, each one can free the shattered
Step unto, Open up
You can undo whatever you do
This sight can make you see through
Whatever can't be seen through
Whomever, Whatever
This sight, can bring light to your feel
The dark is what it will steal
FEEL!
Bring upon the light

Donald Menig

The Song

I look into your face and ask where I went wrong
Knowing it was my fault—how it started with a song
The song led to the smiles, the smiles led to tears
The tears will last forever . . . through all the golden years.
You look just like your father, for months he has been gone
I could have stopped it all if I hadn't heard that song.
In these months I have grown up. Too sudden, all too fast
What I didn't realize that night was that it couldn't last.
The radio was distant and I thought that he would stay—
The last thing I expected was to have you here today.
The dance was finally ending and we drove up on that hill
Everyone was doing it and I thought I might as well
I knew him for an hour, the lights outside were dim . . .
I loved that song playing—I loved it more than him.
As I look into your eyes, it occurs that nothing lasts for long.
I hardly knew this boy, I think. But at least we had a song.

Rosie Zuckerman

The Vertical View

Lord, help me to keep the vertical view . . .
when things go wrong and the good days are few.

When my vision is broken by a lateral skew,
Oh, Lord, keep me strong in the vertical view.

My world need not suffer ill effect,
despite vain rantings of the politically correct.

They corruptly spin, and their pundits spew . . .
as they proclaim this age New.

Though Your truth and ideals they randomly scatter,
in light of eternity, it will not matter.

. . . Because justice delayed is not justice denied,
and, in the meanwhile, I have your peace inside.

I will keep my focus on what is true . . .
and soon I'm restored to the vertical view.

That day has long been foretold,
and is daily proclaimed by the faithfully bold . . .

When the horizon will split with the vertical view,
and, Lord, all eyes will finally look upon You.

Barbara Barrett

His Return

I shall not be moved from this rock
on which I stand.
My faith increases daily; I walk with Jesus
hand in hand.
Greater is the one who dwells within
my heart and soul,
than any trial sent by the one who fools
the world.
No weapon formed against me
will ever cause me harm.
I have Jesus right beside me,
my shield of faith on my arm.
The time is drawing near
the earth will shake on its foundation.
The trumpets will be heard
in every land, every nation.
He will raise his righteous arm
and sin will bow before His throne.
Lift the standard of the Lord
for the battle's already won.

Therese Paterson

I Am

I am an artist painting the lives of those around me.
I am an architect building my life as I go along.
I am a lawyer not afraid to stand up for what is right.
I am a jury member judging others only after
hearing all the evidence and the whole story.
I am a mountain climber climbing my
way to the top, success.
I am a detective solving the mysteries of life.
I am a teacher, others learn from my mistakes and examples.
I am a sculptor molding my life
goals and morals with the passing years.
I am a marathon runner,
full of energy and always ready to face my next goal.
I am a doctor healing those who turn to me
for advice, care and support.
I am a banker, people share their
values and trust with me and gain interest.
I am a scientist everyday finding new data,
experimenting and drawing conclusions.
I am a millionaire, rich in love, life, compassion, and sincerity

Nicole' Freeman

Christmas

What is it nobody knows, but when it comes,
everyone is happy and joyful.
The children are excited about the wonders of the holiday
and what lies ahead.
Will they get what they want or will they just receive love?
No one knows what's going to happen,
that's the joy of Christmas.
When the kids see snow,
they light up with a spiteful spunk in their heart.
That makes them want to jump all over.
When they get that cinnamon taste in their mouths, they go wild.
Their hearts are racing,
they feel like they just had seen Mickey Mouse.

Jessica Pettibone

A Sense of Purpose

To have a sense of purpose;
Means to have pride in one's self,
To give respect to each other,
When one is in need,
To be able to understand,
And lend a helping hand.

To have a sense of purpose;
To be able to love,
And to receive love in return,
Means to be open and honest with one another,
To have a true sense of caring.

To have a sense of purpose;
To live in racial harmony,
With the knowledge of being different,
To let one live as he so chooses,
Without fear of reprise,
When my child and your child,
Can walk the same pathway, side by side.

Joyce Burton

Descending out of Hell

As I descended the staircase,
all my senses could perceive was the embrace of a
new radiant freedom.
What I held in my hands was an
end and a beginning
to me more than to anyone else there
it meant the end of a part of my life that had been as
welcome as death
and much less comforting.

Angela Carol Mitchell

Nor

Yesterday, we climbed a hill.
We climbed a hill, and we were young.
We brought our buckets for to fill,
Just Mary, me, and Miriam.

We gathered huckleberries blue,
And picked the sweet, sweet mountain tea;
Yesterday the Earth was new,
To Mary, Miriam, and me.

"Are we happy?" Mary said.
"I reckon so," said Miriam.
We lay upon a mossy bed, and watched the sky,
And we were young.

Yesterday we had to go.
Yes, it was time, oh, it was time.
We didn't know, we didn't know,
That was the last, the final climb.

Time ushers in a host of things,
The bitter with the sweet, they say,
But notwithstanding what it brings,
We can remember yesterday.

Lenore Shipley

My Dreams

These are my dreams . . . as I see the sunset
I notice the reds and think of your hair
and the beauty of your eyes reminds me of the sea . . .
I continue to dream of a time when I will feel
your perfect lips pressed against mine
and I can almost feel your silky soft skin
as your hand presses against mine
and grips a little tighter for we know . . .
even in my dream . . . this is not a love that can be . . .
I can feel your heart beating in time with mine . . .
our bodies so close we are almost one person . . .
I can taste your tears as we have to say good-bye . . .
so in my dream we never have to say good-bye
we only lie there in each others presence . . .
as I awake I find myself wishing I could tell you . . .
these are my dreams

Jason Richlin

The Day Gone By

A song is sung of days gone by
Here is the woe of today
There is the light of yesterday.

Overcast our day begins
Not a dot of sun to be found
And yet the haze clears,
Not quickly, but as the new day eases into motion,
The light pokes its brightness through the overcast sky
And illuminates our hope with time going idly by
The day is warm and glowy
And so soon forgotten is the past

The day reaches its autumn
The last rays of sun
Stretching across the land in a mournful embrace
And we are sad too
And then it is gone.

We plunge into the darkness that is night,
Longing . . .
    . . . for that day gone by.

Barry Livingstone

Admiration

Beautiful sky
Where whitish clouds dwell
Upon the horizon,
Swiftly moving westward.

Day and night appear
Changed its lovely colors,
Bright and dark
Surround the greenish Earth.

A new day arrives
Light shine warmly on
A lovely face;
Images are getting more vivid to perceive.

Searching carefully on an elegance's face,
A cold wind shivers my bones,
Gives me an annoying headache;
Within minutes, it fades away like smoke.

Motionless as I sit
Mirror reflects my identity,
A look I would admire in the world,
My individual's appearance.

Bihuai He

A Love Lost

In a world thats grown dark
A heart calloused and cold
Leaving no one to turn to
In a world where evils unfold
Born into innocence
We enter with a cry
A living hell awaits us
And we just wait to die
For life is but a tangled web
A battle of lies and deceit
It's a battle for which there is no fight
For it is a battle without defeat!
So entrust your heart to no one
Your reward will be calloused and cold
Leaving no one to turn to
In a world where evils unfold

Marlyn Prewitt

Sullen and Somber

Sullen and somber,
Alone in my temperament, holding back the pain,
Never allowing my weakness to show.
Concealing my thought,
However ample my sorrows were.
Falsely animating happiness
For something remained restrained within.
Weakened was my state,
For a year it developed,
Never did I anticipate recovery.

Petty and naive you are,
Thinking you hold omniscient knowledge
On subjects only experience lends.
Misery and tears you've caused,
Abrasive words and unthinkable actions—
Deeds a best friend would never do.
Years of this deriding,
no solution could I reach.

By chance we conversed,
too many tears have followed.

Jennifer Wagner

Welcoming Insanity

To Richard—take only what God gives you and nothing more.
And only to me my thoughts do roam
Destined to reveal the pain of home
Touch not the soul that breaks in will
Take not the power that corrupts me still

And to my heart only I am true
Forsaking all givers, perchance to rule
I need not your pity, your help, or love
I need only myself, and God above

To me, so does the mind reveal
That all physical has lost appeal
To only thoughts I turn for hope
To give my mind proverbial rope

Carry forward, seekers of my flame
Your destiny of my soul does not remain
Cast off your wants far from me
Cast off you vulgar epiphanies

I hermit to maintain my mind,
And to you, dear friend, I will not combine
So go and dwell in others' concerns
Such is my satisfaction as my insanity burns
        Jennifer L. Mattka

Psychosomatic

Like I swallowed a sledgehammer, handle first.
Huge piece of metal lodged in my throat.
Pressing it out sideways, the wrong way,
and my flesh fighting violently to retain its shape,
my esophagus vainly trying to push the thing down.
Peristalsis?   The handle, wood, going down into my stomach,
rounded edge jabbing me in the gut.
Dull and excruciating.
My anger.
Feels like a million red hot pinpricks beneath my skin.
Porcupine quills of rage. No.
My anger, like lava flowing into all the crevices
between my skin and the viscera beneath it.
The heat builds up but does not burn through.
It will cool and the quills will relax in time . . . soon enough.
        Joy Buchanan

Valentine's Day Ballad

I'm slowly sinking into despair,
What's the thing that brought me here?

A special day for lovers,
Of which I currently am without.

This commercialized celebration of love,
Presided over by Cupid from above.

His arrows fall upon the ground,
And where they fall is where love abounds.

But some hunter he turns out to be,
Neither arrow nor lover has come to me.

So all alone is where I sit,
Waiting for my Cupid's hit.

I'd settle for a little sting,
An overnight, one-night fling.

But a greedy God of Love he is,
He keeps his arrows all for him.

Isn't that just like a man?
        Jessica Black

Essence of Beauty

What is love without the essence of beauty?
Does it exist, is it important, a sense of duty?
For without beauty, no true love exists
And gives no meaning to mourning doves or mists.

Without beauty, all emotions are drowned.
We are all machines, teary eyed and frowned.
All the world turns a dark, hazy gloom.
Now no love can be found; only then is there doom.

Hope is now a forgotten dream,
Beauty is forever deceased, and for eternity there is no gleam.
But when one can look up from dread and see
A ray of light, and behold, beauty to forever be.

Reborn now are all emotions so true.
Darkness is now fading, feelings arise new
For a lady brings faith and peace,
And with her beauty comes reward and gives life a new lease.

This lady's beauty has found a truth in me.
I now have love, and it will always be.
This lady takes my spirit and eternity forward—
I have found beauty; thus love is mine reward.
        Egan Collier

a writer to her work

Dedicated to Spence, Paula, James, Dru & the pig
i keep a thesaurus
i've had since 7th grade
it is my oldest friend
17 years old . . . .
the pages are tattered and torn at the edges
the cover is frayed at the corners
the spiral bound is unraveled
the ink is smudged inside
from years of frantic fingers
racing through my interpreter
who's only goal
is to discover
the most precise way
to allow the outside world
to understand
me . . . .
        Lesli-Jones Tokar Whiteman

My Angel's Footsteps

Many people walk in and out of our lives, and make
impressions like footsteps.

You have walked into my life, and made an impression;
You have walked out of my life, and the impression you have made
will always be remembered.

You always made me laugh,
You always made me smile,
You never made me sad,
You never made me cry,
I was happy when you were near,
and I am sad that you are gone.

I will never truly know how you felt about me,
but I truly know how I feel about you.
You are my angel Shane,
from now until eternity.

I miss you Shane,
but the memories that we have had together
will never be forgotten.
        Kymberli Christian

Worlds Apart

The thoughts, feelings, swirling in my mind
No answer in my mind can I yet find

Show me now, show me why
Wipe this tear from my eye

Let me touch your angel face
Let me hold it in my hands
Let me feel such gentle breath
Please, don't deny me this

One single favor, one simple wish
I want to touch your lips with a kiss

Now in this moment; having everything
Let me hold you close
I'll cherish this moment
Please, don't deny me this

I'm saddened though
We're two worlds apart
And neither can reach the other

Show me now, show me why
Wipe this tear from my eye
        Michael Hall

Single Breath

Through my life and times the world has been
beneath my uncontrollable urge to be free.
To this point, kids, mere children have all been
but a simple form for space.
To fill the void we call our young life,
we have to act responsible, be who you wish us to be.
But I have learned from you that my life shall be
everything I can hope for. Everything you dream of.
If I never live another day may my life be complete
knowing that you are a part of it.
That itself says enough to last an entire lifetime.
But a lifetime to you is an eternity to me.
The eternal bond we share shall be
what holds us together 'til the last words of our breath.
Knowing you, looking back
to see the wonderful time we shared.
The great stories I shall tell my son about you.
How you were an idol, a mentor, and finally my father.
I shall be there for you as you were for me.
No words can describe love except what I write to you,
my father.
        Brian Meloche

No Comparison

The autumn leaves are beautiful,
and the spring flowers so grand
but neither can compare to just the touch of your hand.

The ocean is so wonderful,
with its depths so deep and blue
but Neptune himself
would've fallen in love with you.

The mountains are so refreshing
with their view and fine fresh air,
but I would descend the highest of mountains
to smell your strawberry hair.

I knew from the first time I saw you
that you were the one for me
and when you said you would marry me,
it made me happy as I could be.

Springtime is for lovers,
or so it has been said
but I would give up a lifetime of springs
to spend one winter with you instead.
        Phillip Maynard

Life

Cut in half like tiny blades of grass and frozen
by the chilling winds and snow.
The cry of pain so faint, it can't be heard.
Tears, like mist, fall slowly . . . disappearing in the morning sun.
Trees release their silky cloaks into the soil,
while branches reach for space and sky.
The sky is clear and rays of light find way to earth,
as souls soar out to live in time,
While flesh decays in earthly graves.
        Sharon Parrill

The World Is a Coffin

The world is a coffin.
Being trapped inside with no air,
Bolted tight, and sealed with the kiss of death,
Ruby red lips seal the sentence,
It's all a happy dream.
Is all a giant lie.
And I love you
Is the silent cry.
You're trapped inside with no air,
The energy is zapped from your body.
You see red of your lover,
Black for your hate.
Blue for the passion you see within,
But you see no white.
For the silent cry
Takes all that is pure,
So you lie there lifeless in the coffin you call the world!
        Dessylyn Turney

The Fighter Inside

I was there when you struggled for your first breath.
I was too afraid to wonder if there was a fighter inside.
Right before my eyes you went from bad to worse.
I hoped and prayed there was a fighter inside.
I stood and I watched and I touched.
Trying to spark the fighter inside.
So helpless and alone, nothing else mattered.
There HAD to be a fighter inside.
Holding your hand, secretly talking.
I tried to make you believe there was a fighter inside.
But as I watched you struggle, never giving up.
I knew then and there . . . a fighter inside.
Two years have passed and when I look back.
I see the fighter in me, inside of you.
Like father like son . . . a fighter inside
        Tim McCoy

To Be Reborn

I am thousands of years old
I am tall and thin and bent over
Each time my form changes
Only the color of my eyes remains the same.

From whence I came is to me unknown
From the East, West, North or South
Only in old tomes is my name mentioned
On leaves of parchment is it written.

Who I am I myself don't know
I am laid low and then uplifted
Therefore I can never disappear
When I die I will be born anew.
        Wolf Pasmanik

Between Light and Dark

Break of day or onset of night
Enjoy the seconds, for quick they pass
Tender moments when all feels right
Watch the vibrancy, true beauty, alas
Everyone take a look at nature's true perfection
Immerse yourself as you relax your mind
Notice the revelation of nature's inspiration
Lasting Memories is what you'll find
Involve another, what a lovely scene
Generate romance in your partner's soul
Hold each other close and let nothing between
Those arms will warm you like a mink stole
Affection surrounds both you and a lover
Never underestimate one's passionate intent
Don't be surprised if a flame you uncover
Dusk and Dawn are special one must admit
Accept these words and claim your prize
Rewards will follow as you dare to commit
Know the pleasures of Sunset and Sunrise

John Lampkins

What Is an Angel?

An angel is a messenger of love,
Sent to us from God above,
With wings of silk and white lace,
Gentle eyes and a cherub face.
Their halo is bright and shines like the sun,
Which can never be broken or come undone.
Sometimes an angel can be like you or me,
A disguise that they use so we cannot see.
How different, beautiful, and wonderful they can be.

The angel in my life can be no other
Than my caring and loving mother.
I thank God each and every day
For sending her my way.
And I pray that one day I may be
The loving angel she has been to me.

Manda Rensel

You

I see you in my life coming and going
Why don't you stay in my life
Instead of leaving me in this place
I am all alone
I've let you come and go
It's mostly just watching you from the outside
I see you leaving me again
Today I vow to keep you away
I know in my heart I'll take you back
I love you, that's why I let you come back
You have hurt me by coming and going
Please just this once think of me and what I need
Maybe this time I will shut the door on you
I sure hope so
I want to be normal
I deserve to be normal

Katherine Van Hauen

The Greatest Creation

The greatest creation, created with love,
Was put here with patience and love from above.
Some take for granted the creation it'd be,
But I know without doubt that my eyes they can see.
And my heart even beating can tell me the truth,
With help from my bones that are strong from my youth.
And also my hair and my ears and my nose,
Can tell me with help from my fingers and toes.
Maybe by now with my help you can see,
The greatest creation is you and is me.

Rebecca Faulkner

Golden Tears

As I lie you down to nap I see not just today.
I've shared your past, dream of your future
But who am I to say

What you are, or will become,
Only God does know
He's blessed me with your precious birth
As I may watch you grow

I have been placed by your side,
To share your joyous life
And every tear drop that will fall
I do not always wipe

For you someday will understand that puddles from my eyes
Have been lessons of our time
And truly made you wise

There's many oceans that were filled and many wells gone dry
Fill some puddles with your life
It simply means to cry

No never hide those special drops
They are made of precious gold
Keeping them within your heart
Leaves stories gone untold

Bonnie Rudderham

Ode to Garth

When you grow old and notes you forget,
 take comfort in knowing the people you've met.

You've touched our lives in so many many ways,
 brought happiness and meaning in uncertain days.

We found "friends in low places" while heading to "the dance"
and united as one to take the "shameless"chance.

You send your message so loud and so clear,
 that we shall be free as the change is near.

When "the thunder rolls" and some become "victim of the game,"
we will stand and shout that Garth is the name.

"That summer" in New York brought "the beaches of Cheyenne,"
and left all your fans yearning again to see the man.

Off to Ireland and back the millions did go, but we'll
 forever think of cowboys and boots and "rodeo."

"If tomorrow never comes," let it all be said, that you
 are the man and through your life we were led.

When you grow old with the memories you clutched,
 smile softly and think of the souls you have touched.

Cheryl White

Portrait

Who am I?
I'm me—a composition of atoms, matter and life,
Mixed and conglomerated into one
That others of my race call "Woman;"
Longing, yearning for the thing—the idea—the passion—
That people call "love."
Love.
Not to be in love with love,
But to be in love with a person, a being, a man—You.
For this and only this do I desire in life
On this cold, wicked Earth:
To be with you, near you, and very close to you,
To be wholly yours.
For with you all my most wondrous
And fantastic dreams become true-to-life,
And you become most dear to my heart.

Sheila Harris-Minor

Oh, Father of Mine

As I look back on thee, Oh, Father of mine
The memories of you I will treasure every day
We did some fun things and had a great time
Picnics, cookouts, until the suns last rays

Thanks for the pleasures in life you helped me find,
and all the things I should do and say
along life's sensational way

I know you enjoyed the times that we dined
I enjoyed your zest for life
and the example you so superiorly and expertly designed

All though your life was to short some people would say,
I know you would tell them that God is the very best way

I will dearly miss you oh, dear father of mine
When I see you in Heaven, and others that I love,
 a treasure I will surely find

Nancy Walton

Blank Light (At My Computer)

My Computer hums
It's a repetitive swaying
It is not steady, but is soothing
I take comfort in its never failing song
I glance up at my blank monitor
White light blinds my eyes
Visions begin to dance in my mind
What if my life was blank too?
Yet at the same time I answer my own silly question
For how much you don't see on this white radiating surface
it is still full of life
Commotion and action all so hectic that it comes together in one
magnificent blur
I look back up at my monitor
A blank screen, and the comforting murmur of my computer

Tristan Vick

Twilight Time

Travelling through twilight space,
Through shades of blue and grey.
In the deepening darkness grass diamonds glisten,
And a world in strokes of silence takes pause.

Jason Collinge

Essence of a Woman

The essence of a woman, nothing could compare.
The soft silky feeling of her glossy hair.
The beautiful smile upon her extravagant face.
This sight alone, would make a man's heart race.
Her luscious lips, how they taste so sweet.
This wondrous feeling could never be beat.
The love and warmth I see in her eyes.
Proves to me, she would never tell lies.
There is a sparkle there, like that of a star.
The thought of her is permanent, such as a scar.
The touch of her skin is incredibly smooth.
When I become irritable, it seems to soothe.
And her laugh, that recognizable sound.
Nothing better could possibly be found.
With this woman, my life is complete.
Compared to her, none could compete.

Jason Dunn

The Feat

My shaking hand grows faint at thoughts of you,
I cannot foresee the future ahead.
My lips articulate to cold blue.
But I can see the light you give instead.

You speak words so sweetly into my ears.
Peace flows from my heart's dam in your presence,
Yet you know the intimacy I fear.
There is no fear in love only nonsense.

I have felt this embrace never before.
Passion intensifies my flame of life.
A season I will forever endure.
Passion combines forming one without strife.

I know not what the words that I now speak.
Lost in my heart of dreams expose my feat.

Jeffrey Garner

Emotions

I have traveled back in time to the tears of the past,
they've grown heavy round my heart.

Those images of long past youth . . . .
the mistakes, life makes us pay.

The winds of time are always moving,
we can never repair what was done,
but can carry on and make life better,
for those we left in the sun.

There is great emotion buried within our hearts.
We build walls to shut people out.
We are lonely.

Searching forever in the corridor,
secretly waiting to step across the threshold.

Hiding in the shadows, our dreams slip on by.

We must gamble one more time, take the first step.
We are happy, we are glad.

De Worden

The Grave

Outside . . . grieving and pain.
  Inside . . . cold and dry.
  Outside . . . feeling remorse because a past forgotten.
  Inside . . . hearing the living crying out for me.
Outside . . . wishing it was you.
  Inside . . . thinking death could never happen to me.
Outside . . . wanting me back.
  Inside . . . wanting this not to be.
Outside . . . standing over me.
  Inside . . . crying for reason of no movement, dead.
Outside . . . trying to scream within.

Autumn Norman

The Times that Mean the Most

ME and you have laughed a lot;
But the times that mean the most
Are when you hug and hold me close
We have been through good times and bad times
But the times that mean the most are when you hug and hold me close
We have been through births and deaths and marriages
But the times that mean the most are when you hug and hold me close
I MUST ADMIT THAT WE'VE
BEEN THROUGH A LOT TOGETHER
BUT ONCE AGAIN . . .
THE TIMES THAT MEAN THE MOST
ARE WHEN YOU HUG AND HOLD ME CLOSE . . . .

Fushsia Caldwell

Sun Idealized in You

Inside these eye's, the truth remains.
Desolate or so I thought, until you illuminated my world.
A Dogstar.
Reticent and intrigued, I stare into your eyes' blue.
The moon of my reclusion eclipses with the sun you emanate inside.
Falling through the stratosphere of relentless despair,
We collide.
Cauterizing each other with love.
Enamor.
We hit the ground realizing the Universes decree.
We are divinity.
Stars falling all around our feet.
In reverence, I cry.
The Sunrise falls unfolding its mystery.
Fate smiled onto destiny.
All is serene.
As the thunder starts to roll; I'll remain.
And through the lighting crashing down; I'll sustain.
Reluctant as the rain comes, in time you will understand this love offered before you.
I am the only one. Blind, guided to this love, unconditionally.

Cynthia Wesho

"You Left One Day"

Oh, how I love you so
So much that you will never know,
You left one day without a word to say and
for you always I will forever pray,
You left one day in such a quiet way
as we sat hurting watching you slip away,

If your life were in my hands I know I would
have taken a selfish stand,
I would not have let you go, because you and
mom were the ones to encourage me to grow,

The choice was yours to find forever peace,
but remember the love you left behind was
permanent and not on lease,
You were not just another soldier going home
honor, courage, and commitment were your song,

Yes, you left on my birthday which I have
always known, a day I will never forget
because it will forever and always be etched
in stone . . . I love and miss you Dad . . .

Audery Santana

Shattered Dream

Never again the broken-winged bird
Will fly as it had flown before;
It will fly again, of course it will—
But never with a carefree canter—that can never be restored.

Never again shall I live to dream
The dream that has proven so bittersweet;
I shall dream again, of course I will—
But not that dream—the pain is too much to repeat.

In time the wing of the bird will mend,
And it will fly again, and also sing . . .
And though it will never fly as it had flown before,
It will no longer be the bird with a broken wing.

In time the wounds of my heart will heal,
And I shall dream again, and a smile will be seen . . .
And though I shall never dream the dream I dreamt before,
I will no longer be the person with a shattered dream.

Mallika Khuansathavoranit

Protected

The sounds of the vacuum rival
A calm so pure that I am content.
There is no solicitude in the bedroom
With you.
Lying next to an infection,
I am the vacuum; incapable of matter.
You, the delicious ringworm, burrow
To see the red trickle from my eyes.

As the sun explodes, I will protect you,
Even as your fingers wrap around the
Dagger, sharp enough to slice my tender
Armor. As the fire turns my face black,
And you stab me with relentless possession,
Venus, you are safe.

Michael Brister

The Spiral Dance

I am Kore
the Dark Virgin stirring the Darkness starting the Dance
bringing Light from the Realms of Dark as I alter
I am Nimue
the Young Maiden dancing in the soft green Light
awaking the Nature
bringing Life from the Realms of Death as Herne alters me
I am Mari
the loving Mother bearing all riches for Her Children
and pouring them out unto them
as I set the sails to travel to the Realms of Dreams
in the Dawn I alter
and I am the Nameless Goddess
dark and unknown but knowing everything
I am Wisdom
I am the Light in the Realms of Dark
I am the Life in the Realms of Death
I am the Love in the Realms of Wrath and Despair
I am the Infinite One
I am the Everchanging as I alter
and I am Kore

Nataly Brombach

My Heart

I remained unsure
Of mystery behind the last drink you offered me,
in the middle of night,
under the gleaming moon,
You caught my heart by surprise,
along with my mind,
that was the melancholy of my heart.
You acted more sophisticated,
than Juliet in Romeo's era.
Were you hunting hearts just for pleasure?
Or was your innocence making all the charisma?
But you persist hosting my heart,
so keeping it as your infinite home.
Why do you intend to reside in such ruined sanctuary,
which has been the center of disasters in many occasions?

Mohammad Badri

What a Wonderful World this Would Be!

If all the men in the world were one man;
what a wonderful man that would be.
If all the women in the world were one woman;
What a wonderful woman that would be.
And if all the love in the world were one love;
What wonderful love that would be.

If the wonderful man took the hand of the wonderful woman
and expressed that wonderful love,
What a wonderful world this would be!

Emmanuel Mbobi

The Will to Try Is the Will to Do

I told myself yesterday,
No matter what, don't walk away.
Don't let your feelings get behind,
Close your eyes, open your mind.
Keep your head up through thick and thin,
If at first you fail, try again.
If you don't succeed, don't lose your pride,
Think to yourself, at least I tried.
If you do not try, you have no clue,
The will to do . . .
Remember this through good and bad,
Don't get antsy, don't get mad.
Put your feelings to the test,
Stay together, try your best.
Think to yourself, I can not fail,
For others to follow, leave a trail.
Don't be afraid to ask for a hand,
Ask for help if you can not stand.
If you don't succeed, don't get blue,
The will to try is the will to do . . .

Anthony Montano

Wish upon a Star

If I were to wish upon a star
I'd wish for that wonderful person that I know you are.
And should that wish, one day come true
I will embrace myself, with all thoughts of you.
To feel your touch, and taste your kiss
Would certainly be my dying wish
If only for a moment, to feel the bliss
I'd give my soul, for one last kiss.
Should the dawn of a new day
Bless and smile on our love
Well, I just have to say
We fit together, just like a glove.
And if that day awakes with clouds of grey
To be honest, I have but one thing to say,
We'll get through it anyway.
So now lets smile, and not be blue
For my wish upon a star, is all about you.

Angela Tuhacek

Children of God

The faith of a child,
The strength of You in my heart.

The peace of a child,
The comfort of Your protection on my soul.

The tears of a child,
The cleansing of Your grace.

Lynn Miller

More than Words Can Say

The days are long, and the nights are cold.
How I long to be in your loving warm arms.
Although we are separated by the oceans,
Your laughter rings within my thoughts.
I close my eyes, and wish you with me.
Holding me gently and whispering sweet nothings.
Just the thought of you, brightens up my life.
Just to hear your laughter, my life feels complete.
Just to have you holding me, I am in Heaven high above.
Just to have you loving me, I am the luckiest girl alive.
I looked upon the sky last night, and I saw a falling star.
I closed my eyes, and made a wish with all my heart.
That soon I will be in your loving arms once more.
To be loved and cherished forever more.
The words I say can only express, so little of what I feel.
I could only wish that you can feel the truth.
The truth of how much I love you, more than words can ever say.

Margaret Chu

To Love

Love is beauty and beauty is love,
Eve and Parvatee are symbols of love,
Love, you are the only existence in world so round,
You are the only galaxy that I surround.

Love is the creation and love is living,
Love is the cause of self-conceit,
Love is Ram and love is the Ravan,
Ahh! Love is creativity and love is an awful.

Touching is pleasure; you're the best of all,
Oh beauty! I touch your feet with a respect,
Oh love! You give me freedom from all,
Divine looking your form seems insightful everywhere,
I, a devotee, worship you from the bottom of my heart.

Love is flower and love is romance,
I, you, he, her, we all are lives,
The interaction of these lives,
is the Heaven where love always lies,
Oh love! You are the heavenly love
you are the eternal expression of love,

Hom Nath Subedi

It's You

What do you see when you look at me?
What do you think when you turn towards me?
I see you walking up and down the street
that's when my heart starts to skip a beat
Will you always come to me when you
don't know what to do?
Will you be around when I need
to talk to you?
It must of been the time or date
but being with you is my fate
You're in grade 12 but it seems like
you just dropped by in the mail
I would run an extra mile
just to see you smile
I know I'll never get a chance with you
I know you're going to college but
I just wanted to let you know
There will always be a special place in my
heart for a special person like you.

Jenny Thoi

Acropolis Atop Metropolis

*Dedicated to the architects that created NYCM
and how impressive it is.*
There are gargoyles, gods, saints and trim of lace
carved in stone above your face.
Chevrons, horses, chariots on fire
all eyes can see, if lifted higher.
Lions roar, cherubs dance on air,
All up there.

Pyramids, Aztecs, a cyclops' lair
eagles as though to fly in the air, how proud
all above city streets so loud.

Doric ones display them there,
the wind through Aphrodite's hair.
Amidst the tallest structures of ancient story
there is a glimpse of Old Glory.

Turrets, fortress like, these monuments display
a past how precious, made to last.

Joan Marie Mackin

I Miss My Love

I cry from Hell to the Heavens above.
Why must I be without the one I love.
Must these tears fall from my eyes.
Must I never cherish these beautiful nights.
I lay my hands upon my heart,
feeling as if I were going to fall apart.
I hunger for you only, so precious, so kind.
You are the only one I wanted to find.
I found you there, I couldn't help but stare.
In my heart you are,
from the moment we touched, we both knew we couldn't bare.
You are the light of my life that we are to share.
I take a breath of air, that I wish we could share.
I lay in bed knowing your not there.
Tears run down my cheeks,
wanting to be dried by the hand I long to hold.
I cry once more in hunger for the one I love
to hold me in his arms once again.

Natalie Robinson

It Seems Fitting

One day it seems fitting
A somber mood brought on by life's pressures
Brought on by other's stresses
Melancholic degrees of depression
And the darkness seems fitting

One day it seems
That the feelings are absurd
Death is trivial when life is to be lived
Why would one want to escape from a gift
Such as this?
High arched skies stretch
Across the direct and peripheral
But rain clouds are blowing dangerously closer
As beautiful as they are
Why must it rain now?

So it goes
And it always seems fitting
That the melancholic covers the brightness
Covers the light of a pleasurable day

Kevin Burke

River of Stress

Every time I think things are going alright
Someone comes up from behind me and
pushes me in. I can't swim.
The river's current sweeps me down stream
and makes it harder to stay above water.
Every time I come up for air, there is always
someone behind me in their little yellow raft
slapping me over the head with the paddle
or pushing my head back under.
I can't see. It's murky down here.
The white curtain of bubbles
from my vain efforts blinds me
and makes me lose my sense of bearing.
Which way is up? I can't breathe!
(Yet I can't hold my breath forever.)
Tired, I inhale expecting to breathe life.
To my dismay, my lungs fill with water.
Everything goes black. When I come to,
I realize that my efforts to stay alive
were for what?

Vanessa Ryan

To My Valentine

Thinking thoughts of you today.
To No one else I'd rather say,
I love you each and every day.
This Love we share in such a special way.

I've made up my mind,
This day to call you mine.
You are truly one of a kind.
And I pray you'll forever be My Valentine.

David Godfrey

Drunk Driver

Mommy where is Daddy
Why did he leave
When you say he is in Heaven I do not understand
Please tell me what it means
Why are you always mad
Did I do something wrong
Did I stay up too late or make too big of a mess
Is it my fault he is gone
If I am good will he come back
Mommy I miss Daddy why doesn't he come home

Dannielle Durbin

The Love of Your Life

The one you love, the person you adore.
Who acts as love is a normal chore.
The one who can fill your day with light.
May just be the love of your life.

The one you call your lifelong friend.
The friendship you know will never end.
The one who never wastes a bit of time.
May just be the love of your life.

The one who will always be at your side.
When you are in trouble or just can't hide.
The one who will never put you through strife.
May just be the love of your life.

The one you turn to when in doubt.
The one you know will never pout.
The one you know will never fight.
May just be the love of your life.

The one who loves you endlessly,
With all his heart, with all his mind.
The one will never let you go.
Is indeed, the love of your life.

Amanda Juarez

Afterlife—A Mother's and Daughter's Love

When the moon no longer casts its shimmering glow
And the twinkling stars at night forget to show—
When the sun refuses to shine so bright
And spring stops sending new signs of life—
When winter never again brings cold and snow
And the autumn leaves of fall never show—
When summer never seems to come around
And the joys of all seasons are never to be found—
When rivers cease to flow anymore
And the rolling waves of the ocean stop crashing to shore—
When all life on Earth comes to an end
Then we will be together Mother—Once again . . .

Frances Singleton

The Lurking Loner

As I lurked, around that little old town,
people looked around and frowned,
wondering why not even a cry.
I don't know why.
"Who are you?" they said.
I'm just a loner, asking for some bread.
Please help me, for I'm all alone, without a home.
For day's I've roamed, not knowing where I belong.
I've knocked on door's, that opened and closed,
but that's the life I guess I chose.
Without a word ever being heard,
no one ever asked me what I preferred.
Judge me not, for no one knows who I am,
where I came from or where I'm going to.
I am just a loner, asking for some bread.

Elizabeth Johnson

Will?

Will you take it if I have it to give
Will you leave me if I don't let you breath
Will you hate me if I don't let you go
Will you need me if I stop these shows
Can you feel me when I think of you
Do I fool you when I speak in tune
Do you need me like a desert rain
Can you show me where my pride has lain
Will you want me when my song is gone
Will you guide me if my path is wrong
Will you smell me if I bathe in lies
Will you lose it if I need to die???????
Will you forget me in time
Will you remember these rhymes
Questions from my warping mind
Laced with you and stopping time . . . .

Michael Cross

Through Everything

Through grave misconception, revelations a'dream,
I'll be holding your hand beside this endless stream.
We'll follow its path, to where the river runs deep,
where the sun shines a'brighter, and the finders they keep.

As you blow me away, I'm drawn to you close,
seeking only a fraction, only a dose,
of this love that has long awaited my life,
and has come, to take me away from this strife.

Through thick and through thin, in sickness and in health,
we'll carry each other, with our love and its wealth.
Never I know, shall I leave your warm, calming side,
for this love's only grown, merely half of its tide.

God, I love you, though I'll never enough,
for this love sunk so deep, is endlessly tough.
It's alright though love, for tomorrow I'll grow,
in your arms, head to heart, in the breast of your soul.

Giresh Thani

What's Left?

Your touch settles my breath and I am well.
Too much I ask of you; you turn away.
Poison pours from you lips like hot hell;
Words floor me, and spin my mind in dismay.
I should not think or toil on this, for now
I am all together drained of good thought.
Torn away from me, the platonic show
Of affections do pain a heart that is caught.
Say the words that disagree, I am lost.
In fact, I am void of vision and cannot see
How I lost my way. To where I want most,
I realize now, there I can never be.
I'll write no more, no Eros to inspire
doused are the flames of my passions fire.

Justin Wilds

The Grass

She is like a battle field
I lie wounded in the tall grass

The wind blows softly over my open flesh
and I cringe
not just from the pain
but from the thought of rising to my feet
to see above the swaying patterns of the field
into a vast unfamiliar landscape

I long to stay in these secure confines
to die peacefully
and without the endless reminder
from my future scars

but I know all too well
that the bodies of countless others lay motionless
in the silent innocence of the grass

William Orton

A Poem about a Chatting Friend

An on-line chatter is what you may see
But know this, your friendship is much more to me
As just like glue, our lives may come undone
But with a friend's help you've already won
A positive thought I give to you
Reach for the stars, you should pursue
As the road ahead may be pitch black
A negative thought I will never attack
You know a good friend to find, is hard, they are
That's why our friendship was made on a star
The miles apart, that we may be
I hope I've made my friendship easier to see
Pass as we may or maybe not
Believe in yourself, in my heart you have a spot
Take this as you will, I will never lie
But without your friendship a part of me would die.
Take this on for ages and ages hence
For it is your friendship that has made a loving difference

Laura Minkewicz

American Awareness

I once disliked the way I looked
and then I saw a man without a face.
I once was disappointed because I could not run fast,
then I saw a crowd of people who could not walk.
I once criticized other people born different,
then I saw the hate that bred.
I once was angry because I became nearsighted,
then I saw some people who were blind.
I once complained about our government,
but then I saw a nation that was not free.
I am happy, because I've grown to realize
how lucky I am just to be me.

Duffy Biggs

Good Thought

What you feel is just a feeling.
Like every other feeling comes and goes.

What you know is what you believe in.
A thought, To think; How not to feel, real.

I say Feel, Feel the goodness of your thought.
Find the balance that you've lost.

Love yourself.
Know who you are; And remember.

The good will always find good, for they are related.

The bad will only come in the belief which you created.

Nicholas Johnson

Afterwards

I wake, beads of sweat fall heavily,
Your side of the bed is cold and empty,
I inhale your scent, flowers and sleep,
I see you again, a vision in blue jeans
I remember how you cried, I remember how
fast the tears fell, trying to escape the lying in your eyes.
I remember that sting of betrayal, that feeling of being
the only person who doesn't get the joke,
but laughs in spite.
Love . . . That four letter word symbolizing nothing.
Love, the joy of having, the pain of losing,
the satisfaction of forgetting.
I curse myself for not seeing . . .
I'm destroyed, left with nothing
but memories and hatred.
You smiled and I laughed inside.
You smiled and lied inside.
So now, here I am afterwards, seething,
trapped in my own thoughts . . . afterwards.

Christopher Brown

Final Ride

When I reach into my pockets, I come up with just dust and lint,
Deep in thought with emotions and feelings,
Could she be Heaven sent?

I've had too many heartbreaks.
As well as broken bones.
This dame reminds me that Cowboys shouldn't be alone.

She makes me happy and full of pride.
Jus' like that, on an 8 second ride.
I feel nervous, scared, and want to puke.
As I'm climbing over my last and final chute.

My head is spinning around and upside down.
As though a bull was spinning out of my hand, I'm in the well!.
With all the power, determination and might.
I reach out with a fist of leather and hang on tight.

Y'all see this dame, is a powerful thirst.
Stronger then that of the rodeo, the pounding of the dirt.
This road has led me to much pain and hurt.
I feel absolute confidence, believe me, this is a first.

When you draw your next one,
You never know Exactly what they'll do,
Jus' keep holdin' on an prayin'
Someday it'll be the one for you!

Michael Barnes

Confusion's End

Confusion is where I am;
to move on would be the end.
So when the end draws near
I will be in constant fear
that I will not have the strength
to move on out of confusion.
The moon and sun could be friends
if they could just move on but since they can't
they will be at constant war instead of hand in hand.
The light will never be in balance with the dark that follows,
confusion will always be our home
and there will never be tomorrow.
When the sun is down the moon is up
and the opposite follows there after,
today is now tonight is then,
tomorrow never fills the end
So confusion is where we always stand
until tomorrow if only it would come!

Elizabeth Sheppard

Eyes

It's all in the eyes, all in the eyes
They tell you so much, give away your disguise
wherever you go in a thick fog of lies
the truth can be found in anyone's eyes

I looked in the mirror, I stared at my face
It began to detach and fall out of place
it felt like a mask, like a close binding case
but my eyes were so real and my skin was erased

It's all in the eyes, when we close them to dream
Our souls float away to somewhere unseen
though visions so sharp, so clear and so keen
It's not true and we know 'cause we look without seeing

Eric Lundberg

Only for You

My love is more powerful then all the navy's,
Deeper then the oceans they sail,
My love is higher than the stars, and wider then the universe too
My love is only for you.

My love will stand the test of time
even a 6 month deployment.
My love will stand the test of trails, lord knows we had a few,
My love is only for you

We have endured many things,
on this road we travel on,
but no matter what is yet to come,
there is one thing I swear is true,
my love is only for you

Timothy Franks

What Scares You

What scares you?
Is it the dark?
Or is it a loud bark
Is it doctors, nurses, shots, and needles
Is it a white dove?
Or is it love
Is it getting in a spaceship?
Or having a serious relationship
Is it your teacher, friend, mom, brother, or sister?
Is it your friend Seth?
Or is it death
I bet its a dare
Or is it you're scared to care
Is it school, a job, or a clown?
Is it a sharp knife?
Or is it the reality of life
What scares you?
All of these things scare me and I bet they scare you, too

Scott Cipowski

For Audrey

To my dear sister who walks the path of compassion.
I know one who walks the path of compassion.
I know one who travels the way of love.
She is one who feeds the homeless.
She is one who would rescue a dove.

She has treasure, and she shares it.
She has love that daily grows.
She has light as the dawn as the dawn that wakens.
She has thorns . . . as does the rose.

Angels are her companions.
Kindness is in her face.
Beauty is there . . . if you can see it.
Wisdom is preparing her a place.

Mark Antley

Memories

Sometimes it is lonely when you have been abused,
Sometimes it is hard to forget how badly you were used.
Sometimes it is painful to remember what was done;
The memories of my childhood
that should have been more fun.
The memories of my childhood
that I have wanted to hide,
I pretended that it didn't happen, I really, really tried.
But they keep coming back to me, they will not go away,
The memories that still haunt me, every single day.
Sometimes I have forgotten for a while, or so it seems,
Only to have them come back to me in my sleeping dreams.
The memories of so long ago, when I was just a child,
I wish that they would go away for a long, long while.
But no, they twist and turn
'til they are so entwined,
The memories are forever, always in my mind.

Linda Warren

A New Fresh Young Love

A fresh, young, tender flower pushes its way
Into the brown, gray deadness of early spring,
Spreading its delicate hues of pink and blue,
Still damp from the moistness of the morning dew.
Little does it realize that it's the beginning of a new love,
A love of the mind and soul as well as the heart,
A touching, caressing, walking-in-the-rain kind of love . . .
A New, Fresh, Young Love

Marilyn Huddleston

We

I used a crayon to draw on Locker's clean slate
I'd follow dreams and never hesitate
I took the road that was less traveled by
In hopes finding you, my angel in the sky

I was the boy you turned into a man
Loving you is all of who I am
I'd walk across the desert to get down on one knee
In hopes of finding you, my goddess of the sea

I curse my father each and every day
He moved my body but my heart is here to stay
When my family left I tried to stay behind
Because knowing you helped develop my mind

You taught me how to love and how to learn
And for another day with you my heart forever yearns
I know there is nobody else for me
Because I found my true happiness in We

Josh Cohen

Just One Girl

I'm just one girl in a world filled with hurt,
trying to fit in,
hoping to be noticed,
wanting to be loved,
there's so much I want to say but just don't know how,
so much hurt but I can't find the way out,
I'm just so young but still have it hard,
there's so much to live for,
so many hopes,
so many dreams,
I've never fit in,
always been the tag along,
hoping and praying that someday it will all change,
searching for a way out.

Danielle Cross

Remember When: Our Memories

Zak (my dog)—Remember when you first came home?
In your mouth you held a bone.
Your heart was full of admiration.
We promised to always have dedication.
Remember when we played in the park?
Wouldn't go in until it was dark.
We both knew that it was there,
That strong bond of love in the air.
Remember when you got a bad disease?
I tried very hard to put you at ease.
The light in your eyes slowly faded away;
I knew you were leaving, but tried to help you stay.
Every day I prayed for you; I didn't know what I would do.
Remember when we were the best of friends?
We stayed together up to the end.
One night I wished upon a star,
Pleading you would never be far.
In the end you left me here,
And I know we both had shed a tear.

Nicole Zimmerman

Virginia at Meson Ol'

Oh! Virginia As I look at your face
Framed by the Meson Ol' Pond
Bedecked by gliding ducks
And over-flying sea gulls
I feel mesmerized by the
Tranquility of your personality
That mocks the tranquil pond
/Oh! Virginia In an atmosphere abuzz
With a chattering crowd and
Clanging dining utensils
Against the background of
Other distracting elements
All I hear is your heart and mine
Pumping life-resuscitating love

Atyathoabe Osakpa

Lonely Wake

Solemn solitude overwhelms my images
An animated lover
And a lonely heart
Leave me feeling like I need to embellish the world around me.

Embrace what has been laid before me,
And desire what has not yet been conquered.
I crave feelings that have never been discovered,
And now left to yearn for the future
Hoping to prevail over what my own dreams have only implied.

Kristi Slusher

These Hands

The fingers that play with your hair
The palms that graze you cheeks
The wrists that wear your charms

The hands that help you up
The hands that touch with love
The hands that can be tough

These hands are the ones that hold your heart
These hands are the ones that hold you together
These hands are the ones that carry you through

These are the hands that brought you here
The ones that will never go away
These are the hands of a mother

The hands that play with your hair
The hands of love
Your mother's hands

Jacob Conrad

Forever Untouched

Like a glistening mirror
A star lit sky is mimicked.
A lonely sickle of a moon
Hangs low in the sky.
The silhouette of an aging hill
Watches as the
World goes by.

A valley of crystal waves
Flows silently against
A calm canyon breeze.
The sound of silence is nothing more than:
Waves on the shore,
Crickets chirping,
Or a gentle breeze of a desert lake.
A peaceful shoreline, disturbed by no-one,
Rests quietly in a world of chaos

    Jeffrey Zundel

Mr.

To my family, my wife Rajae and friends
Love . . . .
Love has a meaning in all languages . . . .
You have to give love, if you want to be loved.
You should give it to the entire world.
If you want to have good parents,
Be a good son.
Love your parents.
If you want to have a good teacher,
Be a good student
Love your teacher.
If you want to have good friends,
Be a good friend.
Love your friends.
If you want to have a good wife,
Be a good husband.
Love your wife.
If you want to have good children,
Be a good father.
Love your children.
Hate no one, and you will be loved!

    Abdullah Al-Ghafri

Rebecca

Oh, glorious dawning of the sun
Always so bright and radiant
Oh, glorious sight of her
Always so beautiful and lovely

Her heart so shineth forth
It glows about her
It beats aloud for all to hear
Only God's love doth occlude her own

Oh, magnificent waves of the sea
Always so continuous and flowing
Oh, magnificent voice of hers
Always so calm and soothing

Her hope is heard by all
It speaks of love
It shouts of joy
Only God's wisdom doth surpass her own

Oh, creature of the night, Oh, being of light
Her feelings, felt by all
Her hopes, hoped by all
Her love, hallowed by all

    Joseph Hansen

Imagine

Mr. Pruslin, my mom, my dad, my sister em, and grammy Therese
The stars, the sun, the moon, the sky
The unicorns and centaur's pride
The pixie queens, and fairy brides
Imagine being in a mirror realm
Where peace and quiet is always found
You dip your foot in a gleaming pool
Where the silver liquid is sleek and cool
The pheasant, the mermaid and the merman
The goblins, the trolls, the satyrs, the imps
The scattered cherubs are nice and busy
The sweet little putti give you a kiss
Your heart and your mind are now full of bliss

    Catherine Jones

Life

Make the best of it while you still can.
For . . . you never know when it shall end.
Make sure your loved ones, know they are loved.
That is a really important thing that they want and need to know.
Make the most happy days that you can. Make the best of your bad.
It's okay for sometimes to feel blue or feel sad.
That's just another part of life. Always stay as close
to your friends as you can. You never know when they may be
the only ones there for you sometime, someplace, someday.
Always remember this saying, "God works in mysterious ways."
Because it is very true, you never know what he's gonna do,
or when he's gonna take you away from here!

    Ashlee Cofer

A Tribute to My Elders

See the old man as he slowly walks by,
He gives a weak smile as if to say hi.
See the old woman, poor soul she's so lame,
won't somebody stop and ask her name.
Just a cheery hello how are you today,
would surely brighten these old folks way.
So often forgotten and left all alone,
nobody, nothing to call their own.
Some seem just to wait for their final day,
when our maker above comes to take them away.
Imagine the knowledge that's going to waste,
a repeat of youth most are dying to taste.
So please take the time to give of yourself,
don't place our old folks away on a shelf.

    Judy Seeman

I've Seen Your Soul Before

To Osiris, you are the last piece to my puzzle . . . I love you.
As I sit and watch your face,
you look familiar to me.
As I watch you laugh I try to see,
where you've been, where you'll be.
I cant quite get it, nor can I see,
your body your life your soul, reminds me of me.
As I watch a little longer,
I begin to see, that your soul,
is part of me.
I've finally found what I couldn't see,
that part of you that's inside of me.

True love is unexplainable

    Sarah Blackwell

Missing You

You live in music—each tone I hear
You live in sunshine—in a smile
You live within me—in those tears of mine
which leave my eyes calling your name
They are messengers of my soul
embracing you—my miracle.

Within your gentleness I have found
this long ago lost part of me
I am more whole than ever
because I love
the wondrous you

I kissed a star—up in the sky
yet I am falling back to Earth

Missing you
I will watch the night
for all my life
with different eyes.

Ana Maria Mihalcea

Animal(s) in a Zoo

Trapped, caged, hopeless,
Scared, worried, and powerless
Why do I feel like this?
All these emotions shaping me.
Got me thinking about life, particularly
About how we are all on display for the
Public to see. Casting an ever watchful eye,
Too wrapped up in MY personal business,
Judging me, laughing, pointing, even so far
As to disapprove. And full of reprimands.
How dare they? I ask again, How dare they?
Because even though they are casting many a
Stone, they conveniently forget the faults of their Own.
Looking at me from all sides,
As if I am an animal in a zoo. Not entirely sure
That my future holds such comforts
As the care, food,
Shelter and even love that they receive.
Unfortunately for me,
The animals, they don't even care.

Randy Hogan

I Am

I am terrified
I am scared of bullies
I wish that one person would smile at me
I am about tears and laughter
I am made of sugar and spice
I can be sweet or harsh
Me the lonely animal
Me the stray dog
Me the moon and stars
Me the sun and clouds
I am sugar melting away
I can hide or show myself
I am a butterfly trying to escape its cocoon
I am a flower trying to blossom
I have conquered self confidence
I wait for it to rain so I can shed my tears and not be alone
Me the destroyer or smile maker
Me the cat needing a warm home
But one thing I know is that . . .
I am me, myself and I

Mary Morris

My Apology

After our affray, the day you went away;
My realm just ceased; completely I'd say.
How had our lives gone so astray?
Damn tyrannical rage; that sickening potion.
An inner volcano spewed forth lava lotion;
Hurling me adrift a tumultuous ocean;
Into which I sank down, drowned in emotion.
Through great anguish and agonizing despair;
I could barely cope; would just sit and stare.
Stunned and confused, hurt and dazed;
Struggled to go on; marriage nearly razed.
Thought to myself; I must be crazed.
That you can still love me, I am amazed!
For all the pain I've inflicted
For years and years unrestricted;
I apologize to both you and our daughters
With tears cascading like falling waters.
I am so very sorry; and know why you shun.
Trapped in a web that I myself spun.
I beg your forgiveness; what's done is done.

Mark Guilfoyle

Russian Romance

Scrolling and trolling, searching all night
For the woman of dreams, the one that's just right

My fingers are clicking, the photos at will
In hopes of success, just over the hill

There's blonde, red, and auburn, and strawberry too
My search in vain, 'til suddenly it's you

You jump from my screen, a vision so right
My eyes now lit up, and oh, so bright

My thoughts they are racing, full speed in my head
This woman from Russia, must be in my bed

Not meaning to say, that it's all that I thought
but magnetic attraction, surely we ought

For man and woman, if appeal is so strong
The love is forever, and romance is long

Finding this vision, the beauty that's you
Hope for the future, a love that is true

My search has ended, on this fateful night
If you, my lovely, find me also right

Tell me your feelings, and all about you
And I'll share my heart, and my passions too

Larry Reed

Not Forgotten with Time

A pat on the back
A hug so tight
A kiss on the cheek before bed each night
Things not forgotten with time
Green, green grass of home
Swing low sweet chariot
To his kids he would sing
Plus the ol' rugged cross
Things not forgotten with time
Two horses, a wagon, and him at the reigns
For picnic we'd go on a bright sunny day
More of the things not forgotten with time
On the ground you would fall
Filled with laughter
When his eyes he gave a roll
Things not forgotten at all
In the corner of my mind
In treasured boxes
Are the memories of my father
Whom my love for is timeless

Laurene Bocklage

Innocent Infant

Asleep in my arms, I hold a child
Its breaths so silent, so fragile and mild.
It lays there so still and has no worries
Just living unknowing—never in any hurries.
Its body so small, so soft and new
All others gather to admire the hue.
Oh, how I'd love to be in its place
Doing its own things, yet, forever embraced.
So innocent to evil—not knowing what's wrong
Susceptible but immune—weak, yet, so strong.

Daniel L. Frank

A Magician's Act

Pain emanates from my aura
An overwhelming response to closure.
You will never see the magician again—
No more rabbits or hearts or tears.

There's a ceiling to this hat.
What was black and empty
Can no longer fill with hope or agony.
I pulled a joker out once.

All tricks aside, turn to the acts.
Did they entertain everyone or just you?
I still have that magic touch.
Without my hat I am nothing though.

Nothing will transform me into freedom.
Even the rabbit can't run free now.
I set aside my top hat and wand,
What will you give me for them?

Elisa Lowin

My Fall

It is cool . . . It is quiet . . . Up above, looking down . . .
floating high there's no fool, there's no riot . . .
there's no frown . . .
only zero gravity for an instant . . . then I fall . . .
can no longer fight it . . . can no longer stall . . .
It's exhilarating . . . the feeling's fascinating . . .
The air cushions my form . . .
the sound surrounds me . . . a storm . . .
closer the ground approaches, and I—
I begin to realize . . .
my journey will soon be over—
my purpose has not been filled,
but soon it will as I fall to the ground . . .
my form splattered, with nothing but a light sound . . .
but my fall was not in vain . . . for you see . . .
I am a drop of rain.

Buchele Zipfel

The Value of Togetherness

Thinking back to the day,
when you first realized life was a maze.
Nothing is easy, there is always a task.
You look to the sky as if to ask,
"Is there a way for all to shine through?"
I don't know, but I do need you.
Life tests & retests, dragging you down.
Unanswered questions with not even a sound.
One thing is true, you can't be alone.
You must find someone to help carry the load.
This is why we must start to see,
that we'll always survive if it's you and me.
Two of a kind, beginning to share
one life together without any other care.

Aaron Shepard

As You Enter

As you enter, the room fills then sways
with an astonishing presence.
Silver lights flash and flicker in the
corners of all these eyes as
they are cast upon you.
You are the catalyst, the cause and the effect,
what makes the potential become the reality.
There is this cascading energy
and it pours forth from the deepest recesses
of who you are, who we are.
It pours forth and fills
this empty void of man with its tenacity
with its doggedness.
It teaches the meek of heart
to do what is genuine, what is innate,
what is right.
You are the champion,
inspiration is your weapon of choice,
in this, your righteous crusade to save
humanity from existing without living.

Valerie Rizzocascio

I Love You Mom

A mother is someone you cherish
From morning 'til the sun goes down
She takes away your rainy days
And makes you smile instead of frown

She'll always love you through and through
And help you through the bad times too
She's like an angel sent from Heaven
To make your home a sound, sweet haven

I will love her always and forevermore
Until the sweet homecoming of the Lord
When I will cease to see the tears
That my mom has shed for many years

There never will be pain in that blessed place
My mom will always have a smile on her face
The same smile she gave me over and over again
Except now we'll share it together as friends

Rita Perez

Imagine

Mr. Pruslin, my mom, my dad, my sister em, and Grammy the memories
There were restless nights and cutting teeth,
midnight feeding, how I needed sleep!
The very first step, the wonderful hugs,
the precious smiles, the mess on the rugs.
Hearing mommy or daddy for the first time,
to look in their eyes and see how they shine.
The very first birthday and each one after,
to watch their faces and hear their laughter.
The first bicycle ride, the skinned up knees,
to watch them as they climbed the trees.
The first school day, we're both scared to death,
holding hands and taking a deep breath.
All the games where my daughter would cheer,
my sons on the field in their football gear.
To see them learn and watch them grow,
trying to answer the questions, for things they don't know.
All the good times and all of the bad,
seeing them happy and seeing them sad.
Being there for them when push comes to shove,
always giving to them, my never ending love.
My Children mean the world to me,
I'll always treasure these memories.

Barbara Wilson

Anything Goes Away

What do you do if I turn to you,
Reflecting your rejections?
Man in the street and old wives tailed,
They see your own imperfections.
What if you turned to the lump in your bed,
And it's the lump in your own parched throat. . . .
And all that ever seemed of substance to you
Was only ever less than air and bloat?

Words are words, and I am I,
And only one will never die.
When flesh is forever falling,
It doesn't matter for the lie.

Everything dies
and anything goes.
Where I will stop,
Nobody knows.

Katie Kimberly

Advice from the Angels

Be still about most things,
take your life in stride,
and always show grace
for God is at your side.
Don't speak of your endeavors,
your eager heart's delight,
but let your light so shine
in the darkest of nights.
Keep your children well and warm,
your husband in your heart,
for they are souls that need you there
to give their lives a start.
No matter how low you feel depreciated,
depressed and unequal,
have faith and understand
that you are a special part of a greater plan.
So, hold up your chin
get serious and dig in.
I know you're there, somewhere in there,
come on out and be your friend.

Christina Dyson

The New Pair of Shoes

Minnie was telling the good news
She bought a new pair of shoes
They are black and have a satin bow
They're imported, you know!

They're expensive, she said with pride
Made of costly buffalo hide
Look how they shines
Under the beautiful morning sun.

The children came out to play
And ran and jumped along the way
The boys climbed trees and hopped and jogged
While girls ran after a little green frog

They giggled and laughed for such great fun
They joyfully danced under the sun
They jumped and hopped and ran uphill
And looked for a thousand thrill

But little Minnie is so sad
She couldn't walk, her feet felt bad
The shoes that she had shown with pride
Caused all her pain and she cried.

Haydee Lasco

Last Dance

The nights of passion will never let me go.
Never let me forget our love.
I still feel you against me.
Heart racing, sweat.
Making love every time like it would
be our last.
Little did I know that there really would
be a last time.

Alese Mckinstry

True Reflections

When you get what you want in your struggle for self,
Taking all, and leaving little along the way,
Just go to the mirror and look at yourself
And see what your reflection has to say.
For it isn't your father or mother you'll see,
Whose judgment you must pass.
The person whose opinion counts most in your life
Is the one looking back in the glass.
You'll play the game, and fool many,
and think you've gotten by.
But the reflection in the glass is the true test
If you can't look that person in the eye.
For that reflection will be with you always,
it will stay 'til the very end
And you've passed the most difficult test of your life,
If that person in the mirror is your friend.
You may fool the world down your pathway of years,
And get compliments and praise as you pass.
But your final reward will be sadness and tears,
If you've cheated the reflection in the glass.

Beverly Cook

ME!

Written for my little brother

I am a leader not a follower
I will behave myself and not be rude
I will listen to my teachers and not my friends
I am a leader not a follower
I will not annoy people for them to annoy me
Therefore, I am a leader not a follower
I am not someone who wants to be treated badly
I am a person who wants to be treated nicely
I want people to be my friend
Therefore, I will behave myself, 'cause I am a leader not a follower

Shushawna P. Tam (Age 10)

What Is Love?

What is Love?
It is what I tried so hard to make it be.
It disguised itself and pretended to enter me.

What is Love?
Something too easy to say and very hard to attain.
What is Love? And why did it become so vain?

I realize that Love is only sacrifice,
not feelings, not words, and it has no sound.
Love is pure, it is deep,
and always on the creep.
I pray it will open its heart so that I may sleep.

It makes us surrender the mind,
only to be suspended in time
awaiting its arrival!

Milan Stingily

Texas Roads

With big high Stetsons and shiny boots,
Texas Bears were lyin' in wait.
As night rolled in with wind at their backs,
big rigs rolled headin' dead on straight.

The parade grew as the rigs roared on
or white line fever would slow the loads.
Some twenty CB's crackled to life,
a driver or two wanted off the road.

In the coal black dark of a Texas night,
Bears were waitin' with trucks in their sight.
In the median sittin' ever so quiet,
they got the drivers dead to rights.

All of a sudden with complete surprise,
tough ol' drivers got tears in their eyes.
"Do me a favor, stroll easy down the road,
a truck rolled over with a big, heavy load."

The CB suddenly got awful darned quiet
as the parade so somberly passed.
For one more trucker in the silent night,
that big heavy load would be the last.

Ellyn Kossiski

The Clown Speaks

"Make me laugh," said the man to the clown.
And if I fail, if you still frown?
What if my life wasn't just to satisfy you,
then, sad man, what would you do?
"Please, all you do is bring joy
and smiles. You are a walking toy.
There is nothing else for you to be
if you didn't make a fool of you, for me."
I am more than a red nose;
I am a man behind these clothes.
Can you not see,
that this is not all of me?
"You tell such a good joke!"
But that was truth I spoke!
Now they're content,
laughing at the life I've spent,
and this makeup hides my frown
for someone else needs me, the clown.

Douglas Sullivan

The Rising Sun

From the outside looking in,
You wonder where the world had been,
What has happened since I've been gone?
Have the days just gone on and on?
Does the sun still shine clear bright?
Does the moon still glow at night?
Do people still just live their lives,
From day to day without demise?
I thought the world might just stand still,
While I was sick and feeling ill.
But no time did not stop for me.
It just went on,
Like normal,
As you please.
So when finally recovered,
I had to run,
To catch up with,
The rising sun.

Holly Walsh

Enveloped in the Night

The time of day between sun and moon,
When twilight rises, bespeaking doom,
The time when neither dark nor light,
when evil stalks and good takes flight.

The moon in solemn eerie glow,
Another world, begins to show.
Another place, another land
Where those that dance the shadows stand,

Those that walk the shadows freely,
Enveloped in the night completely,
Watching from the shadows dark,
Waiting for the perfect mark.

But there is one that mortal be,
Who walks the twilight incessantly,
Lured by how the darkness sings,
She courts the night, and all it brings.

She tempts the fates, and in her way,
Lures the darkness, come what may,
Resigned to walk the shadows freely,
Enveloped in the night completely.

Jeannette Doyle

Are Our Dreams Not to Come?

As we all grew,
we started to build interests in things.
We dreamt about the things
that we would want to do.
These dreams
still live with us where ever we go.
But the future
is not what we had anticipated.
Death is soon to come!
Comets, fire, and war will be some reasons of man's extinction.
If this were to happen
what will the dreamers do?
What about the dreams?
Will they lead to death?
What about our lives?
Will we still have fun?
Only time will tell.
Right now all there is to do is sit . . . wait . . . and dream.

Keoni Mahelona

A Love that Cannot Be Known

The world is meaningless today,
not only cold and lonely, but gray.
I speak to you wilderness, and to no one more,
for I wish to cause no sore.
Keep the secret which contains my all,
and protect me from my fall.
I await in this darkness for my love,
who is much more precious than your doves.
These moments I cherish with great desire,
to tell you otherwise, I'd be a liar.
Her beauty shines brightly in the dark blue sky,
to catch a glimpse of her, is to happily die;
sadly I must respect and admit, that her love I am not,
for another has captured her thoughts.
A mask I wear to hide the reality,
for a decision I have made with no partiality.
Time ceases to exist with each glance that I take,
yet the night swiftly leaves as if its life were at stake.
Hush! Hush! And utter no words of your own,
for this is a love that cannot be known.

Ishmael Pessoa

Should It Really Matter

Should it matter if I'm Black or White, Yellow, Brown or Red.

Should it matter if I'm Filthy Rich or Beggarly instead.

Should it matter if my hair is long or braid with beads so tight.

Should it matter if I say pro-choice and you say life is right.

Should it really matter?

To some it matters plenty
To others not a bit,
To those of you who read this,
Here's how to handle it.

Accept me for who and what I am, the same for you I'll do.
For judgement's cast by only one, and neither me nor you.

Juan Requena, Jr.

Breaking Up

The end is so cold and final.
I love you are words of the past.
He's found someone to take my place;
Once first, now I am last.
I'll try to forget him, I promise I will.
Give me time; that's all I need,
To wipe my tears, close my eyes,
To forget his love and this need.
But how, tell me how, can I forget those kisses?
Or the warm embraces we shared?
Or the songs we sang when we were happy?
Or the fun we had being paired?
I can't forget, I won't forget.
All I must do is pray. . . .
To try to forgive him for what he's done.
Then THAT will be my day!

Linda Summers

Angel's Wings

On angel's wings I fly to you,
so innocent and sweet . . . .
everything anew.
Your baby's breath flows across my face . . . .
As I watch you dream of a faraway place.
Please don't feel alone my little one . . . .
for on Angel's wings every night I shall come.
To rock you in my arms . . . .
To dry your tears . . . .
To watch you grow ever more beautiful
with the passing years.

Christine Norris

Battle for Gold

yesterday I saw no sunshine in your eyes
only dark and gloomy green orbs of forboding
desperation has taken his toll on your soul
where the love no longer resides
what took away the light of the knight
his armor always so shiny and bold
for his damsel is no longer his
in his quest for his gold
he lost her
desire and no longer his
for he lingered far to long at the battle within
tomorrow will bring a new battle for him
but will it be worth fighting for he no longer has her
hair of gold
to wrap his heart in when he is home
is the battle within so strong that he lost sight of the gold

Leslie Blume

To Have Known You When . . .

To have known you when . . .
youthful innocence gave forth the chase
and Pandora's box held fast its key,
when all was fair on love's frontier
and gentlemen did court their lady fair,
to have met you under a tropic moon
and gazed upon Heavens unbeknownst,
to have stumbled upon you on mountain top
and breathed the air pure and clean,
to have danced the dance long ago
as Juliet and her Romeo,
to have been the princess to the prince
before the dragon snarled its teeth,
to ride with you along the shore
against the wind to something more,
But, to meet you on this crowded street
seems to diverge so vast a path. . . .

Kimberly Jebb

Silent Compassion

The compassion that brings me to my knees.
The tears I shed, but few will see,
For those who were slain for no reason.
Innocent lives stolen with no meaning.
To say it was their time to reunite with the Light
Is no consolation to those left behind.
I feel the sorrow and the pain;
My tears flow freely, masked by the rain.

The compassion that brings me to my knees.
The tears I shed, but few will see.
The anger and hatred of those who acted.
Their own suffering is not contrasted
By the reality that slaps my face—
Are we evolved, we in this place?
If everyone here could just understand,
We're truly the same—woman, child, and man.

The compassion that brings the world to its knees,
Shed the tears for all to see.

Deb Randolph

Only Him

My love is strange and true, only to him.
Not to be mistaken by anything.
It seems as though his heart is dark and dim,
But my heart is bright and ready to sing.
I know deep down inside his love is true,
Even though he doesn't show it, it's there.
When he is not around, I feel so blue,
So I think of when he plays with my hair.
I don't understand how he cannot care,
Unless he is just hiding everything.
He is so sweet but it is often rare.
It feels as though I'm not his only fling.
I hope that in time he will come to see,
That his love really means so much me!

Lydia Stolfi

A Spirit's Wish

As the sun embraces Mother Earth,
And the moon consoles her through the night,
As the eagle keeps close guard,
So does my spirit reach out to you.

For I am adrift in the clouds,
As the sun, I wish to embrace you.
As the moon, I wish to uplift you.
As the eagle, I wish to keep you safe.

Soon my friend, my love,
We will share a life together,
Share what sun, moon, and eagle have shown us.
Walk the path that is offered to us.

Jean A. Knox

Forbidden Room

The darkness lingers, throughout the world.
Along with the cries and screams for help.
No one will forget the shrill sound of hell.
For it's indented in our minds, can't you tell?

You see, they entered into the forbidden room,
Which was a guarantee of forbidden doom.
They were told the truth, but chose not to believe.
Because of that choice, the whole world must grieve.

They went into the forbidden room which was filled with hate.
It was a room that once you went in;
The old you was never to be seen again.
The deadly substance spread over the world like an eerie mist.
And now,

The darkness lingers, throughout the world.
Along with the cries and screams for help.

Kerri Greene

Why

Why is it every time I dream it is you I see
Why is it that every time I think eternity
I think of you and me
Why was the one time I ever cried was when
you walked out of my life
Why is it I feel you are to be my wife
Can you tell me why
Why is it when ever I let my mind wander
It goes right to you
Why is it when ever we are apart I feel blue
Why do you have the key to my heart
Why are there people trying to keep us apart
Can you tell me why
I can tell you why
You are an angelic goddess
Who makes the cutest of the cute jealous
Your eye's sparkle like waters of a lake
Your smile keeps my wake
Your voice is like a chorus from above
It is only you I love
That is why.

Justin Robinson

My Mother

My mother has been the most wonderful person in my life.
Yes, I mean that. Can you believe?

Mother cares for us before anyone else.
Only she is there for you and for me, of course.
Thank you for my life and for the courage you have given me.
How can I describe a mother who is bigger than life . . .
Enormous amounts of thought have been written about her . . .
Restless minds will continue to do so!

Because a flower beneath the thorn
Always hides the beauty within.
I'm sorry if you thought I was talking only about MY mother.
Pardon me, but I'm not . . .
I am talking about everyone's mother, of course

It's very sad to say,
I believe in God, and yet I have never seen him.
All my prayers go to him without question,
And yet—the only person I can count on is my mother.
Dear God, although I have never seen you,
I ask you to always keep her well . . .
And to all mothers everywhere.

Victor Chavez

Beyond Reason

they take from you what is rightfully yours
Without thought.
Without reason.
Tearing away the innocence.
Causing grief.
Causing strife.
Causing pain.
Do you fight it?
Do you take it?
Its cruel intentions?
Do they care?
No, why should they,
They don't even know you!

Justin Maijala

Joey

I've been hurt many times
My heart has been broken a dozen of times
I say to myself I never want to love again
My heart aches and my mind explores
I search and search but I never find
I look for men but find little boys
When I say you my heart drooped and my eyes opened
I seen love
My pain is gone my search is over
I found an angel so beautiful and so kind
An angel that will not waste my time
My heart no longer aches and my mind no longer explores
We share wonderful nights together
we share wonderful Kisses
We mostly share wonderful love
I give you something money can't buy
I give you my world
I give you my soul

Kathleen Joe

Good-bye

I walk through the halls of the mortuary
Tears falling from my eyes
The loneliness is starting to hit me
I feel your presence is alive floating over me

The room has grown darker
I can feel you leading me to your body
The man pulls the sheet from over you head
I turned my head instantly away
I cannot see your face
I fear that I will have lost you forever . . . but I look at you,
You look so peaceful at that moment

I hear the whisper of you voice saying,
"I love you; I will always love you."
Then I feel your presence relieve itself from existence . . .
All I say is good-bye.

Melissa Keller

Me Forever You

I won't leave your side
No matter how much you hide

I won't judge your decisions
Or blind you from your visions

I'll do whatever it takes
To set you at ease from all of your mistakes

I would never let you down
Or cause you to frown

I'll love you for you
So don't ever feel blue

I'll always be your friend
Our friendship will never end

Crystal Layne

Reflection

As I stare at my reflection, haunted by what I see,
I second guess myself and all I know is "me."
Staring at a person, it seems I never knew,
Glancing back into the past
There's so much that I've been through.
Tears slowly show, as I soon realize what's true
I'm so lost, so far from all I knew.
I touch the glass, reaching for what's real
and coming back empty handed,
Cold is all I feel.
Looking through the glass
A stranger staring back,
Eyes clouded with confusion, recognition's what I lack.
It seems now that all my life
I've been just another person on the outside looking in.
And as I stare at my reflection
so haunted by what I see,
I second guess myself and all I thought I knew was me.

Alyson Fawley

The Thoughts that Run through My Head

Sometimes I sit and lie awake thinking
about nothing and something all at the same time
I wonder what I am thinking but can't even tell myself
I wonder of this and I reflect on that
I don't know why I am thinking
Just that I am
And don't know where I am in my thoughts
I just know that I am thinking.
Like I am in a far off galaxy
But have no clue how, why, or when I got there
Just that it makes sense to me for an unknown reason
Because it is where I am
Doing what I am doing
Although I don't know why
I think I understand
My mind takes over, my body, soul, and hand!

Jason Moser

End of the World

Where will it all be when nothing is there?
What will we all see?
Will we even be aware?
Where will loved ones go?
Will our hearts still overflow?
Will life be there in a different air?
Will our hearts still break with despair?

In this nothingness which we cannot see,
will nothing be the meaning of life?
It cannot be!

The truth is that come one day
the world will end,
and we will have no say.

No election will stop the flow,
No dictator will rule it so!
The world will end.
Where will you be,
In darkness, light or eternity?

Nkechinyere Okereke

My Love

To My Husband David
My love for you is like a rose blossoming in the spring.
Always young, never old.
I'd never leave you out in the cold.
My love for you will never die,
it soars way up high in the sky.
I know I've told you this before,
but I wish to say it once more . . .
I LOVE YOU!

Christine Parish

Innocence and Adversity

It was a product of our innocence and adversity
born from a war; blood, sweat, and tears.
We fought and we toiled
for months and for years
against our predecessors, forefathers
and even our peers.
In a revolution they said could not be won,
but we would not let them take us.
We stood strong
against the unbelievers that sought
to take us to their Hell, homework and chores.
In the end, we stood above the rest
and shouted out to the lawmakers
and even our peers
See Us! Unworthy ones
rise above our fears.
For this is our tree house
our blood, sweat, and tear;
innocence and adversity
for months and for years.

Scott Strain

Are You Ready?

The unknown answer to the most asked question is when
Jesus is coming again
Are you ready for His coming?
Are you ready for the Lord?
Are you ready for your Judgement Day?
If not it's not too late
Just kneel down and pray
Come into my life, please, Lord
The sins You bore on the Cross were mine
Stay with me, dear Lord
I want to be Your child
Walk with me, dear Lord
Every step that I take will be
Steps to bring You closer to me
I now kneel down and pray
Come into my life today
Are you ready for His coming?
Are you ready for the Lord?
Are you ready for your Judgement Day?
Oh, Yes, you now can say
I've asked Jesus into my life today

Tami Rice Olson

Codependence

Only a few are lucky enough to find a pure heart beating
soft and regular.
I've seen it drink in blood like sweet old wine,
soak up anything raw and tingling,
even if that feeling it feels is the
nervous energy of hurt.

It is these cracked mirrors
through which this heart sees itself
so that its fake imperfection is more acceptable than
the beautiful dream it really is.

So for my own sake I will never look on it again,
for there is a hell,
not of fire and brimstone,
nor undisclosed wickedness,

but the hell of watching
my one pure treasure fly
towards Heaven
on broken wings.

Lori Pendleton

In Time

In time you will be a memory owned by past,
because everything nor anything ever lasts.
In time you will be a grain among the dirt,
because every things' home is Mother Earth.
In time you will be of the winds whispers,
and of silences many listeners.
In time you will be consumed in the dark,
and in need of the mornings spark.
In time you will be forgotten like the clouds,
whisked away without any sounds.
In time you will be one of the lost mysteries
wasted away like the beloved seas.
In time you in a sense become time,
and fade back like the summer tide.
In time you will be forever lost,
but in the present forever found!

Chad McAuliffe

Automotive Love

Shall I compare thee to a '69 Corvair? Thou art more fair.
But as for a '57 Chevy, thou doth not even compare.
Being with you lets me love you, oh, so more and more,
but I'd rather ride my Harley and listen to it roar.
I love all my cars, especially my Corvette,
and I'd rather be with it than with a blonde or brunette.
You can pose next to my baby in a polka dot bikini,
but you're not allowed to touch my yellow Lamborghini.
You can sit in the back seat or watch from afar,
as I drag race my hot, V-8 brand-new, convertible car.

Justin Hibbard

I'd Rather Be Fat

Your views
have been squeezed into my brain
until they are melded, and melting
my intelligence, blocking my creativity.
Go jump in the lake!
And take your fat free, washboard stomach,
no pain no gain,
exercise machine worshipping lives
and get the hell out of mine.
The world would rather be
fat
than severely depressed
from you shoving your buns of steel
in our faces.
I will someday
tie up a diet guru
and force feed him blocks of cheese
chocolate bars
whole milk
and Fritos.

Mandy Marchani

Through This Rain

As this rain gently beats down upon my window.
One thought passes through my mind,
why can't you be here?
To see words, wishing it was your eyes
I would look into every morning.
Standing, gazing through this rain
I see the last rose of summer
which is saved in my heart for you.
Wind and rain could never break it.
Protected, I will block all that threaten it,
sacrifice body and soul.
Images of you are twisting my thoughts apart.
Drawing portraits of a shining smile I have never seen.
Let me dream of you tonight, for right now it is all I have.
This rain is still falling, and somehow I hope it never ends.

Richard Pinel

Slice of Life

Sounds I heard while sitting in a flat in Manhattan
As twilight fades to unfamiliar darkness,
piercing noises radiate like tiny sound bites
from a comfortable yet foreign symphony.
Masses of concrete and metal embrace cacophony
like a mother fearful of
loosening her grip on her beloved son.
Dull but ample light pierces the clear stage of reality,
while mumbled voices lend a comforting,
relaxing glow of yesteryear:
a hot, sun-filled afternoon at the neighborhood diamond.
With this, the heavy thud of metal similar to
that of a twenty-pound pipe
dropped on concrete rings through your ears.
Then, without warning,
the edgy, urgent whine of mobile hospitals
smother your thoughts for a brief yet endless minute.

Paul Van Schaick

Valentine

Girl you know it's true,
My Favorite, is no one, but you.
No matter what it takes,
Or how the world shakes.
You will always have a Special part,
Somewhere in my HEART.
Which will always remind me of you,
And give me a reason to come back to you.
Girl, your company is simply the best,
That's why you are special, and not the rest.
Even though you've irritated me a lot,
And sometimes made me real hot.
But one thing has always fascinated me,
Your Natural ability to understand me.
So even if I'm in LOVE with you or Not,
There's something you've got.
Which asks me to stay,
And compels me to say,
Those even if it takes a long, long TIME,
My Future wants you to be my VALENTINE.

Raj Kasthuri

Why Do People Go?

Why do people go away?
Why do people leave?
Why do they say good-bye?
Why is it always hard for us
When people go away?
Why do people go away?

Why do people go away,
When they really want to stay?
Why, oh, why do people have to say good-bye,
When it's always hard to go?
Why do people go?

Why do people die,
When you really wish that person would stay?
Instead of saying good-bye for one last time,
Why do people die?
Why? Why? Why?
Why do people say good-bye?
I wonder why, oh, why?

Kayla Wright

The Kitten

The tiny kitten sat all alone
Quietly sitting all day at home
It sat cautiously, looking around
Waiting and waiting for love to be found
It is a tiny kitten and you should see
How very scared it can be
It may become playful, but then scratches and backs away
Making people hurt, downhearted and gray
It is very sensitive and sometimes quite shy
One little remark can make it cry
People remark on how it appears
Adding and adding to the kitten's fears
It goes to one friend who loves it dearly
This one friend helps the kitten see clearly
It longs for this friend to cuddle it so
But it is afraid, of what I don't know

Julieann DeMeo

Thank You

Who is that child so young I see afar
His clothes so big, his shoes untied and old,
He stands a glow, so bright, a shining star.
Awaiting plans he'll carry out so bold.

The plan he hears, his eyes begin to glow
Then with a start he hangs his head with tears.
How will his family take the painful blow?
He wipes his eyes in thanks for his twelve years.

He watched in pain, his parents leave the house
And walked with hesitation by his Sis.
Cold Chain! He hangs as quiet as a mouse
His final thought, he hopes that he'll be missed.

Give thanks each day for all that's to you
For it may be today that you will lose.

Anne Holmes

Worshipping an Outsider's Life

What a design, what an existence
and the amazing visions of ecstasy
with the compassion inside
the division of radiant moonlight
that brings us together as one in time.

The anxieties and emotions of undetermined signs
brings forth unsteady sadness
the fire within the eternal eyes
gaze upon the infancy of a new birth at once.

It's that innocent and satin bond,
that sent this rush into my peaceful silence,
completely devouring my crystallized serenity.

Every breath of immaculate atmosphere seized my soul,
the vows you sacrifice lie across
the fulfillment you have revealed
that designed my existence.

Marie Korschot

Horses!

I hear a horse neigh,
Give him some hay,
And say,
"I'm going to ride you today!"
But before I do,
I have to clean his stall,
I have to clean it all!
But I don't mind
Because someone has to do it.
When I'm done I'll take out my grooming kit,
Hoof pick, curry, dandy brush, finishing brush;
Now I'll get out all my stuff;
Saddle, girth, bridle,
All my tack,
I put it on my horse
So I can go out and hack!

Jackie Humen

"My Mother's Hands"

My Mother's hands are special; they're always on the run.
They're hardly ever idle, because there's always a job that needs done.
She's even used her hands for entertaining my son.
They are never too busy for picking up a fishing pole;
he says, "G.G.," and she says, "Let's go."
She paints and sews and polishes and creates things so neat!
She's even had to use them for rubbing lotion on my dehydrated feet.
She's soothed my fevered brow with just that special touch.
I never will forget that Mama cared so much!
She's led me down a hospital corridor and pointed out to me,
people who were dying and couldn't use their feet.
I didn't want to walk that day, but she knew I had to move.
If not for Mother's hands, the battle I would lose.
She pushed and gently prodded me and worried in her heart
that I certainly could have died that day and we would have to part.
I love my mother, oh, can you see just how much she means to me?
Someday I'll look back and never will forget,
how much her hands have done for me; she's never failed me yet.

Donna Zabodyn

Picture of My Soul

I am a gaping hole in space,
Looking for a purpose.
Empty . . . I grieve
Ripped open like a letter with no words to express . . . I grieve.
Separated from happiness like an orphan . . . I grieve.
Deceived by my own facade and blind to my own reality . . . I grieve.
Surrounded by bars of despair . . . I grieve.
Locked away by defeat . . . I grieve.
Fallen to my knees in abandonment and lost hope . . . I grieve.
Tears drain my faith, leaving me dry to suffer the drought of my
cracking heart alone . . . I grieve.
Powerless in the cell I now inhabit . . . I grieve.
No cries,
No wails,
Only silent screams . . . I grieve.
No door,
No window,
No way out.
Trapped . . . I grieve.
Self pity puts me to sleep.
I grieve.

Dwight Braswell

Grave Yard Beauty

Droplets of water fall on the petals of the roses
I brought to sit on your grave.
The beautiful sun rises over the cemetery gates,
I wish I didn't have to see it here.
If only you could see the beautiful colors.

As I try to hold back the tears, I close my eyes
and right away the smell of beautiful lilacs takes over my senses.
The memories come back like the smell of the lilacs,
they invade my mind, but only for a second.

As I open my eyes and realize I've been here for days,
it seems like, telling you of my life.
As I try to tear myself away, I feel a single tear roll down my face.
I try not to cry, but it's so hard,
knowing that you are buried
underneath the beautiful soil of mother Earth.

As I sit in my car, I brush the tears away
and pray to God to keep you safe
'til next week when I come back here again.

Andrea Jo Kurtz

Her Love

The morning dew covers the earth as His love covers you
Through the summer breeze in that golden field He whispers through
He is your eyes when the fog grows thick and covers the light
He is that dream that speaks to you and wakes you in the night
Though the waves will crash, they soon will recede
He is there filling your heart, every breath, every need
The true love you wait for is there in His grace
I can see you love Him, it's in your smile, it's on your face
Through every passing second and each fallen rain drop He is there
He is the wind that's unseen, the wind that brushes through your hair
Every leaf on every tree rustles out the sound of His name
The ocean's tides come and go, but His love will remain the same
The sun will set and the stars will shine, a picture in the night sky
I seek His love, for His glory I praise, for His mercy I cry

J. L. Scott

A Friend

Sometimes I feel as though the moon rushes over me
like the waves of the sea.
Sometimes I think that the wind is whispering like the purring of a cat.
And sometimes I feel as though the sun is looking down at me
like the Great Apollo.
And sometimes the stars twinkle over me bye and bye as the
Great Isis guides me.
But mostly when I see the serene sky, I see you my friend—
it is you that brings light to my eyes.
And it is you who dries the raindrops that leak from the ceiling in the sky.
It is you that lends me through the chaos of thunder.
And it is you who smooths the rockiest mountains as I climb over.
It is only you who lay me asunder on my bed of flowers.
And it is you who brings my eyes too see and to wonder.

Elizabeth Kuca

Lost Dreams

The lasting light fades ever so slow,
The wind carries away the only dreams that you know,
You enter a gate the fee is your pride,
And all is lost but your will to survive,
You walk down a path that is new and unknown,
Nervous tension fills the air as you walk all alone,
For a split second there is a break in the dark that is gloom,
What flashes are the dreams you once knew and consumed,
You press on now with hope that your dreams flash again,
So next time you'll hold them until the very end, The moral of this is hold on don't let
go, to dreams and hope when that's all that you know.

Bernis S. Hoskin

The Hole I'm In . . .

Why can't they see me in the hole I'm in . . .
Why can't they hear me in the hole I'm in . . .
I did not get here on my own,
he puts me here while he sits on his throne . . .
I tried to leave, I tried to run away
but it doesn't work, I think I'm here to stay . . .
How will I get there from the hole I'm in,
how do I start from the hole I'm in . . .
I live by his rules unable to speak,
bound by his power or a slap on the cheek . . .
what do I tell them from the hole I'm in,
How do I show them from the hole I'm in . . .
Courage would get me out of this hell
but what would he do if I were to rebel . . .
How do I breathe in the hole I'm in,
How do I move in the hole I'm in,
I've said so much to him but only in my mind,
to believe that he's faithful I'd have to be blind . . .
So I'll probably grow old in the hole I'm in . . . In the hole I'm in. . . .

Lydia Lafollette

Deaf and Brilliant

Dedicated to my daughter, Ericka N. Brown
Deaf and brilliant,
Deaf and brilliant;
not dumb,
as the illiteracy,
Of some.
She hears with her eyes,
and sees with her mind.
It's the world around her
that's deaf and blind!
Deaf and blind
to the true achievements
and accomplishments
of the deaf!

Mary Brown

Bliss

You once held me 'til morning's light
We'd loved each other through the night.
Our passion ardor burning need
Had brought a rapture from the seed.
We loved until the tides rose high
And morning's dawn had filled the sky.
We loved through out Eternity
We loved forever you and me.

Normandie Ducharme

Opportunity

Opportunity knocks,
And she waits for my answer.
I sit down and think,
Weigh out the possibilities,
But when I answer the door,
She's gone.
Then I sit and contemplate
Thinking of what might have happened
If I had just opened the door.

Sheri Lawson

Oleaginous

Oozing Latin,
you smirk through
my pores.
Falsity with class,
you remind me of
a maternal voice
which says,
"Olive oil is good for
YOU."
She became so vexed
When I saturated
my veins.

Jaime Mathis

A Poem for Julia

Remember I love you,
in case we should fight.

A lot more than a little,
and bark worse than I bite.

So in case we should argue,
in case we should fight—

Remember to forgive me,
and kiss me good night!

Todd Schlichter

My Life

The tears fill up inside as I gaze into the deep sky which is never ending.
I feel trapped.
Not knowing what to do or where to go.
I'm trapped forever in this body that is never normal.
I am alone,
having dreams that are a message in a different language,
not knowing what they mean only that they are a sign to me.
My life is like a road which circles, circles, circles . . .
I am crying out, but I have no voice.
There is nothing I can do.
I am not worried,
because I know one day I will be happy once more.

    Norah Stevens-Kittner

The Brook

Visions, Balance of Nature and Life

It traveled many miles . . . stretching longing to continue on its adventure. Although I made a ripple, it seemed quite calm. Then I saw a face . . . the face of a man . . . no it could not be. The eagle called showing a light . . . a way and flew into eternity. It curved . . . it spoke . . . I touched its sacred shores . . . dipping my feet in the water. A mist as spirits seemed to appear within the instant. Onward my body called, as endless as it appeared to have company. Its shape carved out of the mind of God . . . I can appreciate . . . I too can write, I can transform thoughts to words. Words make sentences . . . sentences make communication. The brook . . . oh, the brook . . . brook of life show me on your shore . . . show the sun so that the moon may guide my path. The Brook

    Edward, Monteiro

blooming

leaves fall, i begin to cry
speculating deep, i look for courage.
unknown or death challenge reality
today could be the last, so i fold.

the glow of yellow appears and so
do my tears.
live a broken heart or simply heal thyself.
who taught me to be so sad, i don't know.
yellow begins to fade, i cry some more.
deserted and afraid i look to the sky, the blooming clouds set me serene.

i fold, but today is not the day to fall.
for all other creatures, i live for a reason, to bloom this kingdom.
black came too soon, for i weep, cry, whine . . . gone.

    Rachel A. Perez

Nature

The beauty of the rolling hills,
Framed by white and fluffy clouds.
Big tall trees of green and gold,
In all directions red and brown.
Nature, beauty, all around us.
Onward we go, more we see.
The smell is fresh, the air is clean.
The sunlight as it shines on the deep blue water,
White caps peaking.
Boats are sailing in the ocean, as the birds soar in the sky.
In rolls another wave and on it is a youth,
tall and tan and straight in stature, planted firmly on a board, guiding it into the shore.
Through the hills and rolling mountains,
Along the coast of the vast sea,
Surrounded by beauty, mountains, oceans, and valleys deep.
All GOD made for us in just one week.

    Kelly Misner

Light

Love is light.
So beautiful and bright.
It keeps us going everyday,
Until that light goes away.
Then comes the dark,
Followed by greed.
Then returns the light,
With all of its beauty and bright,
Until that day the light goes away.

    Emilee Dinsmore

I AM

I am the one you look up to,
I am the one that you always knew.

I am the grass beneath your feet,
I am the fate you don't want to meet.

I am the thorn that's in your side,
I am the one who takes your bride.

I am the sky above your head,
I am the words yet to be said.

I am the voice yelling out to you,
I am the cause of what you do.

I am all things, good and bad, for
I am the I am and I am sad.

    Adam Vogal

One's Thoughts

I sit here and wait
as I learn to listen,
I sit here and concentrate
as my thoughts glisten.

I wonder where to start
or if life has an end,
I wonder if it comes from the heart,
or if I even should begin.

I wonder when time is right
or if life is always wrong,
I wonder if love is in sight
or if it came and gone.

Our lives come and go
if things are meant to be,
Before I will ever know,
I can only wait and see.

    Stephen Davis

Pumpkin Tears

Cry or not
time still goes by
stranded sands
of lonely deserts.
I've got the time
to feel the pain.
I'd rather cry
than watch days tire
Inside a soul
of iron.
No risk, no change.
Somewhat deranged
I watch it rain
missing your smile,
Your touch,
You.
(Pumpkin).

    Jeffrey Judson Smith

Poetry War

I try to write poetry . . .
with my blank parchment before me I grab my graphite sword and prepare to battle with
words and emotions as my armor.

The paper laughs at me, striking me with its empty stare. I look away, at a loss for words.

I run my graphite sword over the parchment, tickling the corners with the exuberance of
a child, only to be met with silence.

I pound the paper with my fists and droplets of venom pour from my wounds as I
release my fury with wild abandon, only to receive an empty stare in return.

Finally, I place a tear gently upon its surface, but it beads up as water on oil
and slips silently to the floor.

Undaunted, I madly crumple the parchment into a muddled pulpy mess,
throwing it into the trash.

Breaking my sword in two, I resolve to battle yet another day—
beaten but not defeated in my poetry war.

Kelly Denkins

Journey to Freedom

What is it I search for?
I look into the eyes of a woman in pain.
She cries for help. What do I say?
All words escape me. A shroud of darkness blankets my mind and senses. I cry for help.
A voice within speaks softly—I am here; turn to me.
Time passes—I gaze upon a man near death, his wife at his side.
I look into the mirror of my soul—I am the man, dying within. My cry pierces the dark
veil. I hear the voice within—My son look into the mirror of life. Gaze upon its beauty.
New life springs forth from this death. Come to me—I am your freedom. Take flight my
son—your time has come. Fear not, my child—I am the wind beneath you. I am Life . . .
I am Freedom.

Alan Langlois

Where Is True Love

It seems as though it were yesterday that love walked through my door,
it came and left its mark forever, I almost believed it would do more.
But as quickly as it came to me, it flew just out of reach,
too far for my grasping arms to hold, too cold for my words to teach.
Love is such a hard thing to find, it comes and goes when it pleases—
leaving nothing but broken hearts that quietly weep and cry
out in despair.
It's like a flower that one day is beautiful then the next is faded gone.
Leaving nothing but a bare stem waving in the aftershock, waiting
for something else to come along.
Oh, where is that love that each of us so desperately seek?
When one finds the answer—please, come share it with me.

Carla Durden

Thinking of You

I'm lying here,
thinking of you.
The way your baby-soft hands caressed my back today.
How I heard your heartbeat
as I lay my head on your chest.
How soft and gentle your kiss
a few evenings back
as we tongue-tangled underneath a starlit sky.
How you held me close as we swayed with an overplayed love song—old to the mind,
but new to my heart.
And when I look in your eyes,
I see the starry heavens in all its glory.
I wonder . . .
Am I ready for love again?
Am I ready to face my biggest fear—heartbreak?
Will you rip my heart to pieces?
Or will you mend it with your careful hand?

Laura Colbenson

Alone

I don't know where I am
I don't know why I am here
I wonder if they can hear me
I can hear my voice echoing
Echoing as I call your name
I am here alone
Alone with out you here
I don't know where you have gone
Please tell me where you are
I'm in this loneliness alone
This loneliness called love
I am scared of it
I cannot see where I am
I will be home soon
But I just don't know when soon is
I wish you were here
I call you name, can you hear me?
No
Where are you?
And why am I in this loneliness alone?

Ashley Dryden

Sunrise

Dedicated to my lovely wife, Leighann
the wind has brought me here
so I believe,
traveled from far away
on a warm and gentle breeze

then, as dawn approached
a magic force lured me outside
and what I witnessed
how it would change my life

the sun was rising,
but not like every other day
that very special sunrise
just swept my heart away

disseminating such warmth
like embers all aglow
a spectacular blaze
that could melt ice and snow

a light shown in the eastern sky
filled with sparkling gleam
and though I'm awake, I hope
that it wasn't just a dream

Daniel Garber

Loss—To My Wife's Memory

Unable to sleep
In the bed that we shared
I lay awake all night thinking
I am no longer paired

The pain I feel
Since you have been gone
Has not lessened
With the coming of dawn

You left too soon
So many things undone
A full life to live
A sharing of fun

She was 40 years old
And yet just a child
The sculpture unfinished
The dossier unfiled

She brought me a joy
I could never repay
Oh, Baby how I wish
For just one more day

Leonard Janes

Life

Life is growing . . . up for air and reaching for a hand to pull me out

Suddenly down again, deeper I can see no light, even deeper I go
feeling like I will explode

Fighting, Scratching, trying to call out
but, no one hears. No one sees.

Tensing and then soon giving into the coldness surrounding me

The darkness releasing me while light over comes my path and I am
carried away, floating on a cloud no longer afraid but at peace

At the merciful feet of the king, it is finished, yet I have just begun and
as I lay crumpled at his feet a calm and great release of love
overwhelms me

The understanding and compassion of my king heard my cries of
despair he lifted me up and set me at his feet.

Edith Jackson

Fire

A fire consumes the soul that has been raging for thousands of years.
A fire that has passed through many generations.
A fire that only a few could control and returned unscathed.
A fire that now runs through me.
A fire that only you can change to make your own.
A fire that only you can return from unharmed.
A fire that will change us both to make us one.
A fire that will last for eternity.

Marsha Patterson

You Can't Rain on My Parade

Today is the beginning of a new life For me.
I can see the beauty of the land that Mother Nature sculpted with her hands.

I can feel the sun on my skin, the
Breeze, as it touches me tenderly.

You can't rain on my parade.
Today is the beginning of a new life For me for to utilize all of my potentiality.

I can say No to all the negative things That surrounded my life for so long,
I can say YES to all the positive things that will nurture and enhance my Life, from this day on.

You can't rain on my parade!

Gwendolyn Adams-Evans

What Has Become of Us

If I had to depict this life with just one word, I'd say that it was strange.
That once the puzzle was complete, The pieces would rearrange;
If I had to describe the average person, I'd say that they were stressed.
That each individual had their day of feeling lonely and depressed;
Is it a game that we all play, some hide while others seek.
Do we all want to be the same, or do we want to be unique?
Is there such a thing as true forgiving, or is it confused with just forgetting?
Do we try to erase our mistakes, or just the ones that we're regretting?
When we open our eyes, what world do we see, but the one that we've created.
Is it the enemy or just ourselves that we alone have hurt and hated?
The world outside is a simple reflection of the future we have planned.
We make of life what suits us best, just so we can understand.
We seem to believe there's no way out, that we're marked with a hidden shame.
And still we look to others, for on them, we place the blame.
We all seem to believe that what we feel is right.
But so long as we don't open up, we'll never end this fight.
So keep telling yourself that Time will heal, just hang regrets upon the shelf.
But tell me what good is life, if you can't forgive yourself?

Julie Nigro

The Book of Life

He's Witty and Wise,
With Such Colorful Eyes.
Says he's a Poet,
And he certainly does show it.
But Time has been Kind,
For Wisdom and Rhyme.
With thoughts on the tongue,
From the time he was Young.
Memories are cut in his mind,
Like a knife.
But he's quite a character,
In the Book of Life.

Linda Lanning

I am a Child

I pass through the Carnival
Of colors and bright lights

I walk through the valleys
And narrow streets,
Laughing and crying
Along with the children of the streets
And the rocks and flowers of the valleys

Millions of voices call a name
Nameless, I cry and laugh
With the voices floating in the wind

I walk through the night
And into the day
Gathering bits and pieces
Of a meaning

Through the journeys
I come back to know
That I am a child
I smile as you smile
I cry as you cry
I am a child 'til I die

Murali Patibandla

A Death of Absence

Am I confined
To a blessed gaze
Concealed by her
Ruthless and subtle ways
While threatened
By a constant desire
Subjected to predictions
Of opposite attire
An interrogation filled
With a cowardly decree
A brave man dead
Found late in the evening
A permanent absence
Of general denial
With privacy provoked
In truth, all the while
Persisting the forge
Of a new investigation
Without any sign
Of truth or dedication

Ashley Burgett

Shaina

My grandpa has six children,
my mom's the oldest one.
Shaina is the baby,
and keeps you on the run.

Eyes so bright and blue,
smile so sweet and shy.
If Shaina doesn't get her way,
she'll poke you in the eye.

Whitney White

On the Edge

When I am standing in a room full of friends
But they are really just the background noise
Because I am teetering on the edge of a cliff
That I am slowly falling into
Though I refuse to jump willingly
And if my moments of clarity are all too fleeting
Suppose it is the gravity pull of the magnet at the bottom
Sometimes a voice has the determined melody to break through my thickest fog
It can capture my attention for the eternity of one small second
But the cliff with its deep darkness below changes it to mere echo
And if you chance to catch my eye what might you find in my blue gaze?
Would you know the words to an unfinished song in my head?
Or would you have to turn away from my intensity?
And I might see you standing there—still
to wonder for the briefest moment if you really existed at all
But would I be so forgettable to you?

Heather Talbott

"Tiny Little Hoof Beats"

Tiny little hoof beats echo in the sky—
if you believe in Santa Claus, reindeer really fly.
A dancin' and a prancin' to the jingle of the sleigh—
those happy little reindeer know tomorrow's Christmas Day.
Stoppin' over rooftops where the children sleep below—
tiny hoof beats touchin' down as soft as falling snow,
And down and up the chimneys Santa scurries to and fro—
down and up and down and up as fast as he can go.
And all those little children sleepin' there below—
never hear those hoof beats as soft as falling snow.
But in dreams they dream of Santa where they see him come and go, and in dreams they
hear him calling out "OH—Ho—Ho—Ho—Ho—Ho."
As tiny little hoof beats echo in the night—
tiny little hoof beats echo out of sight.

Vivian Mellon

Painful Partings

The sky grows dark and stiller grey, as my loved ones pass on saying, "So long, good-
bye" It is as though the light and life are gone from all, and only bitter shadows flicker
in the night. People say we must move on, and yet I cannot. It feels of great pain and
sorrow to leave them. So with a knot in my throat and a tear in my eye, I shall hold them
in my heart, they are so dear to me. No person may see the awesome pain and fear I feel
inside my weakening soul.

Amanda Fedie

Looking In

Grey mist rolls in the Valley,
I become lost in thought.
My mind starts spinning unwillingly
and I start to feel sold and bought.

I lose sensation of any feeling and while in the mist, I'm detached from my true being.
Doubts, worries, and fears replace love and peace. As darkness passes over me, I
freeze, I'm paralyzed by trying to release.

Only when others come to break the chains,
I become aware of my insecurities & pains.
I see how I submerge myself in my own misery, knots in my stomach & aches in my
heart. I can't understand my desire to play this part.

Stuck on the threshold at times, I look both
ways. I see the beach, or I look toward the sea. It is only when I look in my heart that
finally reveals to me the place I should be.

Jesse Placky

A Single Rose

I give to you a single rose
A symbol of my love
A graceful flower in itself
A flower touched by God

A flower that is ever so soft
Its petals reaching out
With love and affection
Beaming forth from its heart

I see a single rose for you
I see you in its grasp
Enveloping you with all its love
That love that it has cast

You are a child of God you see
He made the rose for you
He sculpted from his heart
As a gift from me to you

I prayed to God to give you love
He answered me with this
What better way to show your love
Than a single rose of His

I leave you with this wish of mine
For you I ask with love
Are we not a single rose
A single rose of love

Joann Rizzo

The Sunset

Before I go to sleep at night
I look out a window to my right.
Every night
A better sight
To see the sunset in the night.

Alana Cunningham

In Yamgata (Japan)

In Yamagata
the other side of the mountain
a reflection

of a man
he seemed withered and old
hopping, writing

on the snow
on top of the mountain Dewa
BASHO

"The winter sun—
on a snow draped slope
my frozen shadow"

Antonio Gomes

Mother's Prayer

I am so
    glad
To see the
    light
For I did
    call
To God last
    night
But for my
    babes
I must be
    here
So Father did
    send
Me right back
    home

David Wilson, Jr.

Water Lanterns

Leaves fall, decay, making weird patterns thoughtlessly
on the soil encircling still, clear waters where lanterns
of lilies are serenely reflected.
Tall and white, they stand out at this idyllic spot
strangely neglected like the boy standing alone
to see no one knows what.
Perhaps, his reflection, though he be blind?
His world is dark, but he finds delight by the waters
he ponders over lanterns that give light!
His feet in cool waters, they make ripples
interrupting the stillness of his mind's lake
that bears a burden of this world, of the cripples,
of the blind and of the lame who do not know
that he has sight to see his own feeble frame,
nor whomever come to these waters
filled with lanterns' light, bright enough to dispel darkness
of all whom wish to see their frailties exposed, quelled,
them redeemed from the world that thinks this boy is feeble or blind.
He knows, this world is blind!

Sheba Kulothungan

A Friend like No Other

Before you existed just a thought in my mind I knew you had to be mine.
So now here you are such a beautiful creature a sight for sore eyes.
If looks could kill indeed you will, for I have your back and you have mine.
Such intelligence somewhat elegant, but yet no grace.
If you could only see the expressions you bring upon your own face.
You bring such joy to me and others all the way down to your sisters and brothers.
Your presence alone brings such smiles to all our faces
no one could ever fill the places . . .
you have in our hearts, especially mine, as you lie by my side
night after night, day after day.
Where there was I there was you and a few more,
but only the ones you allowed in the door.
Just the other day I thought I saw your face so I dropped to my knees,
you gladly accepted. Never did I think I'd be decepted.
In a split second I felt like a clown as my tears hit the ground
tears of joy, now tears of pain. Or could it have been only an illusion
as stranger's eyes stared at me with such confusion?
No, I'm not crazy, I'm still sane, it is just that you both look so much the same.
I guess I was wrong, now sad for a moment, but not for long.
Now filled with such glory just to be able to tell this story.
That there's another that looks just like you, my precious jewel.
But I'm no fool, for they only a cubic zirconium never to compare again.
To my 4 leg friend, my dearest diamond.

Monique Sykes

Morning Breaks

Morning Breaks . . . my heartbeat fills the silence
Barely awake, I gently shift to face your silently breathing,
still sleeping form
I watch you, eyes closed, mouth slightly open to let the morning air in
I imagine you awake with your blue eyes sparkling and your mouth
gently curved to form a smile
I imagine caressing your cheeks and running my hands through your
blond tresses
But for now I just watch, take in your scent and let you sleep
undisturbed

I wonder what it is about you that makes you want to be with me
I wonder why you are here
I wonder, this morning, as with all other mornings you lie next to me
If I will see you again like this, still sleeping innocently nestled
in my arms
Or will this be the last for me to enjoy my time with you
Or will this be forever, together, we two

Chito Bantug

A Picnic of the Heart

No need to have a park setting,
Or a river to sit by;
You can bring out your special basket
Even if there's no blue sky.
Create the mood for your special love,
Spread the tablecloth of hope;
Eat of life the special things
Like the couple that would elope.
Set out the plates for something simple
Right on your living room floor;
Lay out the flowers and candles
For the one you do adore.
This little picnic of the heart
Is to remind you, it doesn't take much.
It's to show the love you have to give
With a very simple touch.

Christina Ingram

The Game

As I gaze into your eyes
I can see no disguise
With a drop of a tear
In your face I see fear.

Death is a game that everyone plays
It's no doubt that you'll lose
It's a fate you must choose
because you can't go on living the days.

As you take your last breathe
and jump into the sky
Surely you'll die,
If you gamble with death . . .

Unless you have a good hand.

Chad Erickson

Home . . .

Home is where the heart is—
Or so they say.
A house is not a home without love—
Or so they say.

House—four walls & a roof.
Love—a feeling of the heart.
Together—a family & a home.
Divided—a building & alone.

Susan Bottomley

Please Be Mine

Your smile awakens my soul,
As the sun awakens the day.
A kiss and my life is yours,
It seems a fair price to pay.

Your touch is soft and gentle,
As the moon glows in the night.
Hold me and win me forever,
In your arms all things are right.

Your heart is full of emotion,
As the sky is full of stars.
Love me, and we'll have harmony,
There is no greater love than ours

Jody Ho

I Wasn't Looking

I wasn't looking when I found you, with your eyes so bright and blue.
We had many good years together, enjoyed a love so real and true.
Three sons and a daughter, laughter, tears and through it all,
Your love surrounded and protected me like a high stone wall.
I wasn't looking when the years flew by, like a jet in the sky.
We had many years together, our love will never die.
I wasn't looking when I lost you, now my eyes are crying too.
Our time together was too short; how can I go on without you.
I wasn't looking at the Angels, as they took you to Heaven's door.
My tear filled eyes were looking at you, my heart was so sore.
I knew that you were leaving, going to a higher place.
Someday when we're together I'll have a smile upon my face.
I will be looking when that time comes, when again I'll be with you.
Then again I'll be smiling broadly, as I look into your eyes so blue.
All my earthly strife will be over, though I've journeyed long and far.
We will walk the shores of Heaven, and we'll dance among the stars.

Gerry Russell

A Woman's Life

With every day's dawn, brings a new beginning in life
We grow as we learn, and are strengthen by not what we know, but for whom we have become
We love and nurture, we are friend, lover, and fighter
We have gone through pain in our life that give us strength,
and hold on to that which seem so familiar
The loss of a life we hold on to, knowing that somehow it's still there, and the giving of
a life to only let it go.
And we learn that nothing is free but life itself,
and we stop and look back and we learn from our past.
With our heads held high and the strength of a woman we let go of the child that once was
We give without receiving.
We learn broken hearts mend.
That with sadness comes happiness.
When a life is lost, one is born.
And without the strength of God, we could never be.

Loretta Dellamora

Fool's Existence

I sit here thinking, my meaning being this pain I am so drinking.
In so deep as I think of what this simple life could be.
I come to this, a simple kiss upon my lips,
with such indifference to speak a simple truth.
Maybe what I need I could read within the books of wise men.
A solemn lesson. A life without intention, upon the brow I shall envision.
All I strive to see so clearly.
As if a blessing, a gentle caressing upon my troubled brow.
I'll live for love but think of no one upon this simple quest.
My time is long so I shall not linger upon this thought for too long
within this simple frame of mind.
A foot behind, a foot in time moving towards my own perceived existence.
A bright star, not so far. That may eventually be won, by so nobly of a try.
But I'll give into it my one single trick of at least giving it one last try.

Jason Kasner

Wondering

Sitting with a clouded mind wondering where life will take me.
Will it be easy or will it try to break me?
God chose a few friends to accompany me,
but very often I feel like everyone's out to get me.
Used to being alone, aside from my mom and dad,
'cause growing up I learned not to trust easily 'cause I was all I had.
In a way I'm happy I was, even though the days were long.
It taught me not to need anyone and inside made me strong.
I hope this has shed light on the mysterious life of your host,
but for now the shadows that I have earlier stepped out of consume me,
so I embrace them once more to be an enigma, better yet a ghost!

Anthony Anfiteatro

Pain's Passing

If there is darkness in your life,
Pain and sorrow, grief and strife;

Release the harshest pain
There is so much to gain.

Bury it, but not forever:
When the pain is eased, remember.

And as you look on your life now
Remember, pain always passes somehow.

Candida Winterton

Pearl Divers & Prospectors

There are millions of ways
to get lost in the desert, none
to be found, so forget the whisper
of fortunes. The southwest is
half the sea floor, and the sea
where the desert purified itself
to become the sky's mirror,
glittering not with stars but
fool's gold. Even if I owned the net
that held the water, and hauled
the whole of it on board, I would surely
drown, and once more pearls
hatch coral snakes
in the trackless, sibilant dunes.

Susan Baker

My Angel

I have spent,
Many of my days,
Praying for someone,
Who knew just what to say.
Then around the time,
I reached the age one seven,
You came into my life,
And made it identical to Heaven.
The more time,
We spend together,
The more I know,
I want to be with you forever.
I have searched for the words,
That explain how I feel.
And when you hold me in your arms,
It is almost unreal.
I guess my prayers,
Did come true.
Because I now have the angel I wanted,
And that angel is you.

Trish Williams

Many Moods of Earth

Summer storm
Winter winds
Falling leaves
Spring begins

Frozen words
Warm sweet breath
Willow leaves swaying
Cold moon over Earth's death

Fading sun
Falling stars
Night brings creatures
Oceans pause

Mountains move
Water shimmers
Ice melts
Feel the Earth quiver

Tracey Ecker

Two of Cups

Pass the flagon from the Dragon I drink with thee,
In life's circus where the rings are large we tie are barge.
The tide comes in the barge goes up, the tide goes out the barge goes down, I frown . . .
Within the barge the motions less, awareness to confess at rest because of test,
Brings forth a light which makes things right, where is the switch,
what is the hitch, we are in a barge.
The tide comes in the barge goes high a reflection from the ceiling, lets untie this barge and follow this light,
there must be some kind of meaning.
So I pass again the flagon to the Dragon then, I say to thee I see the ceiling, untie that boat and cross that mote the ground is solid here, we walk the path were stones are had my lad, I am glad . . .
We trip we fall be we stand tall, it happens to all, there is a call . . .
Again I say in my way, we passed the test now I rest, I myself have come

Dennis Engley

"Only for Two"

I love to get next to you, and see your eyes glimmer.
Bright sunshine, let it rain, blue moon in my path.
Flowers blooms in the evening, in the shadows of trees,
we lie together in harmony with all around us.
Crickets and owls take their turns next to flowers in bloom,
in shadows of trees we lie.
Twigs and long stem branches,
swing little birds, in the break of dawn.
I see the sky, I turn to you kissing gently your bare shoulders.
slowly I remove petals in your hair of wild flowers broken in the mist.
I fill a basket of those sweet petals with fragrance of perfume
to hold them forever in my silent memories of you.
Make me believe it's true. I want it to last. I want to hold
whatever's there, so it can be locked without us forgetting
how true it was. And for one day we decide to open and let go,
you be the one holding the key, without you
know how much of you is in my heart.

Tadeo Garcia

Intricate Tales of Evolution

As time began many years ago the children of the God took on a new behavior.
As time goes past the children of God have begun a new task in life
as the guides in this new world—this is what is known as
the age of government and what it stands for is the truth.
Unfortunately the wrath of time has soured the way this was
supposed to work.
The ignorance is shown as the so called leaders have begun their wars.
So many young men and women have risked their lives for what—another journey into
the underworld or is this the declaration of
the old world as the scenic views drift slowly by as to disappear.

After the cycle of life has unfolded for this to end as we know it,
we shall separate and go to the area that is known as the age of wisdom.
This known only to the connoisseur as the life of indifference
and to the layman (or layperson) as the life of obstacles.
This makes it very difficult to enhance our intelligence
to the fullest ability, only knowing that there are reasons
that we are only allowed to educate ourselves in this life time.

When all has been said and gone we will have peace on this planet
the one we call Earth and once this happens the God of our world will
have blessed the spirit which we know as Christ the Lord and Savior,
this will be the end of the Earth and of life hoping that all have
lived the fullest of life and have journeys that have all been complete.

Lori Cognasso-Waters

Parents

He sits at the piano, rough loving hands poised over the keys.
His voice resonates with so much character, and so little tune.
She smiles and her eyes crinkle in affectionate admiration.
Even as they laugh together, I see them gaze at each other.
The depth there, and the incredible love they have for one another . . .
I feel privileged to witness such love.
Just by being there, they have taught me life's most important lessons.
I love them so much . . .
And for some reason, I know they love me too.

Heather King

Teachers

Teachers are people like you and I,
until they have little minds
in their garden.
Then they become gardeners in life.
Teaching the little minds all the
joy and beauty a garden
has to give.
When people become teachers
in the garden of life,
they become larger than
any of us.

Kerry Vore

Angels

Angels can be
Near or far
God sends them to this world
Every day of our lives
Leaving them to care for us and
Shower us with love

Yvonne Garcia

Believe

I looked for Love
Until my heart
called me home.

In the silence
Of my room
I was seduced.

By a melody
so tender, so pure
I melted into
A luscious pool.

Swimming breath's current,
On soft lyric,
Into the Infinite's womb,

"Believe in Love.
Believe in you.
Now."

Kimberly Satterfield

Love's Definition

Love is honor
Love is forgiving
Puts others first
Joy found in giving.

Love is faith,
Sights unseen;
Love is belief
Hope borne in dreams.
Love is timeless
Love knows no bounds
Though tides they change
True love goes on.

Love is devotion
Love is true
Love is the life
I've found with you.

Jenny Sego

Things Not Seen

Faith is the substance of all things hoped for but what if I hope for faith?
How do I have enough faith to keep hope alive and how will I hope with no faith?
So without faith I cannot hope for my dreams.
I'm in fear of failure and I fail to realize the fear.
Scared of success yet successful at being scared.
I believe in God . . . does he believe in me?
I want to go to Heaven but does Heaven want me?
I am wrong for not going to church to fellowship with the
hypocrites who judge me . . . "Judge not and not be judged."
However I realize by calling them hypocrites . . . I too judge!
Am I not in the wrong also   LORD . . . I Am lost . . .
A lost soul! I want to be found but know not where I am.
If the truth is what we make it then what is truth and what is lie?
I can not walk. My faith is limited.
I think they tell me I have little faith because I inquire . . . I question
Lord talk to me . . . for real. Show me the way
guide me for I can not guide myself
help me please!!!!!!

Christopher Headen

"Empathy"

Upon entrance, I was impressed with your elegance and your style.
You articulated in speech,
and looked glamorous appearance-wise.
Even the soles of your shoes and every strand of your hair,
you dared to be a lady, you dared to be supreme.
Everything was so put together, groomed and well manicured.
You struck me as being one with class and panache, so bourgeois.
I was so wrong. You fell from grace.
You used your beautiful manipulation of words to disgrace me.
You shocked me. I saw the metamorphosis before my eyes.
For once the wig came off and the makeup was gone,
I saw the true you, your true looks emerged.
A you that's plain and simple, without class or style.
You became an ordinary woman, and given time you became a hag. It's time to say
good-bye, say good-bye mother-in-law.
I thought I would've wanted you in my life.

Clayon Huggins

Think Positive

It all starts with a bright spark from a knight's heart.
Right off the charts, taking flight like a dart.
Hark! Listen in. You'll be glistening, kissing inside yourself.
Glide like stealth technology,
Philosophy, from the skies.
Realize the true dream disguised
through the smoke screen—clean, wise.
Rise like UFOs; analyze what you have chose.
My flows pour your core out like the rain,
No doubt I'mma help you maintain
Your mainframe. Reflect regrets; dissect your brain.
Reject the negative! Let it live and it won't cease
Until you're deceased. Release the leash, grab the beast by the tail.
May peace prevail. I refuse to fail.
Unveil. Think positive. Something's gotta give.
what's your prerogative.
Take it from a desperado; make my motto live.
Think Positive!

Jeremy Kohler

Perfect

Perfect is a sunset filled with gold, orange, and red.
Perfect is the cop who is never bothered by seeing someone who is dead.

Perfect is the ocean, crystal clear and a beautiful blue.
Perfect is the cop who always know what to do.

Perfect are the seasons—summer, spring, winter, and fall.
Perfect is the cop who catches every criminal.

Perfect is the society that understands NOBODY is perfect.
Perfect is the cop that knows he can't be perfect.

Neysa Caron

Life Love

Alone
Thinking of how it will be
How it will feel
Alone
Thinking of people, Human
Thinking not of a specific one, All
Feelings
Alone
Thinking of people, Human
Thinking of us, Human
Peaceful, Manipulative, Intelligent
Complete insanity
Complete love
Alone
Dreaming, Thinking, Concluding
No separation, Human
No separation, Animal
Life, Love
Death, Alone

Michael Matos

Sable

i wish i could
just once to
let you know
not to be shut
up inside this fanciful
facade but to
be free to share
forever . . .unending . . . .
undeniable . . .feeling
never to be hidden
again but i
crawl back into
my shell behind
the Walls

Robert Thomas

Give Me Light

Candle light by the fire
how can I resist to admire
yet I stay still on my bed
with words unspoken yet not said
Give me light throughout the day
show me love in every way
thought of dreams that
have not come true
though it seems that I already knew
another day that is so near
in my head crystal clear
shine your light through my heart
shall I pray we never part.

Jennifer Perla

Remembering and Forgetting

We try to forget
Fearful and sad things,
Also sleepless nights.

Never remembering how bad we felt
Struggling along with problems,
Never clasping reality.

We try to remember
Efforts we put out and courage we have,
Also lucky days.

Never forgetting how good we felt
Savoring each breath of life,
Never entangling truth with lies.

Linsey Carlstedt

My Unknown Place

Someone told me if you think too long,
You'll wander into a place that's unknown. One day I sat and I began to wander.
I wandered into a place where the people were all strange.

They were nice, kind and forgiving, and never said one bad thing.
And they shared with each other and they cared for each other and
They talked continuously.
They talked of love and they talked of peace.
And I had to take a step back and look around because these people seemed so weird to me.

Because in my world the people aren't all nice or kind or forgiving. And the prejudice in
my world is overwhelming.
And so I had to take a step back to see if what I was seeing was true. Because these
people seemed too perfect to be real,
And too right to be wrong.
And then I awoke and my thought was gone.
And I was back into the world in which I described.

A world where there are no perfect lives. But we will soon one day be together as they,
and walk in the same direction and way. But until that day comes, I must not lead my mind astray.
For I still have work to do today.

Erica Fisher

Inevitable

I am willingly drowned by your grace.
Your lips utter symphonic melodies which exists only in those chosen by God.
As I look into your eyes, the universe pauses, and I am finally
embraced with the true meaning of my existence.
Never again confused of the path chosen for me,
I bathe in the emotion that you have saved for many lifetimes awaiting my arrival.
Even the term love is no match for what road has been blessed upon us.
The mere thought of a memory with you brings pleasure to my soul deeper
than the most infinite abyss.
Though the experiences of pain have been mortifying,
they have led to an omnipotent field of peace and happiness,
and as I lie carefree in this field, your essence has wrapped around me
to shield my mind from even the remembrance of hurt.
Your words grace my plate with life long nourishment, and as I gaze into your eyes,
a new universe is created, and I am eternal in only this place with you.
Perfectly matched, it is as if you are DESTINY, and I am PATIENCE.
Together, we are the only future worthy in the Creators eyes.
I will cherish you an eternity after time ends.

Lawrence Williams II

The One

It's his voice, his looks, his touch
It's the way thinking about him makes me feel whole
It's all of those things, plus one
The mysterious emptiness he wants me to find
Me, a complete stranger to his heart
Yet somehow we are connected
The emptiness reaches out to me, and then ducks away in fear
What can it be?
He, the guy I so deeply feel for, or do I not feel for him?
Is it just he that feels for me?
OH! Such confusion, such pain!
I want to reach out to him, but I can't reach out to something that is running
It's so complicated!
But I won't give up
He needs me, and I may need him
I just don't know, but I think it's worth the shallow risk
Maybe it's not all of those things
Maybe it's just him
He draws me in a way no other does
Such a new experience, so frightening
But he loves me, and I think I might love him
I love him!

Jennifer A. Thompson

A Bouquet of Love

If words alone could blossom and grow
from thoughts kept in our hearts,
this poem would be a lovely bouquet
with many colorful parts.

Roses, so sweet despite their thorns,
remind me so much of you.
You've faced many trials in your life,
still your beauty shines on through.

Daisies, pretty and graceful
with faces bright as the sun,
remind me of your cheery smile
well known by everyone.

Carnations, lacy and fragrant,
come in colors of every hue,
reminding me of the many talents
you show in the things you do.

Each separate flower is unique,
not one just like another.
Just as you are special and dear
I'm glad that you're my mother.

Sarah M. Pietz

I Hold to Me So Dear

I need for you to listen
For I want you to hear
Of all the things inside
I hold to me so dear

There is nothing greater
Than having a best friend
The one who will listen
Stand by you til the end

There is nothing greater
Than having a true love
So perfect and so pure
You know it's from above

There is nothing greater
Than having a family
To stand right by your side
When life goes so badly

There is nothing greater
Than having home sweet home
The place you can go to
No matter where you've roamed

Monica M. Robertson

Behind a Smile

I sit here
While the smoke I inhale consumes me
I smile, you smile
But, we still pass each other
Not knowing what the other is thinking
Blow me a kiss
Let me touch your lips with mine
Let our souls intertwine
I'm in love with you
You think?
You see my heart
Do you want it?
You feel my kiss
Do you need it?
I see your face in the smoke I exhale
My lungs feel the pain
My body aches after your touch
Can't you feel it?
Don't you see?
There is more to me, than a smile

Danae Fleming

Decisions

It seems as if forever, I've been sitting on this rock.
A rock that was spewed from the bowels of the earth.
Sitting, contemplating that intangible, elusive, and ofttimes the unattainable feeling, known as love.
A constant fluttering in the pit of my stomach.
A heart racing at a uncontrollable speed.
A mind working overtime.
With only thoughts of you as my constant companion.
I've known the sweet passion and ecstasy of your embrace.
The taste of your sweet lips.
The soft caressing of your hands as they evoke a response from my trembling body.
Knowing that like the coming of night.
Like the sun slipping away.
So must I.
Without speaking of the feelings,
or the love I have for you in my heart.
Being kept alive by your smile, touch,
the soft words you have spoken to me.
So here I sit.
Trying to decide if I should speak of my love
or keep my silence.
Just as the grave keeps its dead.

Clyde Hetrick

Able

Given choice, a Godsend.
To pretend like children and genuinely smile once again.
We arrange the pieces that fall before us.
Strangely conceived how decisions are made.
As if consequences aren't realized.
With carelessness we act, like a game is being played.
The rules designed and expected to be followed.
With that, love is swallowed.
Unlike machines, feelings and emotions dictate the way in which we see the world.
Our role during this age is unknown.
And how could we cherish a desire and take hold,
when we're taught and told who we are.
A dream is cold without compassion.
We will have to risk and not fear to lose.
The ability to choose is prevalent,
to do this discipline is relevant.
The thought, to do so was given.
We must know this in belief, and with faith.
It is how we were constructed in living.

Christopher Sirianni.

Let the Past Be the Past

The morning has awakened me,
With the sun and its gleaming rays,
And the sound of birds telling me, It's a new day,
But the hurt and pain I felt yesterday,
Still lays heavy on my heart,
Knowing that a new day has come
And we're still apart, I begin to feel myself aging inside,
And it made me realize something has to change,
I even look in the mirror and notice,
How hurt has stripped my beauty away,
And I'm so tired of seeing me
Lose bits of myself everyday,
Ain't no use of me feeling bad, about you not in my life,
I'll just use our past to reminisce,
And that will make everything alright,
I wanna thank you for giving me, a past that will teach me
How to do better the next time around,
And a chance to let someone else reap,
In places where I let you down, Let the past be the past
Cause this pain won't last, I'll just pick up the pieces and move on, Because the past has made me strong.

Marc Jenkins

Autumn Leaves

Deep autumn,
Red and crimson. Autumn
Falls, and leaves
Remnant muse
My heart ensues
The flux of the brook, along with autumn
leaves scattering into the riffle
within a flutter
Pearly crystals cloak the tepid,
radiant skies.
Winter advances without admonition
And enshrouds the heart
To a stand still in time
In hope, all shall bloom
Again
The quest for spring's tracks,
Shall I pursue,
Forever

Edmund Fu

My Father's Face

My father's face tells me everything
he wants to tell me like
His face tells me when to stop talking,
or maybe when to talk.
His face tells me
when he's sad, when he's mad,
or maybe when he's tired.
He winks when he's saying, "I love you!"
My father's face says a whole lot.
I love my father's face!

Courtney C. Dover

Last Temptation

With dreams on stilts of endless hope,
the grandeur illusion of splendor
My conscience lost in a fine blue mist
spurred into tempestuous desire

Amid night's claim to peace,
and wearied melancholy feuds
Longing for clever surreal,
I wake to find myself alone.

Jason L. Martin

Fire Child

Stars flying all around
my moon empty and broken
heart and womb, never staying
never taking me to
the glowing orb, fissures
grow inside my soul to
make more room
for the pain
Another death enters the
vessel, housing grief
remorse and blame
Sparks fly around those
shooting stars to
foster blinding faith, to
elevate the fire child
To fall back down to hate

Lieza Clark

I Write

I write love poems
With no lady in my life
I write to hold
The feelings that I have
Even though
My feelings are real
I don't write
What others feel
I write with love in mind
But my own true I have yet to find
Sometimes I wonder am I writing in vain or do others know what I'm saying? Do they
feel my work of are they merely reading words?
I write with no one to give them to
Still I write because I know I have to

       Lorenco Wallace

Amanda

I never understood the meaning of friendship
I never understood why so many people called each other their best friend
I never had a sister, but always dreamed of having one
I never knew what it felt like to have someone you can always go to not matter what
What I did know, was that I wanted, I needed a friend
I wanted the chance to be able to call someone my best friend
I wanted someone to double date to the prom with
I wanted to be able to call someone and talk with them for hours and hours and not get bored

I wanted to have someone to share my secrets with
I wanted someone to gossip with about the most popular or prettiest girls at school
I wanted to have someone to talk about the cutest or smartest boys with
I wanted someone that would go on continuous shopping sprees with me
Amanda gave me that chance
I have had a lot of friends in life, but never anyone I could call my best friend
I never knew what a best friend was, or how it felt to have one, until I met Amanda
It gave me a good feeling inside to know that I had someone other than my family that
has continuously cared about me
It was great to know that I had someone there to listen to me when things got tough

       Michele Monos

Elderly Wishes

Serendipity has a way of dropping into life

when:

Just as life's last breath is about to come, there's rebirth to a new day. . . .

This soul hasn't grown grey just 'cause the hair has. . . .

I got a wish. . . .

I ain't lettin' go. . . .

It will still happen. . . .

So, I ain't lettin' go. . . .

Know what my wish is?

       Rebecca Crowder

Chaos Plays Her Harp

Chaos plays her harp in the key of greed.
Through the centuries examples are seen.
Her tumbling cords that fear has ridden on
has rumbled and roared from twilight to dawn.

Tuned are her strings with a marvelous conception,
but she sings with wonder-lust and deception.
Her song cuts to the heart the breasts of men,
to disrupt the best of friends!

She fed the desire for the fruit that profaned,
and forbade the fire on the offering of Cain.
She bade to inquire old King Saul to shame,
and misled the prophet-for-hire, nearly slain!
Yes, Chaos even led the squires to gamble for His robe, torn in twain!

Thus, it is so my good fellows, that she bellows for the soul in all of us!
With stretched strings she preys upon the weak with cords played in
the key of greed!

       Collin Campbell

A Will? A Way!

The weak are born to wither.
The strong are born to pray.
The weak will curse their lot.
The strong will find a way.

It's easy to aspire
When it's a sunny day.
The test of faith is proven
Under skies of gray.

On whom can you rely?
There always will be two.
Others may be weighed and wanting,
Depend on God, and you!

       Donice Peavy Carter

Matrimony

As two souls combine as one
Destined to wed since their lives begun
Placing on my finger a band of gold
Symbolizing together we shall grow old
In this moment in time
I become your wife
For better
For worst
For the rest of our life.

       Schiquitta Hamler

Surrender

Wash the night with perfumed heat,
Create a mood of madness,
Encase the room and voice my name,
And drive out all the sadness.

One half hour to feed your desire,
Take all of time to recover,
Entangle my life in webs of sweetness,
And convert this friend to lover.

Reach the peak of passion's height,
Plateau for moments and shudder
Embrace my hand and search my eyes
And know that there's no other.

       Daniel J. Held

Racism

Racism is an issue
That hurts inside
You have to take risks
And try not to hide
It doesn't matter what color
Shape or even size
For every new person
There is always a lie
Someone spreads a rumor
That makes you feel pain
And it seems like there's
Nothing for you to gain
Just try your best and
Hold your head high
Because we are all equal
So let racism die

       Shari Henderson

Someday You Will Tell Your Children about a Woman

Someday you will tell your children about me
A woman who went through the bath of love
And enlightened by her sorrow
A woman who lived in the hearts of her children
And memory of her husband
A women who struggled from the crowd
And stood at the stage of success.

Someday you will tell your children about a mother
A mother who nursed her children with blood and sweat
A mother who was her children's favorite story teller and the closest friend
A mother who waited in the stormy weather for her children's return

Someday you will tell your children about a wife
A wife who waited until midnight for her husband to come home
A wife who deeply attached to her man
A wife who dedicated her life to her family

You need not fancy your description but tell the truth
You need not create the passion but show in your action
For I don't ask much from you
Just let your children know that they have the best mother of their own

Xiaoming Qin

Mother Nature's Sleep

As snow flurries fall on a barren ground
You can here the breath of mother nature rattling through the woods
Brief and still you lay in the forest with eyes keen and ears alert
Deer hide amidst the trees like runaways watching you,
Until you see them

As the snow falls harder the occupants of the forest check in for the long winter
You sit and watch peaceful and still as the season transforms the ground and trees

One single log cabin sits in the corner of the woods,
The smoke stack puffs like your grandfathers pipe
And you smell the delicious scent of what awaits inside

As the snowfall thickens you, too, retire to your place of rest,
Just as the animals did
And in all its magical tranquility
the forest sleeps,
Mother natures eyes close and the winter consumes the forest in a sheet of white goodness

Ryan Dunlop

we the people

Us, you, them . . . what's the difference.
the constitution is what divides us.
Blacks from whites, men from women, brother from sister, mom from dad.
The constitution separates us from each other and us as a nation.
We need to come together and fight the capitalist pigs and show them what we can do and we will not go quietly into the night.
We can stand firm, together, as a whole.
As the great Martin Luther King Jr. said in his legendary speech, "I have a dream. I have a dream that my 3 children not be judged by the color of their skin but by the content of their character."   I too have that dream. We need to ban together as a country, a nation, and a whole. In 1776, our forefathers signed a document that said all men are created equal. They wasted their time. If they saw what they fought for, they would cry. They would cry until they finally got what they fought for. Freedom, patriotism, dignity and equality. We the people ask that you break through the clutches of racism, tyranny and our own officials in the pigpen we call, Washington D.C. 'Til then, I leave you and remember to fight for what you believe in, not what you're supposed to believe in.

Justin Tann

goldriver

the goldriver was flowing
with nobody knowing
what lay at the bottom of its bed.

when along came Ben
who had only just then
came out of the bar after a drink.

he slipped from his horse
and you guessed it of course
he·fell head first into the drink.

he floundered about
and trying to shout
went under for the third time instead.

the river of course kept flowing on by
with Ben now in its bed.

(Who cares if Ben is dead).

Victor Foster

Just Richard

For my family and the lord
Richard was just Richard
From the day that he was born,
Down in the Carolinas,
On a cold December morn.

With three sisters and five brothers,,
Who thought he was just fine,
Richard was just Richard,
Our precious number nine.

Richard was just Richard
All through his childhood years,
Loyal to family and friends,
One who always did his share.

Yes, Richard was just Richard
With his own unique personality,
A loving, carefree young man.
A few months short of twenty-three.

When on the twentieth of August
A terrible accident occurred,
Now Richard is just Richard
Sheltered in the arms of the Lord.

Sally Shepherd

When the Sun Sets

When the sun set
Away on the western sky
I think of what I did today
And wonder how I ever got by
Another day I've lived again
To see the setting sun
And if tomorrow is a success
Another race I have won

Natalie Hazelton

The Beginning

The ending is coming near
But that's not what you fear
You say good-bye to your loved ones
You say goodbye to her
Then she runs
Cry at all the things you'll miss
And you start to wonder what you wish
Your head starts spinning
But then you remember
This is only the beginning

Ashley Smith

Eerie Regret

As I lie on my deathbed and await my fate
I feel my blood grow cold

Each breath I take drains the strength from my body
Yet I gasp and fight to take another

My heart slowly beats as it echoes in my ears
As many times as it's been broken, it should have been still for years

My mind races on through the life that I lived
Was I worth remembering?

Will anyone care when I no longer exist? Does it matter? It won't
change the fact that I'm dead

The blood drains from my veins,
It pools on the floor

My soul screams in fear as it leaves its vessel
It's dark, and it's cold

Why did I have to be so bold?
Donna Fernandez

The Wine Maker

You are the wine maker, and I am the grape.
You trample over me a thousand times, as I surrender up my
lormer existence from the vine.
You, with such ease wonder off in search of your own adventures,
leaving me to ferment in such a trampled state.
You may refuse me a thousand times, and lust for one who is a
hundred times more intriguing then I.
Time will reveal all truth, but until then I ferment
in the midst of these grapes hitherto.
Yes! When fermentation and your trampling have made me
perfect, then the time will be right for you to taste
my love with all its glory,
for you to become drunk on my truth, for you to be tied down to me
so you may, for the first time, be set free.
Then and only then you will know what it is like
to become the grape that I am?
For when the grape is crushed and lies in its bloodshed state,
then you will see me too like-wise in my entire splendor and for
no other will you ever long for again.
Lucas Cabrera IV

The Flower

The flower arches its back by the lake,
Stretching toward the sun
Reaching for perfection,
But it is battered by the unforgiving wind.
Its petals are torn from its beautiful face, and its body begins to wither.
Then the gardener gives it a drink.
Ken Isley

still

still glinting in the bright autumn stillness
the hint of an idea of something just over the horizon
something good still there just beyond the line of sight
something good, even now, after everything, still coming out of all this
after all this time
as the slow eye glances sideways between the last rays of sun,
the gaps between the trees and traffic align
to let a flood of memories through,
and for a moment, even in the midst
of all this, even after all and ever,
the world is—still
James Burton

Blank

Painful solitude racks my body like a fever.
The words have stopped, as though dammed up into a tiny pool,
stagnant in the lands of my imagination.

I sit alone. I feel small next to the monstrous pen
that lays before me on the table. It stares up at me
through its piercing gold band, haunting me like the grandfather
clock striking on the hour in the dead of night.

My ideas stay locked; perhaps out of fear, maybe hate.
Yet, this is my passion; which has created a dungeon,
fixed in my mind, keeping me from light.

There is no way out.
My words were once my escape;
they now become my trap, holding me captive each
aching minute I sit before the page.
Cole Coover

True Love

Something has happened that I don't understand;
I'm crying out for love,
Then you take my hand . . . .
You pull me up and help me to my feet—
Oh, how wounds hurt after a defeat!
My eyes have grown swollen from the tears I have cried;
I feel so abandoned, but you stayed by my side.
I go limp in your arms, I give up the fight.
I let go of the pain and you hold me tight.
I look up at your face and see in disgrace,
The print of my hand that had once slapped your face . . . .
And your eyes have grown swollen from the tears you have
cried—When you so loved me, and I abandoned your side.
Michelle Massaro

Eyes of Man

The eyes of men are hopelessly inadequate tools—
So easily dazzled, effortlessly misled—
Three-quarters blind orbs,
seemingly seeing.
And yet they are most marvellous devices,
seeing, infallibly, only what they are told to see, and conveniently
missing others . . .
A patchwork world we do live in!
Bits and pieces of reality and dreams all
strung together at a nice random.
If this abomination, that man can see
merely with his eyes, is true,
what have we been missing? . . .
Have we been groping in the dark,
or simply
walking with our eyes closed? . . .
Emily Wellsworth

Interracial

I close my eyes and visualize the cheerfulness of your heart,
Your happy smile, your sexy style,
and the new love we're about to start.
I visualize new places with many different faces,
Never a hassle about our color or races.
I close my eyes and visualize a place for you and me
Where both of us together will always be happy and free.
Free from the thorns that poke in society's side,
And from its pain remains a shame wherein lovers have to hide.
But you and I are different in that we are proud and strong.
No matter what the world may think, we are where we belong.
So I close my eyes and visualize; where do we go from here?
One thing's for sure—our love is pure, and our hearts forever dear.
Charleston Boyd

Breakfast Thoughts

You were the pebble in the gravel that gives me mold.

What if I disappointed you? I couldn't bare it.
First place, an A+ . . . All or nothing.

You helped me, the lost needle in the haystack.
You were the vision of boundless clouds
Unlimited and whirling around my pinkie.
I lick my finger and taste the bitter blackberry of my father's dreams.

Ammie Elliott

Holders of a Dream

Today the children of our times are dying in the streets,
over colors of a headband, or other stupidities.

The senseless killings every day are surely getting bad, I wish
everyone could just stop and see,
the destruction in our land.

And thousands of little children in the crossfires of our towns,
where there used to be much happiness,
some now are underground.

This violence in our country of the free and of the brave,
just makes me stop and wonder if there's anything left to save.

So let's all band together and stop this violent scene,
for the children are our future . . . . the holders of a dream.

Willis Baldridge

Werewolf

Now you have the license to destroy that which would rend you—
relentlessly stalking to end of the night,
eyes of your quarry now blistered by light,
of shining fangs the moon can only lend you.
Now you have the bitter will to overkill what ails you—
biting and gnawing and grinding to dust,
what you detest and what you can't trust,
'til it's much too small to ever again assail you.

Now you bask in the security that all to come is well—
convincing the world there's sunlight beneath
the shining veneer of your lily white teeth,
which make that winning smile that's born to sell, but
once more you see the mirror'd light, and you reflect as well—
feeling the death that never will die, the strength of the weakness you just can't deny,
you eat out the already broken heart of Hell.

Lloyd Brown

How Can I Be Free?

If there was ever a day that you could see
just how the world has treated me
you would know why I sit so all alone and why I never feel at home
They've taken away something I hold very dear they've blinded
my eyes and deafened my ears
But the spirit inside is what's battered the most to them I am
nothing except the butt of their jokes
They sit there and laugh while I lay here and cry they enjoy the
good life as I gradually die
And I ask once again how can I be free
when everyone thinks they are better than me
My wings have been broken so how can I fly I'm dead to the
world so why can't I die
My questions seem endless and that's plain to see so please try
and give an answer to me
And now that I've asked all the questions I can maybe you can
help me to understand
But you'll probably go on just living your life so I'll keep
singing my song while they keep twisting the knife

David Jay Wech Jr.

My Hero

Father came in and sat next to me on my bed.
He grabbed my withered hand and held it
in his strong, masculine hands.
His strength overwhelmed my weakness, and I began to feel invincible.
I looked at him, and saw a darker complexion than of my own.
The face, which was once young, was beginning to show wrinkles
His blonde hair that was always combed back neatly
was also beginning to show flecks of gray.
The blue eyes that had reminded me of the taste
and the smell of the ocean.
He smiled and made my heart melt.
I always wanted a husband like him; for he was perfect.
My father always had the answers for everything.
He knew just the right words to say, and knew when to say them.

An unfamiliar look appeared to be on my father's face.
I started to see the neatly combed hair falling out of its place.
The strength in his hands started to evaporate.
I started to feel the pains of my body's cry to die.
Fear must have shown on my pale, weary, and sick face.
There were black circles under my eyes,
and what was left of my body was skin and bones.

Niki Hill

Agony

She cannot speak or hold my hand, the photographs just stare,
Frozen in some pleasure's past, that are no longer there.
She worried so about her folks, them getting old and dying.
No one could know that she'd go first, and leave us all a crying.

My favorite sight in all the world was my girl coming toward me.
Her smile would light up everything, and fill my heart with glee.
Oh, special girl, so suddenly all hopes and dreams are gone.
You never got to say the things you would have that next dawn.

She loved all nature's creatures; her car had food for strays.
She was God's perfect little girl, I loved her special ways.
I look up at your window, as I feed your little friends.
Whether furred or feathered, they'll know your love transcends.

You were the greatest thing, sweetheart, to e'er come down the pike,
We'd cuddle in, shut out the world, and do the things we like.
Precious little princess, my always, faithful wife.
Instead of losing you, my love, I'd rather give my life.

Why can't they catch her killer? Doesn't anybody care?
I sometimes want to end it all; hope's bogged down in despair.
My days are long. It's hell to know to have her back can never be
Unless, of course, there is a path to Heaven and eternity.

Robert W. Roth

Where Are We Now?

We are here alone, victim of a raw bone,
stone and steel palace, death without malice,
water without bread, blood runs red,
pain no gain, no rec' when it rain.
Day in day out, argue, cry, we shout.
Brother in need, brother has plenty,
is brother for all or is brother for any?
Sister is alone, no man at home,
children too grown, no father at home.
Where is dad? Is he working late?
Where can dad be, on a secret date?
Sister is tired, sister is beat,
after a hard day at work, now we all eat.
Where will it end?
It isn't the dream, we wake at night, look at us, it's a scream.
Eighty-seven racks all not filled, our goal is limited, must we be ill?
Hang on in there baby, the best is yet to come, maybe.
At least one has a friend, are there any more,
large eyes, big heads, brains that are sore.

Benjamin Ashley

Marion

There are days of different colors, like the sky in all its hue
There are days of different feelings, they are all to be lived through.
For each day is quite important and each color has its own
Reflection in a prism of shades that we are shown
For when this life is over let us proudly say
That in each and every color, we lived the measure of the day
And through this radiant rainbow I always think of you
You're my window and my skylight from whence I have my view
For what are colors in all their glory
If we cannot share our very own story
You're my indigo, scarlet, yellow and pink
Like a piece of velvet into which I sink
And when this life is over and we all turn to light
We'll be each other's beacon through the long, clear night

Marion Heisner

If Only

If only I could keep just one person from falling.
If only I had just one achievement to show for my life.
If only I could stop just one dream from falling or one soul from fading.
If only I had just one moment to look back one
And now that I made a difference.
If only I did just one thing right so that long
After I am gone people will remember me for.
If only.

Lauren Smith

How Can I Explain Her to You

How can I explain her to you,
but to say I've found an exceptional woman

I could say pretty, intelligent, stylish
someone who knows who I am, but that wouldn't explain who she is

I could tell you she has the same quick, quirky, lunatic sense of
humor that I have, but that wouldn't quite do it

Would it explain it better that my heart as well as my body jumps
when I see her? That she is beautiful to me; inside and out become one

That when I joke and make her sides hurt, it makes me laugh
harder (and that she can't take it anymore,
but she wouldn't give it up for the world)

She loves to hear my music
Things that I thought only I could feel, move her to tears,
inspiration, and laughter

Her elegance overwhelms me,
and her sensuousness puts me off balance

But most of all, when she looks at me with love, and her little
expressions that show her soul, I am melted

How can I explain her to you
she is my Diana, she is my love

Michael P. McCormack

Fight Against AIDS

On our borrowed time we take a lot for granted
We see things as straight, and really they're slanted
Our lives are huge, wet teardrops that are awaiting fast to burst
The mystical eyes of rapture lurking unrehearsed
Please pat my shoulder, rub my back, or even stroke my hair
Promise me love and happiness, whatever you can spare
A cherished smile of simple hope; I know my soul will somehow cope
I'll fold my hands, and sputter grace until I'm in a better place
So I'll raise my weak hands from great despair,
And live this time left without a care
Although my vision is now unclear
and my words quite hard to understand
I sit in the dugout amongst a million cheers,
And God's still my biggest fan,
And even though I'm leaving you, you promised to meet me there,
And then we'll share our secrets as best friends
Like we did when I was here

Lisa L. First

Perceptions

Since inception was depression
Deep impressions of immaculate conceptions and pale faces
Imbedded in my cerebellum
Now what's the prognosis
My likeness was sailed from coast to coast
By evil men that resemble ghost
Back lashes to brothers and sisters fresh off the boat
As the caveman gave toast
And to boast
That we were reduced to servitude because their religion we didn't tote
Discovery the gloat
As the masses they came in contact with lay afloat in riverbeds
of blood and gun shells
Straight from hell they came
Walking on all fours like wild dogs looking for the next score
And to add more
Is to state that they were once African
But though recessive genes and glacial adapting
Walks the amoral beast that thinks that He is the
I AM

Darren McLaurin

My Cure

My mind utters with confusion,
simple words I do not understand.
Yet I keep following, as you lead me with your hand.

You lead me past a place of darkness, pain and fear,
To a place where there is no sorrow, but I still can't see to clear.

You direct me to do your will, only your will and ways.
And not to give into what the world has to say.

You embellish my surroundings,
your blessings I endure, to truly take away my pain and confusion, Lord you are my only cure.

Lindsey Flores

The Life Pyre

I needed love, you gave me low self esteem and shame.
I needed to trust, you gave me lies and anxiety.
I needed your protection, you gave me fear and isolation,
Unleashed the beasts in my dreams, Slaughtered my sentry,
sent me running, screaming in my mind, to a world of muteness.
Where fearful things sat incognito behind smiling eyes and faces.
You created a frightening prison for an innocent child,
and threw away the key.
But look! Ive locked it too! From my side!
I can tame the beasts and not be so lonely.
I can take the scraps of life that you've thrown me,
and build a world where children can laugh and play unfettered.
I am the new sentinel of my world. You will not be admitted.
I'm burning the distorted land you gave me,
tilling the ashes into the soil,
Chipping the shackles from my wrists and ankles.
I can feel the simple love I try to give returning through my
hands and feet.
Though my visions are butsimple diagrams in the dust
around my campfire, you will no longer people them.
My dreams are now, just that, My Own!
The Forest Grows!

M. Rebecca Imhoff

All Day

I sit here thinking of you all day.
When I think of you all day,
I think of the great friendship we have.
But now things have changed, now when I see you I get little
butterflies in my stomach.
I know it sounds strange, but still I sit here thinking of you all day.

Jacqueline Fiske

What Am I?

I consist of dreams and wonders,
of wants and of needs longing to be fulfilled.
I am unknown by most, though many claim to know me.
I am not partial to one over another.
I merely run my course.
A sweet smelling breeze am I to some,
Kept deep inside their thoughts.
While fear and avoidance in others I spark,
for they linger on that which is long past.
I am mysterious and full of questions.
To some I am one who crouches low in the hidden depths of
one's mind, waiting to pop out and surprise one.
To others I am a visitor long prepared for; anticipated is my arrival.
When shall I visit you?

Megan Murphy

Strange Customs

They bind their little hands and feet
They say to make them small.
Their customs are very strange to us.
We understand them . . . not at all.

But here we bind their little hearts . . .
By all our customs too.
Day care centers . . . baby sitters . . . Mothers gone . . . and more.
Mothers like detachment . . . no bonding anymore.

Our loss is now affection
And love is out the door
When love goes . . . so does conscience
And troubles in the door.

Our only hope? Renewal
And families must see . . .
That children are most precious!
And their re-spon-si-bil-ity!

Edna L. Ingram

Christmas

A long time ago, a little child was born, from jesters to angels,
they tooted their horn. Under a star, that lit up the sky, he was
born to us all, and for us he would die. He was born to parents,
called Mary and Joe, given the name of Jesus, for all us to know.
He walked through the land, spreading joy and love, and spoke
of a god, he said was above. Then came the day, for us he
would die, he carried his cross, and he didn't ask why. He spoke
to his god, as he hung in the air, my god my father my soul I
bear. I hang on this cross, for the sins of all man, and the word
of you god, that they don't understand. I pray to the god, that
Jesus spoke of, and ask him his will, and some of his love. So
during this season, and those yet to come. Remember the god,
who gave us his son. Thank you and may god bless you all.
Merry Christmas

Jimmy Mojomick

The Tears within My Eyes

For you are indeed my little child, and I can see the beauty that I
created inside you.
As my tears come inside my eyes,
for you will always be my little child, that I created within my world.
For I know the things you face my child. For it was I that created
you to carry that precious smile upon your face, for I too have
those tears that come inside my eyes.
Lord, just hold me inside thy arms so my tears will fade away.
For my tears will always be inside my eyes, my precious child.

Judith Bruce

The One

I knew it from that first day that you'd come my way.
I knew it from that day that you were the only one for me.
I knew you'd be the one to make all of my dreams come true, as I
looked into those eyes so blue.
I was right.
Yes, you were the one who made all my dreams come true, and
now I only want to be with you.
I hope we never part, for I know you have a place deep within my heart.

They said you were too good for me, oh, baby, can't you see
just what you mean to me?
Oh, can't you see just how much I love you?
Nothing can compare to the love we share.
When you're gone my lips long for your sweet kiss,
my body for your touch.
You gave me everything and more and I'm thankful,
so thankful, for you.
You showed me your world, I showed you mine,
and put all the hurt behind.
Now that we've made it this far, we can never turn back.
Now I know that this perfect love will last forever.

Meg Adams

Every Day

Every day, when I awake, my first thoughts are of you . . .
And all the moments shared together, come so clearly into view . . .
When I'm blinded by the tears, somehow we still feel hand in hand . . .
Thanks to that special bond between us, only we can understand . . .

Every day, within my heart, I feel you watching from above . . .
You're still with me, I'm not alone, embraced always with your love . . .
It's the beginning of your grace with God,
and I know it's not the end . . .
Though I cherish, miss you, love you so, my father, my bestfriend . . .

Every day, when I lie down to sleep, you appear within my mind . . .
Of all the fathers who have ever lived,
I'm so blessed that you were mine . . .
Now no good-bye's, no heartaches, just one more thing to say . . .
Always forever, I'll think of you, every night and "Every day"

Mark Shannon Johnson

Eternal Love

I am driven by a restless heart that cannot sleep; caught in an
awakened slumber my eternal love I seek . . .
Carried upon the wings of fate I fly throughout the night's sky;
in search of a foretold destiny that forever binds you & I . . .
Lost to a passion that pulls me further & further to pursue; a
timeless vision that will lead me ultimately unto you . . .
My journey guides me across the water tops over the sands &
the shores; all the while my every breath, my heart, my soul is yours . . .
I am driven by a restless heart that cannot sleep; caught in an
awakened slumber my eternal love I seek . . .

Sarah Bell

Brotherhood

Here we stand at the head of our paths.
So many choices we stand and debate.
But I ask you, as my brother.
No matter what path I choose, will you be at my side.
Trails & Tribulations we must face & go through.
Yet the success of our journey would be so much sweeter,
because every step of the way.
There was you.

Justin Moodley

Snow Coming Down

Wintry mist, powdery bliss, enchanted tears of frost, pebbled sky,
winking eye, shapes of wintry blow.
Drifting pace, silting race, shifting to and fro.
Laughter, sighs, twinkling eyes, glowing cheeks.
Spring's birth, Autumn's end, shadow behind a tree,
glistening ground, crunching sound, moonlight prancing beams.
Angels, snowmen, scarves and mittens, snow ball fights
and sledding mirth.
Sparkle dust, boughs bending toward the earth.
Inner child, dancing wild, round and round.
Filling space, constant race, entrancing nature crown.
Winter's beginning, flakes spinning, from the heaven's they depart.
Happiness felt, tiny treasures in time will melt, drifting layers abound.
Snow falling, snow coming, snow coming down.

Stephanie L. Dejewski

Liberty

The cold of winter edges closer with every stroke of oar.
The ice bites long-frozen fingers and toes.
Stars reflect brightly in the patches of black water
so skillfully mimicking the wintry sky.
The clouded breaths of your comrades fill the air.
The cold freezes the voice in your throat, causing silence to prevail.
Jagged fingers of ice float by the boat; the gentle sloshing of
water occupies the ears of these soldiers . . .
Or does it?
Do shouts of welcome home ring in their heads?
Or does gun fire, the cries of battle?
Laughter, warmth, the company of family and friends.
They have given that up for what?
Seeing close companions being shot down beside you?
Seeing how many men in red coats you can fell until you are
forced to retreat?
No.
They suffer for something greater than that.
Not only do they fight for justice and freedom,
They fight for Liberty.

Katherine McLean

Strength

You think you have everything you need,
career, possessions, and friends but still you have no peace of
mind, nothing to make your worries end.
Every day you wonder how you'll make it,
through the emptiness and pain
Nothing makes it go away, no matter how much success you gain

Making it day to day is very hard, you struggle to get by,
And it's hard to explain your pain to friends,
'cause no one can understand why.
Why you are sad and why you are down,
why you cry for hours and hours
And again nothing makes it go away,
not even them sending you flowers.

Neither your friends nor you can realize how to find that missing link,
The lost piece of your life, that could possibly bring your world in sync.
The Lord wants something better for you, just send him up a prayer,
You can give Him all of your troubles, but . . . do you dare.

He's waiting to relieve the stress in your life, just ask, to you he will give
Pain relief, emotional healing and the courage and will to live.
I know a doctor, a psychologist, a friend, and a counselor
Everything you need in life, He'll give and so much more.

Precious angels, the roads are rough, easy days seem far and few
But just remember you can do all things,
through Christ that strengthens you.

Kellye Frazier

Good-bye Millennium

Hello new millennium, won't you come in?
Blow our ignorant, dull minds with your new technology,
your fresh ideas, your wonderful intelligence.

Disguise yourself as a friend, lend us a shoulder on which to mourn
and weep over past history; help us
with your boldness to say, "Farewell"
to all that was and say, "Hello" to all that is and will be.
Help us all to forget those happy memories we love so much,
just to lay out before us a newer, wackier, more crazy,
powerful contraption of the mind or machine of the world.

Good-bye to . . .
Old musty books, meaningful words,
unforgettable phrases used by unforgettable authors.

War, severe, tragic, bloody, the sounds of explosions
cutting through silent air, like the sharp cutting of a knife.

Baseball, the sound of cheers and shrieks of happiness ringing
in my ears as the home team scores a home run.

Television, the colorful pictures, the unlikely stories,
the creativity and imagination of another being
presented in a lazy, enjoyable manner.
Pollution, dusty black smoke fills the air, enabling us to breathe.

Jocelyn Otten

A Mother's Love Divided

A mother's love divided between the two.
How can it be separate I never knew.
The pain and anger, hurt and betrayal.
A mother's love divided should never be revealed.
You hoped children become something in life,
you wonder what happen because you sacrificed.
You grew older, felt the difference,
you strive to better while the other one didn't.
A mother's love divide between the two.
She rejoiced with the other and left you sad and blue.
Times goes on and days go by, you sit broken hearted and cry.
You did all you could to be the one she loved as an equal.
 yet your tortured because your not part of the sequel.
A mother's love divided between the two,
where do you go what do you do?
You see it from a far, it's tearing you apart.
You try to move on, remember you have children of your own.
Take this word of advice treat your children as equals,
don't be a mother who picks, chooses you'll be the one who loses.
A mother's love should never be divided,
it causes hurt and pain you will never be the same.

Toya A. Coleman

Cause and Effect of Clone upon Christmas

To the believers, non believers, both the mortal and immortal minds,
Please lend me thine loyal faith in truth, therefore, as a non visioner,
Disguised, terrorist imposed, undiscerning response conditioner,
Subsequently, on Jesus name in faith I pray to humanity to please
Lend me thine sacred eye as for to look truth into view to U.S. Congress,
And as believers in virtual reality, behold creation by cloning, look see
Humanity's undiscerning circus of life parades
and vaunt obsessed, yon jest.

To the Christ Jesus, I shall forever believe, lend and serve homage
To thy holy word on thy holy name in service and prayer.
And surely as a believer in Christianity, humanity, and America, on
His sacred word I do, and shall always solemnly swear.
Consequently, on His name in faith I beg Christian preachers.
Jewish Rabbis, Catholic priests to please lend me thine support in my
attempt revelation of an anti Christ and his discern germ clones,
Jesus Christ as the truth, and nothing but truth, so help me, my Lord,
From my skull to my bones.

Dess Vangates

Alembic

It is the perfect time, the time when all is still and quiet and the only sound is your breath in off beats with the wind caging the windows and the moon half-strong and blue trickling over your ears as you lay with your back to me the tousled cover partly pulled up over your sinewy shoulder that sleeps in the milk light.

I drink you in salty, pushing my nose as close as I can without touching smelling your musk eat my earth and my earth eat your musk.

And I know, I know that in the morning I will go home and not shower for hours so that you would be with me all day the essence of you woven into my hands my hair my breasts my purse which has you graffitied all over and will ache when I sit down to do the crossword and shift in my chair and think of you think of your hands and the way they move on me.

Dana Rovang

Are You Ready

You missed the ride, where were you going
can't remember! You got all prepared, and ready to go,
but where, can't remember!
Are you happy or are you sad,
that you are already to go, but can't remember where.

So start to prepare again if you dare,
this time keep up the preparation until the ride comes to your door,
and say, your ride is here.
Just step on board with a smile and much joy because
heaven's doors were open all the time
you just were not prepared to step inside.

Zelda Mcclain

The Star and the Hawk

With never-ending love to my own precious "Hawk."
The palest blush of dawn begins another day
And, low in the west, one brilliant star outshines all others.
A beautiful hawk wheels across the sky, longing for his mate.
Do either of them know they are each other's fate?

The star sends out her shining light across Heaven's deep blue space,
Trying to reach her hawk in flight. The hawk soars high,
And higher still, embracing the wind with his mighty wings,
Reaching for the beckoning star and the siren song she sings.

There is a special majesty in both, this shining star,
And this mighty hawk . . . and a love that has no limits.
But each knows deep inside, that time is not their friend—
That with the passing of the day their light, and flight, must end.

Yet the love that calls to each supercedes any force on earth.
It warms their hearts and feeds their souls,
It's a need they can't resist . . .
And so, against all odds, they know it always will persist.

Helen Mitchell

You

When I was young I had a dream of finding a man who wanted the same things I did,
  And I met you!
A man who would listen when I most needed someone to talk to,
  And then I found you!
Someone to comfort me when I felt down and dry my tears when I cry,
  And then I saw you!
Someone to hold me when I felt I could not go on
or stand on my own again,
  And then I felt you!
I would dream of finding a man who would stand up not only for me, but for himself,
  And that's when my dreams came true!

Susan Hines

Apology (To a Muse)

To you, this day, I pledge away all caution
of the words that I should speak.
Though punished for my crimes without the benefit of time's benign suppression, I cannot claim to lack the flame of speech as if my words were always weak.
So take within your breast that which had always been re-pressed: this, my confession.
Around your light there was no fight against the creeping shadows of the dark Each day and separate day I saw you helped me push away the night's congestion.
But in your lack the horrid black was quick to quench the power of your spark And if left all alone the dark was quick to make it known this bleak suggestion:
"Remit the song; it's been too long—you cannot hope to claim it once again. The folly of your thought is rendered fruitless by the drought of hope's illusion."
And so I ceased the song—increased the magnitude of past forgiven pain. So listen to this song for it has taken far too long to see through my confusion.

Although some naive poets claim to guarantee the beauty of their song, Their first songs can't be blamed; they make it possible for better lines ere long.

Michael Wisebaker

The Giving

Far away and hidden are you, from any. An individual with much potential, but not wanting. Too much is the pain and suffering, too far to go. Let me, feel it too. Let me in. Can it be, you want all of this for yourself? Let me in. Share the cold darkness that you try so hard to hide. And maybe a friend who so loves you, will endure. And then we can climb the barriers of life together. Let us begin. To give the pain is selflessness, to take it from is kindness, but to keep it is unforgiven, since it seems such a waste. To give it up is wrenching—that would mean letting go. And maybe you keep it as punishment for the unsavory guilt you've also taken. In heartache we tend to blame ourselves, not outwardly, but inside, always wondering what we could've done. To change what? Fate? Not possible. Not likely. No. What's done is done. Nothing you do, or think you could've done, will ever change the past . . . You must look to the future. You may think now that nothing will last. And what if it doesn't, what does that mean? Only that maybe you enjoyed your life anyway? And if you believed that love lasts forever, it was a good thing to believe. Love does, but life changes, just as the world will turn. Change is most of the time unexpected. And why do we think that we control our fate? Will we ever learn? Take my hand and walk with me, to a place that's for the living. Leave where you are now, and walk into the light. Join the conscious, have a leap of faith. Someday you may be needed to take the pain from someone else. Then you will become "The Giving."

Dawn Sansom

My Mark in Time

It only takes a minute to stop and give Him praise.
It only takes a minute to show love in different ways.
It only takes a minute to kiss a baby's cheek
It only takes a minute to feel the kind and meek.
But it really takes a lifetime to heal a broken heart.
It really takes a lifetime, but we all must make a start.
We have to make the effort and we have to show we care.
And we have to leave our mark of love here and everywhere.
To act like Christ and spread His word and love our fellowman.
We must act now and follow the Master's plan.
For those who doubt, for those who wonder, what is this master plan? We must live our lives like Him and love our fellowman.

Nathan Walley

Therapy

My therapy occurs whenever I grab a pen
Letting go of my worries, expressing my feelings
until a period shows up at the end
My therapy is sitting in the tub falling asleep to D' Angelo
Which one? Doesn't matter they're both classic as far as that go
But as the steam rises from the water as my mind drifts away
I relieved of any and all troubles stabbing at me that day
My therapy is listening to the soothing words of my woman, my angel
Her presence, affection, and care saving the day from every angle
My therapy is listening the poetic words of my boy, my man
Releasing thoughts, ideas, and eye-openers
That only few can understand
My therapy is giving praise
To the one who has given my all of my days
The one higher than the sky
The one you should never question with such words as WHY?
The one who made the ground we journey on
The air that we breathe
The one who created the trees in order for us to have books to read
The one who created you and me
My therapy is saying thank you constantly to the Almighty.

Willie Parks

Faces

Faces, with all their wrinkles and lines.
Have no bearing on the human mind.
Happiness, distress, loneliness,
They show all this and More!
I can touch your face, your lips, your eyes.
Feel the loneliness, to my surprise.
From your mouth came sweet words of love, togetherness, our place.
In reality, they were lies, from such an honest face.
Our life, our love, our bed, we shared for a while.
Tomorrow, I dread, but my face it must smile.
A heart all shattered, as if it were a puzzle the wind tossed
and scattered. Eyes once like stars,
sparkling in the night feel only a salty drizzle,
such a sad face all full of fright.
Faces, gentle and kind hide many a distorted mind.
A kiss of love, a kiss of death sweet words on their breath so easily,
they deceive the innocent who believe.
Beware of faces all shapes and sizes,
their gentle kiss may brush your cheek, but their lips are full of lies,
still it is love I seek. But face we will smile and go on our way.
Tomorrow just might be our day. We will see face you and me.
Love I wonder is that the right face over yonder?

Kathy Haggins Scott

Let Me Give

What I have may be of no use to you.
You may see weeds, sticks, pebbles in my hands,
Hear trite, mindless words when I speak.
You may drift to memories blessed with sweeter beauty,
My voice may be too Me—
You may long for another's soft, treasured thoughts.

But I spied a yellow flower on the hilltop and climbed to pull it up.
I heard your voice and grew warm telling you.
You touched my leg and I felt it days after.
Let me tumble, say it, shout!
Let me gather all this beauty
and lay it down at your feet:
I love you, I love you!
You are kindness, gazing, praying.
You are manly, cautious, playful, pensive.
Your hands, brow, lips, neck,
Your words, laughter, every moment I love.
Let me give you this love!
Let me give.

Suvi Escareno

Our Four-Legged Little Angel, Maggie May

But a flutter of a heartbeat as you made your way into our home.
Instantly, we belonged to you and we became a Family.
Your love was free and drenched our hearts with every wet, little kiss.
Each day, whether needed or not, you wagged that tail for us
and didn't stop until we were snuggled up that night.
So precious of a heartbeat, we could feel as you slept,
knowing that when you'd awaken, it would be just for us.
So much, you did for us, Maggie May,
making us realize our Heart is in our Home,
and always keeping faith of that union.
Although we had no control of the weakness that overcame you,
we were blessed to be able to give you back to God.
Holding you, as we felt the last precious beat of your heart,
you took with you a part of ours.
To our Four-Legged Little Angel,
you will be graced in our Hearts and Home Forever.

Maria Verkler

Your Flowers

Your flowers arrived on Tuesday,
at a time when I was blue
They were so beautiful, darling,
I just knew they were from you.
They made me feel so special,
they told me that you care
They were saying, "Darling, I love you,"
of this they made me aware
I thank you for your flowers,
that was so wonderful of you
But then darling, it's wonderful you are
and why I'm so in love with you
So, as I look at all the pretty flowers
and the splendor they impart
Please know that I love you
and you're forever in my heart

Rosemary M. Ziegler

Buddies Three

Three young men through life forge,
Virgil, Mel, and buddy George.
Virgil led his senior class,
an artist with a wholesome dash.
Three young men with a unique bond,
all through life and far beyond.
Marriage and families truly blend
these three buddies close as kin.
Each a jewel in his community,
shining brightly for all to see.
Cancer struck Virgil in his golden years,
still Virgil fought on without fear.
Treatment endured in a distant state
while the Reaper stood is silent wait.
Put to rest in the town he hailed from,
the great little town named Albion.
Memories remain as big as life,
his spirit in Heaven reignites.
Skilled to take life on the chin,
three great buddies close as kin.

Vivian Gloff Mollan

Is It Time to Get up Yet?

My life is not over but I live like it was
A secluded, downtrodden spirit in pause
Totally lacking interest in any and all
Completely ignoring my beckoning call
Can I crawl out of depression's black funnel
Or will I continue along this dark tunnel
Do I have strength to turn this around
Ascending to life's higher ground
I've slept ninety hours in the last four days
Yet I am so tired in so many ways

Christopher Lee Johnson

Biographies
of
Poets

ABDELWAHED, MOHAMMED
[a.] Hayward, CA [title] "A Kiss" [pers.] A very special person gives you "A Kiss" and I'm happy to say I found that person. I love you, Marina.

ABRAMS, PETER
[a.] Jacksonville, FL [title] "Flight of a Angel" [pers.] My poem is about lost love and the experience I had with love in my life. I hope readers of my poem will see a little of themselves in my poem.

ACOSTA, LETICIA
[a.] Hialeah, FL [title] "Untitled."

ADAMAIK, SARAH
[a.] Canbbera, Australia [title] "The Wolf's Eye" [pers.] I live in Australia. I am ten years old and I am in grade five at school. I love my home, family and pets. I am a creative person and love to express myself through poetry, art and dance. Sometimes I am inspired to write poetry about something that touches my heart. Other times I get pictures in my head and they won't leave until I do something about them. So I draw a picture and write a poem. Then the picture leaves my head. "The Wolf's Eye" is one of these poems.

ADAMS, DAVID
[a.] Richmond, IN [title] "The Human Race" [pers.] All you see or hear about in this era, are UFO's and aliens on Earth. And every day that passes we are one step closer to space travel to far off places. But yet in the mental of technological way we are incapable of it. I believe that the more we achieve together on Earth, the more we understand regardless of odor, size, or smell, we are truly the same. But now we are not ready for it. We see nothing but wars and rumors of wars, with people of other colors and ways of life. How can one fathom to see the creatures beyond his planet. When on his own planet he sees his own kind an enemy because of his color.

ADAMS, J. HUNTER
[a.] Cedar City, UT [title] "The Magic of the Uninspired" [pers.] As I writer, I express feelings and meaning through the construction of words. Poetry, is given to each and every individual to interpret and understand for themselves, so I will not tell you my interpretation of the poem, that's up to you. What I will tell you is that it is based on love and life experiences, which have since faded away. I hope you enjoy it. J. Hunter Adams resides in Southern Utah as a writer and filmmaker. He also spends much of his time with the world renowned Utah Shakespearean Festival.

ADAMS, JOHN
[a.] Highlands, NJ [title] "A Fire Slowly Dies" [pers.] Poetry, like music, has always flowed through my life. Yet, somehow, neither poetry or music could give me the thing in life I was looking for; romance. This poem is about a special person in my life who give me a taste of romance, even if it was only through my eyes and through my words. Though love was not the final outcome, happiness for her wars and for that I am grateful. Thank you Kerri, for being you.

ADAMS-EVANS, GWENDOLYN
[a.] Ellenwood, GA [title] "You Can't Rain on My Parade" [pers.] When I write, I can place myself into my poetry and visualize what I write about. It is a wonderful feeling and a treasured gift. "You Can't Rain on My Parade" is a positive message to myself that allows me to realize that I am what I make of myself if I close all doors to negativity, by opening all the positive ones. Gwendolyn is a published freelance writer, poet and lyricist, living in Ellenwood, GA. She is a member of the Lexington who's who directory. She has been published in: Quill Books, *The American Poetry Anthology*, *The World of Poetry*, *Winsome Way* Magazine and *Chem Matters* Magazine. Additional credits and

awards: 1986–1989 gold and silver poets award from the World of Poetry. Hobbies: Tae-bo, abstract oil painting, gardening, creative gifts and poetry baskets, Bible reading, organizing youths for non-violent programs, reading and listening to senior citizens.

ADAMSON, SAM
[a.] Terrell, TX [title] "I Beg For Your Love" [pers.] Poetry is my release. My thoughts flow through my pen smoothly as I put my heart, mind, and soul onto a blank piece of paper. That empty paper becomes an ocean of emotions by the time I am finished and is as dear to me as a loved one. But, when writing wasn't enough I went to my mother. Who I love dearly and hope one day I am able to make her so proud of what she raised that all she can do is cry. Thank you mom, I love you!

ADCOCK, ELIZABETH
[a.] Amarillo, TX [title] "Mom and Dad" [pers.] Poetry has been a way for me to express my feelings on subjects that I've normally taken for granted. This particular poem was a Valentine gift for my parents. We live away from each other and I felt it was better than a card. I've always got tear-jerking cards from them and I wanted to give them something special this time. It brought tears to their eyes and continues to tug at my heart.

AGARWAL, NEHA
[a.] Germantown, MD [title] "Winter's Here" [pers.] I think poetry is a special talent that not everybody can find anywhere. With me being a 12-year-old, my poetry life starts off on a boring, winter day. I was thinking of some winter games to play. Somehow, the words just come to me. They just seemed to take place right in my mind. At age 8, I started writing poems on my own hand.

AGEL, CHARLES
[a.] Savade, MD [title] "My Price and Princess" [pers.] Agel, Charles W. III was born on July 18, 1983. He has lived in Buffalo, N.Y. and savage, MD. This poem is about some children who lived next to me in N.Y. I hope it raises awareness about child abuse, I would like to thank my Mother, sister, Noel Cordier, Eddie Lopez, Jessica Corcoran, Cice, my dog Chewbaka, my Goddess, and everyone who has made me what I am, good and bad. Besides poetry I also enjoy art, music and lacrosse.

AGERET, PRINCE
[a.] Cordoba, Argentina [title] "Wonder" [pers.] Born in Cordoba, Argentina, she then moved to the States where she raised her family to three children. While in the States she became acquainted to America writes. My thoughts were influenced by the poetry of Emily Dickinson and Walt Whitman. They inspired me with the profound feeling of freedom and with the sense of belonging to the land, the people and the universe. Back to Cordoba, she published her first narrative, "Vivencias de Paz" (Peace of Living) and later a book of poems, *La Casa del Jacaranda* "Poetry is like freedom, it consists of being the light to ourselves which is feeling free from all the structures of our thoughts."

AL-GHAFRI, ABDULLAH
[a.] Sapporo AK, Japan [title] "Mr." [pers.] I dedicate this poem to my mother Mooza, my father Saif, my teacher, My wife Salemi Rajae, my brothers and sisters, my friends and every one who think of love.

ALASTRA, TOMMY
[a.] Hollywood, CA [title] "Beautiful" [pers.] This poem is about a love that shows no boundaries a love inspired by my dearest Dillian. Thank you for showing me what love is.

ALBELO, BETSY
[a.] Beryn, IL [title] "Enchanted Islan" [pers.] Those nocturnal music notes echo through me, and

they probably will tell I'm old and gray. Enchanted Island represents Puerto Rico. No words can describe the many wonders the Island carries with it. Nothing can replace the vision of beauty that surrounds every natural wonder. A piece of me sits on a balcony at night and looks to the shore, it listens to the waves and melts under a starlit sky. I have my mother to thank for being the wonderful person she is, and for taking me there. I love them always.

ALBRECHT, SYLVIA
[a.] Woodbridge, NJ [title] "Morning Bells" [pers.] This poem reflects the way it was for me for I'm in the autumn of my time, often remembering spring. The plain white chapel with green roof tiles nestled on top of Broad Mountain in the Village of Hudsondale, PA. Sunday morning the bells would ring to gather the farmers to service. I can still hear the voices blending old hymns and see the sprawling valley alive with life. It was a by-gone time.

ALCORN, PAMELA
[a.] Mountlake Terrace, WA [title] "Prayer" [pers.] All of my poetry is inspired by my Lord and Savior. He puts the words on my heart and I write them. This particular poem, I wrote for an extremely powerful and loving best friend, Lindy. I feel my poetry is an inspiration for everyone who reads it, I feel blessed and grateful that I am able to share it.

ALICEA, LORI
[a.] Valparaiso, IN [title] "That's How Your Garden Grows" [pers.] It has been written that, "life and death exists in the power of the tongue." Our edifying words can build one up for a lifetime. And the days of ruin for another with a razor sharp thought. Speaking life to someone is an opportunity we possess with everyday word that leaves our mouth. Remember that words unleased are a feathers in the wind. They can never be retrieved. People's hearts resemble sponges desperately attempting to soak the waters of affirmation. Little effort is required to be a difference. Let us all be mindful that our sentences can be priceless gifts with great worth to it's receiver. It was also written, "from the abundance of the heart, the mouth speaks." May our hearts be the treasures filled to capacity with love, so that we can be the overflow into those around us.

ALLEN, SHAUN
[a.] Wichita, KS [title] "My Love" [pers.] I would like to thank God and my family for their love and support during my struggle to become a writer. I would also like to thank you, the reader, without you, I would starve. Last but not least, I want to thank that one special person in my life. You know who you are. The search is finally over for me.

ALSTON, JACKIE
[a.] Alexandria, LA [title] "Red or White Rose" [pers.] "Red or White Rose" was written in memory of my mother who passed away December 1991. I lost my best friend. During the previous Mother's Day church services, I proudly took a red rose from a little boy's basket. In 1992, I dreaded the tradition of passing out roses; but because of the beautiful memories of my dear mother and the beautiful little boy standing before me, I was able to smile as I took a white rose. I kissed my child's forehead, straightened the beautiful little red rose in his lapel, and prayed that I was his best friend.

ALVARADO, ELSIE
[a.] Bronx, NY [title] "Trickles of Life" [pers.] "Trickles of Life" is an analogy of birth, life and nature. It projects to me a reflection of life's experiences. My thoughts and feelings were inspired by the birth of my children. The sharing within my family, the relationship with my companion, and the examples set by the senior members of my family, my parents. I dedicate this poem to all my family members who are the true inspirations of my creativity. I especially want to

acknowledge my children—Adonica and Edwin Isaiah, Jr., my husband Eddie, my parents Laura and Roberto Sr., my brothers and sister—Robert Jr., George, Dianah, Milagros, and my two nieces Shaguana and Anisa.

ALVAREZ, KRYSTAL
[a.] Union, NJ [title] "Iris" [pers.] I wrote the poem about Iris, my sister two years ago when I was 10. I wrote it about her because when she was born she had many complications. There were times when the doctors couldn't assure us that she was going to be okay. But Iris was a fighter and even though she was small and weak she never gave up. If you ever looked at my sister you could never believe that she went threw that pain. Iris loves to laugh and argue with me but I could never change her for anything else.

AMMONS, VICTORIA
[a.] Hampton, VA [title] "And the Two Shall Become One" [pers.] This poem is dedicated to my God—Fearing husband, Charlie. Our persistent faith and growth in God has enabled us to experience a true oneness. It is important to understand that marriage is more than an "I love you" and goes deeper than saying "I do." This poem represents the words God inspired me write while thinking about how Charlie and I united and became as one. God showed us that he is able to bring two different people after his own heart and spirit into unity "with" his spirit. As helpmate relationship with God, they will experience this unity and the two shall become one.

ANDERSON, ANITA
[a.] New Bedford, MA [title] "The Shutter" [pers.] I enjoy writing, poetry as well as short stories. It gives me an outlet to deal with some of life's situations. The shutter was written when my boyfriend suffered from agoraphobia. He is getting better now.

ANDERSON, BARBARA
[a.] Spring Valley, CA [title] "Have You Heard My Story?" [pers.] Poetry is a voice that is not heard. It is read. It does not have to be understood to be liked and it only needs to be believed in to be loved. I am thankful that I can hear the sound it makes, and love what it says. I wish to thank my family for believing in me. My family gave me roots that allow me to stand strong and continue to grow. I have family that although we are not physically related mean even more to me. I love you all.

ANDERSON, BREANNA
[a.] Hillsboro, KS [title] "Wisdom, Beauty, and Age" [pers.] I wrote this poem because I feel like our modern society has lost sight of the value of the elderly, and the knowledge that many of them possess. The older people in my life have given me an education I could never have learned in school, and I thank them!

ANDERSON, BREANNA
[a.] Hillsboro, KS [title] "The Beat of an Irish Drum" [pers.] I have always loved to research my families lineage, and it leads back to Ireland. I have been raised in a house where Irish music is always playing, and where the Irish drum is always beating.

ANDERSON, DAVE
[a.] Pittsford, NY [title] "Starbird" [pers.] These are the lyrics to a musical composition I wrote in memory of a beloved teacher, Mrs. Hanna Starbird Terrana. With her love and kindness she touched the hearts of many people, including my own. Life goes on and there is everything to think about, but take some time off to remember the people who have helped and stood by you.

ANDERSON, JASON ANDERSON
[a.] Lewisville, TX [title] "The Way You See" [pers.] This poem was written for a friend of mine

who died in a car accident. She taught me to see poetry in a new light. Though she never could read it with her eyes she taught me another way to see. And what she used to help me see through her eyes and heart. This made me not only write poetry but, understand how to feel poetry with my heart.

ANDERSON, JENNIFER
[a.] Middletown, NY [title] "All I Feel for Him" [pers.] My poem "All I feel for Him" is very special to me. It tells about a person that no matter how hard I tried I couldn't change. The poem explains what a painful relationship it was. Poetry has an extremely importance role in my life. I can write about whatever I'm feeling. It's a talent I cherish very deeply. My poetry can make people cry and laugh, and humor is important in life. I also write songs. I live with my father, Harold, Mother, Laraine and older sister Christine. I'm in eighth grade in Minisink Valley Middle School and I'm 14 years old. When I'm by myself I enjoy poetry, singing and listening to music. Music is very important to me. I also feel I have talent in singing. My dream is to become a famous singer. Life to me is a very special gift that should be enjoyed and never taken for granted. We are all blessed to be here so I believed we need to strive for what we believe in and never give up on our dreams. I am determined to make my life a good one. Even though we go through many hard times I know I'll never give up my faith in God. Life is important and I don't plan on wasting mine.

ANDERSON, JOAN
[a.] Woodbridge, VA [title] "A Horse and Freedom" [pers.] I was reared on a farm in Prince George's County, MD; the fourth of five children in the musically gifted family of Kenneth and Lucile Ellis. As a teenager in the 1950's my life revolved around singing and riding horses with my best friend Caroline. Sometimes I would daydream as I watched my horse grazing in the pasture, imagining I knew her thoughts and feelings. Those daydreams (and my mother's poetic legacy) inspired me to write "A Horse and Freedom" when I was only fourteen years old.

ANDERSON, SUSAN
[a.] Madison, WI [title] "Boiling Point" [pers.] Writing is revelation to me. I learn and grow as I write—spiritually and intellectually. Writing also increases my venerability, as my soul takes shape on the page. My vocation? Not yet. My calling? Definitely. I live in Madison, WI, work at the university; and attend University Community Church, whore God feeds me.

ANDERSON, TRACY
[a.] Dearborn, MI [title] "Genuine Love" [pers.] Poetry, for me, is a way to express personal experiences. I believe poems convey individual ideas and are open for each individual to interpret. Mine are simply snapshots of moments in my life. I most enjoy knowing that readers will identify my words with a place or time in their own lives. The breadth of our collective individualities offers limitless interpretations and meanings. I believe that is where the mystery and attraction to poetry lies in all of us.

ANDREWS, STEPHEN
[a.] Orlando, FL [title] "My Love, My Life" [pers.] This is a very special poem to me and my wife. It was dedicated and given with absolute love to my wife on her birthday. I wrote this poem expressing my innermost feelings and deepest thoughts. My wife has truly opened my heart and filled it with love. I have always had some talent with writing letters and poems. But, my wife gave me the love that has been missing all of my life. That is what opened my feelings and expressions to poetry.

ANNIS, JOSHUA
[a.] Mattoon, IL [title] "Darth Vader's Fall" [pers.] My name is Joshua Annis. I live on a farm near

Mattoon, Illinois. I am seventeen years old. My hobbies are reading, writing, drawing, horseback riding and swimming. The poem that I wrote is about when Anakin Skywalker turned to the dark side of the Force, and got into a duel over a volcano with Obi-Wan Kenobi, his former master in Jedi training. This, as you probably can tell, takes place in the saga of *Star Wars*. I used vivid words to try to make this poem sound very dramatic. I believe that poetry expresses the feelings of the soul that the Lord has given to us.

ANUMAKONDA, RAVI
[a.] Athens, OH [title] "My Room" [pers.] "My Room" reflects my feelings about the person I love and the way she changed my life forever. I think she's the most wonderful person I ever met. She began to write one of the liveliest chapters of my life. She painted my life with beautiful colors. I thought I was the luckiest person standing. Then one day, she was gone, just like that. I love her even more now. I know that deep inside, she still loves me. I strongly believe that a time will come when she'll be back in my arms. Till then, I relieve those moments of bliss, that we shared together and her eternal gift to me. "My Room" is dedicated to her and the special moments we shared together.

ARJUMAND, FIRDOUS
[a.] Warangal, AP, India [title] "Unique Creation" [pers.] I am an Indian, doing my graduation in Communicative English and am very much interested in creative writing. To me, poetry is truly the very best way of pouring out all that is inside you, a way that expresses you in the right light; and a way that reaches straight for the reader's heart. My present poem depicts my portrait of a true woman. In composing it my sister, Shagufta, has been a invaluable inspiration to me.

ARMITSTEAD, JANET
[a.] Burbank, CA [title] "Midsummer Swim" [pers.] I was inspired to write this poem after spending a few quiet moments by my backyard swimming pool on a summer evening. As birds cooed softly and twilight deepened, I was struck by the eternal quality inherent in water and its profound harmony with natural surroundings. I have endeavored to capture, in verse, the tremendous awareness of serenity and awe to experienced. I have always enjoyed writing poetry as a means of expressing my innermost feelings and experiences. I also take pleasure in singing. For me, language and song are two of the most natural and joyful affirmations of living.

ARMSTRONG, HART
[a.] Wichita, KS [title] "The Simple Things" [pers.] When I wrote this poem I was on a diet, trying to lose some weight. All I had for supper was one hard-boiled egg, a piece of toast, and a cup of tea. I began to notice that egg, how marvelously it was constructed, what a miracle the shell was. I thought of life's simple things and how God is seen in them if we will only look for Him. I was inspired to write this poem about the egg. And about the bug I saw in my bathroom this morning.

ARTHUR, DAVID
[a.] Colorado Springs, CO [title] "Ideas" [pers.] I started writing at the age of 15, I think, because I was so shy and used it as a form of expression growing older I continued to write, including short stories, a novel, many songs and even a screen play. But, poetry is near and dear to me and "Ideas" is I think, an example of what everyone has said at one time or another. "It was right on the tip of my tongue."

ASHLEY, BENJAMIN
[a.] Newport News, VA [title] "Where Are We Now?" [pers.] In the process of our creation, God breathed into us some of His spirit. It was that spirit which inspired me to look at the conditions of my fellow man; my brothers and sisters, and write this poem. My poem shows what we must endure if we

stray from God's guidance. There are many people in this world today who this poem is talking about. They are in despair, because they have forgotten from whence they were created; in the image of God, to be like God; to become one with God.

ASHWORTH, GEORGE
[a.] Anderson, SC [title] "Happy First Anniversary" [pers.] When I was growing up I had a passion for singing and writing song lyrics. So one day after I married my wife I decided for the perfect gift I would write this poem. Now that it is published in this book I am hoping that it will help me in the field that I have always dreamed of . . . The Music Business. Now I would like to thank The International Library of Poetry for publishing my poem.

AURIEMMA, ANTHONY
[a.] Los Angeles, CA [title] "Princess Sara" [pers.] I am an actor poet living in Los Angeles, prior to moving here I lived in a castle with my girlfriend during that time it seemed that family and friends wanted to sabotage our love, then we began to fade as well in our honesty to each other. Rather than looking at our faults I choose to focus on the lessons of beauty, life, learning and friendship for these are the things that made me noble and wise. Poetry's gift alchemizes life's experiences.

AUSTIN, ARVETTA
[a.] Lewiston, CA [title] "Time" [pers.] "Time" is the most precious gift any of us can ever receive. To live each moment to the fullest with those I love, is saying to God how much His "Gift" means to me. For that reason, "Time" is very special to me, and I hope others will feel the love in my poetry. I love writing and I hope one day I will have the thrill of seeing my two novels. "First Impressions" and "New Beginnings" in print as well. For they, like my poems are truly labors of love.

AUSTIN, NATHAN
[a.] Farmington, NM [title] "How Beautiful!" [pers.] It was autumn of 1998. I was sitting in my work truck in an open field several miles south of Ignacio, CO just east of the Pine River. Several deer were grazing on our gas pipeline right-of-way to the north of me and the leaves on the trees just below the bluffs were sparkling their beautiful different colors from the early light snow that was melting under the mid-morning sun. I felt so thankful to be there to enjoy such beauty and wanted to share it with my wife of thirty years in this poem.

AVISON, IAN
[a.] Whangarie, New Zealand [title] "Fireside" [pers.] To say I place my heart and soul into my writing is my way of showing to the world the truth of my expression that is me. For the words of my writings to dance their reality upon the page I must dip my pen into the heartwell of humanity. There lies the language of emotion which by my guidance I hope to reach out and touch just one reader. To you dear reader I give my heart felt thinks for allowing me this opportunity to express myself, may your way be of love and peace.

AYERS, ANGELA
[a.] Oberlin, KS [title] "Best Friend of Mine" [pers.] This poem was written to express my feelings towards my friends. I recently lost one of my closest friends and I couldn't have to lose another one. I would like to thank Brett for all of his inspiration he has given me. I hope all of my friends realize how important they are to me. You guys make my life worth living!

AYERS, JOSH
[a.] Huntington Beach, CA [title] "Across Forever's Boundry" [pers.] This poem reflects a period of my life when I was wondering whether or not I would ever find that special someone who would make my life complete. There is not always someone for everyone and at the same time there may be more than one person for another person.

BABIJ, DANIEL
[a.] Trenton, NJ [title] "She" [pers.] I feel very blessed by my ability to write insightful poetry. Writing has influenced me from a very young age. I enjoy reading lyrical writings, as well as writing my own material. Growing up in Central New Jersey, the fast paced lifestyled of the east coast is a simple of the experiences that have helped shape my writing. Oftentimes, people are so wrapped up in the "Action" that they almost do not feel the "drama" of life. So I take action in order to instill drama in the lives of those who read my poetry. A lot of our friends, and families experiences are relative to our own. Therefore we can always learn from one another. So I hope you too enjoy poetry, as I do.

BACZKOWSKI, ANTHONY
[a.] Rancho Palos Verdes, CA [title] "Realization" [pers.] This poem exemplifies my philosophical belief that "Love" transcends the elemental universe into a realm that can't be defined. Love gives humanity a glimpse of eternal life. My personal experiences have confirmed my belief that "Love" is undoubtedly the greatest of the human virtues. I want my poem to be an inspiration and a hope to those who read it.

BADRI, MOHAMMAD
[a.] Mobile, AL [title] "My Heart" [pers.] The most pleasant way to express joy and sadness is through writing poems. My special feeling aspires from a region full of natural beauties and streaming springs along with wild roses surrounding the ancient Castle of "Falakolaflak." On a mountain at the heart of Capital city of Khorramabad North of Persian Gulf. I found similarity between poetic feelings and excitement in flying as part of my career. Some of my articles and poems being shared by media internationally. I have also been honored for writing a poem of the legacy of President Clinton named "In Your Presindency." Furthermore, the special poem of "My Heart" reveals some diversity and antagonistic fillings.

BAFIA, RANDA
[a.] Mira Loma, CA [title] "Little People" [pers.] This people was inspired by the birth of my first grandchild. I am passionate about the need to instill positiveness in our children. A poetic verse is an opportunity to express and guide our young people. Instilling in them all that is good, and all that is positive in a world that often loses its focus. It is an opportunity that shouldn't be missed.

BAGSHAW, JEANNINE
[a.] Hochheim Am Main, Germany [title] "The Scent of Love" [pers.] Writing was almost always my way of expressing my emotions. After a very crucial incident in my life, however, I stopped and became laconic and bitter. I had already started to pull myself out of the "hole" I was in, when I met this gentle, intelligent, funny man, who then for the first time in two years inspired me to write. To write this poem. He gave me happiness, gave me wings and thought me how to fly. These words resemble the beauty of our love. Thank you Greg! I am yours forever!

BAILEY, CAROL
[a.] Bolt, WV [title] "A Mother's Love" [pers.] I have been writing poetry for many years. It gives me a lot of pleasure, and is a source of great joy to my life. It's a wonderful way to put feelings into words. This poem is very special to me. I hope it will be enjoyed, by all who read it.

BAILEY, JEANIE
[a.] Houston, TX [title] "In My Dreams" [pers.] This poem was written with a good friend in mind. After thirty years of marriage, she was divorced and entered the dating scene again. "In My Dreams" describes her need to feel loved again. I have been married twenty-six years and can only imagine how people must feel in this situation. I hope others will benefit from this poem also.

BAKER, ANGELA
[a.] Monrovia, MD [title] "My Mother, My Friend" [pers.] Poetry is my life. I've been writing poetry since I was twelve years old. Poetry is the way I express myself and my feelings. I love writing about anything that inspires me. My family and friends have been a big part of my life and I love them all. Thank you everyone who has made a difference in my life!

BAKER, DANIEL
[a.] Winston-Salem, NC [title] "I Remember" [pers.] This poem was written shortly after my then girlfriend cheated on me. This poem has, and always will have a special place in my heart.

BAKER, JAMES
[a.] Groton, CT [title] "My Heart" [pers.] Poetry has had a large affect on my life. I started writing when I was very young. I feel as if it is a stronghold in my life when keeps me going. If ever I need someone to listen to my problems, my notebook has always acted as a loyal friend and my pen has been our way of communicating. I want to tank my family and friends for all their support. Especially my best friend Michelle who has always stood more on back by my side and protected me from my worst critic . . . myself.

BAKER, SUSAN
[a.] Covington, LA [title] "Pearl Divers and Prospectors" [pers.] This poem is in honor of my father, who died at 67 of multiple sclerosis! Now I'm 45, and I also have MS. Both of us loved the desert, and the Pacific Island. In this poem, I tried to hold those conflicting loves as one.

BAKU, YLLI
[a.] Brooklyn, NY [title] "I Don't Change" [pers.] Being myself is what makes we who I am today. Life goes on as the train in my poem moves along its ride. Only when I'm myself I enjoy who I am. Then and only then I feel the pleasure of being me. There's no need to change that. I don't change who I am. I respect it.

BALDRIDGE, WILLIS
[a.] Cottage Grove, OR [title] "Holders of a Dream" [pers.] My name is Willis Baldridge. I'm 30 years old, and live in Cottage Grove, OR. Writing poems are my ways of expressing my feelings about life and events around me. This poem "Holders of a Dream" was written the day after the Thurston shooting in Springfield, OR just North of Cottage Grove. I was inspired by the way our children view life. How much violence children see every day. They don't see what life really stands for. When my two girls grow up I hope they can feel safe in their schools as I once did.

BALEK, PAMELA
[a.] East Berlin, PA [title] "Winter Sonne" [pers.] This is one of many poems that I have composed since my teenage years. It was written for a special person who allowed me to love again after a failed marriage and year of turbulent emotions. The publishing of this poem marks the beginning of a dream for me, one that I hope will continue for years to come!

BALITZ, GREG
[a.] Lawrenceville, GA [title] "Miss You" [pers.] This poem is for someone very special in my life, my father. His strength and commitment to our family is my inspiration. I'll never be able to talk to my father but this way I can immortalize a part of our life. I hope that other people who have had a loss or have a special person in their lives can relate to my love for my father and share this piece with other loved ones.

BALL, CELESTE
[a.] Phoenix, AZ [title] "Dad Was a Quiet Man" [pers.] When my Dad died in September 1999 my sister Marcene encouraged each sister to say something at the funeral. There were a million things maybe I could have said, maybe should have said but I hadn't come across what my heart told me I was meant to say. Then I thought about Dad, his easy chair, afternoons—the poem started to blossom. When I finished I knew in my heart this was what I needed to say. At Dad's funeral I spoke this poem to the gathering. I like to think that Dad approved.

BALL, JENNIFER
[a.] Livermore, CA [title] "Whoever You Are" [pers.] I discovered poetry during my formidable teen years. It was savior them as it is today. I would not be here without it in my life. Art is my life and my life is beautiful.

BALL, LANCE
[a.] Miami, FL [title] "The Union of Love" [pers.] This poem is my expression of encouragement to my sweet fiancee Lynn. After I proposed, I sensed the stress she was enduring while planning our wedding as I started law school miles away. I wanted her to know that our relationship could remain strong and our love continue to grow through our brief separation. There is a season for everything; and this was our dormant period. Lynn is the most patient, understanding, supportive, and loving woman I've known. She is God's perfect gift to me, and I am excited to begin my life with her. I will cherish her forever.

BALLOU, JOHN
[a.] Vallejo, CA [title] "Serengeti" [pers.] I am an artist of endangered animals and in producing a book of my artwork I decided to try my hand at poetry. I created poems to go with the moods and character of each piece of art "Serengeti," is a poem that goes with the face of a Leopard accompanied by Wildabeasts in the background. I have created a book of my artwork and some poems called "Patterns that Connect." My artwork can be found online. I consider writing poetry a priviledge and I will always cherish it.

BANKSTON, MADISON
[a.] Puyallup, WA [title] "To My Husband" [pers.] Having grow up on beautiful Long Island, NY and lived and visited many places in the world, experienced a rich life verse has provided me a way to share those special moments in time with my family, friends and others. I truly believe a thought expressed in verse is from the heart, reaching out to touch even one soul to change it forever.

BANKSTON, MADISON
[a.] Puyallup, WA [title] "If Once But I" [pers.] When we think of finding that one person, our soulmate, in our soulmate, in our many long journeys through our lifetime, well that is what inspired this poem, the hope that somehow we feel a connection even one that spans great distance and time.

BANTUG, CHITO
[a.] Clifton Park, NY [title] "Morning Breaks" [pers.] Inspiration comes in many forms. In this case, it came through fear; fear of losing someone I care about. Then, as I wrote this poem I realized there was no need to fear. She will always be in my heart. For you Kellie, wherever the road takes you.

BARBER, HEATHER
[a.] Adrian, MI [title] "Where Did He Go?" [pers.] I feel that my gift in writing poetry came from my mother, who has also written valuable poetry. (To her) my poem "Where Did He Go" is telling about a woman who's love has left her and she is afraid to love again. I enjoy to write poetry. My poetry shows that there is pain in the world.

BARBER, SANDRA
[a.] Duluth, GA [title] "Secrets" [pers.] I have been writing poetry since I was in third grade. One of the most enjoyable aspects of writing is the freedom to express your feelings so completely. As I look back on my poetry, I realize it tells my emotional life story. It is an accurate reflection of who I was at any given point in time. I live in the Atlanta area with my husband and two stepchildren, two dogs, two cats, one rabbit and a guinea pig. They are all a perpetual source of writing inspiration.

BARBOSA, ARCHIE
[a.] Livermore, CA [title] "Confusion" [pers.] "Confusion" not much to say but the confusion inside my head. A roadblock, so huge to take out with a blink of an eye. My past experiences since I came to America had been rough, so many accomplishments yet so many downfalls! Only time can tell whether I survive, or be a part of the "Bleached" society. Experienced are the most poetic part of your life. You should cherish it, like your mom, dad, brothers and sisters, especially loved ones. Experiences should be your pot of gold, hidden long before the world was created.

BARKER, BRIAN
[a.] Alexandria, LA [title] "Mom" [pers.] Anyone who has ever lost a parent knows how hard it is spiritually and emotionally. I found that the best way to ease the pain was to focus not on the fact that my mother was gone, but rather on all the good times we had together and all the good time we can still have together even though she is not here in person. This poem is my thank you letter for all the times she was there for me in my life.

BARKLEY, JENNA
[a.] Ft. Myers, FL [title] "One Love" [pers.] Poetry has so much meaning in my life. I write poetry to express my feelings about life itself, the way I feel about anything, and about other people. My poem "One Love," is about my Grandmother. This poem commemorates my grandmother for she was a very important person in my life. She inspired me by the courage strength that she had. I wrote this poem so she could see and feel that every one of us is still thinking about her and still holds a place for her in our hearts.

BARNES, BIBBIE
[a.] Blairesville, GA [title] "Harry's Hats" [pers.] My poem was sent to you at the encouragement of my husband, Harry. I was dusting our bedroom furniture. Harry had placed his caps in neat order across the top of the mirror, one hanging on the door knob. Thus, my poem came to be. On the computer I drew a figure holding a stack of various kinds of hats. I placed his poem beside the figure. Harry would soon celebrate his 72nd birthday. My poem became his special card from me. Thank you for publishing my poem. At our age, it makes us very excited and proud.

BARNES, DIXIE
[a.] Clifton, KS [title] "My Baby Girl" [pers.] My daughter, Teresa, took her State Board Nursing Exam and was confident she had passed. One week later, she was killed in a housefire. This poem was written in her memory on the anniversary of her death, February 21, 1999. Teresa aspired to be a geriatric nurse, like me. She was a compassionate caregiver, loved by the residents of the nursing home where she worked as an aide. She gave us a beautiful granddaughter, Regan, who lives with her father in a nearby town. To help other nursing students, we have initiated a scholarship fund at our local bank.

BARNES, MICHAEL
[a.] Clifton, CO [title] "Final Ride" [pers.] I write poetry to express on my decisions in life, based on the facts of the past and present experiences. This particular poem, was written based on leaving the rode "rough life," to commit to the "gentle life" of a family, with my "now" lovely wife (Rebecca.) Faced with uncertainty of what the future may hold vs. what the past has left behind. My "Final Ride" in the Rodeo vs. my "Final Ride" to a fall of heartbreaks.

BARNES, TERRACE
[a.] Philadelphia, PA [title] "I Wonder" [pers.] Writing is a way for me to escape the trades of everyday life, it helps me to relax and clear my mind. This poem is one of many that I have written that escapes the trouble and elevates me to a higher place where I can speak my emotions freely. I hope you enjoy reading it as much as I enjoyed writing it.

BARRETT, ADAM
[a.] Norman, OK [title] "The Curse of Blessing" [pers.] Poetry has always been an invaluable means of expression for me. I put my joys, my pain, my love, and my frustration on paper. "The curse of blessing" is a mirror image of me in poem form. Writing is the way I share my gift with the world.

BARRETT, BARBARA
[a.] Elkhart, IN [title] "The Vertical View" [pers.] Although I am saddened by the world view of our present age, I am strengthened by the abiding infallibility of God's truth and love. I am challenged and grateful to be able to share deeply held conviction through this poem. Perhaps a captured truth or insight will inspire and encourage someone else as well. There are few things as exciting or rewarding at the exchange of ideas and the creation of something which will add some beauty and meaning to the lives of others. The written word endures. What an example God gave us through His preserved message of the Bible.

BARRETT, CHARLES
[a.] Edgewater, FL [title] "Beautifully Perfect" [pers.] My name is Charles Barrett and I am 16 years old. I live in Florida and I don't think of myself as much of a writer. I wrote this poem for a girl who is dear to me. I just want to say that you don't have to be a "writer" to write if someone or something inspires you enough. Also, this poem is for you Brinson.

BARRETT, KEVIN
[a.] Silver Spring, MD [title] "The Shout" [pers.] He resides in Silver Spring, MD. His poem is based on his hospital experience at the young age of eight years old. "The job of the poet, is to fight wars with words. Let our pen be our weapon, let our paper be the battlefield." He has been published previously.

BARRINGER, WHITNEY
[a.] Bismarck, AR [title] "What Sam Gave" [pers.] I wrote this poem because I wanted to see how people reacted to it. Sad mostly, but as a poet you have to see how people react to either correct yourself, or keep on writing that way. Thanks to friends and family, I can write poetry in a way that has a reaction. I don't like to see people throw away my poems saying or acting like it didn't affect them. The key to my poetry is reaction. It shows that the person that reads it, my poetry, and I are alive. Since I am thirteen, it makes me feel really alive.

BARTLETT, TONJA
[a.] Sigel, PA [title] "Frames of Life" [pers.] My poetry, including "Frames of Life," is just simply inspired by life as I experience it each day. I feel that the most extraordinary things are the universe surrounding us, the family and friends around us, and the incredible gifts within us. What else could I write about?

BARTO, STEPHANIE
[a.] Chester, VA [title] "A Maiden's Praise" [pers.] I have always loved reading and writing poetry. This poem speaks of a person who only exists in my dreams. Someone who, through these dreams, I have known since childhood. I would never have

written this poem, had it not been for a very dear friend, who would be mortified if I named him, so I will not. However, I must thank him for encouraging me to write the story of my dream friend and I. This poem was born of that book-in-progress. I hope everyone has someone in their dreams that my poem reminds them of.

BAUMANN, RITA
[a.] Homestead, FL [title] "Three Days in October" [pers.] Born and educated in the U.S. Virgin Islands, Rita Baumann feels richly blessed to have attended St. Mary's Catholic School and St. Joseph's High School, graduating within the top ten percent of her class. Ms. Baumann attended the University of Connecticut, George Washington University, University of Phoenix, and the University of Miami, earning three master's degrees. Ms. Baumann has taught him school English, been a guidance counselor, and a middle school assistant principal for five and a half years. Ms. Baumann now resides and works in Miami-Dade County with her fifteen-year old son, Kai, a junior in high school.

BAVARO, ANGIE
[a.] Boston, MA [title] "Watching" [pers.] I wrote this poem during a low point in my life. I worried about what other people thought of me and not what I thought of myself. This poem is my reflection of myself.

BAXLEY, MICHELLE
[a.] Cottondale, FL [title] "A Chance with You" [pers.] I wrote this poem for a guy that I am now with. For the longest time I want to go out with him, not knowing that he felt the same way. To me this poem means that by expressing my feelings to this guy I was letting him know how I felt and that I just wanted a change to prove to him I could fulfill everything promise. In this small town of Marrianna, Florida, there is not a lot of people who will not be faithful. I will thought and that is what I wanted to say to David. By me entering this poem in his contest he found at how I felt and now we are both very happy.

BAYS, O.
[a.] Miami, FL [title] "Above All You" [pers.] I am fifty four years old, and was a flight attendant for many of them. I have always loved to write. I finally got the courage to send this in and lo and behold you acknowledged me. Having written this poem when I was quite young, I came across it, and felt that I had for the stars and made it happen. I hope those who read it never settle for less. I am an older woman now, having seen the world I still believe in love.

BEASLEY, JESSICA
[a.] Jefferson City, TN [title] "Sickness" [pers.] This poem was written on a College trip to Ireland. The last few nights we stayed in Dublin I started missing my home. All the other students had left, and I decided to stay in and put my feelings down on paper. Although the country was beautiful, there's nothing like home. For years I have been using poetry express my feelings. I have had many losses and gains over the year, and one loss inspired me to start writing. With that one person's love and friendship he changed my life. For that, I thank Mr. Steve Cureton for blessing this world with his son, Brandon.

BEAUDRY, AMANDA
[a.] Barrie, ON [title] "Did You Ever Try?" [pers.] Poetry to me is a way of expressing my feelings. I have always enjoyed writing, it comes natural for me to put my thoughts into rhyme. This poem reflects on how I was feeling at that time. Things were hard and that was my way dealing with it. When I couldn't find the words to say face to face; it came out perfectly on paper. To me, poetry has always come from my heart and has always been 100 percent true to how I feel. I hope there are others out there who can relate. Mom, Dad—I love you.

BEAULIEU, JESSICA
[a.] Welland, ON [title] "Tormenting Yourself" [pers.] A good-hearted woman, my mother, once told me, "To move one person with your words is a life time of happiness." And with these words of advice, that is what I have come on this world to do. My love, for many years has been to write, and move people by my words. "Tormenting Yourself" hopefully shouldn't choose to make shallow conclusions so quickly on others. This poem encourages people to overcome their dark and suffering times, to realize they are not alone.

BELASHUK, VERONICA
[a.] Brentwood, NY [title] "Ronnie's Brother" [pers.] "Ronnie's Brother" by Veronica Belashuk, Brentwood, NY. This poem was written for my brother, the only family I have l left. I wanted him to know how special he was is to me. Family is very important to both of us. I am sure it is important to a lot of people. It is important to let the people you love know how you feel about them. Too many things in this world are taken for granted. I hope everyone who reads this book, is inspired to look at life in a new light. Writing poetry has given me a gift to look at things differently. Reading is our way of "getting away." Enjoy reading this great collection of poetry, and let yourself imagine, dream, and think differently.

BELL, ROSE
[a.] Connellsville, PA [title] "Giving Thanks" [pers.] This poem was written with one very signal person in my mind. A man that came into my life and showed me what true love really is. I would like to take this opportunity to thank him for loving me unconditionally by dedicating his poem to him.

BELL, SARAH
[a.] Portland, OR [title] "Eternal Love" [pers.] This poem is dedicated to my husband who has been an inspiration to my life. Destiny had laid the path to Bryan and fate led me down it; for that I will be forever grateful. Poetry is such a large part of my life because it has allowed me the freedom to share my expressions with others. I would also like to give recognition to my family especially my mother for always encouraging me to write. I have been very fortunate for God has blessed me with many wonderful people and gifts in my life such as my beautiful daughter.

BENGTSON, KRIS
[a.] Raleigh, NC [title] "Slightly North of Broad" [pers.] Life is about having a sand castle of preconceptions built for you and merely watching it crumble beneath the continuous of knowledge, which are formed by words. Words build all that shape our lives. Words are creation, words are motivation, and words are inspiration. The challenge is learning how to channel this knowledge toward your river of dreams. My river was found lightly north of broad.

BENSON, BILLY JACK
[a.] Kapuskasing, ON [title] "Time" [pers.] Most poetry that comes from my often puzzled mind sets itself in a certain rhythmic period in my life since most of my poems are lyrics. Time was written in a matter of minutes with my band, "Tuesday's Father" back in grade nine. We were a bunch of dreamers and all we wanted was a truthful song that actually meant something. I never would have thought that any of our songs would have ever been published. Many thanks to Curtis Dumais and Neil Ng-A-Fook for making this little dream a reality.

BENTSEN, PATRICK
[a.] Riverhead, NY [title] "Dreams" [pers.] My poem is special to me because it tells my life story. In my town not too many people know how to express themselves and with the gift of verse that has been bestowed upon me I have been designated an "outcast." I believe that I am not an outcast, but an unique individual with a gift. Sure it is not shooting a basketball or hitting a baseball. Still I can do something much better and more difficult. I can express my true feelings. Sometimes though it feels like the only way to enjoy my gift is in my dreams.

BERNIER, FARAH
[a.] Randolph, MA [title] "The Gentleman, The Man, The Old Man" [pers.] I am currently a Marketing and Human Resources major at Boston College. I have been writing poetry for as long as I can remember. Everything I've written is inspired by my environment and examples of such leaders as Maya Angelou and Ida B. Wells. I truly look upon poetry as a gift of the writer to others. I feel this way because I believe that no matter who you are and what your situation in life is, there's always at least one other person in the world who relates to you. What better way is there to connect with such relatives, than through poetry? I just hope I can inspire others as I have been inspired.

BERRYHILL, SUSAN
[a.] Benson, AZ [title] "This Person" [pers.] Our greatest adventure in life may be finding our true self, and unlocking our individual potential which probably knows no depth. Unless we intentionally go through some personal refining, we never know what our greatest strengths, of weaknesses, and without discovering the total tapestry of our personalities and lives, we may miss our mark and never become all that we truly can be. Susan hails from Benson, Arizona, has been writing since she was 12, has a professional background in counseling and in the legal field; and says that poetry is the expression of her heart.

BEUGRE, REMY
[a.] Malmoe, Sweden [title] "Reunion" [pers.] My daughter is like two persons in one. Herself and my grandmother who she is reincarnating with the name Amenan. This is a twisted description of the pain that we're sharing of not being with the one we love this is dedicated to Amenan Carol Beugre.

BHAT, ADITYA
[a.] Rockaway Beach, NY [title] "Nightmare" [pers.] I wrote this poem in 5th grade, three years ago. At that time I devoured "Goosebumps" books, which inspired "Nightmare." I'd like to thank my mom for submitting my poem for publication.

BHATTACHARYA, SUDIPTO
[a.] New Delhi, India [title] "I Don't Have a Uterus" [pers.] I was born in 1971 in Delhi. After graduation in English (Hons.) at the University of Delhi, I started working as a copywriter in leading advertising agencies for a couple of years. At present, I am working as a Scriptwriter with a multimedia software organization. Although I am employed, my burning desire is to establish myself as a writer. If I get an opportunity then I would like to devote full-time in literary activities. I am also interested in painting. I am very much influenced by the life and teachings of Swami Vivekananda and mystic Shri Ramakrishna Paramhansa. I had observed that some issueless women were unhappy and suffering from anxiety and social stigma. This motivated me to write the poem.

BICKLER, BRITTANY
[a.] Evergreen, CO [title] "Life" [pers.] Poetry is a very beautiful thing, that I am lucky to be blessed with. Poetry is what I use to express all of my feelings with. It's helped me with many tough times in my life and been a wonderful outlet.

BIGGS, DUFFY
[a.] Des Moines [title] "American Awareness" [pers.] I am thirty-five years old. I live in Seattle, the Emerald City. This poem is an expression of self-realization and a statement of emotional growth. I hope that it shows a spark of the beauty that is within all of us in

this ethnically diverse country. God Bless America, the land of the brave and of the free.

BILBREY, JULIE
[a.] Quilan, TX [title] "My Wings" [pers.] Growing up, I had many obstacles to overcome in life, but because I have always loved to write. I always had an outlet for my feelings and intimate emotions. This particular poem signifies the little girl living inside reminding me of how strong I am, and who I have become by persevering through my past. Today I am a happily married woman with a beautiful home in the country where there is plenty of room to room free. Next to my husband, writing will forever remain my most cherished gift.

BILLING, STEVEN
[a.] Miami, FL [title] "My Long Blond Hair" [pers.] I have written permission from Clairol to use their name in a CD single to be released soon. It's a fun light campy song about beauty. I love Clairol and their products. My stage name is outrageous I encourage other poets to turn their poetry in to songs.

BIRD, CAROL
[a.] West Lawn, PA [title] "Love From A Brother" [pers.] I believe most of my poetry is inspired by God. I now know he gave me a start, telling me to keep things simple and write from my heart. I've been writing poems since third grade as a way to communicate with the ones I love and hold close to my heart. There is a brother of mine who was adopted, lives far away, yet we are so close we write to each other almost every day. This poem is how I know him.

BISAHA, TRACEY
[a.] Tucson, AZ [title] "Hiding Fears Through Shameful Tears" [pers.] I wrote the poem, "Hiding Fears Through Shameful Tears," in my difficult high school years. Like many young persons, I was at a point in my life of attempting to find happiness through many wrong choices. I later found that the guilt of these choices would overwhelm me and leave me empty inside. From the one I was avoiding, I eventually found the peace I was longing for with Christ Jesus on my side, I have been able to forgive my past and live a fuller and meaningful life.

BIVENS, MARREO
[a.] Fruitdale, AL [title] "Your Graduation" [pers.] This poem is a simple poem. I was writing this poem to my sister, because she was graduating from college. I thought that it would be an appropriate work to have published. Poetry is a great occupation to be gifted at doing. I say this because everyone isn't a poet. I don't know who in my family is good at writing poems, but I just know that I can write poems. Well, my family members are as follows: Gwen, Robert, Jeremy, and Tasha Gwen is my mother, Robert is my dad, Jeremy is my brother. And Tasha is my sister. I am from a town in the states of Alabama called fruitdale. It is located about 50 miles south of Mobile. I am a young man. I am only 19 years old. I'll be 20 this summer on June 25, 2000. I'll be attending the University of Southern Miss and I plan to be a Spanish teacher. I love to play football and will be playing at college. Last but not least. I thank God for giving me the talent of writing poems. I know without Him, I can do nothing. This quote here, I will leave. "Stand for something or you'll fall for anything."

BLACK, BILL
[a.] Kingstree, SC [title] "Nightscape" [pers.] We all live behind a mask. Occasionally that mask slips and we allow others a glimpse of the poetic thoughts and visions we usually reserve for ourselves. I am a commercial fisherman spending most of my time battling the sea for a living. While on the water my two main concerns are keeping my boat afloat and catching fish. When I can occasionally take off my "tough guy" mask, I let my inner self express itself

through poetry. I am 47 years old, attended Auburn University in Alabama and now live in McClellanville, South Carolina, a small fishing village. I have a daughter, Cullen, and a son, David and two granddaughters, Jordan and Michelle.

BLACK, JESSICA
[a.] Sacramento, CA [title] "Valentines Day Ballad" [pers.] I find poetry is very therapeutic. I wrote this poem on the loneliest day of the year— Valentine's Day. It's my response to the commercialized, flowers and candy day Valentine's Day has become. I hope people will laugh a little when they read this and then go out and do something nice and spontaneous for someone they love. It shouldn't take a holiday to say "I love you."

BLACK, MICHAEL
[a.] Scranton, KS [title] "The Human Story" [pers.] I write what is given to the pages. I write what I see in the eyes, and what I hear from the hearts of those around me. I put in a pinch of myself here and there. Though I deserve nothing in this life, God has chosen to give this wonderful ability. I thank Him for His sacrifice, and I thank you for your time.

BLACK, RUBY
[a.] Indianapolis, IN [title] "Love of Life" [pers.] I realized one morning that there are individuals who hate taking care of their basic needs and life in general. People rise each day hating each thing they have to do to accomplish a full day. I love my life with the tears, joys, sorrows, sadness and happiness it brings each day. Life is how you make it, change it, except it. What you do each day has already been done. You can add to it, take away from it, change or fix it, but do something.

BLACKWELL, SARAH
[a.] New York, NY [title] "I've Seen Your Soul Before" [pers.] This poem has much meaning to me. My everything Ish was the inspiration for it. As every day goes by he shows me how we are even more one person. I dedicate this to my love, my Ish.

BLAIR, KAROL
[a.] New Providence, PA [title] "Illness" [pers.] For me, poetry is away to express myself in an artistic way. To make sense of some things that have happened in my life, both good and bad. The poem "Illness" is about how life can be so unfair, and trying to figure out why it happens to the ones you love. In troubled times my faith in God and his word gives me strength and keeps me strong.

BLAIR, KAROL
[a.] New Providence, PA [title] "Thankful Poem To You" [pers.] This poem means a lot to me. I wanted to thank God far all the blessings he has given me, in my life. To let him know he is and always will be the first one in my heart. We all should take the time to thank God, and others in our lives. Show more love and kindness, instead of hate.

BLANCHARD, JENNIFER
[a.] Clifton, VA [title] "Can You Love This Cautious Soul" [pers.] There are those who love with everything they have and there are those who believe themselves incapable or unworthy of being loved. We must always give of ourselves, never expecting anything in return—for love is meant to be pure and selfless. If gaining the trust of someone in need takes all the time in the world, then the time spent is always worth it. We will never truly understand the workings of the human heart. It is an ocean and abyss of emotions to deep for man to ever measure. It breathes life into the soul something we can never forget.

BLESSING, FALON
[a.] St. Petersburg, FL [title] "Don't Call People Names" [pers.] What inspired me was my school Palm Harbor Montessori Academy and my class.

But most of all my teacher Ms. Bhana. At one time of my school there was a dose of name calling going around. I remember when Ms. Bhana called us in from recess. She started talking to us and stressing to us. She looked like she was going to cry. I felt really bad and right then I knew I wanted to write something about it so I did. I wrote a poem and that is how I got don't call people names. Thank you, Falon.

BLESSING, KAREN
[a.] Fresno, CA [title] "Storm's End" [pers.] This particular poem expresses the heartache of losing first love and realization that life does go on. The beauty of poetry, for me, goes deep beyond the words on the page to the release of innermost emotions and the inspirational perception of the reader, which is what I hope to accomplish with this poem and others. I would like to thank everyone who has ever been an inspiration to me, for you will always have a place in my heart.

BLISCHE, CORY
[a.] Baltimore, MD [title] "A Rose" [pers.] "A Rose" was written for my girlfriend and I gave it to her on Valentine's Day with a rose. Most of the people around me think I can write very well, and I suppose I can. I am not very optimistic and didn't expect to get published in this compilation. I have always enjoyed writing since eight grade when I had to write a few poems on Depression. One of the poems was slightly comical. It was called "Poo on Shoe." All of my classmates like those five poems and I have written other things since then.

BLUME, LESLIE
[a.] Mitchellville, MD [title] "Battle for Gold" [pers.] Poetry has always been my way of expressing myself when the word could not be said or expressed correctly. This poem was written for Rob, a special man that is very much a inspiration to me and my poetry, as in my children, Jeannette, Cindy and Danny. With their encouragement I have continued to write poetry.

BLUMERT, JESSICA
[a.] New York City, NY [title] "Today Tomorrow Forever" [pers.] This poem means alot to me. It was written for three very special friends of mine. They are Kristen, Angela, and Michelle. These friends have helped me through the best and the worst. Although next year I will be leaving them to go on to a different school and it will be hard for us to stay close. This poem is dedicated to our loving friendship.

BOCK, RACHEL
[a.] St. Louis, MO [title] "When" [pers.] This poem is about my best friend. She is very special to me and I wanted to let her know in a poem. I wrote this and I wanted to share my feelings for my friend with the rest of the world. I hope my poem is read by many people who need to know how true and beautiful a friendship really is.

BOCKLAGE, LAURENE
[a.] Jefferson City, MO [title] "Not Forgotten With Time" [pers.] My father, William Finess Lindsey, passed away a year ago and my love of writing helped to ease my grief! I wrote this poem about him and on a whim sent it in to the contest! I had to shorten it down to 20 lines and though it now doesn't say it all, I know that others will be able to tell what a special man he was! I received my love of writing from my grandmother, Mary Lindsey, and pray that they both can see me and realize how much I love and miss them.

BOHN, DIANE
[a.] Campbell, CA [title] "To Be Free" [pers.] I'm a mother of five children. I love to write poetry. I'm a full-time student. I work with handicap children. This poem was meant for them the darkness they must feel and the light of happiness they feel when they are stimulated to enjoy the light and the struggles they endure.

BOIVIN, TALLIE
[a.] Bangor, ME [title] "Family" [pers.] This poem sincerely captures the essence of my beliefs. To me, there is nothing more important in this world than the ones I love. Family members who inspired me: Shawna, Kyle, D. Shawn, Darroll, and Judith Anderson, Michael, Joanne, Cameron, Matthew, and Danielle Boivin, Eileen Hansen, Rey Prema Tower, Patricia, and Jean Coburn, Husband Richard, and children Maddi and Westt.

BOOKER, SHAVONA
[a.] Cincinnati, OH [title] "Thank You" [pers.] Poetry is my way of re-opening every emotional door, I've closed. It allows me to express myself in the purest way I know. It is true, love, and Grace. I want to thank Alexander Lohachitranont for inspiring me to share this side of myself. For having faith and allowing me to trust others with my heart. Thank you Alex. This one's for you.

BORESI, BEVERLY
[a.] Madrid, IA [title] "Within" [pers.] I have struggled for many years to bring my real self out. This poem reflects the fear, pain and courage used to overcome the barriers that life has imposed upon me. Having suffered from other's wrongs, I learned that sometimes things are not what they appear to be. And that being a product of my environment wasn't the right choice for me. Now that I have tested a world of new feelings; I am finding that to express myself through poetry comes fairly easy to me. It helps to find the child who hides within myself to be safe.

BOSE, TRICIA
[a.] Racine, WI [title] "Daddy" [pers.] "Daddy" was written for my father he was so busy working and putting food on the table and clothes on my back, we never had time together and I was growing up so fast, and we were so close. That he missed alot of me. This poem is one of my favorites because, it quick and short but yet has a meaning to it from the heart and I send this one because of parents that are busy to slow down and look around you. Don't miss the best thing in life, your kids, are a big part of your life forever.

BOTTONE, EDWARD
[a.] Staten Island, NY [title] "Silence Around Me" [pers.] I believe poetry is the true passage into a poets soul. A poet views things with very deep prospective, and searches into the inner core of their heart and soul for passion and truth. Although surrounded by everyday reality a poet can virtually transform into a world of fantasy and imagination still linked to reality to create something powerful and beautiful. My poem "Silence Around Me" was inspired by a women I met years ago who is now my beautiful wife "Donna," one who still inspires me to write beautiful poetry and encourages me to reach for my dreams and that is my passion for poetry.

BOUDREAU, FRANCIS
[a.] Montreal, QC [title] "The Oppression" [pers.] It's quite hard to let the biggest feelings come out with the right words, but in a poem it comes out in the same way that I feel it. There for my poem "The Oppression" reflect my soul and the illness that almost killed me and that afflicts thousand of other person.

BOVEE, C.
[a.] Kaneohe, HI [title] "Moments of You" [pers.] Poetry is a way for me to make visible the contents of my heart in hopes that it may touch someone or that someone may relate. My Heavenly Father has blessed me with this gift. This poem is the result of a special man who with his tenderness and special love awakened my heart and set it a flame. I love you E. M. from the very center of my heart to the very center of yours for eternity. Please share the love.

BOWDEN, CARLA
[a.] Garland, TX [title] "The Love of the Earth" [pers.] This poem is a personification of the wonderful time I had with my first serious boy-friend. We had grown up together and always been friends when we realized we could be more than friends we dated for nearly a year. When the time come for us to move on we both took it very hard. Writing this poem was part of coping. The first copy this poem has many tear stains. This very special persons name is Adam, which means "from the earth," and my name Celeste means "Heavenly." Adam will always have a special place in my heart. We were each others "First Love."

BOWE, DAVID
[a.] Indianapolis, IN [title] "War is Like My Love for You" [pers.] Mr. Marine, my teacher for our poetry unit was my source of encouragement. He told our class to never give up at something you believe in. Thank you Mr. Marine for all your support.

BOYD, CHARLESTON
[a.] Sherman, TX [title] "Interracial" [pers.] The focus of my poem is directed toward "Bigotry." Our society is drunk with ignorance. Thinking that the color of skin or difference of nationality will keep lover's apart. My vision is a sister to Martin Luther King's dream. That all people of the World can live and love regardless. It was Christ who broke down the middle wall of partition between races (Eph. 2:14) to give the world unity. I hope my word's will make a difference in the way we love each other, and see each other as God's creation.

BRADLEY, IAN
[a.] Sparta, WI [title] "You" [pers.] I write to display my reactions and emotions in a tangible form. Using the Art takes great concentrations and a will to create. You must become one with the words till they burn within your mind; only then will they flow from the tip, creating something from nothing.

BRADTKE, DEBRA
[a.] New Castle, IN [title] "The Master's Hand" [pers.] In my poem The Master's hand I was writing about a bad time in my life that did leave some scars that had to be overcome. That part of my life is behind me now, and I continue to write and to share my poetry with friends and loved ones.

BRAEGGER, NICHOLE
[a.] St. George, UT [title] "Will I Remember" [pers.] All my life I have been touched by poems. I feel that poetry can fill our hearts with love, our minds with peace, bringing friends and family closer together. I love to write poetry and feel very honored to have my poem a part of *A Forgotten Paradise.*

BRASWELL, DWIGHT
[a.] Newport News, VA [title] "Picture of My Soul" [pers.] Pure grief is not a glorious experience. It can tear one apart, as it tore me apart. This poem reveals my emotional breakdown. When I lost the love of my life. I dedicate me to write poetry, so to her I owe every word that comes from the deepest depths of my heart.

BRAUER, LEIGH
[a.] Toledo, OH [title] "Love" [pers.] I think being able to write poetry is one of the greatest gift in life you could ever receive. I started to write poems sometime in 99. I started to write poems sometimes in 99. I'm fourteen years old and live in Toledo, Ohio. When my mom was younger she also loved to write poetry. I also love to write poems with my Uncle Jon, we wrote a poem together called "Daze."

BRAXTON, ROBERT
[a.] Plano, TX [title] "Evening with Field" [pers.] The aim of my writing is to be as true as possible. It is a result of the noticeable influence of Robert Frost, specific encouragement from

both my parents, and the unwitting contributions of my brothers and sisters. Thank You.

BRAZIER, ERICA
[a.] Charlotte, NC [title] "My Plea" [pers.] My poetry portrays my life. It mirrors what I have been through, or seen over the course of my years. I unveil my deepest secrets, worst fears, and greatest joys when I write. The poem that I've shared is very personal because it's about coming to my crossroads and facing my inner demons. It is in reference to a time in your life when you know a change must come about and in order for this to occur, a battle between good and evil has to take place. Hopefully everyone who reads my work appreciates it as being my view.

BRENNER, LORI
[a.] Vancouver, WA [title] "Don't Cry Cause I'm Okay" [pers.] As my heart breaks for the loss of my dear child Kassey Oliver, due to Leukemia, four days before her eleventh birthday, I felt compelled to turn to poetry to commemorate her courageous spirit. Forever I will mourn her loss as a vibrant part of my life, but feel joy in the face that her memory will be documented for all to acknowledge her continuous strength and love for life. Thank you for this opportunity to carry on her name. I know she is in a better place now where there is no more pain for her to endure.

BREWER, JAMES
[a.] Nicholasville, KY [title] "I Wonder" [pers.] This poem was originally lyrics to a song I had written, about someone very close to me. I write often as a hobby and a release from stress.

BRICKNER, C. J.
[a.] Tiffin, OH [title] "My Special Friend" [pers.] This poem is dedicated to my husband, Dan, over the past fifteen years, I have collected many special friends (they know who they are), this deserves a special dedication for their support. I give a message to all to not to look at the face value of a friend. Friends come into your lives for a purpose, be thankful that your paths in life have crossed. Cindy is a wife, mother, daughter, sister and student at Heidelburg College (Tiffin, OH). My writing comes from the heart, which we all have experienced; thank you to all my special friends. *Carpe Diem!*

BRICKNER, CYNTHIA
[a.] Tiffin, OH [title] "Wings" [pers.] I dedicate this poem to all the "Wings" in my life: grandma Carol, Mama, Daddy, "Bud" Carol, brothers: Tim and Tom, my husband Dan, my five children (Chris, Jim, Jessie, Zak and Abby), and the rest of my wonderful family and friends. A special dedication for whom this poem was written, Susan (Wing) Galipeau, my forever friend. I am 39, attending Heidelberg College (Tiffin, Ohio) majoring in Psychology. I pray to touch of all those in darkness and bring them back into the light, as so many have done for me. May God's peace be with all of you.

BRINER, GAYLE
[a.] Charlotte, NC [title] "Marriage Counseling" [pers.] This particular prose was written during a difficult period in my life. Through the gift of poetry, I discovered that through pain there is growth. I hope this poem is a blessing to others and provides solace for all who experience endings.

BRINKHOFF, KELLY
[a.] Pleasant Hill, CA [title] "His Sacrifice" [pers.] My inspiration comes from believing in Jesus my savior and God my father. With the help of them, the words and thoughts appear like stars in the night sky bright, shiny and beautiful. Since I was saved and my n ew life began, I have been blessed with peace that I have never known. I now desire to give back to God and Jesus what they have given

to me, love. Through my poems, this is how I have chosen to spread His word and give thanks for His love. Thank you Jesus for saving me on July 4, 1999.

BRISTER, MICHAEL
[a.] Washington, DC [title] "Protected" [pers.] Trying to figure out my role in an ever expanding, continuously changing and constant universe, I'm often lost. As the years arbitrarily increase, I'm realizing that it's all related (de dio), but sometimes the languages aren't the same. Concepts like love, pain, even algebra seem like isolating and intolerable pressure. But than you read a poem, a poem that perfectly describes those indescribable thoughts and feeling, suddenly you're not alone.

BRISTOW, CHARLES
[a.] Thomasville, NC [title] "Winter Morn" [pers.] For Charles Bristow, who was born and raised in rural North Carolina, snow was a welcomed, but rare sight. Charles has always appreciated the area which is his home, and remembered the "Winter Morn" snow-covered landscape through a childhood memory. "Children have the most honest outlook on life, and I feel this outlook needs to be used in expressive writing to capture the truth and innocence of the subject." His faith in God and the south can be seen in most of his work. Originally written as part of a song, Charles shortened the verse feeling that one would be left with a stronger impression if the work was read as a poem.

BRITTON, FRANCIS
[a.] Danbury, CT [title] "Treetops" [pers.] The words in Treetops are little breaths of my life that I wanted to share with others. The hope is that a short journey shared in my life might stir warm memories in theirs. Memories, shared in Treetops are of a boy giving praise to God for creation without realizing.

BRODERSEN, JARED
[a.] Anaheim, CA [title] "Fly into the Sun" [pers.] Fly into the Sun," is about me and my dream girl disappearing from this miserable world. Going through pain in order to reach pleasure. I think poetry means absolutely nothing; it opens your mind, opens doors, reveals surreal and existential elements hidden in the subconscious. We are already dead. You are not reading this right now. The third and final beast has injected this ingredient into your vein while you were sleeping. I have a great father whom I love, a brother, a sister and somewhat of a soul inside of me. This isn't me, I'm not mechanical.

BROMBACH, NATALY
[a.] Duesseldorf, NRW [title] "The Spiral Dance" [pers.] A piece of Pagan Poetry, dedicated to our mother, the gracious goddess. The poem is about her neverending spiral dance, which symbolizes the wheel of life and seasons. I've been a witch for the half of my life now; yet, there's a life long to learn and discover, again and again. One of the most important teachers in my life is my mom, to whom I want to dedicate this poem too, and to all of ye wild and wise Wiccans. May the lady and Lord guard and guide you blessed be!

BROO, KAREN
[a.] Kokomo, IN [title] "Who's to Blame?" [pers.] Although my occupation is an 8th grade student now, my career aspirations are geared towards writing, mainly journalism. My poetry is inspired by my life: family, friends, and God. My family is very important to me because they are what get me through my times of trial. My mom shows indescribable love, and my dad gives love and never ending support. To them I extend my deepest love and thanks for believing in me, and instilling in me the courage and strength to plunge into life.

BROOKS, JENNIFER
[a.] Medford, OR [title] "Only You" [pers.] For the person who has inspired my greatest sorrows and my greatest joys. I will love him always.

BROWN, CHRISTOPHER
[a.] Baton Rouge, LA [title] "Afterwards" [pers.] This poem is universal. It's about the days, weeks and months after a relationship. It's about life. In life there is love. In love there is loss, with loss comes pain (or joy) and from this we gain both knowledge and experience. It's a never ending cycle. A wise woman once told me that, with each relationship we learn more about what we want for our forever. I dedicate this poem to anyone whose experienced life, death or love afterwards.

BROWN, CURTIS
[a.] Lawrenceville, NJ [title] "Slick" [pers.] I have always admired persons who could write great poetry and was consequently shocked when one of mine was chosen to be published! I tend to maintain a "folklore" approach and feel my poems appeal to kids more so than adults, although, what are adults but just big kids? My advice to anyone writing poetry: write for expression and enjoyment, not profit, and submit something occasionally. You might be pleasantly surprised.

BROWN, FITZROY
[a.] Bronx, NY [title] "There's God to be a God Some Place" [pers.] I am an Electrician who love to write and sing. I wrote this poem as a song, and was happy to submit it to your collection to share my belief with the world.

BROWN, LLOYD
[a.] Lebanon, TN [title] "Werewolf" [pers.] I am an adjunct English Instructor at Volunteer State Community College and Cumberland University, both in Tennessee. Much of my poetry comes from dreams, "Werewolf" being an example.

BROWNING, JAMES
[a.] Janesville, WI [title] "Rough Times" [pers.] While I have been writing for 30th years, this has been my first attempt to try to get published. I enjoy sharing poetry even more than writing it. A poet could pen the greatest verse, yet if never shared, it would just be words on paper. It is not the writer that deems his/her work poetry.

BROWNING, TERESA
[a.] Four Oaks, NC [title] "Wedding Poem" [pers.] I wrote this poem as a favor for my best friend's son's rehearsal dinner. I get a lot of cals like that. To me, poetry is the most expressive, intense, feelings that you can expose. If you're sad, angry, hurt, happy, etc., you can utilize these emotions by picking up a pen and paper and letting those feelings out. For me, it's a type of not only enjoyment, it's therapy. My dad reminds me that as soon as I could talk would rhyme everything. He really enjoyed the unique way that I would put the words together. I have always written true and personal poems for special occasions for family and friends. I truly believe God gave me this as a way to express my love to others.

BRUCE, JONATHAN
[a.] Mukwonago, WI [title] "Alone in a Cold, Godless Universe" [pers.] I actually never write much poetry that is meant for the public. Most is dedicated to the ones I care about the most. This one, "Alone in a Cold, Godless Universe" is one that I wrote after a person I cared very deeply for left me. I chose to give it to the public because I want others to know they are not alone in pain, and really, who else was I to give it to? I am sixteen, and not depressed, unlike the poem makes me sound.

BRUCE, JUDITH
[a.] Warner Robins, GA [title] "The Tears within My Eyes" [pers.] After thirty years I have gone back after my G.E.D. Diploma. I have a wonderful husband named Owen and two beautiful daughters, Dona and Carolyn. God has given me a very beautiful talent and that is writing poems such as "The Tears within My Eyes." I have a lot of

wonderful friends but the greatest is my savior Jesus Christ. I attend school, church and many activities within the church. I dedicated this to my family along with dedicating it to God. I want to attend college to improve my writing and to continue to write poems and prayers.

BRYANT, VANESSA
[a.] Coshocton, OH [title] "The Meadow" [pers.] "The Meadow" is very special to me. I'm sure that many people out there can relate to this poem in their own ways. I really feel that things happen in our lives for specific reasons and that we as people get stronger as we go through these things. Poetry has played a very important part of my life as I'm sure it has for many others. Not only has it allowed me to express my feelings and emotions, but it has also allowed me to see a part of myself that I never knew existed.

BUCHANAN, JOY
[a.] Brooklyn, NY [title] "Psychosomatic" [pers.] I have never considered myself a poet, just another sistah from Bucktown, New York (for lay people, that's Brooklyn, NY). I just love to write. Writing, for me, is a doorway into my deeper thoughts and are way to unfetter my emotions. Reading other people's poetry and prose is similar in that it provides a window into the minds and souls of other's and you can see the common threads the almighty has woven through each one of us.

BUCK, KAREN
[a.] Brampton, ON [title] "Battered" [pers.] I have ever felt comfortable expressing my views, or another's in verse. My greatest pleasures in life are my husband, Rod, and my three children, Lauren, Kaitlin, and Brandon, all of whom have received little lines of love over the years. My many interests include reading, collecting books, The Victorian Era, interior design, and gardening. I create and sell Victorian pressed flower pictured, harvesting the flowers from my backyard gardens. As well, I own an internet cardshop, "From My Heart to Your Heart," featuring my original cards. I know not "Ennui." It is not in my vocabulary.

BUCKSOT, PATRICK
[a.] New Bern, NC [title] "Mommas Always Cry" [pers.] This poem was necessary for me to write because my mom has been a real treasure in my life. On the day that my daughter and I were scheduled to return, to our home, after a visit with my parents, my mom walked us to the door. After we hugged, I noticed a little quiver in her lip and a tear in her eye. Although she had always cried at my departure, that moment was forever etched into my memory, and thus this source of my poem.

BUDIMILIC, MANUELA
[a.] Utrecht, Netherlands [title] "Inspiration" [pers.] Inspiration spreads its wings across the tangible realms. To find is highest victories in dimensions of the one's abstract spirit. Connections with appearances give the touch of conceivable, while the rest releases the substance from boundaries, although there was a certain image that awoke these lines of my visions, there is not a singular motif that would stand behind my world of dreams. Should I dedicate this poem to the person or to the beauty in general, may you decide yourselves. My only wish is to give a personal touch to the world of art and freedom. *Carpe Diem!*

BUNCH, ALANA
[a.] Seminole, OK [title] "Love" [pers.] Poetry is like music. It can express so many moods and feelings. Poetry is the song in a writer's emotions expressed in the moment. Poetry is a gift, like loving family or friends are gifts. Poetry can influence and nurture, calm and inspire others. Thank you for the opportunity to express myself to others and to remember my mother and father in a most special way. Also and foremost, I thank my God and Lord for giving me life and love

BURES, CYNTHIA
[a.] Justice, IL [title] "The Love of My Life" [pers.] This poem was written for someone who is very special to me. After several attempts, I know that I have finally found the right person for me. Poetry is one of my several hobbies, which I hope someday can become my career. I enjoy writing than in person. Poetry is simply a creative way to do so

BURGETT, ASHLEY
[a.] Ada, MN [title] "A Death of Absence" [pers.] As a poet and lyricist, I look at and question many different topics in the world today. I have come to the undisputable conclusion that life is not, nor ever has been easy. There are many setbacks and hindrances that keep us from living "the perfect life." After reaching rock bottom, I am finally climbing the ladder back to the top. Poetry is my motivation, the force that drives me. No matter what I am feeling, I can always put it into words. Believe me, it's a good pet to have

BURKE, DIANE
[a.] Philadelphia, PA [title] "Tears Within" [pers.] When I write poetry it becomes a spirit with in me I become one nothing can touch me I don't fill speak or see I'm there but invisible to the world

BURKE, KEVIN
[a.] Council Bluffs, IA [title] "It Seems Falling" [pers.] Poetry is a form of expression to be shared, thus I am overjoyed to have one of my pieces included in this compilation. I would like to thank my various inspirations; for without them, nothing would be possible; My family, my faith, "The Group," Jessi for her unwavering support, and the countless others who have supported my dreams over the years. It is through verse that I express my love for all that each of you encompass. I thank you all

BURKE, TERRY
[a.] High Springs, FL [title] "Tears" [pers.] To touch someone, you must first touch their heart. This philosophy serves me well when I write. I truly believe in touching the heart

BURLAK, EDUARD, JR.
[a.] New York, NY [title] "Wings of My Own" [pers.] "Wings of My Own" is a symbol of determination. It is a message to everyone who dreams and follows their dreams. Never give up, never stop dreaming, and never stop chasing those dreams! For such a determination and ambition can only lead to those dreams coming true!

BURQUE, MICHELLE
[a.] Orlando, FL [title] "I Close My Eyes And Hope To See" [pers.] I have always enjoyed writing. I first wrote this poem at the age of 14. My dream is to become a well known author. I dedicate my first ever published poem to the teachers who encouraged me at Hidden Oaks and Orlando Lutheran Academy. I especially dedicate my first poem to my parents, brothers and sisters and to my loving boyfriend. Most importantly, I thank God for giving me the talent of writing

BURTON, CHARLEAN
[a.] Coldwater, MS [title] "Home" [pers.] Being that I was about to leave home for the first time to attend college, I wrote this poem because my parent's house will always be my home. I hope that everyone who reads this poem can think about what they consider home

BURTON, JONATHAN
[a.] Cincinnati, OH [title] "The Beast" [pers.] I'd like to give thanks to my wife JoAnn and daughter Jasmine who have always stood behind me. Also to my sisters Jeri and Jackie and brother Jim. And lost but not least my mother Evelyn who I credit for my talents and unique look on life. Thanks everyone, Jon

BURTON, JOYCE
[a.] Philadelphia, PA [title] "A Sense of Purpose" [pers.] I began very early as a teenager, writing poetry. My dad was an avid reader of poetry. So I guess that's where I acquired my sense of awareness, through the sensitivity of the words written in poems. Being of African American/American Indian decent, feeling like I was a little different, if not on the outside but on the inside has made me aware of my surroundings. And have made me realize that there is a difference in the way other cultures and races think. So my poetry was and still is a way to express my inner thoughts. My deepest appreciation goes to my dad

BUSS, PATRICK
[a.] Hillsboro, OR [title] "Midnight Watcher" [pers.] To me my poetry is a quite simply a way to express my emotion in a quiet, peaceful form. Which basically means that I have given my heart and soul a path to show their faces to the world. I am dedicating this poem to someone who's spirit has shown me that there are more things in this world than mere beauty. To Lizzie a good friend like no other

CABRERA, LUCAS
[a.] Stockdale, TX [title] "The Wine Maker" [pers.] I am writer from Stockdale, TX. This poem was written in memory of Noelle Kopecki whom I love very much. She has opened my eyes into the world of aesthetics from which life would never be the same without her. Poetry, to me, is not an option or something trivial but is obligatory and universal to all cultures. To live a life without aesthetic appeal would be to live a life filled with banality or rather to live life without color

CACHO, REDENTOR
[a.] San Diego, CA [title] "The Call of Insanity" [pers.] I started writing when I was thirteen years old now I'm eighteen and filled with move experiences. Poetry was what I used or use when I have no control of anything. I let the words go and it focuses everything and I find myself again. Well that's all, oh and I'd like to thank all the people in my life. You're my inspiration and I love you all. Thanks for the inspiration and good times

CADY, TASHA
[a.] N. Attleboro, MA [title] "That Big Lazy Sheep" [pers.] I would like to dedicate my poem to my parents Sean and Tammy, who are always pushing me to do and be all that I can. I'm 13 and live in North Attleboro, MA. I have been writing poems and short stories since third grade. I'm currently writing a full length novel, which I hope to get published as well, I love writing, and reading. I would also like to thank my sister Shelby for her support. I hope someday to be able to capture people through print as so many writers have done for me. Thank you to all my family for your support and confidence

CALDWELL, FUSHSIA
[a.] Brooklyn, NY [title] "The Times That Means the Most" [pers.] This poem is very special to me because it's about people in my family, but mostly about my mother. It also about the different occasions in our life which bought us closer. When my great great grandmother past it bought us closer. When my uncle and aunt got married it bought us even closer. Poetry is something I enjoy doing and in the future I hope to be sending more of my poems. I am thirteen years old in Junior High School which is in Brooklyn. I live with my mother grandmother sister and brother

CALLE, JEVON
[a.] Hinesville, GA [title] "Your Beauty Embraced Me" [pers.] Poetry is a well thought out art form that not many people can ever conceive or grasp the concept of. I have always felt compelled and moved to write, and there isn't a day that goes by

that my solitary thoughts aren't placed on paper. It is to my mother, Barbara, who was my God-sent companion, that I owe this magnificent gift to. It is in this poem, that I express how the beauty of my mother shined out above all things, and embraced my heart, as well as the hearts of many others. I give her my soul

CAMERON, MARK
[a.] Atlanta, GA [title] "Two for the Price of One" [pers.] I am very thrilled and honored to have my poem included in this book. I have enjoyed poetry since an early age and have writing since high school. This is my first time being published. I look forward to contributing again in the future

CAMPBELL, COLLIN
[a.] Hot Springs, AR [title] "Chaos Plays Her Harp" [pers.] As a successful author of "Dead or Alive in the Last Teenage Year" and "Poemstories," poetry plays an important role in developing my writing skills. My poetry is used as a ministry tool to present the mercies of Jesus' love in free verse and songs. My gift is from Him, since age 15. My wife Carmen, and children; Joshua and Angels, also contribute special inspiration. As a Chaplain to the streets on a Harley Davidson, many hearts are touched because of poetry. This gift has even inspired my web site with Poet's Alley.

CAMPBELL, ELAINA
[a.] Lafayette, GA [title] "The Princess" [pers.] I'm ten years old and live on a small farm at the bottom of a mountain. Deer, turkey and other animals play at our pond and in our fields. With all this beauty around me, I've grown to love to draw, paint, write, and listen to music. My poem is about my Granny, who began our farm and lived next door to me, my mother, my sisters, and me. The love of our family encourages me to find the reality of my dreams

CANAVOS, GEORGE D.
[a.] Glen Allen, VA [title] "Autumn" [pers.] The sun which two married people owe to one another defies calculation. It is an infinite debt, which can only be discharged through all eternity. Love, then, with all its delicate splendor, intermingles its divine mirth like the scent of a flower garden. As the perpetual gift of nature, is the panorama of God's art, so ever-fleeting is life that memory cannot always capture the fullness of its joy. We are left only knowing that serendipity serenades a lover's heart

CANDELARIA, FELIPE
[a.] El Paso, TX [title] "Annie" [pers.] I was born and raised in El Paso, TX along with my brother and two sisters. Personally I feel that life is an excuse to meet all kinds of great and interesting people. The people you let in your life whether good or bad will effect you in some way, shape, or form. Some people will make a more substantial mark on your life than others. For those reasons I came up with this poem to forever thank those people who truly cared and loved me for who I am

CANDLER, JASON
[a.] Las Vegas, NV [title] "The One" [pers.] This poem is dear to my heart as is the one. I wrote it for, you know who you are and you know that I love you now and forever

CARDENUTO, ANTHONY
[a.] Mount Kisco, NY [title] "Past sins" [pers.] This poem is dedicated to the 120,000 US residents of Japanese decent, two thirds of whom where American citizens, that were placed into concentration camps during WWII by other Americans. My hope is that we remember an learn now in times of peace that it was wrong. If we do not learn it now, I fear in time of war we will be too emotional once again to see through clear eyes.

CARINO, MARCUS
[a.] Ontario, CA [title] "Sonia" [pers.] As a young person of 17 I have already been through so many trials and tribulations. I was living on the edge a few years ago but always found shelter in my poetry. I feel that poetry is the greatest source of freedom. That is why I was very happy when I found out that I would be a part of this book. I would like to thank the people who have gotten me this far and the people who have given my words meaning. You know who you are—one love.

CARLSSON, KENT
[a.] Helsingborg, Sweden [title] "All Alone" [pers.] I feel the poems is a very good way of getting your emotions out without being forced to say it face to face. A very good thing for us shy ones. I use poetry to let out all my frustrations and aggressions and if I can make only one person do the same by writing these lines, then my message has been headed and my work here is done.

CARNRIKE, JASON
[a.] Glenn Heights, TX [title] "Was There An Eye" [pers.] "Was There An Eye" is a poem depicting the pain of loss and the beauty of a love re-born. The first twelve lives describes how tragic love can feel when it is blindly ignored. I was trying to explain the sorrow as graphically as possible. The last four lines tell of the love that was brought back into my life. I chose only four lives because that's how many days had passed between the love that was lost and the love that was given again.

CARON, NEYSA
[a.] Easley, SC [title] "Perfect" [pers.] This poem is a tribute to my fellow law enforcement officers who courageously risk their lives for little gratitude. May we all continue on knowing that, every day, we do make a difference.

CARREON, JOSHUA
[a.] Arcadia, CA [title] "Love" [pers.] I first would like to thank God who gave me this gift. I also would like to thank my family and friends, who encouraged me to use the talent I never thought I had, for the longest time I did not look forward to writing, yet once I started I could not stop. This poem is not intended for anyone. I wrote this to show what love actually represents, unlike those false marriages that last shorter than an ordinary television series. I am fourteen year old and maybe at twenty you will stumble across some of my other work.

CARROLL, CHRISTOPHER
[a.] Torrance, CA [title] "Wedding Poem to My Wife" [pers.] I have written many poems for friends and family, so naturally I had to write one concerning the greatest day of my life. The verse actually didn't come to me until I several months later all my poetry is purely inspirational with a few refinements. I was reflecting on how I felt during the ceremony, and I was struck by how I was looking up the staircase of the Victorian home awaiting my angel sent from God. After that, the words started flowing. I have written my wife a number of poems, but this one sums up how I shall always feel.

CARROLL, STEFFAN
[a.] Tel Aviv, Israel [title] "Sombre" [pers.] I see poetry as a freedom to express thoughts which to often can evaporate. Poetry gives me unrestricted license to delve deeper to search further into any person, situation or environment I encounter. To piece the outer layer of what is presented to me and to grasp what I see once I peer inside

CARSON, KENNETH
[a.] Lombard, IL [title] "Invitation to Phone Sex" [pers.] This is the first of my poems to make it outside the small circle of friend I share my poetry with and I am very pleased to have it published here. The poem was written for a friend who has a voice that can curl your toes with hello and break your heart with good-bye. Unfortunately, she delivered my invitation but she did like the poem.

CARTER, DONICE
[a.] Columbia, MS [title] "A Will? A Way!" [pers.] Why do I write? I think I write for myself, mostly. If I am sad or troubled, I write. Or, if I am deliciously happy, the words will flow. Sometimes they are the manifestation of contentment and reflection. I am a deeply emotional person who finds writing a release for my poems. Sometimes I offer empathy or comfort with my poems. Sometimes I am inspired to write because, not only in major things, but sometimes in the smallest things my faith in God's goodness is reaffirmed. Oh, I write for so many reasons!

CARTER, DWAN
[a.] Brooklyn, NY [title] "Me" [pers.] I want to dedicate this poem to my family and friends for putting up with my creative spurs and reading my poetry, always. "Me" is a poem that originated from an emotional outburst of pain and confusion. Seized from internal anguish that almost everyone has gone through at least once. This was not planned like other things usually are in life. My poem was a way of letting my feelings escape and eventually overcoming them.

CASS, JAMES, IV
[a.] Angleton, TX [title] "Someone's Valentine" [pers.] My name is James R. Casa IV. I was born in Angleton, a small town in Texas. I am not really a poet, I just wrote for the pleasure. Sometimes it rhymes, and sometimes not. This particular poem was written for my wife, Melissa, from before we were going out, because I was in love with her, and will always be. I would like to give special thanks to her, my mother Carol Cass, who should also be published in this book, and my friends for their support and inspiration.

CASTALDO, RICHIE
[a.] Grove, OK [title] "Night Conjure" [pers.] There are no boundaries to the meaning of this poem. Let it be revealed to you as your soul defines. However, I pray the light of Jesus, the son of God, be revealed to you. I give all glory to my God. For it is He who is the artist and He that has the universe in His grasp. I want to also thank my family—dad, mom, Jeremy, and Maria—whom I love dearly and also my pastors and family at Cornerstone Church. I want to thank Tammy, Amy, Jason, Rachel, and all my friends at Vertex. You Rock!

CASTER, BETH
[a.] Chesterfield, MO [title] "Encompassed in You" [pers.] This poem is dedicated to my Lord and Savior, Jesus Christ, regarding the incredible gift of salvation He offers to all. "Encompassed in You" was originally written for a high school English class assignment. During my sixteen years on this planet, I have been more than privileged to share in the beauty of art and poetry. More importantly. I have been blessed with the eternal salvation that is encompassed in Christ.

CASTILLO, EMIR JOSE, JR.
[a.] Los Angeles, CA [title] "Ode to the Homeless" [pers.] This poem is for all the forgotten souls who live in the streets of "Any Big City" USA. We can think of thousands of excuses why we don't want them in our lives. Why we shoved them at the back alleys and dark corners of the city. This serves as a reminder that deep in the city, our forgotten brothers and sisters are freezing in the cold, and hungry not only for food but for love and caring from the fortunate ones like us. What happens to the rest of us at the end of the day? We come home to a nice, warm and cozy place after a long day's work

CAUDELL, NICOLE
[a.] Newtown, PA [title] "On Your Dawning" [pers.] I am a senior in high school. But, most importantly the granddaughter of a war lord, looking forward to an affair with words for the rest of my life

CHALKLEY, IRENE
[a.] Columbus, GA [title] "Courage" [pers.] Life started in Athens, Greece. The daughter of Michael and Anastasia Ikonomidou Vamvakeros. The brothers were Alex and Alkis. The home atmosphere exuded integrity, intelligence and insecurity. The husband, Frank Chalkley, was American, and the only son Michael married Nancy Floyd. The two grandsons, Alex and Nicholas fascinate my soul, as their vastly different characters exhibit their diverse ancestry. As a participant is an essential ingredient of spiritual growth. My poem, "Courage," expresses my feelings about the different kind of courage it takes to face and conquer self

CHAM, JUN
[a.] Burnaby, BC [title] "Friends are a Joy" [pers.] This poem is created with the power of friendship. Friends to me are very important because there are many things in life you can't just do it alone. I owe everything to a very special friend; although I don't know her long enough as a good friend. Her name is Su Ching Wong. Here, I would like to thank he's gratefully and also to be support of my friends and family

CHAMBERLAIN, PATRICK
[a.] Columbia, MD [title] "Incomplete" [pers.] Expression of self is a way for me to transcend from the harsher realities I've experienced in my life I am a student at the University of Maryland, and I'm pursuing my bachelors degree in economics. I dedicate this to all of my friends and family, because without them I would be "Incomplete" as well

CHAMNEY, HALI
[a.] Regina, SK [title] "Going Home" [pers.] I am a 28 years old, wife, mother of three young children and a registered nurse. From the time I was about ten years old, I found poetry to be the most effective means of expressing my emotions and thoughts. I am grateful to God for this gift of literary expression and thankful for the opportunity to share my poem "Going Home." My hope is it will reach even just one persons heart

CHAN, ROSALYNNE
[a.] Richmond, CA [title] "Mirage" [pers.] There's a certain element in poetry that connects me with them. When I started writing my own poetry, the connection grew stronger. I cannot explain this connection, but the best things in life are better left unexplained. Poetry is just a piece of the puzzle to solving the mystery of one's life—normally the writer's life. And even though I may never solve this riddle, maybe someone else who reads poetry can

CHANG, PETER
[a.] Temple Hills, MD [title] "Poem of Picnic" [pers.] Peter K. Y. Chang was the winner of Fallot poetry competition, poet of Merit of American Poetry Association, and Poet of Merit of International Society of Poets. As a bilingual writer, he also earned the grand prize of Chunghsing Literary Award, held by Taiwan Writer's Association. The details of his Chinese works are on ROC National Library website.

CHATTMAN, JACOB
[a.] Carefree, AZ [title] "The Winter Has Set" [pers.] I try to use my words to make you think about yourself good or bad it doesn't matter as long as you are thinking

CHAVEZ, VICTOR
[a.] North Hollywood, CA [title] "My Mother" [pers.] My name is Victor Chavez Pena. I am a native of El Salvador in Central America. As a kid, I have always wanted to become a writer and the passion is still there. Now, I am a supervisor for a company called investor management trust in

California. One day my daughter told me that she needed to present a speech at school and with my mother and wife in mind . . . I wrote this poem. I wanted it to be powerful of passion. So every mother that heard it will feel important. About me, well . . . let's just say that you have enjoyed my work and that you like my poem just as I do

CHESBRO, ELDON
[a.] St. Petersburg, FL [title] "Roses" [pers.] Why I wrote Roses. I am a retired businessman now living in a rural community, where relationships are in integral part of the social Fabric. Lori also is a member of this community. The subject of the poem "Roses" in Pandora, a name I choose for Lori as a poetic deceit. As we know the Greek goddess was charged with the care of a box containing the blessings, ills of the world. Curiosity led her to open it, thus releasing them into the world. For me Lori depicts this persona. Her curiosity leads her to a complete openness in her approach to life. Sometimes this openness leads me to ponder the necessity of summoning 'hope' the only blessing, ill left in the box at its opening

CHEVERE, VICKIEY
[a.] Oklahoma City, OK [title] "Untitled" [pers.] This poem represents heartbreak, not only in someone else, but in yourself as well. Very difficult to truly love someone when you don't love you. Sometimes it is too late to understand that completely. Through the eyes of a poet, life becomes less simplistic, as one might float through it. Poetry is a way or expression as well as release. Everything I write is true, all the emotion is very real. I thank God each day for this gift. Trust in the Lord, and allow Him to lead, trust in yourself and you will succeed, believe in yourself and you'll find your way, look toward the heavens and hold on when you pray

CHINIGO, STEVEN
[a.] Westerly, RI [title] "Where I Find My Heaven" [pers.] Back in 1999, I was engaged to be married and I wrote this particular poem. It came straight from my heart one day when I was at work. It's amazing how when you think about loving things, only lovely thoughts can flow. We are no longer engaged, but the poem will always be close to my heart because it came from the overflow thereof. I was introduced to poetry by my English teacher, Mrs. Serra of Westerly, RI. I want to say thanks to her for instilling the goodness that is in poetry, you've truly made a difference

CHIRA, ADRIAN
[a.] Chicago, IL [title] "Memories" [pers.] The poem is about being an ocean away from the loved ones. It's about feeling alone in a new country and living on those memories that once brought you so much joy and so many smiles. It's about longing for those times and wishing to rewind the time back . . . moments are so precious . . . that we need to treasure them and live them to the fullest because all that's left behind is just . . . memories!

CHIU, SUSAN
[a.] San Antonio, TX [title] "Dying Angels" [pers.] I have the unique privilege to work in a job I love. I am a counselor in a Juvenile Probation Department. Too often I have found the behavior observed has little to do with the child's underlying difficulty. Unfortunately, these kids are often shared by puritive school and community staff. Although my teenage years preducate much empathy for victims who are re-victimized, I now see individuals must choose to move from underdog to champion. It is more than chance that most of my relatives have also chosen to be lifelong champions of the cause of their choice

CHONG, SHING
[a.] Richmond, BC [title] "Maze" [pers.] I was born in London, England in 1979. I spent fourteen years

living in HongKong when young and then moved to Vancouver, Canada in 1993. I graduated from St. Margarets School in Victoria, B.C. in 1997. I'm currently studying in Simon Fraser University in Vancouver, B.C, majoring in Econonmics. I write novels, drama, and poetry in both Chinese and English.

CHOW, SONYA
[a.] Fremont, CA [title] "My Star" [pers.] My poem is very dear to my heart. I wrote this poem about my soulmate "My Love, My Star." Hopefully those of you who read this can relate to my poem. It's about the feeling one gets when one realizes that they have finally found their other half. After an experience like that life will never be the same. I am very proud to share my poem I could not fit my whole statement in the space provided. So I will continue my statement here with you, enjoy!

CHRIST, DARLENE F.
[a.] Cobden, IL [title] "Together Forever" [pers.] This poem reflects someone who is very important to me, whom I have learned from and who has inspired my life. I hope others can touch somebody's heart with my poem, and relate to my love for this special person. My husband

CHRISTIAN, KYMBERLI
[a.] Kirkwood, MO [title] "My Angel's Footsteps" [pers.] Poetry has always been a type of sanctuary for me to release my innermost thoughts and feelings. After the death of my friend Shane, I was confused and felt that life was short and unfair. But now I know why Shane and I crossed paths; to teach me a lesson . . . Don't drink and drive. Cherish what you have today; if tomorrow never comes

CHRISTIE, SEAN
[a.] Mayville, ND [title] "Beauty" [pers.] This poem was written with my incredibly wonderful fiancee Jenny in mind. I met her while we were both attending Mayville State University in North Dakota. This is dedicated to her

CHRISTOPHER, ALEXANDRA
[a.] Silver Spring, MD [title] "Think About Me" [pers.] This poem was written to express appreciation for my life, husband, and our sons. It is dedicated to the people I have met throughout my life, and I offer my utmost gratitude for their kindness and deeds. I would not have learned to smile again without their friendship and belief in me. After the sadness and hurt of years of negative conditioning I finally realized that with God's assistance, I always had love to share. To my family in the United States and in Ghana and to all seeking silver livings in dark clouds Think About Me is my gift of hope and inspiration

CHRISTOPHER, PATRICIA
[a.] Lebanon, OR [title] "Wonders of Our Farm" [pers.] Poetry came from mom. She is gone now. Poetry lives on in my sister Nancy and now I find I can do it too. What a surprise to our friends Mrs. Fern Pratt Julian Packard who gave us a chance for our dream of a farm. Thank you. To my husband Billy Jack, our sons John, Mark, Robert, daughter in-laws Karen, Rhoda, Beth Grandchildren Samantha, Bobby, Ariana, Joshua, new baby to be and future grandchildren. I love you all and always remember take time to look and listen. The wonders you will see and her

CIPOWSKI, SCOTT
[a.] Hoffman Estates, IL [title] "What Scares You" [pers.] My poem "What Scares You" is really about my life. The past six years have been rough in my life. Four years I went through kidney failure, I was scared of doctors, nurses, and most frightened of shots. After the hard years in the year of '98 my dad gave me one of his kidneys. Then the last two years I've been ever so scared of death. Two of my

grandparents have passed away and it's been very hard. So looking back over the rough years is what inspired me to write this poem. And I would like to dedicate the poem to my loved ones all around me. Especially to my two grandparents

CIPRES, LISA
[a.] Chino Hills, CA [title] "Life's Too Short" [pers.] This poem was inspired by my Mom, grandma, and fiance. Mom and grandma would always tell me, "life's too short to be sad or upset with your loved one's because you never know from one moment to the next." I would never want to take for granted the time I have with my family and friends. God has his plan for each of us. He doesn't want us to live in fear, but to live in happiness and to love unconditionally, just as he love us. Life is too short, we have a choice not to make it too late

CLARK, JEFFERY
[a.] Cullman, AL [title] "Prize" [pers.] This poem reflects the guilt that I myself feel concerning my children and the lack of time I spend with them. Like many others out there I tend to be caught up in trying to better things for us as a family the whole world needs to slow down and rearrange our priorities

CLARK, LIEZA
[a.] San Jose, CA [title] "Fire Child" [pers.] Writing has always been a release for me. It has gotten me through much that life has dished, I love the Catharsis that takes place when you experience something difficult and then transform it into a thing of beauty via the written word

CLARK, LISA
[a.] Chillicothe, OH [title] "Open Your Heart to Me" [pers.] Thank God, Jesus Christ, my parents Linda Geffers and Samuel Jeffers Sr. though I tested their wills many times through the years they never gave up on me. My life's journey has just begun. Every day past present, future, was, is, maybe not be perfect with guidance love, forgiveness of each owns way, there will be a time. When all is known, let my words pass on faith, hope and unconditional love. Let angels sing to another whose soul can be free and saved through the prayers of these words. Let them see the guiding light as I have

CLARK, NICOLE
[a.] Suffolk, VA [title] "The Clock" [pers.] I am nineteen and currently a college student. The art of music and poetry are very meaningful in my life. This is a rather dark poem expressing my concept of time and our inability to escape it. Time is something that everyone lives by. It's always in demand, and yet, it is wasted more than anything. Everything that we do in life whether we realize it or not reverts back to time. We are slaves under its control. The only way for us to escape time is for time to stop . . . and the only way for us to make time stop . . . is for our own clock to stop ticking

CLARK, PAULA
[a.] Omaha, NE [title] "Mary's Dirge" [pers.] I'm a wife and mother, as well as having a full-time career as an RN. I hold a B.S.N., which I earned in 1998, through encouragement from my Aunt Mary. This poem is an honor to that Aunt, who inspired me throughout much of my young adult life to aspire to what and where my heart and mind guided me. The text in this poem reminds those who knew Mary, what she was all about. She left an impression with every person she touched in her life. My hope, is that for other reading this they will be touched, vicariously through this words

CLAY, CENETH
[a.] Masonworth, PA [title] "Aunt Mary Ann" [pers.] This poem is very special to me because it talks about a very important person that I love dearly, my aunt. Aunt Mary Ann was the one who

got me interested in writing. She always told me to go for your dreams. No one can stop you. Then when she died I couldn't talk without crying. So I began to write everything down. I wrote the poem one day and placed it in a frame. I saw the contest and entered it. I know that if she was here today she would be very proud of me

CLEGHORN, PEGGY
[a.] Winthrop, AR [title] "Conquer and Divide" [pers.] All of my life I have written poems and short stories for family members. Poetry just seems to flow from my heart freely. This poem was written while I was going through a very emotional time ten years ago. I was newly divorced, had started nursing school, and was a mother of two boys, ages 14 and eight years. It was a tough time for all of us, since nursing school demands 80 percent of your attention. This poem was written in my room as I stared at the sky, praying to make it through school, provide my boys with a better life, and for the pain to heal. It was a dedication to my sons Matthew and P.J. a promise of new beginnings. I graduated nursing school in 1991 and remarried that same year to a wonderful man, Mark. We live in Winthrop, Arkansas and together have built a wonderful life raising six children. I am a L.P.N. and CFO of our farm. My husband is a supervisor for Georgia Pacific Papers, and CEO of our farm consisting of 200 acres, cattle, horses, and hugs. Poetry is a very important part of my life, and this poem is especially important to me because I did conquer all the challenges I was faced with and made my life better. I was able to divide, separate the difference of hearing I love you and actually knowing the meaning of I love you. We have built a wonderful life, and my boys are now grown, responsible young men. I wish to dedicate them for their love and faith in me

CLIFFORD, TONI
[a.] Lafayette, LA [title] "Muted Whisperings" [pers.] Once in a great while, a life altering event occurs. We make choices to either collapse to our knees or brush ourselves off and go on proudly. I choose to go on. Were it not for love, family and friends, I don't know if I would have the strength. But I do. Finally, I do

CLYMER, JENNIFER
[a.] Anchorage, AK [title] "Weeping Willows" [pers.] I am a student at the University of Alaska Anchorage. I am majoring in Journalism and Public Communications with a degree in Public Relations and Advertising. I have loved to write my whole life. I have always felt it was the best way to express myself. Weeping Willows was written when I was dealing with the pressures of being a young teenager. I hope you enjoy my poem, I look forward to writing more for you to read

COARD, DONALD
[a.] Stephens City, VA [title] "What is Love" [pers.] Poetry is a way for me to express my emotions and feelings. Most of the poems I write are from personal experiences, so writing just kind of comes naturally for me. My English teacher at Sherrando High School, along with my mother, have encouraged me to pursue my writing talent to a higher level and that's what I hope to do with the publication of this poem

COBURN, ANGELA
[a.] Florissant, MO [title] "In a County Jail" [pers.] This poem was about an experience in Capte Girardeau, MO, in which I was falsely arrested for assaulting an officer. I couldn't express my feelings verbally so I documented them in this literary piece. After unfair treatment and a lengthy court battle, I returned to St. Louis to continue my education. I later received a Bachelors of Arts in Communication and a certificate for Writing from the University of Missouri-St. Louis. I also re-

ceived a Certificate of African Studies from the University of Ghana-Legon, in West Africa

COCHRANE, DIANA
[a.] Cheshire, MA [title] "Long Distant Chances" [pers.] I have written poems since I was 15 years old and I'm now almost 33. I finally took a chance to enter one of my poems and I'm so glad I did because now it's being published. This poem is for all those people why are in a long distant relationship and the chances they take to get there. It is also about being long distant friends of the opposite gender who decide to only remain friends forever. This poem has special meaning to me and it's from my heart.

COFER, ASHLEE
[a.] Fredericktown, MO [title] "Life" [pers.] I was inspired to write this poem because of my best friend's being in and out of the hospital and with expectations of him soon passing away. He has endeavored more than you could imagine for one human body to withhold. I'm very much love and enjoy, writing poems. I write them on the main basis or subject of reality or love. I'm hoping that each person that reads this poem, for their hearts to be touched to the extent of giving them another way of looking at life. I would like to dedicate this to Kara and her dad

COGBURN, ANGELA
[a.] Evans, GA [title] "Secret Place of His Presence" [pers.] If was by abiding in the secret place of God's presence where I received the gift of writing poetry. Seeking the face of God and spending time in His word is the avenue in which the words flow. The poems are his, and I am the vessel who holds the pen of a ready writer. My desire is that others will be encouraged by the poems God has given me. Also, my hope is that the readers will be challenged to seek a deeper relationship with their Heavenly Father

COHEN, JOSH
[a.] San Francisco, CA [title] "Financial Analyst" [pers.] Josh Cohen is a financial analyst for Deutsche Banc Alex. Brown in San Francisco, CA. He also serves as President of a non-public organization. Developing Minds, which aims to provide educational resources for children in need. His poetry reflects his goal of the love and emphasizes his value of relationships.

COLEMAN, KRISS
[a.] Champaign, IL [title] "Indifference" [pers.] Kriss Noelle Coleman is from Champaign, IL. She is a dedicated mother of three. "I dedicate this poetry to my family. They taught me the real import of indifference. I would like for my children to grow up in a world where the tone of their skin, or the origin of their background has no influence in how they are viewed by the world. If I can instill in them an attitude of indifference toward prejudice and hatred, toward ignorance and deceit, then I have accomplished my goal of making the world a better place for all of our children

COLEMAN, TOYA
[a.] Cleveland, OH [title] "A Mother's Love Divided" [pers.] I'm so very thrilled my poem was selected, this is something I will cherish forever. I will be leaving something behind that the whole world can share for generations to come. That from the heart touches the heart. I hope that everyone who reads my poem will feel the same. This poem is dedicated to my family. Claudine, Sherman, Ebony, Glenn "Thank You" so much for believing in me

COLEMAN, TRACEY
[a.] Halifax, NS [title] "Friends Forever" [pers.] Tracey Coleman, Nova Scotia, Canada. To my readers: My poetry allows me to express my thoughts and emotions freely without judgement. My "Friends Forever" poem goes out to a special woman named Phyllis. She will always

be my guiding light into the future. Phyllis provides me with faith and love to never give up. Thanks me, love Tracey

COLLIER, EGAN
[a.] Grove City, OH [title] "Essence of Beauty" [pers.] This poem, along with much of my other poetry, was inspired by my fiancée, Alissa. She is the greatest gift I have ever received and she has brought our emotions in me I never knew I had. Essence of beauty is a dedication to her and everything good that has come from our relationship. Having a loved one has done wonders for my writing, and I believe that love is the greatest inspiration a writer can have

COLLINGE, JASON
[a.] Vancouver, BC [title] "Twilight Time" [pers.] In an insane world where most people live and die without a glimpsing a single dragon there are still some who keep alive the flame of belief and hold if close to their hearts. This poem commemorates those quiet times between day and night when, in the halflight, we take the time to relax and perhaps to dream. It is written for and dedicated to the hardest working dreamer that I know, my fiance, Tania. She is my inspiration, she is my joy, she is my love and my life.

COLLINS, SHONN
[a.] North Plainfield, NJ [title] "How Do You See Me" [pers.] Poetry is special to me because it helps me to connect to myself, to others and to the environment. Poetry allows me to reflect on my life's journey. Poetry allows me to take fragmented images in my mind and create whole pictures and in the process I gain a new understanding of who I am. I love words and I can't imagine my life without them

COMANIUK, LEN
[a.] Vancouver, BC [title] "Poem of F" [pers.] There is arrogance by which we live by. Ignorance ensues. With my threat of death an altered new clarity grows inside. I dedicate the "Poem of F" in life to "Family and Friends." Opportunity is not a lengthy visitor. Realize we're all dying from the moment of birth. Determined, I will be an accomplished writer with mantra "I think therefore I am." Scribe of thought, experience and observation. I'm ever grateful for being taught how-to. 41; male; Canadian of Romanian, Polish ancestry. Prairie boy migrated Westcoaster. Officer worker dabbling in a life's passion: Writing Albeit late, I am.

COMENTALE, CAROLYN
[a.] Burgaw, NC [title] "Your Soul Knows" [pers.] I was inspired to write this poem out of love, loss and a need to make everyone who reads, this, aware of how fragile and unpredictable are our lives. My children, John, Jake, Joseph, Anna and Terri, and my grandchildren, Beth, Anthony and Andreja, have bear such a blessing to me. Although I lost my husband and my Joseph in 1996 and 1997, respectively they continue to be. A great part of our lives. The memories of them keep them alive in our hearts. Every time I see my son's beautiful twins, Anthony and Andreja, their father and grandfather shines through, full of life, free of spirit. They live on! Deep inside all of us, we know the right choices to make the right thing to do. Every decision we make, if it's made conscientiously for the love of all God's creations, it will never be the wrong decision. Make every moment count. Have no regrets

COMMISSO, MARLENA
[a.] Maple, ON [title] "Life After Death" [pers.] This poem is very special to me because it is a reflection of my religious faith. My heritage has inspired me to embrace my faith through my writing

CONCEPCION, EBENEZER
[a.] Union City, NJ [title] "An Albanian Boy" (Kosovo) [pers.] I wrote this poem to convey the message that we many times are confronted with situations that overwhelm us in such a way that we don't know what to do or where to turn to. Then, because of these devastating circumstances, we look for a solution in the power of our social positions, financial status, or in other living beings who eventually betray us. But we must take time to look within ourselves so we can find the true hope that we can only rely on, which is the love and faith that God has given us. This is what the Albanian boy learned to do even though he was faced with a future that promised him nothing that his little heart desired

CONLEY, DANIEL
[a.] Porland, ME [title] "Street Gangs Vs. War" [pers.] I have worked with homeless adolescents here in Maine for 12 years. "Street Gangs Vs. War" was written to release pent up emotions (as I often do), after I was reminded of the senseless, yet valiant efforts of friends who died in Vietnam, compared to the senseless, honorless, violence of gangs. This after a young client was badly cut by gang members with Mechetes

CONNOR, SI
[a.] Thomson, GA [title] "A Child's Grasp" [pers.] For Ryan—that we may both come to know Sinn Fein

CONRAD, JACOB
[a.] Falconer, NY [title] "These Hands" [pers.] I just wanted to find some way to show my appreciation to the one who brought here. My mother is the most special person in my life. Like most, she was there when I needed her most. She was always loving and never failing. So I just wanted to tell how much I love and appreciate her. Thank you Mom

COO, PATRICK
[a.] Glendale, CA [title] "Special Friend" [pers.] I have often wondered whether people meet by chance, or if perhaps people's lives cross paths for reasons we may not always know. It was electronic words that drew our worlds closer together, and hopefully by poetry I can begin to express my love for my friend. This is the first poem I have ever written, but with special and inspiring friends like Carla, I doubt that it will be last

COOK, BEVERLY
[a.] Portsmouth, VA [title] "True Reflections" [pers.] I started writing when I was very young. I would write all my thoughts down on paper. It seemed to somehow unclutter many of the thoughts that confused me in my life. My mom said the world find little notes I had written to myself all over the house. Eventually with the help of my best friend and confidant, my sister Cassie, I realized I could express my feelings in stories and verse. I find writing poems very therapeutic. I turn to my poems often to remind me of who I am, where I've been and where I am today. Writing poetry gives me an inner peace. I wrote this poem, true reflections for my oldest daughter, Adrienne when she left home to go away to school. I realized she was carbon copy of me at that age. She was making some of the same mistakes I had made in her struggles to find herself and her own identify. Ironically, as a child growing up she also wrote notes to herself, kept a journal and today finds solace in writing poetry the same as I and my beloved sister. True reflections is a poem written from my heart

COOPER, PETA
[a.] San Francisco, CA [title] "Whom Am I?" [pers.] The poem I wrote was from my American lit class. The assignment was to describe who we are. To get to know the real me you have to read this poem. It's amazing that writing can get down

to one's inner most feelings. This poem sums up the person I really am. The quote "A dream is a wish your heart makes" is a special quote that I will always keep with me. Through the bad, the good, sorrowful times, and bone crushing times that quote has never left my heart. Always remember it's OK to be different. The uniqueness gives our world a spicy kind of flavor

COOPER, ROBERT
[a.] Lancaster, TX [title] "Black Vison" [pers.] This poem is dedicated to my wife Shelly, my daughter Chandlar and my unborn daughter Madison. This poem represents the struggle of our people. I hope this poem inspires someone

COOPER, DONALD, JR.
[a.] London, OH [title] "My Dad, My Guiding Light" [pers.] My mother died a few years ago and even to this day I can still feel the same hurt I felt the day she passed on. But over the years we seem to forget the ones that share that hurt. As my dad and I we're sitting on the porch talking one day, I, for a moment couldn't hear the words that were rolling off his tongue; but the ones that were coming from his heart through his eyes. I found myself listening for the first time the hurt from the memories we both still share. That afternoon I realized that over the years I had not told my dad what his love has meant to me. This was what inspired me to write this poem

COOVER, COLE
[a.] Sleepy Hollow, IL [title] "Blank" [pers.] As someone who has been writing since I was able to hold a pen, I like to think that I have been chosen as one of the few individuals who was given the gift of the written word. This particular poem is one which expressed every writers menace, writer's block. When I wrote this poem. I was attempting to break a bad case of writers block; I guess I did! To all the young writers: never let anyone tell you that your writing is too straight forward, or too abstract; There is no such thing. Write what your heart tells you to and with a little hard work/effort, you will go far!

COPELAND, CLAY
[a.] Craig, CO [title] "What's in a Song"

CORBETT, JAMES
[a.] Rocky Hill, CT [title] "Under the Sun" [pers.] I wrote my poem as a vindication for the creative genius that is poetry. To find out that it would be published was a vindication for me personally. It is verse that only we hear. It can be a moment of humbleness that only a poet can know. I feel that poetry rages through me at times, for it is the deepest expression of feelings and thoughts I can show. It is my deepest passion. Your acceptance of my poem to be published warmed the heart of a young man hardened by the cold steel that can be society

CORDELL, DAVID
[a.] Murphy, NC [title] "Mom" [pers.] The reason I wrote this poem is because no matter what happens in my life my Mom has always been there for me. I know I don't have to tell her how I feel and usually don't but she always knows. Mom, Sharon, is my support, strength but most of all my "friend." I am a University of Knoxville graduate. I have a brother, Jamie, who is presently attending Georgia Southern University at Statesboro. My family is very close we are each others support system

CORDOBA, LORENA
[a.] Surrey, BC [title] "Nature's Quarrels" [pers.] Although your life may seem simple, your inner self is abundant. Shortly after I wrote Nature's Quarrels, I woke up to find my energy not there, I felt paralyzed. I heard a high pitched voice cry "of no"! That was my ego. At that moment my energy returned. I have now experienced visions, tunnels, light, and other planes of existence. Inside

each of us is an energy field that has chosen to live. We all have a purpose in life. It is in our best interest to strive for higher consciousness, and prepare ourselves for the afterlife. It is an honor to share this with you

COSTELLO, ALEJANDRA
[a.] North Potomac, MD [title] "The Next Step" [pers.] "The Next Step" was written for someone special in my life: my role model and my sister. As my sister reached the point in her life where she would graduate high school and move on, I decided to write a poem. Poetry is an essential aspect of my life. In my opinion, I think writing your feelings down in a poem is the best way one can express themselves amongst all others. I am grateful to God today, for sharing this wonderful gift with me

COWDRICK, DAVID
[a.] Santa Fe Springs, CA [title] "She Cries" [pers.] For Monica Coto, my love and inspiration, and my parents, David and Rachel Cowdrick, for giving me the best of everything

COX, JENNIFER
[a.] Chattanooga, TN [title] "Window" [pers.] This particular poem was constructed in a mere seven minutes. I work as a behavior modification coordinator with special education students whom have been coded seriously emotionally disturbed. This scene included me zoning out for a moment as I collected my thoughts while. I intervened with a child in crisis

COX, LINDA
[a.] Cassville, GA [title] "Dream" [pers.] In my opinion poetry is a wonderful way of expressing your feelings and emotions. I wrote this poem because in a dream things can always be the way you want them to be. When I'm writing poetry I can forget all my troubles of everyday life. Poetry is my way of saying what I need to say about the way I feel

COX, SHEILA
[a.] Walnut, CA [title] "Him" [pers.] It is my belief that all things are through Christ. This poem is in remembrance of that belief as well as a dedication and oath to my father, God, Jesus Christ. For it is He that plays the song of poetry in my heart to sing to you

CRADDOCK, DAWN
[a.] Browns Mills, NJ [title] "Two Lonely People" [pers.] This poem inspired me when I started to play card on the internet. So many old young even children out there men woman all. I sat down and wrote this for all the lonely people in the world I didn't realize how many till now. So this is for all our lonely people, this is for you enjoy

CRAFT, CHRIS
[a.] Portsmouth, OH [title] "Eternal Dream" [pers.] Born Portsmouth, OH. My parents are Ervin Stanley Craft Jr. and Cyndelia Craft, and my brother Stanley Scott Craft. I worked at Festival Foods New Boston, Ohio and I work for my brother making ornamental concrete. Education Portsmouth, East High Class of 1998 hobbies playing trumpet, guitar and bag pipes. Poetry is a way in which I am able to express my thoughts and feeling. I hope poetry will always be a part of my life

CRAVER, DEBORAH
[a.] Eagle River, AK [title] "Strength" [pers.] This poem was written to honor my dad, James F. Reavis, Sr. Who is diagnosed with ALS or Lou Gehrig's disease. It has been hard seeing this vibrant tall man deteriorate physically. Yet the high character that I admire in him is still strong. The disease has not diminish what he means to me. My poem, "strength," is an expression of that admiration

CRAWFORD, JAMES
[a.] Raleigh, NC [title] "I'm Invisible" [pers.] First, I would like to thank God for the soul he has given me. I didn't think of myself as a poet when I wrote "I'm Invisible" because this was the first time I've ever written down my feelings. I was stressed out, mod and depressed so I started writing and instantly I felt the power of poetry. It felt so good. I was relaxed and felt the stress leaving my body. I knew I've found a new medicine for my stress and it is called poetry!

CRAWFORD, MARNEE
[a.] Cordell, OK [title] "Reflections" [pers.] This poem symbolizes the necessity for me to daily "take stock" of how my actions and words reflect to on lookers. My daily walk with Christ is important to me and that's what I want others to see. This poem reminds us all of the need to review our own lives and what type of messages we are "reflecting."

CRAWFORD, MARNEE
[a.] Cordell, OK [title] "Home at Last" [pers.] This poem symbolizes my journey out of my past child like relationship with God into a more meaningful walk with Christ as an adult. It gives me a sense of peace that we are together in my life's journey and a calmness about my future

CRISAFULLI, KIM
[a.] Oakland, NJ [title] "Vietnam Vacation" [pers.] I was 12 years old when I wrote this in 1971 as I watched the men getting off the plane from Vietnam I cried and wanted them all home as soon as possible. I put my feelings on paper at that time thinking if I wrote it down, it would happen faster. I can remember one man getting off the plane and saying. He just wanted the rest of the men home. I cried myself to sleep that night. I will never forget the feeling I had that day for our, brothers, husbands, and friends

CRISPIN, CHELSEA
[a.] Matthews, NC [title] "Only Second Best" [pers.] The good thing about poetry is that it can be used by anyone. It is a good way to show your feelings and emotions through simple words. It's amazing how at once a single thought or feeling could be turned into an inspirational poem. Poetry is never wasted. No matter what the poem is about or who interprets it, everyone can relate to it in some way

CROMER, WENDY
[a.] Greenwood, SC [title] "A True Friend" [pers.] Poetry is a self expression release for me. I have a very difficult time expressing myself verbally. When I write it in a poem I can truly be myself. I enjoy writing poems for people and special occasions. Poems can make people laugh, cry and also help difficult times

CROSS, MELINA
[a.] Montgomery, TX [title] "I Have Met An Angel" [pers.] At the time that I wrote this poem I was fortunate enough to be able to share it with my grandfather, Walter Ray Harrington. I can still see the look on his face so perfectly in my mind. A face of tremendous pride as tears flowed down his cheeks. My grandfather no longer walks on this Earth with me he has now permanently acquired his wings and halo. So you see "I have met an Angel," I hopefully this poem will provide others with a way to share special thoughts of their grandfathers

CROSS, MICHAEL
[a.] Gorham, ME [title] "Will?" [pers.] Poetry has always been an escape for me. Whether I am writing from personal experience or trying to capture how I might feel if someone else's pain were my own. It always ends up making me feel like I can face a bad day, or deal with one. One very important person in my life was moved by words

and I crave now to move more people. I have my own meaning here but it's open to your thoughts. Open your mind and read on my friends

CROWDER, REBECCA
[a.] Antioch, CA [title] "Elderly Wishes" [pers.] The elderly have wishes, dreams, hopes and visions. To make their final living wish come true is the mission of An Elderly Wish Foundation! This foundation began in Dee of '98 for the respect of all those living long lives; and in honor of Elizabeth P. Baudino McWhorter; a nurse veteran of fifty years; a fine example of the endless unconditional caring our lives can reach too. God bless the elderly and may this merely be the beginning of celebrating and validating their wishes. I hope this poem inspires many to ask their elderly ones "What can I do for you now?" This is the circle of life

CUADRO, DANIEL
[a.] Fairfield, CA [title] "Carolina" [pers.] Dear Dad, I dedicate this to you, in memory of your father . . . I'm sure that if you could have written this, this is what you would say. Hopefully you find comfort in this poem, and that every time you read it, nothing but happy memories came back

CULBERTSON, FRANCES
[a.] Eudora, KS [title] "Eyes" [pers.] This poem is dedicated to Amber Lee Ann Decker and Timothy Andrew Decker, my grandchildren. May their lives be totally focused on Jesus with total trust in his care. Love, Grandma Culbertson. It is my hope see you in Heaven (my special guy) (cupcake, Ruddy Roo, sweetheart).

CULBERTSON, JOHN
[a.] Anderson, SC [title] "A New Day" [pers.] I started writing poems as a teenager. While working at the post office I wrote poems about special events and retirements. I never thought I'd get one published. I'm now retired and enjoy traveling, fishing and playing golf with my wife Azahee. We have seven children and fourteen grandchildren. I firmly believe that God directs my life and I try to follow his teachings daily. He has blessed me with whatever talent I have. I thank the International Library of Poetry for giving me this opportunity!

CULLUM, CLIVE
[a.] Harlow, Essex [title] "Words at Rest" [pers.] I was born in Harlow, Essex in England in the mid 1950's. The poem represents to me physical bond between people how it sometimes transcends verbal communication. Though it is only one layer in the rich seam of human relationship!

CUNNINGHAM, ALICE
[a.] Locust Grove, GA [title] "Thirsty" [pers.] Poetry illuminates the darkness and is always explaining things. Sometimes hard truths and other times acting as a gentle reminder of the hundreds of small miracles that clutter every inch of space and yet somehow manage to go unnoticed. Poetry helps me to stay focused on the important things, such as seeing the magnificently colored arch of a rainbow and not that illusive mirage of a pot of gold at the end of it. This poem "Thirsty" is about expectations and how our perception is indeed our reality

CURRY, ERICA
[a.] Oakland, CA [title] "Baby Bird" [pers.] "Poetry should tell a story." At 21, I embarked on a courageous adventure on the Hawaiian isles where I became deeply inspired to compose my life story in a book of poetry. The book is entitled "Love, Spiritually, and Identity and the poem "Baby Bird" is my description of how nature teaches us about growing up and becoming an adult. The idea came to me at the same time that I watched a baby bird flying away, for the first time, from its mother's nest

D., SAPPHO
[a.] Glendale, AZ [title] "Lovesick" [pers.] Lust, Magic, Beauty, and Love are Poetry's gifts. My voice has been heard as the high priestess Sappho of Audromeda.

DAEHN, MARTA
[a.] Rochester, MN [title] "A Fairies Dew Morning" [pers.] Minnesota is my home, and I am 12 years old. My mother read books to me at a very early age. Later on she encouraged me to write. I like to use words that flow and do more than just describe—words that create pictures in your mind. This poem is for my mother, my grandmother Marilyn, Lauren, and Maja—people very special to me

DAHLE, NANCY
[a.] Gresham, OR [title] "Penny" [pers.] This poem is very special to me. I have always considered it my "baby." It is a poem about my mother. She passed away of ovarian cancer, just one short month before my sixth birthday. She had a great influence on my life, and will live forever in my heart

DALY, EVAN
[a.] Spokane, WA [title] "A Dog's Fetish" [pers.] My English class assignment was to create a poem from an object's point of view, without saying what the object was. I had some trouble at first, then I looked down. There was my miniature dachshund begging me to throw her ball. Then I had an idea! Why not write about being a ball? The next day in English I read it in front of everyone. My poem was the only poem that stamped the entire class

DANDRON, JEREMY
[a.] Ft. Gordon, GA [title] "Self" [pers.] This poem is very special to me. It is a moment in my thoughts that no one else can see. It is a moment in my thoughts that I want everyone to see, not just me

DANIELS, VICKIE
[a.] Vale, NC [title] "My Love" [pers.] This poem was written for a special man, who came into my life. He is so gentle and compassionate. Gary made loving him so easy. He is appreciative of everything that I do for him. After almost losing him to an heart attack made me realize this. This poem let me express in a small way how much I love him. Writing poems seem so simple for me when faced with all kinds of life's obstacles. This is an "Awesome" gift from God and I'm thankful to be able to express my feelings through my poems

DAUB, ROGER
[a.] Des Moines, IA [title] "Call Upon the Name" [pers.] Retired Federal Employee. Former US Marine. Happily married for twenty-six years. Christian, who puts God above all else. Loves family, especially two year old grandson. This poem was given to me by inspiration. My prayer is that it will cause others to know how much God loves them

DAVENPORT-WESTON, NATHELIA
[a.] Jessup, MD [title] "I Cried a Smile" [pers.] This poem was inspired by the love of my life, Mr. Mare R. Weston. It serves as an illustration of the emotional roller-coaster falling in love can sometimes be. I dedicate this poem to the one who taught me to learn, love and appreciate the beauty of well strong words. Like strands of exquisite pearls, these words bring joy. That person is my ever loving and supportive mother, Mrs. Katie K. Davenport. I love you, lady.

DAVIS, GLORIA
[a.] Franklin, TX [title] "My Child" [pers.] This poem was written for my youngest daughter, Leslie, as a wedding gift. Her wedding day will always be the most important and memorable day in her life. I hope that my words will be one of the cherished reminders of that very special day.

DAY, CARI
[a.] Port Orange, FL [title] "The Mighty Hurricane" [pers.] I am just an average thirteen year old girl. This poem was an assignment we had for our language arts class. Our teacher said to write the way we felt about hurricanes, since we live in the way we felt about hurricane season. To me, hurricanes are bringers of destruction, so fierce and strong. I'm thrilled I got a jump start on my writing career! I've always enjoyed writing poems ever since I learned to write. I dedicate this poem to my teacher, Mrs. Bacon. Her enthusiasm and passion for everything, has inspired me, and I'll remember her always

DEATON, SUE
[a.] Cordova, TN [title] "My Special Friend" [pers.] A dream come true a special tribute to all my friends, each one very special in my life. Just wonderful way to express my "wishes, wants and dreams" and say "I Love You"

DEBACKER, CAROLYN
[a.] Huntsville, AL [title] "Feelings" [pers.] Hi, my name is Carolyn DeBacker and this is a great honor for me, cuz I have never in my life had an opportunity such as this. I live in Huntsville, Alabama. The story behind this poem is: Recovering from child abuse to my present life today. Where there is a will there is a way. Thank you for giving me a chance

DEBROUSE, CHRISTINA
[a.] Dearborn, MI [title] "Stronger Than Steel" [pers.] This poem was written as part of a birthday gift for my sister, Michelle. No matter the physical distance between us, I feel she is with me always. For me, poetry is the most expressive means of communication. A person writes poetry without editing the words due to a facial expression or interruption. It allows a continuous flow of feeling and true honesty for the writer

DECHRISTOFORO, JULIA
[a.] Eureka, CA [title] "Solitude from the Moon: A Villanelle" [pers.] I am honored to have the opportunity to share my work with you. Poetry has always been a part of my life: illuminating moments of enlightenment and cradling moments of profound sadness. I hope my voice has touched you. I would like to thank my parents for their unending love and support. I would also like to thank my love, Terrence, for always showing me the reflection of my heart

DECK, OLIVIA
[a.] Ft. Wayne, IN [title] "The Man" [pers.] This poem is extremely important to me. My relationship with God is reflected in this poem. I often do sit and think about Him coming again. I imagine what it would be like in many different ways. Ever since about 7th grade I have many questions about Him coming. I now understand a lot more about the rapture. I would like to thank my parents who have been very supportive and my English teacher Mrs. Drerup and also Kathy Sherman for helping me realize that I have such a wonderful talent

DECKER, GLENNA
[a.] Munday, TX [title] "The House of My Youth" [pers.] I lived in Vera, TX until 1960, a small rural community about 15 miles from Seymour, to where we moved. "The House of My Youth" is written about our family home in this small community. I wrote this poem while looking out at it as I drove along the highway, and memories of me and my family flooded over me. Poetry and songwriting have allowed me to express my feelings in all types of situations and deal with whatever life has handed me. I thank God for giving me this gift

DECKER, TERRA
[a.] Mt. Juliet, TN [title] "My Love" [pers.] I am 13 years old and I am home-schooled. I often dream about my future husband. My parents have prayed for him my whole life. I am looking forward to being a wife and a mother one day. I believe it is the highest calling on a woman's life. I thank God forgiving me these words to share with the world

DEJEWSKI, STEPHANIE
[a.] Lynnwood, WA [title] "Snow Coming Down" [pers.] Poetry is my voice when I cannot speak; it is song in harmony with my nature. Writing verse has always been a part of my life and my beloved pastime as well as communing with nature. "Snow coming down" was inspired while watching the snowfall and reflecting on the mirth it brought to my brother and I as children. I grew up mostly in the Midwest, served honorably in the U.S. Navy, and am currently attending the art institute of Seattle. My love to all those who are special to me and blessed be those who searched for peace

DEJUMO, LANILYN
[a.] Kowloon, Hong Kong [title] "The Bride" [pers.] If not reading my own personal collections of poetry, I write about anything that comes into my mind. I believe that everyone can be a poet. Poetry is not taught nor learned. It comes from a person's heart and imagination. A picture of a bride in a magazine prompted me to write this poem. Every woman wishes to walk down the aisle someday, radiant with happiness and beauty. "The Bride" is for my sisters, Leila, Loida, and Leslie, who live in the Philippines

DELARM, JOHN
[a.] Prospect Park, PA [title] "I'll Be Standing By Your Side" [pers.] I also write music which in turn is poetry. Which both has helped me in hard times. My poem "I'll Be Standing By Your Side," is a poem I wrote for my brother who drowned when I was sixteen and he was fourteen, and basically I never really said good-bye. So treasure the people who surround you, you never know when they want be around to say the things you want he or she to know. In other words let the person know what they mean to you before it's too late

DELGADO, ELIZABETH M.
[a.] Covina, CA [title] "My Love" [pers.] My name is Elizabeth Miriam Delgado, and I'm 15 years old. I live in Covina, California with my family, and pets. I'm still in High school, and trying to do my best. I started writing last year sometime. It was my freshmen year, and things were getting a little hard in some ways. So I just started writing to release my feelings, and it became a thing I just did. Some people told me I was good, but I didn't believe them . . . I never was that good at writing before, I guess I am now a little. Enjoy the poem

DELLAGROTTA, WILLIAM, JR.
[a.] North Kingstown, RI [title] "February Chill" [pers.] This unique opportunity makes me want to write something to cling to over time; instead I say "Let's Enjoy Life Together!" Poetry remains strong when it enhances our music: "Songs keep our hearts big; let the music play."

DELLAGUARDIA, ANNEMARIE
[a.] Arvada, CO [title] "My Uncle" [pers.] I started writing poetry when I felt depressed. It is away for me to get out my feelings and express how I feel. I wrote "My Uncle" when my Uncle Phil; who had Hemophilia, died from complications with aids. When he died, I thought I lost my companion. I felt we shared a bond that no one else in my family could share. We both have blood disorders, and I feel that when he died, he gave me all of his strength so I could fight against my blood disorders just as he had done

DELLAMORA, LORETTA
[a.] Salinas, CA [title] "Womans" [pers.] This is a poem about my life, I have enjoyed writing poems and music since I was thirteen. This poem is for all my family and friends who believe in me and helped me to become the person I am. To my daughter Shannon for her strength, my son Michael for his courage, my son Joseph who makes me laugh and my husband for all his years of devotion and guidance and love. My mother for being there and my father who watches over me

DEMEO, JULIEANN
[a.] Yonkers, NY [title] "The Kitten" [pers.] I wrote this poem in my early youth. It is a good representative of how I felt back then. Since this is my first publication I am glad that one of my first poems is being used. This poem signifies the beginning of my story . . . and, oh, what a story it is

DENES, CSILLA
[a.] Bronx, NY [title] "Friends" [pers.] This poem means so very much to me and I keep it close to my heart. It is a poem which glorifies those people in our lives, who stick by us at all times, through thick and thin. It is very difficult to find people like that these days, I was very fortunate in finding some who inspired me to write this poem. Because of this, I'd like to dedicate this poem to Emese Keri, Nicole Truman, and Angelica Cotto. Thank you for being there for me through everything I went through. I want you to know that I value your friendship greatly. I love you guys and God bless everyone!

DENKINS, KELLY
[a.] Grand Rapids, MI [title] "Poetry War" [pers.] I owe any creativity that I have to my husband and fellow writer, Robert Earl Reeves. My love for him and God have and are my driving force. A special thanks to my mom Dawn Halfaday, and children, Michael, John, Phillip and Jessica for without them in my life I wouldn't need to "escape" into my writing! But I love you all anyway

DENNISON, ELAINE
[a.] Tucson, AZ [title] "Happiness Today" [pers.] The early morning I wrote this poem was going to be a harder day for me. Being able to write this poem on happiness today made me feel happy for this very day and realize my blessings. My mother helped me memorize the loved poem, "The Touch of the Master's Hand" by Myra Brook Welch when I was eleven years old. Poetry, music, and stories (read by my mother and grandmother) have been an important part of our family when I grew up and now

DENT, CHERRYL
[a.] Ermington, NS [title] "My Fire" [pers.] To me love is a fire as it has times when it's raging and times when it seems it's gone out but just a spark tells you it can be rekindled this poem is dedicated to my husband Vince, the roaring flame in my fire! "May the fires always burn here in Australia"

DERRY, MAXIE
[a.] Shafter, CA [title] "The Lady" [pers.] I have always used poetry to express myself when sad, or happy. This poem was for someone who was special in my life; just like my poetry

DHEER, SACHIN
[a.] Philadelphia, PA [title] "Seasons" [pers.] I wrote this poem after having lost my mother to cancer at a very young age. I soon realized that my work had a more general appeal: it served as a reflection of my feelings about other meaningful relationships in my life. Ultimately, my original inspiration, my mother, led me to pursue a career in medicine. I am currently a fourth year medical student at the University of Pennsylvania. I intend to continue my training as a Radiologist, perhaps further specializing in Interventional Neuroradiology

Di BONAVENTURA, CRISTINA
[a.] Bullhead, AZ [title] "Black Velvet Nights" [pers.] Poetry is definitely a gift. I have been

writing for about 12 years. I started writing poetry after having read and enjoyed Christina Rossetti's work. I feel deeply passionate about the creative expressions of one's innermost feelings shared by painting a mental picture with words. Poetry is how I have been able to express myself and also how I have personally been able to work through some very tough trials in my recent life. I thank God for the gift he has given me to be able to share with others

DIAZ, DAWN
[a.] Selma, OR [title] "Mother" [pers.] I am 12 years old. I live on a mini-ranch in a small town in Southern Oregon with four relatives and a friend along with horses and dogs. I am in the seventh grade and I am home-tutored My hobbies are writing poems and drawing. I like poetry because I can sit back and express myself. Poetry is a way of telling someone how I feel without having to tell them to their face

DIERICKX, JENNIFER
[a.] Palmdale, CA [title] "The Bad Dream" [pers.] As a poet and artist I use both mediums not only as a profession to express my views and feelings, but to commemorate moments held clear to me. My poem "The Bad Dream" is inspired from a childhood memory. Not only do I dedicate this poem to my beloved mother, but to all mothers. A small, simple ode to their ability to comfort which is truly a gift of motherhood

DIGGS, FRANCENO
[a.] Glen Allen, VA [title] "Unravelling Our Thoughts" [pers.] Many minds are baffled by the obstacles of daily routines and find no time for relief. My husband, Kermit H. Diggs, Jr. amazes me with his daily demeanor of contentment. I realize that his mannerism has been a rue blessing for me, since I have a tendency to worry. I wish to dedicate my poem "Unravelling Our Thoughts," to those who are discontented and have neglected to appreciate the surrounding goodness and beauty of nature

DINSMORE, EMILEE
[a.] Birmingham, AL [title] "Light" [pers.] I write when I am sad. I believe writings is the words of the soul. When the soul is eager to communicate, you write. My poem is about the pains and emotions that occur with love. The light is the happiness that comes with love where's dark is the loneliness. It debates the pros and cons of love, which there are many

DIXON, KATHY
[a.] Gene Autry, OK [title] "I Beat Quietly Now" [pers.] This poem is one of several hundred, written over and throughout a lifespan of forty-four years. To accompany these poems are two full-length novels. The first entitled, "The Search for Good Mother," and the second, "Multiple Me." I am very grateful for the outlet of writing, as it gives me away to cope and to survive. Being able to take the chaos around me and turn it into something with form and beauty is completely satisfying to me, and is also my reason for living

DOEHRING, ERIKA
[a.] Coquitlam, BC [title] "Have You Ever" [pers.] I believe, deeply, that everyone has a soulmate. Many people never find each other. My mom married her soulmate, my dad. Less than a year later daddy passed away. I dream of loving a love that steals my heart, laughing a laugh that captures my soul, and being kissed a kiss that touches my heart. I dream of my soulmate. But hey I can wait after all I am 13

DOOLITTLE, LILLIAN
[a.] Gray Court, SC [title] "Children of the Time" [pers.] This poem is to all the children I've taken personally known and one's I've yet to meet. Whether in Newspaper articles or on life's journey. For my brothers Charles, William and Wendell

in Long Island, New York who have all made it through childhood and have children of their own. "Watch over them! Show them you do care and let them know they are loved every day . . . so in return they pass this on to their children . . . "And to my son Adam, whom I truly cherish and love, "My gift from God!"

DORAN, LYN
[a.] Pittsburgh, PA [title] "The Puzzling Soul" [pers.] Poetry is a window into our very soul. It's an emotional need to be heard, to ease our pain, or to comfort ourselves and others. Life's daily struggles and joys, are mirrored in poetry. My poems have reflected this since, I was a teenager. I appreciated this opportunity to share this poem with your reader. Also, to those who have encouraged me, I hold you dear.

DOROSLOVAC, BOB
[a.] Akron, OH [title] "Good-bye Little Angel" [pers.] As music seems to be the soul's own speech, so a poem, I believe, bares the emotions of a fragile heart, whether scarred, or elated. This poem is about our little angel, Ashley, who left us so quickly! And even though there's nothing of this world that can replace a child's hug and the joy it brings, nor equal the grief after losing a little one, yet a poem seems to fill the heart with a language of its own. May this poem be an inspiration to others who like us, had to say good-bye too soon

DOVER, COURTNEY
[a.] New York, NY [title] "My Father's Face" [pers.] I am 16 years and I have always loved literature and poetry. Poetry is a part at me and complements of others. This particular poem is very special to me. It is about the most important man in my life, my dad. I have notice over the years that he does not talk much about things as they happen. But, when I look into his face and deep into his eyes, I can see what he is thinking, feeling, or even saying to himself. I feel that I have a unique and special bond with my father that doesn't require many words. My dad is very special to me and I love him with all of my heart!

DOYLE, JEANNETTE
[a.] Calgary, AB [title] "Enveloped in the Night" [pers.] Jeannette Doyle currently resides with her husband in Calgary, Alberta Canada. The inspiration behind her poetry stems from her hobbies; reading fantasy and horror, as well as, an interest in role playing and vampire folklore. "Enveloped in the Night" was written after one such roled play where in her character existed between the state of humanity and becoming fully embraced by her vampire sire. However, it is the author's belief that everyone exists spiritually between the time when darkness has not set, and daylight has almost fled. Everyone walks the twilight and some yearn for the darkness

DRICKER, JESSIE
[a.] Portsmouth, NH [title] "The Fantasy of Love" [pers.] Love is the best feeling that anyone can experience. Unfortunately, it almost always ends in hurt, not happiness. Sadly, it's not the happiness but the hurt which stays in our hearts the longest. I wrote this poem after my life seemed to crumble, and afterwards, my poem brought me a sense of peace. I dedicate "The Fantasy of Love" to anyone who has loved and lost, for they are not alone

DRIGGERS, JOYCE
[a.] Trent, TX [title] "Treasure" [pers.] Poetry is the form of expression I use to share events and emotions experienced in life with others. The poem "Treasure" is about a gentle feline (named Rascal) that now resides with me and has a special place in my heart. Previously, he was an unloved barn cat (used to control mice and snakes) that had three different owners within a year. He had never known the security or amenities of an inside home.

The poem is displayed with his picture amongst the other beloved family members portraits. I believe love is a gift from God, to be treasured

DRINAN, MIKE
[a.] Virginia Beach, VA [title] "Mother" [pers.] My poem "Mother" is not about my mother. It is thoughts of a child or a teenager that is undergoing a dramatic change in their life. Therefore, I would like to dedicate this poem to Tim, Kristin, Danielle, Astin and to myself for not losing track and for not forgetting who truly cares for them. I love you all

DROLLETTE, LORETTA
[a.] Plattsburgh, NY [title] "Winter Blues" [pers.] Poetry has always played a large part in my life. It helped me to express my myself when words spoken out loud were not enough. Poetry enabled me to create places, people, and feelings and put them, into a world of their own

DROPMANN, DAMIAN
[a.] Sydney, Australia [title] "Waters Choice" [pers.] Being a metaphoric representation of Gods grace, "The Waters Choice" was my first poem ever. Written for the eyes of others, it is a portrait of our heavenly gift painted using Earthly wonders. It was written so that others might understand his faith given salvation and most of all to give praise to our Lord Jesus Christ using the gift he has given me

DRUM, WAYNE
[a.] Valrico, FL [title] "Just Ask Your Children" [pers.] A special lady who loves and cherishes her children dearly inspired this poem. As a mother of two sons, she gives so unselfishly of herself for them. She's always involved in their lives at home, at school, in outside activities, in every way a mother should be. She reminds me so much of my own mother, Janelle "Susie" Drum. They both exemplify motherhood. This poem is dedicated to both of them and do all the other wonderful moms who make their children a priority in their lives. God bless you all!

DRYDEN, ASHLEY
[a.] Bolivar, MO [title] "Alone" [pers.] The meaning of life to me is love. There are certain people that I have almost time and time again, and I know that if I did lose them I'd lose everything I ever thought I had; love, happiness, peace, and everything a person needs to live. This poem describes the feeling in my heart when I don't have them with me, and how I would feel if I ever did lose them forever. They know who they are and that I'll always love them. They hold a place in my heart that can't ever be replaced by anyone

DUCHARME, NORMANDIE
[a.] Sarasota, FL [title] "Bliss" [pers.] Though the magic of poetry has been a vital ingredient my life, it was the spiritual reflection of John C. Huebner, who brought forth the crystalization for the birth of "Bliss" . . . a friend who became a lover . . . a lover who became a Twin Flame.

DUCHESNEAU, CAROL
[a.] Oxon Hill, MD [title] "A Rising Hope" [pers.] I feel I owe my talent to my parents because it is their creativity and intelligence I inherited. My father, Herve Duchesneau, has written and published a small book of religious poetry. My mother at one point in her life was studying to be a teacher. As for myself, poetry is a form of self-expression to me, making me versatile in what I write my poetry because of this particular reason. All expressions are parts of me. I have been encourage by friends and family to publish my poetry and this occasion has given me a chance in that direction

DUGRE, MARK
[a.] Brockton, MA [title] "Rid the Fear and Turn the Key" [pers.] The ability I've displayed being

capable to manipulate words and while doing so having them sound good going in through the ears and soul together with some sort of meaning is a gift that the man upstairs has so graciously bestowed upon me. Poetry is a via of expression for those who feel they have a great deal of varying opinions on life and all of its experiences. All poetry is a means of conveying all those varying opinions in a sugar coated way. Not everyone listens when you speak, you would be surprised how many listen when they read. R.I.P. John Lennon!

DUNBAR, SAMANTHA
[a.] Bethel Island, CA [title] "The Unicorn" [pers.] This poem is very important to me because it was the first poem I ever wrote. It is about a friendship that is lost in reality and is found in the heart. I also agree that to be able to say that you have very special feelings for someone in rhyme, or verse is a gift. To be able to express your feelings for a personal value in writing from the heart helps you with life, friends and school. It makes me happy to be able to express myself through poetry

DUNLOP, RYAN
[a.] Coto De Caza, CA [title] "Mother Natures Sleep" [pers.] This poem is about a person very dear to me, in this poem I try to create an image of that person in a setting I enjoy. The winter time is that place I set out to make real for anyone who hasn't experienced it or loves it as I do. The person in the poem is watching the surroundings and is in a peaceful state. I hope this poem can show others the magic that can be seen, in such simple things

DUNN, THOMAS
[a.] Phoenix, AZ [title] "Hangman" [pers.] I am an anthrophobic 17-year-old. I derive my imagination from my only fear: people. My poem shows fear of hypocrisy. Hypocrisy is a necessary part of everyone. I would like to mention some people for working hard at being my friends. They are Leslie Ringen, Aubrey Sjol, Mike Boger, Heather Boe, Hannah Theis, Anne Theis, Sandra Boe and all her family

DURDEN, CARLA
[a.] Cataula, GA [title] "Where Is True Love" [pers.] During a humanitarian aid trip to Sarajevo, Bosnia, my heart was broken for the many I saw troubled in this war-torn area. The children's hollow eyes were filled with great despair as they searched hopelessly for someone to show them true love and the meaning of life. They spoke of families once happy and thriving, now shattered and impoverished by war. Their world had quickly changed and their hopelessness encouragement me to share the one who is true, love. This poem was written through the eyes of an actual war-orphan who witnessed his family's death.

DYKE, CRYSTAL
[a.] Harrisonville, MO [title] "Life" [pers.] Of all the poems that I have written "Life" is my favorite. I wrote this poem because I am a fan of professional wrestling. I feel that their story lines pertain to everyone's life

DYMARSKY, IRINA
[a.] Warminster, PA [title] "Red Rose" [pers.] Second Period English we receive our assignment, a poem I automatically turn to the easiest solution, to write something and hand in whatever that might be unlike anything I expected I turned in a sonnet. A sonnet composed of fourteen lines with a final, independently rhymed couple that makes a unifying climax to the whole. Many female writers choose to write about those, of the opposite sex. Who have broken their hearts, but not I. I chose to write about those males, "Romeo," who completely give themselves up and get rejected by their love

EALY, M.
[a.] New York, NY [title] "Almost, Juliette" [pers.] Poet, playwright, director, and actor M. Ealy lives

on the East Coast after stints in the Midwest and the South. A strong believer in the power of the written word he writes "Almost, Juliette" and other poems with the same topic to make love action packed and not just legendary

ECHEBARRIA, DANIEL
[a.] Reno, NV [title] "See Me" [pers.] When I write, I just put down what's in my heart. I feel, then think, then write. I try to convey my innermost thoughts and emotions through the words. The poem, "See Me," was written during a troubled time in my life. Sometimes, one line of a poem can mean as much as a thousand fine speeches. So look at my work. Make a decision about it but in the end, the only person who it really matters to is me

ECKER, TRACEY
[a.] West Middlesex, PA [title] "Many Moods of Earth" [pers.] The words of poems can stir many emotions deep within. That is why I call it soul writing. Everyone of us feels happy, sad, angry, alone and broken hearted at any given time in our lives. Just like the words of a favorite song, poems can soothe a soul or help heal a broken heart. Being able to share my soul writing, knowing that some where out there someone identifies with my words brings me great satisfaction. It's like having a friend who understands how you are feeling. Many moods of Earth is my way of paying tribute to our ever-changing Earth. It almost seems as if Earth also has emotions and is sharing them with us every day

EDISON, BRITTANY
[a.] Sharpsburg, GA [title] "Daddy's Little Girl" [pers.] This poem is special to me because I wrote it for my Dad. He is a very giving and unselfish person. He works very hard to give me and my little sister the things we need. This poem was my way of telling him, "Thank you" and "I love you Daddy." Poetry is the way I express my feelings. I hope my Dad realizes how much, I love and appreciate him

EDVARTSEN, STIG
[a.] Olney Bucks, United Kingdom [title] "Cliff" [pers.] This poem is for my grandfather and for my dad. Two people who taught me to love the sea without using any words at all. It's also for all friends, far and near, who let me write and who seem to enjoy it. Mr. P., Mr. T., Mr. R., and Mr. F. deserve special mention. Honesty and truth have no value without compassion.

EDWARDS, AMY
[a.] Zephyrhills, FL [title] "Heart Bond" [pers.] Heart Bond was a Mother's Day Gift, it was written as an expression of love to someone very important in my life: my mother. Her strength and courage have inspired me, and this poem is a gift to her and to all mother's

EDWARDS, DEWELL, JR.
[a.] Wichita, KS [title] "Little Kids" [pers.] My interest in poetry began when my Jr. High school teacher Ms. Vashti Lewis, suggested that I read "The Complete Poems of Paul Lawrence Dunbar." I was amazed at how "Whitty, Ethnie, and just plain fun to read his poems are. I live in Wichita, Kansas. I am a musician, song writer, and I am an artist. I started writing poems three years ago. I am forty-five years old. I hope that my poems will be fun to read, and will inspire and motivate our children today to read that first poem, and get "hooked." Just as I did

ELDRIDGE, DORAN
[a.] Gillette, WY [title] "Paradise" [pers.] I was in high school in 1946 when I wrote this poem, our English teacher told the class we had to write a poem or story for the class and the best would get published in the weekly Local News Record, mine was chosen and printed 1946–47 I kept it all these years in a scrap book, so when I saw the contest more mountain top on my computer. My

wife suggested to send in my old poem, so this year we are having our 53rd high school class reunion. I thought it would be neat to show my poem published in a book. At the time of writing the poem I was looking to getting out of school for the summer

ELLIOTT, AMMIE
[a.] St. Clairsville, OH [title] "Breakfast Thoughts" [pers.] This poem is a thank you to my father, Alewyn Elliott, who always encouraged and pushed me to do my best. He's been a great influence in my life. I dedicate this, my first published work, to him and the rest of my family, my mom Rhian, Sarah, Jim and Kathie, who have always been supportive. I would also like to thank Robert Kinsley, my professor at Ohio University, for his help and encouragement in regards to my poetry

ELMLINGER, ROBBIN
[a.] Wichita, KS [title] "A Child's Dream" [pers.] I wrote this poem for my children, Amy, Christopher, Justin and Samuel. They go up so fast, one minute their babies the next their grown. They want to grow up to fast

EMANUEL, EDWARD
[a.] Centreville, VA [title] "A Moment to Forget" [pers.] Born and raised in Revloc, PA. Retired from the US Marine Corps after 28 years of service. Currently living in Northern, VA. "Today is tomorrow, so live for today and the past was your education."

EMM, NICK
[a.] London, UK [title] "The Eternal Question" [pers.] For me, poetry cannot be understood completely by being read. It must also fulfill its primary function, like music, as a spoken art form. This poem especially requires this. Like life itself, we are often so blinded by visual experience that we are deaf of what is beyond the visible world. On first sight, this poem seems incredible—without form and void, meaningless. Read aloud, however, starting at the heart and working outwards, its regularity and meaning soon become audible, symmetrically growing at a solid, iambic-trochaic pace. Until finally, beginning, middle and end harmoniously rhyme. The answer, perhaps?

ENCARNACION, TABITHA
[a.] Howell, NJ [title] "Choices" [pers.] I've always loved to write, especially poetry. Teachers always complement my work. I love to write poetry for a couple reasons. One it's a way for me to express myself, two it shows me that I am good at a certain thing. And three in a way, when I look back at what I have written. It speaks to me in a way. Even though I'm only eleven years old, my youngest brother says I can be a poet. He really doesn't like poetry that much but he really likes my poems. I get my inspirations from my family and my 6th grade teachers Nicole McAfee and Steve Milkowski. Some of my hobbies are writing poems reading books, dancing, shopping, hanging out with friends, playing with my brother Joseph, and calling my cousin Andrew

ENGEL, JESSICA
[a.] Shirley, NY [title] "A Poem about Color, Elves, and Spring Time" [pers.] Originating from a short story I had written, "A Poem about Color" adds to the love of a grandfather reciting his age-old favorite fairytale about the changing of the seasons to his grandson. To me, poetry defines the person. It affects the atmosphere of the very room in which it is read. Through poetry, the brighter and happier aspects of any life can diminish the darkness that hovers around the bend. I enjoy focusing my writing in that happiness. A person smiling after reading one of my poems only contributes to the light I wish to send out

ENGLE, JUSTIN
[a.] Pueblo, CO [title] "Contemplation 1" [pers.] I want to say something deep and profound about

my poem, but I would prefer that it find a place for itself in your mind, so that you can use it as a mirror, and remember the places you have been. I would also like it to be of some help to those of you who think that you will never get over the loss of someone close to you, or that you will never solve your problems. You will find your way, and as trite as it sounds, life does go on

ENGLEY, DENNIS
[a.] Clearfield, PA [title] "Two of Cups" [pers.] Dennis Engley is a disabled American Veteran from the Vietnam Era. He is an artist, a bard and a craftsman in clay, wood, and way. He as well study's and practices the art of Metaphysical Sciences, and says he lives every poem he writes.

ENGMAN, AMY
[a.] Norfolk, VA [title] "Gaia's Plea" [pers.] This poem was written after attending a National Conference on political activism. I hope my words inspire others to become activities. My life is dedicated to change and the ending of oppression. This poem is about giving a voice to the voiceless. I hear the song of the earth and write her words

EPPLER, TERI
[a.] Riverton, WY [title] "Love Is Like a Rose" [pers.] Poetry to me is an outlet of emotion. It is a beautiful gift to be able to write down one's feelings in verse. My poem "Love is Like A Rose" is about regret. I compare love to a rose because, like love, a dying rose is beauty fading away. Sometimes you don't realize somethings beauty until it's gone. We all have regrets. To say we have no regrets is to say we have not lived at all

ERIKSSON, ERIC
[a.] Stockholm, Sweden [title] "Read it from Me" [pers.] This poem is something I want to everyone to read to themselves. It can mean so many things, depending on how you read it. Only you decide how to translate it. My inspiration comes from so many places. Among other places my strength in this life my shepherd and protector. The poem takes up the very unexplainable subject love. I hope that one day it will become clear to me. I can see so much in it and that is also why it is so special to me

ESCARENO, SUVI
[a.] Gresham, OR [title] "Let Me Give" [pers.] I wrote this poem for Dan. His twenty-five-year-old goddess-wife Kathleen had died suddenly of cancer, living him alone to raise their beautiful baby, Hannah. I had moved into Dan's church congregation three months before Kathleen died. I had been divorced, living alone with my daughter Laila for two years. After mourning several months, Dan called me. Our year-long relationship resurrected emotions in me that had been dead for a long time. And though Dan's heart was still dead, I could see he enjoyed our time together immensely

ESQUE, RICKEY, JR.
[a.] Huntington, WV [title] "The Rose I Left Behind" [pers.] I started writing poetry is 1998 when I was twelve. It was like a bullet hit my head. Both my friends and maybe my little brother have supported me into writing poems. It's nice to write a poem and dedicate it to anyone or anything special. It gets to express what you feel. This poem was actually dedicated to my favorite object, a star. It was like describing a beautiful object in the night using poetic form. Telling a person how special they are through a poem is a very creative thing to do. I'm very proud of this poem for being able to be published.

ESTRADA, JESSICA
[a.] New York, NY [title] "This is the End" [pers.] First off, I'd like to say thank you. Poetry is a form of writing that is beautiful and grows within an individual I'd like to give thanks to my parents mom, dad you guys are the best. I love you. This

poem is mostly dedicated to those that I've lost no matter how much you try to change, how you look, you still can't change who you love. So cherish the love you all have.

EVANS, ELAINE
[a.] Attica, IN [title] "The Race" [pers.] I wrote this poem about the events of April 12, 1998. I left the father of my child, my ex-husband, that night. I have grown stronger, and my beautiful baby girl is becoming a toddler; her gleeful eyes inspire my hope. I am now pursuing my dreams: acting, writing and being a mommy. Though my decision was painful, I had to leave. Too many people are trapped, but change is always possible. In order to save your life or that of a child, know this: there is no better choice.

EVANS, SALLY
[a.] Amarillo, TX [title] "Zinnias" [pers.] Writing poetry is a new experience for me. I find that it helps me to express the pain of life as well as the joy, and that my own soul is nurtured in the writing

FACIANA, PAUL
[a.] McHenry, IL [title] "What Are Mothers For?" [pers.] Poetry for me is a release of emotion not shared at the moment of an activity but after reflection on the event. Although I have been writing for 40 years any most of my works are song poems this my first publication and release of any of my material to the public. My wife Annie has been the greatest source of inspiration for me. I may now see if any of the other 700 or 800 writings can be used by others

FAIR, DAWN
[a.] Chester, MD [title] "Haunting Dreams" [pers.] My poem is a release from a dream I had. It helped me tackle the feeling I felt by releasing these intense thoughts on paper. My poetry tends to reflect my emotions on a direct level and other times very much indirectly. However this poems expresses my subconscious via a dream and, as someone said, it's very honestly emotional

FAN, YU
[a.] Jersey City, NJ [title] "Study at Pace University" [pers.] As I've been planning to study in US for my M.B.A. degree long time I'm so excited when I finally realized it and arrive at Pace University NY. This poem is a gift to myself to memorize all efforts I devoted and it's a self encouragement as well

FARAZMAND, SAMAN
[a.] Burke, VA [title] "The Flower" [pers.] Poetry to me is away to express my innermost feelings and emotions. This particular poem was written during my parents divorce at the age of 9. I have always used poetry to express my love for God and the people I care about. Maybe one day I can publish my own book a poetry. Until then remember that "Ignorance is an evil that eats away from within

FARMER, DONNA
[a.] Athens, TX [title] "It's Midnight And" [pers.] Because "It's Midnight And" is a highly personal bit of verse, I feel any explanation would deter readers from making "Midnight" their own. Therefore, I present it without explication. I hold a Master of Arts in English, have taught speech and drama, multiple levels of history, English and Creative Writing, participated in the University of Houston Inprint Seminars, Rusk County Poetry Contest, San Gabriel Writers League Conference, and belong to the Austin Writers League. My poetry has been published in Sigma Tau Delta's The Laurel at the University of Texas at Tyler and my essays as newspaper columns

FARMER, LYNDA
[a.] Crenshaw, MS [title] "Are We the Same?" [pers.] I have always written my thoughts and

feelings down on paper. It makes me feel better somehow. I can say things that I might not otherwise have the courage to say. My life has been good, God has been gracious and generous to me. The words I put on paper help me to express my love for him and all the things he has given me, as well as to all mankind

FATTORINI, STEFANO
[a.] Montreal, Canada [title] "Life" [pers.] Born in Ontario, Canada on March 1st 1981 and having lived in Montreal, Canada since August 1981. I was inspired to write a poem two years after having read one that really touched me. On an occasion of sadness I put my thoughts to paper, then began the poetry stream that emerge from the Lake of my Life

FAVATAS, DIONISIOS
[a.] Rochester, NY [title] "Cold" [pers.] I cherish life in its many aspects. I have seen the world through many perspectives. I was the young man living in Greece; I was the man who traveled the world; I was the young man who heard the voices, the cheers, the shouts to make myself who I am today. I feel that poetry is my release. My emotions, happiness, sadness, love, anger, etc. are my poems. My poems are alive and my life is an open book for all those who are interested. I am greatly honored for being selected, and I appreciate this opportunity

FAWLEY, ALYSON
[a.] Ft. Lauderdale, FL [title] "Reflection" [pers.] Being a teenager is an overwhelming if not scary experience, that at sixteen I have first hand experience with. My writing helps me to understand myself better in this confusing time of my life. I hope to be a writer when grow up and writing poetry is a kind of practice. This poem was written at the beginning of high school, when I was placed in a new environment with new people and feeling very small in a big place. It was a time when evaluating myself as a person was needed and self reflection helped to clear somethings up

FAY, JANA DELAUNE
[a.] Spokane, WA [title] "Sanity" [pers.] I live in Spokane, Washington, with my husband and three cats. I enjoy reading, playing my piano and gardening. I have a B.S. from Marylhurst College (Marylhurst, Oregon) and recently earned an M.A. from Gonzaga University in Spokane. Playing with words has always held special fascination and much enjoyment for me. I take pleasure from the challenge of selecting the word ripe with meaning. Sanity was written during a time when someone I love was desperately struggling against depression. This experience made me aware of how fragile the human psyche really is, causing me to research and learn more about mental disease. My hope is that those who battle depression will have the love and support of family and friends to anchor their sanity

FEDIE, AMANDA
[a.] Mondovi, WI [title] "Painful Partings" [pers.] My poetry reveals my emotions that, normally, I don't tell anyone. I feel more comfortable expressing them in my poetry. This poem is special to me because it is actually talking about some relatives that I miss and wish they were here to share my joy

FERNANDES, JOSEPHINE
[a.] Bombay MA, India [title] "Wish You Were There" [pers.] I have risen from the ashes of a broken life, made torturous by an alcoholic husband and wife basher. I made a success of my life and that of two children, son, Kevin and daughter Sandra both married and living in homes of their own. 'Cause I believe that tough people last, touch situations don't. I am a diploma holder in International Marketing and Export Management, Personnel Management, Public speaking and presently learning jazz dancing. I hold a position of Sr.

Executive (Export), and have traveled worldwide. I live alone in a beautiful house, and in my poems I express my innermost feelings and emotions. I have written several poem in the last 15 years. Wish you were there is my all time favorite, it is dedicated to the man of my dreams, whom I have yet to see in flesh and blood, since he lives only in my dreams . . . I believe that someday he will come to me. To share in my aloneness, and make me complete

FERNANDEZ, DONNA
[a.] Silver Spring, MD [title] "Untitled" [pers.] I wrote this poem in the deep throes of depression. It was a dark time in my life when I felt so lost and unwanted. Poetry has allowed me to express my deepest, feelings. It has allowed me to explore these feelings and make realize that my children don't deserve such a cold memory of their mother. For this inspiration to live, I thank my children—Aaran and Steven. Poetry continues to be an important part of my life. It is an outlet for my pain, grief and joy

FIELDING, MARJORIE
[a.] Brandon, OR [title] "Illusions" [pers.] The territory of "Words" in relation to conceptualize experience at the threshold of breathing life, are the after. Thoughts used, as we cross-over to what lies before us on our earth walk. For me, writing has a will of its own. It pushes me into the luxury of solitude I swear I cannot afford. Like everyone else I am caught up in the swirling maelstrom of survival. Writing helps me evolve. To let go experience the mystery of my own life. I appreciate "words" and hope that sharing will come full circle

FINEDAY, REBEKAH J.
[a.] East Grand Forks, MN [title] Untitled at This Time" [pers.] I grew up in beautiful Cass Lake, MN., blessed with inspiring mother who writes songs, a loving father who writes inspiring letters and anointed messages from the pulpit, and six brothers and sisters who have been very influential in my life I love you all! With diverse personalities in my beautiful family, growing up on the Rez, and many encounters around the world through the Air Force, God has given me opportunity to share with you events in life as you would see them from my souls view. Thank you, Niij and Radar, for your encouragement

FINESTEAD, BETHALENE
[a.] Granger, IA [title] "Quilt of Life" [pers.] Born, July 11 1938 at Chariton, IA. My parents were Aldo and Eva Ellen Crandall. I'm married to Lowell Alan Finestead, on December 27, 1959. Our Children are Ramona Rae, Ellen Dawne, Arlan Lee and Tanya Doreen. I am a retired Lower Elem. Teacher. Along with God, my husband, children and grandchildren are the center of my life. I consider myself a professional volunteer, helping children and the elderly. I enjoy all kinds of crafts, gardening, indoor flower and being with people thus representing my patches of life. I believe our creator instills the talents so we may live a wholesome life. My writings come from the depths of my "inner being" which I believe ore generated by God

FINLEY, MARK
[a.] Clarksville, TN [title] "Twilight Rose" [pers.] Normally, I am not a very intense poet. I am usually hindered by meter, rhyme, and technicalities. True poetry comes from heart-felt inspiration. I can honestly say that the love of my life being out of my reach for so long inspired this poem. She is my most precious treasure, and time and distance will never separate us. God has preserved our love for this long. Maybe he sustain us through eternity. I love you, Elise

FIRST, LISA
[a.] St. Louis, MO [title] "Fight Against Aids" [pers.] I write alot of poetry, but this particular piece of writing was written with a special friend in mind. He was a very loving person, and somehow I feel that he's watching over his friends. This one's for Luther

FISCHER, JIM
[a.] Joliet, IL [title] "The End is Near" [pers.] I'm 14 and in the 8th grade. I live in Joliet, IL. I started writing short stories but could never connect. I found my true calling, poetry. I write poems still and I hope to write in the future as well

FISCHER, KORYNTHIA
[a.] New York, NY [title] "Darkness" [pers.] I love to write poetry brings out my creativity. My inspiration in writing is life. The poem "Darkness" is one of my best thus far, this poem helps others know that they are not alone in their sorrow

FISHER, ANN
[a.] Fruitland Park, FL [title] "True Friends" [pers.] I lost my best friend, my husband Foe in January 2,000. The poem "True Friend" was written in memory of him, and as a tribute to all the family and friends, old and new who have stood by me during this difficult time

FISHER, ERICA
[a.] Birmingham, AL [title] "My Unknown Place" [pers.] I believe the talent that I have to write, is a gift from God. This poem is my favorite, because it illustrate a perfect world. In that world there's no killing, and the people actually care for each other. I know our world can never be that perfect, but if we all try we can make it a little better

FITZPATRICK, SUZANNE
[a.] Kazoo, MI [title] "Sky" [pers.] Nature is my solace, without it I believe no passionate inner spirit would exist. Simple acts such as watching the sky or a walk in the woods can certainly calm my soul. Even when very young I took an extra interest in my surroundings. Poetry came to me as soon as I could read and write. Written when I was a child of eleven years. "Sky" has always been one of my favorites. My husband Tim choose this work from a large assortment of poems on all aspects of nature. Enjoy!

FLEMING, DANAE
[a.] Richmond, VA [title] "Behind a Smile" [pers.] Military brat from Oakland California, now in Richmond, Virginia. My travels have given me experience of people and planes. That has a great contribution to me being such an open-minded individual, that can still relate to the whole. I believe experience is life and life is poetry. I write for real people, who do real things, because I have experienced what they are going through or will encounter. Hell, I'm going through it (youth). Some have forgotten where they came from, but not me. I embrace it, keep it real and share it through my pen. For Shawn Fleming my nephew

FLETCHER, VINSIN
[a.] McDonough, GA [title] "Love Slave" [pers.] I write poems to enrich, encourage and or inspire one's life. This and most of my poems are for female readers, especially those who desire a knight coming to their emotional rescue. As a single male wanting to be married, I think a man isn't a man unless he pampers his woman

FLOBERG, SARA
[a.] Cheyenne, WY [title] "Hell" [pers.] This poem "He" was originally written as a class project for my Sophomore English class. When I wrote it I was thinking of my past and what I have gone through. After I was done, I realized the way I had written it, that each person who reads it will find a new meaning which fits their life to matter what their situation is. I hope when your read it you can apply it in your life in your own special way

FLORES, LINDSEY
[a.] Sand Springs, OK [title] "My Cure" [pers.] I believe that the ability to write poetry is a gift from God. At fifteen years old, God has given me this wonderful gift, and I thank Him for that. "My Cure" explains that God truly is the ultimate healer, only He, through His son Jesus Christ, can take away all of your pain, sorrow, and confusion I can only pray that those who read this poem can come to this wonderful realization also

FORD, JOSEPH
[a.] Ft. Valley, GA [title] "Love Lost" [pers.] My poem was inspired by my everyday life. Indeed, my experience with my love interests had a great influence on this and all of my work. I believe that one cannot truly express him or herself in words when one has had that motivating experience. My name is Joseph Ford, I was born in rural Georgia. I have two daughters and two sons: Cedric, Ieshia, Odez and Caresse. They too are my inspiration. I love them dearly!

FOSTER, DANIEL
[a.] Grand Anse, Grenada [title] "Ray of Light" [pers.] I have found that poetry is a gateway in releasing emotions that one has inside. My poems are personal ones, others are purely imaginative. This poem "Ray of Light" is one of imagination, and I sought to write something different and unique; something people could even possibly relate to. Though I still consider myself a novice in poetry, I always believe that with imagination, anything is possible, and this is not only limited to poetry writing

FOSTER, LAKICIA
[a.] Miramar, FL [title] "Night" [pers.] "Night," depicts the very basic darkness of lie, darkness that so often becomes despair. We can spend our lives trying to understand ourselves. We build characters based on lies, make mistakes, experience pain, and live in fear, until we become swallowed up in our desperate struggle, to be free from a world off our own creation. Life doesn't have to be that dark. There is so much light in our existence, but the key to living it is letting go of the darkness and accepting the light that Jesus Christ is. We do have a Savior, who seeks us in love. I know

FOSTER, VICTOR
[a.] Kent, UK [title] "Goldriver" [pers.] Victor Foster sometime poet, practical Jokfa and poker player. Lives in Bexley, Kent, United Kingdom. Russian mother and English father, probably accounts for the sense of humor. I only write poetry whilst waiting for a good poker hand. Therefore I have lots of poetry, all about Ben and the river that took his life (Poem in this book). Maybe it's not a laughing matter, but it made me laugh when I wrote the poem, a combination of too many Jack Daniel's and bad poker hands

FOUTY, LEONARD
[a.] Rockford, MI [title] "Maple Leaf" [pers.] I love writing poetry about the beauty I see around me. Many times they are nature themes, many times introspection and other times just pure fancy. I want to touch deep emotions when I can

FOX, CARROLL
[a.] Ft. Myers, CA [title] "Down in Liquor" [pers.] Wrote this poem after a friends death stayed drunk for three months. If you read it you will know what it means missing verse in poem it is: Face your problems as they come no pity, no tears

FOX, GAIL
[a.] Bay City, MI [title] "Elizabeth" [pers.] I have always had a special love for the elderly. So when I became a registered nurse, it only made sense to work in a nursing home. I care deeply about all 27 of the residents that are under my care but I am especially fond of dear sweet Elizabeth. She is

86 years old and use to be a 3rd grade teacher. Elizabeth has Alzheimer's disease but to know her is to love her!

FRANCIS, DEBRA
[a.] VA Beach, VA [title] "The Sailor" [pers.] As a newly wed and very new to the military lifestyle. When my husband left for his first deployment. I found myself thinking of how much I missed and longed for him. In time I found that writing my feelings in poetry helped ease my loneliness. Writing "The Sailor" is my way of expressing my love for my husband. It is my love for him and his duty to his country that made this poem possible. It is a poem of love and strength. I hope reading "The Sailor" touches your heart, and leaves you thankful to be near the ones you love.

FRANK, DANIEL
[a.] Lake Bluff, IL [title] "Innocent Infant" [pers.] Born in 1969, in Kenosha Wisconsin. I never knew I could write poetry until in 10th grade we had an assignment in English. That started it all. "Innocent Infant" is one of my favorites because in life everyone is in a hurry yet when it comes to holding a baby everything slows down

FRANKS, TIMOTHY
[a.] Everett, WA [title] "Only for You" [pers.] I am currently serving in the U.S. Navy in the Pacific North West. At the time I wrote the poem, my ship was on deployment to the Persian Gulf. I wrote the poem to my wife, Kim, to let her know that my love for her is eternal, and that no matter how many miles separated us, nothing and no one would ever change that

FREDRICK, ROY
[a.] Jonesboro, AR [title] "Sins of the Past" [pers.] Poetry for me is an escape, a view of reality with an eloquent twist. This poem is exactly that to me, in that I indeed often feel down trodden and alone thus cursing my very being. Although I do lean towards the darker side of life, I feel that this is where the best inspiration is found

FREEMAN, DONALD
[a.] Coronado, CA [title] "Times Slipped Away" [pers.] I was born in Alexandria Virginia to Colonel and Mrs. Bruce Freeman. I graduated the US Naval Academy and currently serve as an officer in the US Navy

FREEMAN, HEATHER
[a.] Fort Collins, CO [title] "At Night" [pers.] I wrote this poem for my friend Cindy. I've never actually met him we've only spoken on the phone and through e-mail. I wanted him to see all my love for him and how important he really is to me. It's just a small way for me to say thank you for always being there

FREEMAN, NICOLE
[a.] Shelton, WA [title] "I Am" [pers.] The poem "I Am" portrays the qualities every person has, but only few use. People seem to limit themselves by their background, or heritage. I hope the poem "I Am" changes peoples outlook on life

FRIEDMAN, RACHEL
[a.] Boynton Beach, FL [title] "The Emotions of Big Words" [pers.] I believe that everyone is a poet if they just open up a little. Poetry to me comes from deep down within your soul. I started writing because it was the only way I could express myself to others. Poetry is such a beautiful thing. I just wish more of us would open our minds and souls and just write what they are feeling

FU, EDMUND
[a.] Beaufort, SC [title] "Autumn Leaves" [pers.] I have Tourette syndrome. After years of being told I'm nothing. I've finally decided to believe in myself. I would like to thank my mother, for being with me through my downs. Also for her gift of art.

I would also like to thank my friends from the Tourette Syndrome Chatroom. Who have given me the inspiration and friendship to last a lifetime.

FUGLESTAD, LINDA J.
[a.] Bethel, VT [title] "When it Hurts to be Held" [pers.] I began writing as a young child and have been encouraged by my wonderful family and these, beautiful green mountains to continue expressing myself in poetry and stories. Sometimes, when feelings are difficult to express, writing is the perfect outlet. This poem was inspired by an amazing man who stole my heart, then sadly, gave it back. I actually wrote this poem in high school but lived it two summers ago. That summer etched these words into my soul. He knows who he is. He's my best friend. I also have four incredible daughters who inspired and complete my world.

FULTON, DARA
[a.] Brooklyn, NY [title] "Meta-Me" [pers.] My poem "Meta-Me" expresses the formation of a rock and the outcome of my life. The unknown material is formed to create an everlasting impression to its environment. My life is a rock because it's a constant change. It also represents who I was, who I am and what I'm about to become. I feel the connection I have for the earth is as powerful as a rock. It symbolizes my personality, my spirit and overall my life.

GALAWAY, RICHARD
[a.] Beaverton, OR [title] "Winter" [pers.] I write poetry as a way to express myself and my emotions. When I write, it comes straight from my heart. I also write poems for people. This particular poem was written for my aunt for her birthday.

GALGANO, MARY
[a.] College Park, GA [title] "Dog Days" [pers.] Writing has never been an option. It is as necessary for me as water and air. From the first time I could hold a pencil, every emotion I ever felt found its way to paper. It is not uncommon for a poem to wake me in the middle of the night demanding its voice through my hand. As a working mother of five, supporting my family took precedence over a career in journalism, but after a life-threatening 'bout with cancer at age 29, followed by a long recovery period and eventual divorce and bankruptcy, I reprioritized my life. If I can elicit one nod, tear or chuckle, or just an empathetic sigh, then I am doing what I was meant to do. The tangibles in this life are very fleeting. Relationships, health, material possessions all come and go. The concrete of my life is measured by the ability to leave my words imprinted on your mind and scratching at your heart. All else is chaff.

GALLAGHER, MICHAEL
[a.] Oakhurst, CA [title] "I Wish" [pers.] I feel that "I love you" is a very powerful phrase. This poem shows that. It shows my caring for a special someone and that someone not seeing it. When I wrote this poem I believed whole hearted that this special person would see that I cared for them. They didn't, This poem is so dedicated to my true love.

GAN, STEVEN
[a.] Doylestown, PA [title] "The Kiss" [pers.] The author of this poem, Steve Gan, has had more than his share of heartbreaks. Forever the optimist, he continues his search for that one girl to complete his life. He will know in an instant by her kiss that he has found his true soulmate. This poem is dedicated to Sally, a woman who's life are like the finest wine. For it is with her that he wishes to start life's journey and adventures.

GANGADHARAN, NICHOLAS
[a.] Bloomfield Hills, MI [title] "Feel" [pers.] I would like to dedicate this book to my mother, Constance, my father, Vellappillil, my sisters, Anna and Chinna, and to my great aunt, Maria. I love them all.

GARAY, SARAH
[a.] Temple, TX [title] "Voice in the Wind" [pers.] This poem speaks of the many times the distance that separates my fiance' and I saddens my heart. But my August of this year the distance will be no more and we will be together, "until death do us part." I love you Brian.

GARBER, DANIEL
[a.] London, AR [title] "Sunrise" [pers.] I was born in Germany and came to the United States as an exchange student. Later, I returned to live in Arkansas to attend Arkansas Tech University and to enjoy the rural setting. As soon as I wrote my first poem I became fascinated with poetry. It allows me to express my thoughts and ideas in a way I can't with plain prose. Most of my poems were in German. "Sunrise" is one of my first poems in English. My loving American wife, Leighman, who was then my girlfriend inspired me to write this poem, so it means a lot to both of us

GARCIA, TADEO
[a.] Miami, FL [title] "Only for Two" [pers.] Poetry is the finger print of our souls, you might be driving or just woke up from a long night sleep, and you start to write verses in your mind and you can't wait to put it in writing. "To read a good poem, is like savoring a delicious recipe all the ingredients are combined to enhance our tastebuds and tickle our palates would be like the preferences of ones poems..

GARMAIZE, JEANNE
[a.] Anchorage, AK [title] "A Sacred Trust" [pers.] This poem to me in its entirety after visiting the home of a very wealthy and, ostensibly, very religious man. The walls of the "family room" were lined with mounted heads of animals from all over the world. Some were endangered species. I anguished over how he could kill these beautiful creatures. In Alaska, Native people hunt to survive and to preserve their ancient way of life. They honor the soul of the animal who gave life to sustain theirs. I find no honor at all in murdering God's creatures for vanity.

GARNER, JEFFREY
[a.] Malibu, CA [title] "The Feat" [pers.] If you can relate to my poem "The Feat," then you have truly loved another. "The Feat" is dedicated to my soulmate Michelle Rihovsky. Thank you God for your blessing and unconditional love.

GARRETT, TIMOTHY
[a.] Summit, NJ [title] "Passed Over" [pers.] I think that we all have mourned the passing of a family member, friend, lover, race to natural or unnatural causes. After they have left our common plane, we wonder why they were taken, why we were not. My poem doesn't end with "a gracious quiet" because I feel the question must be asked, "Why Had a I been spared?" We were spared so that we will remember that abuse and discrimination are still with us and that love and diversity must persevere.

GARRISON, ROBERTA
[a.] Charksburg, OH [title] "From the Moment" [pers.] This poem was inspired by the birth of my son, who has been my inspiration for several years now, but it was brought back to life at the recent birth of my granddaughter, Courtney, and it is dedicated to all the young mother's of the 21st century, along with a special prayer for them and their children.

GASSMANN, VIRGINIA
[a.] Cleves, OH [title] "Another Day" [pers.] Many of my poems are quite bleak, due to traumatic events which took place during my childhood. However, this poem was written as I began to see a light at the end of the tunnel in my search for peace and happiness. It is my hope that this poem will inspire others to seek the light at the end of their own tunnel.

GAVRILCHUK, KATY
[a.] Fulford, QC [title] "Life" [pers.] I'm 13 years old and live in the Eastern Townships. When I write poems, I don't think of what to write, I just write poems, I don't think of what to write, I just write what's on my mind, or what my soul tells me to write. I love poetry because it helps me to express my feelings about life. When people ask me, "what's the meaning behind your poem, "life," for some awkward reason, I'm not able to explain. I guess I can't really put it into words.

GELINAS, SARAH
[a.] Manchester, NH [title] "Silent Walk" [pers.] I wrote this poem for my husband Spencer before we were married. I wanted him to know how much I love him and his companionship. He makes this "Silent Walk" possible every chance he gets.

GERARD, MICHAEL
[a.] Blaine, MN [title] "Sorrow" [pers.] I could explain the message I was trying to convey, but I'd rather leave that up to the reader. Poetry, to me, is what you make of it, and shouldn't have to be explained. I want people to draw their own conclusions on my poem, because ultimately the meaning is left up to them. Writers often talk about writing what you know. All we truly know in this world is ourselves, and everyone is their own individual, with varying opinions. I want people to use their imagination, rather than be bogged down by literal meanings and definitions

GERLACH, TAYLOR
[a.] Louisville, KY [title] "Call to Arms" [pers.] The poem I wrote had a great deal of meaning to me. I wanted to dedicate it to the soldiers who fought and died in the Civil War. I believed this poem would somewhat bring back the memory of these brave men. What those men did for our country is what is known as the ultimate sacrifice—Death! So, this poem was in memory of the great men who fought and died in the Civil War

GHOULEH, SAMMER
[a.] Oak Lawn, IL [title] "Beautiful Children" [pers.] Sammer Ghouleh is a distinguished inspiring poet. She has been recognized for her love of poetry and art. During her university years, she published two book and entered many poetry contests. She is also an established artist, well (recognized) by many. Her most recent book is called treasured misfortunes. Sammer proudly dedicated the book to her daughter who is suffering from the crippling birth defect of Spina Bifida, as well as to all the beautiful children of the world who are suffering from special needs. Proceeds will be donated to the Illinois Spina Bifida Association, which is dedicated to uplift these children from their burdens.

GIANGRANDE, PHIL
[a.] Ft. Lauderdale, FL [title] "Silence and Strength" [pers.] I love the written word, I always have. Poetry, can be the written word in its most powerful form. A well crafted poem can transform and enlighten as easily as it can entertain and soothe. There is something for everyone because everyone has a little bit of the poet inside

GIBBENS, LAURA
[a.] Kansas City, MO [title] "Silence" [pers.] Poetry I think is just a way, the best way I know how, to express myself, until I realized that I could simply write down what I felt. This poem is about how some people feel when "the popular one's get to them. I just tried to explain, the best way I knew how, that no one is better than anyone else. I would just like to thank my brother Patrick and also Christina, and my parents and grandparents, and to my friends especially Christy, Larissa, and Sammy and of course our great God above

GIESEN, HILDEGARD
[a.] Solingen, Germany [title] "Spring" [pers.] After nearly 25 years of working as a pharmacist I went back to university to study English. I have always loved poetry. By reading poem I compensated for my world of science. Walking on a beach, sitting at the rim of a canyon, working in my garden—all these things offer the chance to rearranged my thoughts. I appreciate your publishing of my poem and thank you for the possibility to share my thoughts with other people

GILES, LINDA SHOWS
[a.] Chino, CA [title] "The Shadow" [pers.] This poem was inspired by my son-in-law, Albert, who has faced many challenges in his life. Through the love of my daughter, Jill, he found the determination to overcome the adversities of the past and the courage to reach out for his dream. I dedicate this poem to both of them and to all of those who have learned, or have yet to learn, that the strength of love can light the way to overcoming whatever obstacles may be placed before us

GILMORE, MICHAEL
[a.] Oceanside, CA [title] "Tomorrow's Shattered Mirrors" [pers.] I'd like to thank the judges for their decision to include my poem in this anthology. I'd also like to share my deepest respects for Marvy, a friend of mine who inspired in me the emotions expressed within these words. Without her this poem may never have been written . . . I only hope something can be learned from her pain and sorrow as I have tried to represent them within these words

GIUNTINI, WANDA
[a.] Medford, OH [title] "Run Away" [pers.] My poem is a thought which was conceived in the mind of a confused young girl on the day she succumbed to peer pressure. She was torn between a love for family, and trust for a friend who convinced her that the test thing to do was to run away. The Lord Christ has truly blessed my life with a husband of 21 years (Mark) a beautiful, creative daughter (Laurie), a charming son-in-law (Derek), an adorable granddaughter (Kyla), and a bright, artistic son (Mark Jr.). I am very proud of my family and all their accomplishments

GODFREY, DAVID
[a.] Warner Robins, GA [title] "To My Valentine" [pers.] This poem is to someone very special and along with the poem, she is very precious. I wrote this poem for the sweetest lady in my life that has given me so much. My dearest girlfriend. The words of this poem are from the pages of my heart to hers. And I am happy to be able to share them with all those that read. These few lines. To my valentine is the name of the poem for several reasons. The main reason is that I wrote this poem for her first valentine's day together. I am so thankful to God, because he gave me this awesome ability to express my love for my girlfriend in a unique way

GODFREY, TERRILYN
[a.] Mansfield, MA [title] "The Open Door" [pers.] A love of words and expression has always come easily to me. Poetry is a wonderful way to express the intricacies of life. I am a naturalists, gardener, writer, business owner of a garden/ floral shop called Thyme in Garden in Mass. There is so much to write about in this awe-inspiring life of ours

GOLDAPP, CAROL
[a.] Omaha, NE [title] "Her Eyes" [pers.] This poem is dedicated to Sandizielinski. It's her eyes, I wrote about. I looked at her beautiful blue eyes one day, and they showed so much. The next thing I new I started writing "Her eyes." I truly love you Sandi. My inspiration for writing comes from the BeeGees' Andy Gibb. They gave us beautiful Lyrics, that can really touch our hearts. I read, that if you can write something, and it reaches someone's heart, you have a gift. I also want to thank my soulmate, Kim Zielinski for pushing me to write. My parents Carl and Donna Goldapp. Thank you to the brothers Gibb

GONZALEZ, MARGARETT
[a.] Largo, FL [title] "Nature's Gift to Remember You" [pers.] Poetry is like my soul mate. The patient friend who is always there to listen, to be my confidant, to never judge or criticize, and can recall everything I've said. It is always glad to see me regardless of our time spent apart. We are always able to pick up where we've left off as if no time has passed, we never outgrow one another. Poetry has been this to me for fifteen years now. Whenever I read my earlier works, It's like reminiscing with my friend while we're looking at old photos of ourselves together

GOOCH, TOMMY, III
[a.] Danville, AR [title] "Missing You" [pers.] This poem was inspired by Mizu a role playing partner. I would like to thank Lady Mizu for her inspiration, and my parents for their support. I live in Danville, AR. I am a 9th grade student at Danville High School. I enjoy hiking, role playing, and contributing to people around me

GOOD, WILLIAM
[a.] Colorado Springs, CO [title] "Reality Returns" [pers.] Nearly two years before this publication these words mysteriously rolled of my heart onto the paper. Somehow these words captured the essence of the human search for intimacy. In a moment of spiritual ecstasy I seemed to have "found what I was looking for" as Bono sang. Yet my understanding was not made complete until I met the one. A year after writing "Reality Returns" I asked Nikki to marry me, the earthly beauty who brings harmony and contentment to my world. To her I dedicate this work and give my heart. *Coram Deo!*

GOODMAN, LAURA
[a.] Honolulu, HI [title] "Reflections on Growth Through Mr. Ameen" [pers.] I especially thank Mr. Ray Ameen and Andrew Ameen for the inspiration behind the poem

GOODYEAR, EVELYN
[a.] Marion, SC [title] "Lost Love" [pers.] This poem is very special to me. It was written in 1988 in memory of my husband, Otis Sr. who left home one morning never to return. He left me and four boys behind to bear the pain of his life being snatched away by a bullet. This poem somehow helped me to get on with life. We miss him dearly. I am an educator of twenty-eight years who reside in a small town, Marion, SC. I reared four boys and have one grandchild. I enjoy writing poetry, reading, public speaking, singing and teaching. I thank my four sisters, four brothers, my mother, children and friends for their continued support as I continually struggle with life's obstacles. I hold a Bachelor of Arts degree, and a master's of education with a minor in Elementary Education. I'm currently teaching composition and rhetoric to College freshman, and working full time teaching freshmen focus at Marion High School.

GORDON, KRISTOPHER
[a.] Cross, SC [title] "Love" [pers.] Poetry has become a way of expressing my feelings on certain aspects of life. This poem expresses some of the happy times in my life, and a conflict in ways that my sister and I view the word and feeling of love. My poetry is a gift that I am thankful for every day. I just hope that this poem can touch people as it has touched me

GORSCHEK, TONY
[title] "Going Home" [pers.] As a species we are capable of such wonderful dreams, and such horrible nightmares. Poetry is one way of expressing our unique traits as a race. The poem "Going

Home" is my nightmare expressed in words. Thank you mother and father for having me. Thank you sister for being there.

GOSI, LANCE
[a.] Gaborone, Botswana [title] "My Love" [pers.] I am a Dyslexic teenager and although I may not be able to spell words correctly, I still enjoy playing with words. I enjoy the challenge and expressiveness of words, and I love the subtleties and symbolism that can be achieved with words and poetry

GOTSCHALL, BENJAMIN
[a.] Atkinson, NE [title] "It's Drowning" [pers.] During our lives we constantly experience reality; that is to say, our thoughts and feelings are just as real as our actions and the events going on around us. The only things that consciously try to do by writing is capture pieces of my own reality, whether they are dreamed, experienced, or imagined. Initially, my poetry is just that mine, but I choose to share it with others with hopes that they might be able to use those bits of reality captured on the page to view life in a different way than they had before

GOTTFRIED, MICHAEL H.
[a.] Punta Gorda, NJ [title] "Growing Old" [pers.] I was born and raised in Newark, New Jersey. After graduating from college in 1968, I spent two years in the Army. It was during this time period that I wrote "Growing Old." Though I have written numerous poems since then, "Growing Old" has always been my favorite. It was my first attempt to express the feelings that I had about life, and how fleeting it seemed to be. I now live with my family in Southwest Florida, where I work as a Probation and Parole Officer. Poetry.com has given me a chance to share my favorite poem with others, and for this I am very grateful

GRABER, GARDNER
[a.] Reseda, CA [title] "Lover's Glory" [pers.] Poetry is a double edged sword. It not only says something meaningful, but it does so in a beautiful way. This poem deals with hidden secrets that become exposed to the light. These secrets can destroy the delicate relationship we cultivate throughout life

GRAHAM, IANA
[a.] Brooklyn, Ny [title] "Broken Daffodil" [pers.] Growing up in Brooklyn, you endure many hardships, especially when you are female. Poetry allows me to break through and find an exit to everyday stress and problems that come along when you are a teenager. I first started writing poetry because it was a way to alleviate problems from my mind. I continued to write poetry because it is a way for people to find out who I am. I believe that poetry is like an onion: the more poems you write, the more layers you peel away until you expose the soul of the poet

GRAHAM, MATTHEW
[a.] Gallup, NM [title] "Time to Go" [pers.] This poem is one of many, but it is one of my better poems. I wrote this for the friends that I have lost, to friends that have lost someone very important to them, and to any one else who needs a poem to let them know friends are not gone forever

GRANT, SHAR
[a.] Los Angeles, CA [title] "Madonna and Child" [pers.] For Maia Rhea and her mother for making art out of motherhood

GRAY, ALETA
[a.] Woodbridge, VA [title] "Deceitful Games" [pers.] I would like to thank my parents for all their support and encouragement. Also I would like to thank, Lem. I love you Teddy Bear, for all his love and support. Last but definitely not least I thank Jen for whom I wrote this. Without all of you I would not have made it this far. I love you all!

GRAY, NICOLE
[a.] Clifton, VA [title] "Confusion . . . Madness" [pers.] To me poetry is an insight into the inner self. It's a way of expressing feeling and emotions freely through use of word imagery. These feelings may not always be bright, cheerful ones so often portrayed in verse as can be seen by my poem "Confusion . . . madness." For me poetry is a passion and a window into the author's soul

GRAY, STEPHANIE
[a.] Flemingsburg, KY [title] "Ode to a Cat" pers.] This poem was written in my Advanced Poetry class in graduate school. It is a special poem for me because it is about my pet cat which I have had since 1991. It is also special to me because this is the first time I have had one of my pieces published. It is very exciting for me. I am a high school English teacher and I enjoy sharing my poems with my classes when I teach poetry. I hope that in doing so, it will show my students my enthusiasm about writing and will help to pique their interests

GREEN, BRANT
[a.] Charleston, SC [title] "Biological Classes" [pers.] To explain what brings about my poetry, at least 99% of the time would have to be loved for life. My creative talents are at their peak when I am tired or about to fall asleep. All my poetry comes from my emotions at a particular moment in the day, whether it is at night or day or about love or hate. I enjoy writing poetry, it helps to release my emotions more easily than through oral communication. I attend The Citadel, The Military College of Charleston South Carolina, class of 2001

GREEN, NICHOLAS
[a.] Maidenhead, United Kingdom [title] "Parallax" [pers.] My motivation is existence itself. Whether it's a poem, an arch, a symphony or a lever, the unknown is made knowable by the courage of creation. As individuals and as a species, the dark is only pushed back by the humility that originality imbues, and the awe that lies beyond it. Creation is my psyche breathing, and my life is oxygen debt

GREEN, NICK
[a.] Boca Raton, FL [title] "The Path of Life [pers.] This poem not only shows my views on life and the human race, but it also shows that even young teenagers can look at the world in a serious and poetic way. It isn't age that counts, it's emotions and heart. Even the youngest child can be a poet, if they wish

GREEN, LARRY, JR.
[a.] Philadelphia, PA [title] "Misery's Passion" [pers.] Poetry to me is so much more than letters and phrases, but one's most sincere emotions detailed within literary prose. For if I can search within myself and in written word express my innermost secrets, desires, and hurts, then and only then have I personally attained true "poetry."

GREENBERG, JASON
[a.] Chicago, IL [title] "Insomnia" [pers.] Insomnia affects 50% of the population. As a student, I experience insomnia. The feeling of being tired all day and not being able to go to sleep, are symptoms. People who suffer from insomnia can relate to my poem. This poem means alot to me. As a poem with a learning disability in writing, I have risen above the hardship and have written a poem. Those with learning disabilities can draw strength from the idea: The human spirit can take one beyond the naked eye to wonders only the heart can see. Stay strong and accomplish great things

GREENE, KERRI
[a.] Estacada, OR [title] "Forbidden" [pers.] I am fourteen years old but have been writing since first grade. It's always been my dream to have one of my pieces published. I wrote forbidden room

because of all the hate that this world is filled with and because it affects us all. I hope that other people will like my poem as much a I liked writing it

GRENFELL, CHELSEA
[a.] Bloomington, CA [title] "Grace" [pers.] My poem is an appreciation of the place in my mind where things are what I want them to be. It's a place where I take the greatest things of my imagination and combine them with the greatest things in life. The happiest people have created this inside themselves and live every day. If you have taken any step into transforming your dreams into reality, you've already been there. Though that is what my poem is based on, I cannot say the complete meaning of it. Only you can determine that. I'm 15 years old and live in Southern California

GRETTER, ROBERT
[a.] Mountain Home, AR [title] "If Only Moments" [pers.] I live in Mountain Home, Arkansas were I was fortunate enough to meet the true love of my life, I wrote this piece and others for her under the pen name Linda Sue's Wordsmith. I feel blessed in one being able to meet her and two being able to express my love for her. I think this is how love should be. All encompassing in the wonder of it. You can look for cards with my poem at Linda Sue's Wordsmith

GRIFFIN, ELIZABETH
[a.] Weogufka, AL [title] "God Knows" [pers.] I am new to poetry and I just took a chance at sending this one in. I had no idea it would actually get published. I started writing when I was 14 for a class project and discovered I really liked expressing my feelings in a meaningful way. Now that I am 15, I can't believe one of my poems was published. Thank you so much you have no idea how happy I am

GRIFFIN, MICHELLE
[a.] Mt. Vernon, WA [title] "Thought Alone Forever" [pers.] I have been writing for quite sometime now, writing has always been away for me to express myself on my deepest feelings and emotions. Poetry has been a release for me. When I feel blue or have had an ended relationship. Relationships are very important and most people take them for granted, this is where thought alone forever comes from, somewhere deep inside where you have been hurt. I have written many songs and poems on the matters of a broken heart. To some this may bring up old feelings of unrequited love, to others the feeling of loneliness

GRIFFITH, REBECCA
[a.] Glendale Heights, IL [title] "Love is Invisible" [pers.] This poem was inspired by a special person in my life, J.D.N. The phrase "Love is Invisible" appealed to the writer in me and the words just poured onto the paper. I enjoy writing poems to describe my feelings that I have experienced. My poetry comes straight from the heart, as all things should. I hope that others will enjoy this poem as much as I have enjoyed writing it. I would also like to say to my father, stepmother, grand father, brother, and J.D.N. I love you and thank you for your support

GRINDSTAFF, ELIZABETH LEAH
[a.] Marion, NC [title] "Aleia" [pers.] This piece was initially intended to be kept privately locked away in my journal . . . to be viewed, on occasion, by my eyes only. To be felt in my heart alone. But now, I find that sharing the memory of my best friend with all who care to know her is of the utmost importance to me. For I truly believe that the only sure way for one to die is for one to be never remembered. I remember you with joy, Aleia . . . and now you will live forever and for always!

GRISON, DEBORAH
[a.] Chicago, IL [title] "The Taste of Love!" [pers.] I began my relationship with words thirteen years ago as a sophomore in high school. Since that

moment, I have carried my love for words (poetry) inside of my spirit and soul like a mother carrying a child in her womb. When it comes to poetry, I wait in anticipation of what the creator will birth inside of me. My dream is to write books about various things. My first challenge is to self published and executive produce my first book of poetry entitled "The Attic" and a C.D. with the same name to compliment the book. Peace to all poets everywhere

GROFF, MATTHEW
[a.] Leola, PA [title] "Ormalu" [pers.] There is value in rejoicing in the moment without obsessing about forever . . . sometimes. New love can be this free, when entered honestly

GROSS, SAMUEL, JR.
[a.] Springfield, VA [title] "Free Dume!" [pers.] I am a self-employed architect which finds creative expression in several media. Creative services seek instinctive freedom to achieve the appropriate solutions. But seeking that freedom discovers infinite obstacles where, one is never sure his creation is free

GUDGEL, JACK
[a.] Bayard, NE [title] "My Testimony" [pers.] My deep appreciation for what God has done for me was the inspiration for this poem. My prayer was that He would "give me a song" that told three things: What I was, what He did for me, and what He will do for you. I believe my prayer has been answered. "My Testimony" has been set to music, though never published. I pray it blesses you as it has so many others

GUDMUNDSSON, KRISTJAN
[a.] Vestervig DK, Denmark [title] "The Quest" [pers.] This poem is very special to me, as it commemorates two people that where very important to me: my grandparents. Their courage and strength have been inspirational to me. After there death I started to think about what the meaning of life? Well nobody knows, and nobody will ever find out, the answer that we look for is buried in Ancient history and will forever more remain in ancient history. I hope that you dear reader will find as much joy in reading poetry as I do

GUILFOYLE, MARK
[a.] Sand Point, MI [title] "My Apology" [pers.] I am an osteopathic physician with additional training in Radiology and enjoy practice in a rural setting in Michigan. I have memberships in Intertel and MENSA; International High IQ Societies. I gain satisfaction in helping people achieve maximum health and longevity by operating a home-based Internet heath shop. This poem was written during an emotional low-point in my life. My wife had left me for several months due to repeated bouts of quarrelling and domestic aggression. During therapy, I wrote the apologetic verse. We reconciled and restored our relationship, and are now quite happy again

GUILFOYLE, MARK
[a.] Sand Point, MI [title] "The Origin" [pers.] I wrote this poem after reading a book by Carl Sagan; entitled Pale Blue Dot. All of the elements an earth; and hence within ourselves, were derived from a super nova stellar demise. Also, I make reference to the Big Bang theory of Cosmic evolution. Poetry is the condensation of thoughts and emotions expressed eloquently. I write poetry as a method of introspection; and also to give outlet to my creative instincts. I thoroughly enjoy carefully crafting the meaning, mood, meter and rhyme of every line. Other interests include reading, photography, kayaking, and internet marketing.

GUNDELACH, CARRIE
[a.] Depere, WI [title] "Take Me Away" [pers.] Poetry has always been a way for me to express myself. It's also an interesting way to place myself in the shoes of others. Poetry to me is the opportunity to see things in a new or different light

GUNTER, RENNISE
[a.] San Jose, CA [title] "Daddy's Home" [pers.] My inner most thoughts and feelings come pouring out in words when I think about my husband Bill, my two year old daughter Samantha, and my one year old song Cole. They are the light of my life, and they make each day a precious gift. I truly savor each day I spend at home with them. My poem "Daddy's Home" gives readers an idea of the importance of having a Daddy really is. My babies love their Daddy and I enjoy writing poems to express to the world about their special relationship

GURULE', JEFFREY, JR.
[a.] Pittsburg, CA [title] "Your Father in Me" [pers.] I don't write for myself, I recite for the people, and society to possibly point out its evil. And I'm not a rapper nor a poet I'm a prophet. But if I proclaim it, they search for the flaw in it, so they can try and excuse it as just music but it's like the news with more truth in it

GUTIERREZ, CYNTHIA
[a.] Godwin, NC [title] "Seasons of Love" [pers.] This poem is special for it tells the story of one person love. As it begins until it reaches him. And how that love is forever. Poetry is a gift given to many, yet used by few to express everything within our world be it good or bad. I use poetry to fill greeting cards for friends and family, letting each individual be my inspiration by listening to their hope and dream. Other poems flow to me like water in a spring just wanting to be free. And I am the lucky one to write it all down

GUZMAN, OLIVIA
[a.] Plano, IL [title] "Look Into These Eyes" [pers.] This poem is special to me because it's the first poem I ever wrote. This particular poem for me, expresses my feelings for the man I love. I want him to know that when I say the words "I do," that it will be for life, and this is a promise I will hold dear to my heart till death do us part. Thank you ILP for giving me the opportunity to let others read my poem and may it touch their hearts the way it does mine. God Bless!

HACKETT, APRIL
[a.] Durham, CA [title] "Tears" [pers.] This poem is very special to me. When I wrote this I was very depressed. As I wrote "Tears" it made me feel better because I got my feelings out. Whenever I'm sad I always write a poem down. It makes me feel better. I've always loved poetry it's my hobby

HADDIGAN, LUCEAL
[a.] Troy, AL [title] "Dream" [pers.] I began writing poetry when I was a young girl age 13. "Dream" was my first piece of work. I had my first boyfriend, whom I was deeply in love with and he broke my heart. I have written poems and short stories throughout my life all are very personal to me. My stepmother Nadine Brooks is one of the few whom I have shared my writings and feelings with. She always told me I should send some of my work in that it was good. I always told her no I was scared to share who I was and my life with anyone. Nadine passed away Feb. 1999 and because of her I have had my first poem published

HAGBERG, CHRISTOPHER
[a.] Hayesville, NC [title] "Everything" [pers.] Variety is the spice of life, and I believe in variety. I write what I know, and living in a small town, there isn't much else to write about. I enjoy the simple things and I feel this poem reflects that. It also describes exactly how the love of my life, Stacy, makes me feel

HAGER, TAMMY
[a.] Streetsboro, OH [title] "Through My Eyes" [pers.] I thank God every day for giving me the gift of writing poetry. And I want to use this gift as a way to glorify him and him alone. Without him I would have nothing and be nothing. When I started "Through My Eyes." I had the intentions of writing it about God's creation, little did I know it would be through a blind person's point of view! Needless to say I am more appreciative of seeing God's surroundings. Because we never know when God will close the door on our ability to see, and open the door to new things

HAGLER, ANGELA
[a.] Rockwood, TN [title] "Life" [pers.] My poetry is a very special part of me. I'm a Tennessee housewife who loves trying many different things. I have had photo's published with The International Library of Photography and just finished writing my first novel titled "Stormy." My husband Jerry and I love camping and hiking in the Smoky Mountains. My Grandson Alex is the love of my life. I hope you enjoy my work

HAMAKER, JESSE
[a.] Yreka, CA [title] "Life" [pers.] Grizzled Old mountain man, eighty years old, a retired forester, always macho, having been, a miner, logger, rancher, martial arts, bar bouncer, also a combat airborne WW II, always interested in new challenges, had a book of 180 pages published, poems, prose and stories at 78 years "the rural philosopher" my writing is spontaneous, akin to automatic influenced, I think by my dead sister or mother, have two grown children who are very successful, married my wife is also a vet WW II. I am very active and intend to wear out not rust out Born November 25 1919 at Newcastle, CA

HAMLER, SCHIQUITTA
[a.] Owings Mills, MD [title] "Matrimony" [pers.] I am a 27 years old reservationist and have a five year old daughter "Marissa" who is my inspiration. Poetry is a way of putting in writing visions within my head such as this poem which is a fraction of a larger poem that describes in detail from the thought of, to the final acts of a wedding. It would be a pleasure to have this poem be a part of weddings throughout the world. I have a collection of poems which I would like to be printed or to become songs in the near future! Signed an undiscovered poet

HANCOCK, RONDELL
[a.] Norfolk, VA [title] "A Rose" [pers.] This poem is for all the ladies who have given so much while asking so little in return. They give life and keep giving until the end. Thank you from my heart. This poem is dedicated to my wife Laura, all ladies in the world my inspiration comes from all the ladies of life. My mother, wife sisters, touched me deeply. I have learned that to give all you have, and do it with a smile is more than any man could give. Thanks for always being their when I needed you

HANDSAKER, MICHELLE
[a.] Nevada, IA [title] "Eternity" [pers.] Writing poetry is my cherished gift from God. It enables me to touch people and connect with them in a pure and unspoken manner. My words may come from my mind, but always by way of my heart

HANEY, ANDREW
[a.] Boswell, OK [title] "The Wall" [pers.] 19 year old National Guards Men. Attending University of Oklahoma in Fail of 2000. Grew up on a small ranch in South East Oklahoma

HANNA, RENEA
[a.] Rawlins, WY [title] "Winter Blankets are Needed" [pers.] I love poetry and enjoy writing it as well as reading it. In this poem I wanted to capture the joys and sorrows of winter. At the end I recalled how our fathers used to complain, "I used

to walk through six feet of show etc." Also the world can be a cold place while walking through it and sometimes we need to cuddle up in a warm winter blanket. I hope you enjoy my poem and love poetry as much as I do

HANNER, RONALD
[a.] Winder, GA [title] "Day's Journey" [pers.] For the pat few years. I have wondered how I, a 48 year old truckdriver would leave a mark for he world . . . something that says, "I was here." A little over a year ago, from out of the blue, I started writing poetry. "Day's Journey" is the second poem I ever wrote. I am honored to be included in this anthology, and a little dumbfounded at the same time. I dedicate this to my love, my inspiration, Anita. I love you very much

HANNINGTON, KAREN
[a.] Exeter, PA [title] "Battle Cries" [pers.] In my life I have met people who have left a lasting impression on me. "Battle Cries" was written after a difficult period with a friend who is extremely important to me. I am grateful that this poem was selected for publication. It is dedicated to my friend who taught me patience, courage, and the value of true friendship

HANSEN, JOSEPH
[a.] Monument, CO [title] "Rebecca" [pers.] A wise man once told his lover that if love were happiness then he was the happiest man alive. I never had a romantic relationship Rebecca Reynolds; but as a friend, she still helped me to feel loved. When Rebecca passed away her friends and family were devastated. We have vowed never to let go of her memory. As part of the commitment I have made, I have written this poem in a hope that as others read about Rebecca, they will remember her as I do, beautiful

HANSON, WILLIAM
[a.] Oconto Falls, WI [title] "Stew" [pers.] I based this poem on same childhood experiences involving the neighborhood kids, summer evenings, and a few targeted gardens after playing basketball. What if it was Gods garden? Obviously he would know who the culprits were despite their best efforts to disguise themselves in angel costumes. What would he do? You decide

HANSON, WILLIAM
[a.] Oconto Falls, WI [title] "Missing" [pers.] This poem is just about a memory, triggered by certain circumstances years later. I was shooting pool in a low lit bar next to a couple of red neon beer signs. In the other side of the room the door was open and I could see out onto the street which was facing west. The sun was setting and it was raining and it reminded me of a girl I once spent time with. Where is she now?

HARDRICK, JOI
[a.] Decatur, GA [title] "Mother" [pers.] This poem was written in dedication to my mother and to all the mothers who give to their children the courage and strength to strive for their dreams. It is a thank you for being who she is my inspiration and for allowing me to be inspired by her. I have always been fascinated with the beauty and majesty of words and through words I try to give others the same gift that I received

HARDY, IAN
[a.] Padstow, NSW Australia [title] "Reflections" [pers.] Poems to me are windows to the soul of the creator

HARE, MARCH
[a.] Freemont, CA [title] "Awaiting the Bolt" [pers.] When yearning comes, it comes in song, a lilt, a beat, a throb . . . A sailor's night, a lighthouse long, a whistle, a laugh, a sub . . . Whether it is yearning, union, loneliness or joy, poetry is it for March, who ranges

from March the Monk to being the March Have. March writes musical lyric, and the book of poems he propose to publish is aptly titled "Now Songs Old." He travels between the West and the East, and hopes that, like the name he has chosen for himself, his songs will be free of a background, yet mean something to all who read him. His real name, finally, is Padmahumar. He is twenty-nine years old, terribly restless and intense.

HARGRAVE, JAMES
[a.] Parachute, CO [title] "Life's Theme" [pers.] Writing poetry means everything to me. It is one thing I can do well. It is easy for me and it has rescued me from many a tormented night of loneliness. I have been admitted to Psychiatric hospitals many times as I struggled to gain balance and calm in my life. It is the contention within my soul that lingers in my poetry. I enjoy it and I enjoy sharing it with others. I am a thirty three year old single male from Grand Junction, Colorado and hold a B.S. degree from the University of Texas at Tyler

HARMON, STEPHANIE
[a.] South Portland, ME title] "O.U.I." [pers.] My poem was inspired by Mothers Against Drunk Driving. My heart goes out to everyone that has lost a loved one to that terrible fate. I would like to thank my family for all the inspiration that they have given me through good times and bad. Kaitlynn, Sullivan, Andy, Mom, Rick, Kelley, Christopher, Courtney, Jeanine, John, and Nana Jo, I love you all. Michelle and Nona, I love and miss you both dearly, although you are no longer with us, we will cherish your memories and your spirits will always live on in our hearts

HARPER, KENNETH
[a.] Bloomington, IN [title] "Messenger" [pers.] I think that people have forgotten how to get along. I took an angel's perspective to take a look at the world in this poem to remind everyone that there are bigger things thanks out there and we'll never get to see them unless we all work together. I get my creativity from my mother, who always has an idea. I love her and would like to thank her

HARRIS, STEPHANIE
[a.] Yuma, AZ [title] "The Ocean" [pers.] I'm nine year old. I like this poem because it describes how the ocean is like God. God is very special to me. God wants us to honor Him so I honored Him in my poem

HARRIS-MINOR, SHEILA
[a.] Richmond, VA [title] "Portrait" [pers.] I have always sensed that writing, as a means of communication, could be a view into one's soul. This poem is particularly demonstrative of that idea. It has captured some of my innermost feelings, since my having first experienced "Love," nearly thirty years ago. The poem was meant to suggest that love can be very painful at times. However, as painful as it can be, there is still nothing on Earth that can compare to the exhilaration that one feels, when love is new and without complication

HARRISON, JUDY
[a.] Lakewood, WA [title] "A Dove" [pers.] This is only my second poem. They came through the spirit of Jesus Christ, in answers to prayers. He has given me peace and helped me to turn my worries over to Him. Judy Harrison Tacoma, Washington

HARRISON, LORA
[a.] Cairo, GA [title] "Let's Go to the Zoo" [pers.] At age sixteen, I pieced together this poem for the children I might one day have. It's very special to me, as simple as it is, because the poem symbolizes the love I had for my children years before their births. Today, Elizabeth at twelve and Chevy at four, my children know the poem almost by heart. I often like to picture them telling its tale to my grandchildren. If there's one way a mother can hope to live in the hearts of her children forever, it's within a poem written by her just for them

HARTZ, LESLEY
[a.] Fullerton, CA [title] "For You" [pers.] Only lately have I become more open to expressing myself. However only in my writings can be true feelings be said. I wrote this poem for Phil. The love in my life. Together we have experienced pain, and together we will gain strength. I want him to always know I am there for him and love him

HARTZELL, KATHRYN
[a.] Riverview, FL [title] "Soul Mates" [pers.] The ability to give love, is a gift, to receive it, a blessing. My blessings are my inspiration. They are, my mother Mildred Tripp, my husband Robert, my children Jamie, Laura, Ray, Patty and Kathy. Further blessings include grandchildren, William, Sarah, Megan, Devon, Stephen, Jasmin, Jade, Butter, Christian and Angelo. This particular poem is for my "soul mate," Robert. Thank you Bob, this one's for you

HAUGE, DANIEL
[a.] Harrison, AR [title] "My Heart's a Paper Airplane" [pers.] The inspiration of this poem came from my life. At the age of 13 months, my twin brother and I were put in foster care, for reasons too hard to talk about. The couple that took us in, gave our life's new meaning and at the age of four, adopted us. Now we're 18 and soon we will be on own, and through poetry, music or song. We too, want to pass this love along!

HAWKINS, DORIS (DEE)
[a.] Lamar, CO [title] "There is No Pain Today" [pers.] This poem is dedicated to my father, Leonard Blundell. I wrote this poem the morning after he had died, which was also my 31st Birthday. He will always be apart of my life. Also, my husband, Earl, who without his support, I would not have made it through the last five 1/2 years. Thank you for this chance

HAWKINS, WINIFRED
[a.] Cayuga, IN [title] "The Hill in 1923" [pers.] My family owned that "community hill" that different seasonal joy did fill. Our land edged South of Central Park, Yard, two branches, hill provided such a lark. Thinking thoughts in rhythmical composition. Of places, people or what caught my attention. Being eighty and asked of events of old, write it too, though we like to be told. Starting with "the hill" then thoughts did flow. Even good of "The Depression" you know. Entered the contest, with this first of series see classed as semi-finalist, just overawes me. Well, that about tells it all . . . writing and entering, I've had a ball

HAWKS, RICHARD B., III
[a.] Dallas, TX [title] "Don't Let the Devil Use You" [pers.] This poem was spoken into my spirit by God's precious Holy Spirit for the purpose of enlightening Christians on one of the devices of Satan. Jealousy is too prevalent in the church of today. And I hope this poem along with many others that are inspired by our Lord and Savior Jesus Christ will also have the opportunity to be seen and read worldwide by way of the publication of your book and other books. I'm just thankful that I've been blessed with the opportunity for my work to be published in your wonderful publication. May God continue to bless you

HAWKSHEAD, JOHN
[a.] Jefferson, LA [title] "The Hospital Lounge" [pers.] With this poem I wanted to create a sense of the despair that one finds in hospitals, even those with the most advanced life saving technology and skilled professionals. I have mainly written poems for my wife Becky to express how much I love her; with "The Hospital Lounge" I was attempting to go in a different direction

HAWTHORNE, MICHELE
[a.] Apache Jct, AZ [title] "For the Love of

Him" [pers.] I wrote this poem for the love of my life, my lover, partner and friend. I have been writing poetry since I was nine years old but this is the first publication. I hope to write many more, in many years to come. I hope this piece brings enjoyment to all

HAY, DEBORAH
[a.] Portland, OR [title] "My Love" [pers.] The poem "My Love" was written truly for that, My love. It was written with the deepest feelings for my one and only true love. Therefore, I must dedicate the poem "My Love" to my wonderful, loving husband, William R. Hay III, because the feelings in the poem would have never been there without him. I would also like to thank you for the opportunity to share my poem with the whole world as everyone in the world searches for but rarely finds the kind of love expressed in my poem

HAYES, REJJI
[a.] Brooklyn, NY [title] "Xitrenka" [pers.] The title of my poem "Xitrenka" means devious lady in Russian. The works of Pushkin and a former loved one inspired me to put forth this effort. I have been writing poems since the age of fourteen, but never deemed any of them as worthy reads. For me, poetry is a clever and creative way to express my thoughts

HAYNER, TINA
[a.] Washington on Courthouse, OH [title] Through the Eyes of My Child" [pers.] Poetry comes easy for me, a gift from God. This poem was wrote for my oldest child, to show her I know the hurt she fills. I hope a missing parent reads this and makes a special visit to a child that's waiting. To both my children I love you! Mommy

HAZEN, JOSEPH
[a.] Memphis, TN [title] "Inventing The Wind" [pers.] I am sixteen years old, and have been writing as a form of release for years now. But the joy I got from this surprise winning the right of publication in my first contest indescribable. I want to thank the people have encouraged and inspired me so far: Rachael, Meagan, Zach, Adam, Katie, and others. Finally, I want to thank my father, without whom I would, quite literally, be nowhere

HE, BIHUAI
[a.] Long Island City, NY [title] "Student" [pers.] I see poetry as a way of expressing my innermost feelings or how I perceive every aspect of life differently. In poetry, we have to visualize the meaning behind every line. We have to read it couple of time to understand what the authors are trying to imply. I always encourage my friends to write poems but after they heard "Poetry," an unpleasant posture strikes upon their faces. I am sure writing is a gift and most people possess it within their characteristics, waiting to exit its potential impact upon the readers

HEADEN, CHRISTOPHER
[a.] Greensboro, NC [title] "Untitled" [pers.] This poem is a prayer for faith. I believe that it takes a lifetime to write a poem and I owe all of my literary works to those whom I encountered throughout my years. Therefore, I want to thank God for giving me the strength to turn my adversities into my ambitions. Thank you mom for being there with me through it all! I love you. I also want to thank my pops for giving me the element of hard work and perseverance. And to all others who have left memories in my past and footsteps in my heart . . . Thank you

HEATH, TAMMY
[a.] Charlotte, NC [title] "A Woman One Day"

HECK, ELISABETH
[a.] Miami, FL [title] "Smothered" [pers.] I was born and raised in Miami, FL. I am preparing to move out of my parents home and cross the

country to San Francisco, CA. Poetry throughout my life has been one of my few emotional outlets, and I hope that will continue in the future as I embark on the greatest adventure of my life

HECKMAN, ROBERT
[a.] Findlay, OH [title] "Hand in Hand" [pers.] Often in life, when the hard times seem to overshadow that which we know and love, it is easier to express feelings in verse or melody rather than in verbal language. This poem came from one of those times. How clear thoughts can be when expressed in writing or music

HEFFNER, KATHRYN
[a.] Shickshinny, PA [title] "Sunshine Valentine" [pers.] Always enjoyed writing but nothing serious until recently. The eldest of five daughters. Our mother Frances Daniles died unexpectedly in June, 1999, which left us devastated. Mom was my inspiration to begin writing again. My poems were my outlet of dealing with my grief. Sunshine Valentine was written for my sisters. We have always been close but our love is now more special than ever before. Graduate of Penn State University-Paralegal. Enjoys writing, cooking crossword puzzles, crafts, and NASCAR racing. Resides in Shickshinny, PA with husband, Paul and sons, Christopher and Justin

HEIDEBUR, AMANDA
[a.] Lonedell, MO [title] "The Night Time" [pers.] I think it's a gift to write poetry, and my mother and a couple of friends encouraged me to write my poems. "The Night-Time" relates to the forest at night. It tells a typical setting of a forest and tells what was happening as day turns into night. It also describes me as sort of being alone, because I have very few friends, and people like to tease me. I try to put my feelings into my poetry and think of what is going on in the world. I try to understand life in general and I read a lot of books. I'd like to thank my best friends Alicia Barahas, Erin O'Briskie, Mrs. Schlafer, Mrs. Hografe, and all my teachers I've had. I'd also like to thank my favorite band NSYNC for inspiring my inspiration and for helping me get through some tough times. I'd also like to thank my family for all their encouragements and help throughout the long and crazy years. I am 15 years old and I live in a small town called Lonedell and it's in Missouri. My hobbies are spinning records, playing sports, collecting stuff, hiking, biking, listening to music, and having fun with my friends and family, I also like swimming and doing dangerous stuff. I'm going into high school. I would like to become a writer or a Marine Biologist, so in my spare time I study. Thanks for giving me the opportunity to write this

HEISKELL-SIMMONS, DEBORAH
[a.] Louisburg, KS [title] "When" [pers.] I wrote this poem for my husband for Valentine's day. I think it is a very important part of life to tell loved ones how much we care or miss them. Something that too often gets over looked in life. I started writing poetry at a very early age to express my feelings or thoughts. My inspiration comes from all I do in life. Our ranch with our quarter horses, my husband, and God's gifts are inspiration enough for me. It has also been a life long dream to become a published author. May this only be a start

HEISNER, MARION
[a.] Westlake Village, CA [title] "Marion" [pers.] The poem "Marion," was written in 1985 by my late husband Marty Sugerman. He wrote it for our anniversary. I treasure his poetry and this is one of my favorites. Marty died in 1988 but his poetry stays with me always

HELD, DANIEL J.
[a.] Key West, FL [title] "Surrender" [pers.] My poem, "Surrender," is dedicated to a woman I have known since childhood, written shortly after we

decided to take our relationship to the next level. I write poetry about various topics, but romance has to be my favorite; perhaps because it is the easiest for me. So easy, in fact, that this one was written while waiting for an oil change! Proving once again, that inspiration can hit at any time. The key is to get it on paper during the moment, no matter where you are or what you maybe doing

HELLER, KAONOHI
[a.] Keaau, HI [title] "Headtrips" [pers.] "Headtrips" is one of many poems I was inspired to write during my educational experiences at Hawaii Pacific University and the application of theory and concept in real life situations my study of abnormal Psychology provided me with the understanding of people who were labeled crazy as well as my own personal experience of Headtrips. To all the poets who give words to the messages of our time . . . share your voice of truth that others may know the spirit within, themselves and give it flight

HELMKAMP, EMILY
[a.] Lafayette, IN [title] "My Best Friend" [pers.] I am a freshman in high school in Lafayette, Indiana. My poem was inspired when we had a project in my English nine class. I continued to write poetry after the project and decided to write a poem for my lifetime best friend, Erin Weatherwax. I wanted to write a poem to give to her to let her know how much I cherish our friendship. My sister was the first person to inspire me to write poetry. I've always admired her talent to write poetry. I feel poetry is one of the best ways to express yourself

HENDERSON, JAMES
[a.] Dublin, VA [title] "Distant Drums" [pers.] It is not by my hand, but he that guides my pen. For he mellows the heart and stirs the soul. For he reaches deep within, where I cannot, as boundless are his wonders to behold. For in retirement it is our gift to you

HENDERSON, SHARI
[a.] Simi Valley, CA [title] "Racism" [pers.] Life doesn't always go as planned. Mine fell apart. I was put in the system when I was sixteen and had been moved to a multicultural placement. The third day after my arrival I was accused of being racist. I never really understood the power of accusation until that day. That same night sitting in my room crying I realized I was being discriminated against, that the racism was against me. The pain, anger, and frustration I felt was released through my fingers to create a written piece of art. Thank you for letting me share this realization with you

HENNIGER, MARTHA
[a.] Elgin, Kogleo [title] "Clinical Depression" [pers.] My poetry is not always so dark. But I join the ranks in this poem of people who have had clinical depression and have been frustrated by the judgments of those who have not

HENRY, MARGO
[a.] Branford, CT [title] "Ceaselessly Flowing" [pers.] Poetry is as essential to me as breathing. It allows me to completely savor the moment, through all the senses. And if I allow the verse to flow naturally through me, then something magical happens and I become aware of the evolution

HENRY, SHIRLEY
[a.] Glastonbury, CT [title] "Freedom's Home" [pers.] I am a mother of seven children twenty grandchildren and the great granddaughter. I started writing poems when I was real young which I get from my grandfather. I wrote this poem because I see how far we have come in not putting in God we trust anymore which made our country a much better land when we did. I am retired for the time being, my hobbies are drawing playing scrabble, cards. I live in Connecticut

HERNANDEZ, JESUS
[a.] Oxford, AL [title] "All Hallows Eve" [pers.] I want to take this chance to thank someone very special to me. She has helped me in more ways than she could possibly think of. She has also inspired me to do the best I can at whatever I do. She means more to me than anything in this world. I just want to say thank you to her for all that she has given me and everything she has done for me. I love you, JSC.

HERNANDEZ, MANUELA
[a.] Glendale, AZ [title] "Man in the Back of a Pickup Truck" [pers.] My name is Manuela Rios Falcon Hernandez I was born on February 22, 1939, in Rio Hondo, Texas. I always carry a pencil and pad, because I write about the people I see around me. The young man in my poem I saw one morning as I drove to work and this is the way I saw him. My husband was a migrant worker and I've tried to write down my impressions of life as I see them. Thank you for including me in your publication I have never felt, that I would get recognition of my "scribblings," with love sincerely Manuela Hernandez.

HERSHBERGER, LINDA
[a.] Jacksonville, FL [title] "A Real Life" [pers.] A young life fell deeper into worthlessness because of verbal abuse in childhood. Then a relationship of betrayal. Feeling suffocated inside four walls, my only escape was out into the vase open space. A lonely walk through the quiet forest and compelled me to sing to the birds in the trees, which then became my captive audience day after day. Nature seemed to open doors of awareness of someone greater than myself. By walking into the meadow the breeze and sunshine flooded emotions, a cry to God brought peace to an anguished soul and purpose in life began

HESS, JOSHUA
[a.] Swartz Creek, MI [title] "When We Live" [pers.] Now 21, the poem "when we live," came to life at the age of 14." When we live is one of lighter poems I have written. Many of my poems are dark and angry, some, inspiring and colorful. Like Life. The world has good and bad to offer, ups and downs, blissful states of mind, and severe depression. I choose to explore them all. I hope one day to have a book of my own published, and to write songs for other artist as well as myself. So . . . remember my name

HEUER, JEANNE
[a.] Shoreline, WA [title] "Feel the Magic of the Moment" [pers.] When drifting into a deep state of euphoria, a vision of a moonlite evening one summer long past, was the inspiration behind the creation of my poem. This is the first poem that I've had the courage to enter in a contest or share with anyone. When my poem was selected for publication, it was a joy beyond my wildest imagination to have such an honor bestowed upon me. Writing my poem was great fun and I hoped to share my passions with others. Yes, feel the magic of the moment

HIBBARD, JUSTIN
[a.] Millersville, MD [title] "Automotive Love" [pers.] Girls have always had a higher priority in my life than automobiles. That's why my friends and I find this poem so humorous and ironic. I wrote "Automotive Love" in 1997 when I was sixteen. While I was reciting quietly to myself the beautiful, romantic words from Shakespeare's something about comparing a woman to a car. And while his words broke my mood, they sparked creativity inside me. During the class that followed, I began writing this poem in an attempt to arouse many laughs for years to come

HIBBERT, LENKA
[a.] Central Islip, NY [title] "Cowboys and Indians" [pen.] I wrote "Cowboys and Indians" during a time of hardship and struggle. I longed for the rosy glow of my youth when childhood was innocent and carefree, when it was full of hopes and dreams for the future. I mourn the youth of today who do not have the privilege of a whole, loving family; a safe, warm, childhood and a chance to dream. Children of today grow up too fast

HIGHT, AKILI
[a.] Inglewood, CA [title] "Eternal Life" [pers.] Poetry is an expression of life, through emotion and thought. My poetry changes as I change. I often look back at a piece that I felt was some of my best work in previous months, and can't believe I wrote it. As the universe evolves, so do I

HIGUERA, JOSE
[a.] Los Angeles, CA [title] "Solitude" [pers.] I wrote this poem to express the feelings I carry with me everyday. I feel like there are some things I cannot do and that I can only wish I could do. I wrote this poem to let out and show those feelings to all who read this poem. To me, writing poems is more effective to communicate deep feelings than talking about them or writing essays about those feelings because the poems can communicate a wide range of feelings and ideas in one small space and can last a lifetime in the reader's minds

HILL, JENNIFER
[a.] Orleans, ON [title] "Windows of You" [pers.] I guess my love for poetry started when I was thirteen. I had a wonderful English teacher who opened a whole new world to me though the works of Robert Frost and Alfred Noyes. My work will forever be a testament to that gift she gave to me

HILL, MARTHA
[a.] Norfolk, VA [title] "The Realtor" [pers.] Writing is a God-given gift I appreciate, being grateful both my parents encouraged reading at a very young age. My late Father wrote for his own amusement, but did have pieces published. Therefore, this publishing is in honor of him. Inspiration is all around me living on the beautiful southern shores of the Chesapeake Bay with my eighty year old mother, three cats, Cleopatra, Peaches, Sugar, and my Soulmate, Tom. As a Real Estate Broker for seventeen years, my poem expresses "Reality" of the profession and great satisfaction received by helping people achieve their dreams and goals

HILL, NIKI
[a.] Colorado Springs, CO [title] "My Hero" [pers.] For many years I did not know how to express my innermost feelings, nor even my simplest thoughts. Poetry was my way of releasing all the pain and desperation, anger and rage, ecstasy and tenderness; that I had concealed from the ones that I loved the most. Since my diagnosis or rheumatoid arthritis, I have had to overcome many obstacles. My disease has taught me a great deal-like how to open my eyes and see how privileged I am to be apart of my family. They are my tower and mighty crag. I dedicate this poem to my family

HO, JODY
[a.] Pasadena, CA [title] "Please Be Mine" [pers.] This poem is very precious to me since it is a beautiful poem on love. It shows what a young girl would think about love and proves that not only adults have special moments and feelings, I think poems are wonderful ways to express out your feelings, though it is only a few paragraphs long

HOBBS, DIANE
[a.] Milan, NM [title] "Shadow in the Trees" [pers.] Poetry in all its dynamics will never be replaced, or forgotten, for it lives in the hearts of each one of us. "I Am The Shadow in the Trees," because my poem reflects my life as it may be. Fair Maiden Kaelin, was born on July 27, 1957 on Long Island, New York and currently lives in New Mexico.

The beautiful Modern Art pieces I create with mirrorized colored aluminum and mirror are my forte

HODGES, KELLIE
[a.] Hartsville, SC [title] "Hurt" [pers.] I would like to say thank you to the fifth grade teacher who encouraged me when I brought her my first poem. Thank you Mrs. Moses. To my husband, Nick, I love you very much and I am proud to have you by my side. To my children, Kyle and Nicholas, I love you dearly and wish you nothing but the best in life. And last but not least I need to thank my mom and dad for always believing in me. I love you all and keep you close in my heart

HODGSON, CARMEN
[a.] Auckland, New Zealand [title] "Infatuation" [pers.] Poetry came early in life, memories of a hurtful teacher not believing a child could write the limerick, is now a fabulous compliment. At eighteen I found my best friend (via words), Ella Wheeler-Wilcox. Although I have been unsuccessful at finding move of her work in New Zealand, the book I have is a beloved companion. This poem, I wrote at the age of sixteen for a dear friend. I am sure Murray can appreciate it move now, 12 years later

HOFER, BENJAMIN
[a.] Obenburg, Switzerland [title] "The Way Through the Life" [pers.] "The Way Through the Life" is very special to me. Because of the following reasons: First and most reason is, that I wrote that poem for a person who is so important in my life, for Jayne and first true love. She gave me strength and power to change my life finally. I don't know how to thank her for all that and especially for inspiring me, so I like to dedicate this poem to Jayne. Second reason is that this poem was my first experience in writing about my feelings. Last reason is that I'm still learning English and the success of this poem will motivate me to learn English even more intensive

HOGAN, RANDY
[a.] Waukegan, IL [title] "Animals in a Zoo" [pers.] I'm really excited, since this is my first poem that I've written outside of school. I want to dedicate this to Mom and Dad Brad Jr. Sarah Grandma and my friend James Spencer who is a wonderful source of support and insight, I'm lucky to have met him. Thanks buddy. I plan to write more poems as well as short stories. I hope you enjoy my writing. I wrote this due to personal problems. So it was reflective of my feelings at the time. Thank you for taking the time to read it. (Also thanks ILP.)

HOLLERMAN, JUSTIN
[a.] Masury, OH [title] "Heavens Sea" [pers.] I wrote this poem from a very special person in my life. Leslie Suchy, I will always be here for you

HOLLEY, ASHER
[a.] Granby, CO [title] "The Light Within the Darkness" [pers.] You know I'm there and yet I'm not, you see me every day and yet you never do. A ghostly apparition made up of digital emotions I am, and yet I'm stronger than most, and wiser than most, and frighteningly more alive. I dream, yes I dream, of unhindered actualization of thoughts where will and becoming would be one. I dream of a past to be with moments of ending and seeds of beginning. I do this alot: dream. That's why I'm made out of pristine glass, I'm always far away. I'm easy to break if only you could reach me with your clandestine thoughts, distance is my shield. Yet it is my barrier, through which every once in or while my screams get through. What am I screaming about, you ask, me hidden in my labyrinth of mathematical chaos? I'm screaming, "I am the unforgotten"

HOLLIN, HANNA
[a.] Naperville, IL [pers.] "Your Gone" [pers.] My feelings about poetry are very strong. I have loved

poetry all my life. I think that a flow of emotions can burst to of a person who writes. Poetry is like art the only enemy is taste. I think this poem can be used in different, context. It can be a lost love, someone who passed away or a family member. My cousins and I used to be close, but now were not. They used to be best friends. I love them so much! This poem reminds me of them

HOLLIS, MADELYN
[a.] Hohenwald, TN [title] "To Be Left Behind" [pers.] My husband loved and encouraged my poetry. He was the backbone of my world. His death recently left a void for the children and me that is indescribable. "To Be Left Behind" address that emptiness yet looks forward to the day that we will be able to draw from the memory of his love and build our new beginnings

HOLMES, ANNE
[a.] Zionsville, IN [title] "Thank You" [pers.] I am a freshman at Purdue University studying Elementary Education. My poem thank you was my way of expressing my then 12 year old brother's last night with us. Today he would be 16 years old. The "Sis" mentioned in the poem is me. I was the last person he talked to. The two of us were very close so the poem is written solely from my heart

HONEA, ERIC
[a.] Atlanta, GA [title] "Huh?" [pers.] There must be something more to see, in this reality. Something more than our eyes realize, innocence while in our youth, we grew up and turned our backs on the truth. Tragedy comes to those who choose this world but lose their souls, while open minds are left behind to explain the seasons, the changes, maybe it's about love or lock there of.

HOOSER, BESS
[a.] Seymour, TX [title] "My Long Journey" [pers.] The most emotional moments in my life have found expression in poetry. I am a 72 year old retired bilingual/ESL specialist. I sincerely hope will speak to the hearts of many, and let them know there is a big world to be discovered. I recently accompanied a team of doctors and nurses to a village in the mountains near a guerilla stronghold in Guatemala. For 16 days I translated medical instructions for nearly 2000 patients. This poem was written in my hotel on our last night in country to share with others my feelings about our experiences

HOPKINS, ROSALYN
[a.] Fayetteville, NC [title] "The Youth Offering, The Youth Redeemed" [pers.] I wrote this poem for a beautiful young lady with very sad brown eyes. I told her that one day, the poem would be published and that I would dedicate it to her. So, D. Mc., here is your poem dedicated with much love. You are yet in my prayers. If we never meet again, remember, God always knows where you are

HORSLEY, JAMES
[a.] Leesburg, TX [title] "Butterfly" [pers.] I am a writer of poetry but Sea Art Studio is my life. I am a sculptor of clay sea life is my subjects. Both creative forms are an extension of my soul. My poems are my emotions of loving a girl. My sculpture is my expression of pleasing her. My life, my world revolves around a girl I haven't found. This is my message in a bottle

HOSEIN-HOUSE, CHARLEEN
[a.] Seattle, WA [title] "Delusions" [pers.] Writing poetry signifies the need for me to see beyond the outward appearance. "Delusions" was written for those persons who have been overlooked by the irrelevant, not by what the self-less nature of the soul can possess. Most often the beauty in people is clouded, by our own assimilations. Writing gives me the opportunity to go on with living, learning and experiencing the many dimensions in "being human." Generally, I believe, something pleasing can be found most obscure

HOSKIN, BERNIS
[a.] Fontana, CA [title] "Lost Dreams" [pers.] Poetry is an outlet for me. Through poetry I creatively express emotions such as anger, happiness, and or depression. I believe I am blessed with the talent to write poetry. This is my opportunity to share my talent with the world. Lost Dreams is the first piece of literature I present to you

HOTOV, ANDREI
[a.] San Francisco, CA [title] "For Here or to Go" [pers.] I was quite surprised to find that my poem was picked up. The English is my second language after Russian, so I tried to write some poetry in English and people lived it. The history of this poem is sad and romantic. It's about a girl and felt in love from the first time I met her but I could never get into relationship with her and her heart belongs to someone else. She used to work in one of San Francisco coffee places. So in the morning I stopped there for a cup of bad coffee just to see her and to say a few word. The story goes more complicated and I have a good poet for my future story with more details

HOWARD, ADDI
[a.] Lumberton, TX [title] "Fear" [pers.] This poem entitled "Fear" was inspired by my four year battle with an eating disorder. Anorexia kept me bound in paralysing fear. I was afraid to eat and most of all, afraid to lose control

HOWARD, ROBERT
[a.] Grand Rapids, MI [title] "Let's" [pers.] I have been writing since I was in high school and I am currently working on a novel, which I hope to finish in my lifetime. Writing poetry, for me, is mostly spontaneous, I like to send cards to family and friends with my original poems. Nothing says I love you better than an original poem

HOWARD-BRIGGS, RUTH
[a.] Middletown, OH [title] "Exhausted" [pers.] This poem is a work straight from the heart. I experienced quite a bit of pain during the time period in which this poem was composed. Since then I have recovered and am able to deal with love in its purest form

HOWELL, TIA
[a.] Cherryville, NC [title] "The Greatest Joy" [pers.] Many of the poems that I write are prayers. I wrote this poem at 3:20 am one morning. Some things were not going right in my life, so I began to pray and then I started to write these words. I named it "The Greatest Joy" because at the moment that I finished the poem, I knew just how much God loved me, and I knew for a fact that I was saved; and that is indeed, the Greatest Joy of all

HUANG, BENJAMIN
[a.] Mobile, AL [title] "The Four True Elements" [pers.] I wrote this poem in honor of Philosophers, lovers, those who hope, those who have died, and those who are born. I commemorate this to my two friends Helen Petersen and Alyson Gamble, who inspired my writing I hope others are lucky enough to have poets to learn from as I did. Enjoy the poem

HUBER, LETICIA
[a.] San Diego, CA [title] "Oh, Laughing Star" [pers.] This poet is a spirit, passionate love of words and their most basic meaning; of the way they travel; the power they have. The gifts they bear. I love the minds that think them, the people who use them, the things they name. And more than all, I love the source of all words ever said and to be said and thought. Poems are a good connection to that source

HUCKABY, BENJAMIN
[a.] Chesapeake, VA [title] "Secret Places" [pers.] I have been writing poetry off and on for most of my life. Throughout my life, I been able to

express my feelings much more clearly with poetry. This particular poem was written during a very lonely point in my life. My wife had died and I was depressed

HUCKINS, BRADIE
[a.] Colleyvile, TX [title] "Perfect" [pers.] This poem was written for a school report and I decided to send it in. I love writing poems, and they let me get my feelings out on paper. My mom, dad, and brother have a long influence on my life, and I love them very much. I also very much appreciate the encouragement of my friends. Their support has made such an impact on me. My family and friends don't know how much they all mean to me

HUDDLESTON, MARILYN
[a.] Canyon, TX [title] "A New Fresh Young Love" [pers.] Daughter, sister, mother to five miracles, grandma to four little ones, niece, Cousin and Friend to many. Ph.D., Financier, author. Recognized for life accomplishments: Who's Who in American Women, Who's Who Women of the World, and Who's Who in the South and Southwest. Thank you first to God, for this special gift. A special thanks to the selection committee for publishing my work. To mama and Uncle father Jim for your untiring efforts and motivation. To my husband of 25 years, my inspiration, and for whom this prose was written. Poetry is . . . the beacon by which we find our way.

HUDSON, JOSHUA
[a.] Pensacola, FL [title] "Gravity" [pers.] Obviously, I was deeply frustrated when gravity came out of me. It had to be released however, as my heart was with another far away. Her face was too painful to even think about, and her touch . . . ouch! Sex was too easy to write about when I sat to put pen to paper, but this feeling . . . thank you

HUDSON, LATISHA
[a.] Spring Valley, CA [title] "Not to Worry" [pers.] My poetry is an expression of my life, thoughts, experiences and beliefs. When I write, I like the readers to decide what it is about. I have learned that people can often see or read the same thing and have different thoughts. As long as my poetry touches someone, I have done my part. I dedicate the first publishing of my life to my deceased uncle, Larry Akins. He made me believe I could accomplish anything, and by God's grace, I have done this

HUEBNER, KRISTEN
[a.] Hay Lakes, OK [title] "All Alone" [pers.] This poem is important to me because I wrote it after the man I had loved so dearly only pretended to love me and then took off with my best friend. I hated them both for what they did to me. This verse is my way of what they did to me. This verse is my way of learning not to love someone just because they claim they love you. I live in a small town called Hay Lakes in Alberta. I attend New Norway School and I am in grade 9, I started writing poetry when I was about 13. My first poem was called "The Birds and the Bees." I have three sisters, Jody, Amy, and Kelsey. I have a very strong relationship with the inspiration to all of most of my poems, his name is James and He is the most important thing in my life

HUGGINS, CLAYON
[a.] Queens Village, NY [title] "Empathy" [pers.] I was born on the Caribbean Island of St. Vincent and migrated to the USA at the age of nine. I graduated from Marist College with a B.Sc. degree in finance and now work as a Risk Management Analyst. I live in Queens, NY with my gorgeous daughter, Zoe Giovanni. I've always wanted to be a writer and have written several poems and short stories but never published. This particular poem is important to me because it was inspired by

several people who are experiencing difficulties with their in-laws; You're not alone. Hello to my family in Florida, Canada and NY

HUGHES, NICOLE
[a.] Niles, OH [title] *"Te Quiero Mi Amor* (I Love You My Love)" [pers.] During the time in which I wrote this poem, it seemed like all of my friends and I were going through the same type of situation, where we really loved someone and they left us and the smallest things were what we remembered and missed I'm sure many people will be able to relate to it and I hope some people may get some comfort from it knowing that they've not the only ones who may be feeling this way. I hope my first published poem is enjoyed

HUMBERT, ERICA
[a.] Fontana, CA [title] "My Mistake" [pers.] I wrote this poem because it seemed to express my inner-self. I was going through the stage where, everything I thought, seemed to come out in a "Romantic" sense. I was always thinking about what it was like to fall in love, and the struggle that would come along with it. I received this special talent from my mother, and I love the fact that I can think as a poet. So I hope that I could carry on this special talent and share my ups and downs, with my great family and friends

HUMBLE, NEELY
[a.] Mesquite, TX [title] "I'm Sorry" [pers.] I love to write poems, but I don't write them from personal experiences. I mostly just make them up off of the top of my head because it is easier for me. People think that it is amazing that I have such a wonderful talent and I am only 13. I don't think it is all that amazing because I believe that everybody has a gift. Some people just theirs sooner than others

HUMEN, JACKIE
[a.] High Bridge, NJ [title] "Horses!" [pers.] One of the reasons why I wrote "Horses!" is because I love to write and I love horses. It is especially rewarding when you can combine the things you love together. It is very inspiring when you walk into a barn and smell the sweet smell of feed and when you hear the soft snickering of horses. I imagine the magnificent beauty of a horse galloping around his pasture. Anyone who has ever experienced this is a very fortunate person!

HUMPHREY, ANNA
[a.] Santa Ana, CA [title] "Love So True" [pers.] "Love So True" is a poem that my rustling leaves, bird's songs, as well as everything else He has created. Before I became a Christian there was avoid now that loneliness is filled by my true-love, God. I wish for everyone to come to know Him personally, to fill that void in their own life. Nothing else on Earth can take His place. There is place and security in knowing God loves you and will always be with you. Give Him your heart today

HUMPHRIES, JACK
[a.] Gulfshores, AL [title] "Mom, Jesus, and I" [pers.] I wrote this poem while sitting at the hospital with my mother. She did of cancer two weeks later. I am honored that it is being published. I hope everyone that reads it can be uplifted. I love to write music and poetry because it to be printed in. Between darkness and light is what my poem is about. There is a lot of darkness in this life, but if we walk in the light of Christ we can see our loved ones again

HUNTER, DARYL
[a.] Plantation, FL [title] "Her" [pers.] The poem "Her" was written in January 2000, during my sophomore year of high school. My English class was studying poetry that semester, and I found I really enjoyed it. I decided to try my hand at writing poetry and "Her" is what resulted from that. I was 15 when I wrote "Her," and I hope to continue writing

HUTTON, MONTIE
[a.] Apple Valley, CA [title] "Hearts Distance" [pers.] I dedicate this poem to Maggy who bridged the distance; to Courtney who inspired me to cross; to my Dad who showed me the way and to all of those who took my risk to love, I commend you for truly the only risk we take is the one not taken

IANNONE, MICHAEL
[a.] Pensacola, FL [title] "Cradled in the Arms of Jesus" [pers.] My poem was inspired by television news of tragic deaths from plane crashes and natural disasters. To console remain loved ones I believe when we pass on "we are cradled in the arms of Jesus." I have a masters degree from U.W.F and complete studies for a doctorate, Florida State University since becoming disable I've renewed my passion for writing poetry, the flaming candle of life that will never flicker out. I dedicate my poetry to the two candles of my life my daughter, Kathi Iannone and my grandson; Bricen Trace Iannone

IGIC, RAJKO
[a.] Chicago, IL [title] "Are We Inferior to Dolphins" [pers.] Dudley Herschbach was inspired by Leo Szilard's book, *The Voice of the Dolphins*. Herschabah was fascinated by dolphin society. If a dolphin becomes unconscious or injured, others rush to its aid, float it to the surface, and it can breathe. Otherwise, the injured animal would drown. The dolphins have a communications system that helped them to develop a "group mind." Perhaps the behavior of dolphins could teach us to enhance our own capabilities, suggested Herschabach. In this era of increasing communication among people's all over the globe, we hope that "The Voice of the Dolphins" will be widely heard

IMHOFF, BECKY
[a.] Madison, WI [title] "The Life Pyre" [pers.] Poetry has been a powerful tool, for me, through recovery from childhood sexual abuse. This particular poem has been revised several times as I moved through my healing. I hope that it can reach out and take the hand of other children, young and old, who need encouragement through the dark channels of recovery. There is hope and strength in numbers, breaking the silence is the hardest part, but the first step to peace and new hope

INGERSOLL, LORRAINE M.
[a.] Peabody, MA [title] "Steve and Ernie" [pers.] I just love children. When I saw the look of love on the face of my son Steve and on Ernie's for him I knew I had to have that moment in time forever. To answer his four year old question, I am his friend. At 42 years old Steve is a happy well-liked man and father of two children I am so proud when strangers tell me. Steve is a great guy "Well I say he takes after his father and mother!" Me? I also love science a have the great curiosity of a "Cat!" I must know all I can about life, liberty and outer space. Someday I will write a book on "memory" and how it is created. My theory is now, since 1977, in copy right and the library a congress waiting to be discovered. I love live especially family. You're never alone as long as you have then and your God

INGRAM, CHRISTINA
[a.] Kensington, NH [title] "A Picnic of the Heart" [pers.] Poetry is a way to express ones feelings and emotions. A way of putting down on paper what one maybe hesitant to say out loud. The receiver of a poem can accept what is being said more readily than if being told face to face. Poetry to me is like looking at a wild flower filled with beauty and a silent song which holds a hidden message. The receiver in turn must find the message in order to receive the blessing. A Picnic of the Heart has a simple message but a powerful outcome if accepted

INGRAM, EDNA
[a.] Tupelo, OK [title] "Strange Customs" [pers.] Poetry is a lovely way to express your innermost thoughts and concerns. I feel that this poem depicts what partly contributed to declining in our nation

INGRAM, JAMES
[a.] Virginia Beach, VA [title] "An Ode and Finly Farewell" [pers.] Poetry is a hobby for me and I enjoy it. "An Ode and Finly Farewell" was written for co-worker whose little fish died. Several co-workers had fish and when one died, I would create an ode to some of them and e-mail it throughout the firm as humor. Poetry is an escape avenue and stress reliever for me. I also use it as an attempt to capture human emotions. I have done tailored at the request of friends who expressed an appreciation for my efforts to understand and explain their emotion from a Layman's perspective

INGRAM, MICHELLE
[a.] Columbus, GA [title] "Reality" [pers.] I was young, finding my own way in life from underneath the security umbrella of Mom. I was "wet behind my cars," yet keeping my head above water . . . .breathing, surviving and receiving healthy doses of challenges. Before anyone steps onto a path of uncertainty, understand "Reality" first

ISLEY, KEN
[a.] North Bend, OR [title] "The Flower" [pers.] When I write, I write from the heart, inspired by family, friends, and events in my life. I love poetry because it enables me to express myself in ways I can't do otherwise. My poem "The Flower" is about the many struggles we face in our quest for perfection. One day life is fine, and the next you don't think you can go on, until finally that special someone comes and lifts you from the depths. I would like to thank my gardener, my personal Lord and Savior, Jesus Christ, for that life-sustaining drink of living water

JACKSON, CHARLES
[a.] Turlock, CA [title] "Time and Again" [pers.] Charles A. (Tony) Jackson is the adopted son of a prominent Turlock, CA, family. Educated in local schools and graduating from University of the Americas, Mexico City in International Relations, and Fresno Pacific University in Mathematics Curriculum he has taught in Turlock for 30 years. His poetry is inspired by feelings found in the diverse situations and people that surround him. His work spans almost ten years. "Time and Again" honors his love for W.E.B. and his profound feeling that they have their lives woven together for time immemorial

JACKSON, EDITH
[a.] Craigsville, WV [title] "Life" [pers.] This poem is a very special to me, as it commemorates someone who I loved and cared for deeply. My aunt Marie. This poem reminds me of the way she struggled with faith and death

JACKSON, JEFFERY, JR.
[a.] East Point, GA [title] "Letting Go" [pers.] It seems like yesterday when I first picked up pen and paper. Now, twenty years have passed and my love for the craft has flourished. My poetry is my journal to the world a world of enchantment, heartache, and self-fulfillment. As a child born in the City of Atlanta, Georgia, my passion to learn and express myself through poetry has been a lifelong challenge. Through poetry, I am able to express myself in ways my soft-spoken tongue could not. I am able to show courage through adversity, triumph over victory, and an undying love for others

JACOBA, CHRISTIE
[a.] Battleground, IN [title] "Help Me" [pers.] I was born in Lafayette, Indiana on December 11, 1971. This poem, I like many others is my way of expression without having the ordeals of talking to people. I've been reading poetry ever since I've known how to read. Even with nine brothers and

sisters I've found books to be the true best friend. Married on March 12, 2000 to David Jacoba I have finally found the happiness that every person deserves. My new family of David, Chad, and Courtney have become the world to me. I love them all

JAMES, DON, JR.
[a.] Chicago, IL [title] "A Run in Her Stocking" [pers.] This was a fun look at how one man views the entertainment industry. I enjoy poetry as an escape from the computer industry and hope everyone gets a chuckle from this poem

JANES, LEONARD
[a.] Bayonne, NJ [title] "Loss—To My Wife's Memory" [pers.] When I first met my wife, I wrote syrupy love poems to her. She was the most important person in my life for 17 years. I just want people to know how much I miss her and this poem expresses in print how I feel much better than I could ever say. And if it touches someone, I know she'd be pleased

JANOSIK, DANIEL
[a.] Columbia, SC [title] "Hostia" [pers.] The most significant even in our history is that the God who created the universe humbled himself and became a man in that same universe for our sakes. This poem seeks to portray that mystery visually. The "woman" in spirit sleeves represents the Spirit at work. The "lotus petal" represents Christ as He becomes incarnate (wraps Himself in flesh) and literally becomes a creature in the world that He created. T. S. Eliot called Him the "still point of the turning world," and as we reach for Christ He will be found in the "stillness" between two beats or two waves two points of finitude "containing" the infinite

JARRETT, MARY
[a.] West Keansburg, NJ [title] "Dear Oprah with Love from Mary" [pers.] Oprah is an inspiration TV talent. Her shows have helped me so many times. I wrote this poem as a tribute to her for all the lives she has touched. Having a poem published has always been a dream of mine and I hope someday my daughter Rachel can read it in this book and see for herself that dreams do come true

JEBB, KIMBERLY
[a.] Cabot, AR [title] "To Have Known You When" [pers.] Since ancient times the soul has sought out various forms of expression. We seemed to recognize how the art of writing could provide a common bond between people. The evolved written verse provides us with a vital link in better understanding our human emotions. Poetry is my outlet and personal portrayal of the vast array of emotional, physical, and mental experiences that life offers daily

JEFFERSON, GARY
[a.] Muncie, IN [title] "A Tear for Two" [pers.] There are two types of poems I write one being creatively planned, manipulated and recreated until I am satisfied and the other (as this one is), being pure revelation and straight from the heart. It flows from the pen as if it were already created before hand. Life can get hard, but as Christmas we must realize our God, (Jesus Christ) has suffered more. I am a member of the Church of Jesus Christ of Father-day Saints. I am an artist and a writer. I wish to use my talents to bless the lives of others, to please the Lord in doing his will. Poetry can be a powerful way to express one self to others. It has the power to capture our imagination, inspire our minds and touch our hearts. I believe all forms of art has the ability to lift the souls of man

JENKINS, CLANE
[a.] Phoenix, AZ [title] "Lone Wolf" [pers.] Lone Wolf was written in a fervent moment of some unknown inspiration. The poem its words and its flow, not only represent a part of me that very few

know about, it also projects an image of who I wish to become. The character in the poem is struggling to preserve the world and its reality when it has already become a floating illusion in the minds of men. He not only struggles but hunts as well, revealing a determined warrior completing his task. It ends with the poem only being a vision in the sleeper's eye. I hope you enjoy

JENKINS, MARC
[a.] Cleveland Heights, OH [title] "Let the Past be the Past" [pers.] If write about real life experiences, whether it be my own or someone dear to me . . . people will relate . . . I just want to get my lyrics out there because it's a lot that still has yet to be said!

JESSUP, VERONICA
[a.] Woodstock, GA [title] "Weather" [pers.] I was born in Georgia on January 2, 1985. I go to Woodstock High School. I am very atlethic. I am a black belt in Choi Kwang Do. I also played Volleyball for my high school. I would like to give a special thanks to my 7th grade teachers: Casey Shull, Stacy Gerker, Lorin Cook, and Robert Daniel. They are the ones whom helped me get out of the "bad" crowed an realize that not everything revolves around your peers. Also thanks to everyone who read my poem

JIMENEZ, JOLENE
[a.] Rancho Cordova, CA [title] "I Believe" [pers.] Behind the story of this heart warming poem is dedicated to the love of my life: Jaroslav M. Turner, for this poem was written from the inspiration and the vision of love towards him. This love has made me reach a new plateau of fate and gloriously magnified my life. Taking by breath away when I heard his voice on the phone. Even to this day, I continue to write more poetry about our perfect love that started with a touch of a keyboard. As for one day to continue the happiness with no worries

JOE, KATHLEEN
[a.] Coquitlam, BC [title] "Joey" [pers.] This poem is very special to me because I wrote it for a very special guy named Joey. I thought that a poem would show my love for him. I'm very proud to have this talent. I got this talent from my father, who has wrote alot of poems thought his life. I'm only a 13 year old and have been writing poems since I was 8–9. The poem show my feelings

JOHNSON, ASHLEY
[a.] Hinesville, GA [title] "God Sent Me an Angel" [pers.] My Grandmother was a very inspirational and spiritual woman. We were very close to each other. When she became terminally ill and my mother her to live with us, I was very instrumental in her care. At the time of her death I wrote this poem to go on her obituary. I had the complete assurance that an angel was with my grandmother throughout her illness. This gave me comfort knowing that God had sent her a special angel

JOHNSON, BRENDA
[a.] American Fork, UT [title] "Survivor's Tale" [pers.] Having my writing published was something I've never even dared to dream of. Things like that only happen to people like Robert Frost, not fifteen year old girls from Utah. I entered my poem into this contest because I thought I could learn something from the experience. I did, I learned not to let go of dreams, no matter how impossible they seem. It can even happen to fifteen year old girls. I also learned that no one can make it without the support of their family and friends. I love you all. Thank you for not letting me give up

JOHNSON, ELIZABETH
[a.] Welaka, FL [title] "The Lurking Loner" [pers.] I am 48 years old, married for 31 years, to Alfred V. Johnson Sr. a correctional officer. The mother of 31 years old Alfred V. Johnson Jr. one

12 year old Jessica Nicole Johnson. One of nine children born to Daisymae Graham of Welaka, FL. Life is precious, give to others and expect nothing in return. Open up your heart, to people in need. This story is based on the true story of a old man who was all alone, with no real home or bread to eat. The old man is now deceased, but at least he died with some dignity

JOHNSON, EVELYN
[a.] Wasilla, AK [title] "His Life" [pers.] This poem was written about my father. He is gone now. Every time I read it, which is often. It brings tears to my eyes. I can feel his presence, I can see every move he makes, and every step he takes as he walks down that lonely road to feed, water and care for his horses. I know every horse and animal lover that reads this, are the only one's that know and understand, how much love that one person can fully give to their animals. Hope this poem enjoyed by all who read it

JOHNSON, JANE
[a.] Brooksville, FL [title] "I Am Unique" [pers.] My poetry is influenced by my surroundings my emotions, my family, and my relationship with God. Raised on Long Island along with eight siblings, Dad died while mom was eight months pregnant with her ninth child. Cathy, Laurie, myself, Buddy, Mary, John, Ken, Rick and Veronica, together we made memories and now I write them as poems. My husband Dave and I, married 29 years, have two children, Jennifer and Jessica, one grandson Jacob and Ethan is due in June. Dave is why this poem was written, he makes me feel like I a special just being a women, is unique!

JOHNSON, MARGARET
[a.] Jacksonville, FL [title] "Halls" [pers.] This poem has two very deep meanings to me because it is very much a reality to me. I leave its meaning up to the readers, but it is only I who knows its true connotation. I would like to give two sincere thanks to my mother and father for everything they have done for me. I love you guys! Enjoy and thanks to all

JOHNSON, MARK SHANNON
[a.] West Des Moines, IA [title] "Everyday" [pers.] Coping with death, is the most emotionally strenuous instance one can endure in their lifetime. "Everyday," was written in honor of my father "Bodie" Duane Joseph Johnson, to immortalize my love for him. Most everything I am came from something he had bestowed to me, most importantly my belief in God. Without that life has no meaning. He always hoped I would choose writing as my means I hope he would be proud to see my work published. It is my sincere wish that people relate to my words that remind everyone to remember those how gone, "Everyday" God bless

JOHNSON, NICHOLAS
[a.] San Francisco, CA [title] "Good Thought" [pers.] Poetry is my remedy to a better life. A God given gift, which swims inside of me. Inherited by my ancestors Greek Philosophy. No one is perfect, yet I believe we all can be better. Poetry has helped me become that better person. Words are powerful, therefore, they should be written in positive form. This poem simply reflects on the power of good thought. Think good and good will happen. I was born and raised in San Francisco. Where I reside and write my poetry

JOHNSON, RECHE
[a.] Gainesville, FL [title] "Halfway" [pers.] This poem reminds me that life is full of compromise regardless of who you are and where you come from. In recognition of "the gray area" called compromise and to my loving family for educating me in this area of life, I humbly give you "Halfway." May everyone take comfort in the halfways life has to offer

JOHNSON, WANDA
[a.] New Orleans, LA [title] "My Knight" [pers.] Poetry is a very special gift to me. It allows me to express my feelings about people and things in a very unique and wonderful way. My poem "My Knight" is a perfect example of that. I wrote it to express the love and respect I have for my husband and the reasons why I love him. It is my sincere wish that my poem will inspire and motivate others to tell the people in their how much they care for them, because life is too short to take it for granted

JOHNSON, WILLIE
[a.] Birmingham, AL [title] "Through My Eyes" [pers.] I started writing at age 10. I consider writing to be an excellent way to explode my feelings and share my concerns with others

JONES, CATHERINE
[a.] Danvers, MA [title] "Imagine" [pers.] Writing is my favorite thing to do. I was first encouraged by my 3rd grade teacher, Mr. Pruslin. My mother says I have the heart of a writer and my dad's encouraging too. Poems just come to me like a clap of thunder. Receiving this letter was a gift. You see, all real poets only need, a pen and paper to make their dreams come true. Someday, if I get far in the writing field, I'll say . . . thank you so much poetry.com you gave me my start in writing

JONES, EDDIE
[a.] Atlantic Beach, FL [title] "Our Love Belongs to Us" [pers.] This poem was created as a gift for a very special lady: Ms. Gail C. Campbell, who continually encouraged me in my pursuit of this art form. Her love, inspiration and moral support were instrumental in me writing this poem. I also want to thank my family and sisters: Ms. Demetria Wells who also encouraged me to continue writing poetry. I hope this poem will be an inspiration to others who have been inspired by caring people in their lives. Because love is the most precious thing in God's creation

JONES, GORDON
[a.] Toronto, ON [title] "Gone Fishing" [pers.] I don't know where my poetry comes from it just comes from with inside and I just sit down and write. My only hope is that the other people that read my poems can put themselves in my place and enjoy and feel what I feel in my poems. I learned a trade at 18 years old I was a lather now they call it carpenter I loved every year of it. I have four children Sherry, Gordon, Cindy, Robin and they blessed me with 11 grandchildren. It's no wonder why I feel so good

JONES, LISA
[a.] Mechanicsville, VA [title] "Untitled" [pers.] Everyone has, at one time in their life, lost a friend or loved one. It's sometimes hard to find just the right words to say to the bereaved. When the life of my friend, Ben, was taken in a tragic house fire, I felt compelled to write a poem that would help ease the pain of such a great loss and bring comfort to Ben's family and friends. "Untitled" is dedicated in honor and loving memory of Benjamin R. Hancock and it celebrates the life he is living now, in Heaven (March 19, 1981–February 9, 2000).

JONES, MANDY
[a.] Southside, AL [title] "Why" [pers.] Poetry is a therapy for me. Some people do it for fun or for someone else I do it to get things off my chest. The poem you just read had to do with a guy I used to date, about the night we broke up and it was my first poem. All of the poems I write have to do with relationships mostly mine. I didn't start writing poetry till November last year (99). When I was 13 I have a notebook for English and I couldn't write one poem and now look at me

JOSHI, PANKAJ
[a.] Kathmandu, Nepal [title] "My Alternate Self" [pers.] I grew up in a very supportive family and with books all around me. During my childhood, I sought answers in those books, to the queries that surround the inquisitive mind of a child. And I was drawn into a bit of philosophy, which projected life in its metaphysical glory. To express and explore that seamless boundless existence called life. I couldn't have found a more reliable ally than a piece of poetry. In this poem, "My Alternative Self," I crave for an existence, which probably I would never be. It is the one which has answers to all the queries and remedies to all the sufferings in this world. It is a vicarious outlet to the empathic soul that resides within every human being and me

JUAREZ, AMANDA
[a.] Dallas, TX [title] "The Love of Your Life" [pers.] As a hobby, I have always loved reading and writing poems and stories. One of my lifelong dreams was to have one of my poems or stories published. So ever since I was a little girl, I have been writing poems for my school newspaper. I thank God for this special gift He gave to me, and without Him my dream would have never come true

JUMP, BRIANA
[a.] Eudora, KS [title] "My Love For You" [pers.] My name is Briana Jump and I'm from Eudora, KS. I'm 14 years old and the poem that I wrote is about a very special person. His name is A.J. McLean. He is a member from the band the "Backstreet Boys." In this poem I expressed the way I feel about him, even though I've never met him. That would be a dream come true for me, just like having one of my poems published in a book. I would like to thank him because he inspired me to write this poem. Even if he doesn't ever read this, I'm very thankful that I have this chance to share my poetry with so many people

KAESTNER, ELIZABETH
[a.] Bellmore, NY [title] "At One with the Earth at Death" [pers.] Live, live, live! Live a saturated life for all we know, this is it!

KAMARAH, SHEIKH
[a.] Richmond, VA [title] "Rhythms of Pain" [pers.] I am a Sierra Leonean, educated in Sierra Leone, England, and America. I am at present an assistant professor in the department of Languages and literature at Virginia State University, Petersburg, Virginia (U.S.A.) teaching Linguistics, writing and literature. This poem is my way of capturing and freezing on the page, the horrible images of the brutal killings in my country, Sierra Leone, as a result of the Rebel War. The war ripped the fabric a human dignity and decency off the face of my once peaceful country. Poetry is the net of words that effectively captures the intense emotions that I feel.

KANNO, HIRO
[a.] Villanova, PA [title] "H.E.R. Theme: Among the Stolen Moments" [pers.] This is one of the purest qualities of Hiphop in its Essence and Real. My inspiration was from a true MC, Commons three albums. Resurrection. One Day it'll all make sense, and like water for chocolate. When "her daddy would beat her, eyes all puffed (common), artists like Common, Blackstar, and Blackalicious brought back the soulful element of hiphop. This poem is dedicated to the underground Mrs. who doesn't receive recognition in the media but maintains their integrity nonetheless

KARIDIS, MARIA
[a.] Bogota, NJ [title] "Tree Climbing" [pers.] "Tree Climbing" delineates a turning point in my life, an inevitable turning point in everyone's life—outgrowing a dying childhood. When words of term papers, a job, universities, and a driver's license are so often heard and spoken, childhood is subconsciously mutated from life to memory. By the time realization of this mutation occurs, the person has grown, and the childhood waned. Per-

son and childhood are no longer compatible. Now, at the age of seventeen, I am experiencing the difficulties of being that person

KARIM, RAHMAN
[a.] Rocky Mount, NC [title] "Your Love Makes Me Weak" [pers.] I would like to first thank God then secondly give my love to the only women who has always and will always make me weak, I would also like to send out my love to big "D" the earthquake and the funk Dr. D.D.S. and Mel Blunt. My greatest appreciation goes out to my loving mother, Merry and the man who gave me this mind. . . . Omar to the reason why I live, the words yaz and rashed.

KASNER, JASON
[a.] Post Falls, ID [title] "Fools Existence"

KASTHURI, RAJ
[a.] Norwood, MA [title] "Valentine" [pers.] The speciality, this poem holds for me are due to the following: 1. It's my first poem 2. First one I ever wrote for someone special 3. Had written it six years pack on a bus, travelling and the dark day 13th feb. 4. Finally wanted to prove myself that I can be poetic too. Even today after so many years when I read it, I realize that is was a pure reflection of my feelings, genuinely and honestly expressed in words

KAVA, MIKE
[a.] Rapid City, SD [title] "Fear of the Forgotten" [pers.] I consider myself a decent writer who does it whenever I can. When my brother died on March 29th about 8:00 p.m., four hours before my birthday (March 30th), I was torn up. The last memory I have of him was an argument we had when I was home for spring break. The next thing I know he was killed in an accident. The pain of our parting, does and always will haunt me. I owed him and tried to pay him his do the best I could! To my brother I say: Forever Peace!

KELLY, SEAN
[a.] Stockertown, PA [title] "The Night Before Thanksgiving" [pers.] I wrote this poem in the fifth grade and got an A+ on the assignment. Now I am in the sixth grade and my favorite subject is English Literature because of my wonderful teacher Mrs. O'Callaghan and because I am reading some excellent books, and have started to write my first book. I am an eleven year old who really loves to write. The one thing that really inspired me the most for this poem was Clement C. Moore's "The Night Before Christmas," from which this poem is based

KENNEDY, BRIAN
[a.] Burlington, VT [title] "Observations of the Oil Man" [pers.] This poem was written about a summer I spent in Illinois. Two years later I was enrolled in a poetry workshop and I needed to have something written for the upcoming class and I jotted it down five minutes before the class started. This poem, for me, expressed succinctly the entire experience that I had had. I have never considered myself much of a poet, but writing is something I consider to be a very cathartic experience. This is why I think I will always do it, whether it is fiction or poetry

KENNEDY, LATISHA
[a.] Sumter, SC [title] "Trust Him" [pers.] "Trust Him" depicts a time when we may at one point in our life, feel as if we're alone or without hope. But, I'm a witness in that we're not alone and our hope can be found in Jesus. Just place your trust in him and he can see you through. My poems are a gift from God and are written to encourage all, while glorifying Jesus. I pray that this poem will bless and encourage all that read it

KENNEDY, NATALIE
[a.] Ponca City, OK [title] "February Sorrow" [pers.] I have been expressing myself through

poetry from the time I was about six years old. I have always been very artistically inclined in all the visual genres from drawing and painting to writing poems and stories. But, I, not being a very outwardly emotional person, poetry has always been my greatest release. It has always been a dream of mine to be published. I always felt sure that someday I would be, but I never knew it would happen so soon. I feel that this is one of my greatest accomplishments to be published by the age of fifteen

KENT, MARY
[a.] North Beach, MD [title] "The Servants Sing" [pers.] Communion service at my church has always been a beautiful part of worship for me. The altar especially adorned in white, enhanced by candlelight, heightens my anticipation of sharing. This particular Sunday as the pianist plays, a choir consisting of senior members processes down the aisle. The church becomes magnificently filled with His presence. This is a tribute to those people, who established a place for me to come to and for me to be nourished by His love

KERN, RUSSELL
[a.] Philadelphia, PA [title] "Of Me" [pers.] Audible Eerie is a traveling gypsy-bard. After an unpleasant performance for the king of Bix, Audible was cast out of the land. It seems as if he made a pass at the Queen. With any luck audible will find his way home, but who knows what adventures are in store for him on his journey back

KERR, ROBERT
[a.] Jonesville, SC [title] "Broken" [pers.] Well, I will say this. The poem is about, partly, my first love and how I messed it up. But that's life, you're only young once and being ignorant is part of that experience. If I saw her today I would probably breakdown and cry, and tell her for once, what she truly meant to me

KESSLER, BONNIE
[a.] Pawcatuck, CT [title] "Two Minutes—Prayer of a Firefighter" [pers.] This poem, "Two Minutes—Prayer of a Fire Fighter," is in dedication to a good friend. His efforts with local fire departments and his commitment to helping others was the inspiration for this poem. Poetry is my outlet to express my innermost feelings and it is truly a gift to be able to share my writings with you. JPM, this is for you and all the other fire fighters out there

KHADER, SHABEER
[a.] Newark, CA [title] "A Vision of Beauty" [pers.] I hold this poem very close to my heart. Everyone of us dreams of that special someone. This poem describes one such special person she is the kind of person every heart years for and a lucky few find. I would like to dedicate this poem to my loving family who have always loved and supported me. I thank God for this talent and hope to use it to bring joy into people's lives or at least put a smile on a few faces

KHAMBHAMPATI, SHIVAJI
[a.] Laurel, MD [title] "Aroma" [pers.] Being a doctor of Medicine, I love my profession and the life around me, perceiving both sorrow and joy as one. A loves of God and the powerful mother nature. The idealist in me likes to see good in anything. For me nature is unity. Without markings, one beautiful power the mother nature unveils year after year is the spring season. The sudden explosion of tender green leaves and the amazing colors of the blossoming flowers on any eventful morning—is a joy unfulfilling. This infinite amusement gave all the inspiration to pen this poem a tiny dedication to her mighty honour.

KHUANSATHAVORANIT, MALLIKA
[a.] Bangkok, Thailand [title] "Shattered Dream" [pers.] "Shattered Dream" isn't a poem about despair. It's about hope, love and having the

courage to dream again after you fall. I owe my own courage to two people, my pillars in every storm: Raser best friend, fellow writer . . . I couldn't have done this without you. Oh my you shatter the darkness, enabling me to believe in myself. With you, I can catch shooting stars. Writing illuminated a part of me usually hidden away. I want to thank poetry.com for making it all possible, for letting me shine and giving me this opportunity to touch the world with my writing

KHURANA, ANSHIKA K.
[a.] Bangalore, India [title] "Upon True Love" [pers.] This serious impassioned love poetry, speaks of human powers in love, and making the union of two human beings in love, apprehensible. I dedicate this poem to the one true love who has been my courage and strength, making a vast difference in my life. I shall always be grateful to my family, especially my mother for her encouragement, support and belief. Poetry to me is a medium of exploring uncharted areas of emotions, and the ability to view life differently

KIDD, CHERYL
[a.] Altoona, PA [title] "What the Bible Teaches" [pers.] The poem I wrote has been a gift from God. And without going through trials in the past months, I would have never been able to write. I thank God for giving me the knowledge and ability to write, secondly, without one very special friend, that has been an inspiration, has taught me to let God work, and believed in me. He read scriptures to me even when I didn't want to hear. He always stressed to read the bible. He never gave up on me. So I thank you Pastor Gary Dull and dedicate this poem to you

KIESINGER, SONYA
[a.] Kreamer, PA [title] "Brown" [pers.] I'm the writer of the poem "Brown." The reason I started to write poems is my teacher's encouraged me by making me write poems for home work assignments. I'm currently in eight grade. I go to Middleburg High School in Pennsylvania. I do have some poets who's work make me want to write poems and they are William Shakespeare, Edgar Allan Poe, and Phillis Wheally. I never thought I would have the chance to have one of my poems in a book. I want to thank my family for encouraging me

KINDLE, CHARLOTTE
[a.] Tacoma, WA [title] "The Last Poem" [pers.] I have been writing short stories and poems ever since I learned how to write. It just always came naturally. Most of my poems are well over twenty lines, so not all are submittable. As for their content it has always been very dark, dreary even. I can only write what I know and feel, or have experienced. The last poem I was very pleased with. I am very critical of my work, and rarely share it. This was the first time I have ever shown my work to anyone, besides close friends. Thank you, yours cruelly, Charlotte Kindle

KING, CHRISTOPHER
[a.] Albany, GA [title] "Message of Conviction" [pers.] I wrote "Message of Conviction" to remind myself of the enormous burden I carried in the past. Though the time between my conviction and acceptance of Jesus Christ as my Savior, Mentor and friend was relatively short, it was a hellish few weeks and even then I wasn't rid of the burden until a good while later. This poem is a reflection of my mind set during that trying time and continues to be a reminder even today. Those of you that know this feeling of conviction, I do hope this poem will help you throughout your own journey

KING, JASON
[a.] San Diego, CA [title] "I Don't Miss You" [pers.] After a tough break up, one's emotions can surge, filling the mind with pain and loneliness. Anyone who has had a learning experience like mine can definitely connect with my swirl of

emotions. Being only 18 myself, I can only dream of that which lies ahead. I just hope that I can remain happy in my current relationship with my very wonderful girlfriend, Teresa. Jen, if you are reading this, thank you for the inspiration. Well, to sum this up, falling in love is the best or worst thing that can happen to you. I highly recommend it

KING, JENNIFER
[a.] Holley, NY [title] "The Pointless Existence Of Life" [pers.] I'm a 14 years old girl from Hamlin, NY and a freshman at Kendall High School. One of my interests is maybe someday becoming a veterinarian. I am starting to become fluent in Spanish. In my spare time I like to draw and paint ceramics along with writing poetry. This poem is describing the way how in school everything is a popularity contest. If you're not popular, the popular people dislike you and treat you like an "untouchable" and this makes you feel like you have no friends. Many thanks to my family for supporting me in everything I do

KINGSBURY, VICTORIA
[a.] Ashaway, RI [title] "Me" [pers.] I, Victoria Ann Kingsbury was born Aug. 21, 1989 in Westerly, R.I. I am in the 5th grade and wrote this poem in the morning program at Ashaway School. My favorite pastime is drawing Chinese dragons, but I also read a lot. My favorite author is Bruce Coville. In 1999, I won the school spelling bee

KINNEY, MICHAEL
[a.] Mobile, AL [title] "Songs of Silence" [pers.] Poetry is more than just an expression of a thought, or a story or a belief . . . it is more a medium that transcends the spoken word, that breaks down the barriers of social interaction and confrontation, and gets to the heart of what is real and pure

KINSEY, ROBERT
[a.] Morriston, FL [title] "Wishes?" [pers.] Writing is my release when life's troubles seem to overwhelm me. Being a construction worker I seldom get the chance to share my poems with anyone other than close friends and family "There is no greater gift than to touch the heart of another or bring a smile to their face."

KIRKWOOD, PETE
[a.] Helper, UT [title] "Angel" [pers.] "Angel" This poem is a poem of hopeful love. For one day I hope to meet a women I can love and cherish for all times. As described in this poem of mine

KITTEL, CLAUDIA
[a.] Yucaipa, CA [title] "Whose Will?" [pers.] I love praising the Lord, and my purpose in life is telling people about Jesus and His love for us. I wrote this poem to help a young woman whose boyfriend had just passed away, so she would stop blaming God

KLAKAMP, CHRISTOPHER
[a.] S. Amherst, OH [pers.] I originally wrote this poem for a pro-life contest in high school. I enjoy converting my personal experiences and views into poetry in an effort to share my emotions with others in a simple but powerful way. I would like to credit my parents, Kay and Chris, for giving me the opportunities to have the experiences that I have had in my life. Events throughout my life are generally where my thoughts, ideas, and emotions come from. I never would have thoughts one of my poems would be published. Having my work in this book is like a dream come true. Thanks!

KLINE, ROSE
[a.] Monroe, LA [title] "On Meeting" [pers.] This poem was written for my husband of 18 years. He was inspired and encouraged me to nurture my spirit. As a social worker, much of my energy is directed toward helping others. Writing is the primary way I keep my life in balance. I hope that my poem reflects way I keep my life in balance. I

hope that my poem reflects my belief that relationships are the most important thing in life

KNIGHT, ROBIN
[a.] Newton, Australia [title] "First Hyacinth" [pers.] Robin Knight lives in Geelong, Australia, and trained as a teacher and librarian, working at primary, secondary and tertiary levels for 30 years until retraining as a pharmacy technician on 1993. She has always written poetry, and advocated poetry, and conducted a successful Poetry-Writing course of the Education Department of Victoria's Talented Children's Program in 1981. She currently operates a rural-centre Pharmacy/Giftshop at Bannockburn, Victoria, with her pharmacist husband, between trips overseas to catch up with internet friends and gather data for an online travel diary.

KNOX, JEAN
[a.] Temple, TX [title] "A Spirit's Wish" [pers.] This poem is very special to me, because it is the first thing that I wrote since I had a head injury. From special equipment and encouragement I would like to relate my love and thanks to Kyla C. Sherrard and her family

KOBUS, DAVID
[a.] Jackson Heights, NY [title] "Maybe "Then" [pers.] "This poem is a direct result of my taking a good look in the mirror. I realized that all of us have something special to offer the world, if only we believed in ourselves. I would thank my family for all their love and support. I also want to thank Courtney for proving this point for me

KOHLER, JEREMY M.
[a.] Bronx, NY [title] "Think Positive" [pers.] This is a verse and chorus from my first complete song. As a teen, I performed this rap in front of 2000 students at an anti-drug rally in NJ. I love this song! It helps people "Think Positive." I am twenty years old. Since my early teens, I have been using songs, rhyming, and rap to express my feelings about the world and my problems. Usually, I compose out loud while I am performing freestyling. If I like it, I write it down. I think rap is the poetry that today's youth relates to

KOLOMBATOVICH, KATHERINE
[a.] Franklin Park, NJ [title] "Mist of the Meadows" [pers.] I feel fortunate to have the ability to write this work of art. My inspiration comes from my friends and family. I dedicate this poem to my mother and father for without them my writing would not be possible. Also to my younger sister who I hope will be able to fulfill her dreams someday

KOPILCHACK, JUNE
[a.] Royersford, PA [title] "What Harm Shall Come of Me" [pers.] Growing up in a small town in Pennsylvania, near Valley Forge. I started to read poetry when I was in high school. I started to write poetry about that time also. I enjoy reading and writing poetry, it has special meaning in my life. I have two children, a daughter, Allison who has two girls, Alexandra and Emily. My son, Bradley, has a daughter also, her name is Felicia. I read poetry to my granddaughters and who knows someday they may write also

KOSSISKI, ELLYN
[a.] Organ, NM [title] "Texas Roads" [pers.] Texas Roads was inspired by my days driving a big truck. Driving through the night, there were many times when I ran with the "parade" looking out for "full-grown bears." Yet, it seemed the two worlds, so often at odds, come together when there was an accident. Off the road now Texas Roads was inspired by my days driving a big truck. Driving through the night, there were many times when I ran with the parade looking out for "full grown bears." Yet, it seemed the two worlds, so often at odds, came together when there was an accident. Off the road now and living in New Mexico, I

wanted to express my gratitude for the thousands of drivers who make our world work as well as it does. At 53 years old, the siren song of the jakes still beckons but, until I drive again, my heart remembers through poetry

KOSTICK, TARA
[a.] Saginaw, MI [title] "Without Love" [pers.] With poetry, I am able to explore my inner feelings, and in doing this, I can understand myself a little more. Poetry is my deepest passion, and I've written down such deep thoughts that surprise others who read my poetry, when I reveal my sensitivity. I am a very shy and quiet individual, and by writing poetry, I'm able to express myself better with pen and paper than by conversation. Whenever I need to escape or I'm just feeling angry with myself, I reach for my pen and paper and immediately release my emotions, trying to overcome my fears and my pain

KRALL, MARK J.
[a.] Washington, PA [title] "Searches" [pers.] Healthy mindedness should be a continued guest as this is paramount for optimum human performance. For me, creating a poem has therapeutic effect in that it may provide a sense of closure to a topic. Particularly unresolved ones. But writing poetry is always a good means of expressing emotional disposition no matter what my attitude is regarding a subject. Putting a related set of thoughts down on paper to reflect upon also serves that basic human need to communicate, without the task of perhaps laboring through a difficult conversation and getting side tracked from what you'd otherwise want to get across

KRAVCHAK, DEBORAH
[a.] Virginia Beach, VA [title] "Taking Out The Trash" [pers.] Taking Out The Trash" is one of my very first poems. Written at a crucial point in my life, these are not simply words laid to paper, but an actual account of me letting go of all the negative influences in my life. After completing this poem, I have been able to move on and begin writing more and more poetry, concentrating on all the beauty we are all truly blessed with

KREMER, BARBARA
[a.] Anchor Point, AK [title] "Time" [pers.] I was raised in Alaska. I am married to my childhood sweetheart, who inspired this poem. I have two wonderful boys A. J. and Peter, who keep me young at heart. I would like to dedicate this poem in loving memory of my sister; Heather Harris and to my husband with whom time stands still. I'll always love you"

KRUEGER, JAYMIE
[a.] Schaumburg, IL [title] "Flames" [pers.] I have been writing since the age of nine. I am now 14. To me poetry is just the song of life. When I write, I tend to use words that help reader to visualize and really feel the poem. This poem is about the anger and hurt, I once felt when someone said unkind, painful words to me

KRYS, JAIME
[a.] Kitchener, ON [title] "Angel Bells" [pers.] I am often described as an emotional person by the people closest to me. Though, to be honest, I would not want to be any other way to experience emotions means to be alive. My advice to anyone is to pursue your dreams and support others in the pursuit of theirs I thank my family and friends, new and old, for their continued love and support. May all your dreams come true and always reach for the start much love always

KUCA, ELIZABETH
[a.] Jersey City, NJ [title] "A Friend" [pers.] "A Friend" was written with the thought of the best qualities my close friends have shown to me. This poem is my favorite one that I've written and is very dear to me. May it commemorate friendship for a lifetime

KUEBLER, KATHRINE
[a.] Ossineke, MI [title] "Anonymous" [pers.] In my 18 years of life my imagination and sensitivity have been my greatest assets. I believe they show in this poem that even if I haven't experienced something myself being sensitive to those who do experience it every day is important. One of my strongest beliefs is that to truly be kind one needs only to have compassion. I thank all those who have taught me life's many lessons but especially the man who inspired me to express these lessons in poetry and appreciate their beauty. My poetry teacher, Mr. Koch. God bless

KULOTHUNGAN, SHEBA
[a.] Waxahachie, TX [title] "Water Lanterns" [pers.] Poetry and poetry writing touch the deepest recesses of my life—my faith in God, my family, my purpose in life, and the ideas that make or break my world, my land, my people. So my poems are my reflection, my lanterns of the night and my lilies of the day. This poem, "Water Lanterns" is meant to enlighten our dark world that does not see "like the blind boy" This crippled world's true image captured in his own reflection, the meaning of life revealed in the lilies, and the hope of life afforded by the waters. The poem is a plea to "see" and hold up our lanterns

KURTZ, ANDREA
[a.] Orland, IN [title] "Graveyard Beauty" [pers.] I feel poetry means a great deal to me. It's a way I can express my feelings, and got it out. My poem, "Graveyard Beauty" is about a friend of mine that died. And now, instead of seeing her in better places, I visit her in the graveyard. I described the graveyard I visit her in every week, and the thoughts I think while I'm there

LABAY, DAVID
[a.] Boerne, TX [title] "Theory of Everything" [pers.] As a music theorist, I analyze the patterns of human emotion translated into musical notation. Like my favorite song on the radio, I have always wondered why I love to hear certain patterns over and over again. When I learned that the entire universe is musical in nature, I wanted to know what pattern was God's favorite. Then I would know God's music theory. If our music can be used to heal the human body, maybe God's music will cure the diseases of mankind. But we will have to work together and listen to each other to sing it

LAFFERTY, BLAIR
[a.] Reliance, SD [title] "Memorial to Columbine High" [pers.] Poetry is truly a special way to express yourself. I wrote this poem after learning about the tragedy, through a school report. School safety is a very big issue that I believe has its place in many people's lives. The columbine shooting, in a sense, was the one event that finally brought attention to this particular subject. Though I knew no one from Columbine personally, the stark agony and deep emotional pain truly affected me. It gave me a new perspective of life; live life to the fullest, you never know when it will end

LAFOLLETTE, LYDIA
[a.] Yellow Springs, WV [title] "The Hole I'm In" [pers.] At one point and time in my life I was in that hole. I want to let other women out there in the same position know that there is a way out of it. It's not easy but you can do it. I did! Everyone has the right to be there own person, make their own choices and have a life. Believe in yourself. You can get out of the whole!

LAMB, DEBBI
[a.] Pavo, GA [title] "Men, So Many, Too Many Men" [pers.] This poem is dedicated to the man who breathed new life into my existence. At a low point in my life, I started college and met my Renaissance man. As my English professor, he encouraged me to express myself in poetry and

short stories. As a kindred spirit, he inspired me to celebrate my individuality. When he resigned his teaching position, I thought I might lose my newly discovered freedom of expression. Instead, I realized that the spirit behind his lessons would forever linger in my soul and occasionally manifest itself in the form of poetry

LAMBERT, SANDRA
[a.] Sheridan, OR [title] "When Dreams Sleep" [pers.] Poetry is a special part of my life. It is my way of expressing the joy that I find in the world around me and provides the perfect channel to show the love and affection I feel for those closest to me

LAMON, COLLEEN
[a.] Yuba City, CA [title] "The Sleep Fairy" [pers.] "The Sleep Fairy" is dedicated to sleepless children everywhere. This poem was adapted from a bed time story which I created to help my two children, Tyler and Connar, fall asleep. To this day they believe the Sleep Fairy visits them and leaves them small treats by night, and sleeps in our garden by day. There's no such thing as too many friendly fairies!

LANDERS, BUCK
[a.] Calvert City, KY [title] "Past It On" [pers.] I hope my poem might encourage a couple of people to listen to what an elderly person might try to share with them. Then try to encourage a child or teen to learn about their family, and their heritage, to learn, and teach a skill that could be handed down from one generation to the next

LANE, MICHAEL
[a.] Richardson, TX [title] "So You're in Love" [pers.] I actually wrote this poem while dating in school. It seemed like everyone would just throw around "I Love Him/Her" so quickly, it always made me wonder why. Why do you think you are in love? I'm also a musician and hope to write this poem into song one day

LANE, MONICA
[a.] Lorman, MS [title] "Music Can Open Windows of the Mind" [pers.] I have always been a lover of poetry and music. I feel that both of them play an important part in my life. Music calms me and poetry expands my imagination. I am a native of Lorman, Mississippi. I have obtained a Bachelors of Science Degree in Psychology from Alcorn State University. Presently, I am continuing my studies in Guidance Education. I hope to use poetry as therapy. I have ambitions to become successful as a poetry writer. My hobbies are; reading, writing poetry, playing piano and listening to music

LANGLOIS, ALAN
[a.] Keene, NH [title] "Journey to Freedom" [pers.] This poem is an abridged version of a poem I wrote at the end of an eleven week Clinical Pastoral Education experience. This CPE experience focused on the individuals as a minister, drawing on both the strengths and weaknesses in the clinical setting. I discovered my yearning for personal freedom as I gazed intently on my shadow side. Freedom arises from recognition and acceptance of personal weakness

LANNING, LINDA
[a.] Tahlequah, OK [title] "The Book of Life" [pers.] I wrote this poem for and is in memory of "Burl White," a wonderful poet. God bless all you poetry lovers. The ability to express your artistic visions of people, life and love, is a power which lifts us all to a higher appreciation of the art of poetry. My next poem will be in memory of my beloved grandmother. I would like to thank my family (Gary, Stephen and Daniel) and my friend (Bud) for all the support

LAPOINTE, CHRISTOPHER
[a.] Yorktown, VA [title] "Le Sourire" [pers.] I am an aspiring poet, and am thrilled at the opportunity to share what I love doing with others.

This is the first time anything I have written will show up in a National Publication, and I am overjoyed at what has happened. The poem that is in this book is about a girl that is very special to me. I still dream of kissing her smile and drowning in her eyes. Thank you

LARKIN, MELANIE
[a.] Oklahoma City, OK [title] "Farewell" [pers.] This poem was written to someone, whom I loved a great deal. Dayton Edward Meiner. He was one of my closest friends. He took his own life November 8, 1999. I never got the chance to tell him how much he meant to me, or how much I loved him. But now in my heart, I know he knows. And I would like to thank his stepmother, Carolyn Meiner, for helping me to see that. I love to write and I would like to thank all who have encouraged me and who believe in me

LARRABEE, ANGEL
[a.] La Center, WA [title] "My Father's Spirit" [pers.] My poem "My Father's Spirit" is my account of what happened and my feelings about my father leaving me so early in my young life. I came into this gift of writing poems in my mid thirties. There have been times in my life that have been difficult and some of my poem help me reflect on how I was able to get through them, and how I viewed these troubled times. This poem is my way of letting everyone know that those near and dear to you are always going to be near and dear to your heart, even in spirit

LARSON, SARINA
[a.] Howell, MI [title] "Until You" [pers.] Writing poetry is my way of releasing the emotions hidden inside me. This poem was written for my first love, Curtis, who I have learned so much from. He is my hope and my strength, and will always be in my heart

LASKY, HELAINE
[a.] Oshkosh, WI [title] "Insight" [pers.] The insight I received while writing this poem came through me from a higher energy. We are all I and therefore whatever I perceive from other is a mirror of me. This poem was a gift sent to me that I am grateful to share with others

LASLEY, CARLYNN
[a.] Canton, MI [title] "Wish Upon a Star" [pers.] I began writing poems the first time I fell in love. I was surprised how easy the words came to me. Now because of that experience plus more, I've been able to express my thoughts, and feelings through poetry. They're not all about me, but the whole world. I've written poems about different things such as abuse, rape, abortions, drinking and driving, death, suicide, murder, depression, love, heartbreak, friendship, family, and the greatest feeling in the world-happiness. I'd love to share these with the whole world because I think so many people can relate

LAUVER, NED
[a.] North Ridgeville, OH [title] "The Boxer, With Apologies to Paul Simon" [pers.] This poem is based heavily on the song: "The Boxer" by Paul Simon. We suffer the cuts and bruises on a daily basis, that something sits within us all that makes us stand and continue the fight. Special thanks to Shannon because this boxer needs you

LAWSON, SHERI
[a.] Rio Linda, CA [title] "Opportunity" [pers.] This poem expresses what I used to always feel like inside. I used to sit and think about every opportunity that came my way, but by the time I would come to a decision, that opportunity would be gone. Now, whenever I start to ponder on an opportunity, I think of this poem and jump ahead and take that opportunity. My hopes are that this poem will help others enjoy their life the way I have enjoyed mine

LAYTON, HELEN
[a.] Palm Harbor, FL [title] "Alone" [pers.] This poem is dedicated to my husband Jessie E. Layton. He is without a doubt my true soulmate, whom I love with all my heart and soul

LE, THOM
[a.] Fontana, CA [title] "Poetic Lyrics" [pers.] Poetry shall forever be in motion. As the world forms, societies change and witness clash. I have grown up in a society where love coexists with sadness both elements have made my life, completing fully as the yin and yang. Expressing my feelings of life through the gift of a poem fulfills my needs like eating and sleeping. I appreciate the inspirations life has given me, therefore I thank each and every one

LEAKE, RANDY
[a.] Hobbs, NM [title] "Life" [pers.] As a recovering alcoholic of twenty-two years sober, and an Egomaniac the words of this poem share a new perspective of life. This is a coming out experience; from darkness unto light. A surrender of as much self-will as possible, "One day at a time." The recognition that strength and wisdom come through surrender

LEBLANC, CHANTAL
[a.] Gatineau, QC [title] "What If" [pers.] What If . . . is dedicated to all of who have the same insecurities as I. And thanks to Mom, dad and my boyfriend Dany for being patient with me as I search for the answers

LECLAIRE, JOLENE
[a.] Luxemburg, WI [title] "Gods Creation" [pers.] To my late husband Eugene, who gave me so much encouragement in life, I would like to dedicate this poem in his memory. Most importantly, I thank God who gave me the talent to accomplish this

LEE, JENNIFER
[a.] Richmond, BC [title] "Avatar of the Sun God" [pers.] Normally, I have great difficulties when writing poetry. It takes a substantial amount of inspiration and motivation for me to feel comfortable expressing how I feel in a poem. I am very ecstatic and flattered to have found both my inspiration and my motivation in my fiancee. This poem is dedicated to him, and to the incredible ways he has shared, and still shares, himself with me. Every day, he honors me with his undying devotion, loyalty and love. This is my way of thanking him, and trying through this poem, to show him just how much I love him

LEE, PATRICIA
[a.] Odessa, FL [title] "Always with Me" [pers.] Every life experience entails a story. I feel that poetry enables us to share our stories and express unfeigned feelings regarding these experiences. Once, as a child, I gave my other a ceramic plate which bore a beautiful poem. The memory of her tearfully reading it aloud has been my source of poetic inspiration. My poem reflects a part of my story. It is about moving 1,200 miles away from my Aunt Pat Naples, a woman I love and miss spending time with. Although I am unable to physically see her, she is "Always With Me" in my heart

LEE, TESSA
[a.] Ewing, NJ [title] "Wake Up Children, Your Moon Mother Weeps" [pers.] I watched her and thought about how nice it was knowing that the moon has always been there and will always be there. I felt secure knowing her cycles and comforting knowing that her wisdom and reliability will always be there to guide me through the chaos in my life. The moon is everyone's grandmother. She watches over all of us and guides us if we let her. I fear the world is forgetting the wonderful gifts that this universe offers

LEFTWICH, HILLARY
[a.] Colorado Springs, CO [title] "My Only" [pers.] This poem describes the anguish a person can

experience after losing someone they love. The transition period after a passing and before acceptance is often one of a dream like quality, one where existence is only experienced in obscure fragments. Dreams can suddenly twist into a reminiscent reality. This poem is dedicated to a friend who took his own life, but sometimes continues to live on in my dreams

LEGERE, JAMES
[a.] Torrance, CA [title] "Dear Mama" [pers.] Raised in a relatively poor family. I spent many years accumulating materially what was missing in my youth. Getting and staying out of my own way was necessary to realize that creativity for me comes from learning to make what you need out of what little you have. We are products of our experiences good and bad. Nothing is by accident. It's what we do with these experiences that sets us free

LEGG, PAMELA
[a.] Cross Lanes, WV [title] "The Storm" [pers.] Poetry has become my release. It is the only way I can effectively explain what I am feeling inside. I would like to say that I owe everything to my darling like boy, Christian Ray

LEMON, MICHAEL
[a.] Alexandria, VA [title] "Beauty By Name" [pers.] The story behind my poem, "Beauty By Name." There have been moments in my life when unexpectedly, I found myself overwhelmed by beauty. On this particular day, I was at a loss for words and unable to express my feelings to the woman that inspired them. I was afraid that I would be unable to convey the sincerity of those feelings or that they would be misinterpreted for more than what they were. So, I chose instead to use them for inspiration for my writing. I'm also pleased to say that the woman who originally inspired this poem, would later become a good friend

LENARD, L.
[a.] Havertown, PA [title] "Paragon"

LEPE, JOSEPH
[a.] Long Beach, CA [title] "Spiritual Death" [pers.] I am from Long Beach, California. Originally this poem was part of a larger one that was not titled. I had written "Spiritual Death" over two years ago, when I was twenty one. Publication of my poem has encouraged me to write a short story. I am proud the share my story with the rest of the world, for which my goal for writing "Spiritual Death" was met. Keep journals and write whatever is on your mind. The best sessions I have found are at two a.m. Even engineers can become poets also

LETOURNEAU, PETER
[a.] Auburn, ME [title] "Ode to Y2K" [pers.] Encouraged by family and friends, I have long authored poems on a no-fee basis for important personal and business events in the lives of others. "Ode to Y2K" was done on a whim, but may signal an unexpected turning point in moving from amateur status to poet for hire.

LEUCUTA, TRACIE
[a.] La Crosse, WI [title] "Elektracoustic" [pers.] I have long been an admirer of the music of Andreas Vollenweider. His brilliant melodies have moved me and given me peace in times of need. This poem is written from the point of view of his instrument of choice the electracoustic harp. It is my thanks to him and the other amazing musicians he has worked with for the many hours of joy their music has given to me. Your presence on this Earth is truly a blessing!

LEVEEN, AIMEE
[a.] Charleston, SC [title] "Valentine" [pers.] I feel that being able to write your feelings in verse is the best way to express your feelings. When I have an idea, I feel I must copy it down on paper to type later. Before I did this, I lost many great ideas. And

I am advising people who would like to become poets to write down their ideas before they lose them. I have always taken great pride in my work, and I am happy to see my work take place in your book. Poetry has always been something that comes easily to me

LEVY, DEEDRA
[a.] Mississauga, ON [title] "Death of a Salesman" [pers.] Poetry has played an essential part in my emotional and psychological well being for most of my life. I have been able to channel my anger and use it to create something beautiful. My poem, "Death of a Salesman" was written during a particularly painful part of my life when I was, once again, disappointed by the one man I should trust: my father. As I read and reread this poem, it becomes clearer that I am better off without him . . . a type of "literary healing" I suppose

LI, JILL
[a.] Amsterdam, Netherlands [title] "God of Silence" [pers.] Poetry has always given me much pleasure and has been a great comfort to me throughout my life. In writing poetry, I want to communicate an idea or feeling to the reader, and, most importantly, to touch one's heart and mind as poetry touched mine

LIEBOW, JOANNE
[a.] Beachwood, OH [title] "Light" [pers.] Poetry provides direct access to my feelings and brings me the words I need to turn my feelings into thoughts for you to examine, take to your heart, or just say, "I don't feel that way." Poetry is my venue (or avenue if you wish) to track and trace the feelings in my heart into my head and convert them into words. Poetry is the key to my imagination, hope and everything I think and feel that moves us all into tomorrow we can share. Poetry is my light

LIGHTBURN, ARIFAH
[a.] Tampa, FL [title] "Anger" [pers.] If I had to choose between poetry and oxygen, I would die always, as my life could not be lived without one or the other. Like oxygen, poetry, I believe, is one of the greatest of gifts. Like truth, it seeks no reward; it asks for no praise. Poetry just is. It is a medium through which life's most problematic questions are answered. In man-made words, poetry captures abstracts, and guides me through this journey of life when the inexplicable threatens. I hope that through my mystical enlightenment I have shed a little light in someone else's corner of the world

LINDENBAUM, MICHAEL
[a.] Victorville, CA [title] "Will You Be There in the End" [pers.] This poem holds a special place in my hearts as does all my work, but I am hesitant to show my talent often. It express the strong need to have someone special in our life and the memory that two people share when they are truly in love. Remember that there is nothing more real then the emotion of love and nothing can compare to the joys and laughter it brings. In this world true love can be hard to find. But I believe everyone will have there chance and only the sincerest loves will be there in the end

LIPSCOMB, HEATHER
[a.] Travelers Rest, SC [title] "Lab" [pers.] I am a 13 year old girl from SC. This poem was inspired my by dog Lab, a labrador. He died at the age of 13, in 1999

LISS, ANDREA
[a.] Bensalem, PA [title] "Inner Reflections" [pers.] Reading and writing poetry has always been a pleasant diversion to me. Poetry is a powerful means of expressing emotions on an endless journey into the world of imagination and creativity. My grandmother's memories impacted my writing techniques, whereas my children continue to be the source of inspiration. I am fortunate to have my poem

forever immortalized for others to see and enjoy. I can only hope that others will the same enthusiasm and be a part of the wonderful world of poetry

LISZANCKIE, RICHARD
[a.] Eatontown, NJ [title] "How Blest I Am" [pers.] Poetry is an opening of the mind and spirit. It allows, as no other literary form does, ones expression to be limitless. It speaks from the heart, it is guided by mind, and explores the depths of being. Any subject can be treated with verse, poets possess an internal eye that sees situations from many perspectives. This work looks at a life that unknowingly shaped part of my existence without cognizance of that fact. It is written from how my spirit viewed it, never fully understanding the influence, but ultimately being fitting from it. I have trade marked intellectual properties, for promotion and pedagogical purposes, but poetry provides the stimulus for thought unlike any other format in literature. Additionally, I have had previous teaching experience as an assistant professor of marketing at a private university. Other experience includes an assignment as an executive at a major network. Each help provide ideas for potential publications

LIVINGSTON, BARRY
[a.] Concord, NH [title] "The Day Gone By" [pers.] This is a special poem dedicated to my 10th grade English Teacher, Claire Gassett. We covered a section on poetry during a time of my life when I attempted suicide. Her voice and the poetry she read were all I could hear when my world was black and silent. Thank you Ms. Gassett

LLOYD, KASEY
[a.] Lake Luzerne, NY [title] "Emotions" [pers.] This is the story of my first love; and the after effects of the break up. It is what everyone goes through at one time or another. If this helps just one person it is good enough for me

LOFTIS, LORI
[a.] Orlando, FL [title] "Lonely Lover" [pers.] I feel that poetry is an expression of what is going on in your inner self at the time it is written. "Lonely Lover" expresses the loss of past love and the desire to find that one special "prince" that will be there for me today and always. I dedicate this poem to my two very, very special princes, my sons Kori and Ryan without the past loves I would never have been so greatly blessed by having such wonderful young men like them in my life that lift my spirits and support me in whatever I do. I live in Orlando, Florida and work as a paralegal. I enjoy escaping to the ocean when things seem tough as the ocean is serenity to me just to sit, watch and listen to the waves roll in and out

LOGAN, CHRISTOPHER
[a.] Chatsworth, GA [title] "Ultraviolet Screams" [pers.] Dreams are our spirits way of talking to us when we are asleep, Poetry is the way it talks to us when we are awake. Poetry is when our spirit takes emotions, thoughts, and passions out of the toychest of our souls and plays with them. I believe God has given me a small flickering flame for words, my goal is to return that flame to Him burning greater and brighter than when He first gave it

LOMBINO, MARY ELLEN
[a.] Doylestown, PA [title] "Dreams" [pers.] Dreams come to us all but the ones that have significant meaning are the dreams we wake up with. Thank you mom for making this happen. Without you none of this would have been possible. Phil, see a penny pick it up! Dad I am proud to have you as my father for all that you have accomplished

LOPEZ, AQUILAH
[a.] Evans, GA [title] "Rebirth" [pers.] This poem was written as I began to withdraw from a State of depression. It was with the help of family and

friends that I made it through, as well as by writing poetry. I have been writing poetry since I was at least 13 years old, and find it to be a great release. Most of the poems I write have to deal with a situation I am faced without that time, and I truly believe writing poetry helps to soothe my soul. I also enjoy making web pages, which I hope to one day make a career of

LOTT, TINA
[a.] Orlando, FL [title] "Someone I Know" [pers.] All my poems so far, have been inspired by an incredible man that has touched my life and my heart and taught me so many things. A man that accepted me the way I am and showed me how it feels to really be loved. This particular poem was just me feeling sorry for myself after the breakup. Even though we broke up due to circumstances beyond our control, he was not someone that used me. He is too wonderful for that. Rex, thank you so much for all that you have given me. I'll always love you

LOUNSBURY, COURTNEY
[a.] Espanola, NM [title] "Frozen Dream" [pers.] I've been writing poetry for as long as I can remember. Whenever I have felt as though I could not verbally express myself, I would write it. Though not said until now, this poem was written for my father; the only person who has stood by me and believed in me through thick and thin, no matter where we've lived and what we've been through. No matter what anymore says, he will always be my hero. Thank you *Mon Pere*!

LOVE, GENEVIEVE
[a.] Port Jervis, NY [title] "Hero" [pers.] I wrote this poem for my mother, for Mother's Day. I wanted her to know how much I love and respect her, and how her courage, strength, and love inspires me. I hope I can be as good a mother as she is when I grow up. I love you mom

LOWER, ELIZABETH
[a.] Mexico, MO [title] "Too Early" [pers.] Poetry is a love in my life; it has always been a dream of mine to have a poem published. I dedicate this poem to these beloved people: my husband Brad; our son Jordan; my brothers Jim and Bob Mercer and Bob's family; my parents; and friends Cheryl Bell, Lance Fetterhoff, David Goodman, Mary Ann Fite, Debbe Jones, Debbie Klumpp and Teresa Stone. Most of all I want to thank God, who has blessed my life with special people and a special gift

LOWIN, ELISA
[a.] Omaha, NE [title] "A Magician's Act" [pers.] I love to write poetry. It serves as an outlet for my emotions, allowing me to keep inner peace. I wrote this poem softly after I achieved closure from a damaging relationship. My poems allow me to look objectively at my life and move on

LU, ANDY
[a.] Vancouver, BC [title] "Bird. Cage. Sweety." [pers.] This poem is for someone who I really loved! John was the only person I only like, but I am just a bird that he would never capture. However, I still want, thank him for letting me be a small part of his life

LUCAS, ANDRES
[a.] Queensland, Australia [title] "Writing Without U" [pers.] Inspired by the book "Cuentos Para Pensar" by Jorge Bucay, this poem is to all the girls I've loved, to the girls who've loved me, to the ones I've treated wrongly and rightly, and to all the girls who said "No!" I'm just another confused mortal who thought life and love were meant to be easy, and just made everything harder trying to make it "right." I now believe in karma (and rightly so I should!), and I apologize to everyone I've hurt, either physically, mentally or emotionally. I love you all!

LUCIANI, ALICIA
[a.] West Babylon, NY [title] "Facets" [pers.] Played by eighty-eight keys, attached to a cordless phone, with sounds of today's CDs, and sung unto me; are all but a given to this thirteen year old Love is the swing that propels the soft sphere that allows me to dance the bases. Allowed am I only after the completion of my studies. Enhanced by the computerized world and today's net. Now most pleased with oneself all is needed but to shop, shop, shop and dress

LUGA, MELISSA
[a.] Hilo, HI [title] "Death of a Star" [pers.] I am nine years old and a third grade student at the Kamehameha Schools, East Hawaii campus. My class was studying the phases of the moon. My teacher, Mrs. Loo, suggested we keep a moon journal for one month to help us record the phases of the moon and to describe the evening sky, stars and sounds. While painting in art class, I made the connection of how the drops of paint were similar to what I saw. This poem shares my memory of the night my mother and I witnessed a super nova, or the death of a star

LUJAN, MAYA
[a.] Anaheim, CA [title] "Voice in the Wind" [pers.] This poem is an expression of life's experiences, whether good or bad. It's amazing one word can have so many meanings. I think "Poetry Reduces Stress." Whenever I have a thought I write it down and add to it later. My husband art and daughter Dominique have also encouraged, and we are all very grateful to the committee for choosing my poem for their book

LUMIA, SANTO
[a.] Palm Beach, FL [title] "A Wife By Any Other Name" [pers.] The oldest of seven children, born in New York City. Inducted into the Army in 1966 at the age of twenty. Served Vietnam in 1968–1969. Retired in 1997 (Colonel). Education—B.S. in Accounting; M.B.A. I never gave poetry a second thought until a couple of months ago when a friend (a poet) inspired me. I went home that evening thinking about her work and wrote my first poem. This is my second poem. In these few verses, I attempt to capture how my wife of twenty seven years has supported me and helped to keep me focused

LUNDBERG, ASHLEIGH
[a.] Mill Creek, MA [title] "Reminiscing Through a Teens Mind in Relationships" [pers.] I think that it's strange when it takes some tragedy to have some creativity at times. My poem was actually written when I was quite upset, being in a bad mood sent it into a contest. Weeks went by and I received a letter telling me my poem was to be published. My family and I then laughed, since on my own I never would've considered submitting my poem. I feel inspiration is always there in different ways, you just need to learn to channel it correctly

LUNDBERG, ERIC
[a.] LaHabra, CA [title] "Eyes" [pers.] Nothing is more wonderful or exciting than inspiration when it hits, and nothing is more rewarding than setting that idea free before it dies inside your little mind. I love poetry for the truth it can convey and how simply and eloquently yet so completely it can encapsulate that truth

LUNDGREN, THOMAS
[a.] Torrance, CA [title] "Something Unique" [pers.] The World of Literature spins on perpetual motion, as inspiration fuels creativity, then responds by creating more inspiration. Life and Death, perpetual and unique, in their own right, have inspired writers since the beginning. Likewise, the death of my father, inspired me to create "Something Unique." Although the poem gives off a chilling sense of death, its message is of warmth,

through remembrance, which allows us to continue on. Our time here is short, death is forever, enjoy the poem, enjoy your life

LUTSENKO, BORIS
[a.] Philadelphia, PA [title] "Different?" [pers.] I'm the author of the poem "Different?" I'm 13 years old. I live in Philadelphia, PA but I wasn't born here, nor the USA. I'm a Russian immigrant. In June 1997, I came to this wonderful country to stay, to learn, to live and most importantly I try my best to do it. I even received a presidents education award in 1998. From the two 1/2 years of living in US, I can easily say that this country exceeded my expectations and my dreams. I hope my will inspire you because it certainly inspires me

LUTZ, JEAN
[a.] Lafitte, LA [title] "View from the Cross" [pers.] In "View from the Cross," I wanted the reader to come to believe that Christ gave His life so that every individual, from His death until His return could know Him personally. Jean is a retired clerical worker. Proud mother of three sons, loving grandmother of three grandsons, three granddaughters. Enjoy writing Christian articles and poetry, and surfing the net.

LYONNAIS, LILLIAN
[a.] New Bedford, MA [title] "Surprise" [pers.] The idea for this poem originates from being fortunate to have a friend named Sara. She now resides in Hawaii. I have traveled to Hawaii a couple of times Sara's the one that gave me the encouragement to travel. She's an avid traveler and I miss her dearly. Just the thought of being in Hawaii with Sara brought this poem to mind

MACKIN, JOAN MARIE
[a.] Kearny, NJ [title] "Acropolis Atop Metropolis" [pers.] The inspiration for my poem was due to the many years I worked in New York and how my appreciation and admiration for the architects, Engineers and construction workers grew each year. I especially enjoy the artistry that was created even in the most remote place. Special attention to detail was due to the fact that my dad and others in my family worked in New York construction for many years. Poetry has always been an enjoyment to me as well as my personal way of Journaling experiences and stories. I've been fortunate enough to travel with work and experiences different cultures and people. This can also be found in my other loves, painting and photography

MacLAREN, ASHLEY
[a.] Whitefish, MT [title] "Fire" [pers.] When I feel emotions, passion and pain I get an incredible feeling inside me. It works its way through my body. This poem is the product of the fire times I felt this hunger to write. I feel powerful like I can almost manipulate words to say what I feel. It gives me a sense of control. To have someone understand this is a way for them to understand a part of me that not many people can get to. To have even one person relate to me in that way is for me to have truly lived my life

MacMILLAN, JAN
[a.] Dover, NH [title] "Dreaming" [pers.] When I write poetry, it's usually a reflection of my inner self doing its best to express my feelings with pen and paper. Most of my poems have been written to, or about my loved ones. It's one of my ways of sharing my love with them. A few of my poems have gone with "the mood of the moment" as in my poem "Dreaming," where I must have been feeling the need to escape that day! I reside in New Hampshire with my three children. Doug, Bryan, and Lindsey, who wholehearted cheer me on with my poetry writing

MADISON, HANNAH
[a.] Northwood, NH [title] "Through Your Eyes" [pers.] I am very proud of this poem and I really

like it. It is special to me because it inspired a couple of my friends to write poetry. I am glad to be an inspiration to them so that there will be more poets in the world

MAGALONG, CHOYA
[a.] San Antonio, TX [title] "This Gift" [pers.] To me, poetry is very important. In poems many treasures can be found. Poetry has the ability to make you laugh and at the same time cry. Two of life's greatest tributes can be found in poetry; the power of words, and the power to use them through thought, "This Gift," to me, helps convey these such treasures that God has given to me. Through God's love, he takes us from the darkness of our lives and brings us into the light!

MAHELONA, KEONI
[a.] Kapaa, HI [title] "Are Our Dreams Not To Come?" [pers.] This poem talks about all the children of the new millennium. Will these children have a future? The bible states that the Apocalypse is soon to come. If this is true, then these children cannot fulfill their future dreams. All they can do is wait in terror, hoping that they'll have a future. I am one of those children. I take these hypothesis about the future seriously and I do not want them to come true for they are not my dreams

MAHNERT, KAI
[a.] Tralee Cty Kerry, Ireland [title] "Feelings" [pers.] I have lived in many different places all over the world, such as Germany, Ireland and Australia. Writing has been a tradition in my family for generations and for me it is a very personal way of expressing my feelings about myself and the similarities of people from different cultures. This poem was written a few years ago in Brisbane, Australia, where I was doing research on Celtic Mythology. In my time there I made a lot of discoveries about myself, the most important being that I love my family. This poem is dedicated to them

MAIELLO, BONNIE
[a.] Nanuet, NY [title] "Trusted Friends" [pers.] Poetry is a way for me to express my feelings. "Trusted Friends" came to me, and other poems during a difficult time in my life. I am thirty-four years old and I live in Rockland County, New York. I have been married to a wonderful man Joseph for twelve years. Together we have three beautiful daughters Ariel, Jessica, Chelsea and Joe. You make my life worth living. You are the poetry in my heart

MAKOSKI, CALIE
[a.] Poland, OH [title] "Swing" [pers.] Writing poetry. I, one day, hope to become an author for children's books because I love to write adventure and mystery stories

MALDONADO, CURTIS
[a.] Milwaukee, WI [title] "Psychedelic Dreams" [pers.] I've always been someone to shell up inside. I've never expressed how I truly felt to anyone. Poetry gives me a way to step outside myself and witness the true feelings in front of me. Poetry allows me to express my feelings without prejudice, criticism, or the other harsh realities of the world in which we live. I guess being both Japanese and Puerto Rican allows me to view the world around me in a different perspective. All the feelings I have inside, all the different perspectives on life, they all roam out in my poetry. We all have at least one way to release our feelings and emotions in life, and poetry is mine

MANESS, BARBARA
[a.] Corinth, MS [title] "Something About Love" [pers.] Poetry is my hobby and makes me happy. You can write what you would never say. I write mostly about people and their trails. I try to make them feel better. I am a grandmother that loves life, family, friends, animals always trying to share love with the world God's love

MANN, MICHELE
[a.] Herndon, VA [title] "Enhancing My Senses" [pers.] I was inspired to write this poem for Valentines Day. I wanted my husband to know that he helped enhance all of my senses. I love you, Tom

MARARA, EMMANUEL
[a.] West Sussex, UK [title] "How" [pers.] There are many perplexing things in the world around us. As inquisitive people we all ponder about why and how things are the way they are only to find a humbling answer. Things are the way they are because they are. Poetry seeks to show purpose rather than reason. I wrote this poem in an attempt to come to terms with a lot of mysteries in my daily life. I hope it encourages an acceptance of life as it is. We are after all mortal and cannot be in enlightenment all of the time

MARCHANI, MANDY
[a.] Moundsville, WV [title] "I'd Rather Be Fat"

MARQUEZ, MARIA CORINNA
[a.] Charleston, SC [title] "Orgasms of the Soul" [pers.] Eclecticism is a constant in my poetry. I can write from surreal poems, to erotic ones, to violent ones, to reflexive ones, and everything in between. For me, poetry is one of the best ways to communicate who am I, and what's going on through my mind in a particular time. "Orgasms of the Soul" is a poem of "Erotic-Surrealistic Philosophy"

MARSHALL, ROBERT
[a.] Lynchburg, VA [title] "On the Small Pebbles" [pers.] The way we use language as human beings is amazing. Not only do we use it to communicate our thoughts and feelings, but we can also use it to evoke images and emotions in others. No other animals are able to communicate with that amount of depth. For me poetry is a very powerful part of being human because it is the most eloquent and beautiful use of the gift of language

MARTIN, JASON L.
[a.] Overland Park, KS [title] "Last Temptation" [pers.] I truly believe, a day that you do not learn something new about yourself and the life you lead, is a day utterly wasted. I suppose that this statement is the basis of my poetry. It is a daily journal complimenting my growth in this life. Each poem is created by the "Life Lesson"; the quintessential learning tool. Losing Unharmed Charm and The Last Temptation are my finest examples. A native of Little Rock, AR. I now reside Overland Park, KS. I am a graduate of Arkansas Tech University, receiving a Bachelor of Arts in Speech Communications and Political Science. As it continually does, my life has thwarted me in to another direction. I am currently pursuing a Bachelor of Science in Telecommunication Management (Networking), at Devry Institute of technology. Sometime in the near future, I am planning to publish a book of my poetry. Currently I am taking in as much as I possibly can, learning the lesson

MARTIN, MICHAEL
[a.] Brea, CA [title] "Silently" [pers.] This poem is special to me because it brings to life my worries about the rain forests. Poetry means a lot in my life. It let me express my inner most feelings. If it wasn't for my mom, Cheryl Crossley, I probably wouldn't have wrote this poem. I like to skateboard, play video games, and play football and/or basketball

MARTIN, MICHAEL
[a.] Goshen, IN [title] "The Eagle" [pers.] I stand in awe of this magnificent bird! I feel this poem is an analogy to a Christian. Isaiah 40:31. The first four verses are symbolic of the beauty and freedom in Christ after one has become born again. The second part symbolizes the way God cares and provides for his children. And in the last part, peace and rest to those who are totally surrendered

to Christ. I inherited this gift of poetry from my dear mother. I also appreciate my ninth grade teacher who encouraged me in this area, for out of that this poem was born

MARTINEZ, ALYNNA
[a.] Huntington Beach, CA [title] "Blue" [pers.] Perception kills the truth embarked in my heart. Miss interpretation caused words of love to be words of hate. I wrote this poem knowing we interpret things different and what I feel may come out wrong. So please do not listen to my words but hear my heart's cry. I dedicate this poem to all of who have been misunderstood, because communication is a language it's a battlefield. Especially when the battlefield is in front of the mirror

MARTOCCI, CHRISTINA
[a.] Dallas, TX [title] "They Lie" [pers.] Only a select few have ever read anything I've written so naturally, I was afraid of rejection and hesitant to submit my poem for possible publication. Many thanks go to my family and M.F.M. for their support and encouragement. This has been a thrill to my creative spirit. I never knew I could be so proud of myself. What a tremendous confidence builder. To my son, Nicholas, M.L.H. forever and always

MASTERS, MELISSA
[a.] Gary, TX [title] "You and My Dreams" [pers.] All my poetry was inspired by someone special or something special. Each poem has a different meaning about it. "You and my dreams" was more of a feeling I had one night. I wrote it down and it became a piece of art. I started writing at age 13. I had a dream the night one of my good friends past away "Chad Webster" and I wrote it down and it become a poem. I only write what inspires me. I have over 90 poems already written and one day I want to publish them all in one book. When I grow up I want to be a famous writer and I want everyone to like my work. I normally write of my living room table where it's quiet. It's a comfortable place for me. Because I can focus on my work and my surroundings are comfortable to me. You and my dreams is a dedication to Jon. I love you and thank you!

MASTERS, SEAN
[a.] USAFA, CO [title] "Eagle's View" [pers.] "Eagle's View" is a great poem! It invokes feelings of freedom and comfort. This poem also expresses a powerful message of faith

MATA, VIRGINIA
[a.] Laredo, TX [title] "Only God Can Judge Me" [pers.] What inspired me the most to write his piece of poetry is the fact that so many people insist on judging others. Since I'm a 14-year-old eighth grade student at L.J. Christen Middle School, my goal was to motivate such judgemental people to not critique others as well as keeping comments to themselves. My poem is more of a piece of advice for teens to ignore such comments in order to avoid further discrimination. I, myself, intend to place in action my own advice and set a perfect example

MATHENY, EMILY
[a.] Murfreesboro, TN [title] "Help" [pers.] Writing is one of my hobbies. I feel it is the best way to overcome my deepest fears and express my simplest joys. I have to give thanks to my Dad, who has inspired and encouraged my writing. Writing is a great satisfaction and alot of fun

MATHIS, JAIME
[a.] Berkshire NA, England [title] "Oleaginous" [pers.] I have always thought my face too round, my rear too big, and my vocabulary too small. My face I can do nothing (naturally) to change, my rear I can do little to change, but my vocabulary I can do a plethora of things to change. Life is simply an exercise to charge what you can and realize what you cannot

MATIAS, RAMON
[a.] Miami, FL [title] "The Final Lover" [pers.] I never believed poetry should be explained. For me a good poem is one which no one understands completely, not even the author knows the complete meaning of the poem. "The Final Lover" is an example of that, I wish I could explain the meaning behind what I wrote, but I can't, the poem should have a personal meaning to the reader. Now, a little information about me. I am an eighteen year old male, and am currently attending Florida International University. I am studying Psychology, but my real dream is to become a writer

MATOS, MICHAEL
[a.] Manteca, CA [title] "Life Love" [pers.] Thanks to everyone in my life, especially the ones furthest from me

MATRAS, CHRISTOPHER
[a.] Charleston, WV [title] "Angels in Disguise" [pers.] I wrote this poem to show how I view someone extremely special to me, my girlfriend! Throughout the past years, she has become the best friend I always wanted and the girlfriend of my dreams. She has taught me many things about herself as well as myself, that I will carry with me for the rest of my life. I love her as both girlfriend and my best friend forever

MATTHEWS, JOHN
[a.] Little Rock, AR [title] "The Wild Duck" [pers.] In 1967, age 35, Asst. Dir. of the Ft. Lauderdale Civic Theatre, immersed in the production of Ibsen's "The Wild Duck," I wrote this sonnet from '68 to '70, I obtained an M.A. in communications/creative writing, institute to Allende, San Miguel de Allende. In 1957, I became a realtor. From 1970 to the present, I continue in that profession

MATTKA, JENNIFER L.
[a.] Kitchener, ON [title] "Welcoming Insanity" [pers.] To me, poetry is a passionate energy that wells up inside you and must be released. My work reveals itself as I am forced to conform to the many toils of North American living. It is drawn from love, loss, and feelings of complete despair or total euphoria. My work is therefore an expression of strength and not of need

MAU, DHANI
[a.] Seattle, WA [title] "I Am Sitting Here" [pers.] This poem was for an assignment in school for my writing class. We went to a small park near the school. We were to write observations in a poetry form. If was to be a fall poem. I really enjoy writing poetry, recreational and for my writing class. I thank my writing teacher for giving me the opportunity to write this poem

MAXWELL, JASON J.
[a.] Levittown, PA [title] "Where No Shadows Fall" [pers.] I wrote this poem just a few months before my 18th birthday for my girlfriend of eight wonderful months, and then presented it to her on Valentine's Day. I hope you enjoyed this poem as it meant a great deal to me when it was chosen to be printed in this collection. If interested in any of my other work, it can be found at my website.

MAYNARD, TRENT
[a.] Surrey, BC [title] "Set Sites Higher" [pers.] This poem is very meaningful for me because it is my emblem of hope for the future. In our society, so many people have such little hope and give up so easily. I wrote this poem to show these people that through God's help and through setting achievable goals they can escape from their binding struggles and move on into a bright and successful future. I would like to thank: God, my parents, my grandparents, Tracey, Richard, Melissa, Sarah, Pam and all my other friends and family. You have all contributed amazing things to my life

MBANEFO, JIDEOFO
[a.] Chicago, IL [title] "At First" [pers.] Jide' Mbanefo was born in Washington, D.C. in 1977. He grew up in Bethesda, Maryland as his parents worked for the United Nations. Travelling with his Nigerian family through Africa and Europe influenced much of Jide's work. However, his evident love for nature is rooted in his participation in the University of Michigan's New England Literature Program. The curriculum unites regional authors to the outdoor life that influenced their work, Jide' graduated with a B.A. in Psychology from Michigan in 1999. He lived briefly in Chicago and currently resides in Northern California

MBOBI, EMMANUEL
[a.] Toledo, OH [title] "What a Wonderful World this Would Be!" [pers.] The motivation behind this poem is the apparent lack of love in the world today. Even the one institution called marriage in which love is supposed to thrive, it has lost its luster. Love has grown dim and seemingly so far away that nobody seems to know what its real meaning is. Many things have been done in the name of love even killing. If we could all give love a chance, it might be a prelude to a utopian society

McAULIFFE, CHAD
[a.] Somersworth, NH [title] "In Time" [pers.] Being a teenager is not an easy thing from my experience. The world reveals more secrets and wisdom each day. This makes life extremely difficult to keep up with. But one issue that I keep confronting myself with is death. Many people have different opinions on this touchy subject and I just decided to put my thoughts simple and direct. This poem is dedicated to life and my Lord God. I thank my family for supporting me every day of my life and hope you enjoyed this poem

McCARTIN, DIANNE
[a.] Anderson, CA [title] "Please" [pers.] Everyone, at some point, has someone they love or care for deeply. But, with love and relationships come confusion. When I wrote this poem, I was confused with the relationship I was in. I feel that everyone has a different path they choose to release their emotions. Some people listen to music or take a long drive, but I choose to write poetry because feel it is the only way I can truly release my emotions

McCARTY, JOSHUA
[a.] Chicago, IL [title] "Neverland" [pers.] Prose and poetry is important to me, as it is the medium in which I have chosen to express myself. I hope others will come to an understand about what I say, and I wish well to all those choose the same path

McCLAIN, ZELDA
[a.] Lockport, NY [title] "Are You Ready" [pers.] "Are You Ready" This poem is one among many that can fulfill, open, close and make my life see it full potential. Am I ready, no not yet I'm still preparing myself to fulfill my life. I can walk, I can talk, I can see, hear, smell, touch, feel and it's all of me, with poetry I am happy, sad, disappointed etc., but through it all I can rejoice because poetry can open up apart of my life that I need from myself and fill the darkest part with light and then I lie all over again

McCORMACK, MICHAEL
[a.] Elkins Park, PA [title] "How Can I Explain Her to You" [pers.] "One day I realized, the artists will save the world. Though their gentle strength must withstand the harshness of a real world, it is through their works that others will have insights." I wrote this poem for my wife, Diana, shortly after we started seeing each other because it expressed what I felt in my heart. I was blessed to be able to read it to her during our wedding ceremony. Thank Diana, for being my inspiration

McCORMICK, DENNIS
[a.] Ridley Township, PA [title] "Accident" [pers.] My name is Dennis McCormick and I am ten yeas old. I go to Grace Park School. I wrote this poem when I was nine years old. It is about my oldest brother Bobby. He was coming home from Baseball practice when the car he was in slid off the road and hit a tree. I remember feeling very scared that night while we were waiting in the hospital emergency room. I have a mom, dad and another brother, Sean. And I love them all very much

McCOY, CYNTHIA
[a.] Tallahassee, FL [title] "Emily" [pers.] "Emily" is a poem about someone with whom I shared a bond that felt so unique. For a brief moment of time, we taught each other what it meant to be human: to love and be loved. Although we have grown apart, this poem is my fond remembrance of our time together

McCOY, TIM
[a.] Bexley, OH [title] "The Fighter Inside" [pers.] This poem was inspired by my son, Ryan Patrick McCoy. He fought and struggle to survive his first few days of life. Unlike cousin Curran, he won his fight. I truly believe that the quality of a newborn life is not measured by its length but by the love that is given and the love that is received. I dedicate the poem to my son Ryan and my niece Curran. She was here in a short while but she touched all of our hearts for the rest of our lives

McDADE, MELODY
[a.] Fort Meade, FL [title] "Come to Me" [pers.] I wrote the poem to my husband Brian expressing how much I love and need him. I know it is the Holy Spirit through my believe and trust in Christ Jesus who gives me the words to express my thoughts and feelings of people dearest to me. I want to thank my mother Olive Peryer, my sister Yvonne Fleury, my son David Fullmer and especially my dear friends Chris and Anna Paul for years of encouragement and Anne Maddy for always being there when I need her. Once again thank you. I love you all so very, very much

McDONALD, BETHANY
[a.] Hopedale, MA [title] "Homeless" [pers.] I attend Hopedale Jr. Sr., High School. I enjoy nature, animals of all kinds. I play the piano and violin, love to read and write poetry in my spare time. I go to Boston often and see homeless people and I feel very badly for them, especially in the winter. The poem had been going around in my head and I finally found time to put it on paper. I am very excited to be in this contest and to have my poem published. Poetry means a lot to me

McDONALD, GEORGINA
[a.] Norfolk, VA [title] "Alone" [pers.] I wrote this poem when I was sixteen years old. I was at the time experiencing a little but of depression. I decided to write my feelings down in the form of a poem. I have written other poems, but by far it seems everyone that I let read this poem has complimented me and has told me how I should put a book together. Well, now almost five years later I finally took that first step. I want to thank everyone who was there with me for this, especially my Mom and my friends here in Norfolk, Virginia. Thank you to you all, you all are my inspiration

McDONALD, JASON
[a.] Dallas, TX [title] "Caustic Emotions" [pers.] I am currently a junior at Greenhill School and am 16 year old. Caustic Emotion is about my mother, and is an example of one of my many poetic attempts to come to terms with her death. Because it's definitely one of the negative events in my life, I try not to think about it. A myriad of bad things happen every day, but I've found that focusing on those things does absolutely nothing to ame-

liorate your current situation in life. Instead, it only acts to take time away from pursuing what actually makes you happy

McELWEE, LINCOLN
[a.] Santa Barbara, CA [title] "Awake Within Me" [pers.] I wrote this poem as a prayer to God. My prayer is that He will show me the meaning of living each day to its fullest. I know there is a potential within me for greater things and with this poem. I am asking God to awaken that potential

McENERY, KATIE
[a.] Oak Forest, IL [title] "Friends Forever" [pers.] This poem was a reflection of how I felt concerning friends who had become an important part of my life during my high school years

McGHIE, DIANE
[a.] Taylorsville, UT [title] "My Soul Weeps" [pers.] I have always loved to write poetry. I believe it's a way of unlocking one's inner feelings. I'm most inspired to write, when enjoying hobbies, such as running or biking, "My Soul Weeps" is dedicated to all those hopeless romantics out there, who have ever felt the hopelessness of an unobtainable love. I thank my parents and family for the support they've shown. And their encouragement to continue to write. But most of all, for their unconditional love

McHUGH, SARAH
[a.] Wixom, MI [title] "China Doll" [pers.] Poetry is a gift. I feel that when a person receives this gift, they should use it to their up most ability. My poem "China Doll" holds a very dear place in my heart, it is dedicated to my best friend. This poem not only describes her looks and personality but her strength and how she can make others feel good about themselves

McINTOSH, PATRICE
[a.] Clemson, SC [title] "On My Own Two Feet" [pers.] Even though I deny it constantly, I in definitely a daddy's girl! As most teenage daughters do, my father and I are constantly "Discussing" my life, whether it is about boys or school. This poem, "On My Own Two Feet," tells about the normal frustrations between father and daughter. The message is this: "Daddy, I'm 18 years old and I'm graduating June 2, 2000. It is time you let me stand on my own without your offered hand." I don't think that I'm the only daughter who has felt that way about her father, and I do know that it is a difficult task to break away from the loving hand of parents. I suppose I will always be daddy's little girl. But I want daddy to realize that his little girl well, she ain't so little anymore. I'm eighteen years old, about to graduate with the class of 2000. My daddy has taught me all that is going to carry me through the rest of my life. For this, I say thank you, Daddy, I love you

McKELLAR, ASHLEY
[a.] Whippany, NJ [title] "Dreaming Through the Eyes of a Youngster" [pers.] "Dreaming Through the Eyes of a Youngster" was a poem I wrote when I was in fifth grade. I have always been fascinated by dreams and this is what got me interested in writing about this topic. My mom has always enjoyed writing poetry and she is who inspired me to write poems. I dedicate this poem to my family, whom I love very much may all their dreams come true!

McKINSTRY, ALESE
[a.] Irving, TX [title] "Last Dance" [pers.] Poetry is my way of expressing myself; it's how I let loose those powerful emotions inside my heart. It is everyone's dream to find someone they can spend the rest of their lives with; sadly some spend their whole lives searching for that someone. I have found the love of my life. I find myself very lucky. I am completely in love with this person. When I wrote this poem, I thought about my love. How

could I live without you? If there was a message in this poem, it would be to treasure every moment with the love of your life. You never know when it will be the last dance. Baby don't worry, we have many more to come. I love you

McKLOSKY, DAWN
[a.] Fort Collins, CO [title] "Gone" [pers.] This poem was written to explain feelings known by me and only me, felt for a friend and lover. A poem he asked for but never received. I hope one day he may read this . . . and know that he was the one, the only. It's a thin line between love and hate. Good luck and nothing but the best M.S.

McLAURIN, DARREN
[a.] Birmingham, AL [title] "Perceptions" [pers.] This poem is a reflection of my inner most feelings. It is a political and moral statement about the worst Holocaust in human history, the African slave trade where millions of my ancestors died by the hands of Europeans. It was imperative that I submitted this poem out of all the others that I have previously written. Because we (Africans/Americans) have escaped physical bondage only to find mental bondage waiting around the corner. This poem was written for my brothers and sisters as a wake-up call to why we are here in America today suffering just like the slaves that walked onto the dock approximately 400 years ago and for true equality we still have so far to go

McLEAN, KATHERINE
[a.] Riverton, UT [title] "Liberty" [pers.] I have always had a difficult time expressing myself through speech, so I am extremely grateful for my poetic abilities. I am embarrassed to say how much my poems are written for me than anybody else, but it is so. Even if my poems are write rather selfishly, there are people in my life that have given me this gift. I am grateful to my parents for pushing me to get my pen moving again and my 8th grade English teacher for giving me the opportunities to do so. I only hope that everybody can find a way of expressing themselves and have all of the encouragement I've received

McLEAN, SHARON
[a.] College Station, TX [title] "I Am" [pers.] I feel that poetry is a gift from Almighty God. With such a gift, I can allow my imagination to run free. There are no limits or boundaries. "I AM" is a poem that allows me to see things from within a mirror. From "Within" is how I view people and life, getting the "Real" perspective of things. For encouragement from my family and special friends, to them I wish many blessings and much love. Must importantly, I thank God for His love, grace and mercy

McLEOD, MICHELLE
[a.] North Bergen, NJ [title] "Where Have We Gone?" [pers.] When does one write poetry? Either because I love or desperation? To capture a moment of loss or gain? Is there anything worse than losing a true love? I don't believe there is any way to say certain things out of desperation without a poem or song. Poetry captures the heart strings because of the images left behind. My soulmate knew we were headed for a fall. We needed to go back and be ourselves again. I love you, my soulmate; today, tomorrow, and for always! Thank you for coming back

McNEAL, JOEL
[a.] Juniper, GA [title] "A Great Divide" [pers.] I often use poetry to help me explain my emotions towards issues that plague society today. In this poem, I have found solitude in knowing that although people of different nations, races, and ethnic often find themselves very far apart (like a great divide), some can find a way to be very close (despite their differences). And for those that fail to see how similar and close they really are, they're ignorance and ethno-centrism prevents them from (really) living

McNEILL, DONNA
[a.] Englewood, NJ [title] "Footprints" [pers.] This poem was a spiritual awakening to become more conscious of "self" and my surroundings. I hope that this poem will be an inspiration to those who continuously step on mines to become more consciously aware of "self and their surroundings, and to know that no matter how many mistakes you make in life, with faith, you truly can change the pattern of your footprints

McPHERSON, BRIAN
[a.] Tulsa, OK [title] "First Day of Fall" [pers.] For D.L.M., 1940–1999. I miss you, Dad

MEDIG, BRAD
[a.] Orillia, ON [title] "The Eleventh" [pers.] I am 14 years old, and live in Orillia, Ontario. The poem was initially written for school as a remembrance day poem for a contest. This is important to me, as I had great Uncles and a great grandfather who served in the war

MEIZLER, MARCY
[a.] Dearborn, MI [title] "Heart Beat" [pers.] Poetry is very hard to write but when something dramatic happen, it comes naturally to me. This poem is a love poem and was hard to write because I can't say I've experienced real love. My friend Sabrina inspired to start writing poems and I'm very happy for that. Writing is my favorite way to express my feelings for someone or something. And I'm very happy to have this talent

MELCHER, DON
[a.] Merrillan, WI [title] September" [pers.] I think poetry is an expression of the spirit. It comes from deep within and cannot help but communicate something important about the poet, as well as the message he is trying to convey. I think everyone possesses an appreciation of beauty and is therefore capable of writing poetry

MELLON, VIVIAN
[a.] Wilmington, DE [title] "Tiny Little Hoofbeats" [pers.] Poetry flows like music in motion through my heart. Oh to be a child again. My imagination can faintly hear those tiny little hoofbeats a-dancin' and a-prancin' to the jingle of the sleigh.

MELOCHE, BRIAN
[a.] Whitmore Lake, MI [title] "Single Breath" [pers.] Looking into the eyes of my father as I was writing this was the support I was looking for. From the different aspects and point of views we share as a father and son relationship I figured that with all his hard effort, part of mine was missing. As so the poem goes, a tribute to the one who has been there my entire life and forever, the title entrance begins a single breath

MENARD, FRANTZ
[a.] Bridgeport, CT [title] "A Love Letter" [pers.] This poem is dedicated to the true girl love so dear, Nicqueva Nelson I was inspired one night to right a poems of a love letter, therefore I wrote one. Nicqueva is everything to me and more. I can't wait to show her this poem. I've been writing poetry since I, was twelve years old. I also write stories, act, model, cook, and also everything a young teen loves to do. Basically, I hope someone extremely important sees my work and my profile and calls me for further and future works. I'm only fifteen but got alot of talent in me. I just want to say, I love you very much Nicqueva and by prayer and the will of God, anything and everything will happen

MENIG, DONALD
[a.] Hillside, IL [title] "The Great Sight" [pers.] I wrote this poem on the night, my little brother was born. The Great Sight is a generalization of all powerful sights that can open your eyes. This particular sight was the birth of life. The life that flows throughout everyone and everything. I try

to give a message or inspire those who will listen. I hope someone will benefit from this piece of my work. I am an artist. A musician at heart. It is my true way of communicating what I feel. It is my gift and I am honored to be able to share it with you

MENO, JULIA
[a.] Jackson, WY [title] "Two Trees" [pers.] I feel that the hardware of one's soul can be found in poetry. I am continually awed and inspired by natural environments and landscapes. There is nothing better than feeling a connectiveness to all things

MERCER, MICHAEL
[a.] Webster, TX [title] "Leah" [pers.] I found my gift of poetry because of Leah. There has been no other woman in my life who has inspired me like she has. God is glorified through her. This poem is a screaming whisper about how God works in the lives of His people. Leah, my sweetheart, directs me back to Christ when I lose my focus. She is truly a disciple of His. This was my first poem to write. I can now use this God given gift to glorify Him

MERRINGTON, JASON
[a.] Calgary, AB [title] "A Tree" [pers.] Poetry, like all forms of knowledge, is meaningless. That is unless it's applied into practical action! "A Tree" is an attempt to inspire care with action. We all see the insanity in slaying our world's forests in absurd commercial proportions, while sacrificing the precious life giving properties trees provide. Some are currently trading our rainforest medicines, wild life, and yes, our own life sustaining oxygen for a wind blown advertisement, or yet another yearly phone book, which sarcastically I'm sure, will soon replace the internet. I'm not just a Canadian musician and college student, I'm a resident of planet Earth. Create and motivate practivity, not insanity

MERSING, KRISTIN
[a.] Neville Island, PA [title] "The Liquid World" [pers.] This poem actually has a very weird story to it. One night I was feeling ill so I went to bed and the poem is a summary of my dream. I would also like to say that I dedicate this poem to my dad. He unfortunately never got to see this day but I know he's watching me from Heaven and he's very proud. Fare thee well father, until we meet again

MESSINA, LISA
[a.] Valley Stream, NY [title] "You" [pers.] I always found it hard to "say" what I was feeling— so I started "speaking" through my poetry. This poem was written for someone who is very special to me and will always hold the special place in my heart; no matter what happens

MICHELA, MICHAEL
[a.] White Lake, MI [title] "Hannah" [pers.] This poem was written in honor of our daughter Hannah. Even though she was unable to breathe the breath of life, our hearts will always hold a place for her. I have found that poetry allows me to express myself in ways that words sometimes cannot reflect. There is no greater peace than to sit back and write poetry from your heart. Hannah we miss you so much. Love, Mommy and Daddy

MIHALCEA, ANA
[a.] Los Angeles, CA [title] "Missing You" [pers.] Life is a mystery. Our consciousness cannot even grasp the intelligence of nature, neither can language properly describe it. Poetry, just like music and art can touch emotions and surpass the restriction of the logic mind. In this process we gain access to that which is infinite, unspeakable and miraculous. This is what can never be seen or understood but our human heart will always long for

MILES, EDGAR
[a.] New Braunfels, TX [title] "Grim Reality" [pers.] "Grim Reality" is actually a song that I wrote for my band, die daily , and is one of my favorites. It represents the need for brutal self honesty, the defiance of mediocrity, and the embracing of one's dreams

MILLER, CAROLE
[a.] Hershey, PA [title] "What is Love?" [pers.] "What Is Love?" is dedicated to my family; to John Mingo and family and all the loving people who come to find comfort and peace in their hearts through the loss of a beloved one on in memory of Pets

MILLER, JAMIE
[a.] Portland, OR [title] "Cared By You" [pers.] This poem expresses the emotions of a woman in a violent relationship and describes how she finally breaks free on her own to discover what true love and true caring feels like. I feel that all women can benefit from knowing that love is not a control and submission process and that caring is just as important as loving. At the moment, I am a student at the University of Southern California and I'm studying psychology. Poetry is a hobby all humans should be interested in and, while I'm on the subject, all humans should have dogs as well

MILLER, RANDY
[a.] Marion, NY [title] "Questioning Life" [pers.] I think poetry is a healthy means of communicating thoughts and ideas. By the simple flow of a pen, you can accomplish so much. Whether it's releasing feelings and emotions from deep down inside, or simply expressing some thoughts you have. Poetry is an art, and to become a poet you must learn to be an artists. Also, don't ever think you cannot become a poet, because anyone can. It just takes a little patience, and persistence

MINGO, JOHN E.
[a.] Belmont, NH [title] "Love" [pers.] My poem, "Love," was inspired by my family, Carole and Ken Miller and the many thousands of folks who share in the same loving feelings for their beloved ones who come to "In Memory of Poets.Com" which is dedicated to my cocker spaniel, candy, who gave so much love and understanding to me through a very difficult time in my life

MINKEWICZ, LAURA
[a.] Tonawanda, NY [title] "A Poem About A Chatting Friend" [pers.] I owe a very special thank you to James Candore, for if it wasn't for him this poem would have never been written. He has taught me more about life in the few short months that I have known him, than I have ever known. He has helped me search for my inner peace and to be happy with myself which in turn has made me a much stronger person. To him I will always be grateful

MIRCHANDANI, CHERYELONA
[a.] Baltimore, MD [title] "Pain to Gain" [pers.] This poem is dedicated to my family whom I love beyond words. Naresh, Shannon, Daniel, Katie, Sara, Nanak, Joshua, Michael, Ruben, each enhance my life beyond measure. I thank God for them, Carter and his parents Rev. Gordon Clews and his beautiful wife Eleanora whom have both rejoined each other in Heaven. I pray that God will shower each of them with all they need o be happy, healthy, and full of His love always. God Bless my mom, Joan Chambers and Mother-in-law Sushelia Mirchandani with peace, love, and healing for a long life. God Bless all that read this

MIRCHANDANI-SANCHEZ, JOSHUA
[a.] Baltimore, DE [title] "Who Makes You Tired?" [pers.] My name is Joshua Mirchandani-Sanchez. I am a ten-year-old student at Millbrook Elementary School in Baltimore, MD. I have many hobbies such as writing poems and stories, drawing, helping my papa work on cars, raising my dog Pugzy, and hermit crabs, watching videos, and playing games and sports. Also, I love spending time with my family (my papa, Naresh), my mama, (Cheryelona), my brothers and sisters (Shannon, Danny, Katie, Sara, Nanak, Michael), and friend (Ruben). I love collecting things (Pokemon cards and stamps), and traveling. I want to dedicate my poem to my mama who put poetry in my heart

MISNER, KELLY
[a.] Lompoc, CA [title] "Nature" [pers.] The ability to have been able to have written the poem "Nature" is a gift from God. I have been very blessed not only with the gift of writing but also with a loving family that is always encouraging me. My hope and prayer is that this poem helps you to seek the beauty in nature that God intended for you to see. If not take a good look around you again

MITCHELL, ANGELA
[a.] Nashville, TN [title] "Descending Out of Hell" [pers.] I have developed a very high standard for what I consider to be "good" poetry. I never thought that anything I wrote could fall near that category, so I was very surprised to be included in this book. I want to thank my high school English professors for introducing me to poetry in a way that inspired me to strive for a higher standard. I also want to thank my parents and Frank for giving me the confidence in myself to submit my work. If anyone would like too know the story behind my poem

MITCHELL, SARA
[a.] Anacortes, MA [title] "My Unquiet Mind" [pers.] I am 18, and a college student of pre-made poetry and writing of all types have always been a very important and powerful outlet for my feelings my poems are always written through stream a consciousness, and are rarely revised, this particular one took five minutes, but is still very significant in relaying my emotions. I've been writing poetry since I was about 12 years old, and find it my favorite release and expression

MITTI, CARYL
[a.] Oxford, MA [title] "The Child Within" [pers.] Deep within all of us is a child. For many of us childhood was not a carefree time. Many had to bury their child in order to exist. The child within was my way of releasing my inner child. It has allowed me to forgive the past, enjoy the present and look forward to the future

MOJOMICK, JIMMY
[a.] Kearny, NJ [title] "Christmas" [pers.] My name is Jimmy I am a 46 year old male and ever since I was told that men don't cry when my older brother Tony was killed back in 1970 I started to write what I felt on paper and many of those that would read my words would cry for me many told me mainly my dad who pasted away in 1991 I should try to share my poems with others so if my poem "Christmas" is published I would like to dedicate it to both to my brother and my dad as my tears on paper

MOLCZYK, KELLY
[a.] Lavista, NE [title] "A Lyrical Formation" [pers.] I like writing in ways to get people to think. It exercises the mind. It opens you up to new possibilities. Poetry is painting. It's painting with words. And sometimes, when look at it from different angels, images are endless

MONK, MARCH
[a.] Lawrence Ville, NJ [title] "Remembering Dreams" [pers.] When yearning comes, it comes in song, a lilt, a beat, a throb . . . A sailor's night, a lighthouse long, whistle, a laugh, a sob. Whether it is yearning, union, loneliness or joy, poetry is it for March, who ranges from March the Monk to being March Hare. March writer musical lyric, and the book of poems he proposes to published is aptly titled "New Songs Old." He travels between the West and the East, and hopes that, the name he has chosen for himself, his songs will be free of a background, yet mean something to all who read him. His real name, finally is Padmakumar. He is twenty nine years old, terribly restless and intense.

MONTANO, ANTHONY
[a.] Las Vegas, NV [title] "The Will to Try is the Will to Do" [pers.] "The Will to Try is the Will to Do," a philosophy I have lied with ever since. I was old enough to know the difference between the words "I can" and "I can't." Both can be use constructively. "I can" be anything or do anything I want, but "I can't" stop writing my poetry, my stories, my life. To me there should be no such words as "I can't." I can't do this or I can't do that my friends can do anything you put your mind to, if you just try. This poem is the first poem I have that is now published, which is proof . . . the will to try is the will to do . . . thank you

MONTEIRO, EDWARD, JR.
[a.] Port Chester, NY [title] "The Brook" [pers.] "The Brook" long nature walks, that's my inspiration and a vision in a dream. People, nature, life they all make and set a mood within that opens my mind to receive. A love of life and the cone of my life, I can't wait to share more with you, I have pages more. Love, life and happiness, "God Bless"

MOODLEY, JUSTIN
[a.] "Columbus, OH" [title] "Brotherhood" [pers.] Poetry is a great way to capture ideas and emotions. My poem "Brotherhood" was written for two positive role models I had in my life, my brothers Ryan and Sheridon. They were the only men I could ever really look up to. The lessons they have taught me, and their actions have directly shaped me. And the greatest thing they've given to me are the unconditionals. Things like love and respect have helped me through obstacles in my life. So this was my way of saying thanks

MOODY, VANESSA
[a.] Centerville, GA [title] "Waste of Time" [pers.] Poetry has always been something I have done for myself. Rarely have I shared my writing with anyone. All of my art—writing, painting, drawing, and music—fill my life and keep me going. I strongly agree with Anipefranco, because I too feel that "Art is way I get up in the morning." I hope that my work helps someone else get through their day, as it has certainly helped me get through many of my mine

MORALES, DEBBIE
[a.] San Francisco, CA [title] "Bad and Good Come Together" [pers.] After only being on this Earth for 15 years, I have come to understand that life is full of surprises. This poem states my point of view of life and some of the things that are a part of life. Since life is not made up of only good things nor only bad things, I thought fit to include both in this poem.

MORALES, ERASMO
[a.] Needville, TX [title] "A Message to Remember" [pers.] This poem is unique in the sense that anyone who reads it can somehow relate to it and feel the meaning of it. I'm not a poet nor a writer. It just so happened that on one of the worst day of my life, I picked up a pencil and started to write. I didn't have a point to make or any sense of direction, I just wrote. When I finished and re-read what I had written, I couldn't believe my eyes. On the worst day of my life, I created the poem "A Message to Remember . . . ," and for no reason at all or so I thought, but God on the other hand, did have a reason. Be blessing me with the ability to write this poem, He showed me that the best days are yet to come if I stay faithful to him and love him forever

MORALES, MARIO
[a.] Austin, TX [title] "Emotions" [pers.] After many miles and roads, my soul has found its voice. In writing I deliver what I feel, what I see or what I think. It has always been my dream to share it with you all

MORDOH, MICHAEL
[a.] Ringoes, NJ [title] "Daydreams Vanish Like A Withered Flower" [pers.] This poem is about loss, a loss of love I've been searching for, and have never found. We as people strive for happiness, whether it be in work relationships, or whatever. This poem is for anyone who has ever tried to find that special something or someone and failed, I find myself worth in, and a sense of happiness from writing, as well as the music bands I play in. Although I make and have no money, without the above hobbies, I would have been dead a long time ago

MORGAN, BRITTANY
[a.] Rome, GA [title] "The Lost Girl" [pers.] I am 14 years old. I wrote this poem, "The Lost Girl" when I was going through a very difficult time in my adolescent life. There was no ne that I could share with and even if there was, I couldn't find the words. Writing is my passion so I put all those feelings into this poem. Things are wonderful now but deep down "The Lost Girl" will always be a part of me. If I could give advice to anyone who can relate to my feelings of being lost, I'd say "don't give up!" Being lost isn't so bad because you get the happiness of being found one day. It will come

MORRIS, DAVID
[a.] Los Angeles, CA [title] "Union Child"

MORRIS, MARY
[a.] Snohomish, WA [title] "I Am" [pers.] This poem is a gift that I did in my language class. My teacher Mr. Donhue and my mother have inspired me and I've always wanted to be a writer

MORRIS, TED
[a.] Winlock, WA [title] "Rooster and Arrow" [pers.] "My career as a writer is predominantly based as a lyricist. This poem, I assure you, was written for prose, it was, however, a song for a while! I received my diploma in special publishing, from The Institute of Children's Literature one month prior to the notice of the publication of this work! A benchmark in my career. Thank you for reading!"

MORRISON, KYLE
[a.] Chicago, IL [title] "Hive" [pers.] Poetry has always been a great release for me a chance to unburden myself from the things in my life that can seem too much to handle. I thank my family and friends for all the inspiration and support they haven given me throughout my life. Without them, I would not be able to accomplish all the things I have done so far

MORTON, VERONICA
[a.] Loveland, CO [title] "Shadows" [pers.] Poetry has always been a great escape for me. It helps me express my hidden feelings. This poem was written after my "Crush" broke my heart. I write most of my poetry after painful experience whether it be the death of a friend or a broken heart. Poetry helped me to overcome these struggles and gave me strength. My strength also comes from my loving and supportive family and friends who I always hold close to my heart

MOSER, JASON
[a.] Womelsdorf, PA [title] "The Thoughts That Run Through My Head" [pers.] I live in a small town in Pennsylvania and I am a senior in high school. Over the past years I have found poetry to be the most expressive form of my thoughts and emotions

MOSS, GLENN
[a.] New York, NY [title] "September Hints" [pers.] Like anyone who write, poetry or function, the "need" to express is deep. While not always an easy path to find (and rediscover) the search for words to match feeling and internal imaginary remain, essential and forever journey, this poem reflect, autumn moment imagined and desired. I hope the reader find, something to light or watch a moment. As a business affairs executive in the media creative process to everything I do negotiating writing, plannings. The effort has made a difference

MOYER, LYNNE
[a.] Houston, TX [title] "I Could Not See the Love for the Tease" [pers.] The angels inspired me to write poetry in response to my request for a vehicle to make my heart sing. I am a pharmacist by profession and the ability to make your own heart sing creates a powerful momentum for life. Rejoice in the ride!

MUCHA, GREGORY
[a.] San Antonio, TX [title] "Becky's Twist" [pers.] My family has been gravely impacted by the effects of alcoholism and mental illness. What I've tried to do in this poem is encapsulate one of many moment in the life of an alcoholic and communicate the letter devastation, denial an deadlines of the disease to both unaffected and, hopefully the stricken

MUDGET, JAMES
[a.] Hudsonville, MI [title] "In the Name of a Better World" [pers.] This poem was written as a cry for a better world to live in. I welcome comments on my writing.

MULLIKIN, KEVIN
[a.] Mt. Pleasant, MI [title] "Unrequited Love" [pers.] When you love something so much, and it does not love you back, it hurts. This poem was my creative outlet for the pain I experienced. Originally I wrote the poem in French for a writing course I was taking, but I had to translate it as the majority of the class did not speak the language

MULLINS, PAUL
[a.] Webbers Falls, OK [title] "Summer Breeze" [pers.] Poetry is a big part of my life, this poem is about someone who was very special in my life. That I remember from time to time. I am a painter of oils, and a recording artist with my current band Insomnia and a previous band Hellrazor. Special thanks to Ashley Jean Mullins (young), Raven Siara Mullins (Young), Sandra Stone, Rhonda Mullins, Bobby Isbell, Farrel Isbell, Scott Shell, Terry Ward, Allen (Devo) Powell, Frank Perry This poem is dedicated to Earl Menie, Evylin Menie, Ashley Jean Mullins Raven Siara Mullins, Geraldine Mullins

MUNGO, NICHELLE
[a.] Brighton, MA [title] "My Deliverance" [pers.] This particular poem deals with betrayal, anger, and eventually the release of anger. As bold as this work is, my prayer is that it helps to release anger from the millions betrayed by ones closest to them. Born into a family of anointed preachers, musicians, vocalists, artists, actors, and writers, I in no way feel as if this has anything to do with "me." Whether I'm writing a song, poem, or musical score, I realize the anointing comes from God alone as the inspiration to do such comes from sensitive experience

MUNVES, JONATHAN
[a.] Austin, TX [title] "Train of Thought" [pers.] My poetry is the way in which I explore life. I strive to express the supernatural which exists within the mundane. In poetry, as in life, the depth and richness of images as well as experience is as important as the specific content of the experience itself

MURDICK, LAURA
[a.] St. Peters, MO [title] "I Just Want to be Happy" [pers.] I came to the realization that life is full of pain, and a need for happiness at a very early age I have so many feelings, most sad, and the only way to get them out is through poetry. I never really thought my poetry was that good, or anyone would really like it. Being 15 years old, I didn't think my poetry would ever really have an effect on anyone but maybe someone feeling lonely, and sad, will realize their not alone as they read this. I dedicate this poem to my English Teacher Mrs. Kathy Fox, who has always believed in me

MURPHY, KRYSTAL
[a.] Orwell, OH [title] "Beautiful Land" [pers.] This poem is dedicated to my grandparents: Linda and Joseph Gribble, and boots reed. Thank you for all of your encouragement. I love you

MURPHY, RYAN
[a.] Florence, OR [title] "Princess" [pers.] I am a firm believer that poetry is the heart's voice and that the truest and purest comes from the strongest feelings, like one's love for a sister who has wondered away. Tara, I pray that you and anyone else in the same circumstance will hear the voice of mine and God's love for you in this poem. All thanks to God for the gifts of words and a special thanks to a special person. Heather, without you none of this would have happened. My gratitude and love for you always

MURRAY, MEGHAN
[a.] Ashcroft, BC [title] "Suicide" [pers.] Poetry is something I started going when I was very upset. It allowed me a way to vent all of my anger and feelings. Now poetry is something I do because I love to. Writing poems has become my way of expressing myself and sharing my feelings with others. It was my way of telling about my loving father who recently passed away, and telling people of the hurt I've been carrying. There's no special meaning behind "Suicide," it's just something that came to me one day. Poetry is my way of leaving a mark in life

MYERS, PATRICIA
[a.] Arroyo Hondo, NM [title] "Illusive Valentine" [pers.] I was told not long ago that in this life I have a twin flame—a twin soul. I contemplated this message at great length. Being single and twice divorced I found it required deep scrutiny of my intimate self. I wrote this poem as an answer to my own quest. You see, I believe in love and all things possible expect miracles

NAIL, TARENA
[a.] Tecumseh, OK [title] "Music Around the World" [pers.] This poem was written for a friend on a moments notice. However, between its lines appear my life's philosophy, that "everything is beautiful in its own way." We cannot always see the roses for worrying about the thorns, but what is important is that we know they are there. Beneath every flower of personal growth and development lies the root of personal pain and embarrassment. What the orchestra plays tomorrow depends on how one dictates the music today. Live life to its fullest, choose to be happy. Listen for the music in the world around you!

NARD, STEVE
[a.] Thayer, IN [title] "Rime of a Hypocritical World" [pers.] This poem expresses one of my biggest grudges I have with society. Hypocrisy to me is the world's greatest flaws. The poem gave me the chance to search through society, and find the true "False" powers who pull strings like masters of puppets. The common folk are puppets in a world controlled by so few and influenced so easily by the government and church, corrupt with greed, envy pride or sloth. My poem was also away I could get my point out, and open some people's eyes

NARKIEWICZ, PAUL
[a.] Redford, MI [title] "Same Old Night" [pers.] I attend Wayne State University in Detroit Michigan. I'm working towards my bachelors degree in English. I enjoy writing and hope to become a writer someday

NEAL, BOBBY
[a.] Huntsville, AL [title] "Positively Broken" [pers.] I write to express how I feel about certain situations in my life. I've been writing poems, or at least trying, for eight years. Writing poetry helps me in my most desperate times. I was inspired

to write this poem by my broken heart. Something happened between myself and my former love. Everything that happened between us was my fault. I just refused to believe it. I always felt afterwards that she hated me and wanted to drag me down. It was my own conscience that pushed these thoughts into my head, and I realized it all too late

NEAL, MARY
[a.] Colorado Springs, CO [title] "This Tree" [pers.] On a point of hill, all exposed, stood one pine tree alone. I rode the branches of that tree in March winds as a young girl. The image of the tree represents me, anchored on a hill, and extending my arms to embrace God

NEAL, VALERIE
[a.] Bronx, NY [title] "The Race I Must Win" [pers.] My life changed at the age of 49. My nineteen year old daughter was crushed to death by a 35 foot tree. She became a hero on September 1, 1998. Her death attracted mass media attention. She died saving her brother. I wrote my poems in remembrance of her. I am now raising her daughter and living her dreams. Dreams that she can no longer feel. Losing her was like losing my right hand. I am presently going to law school. My goal is to start a Aisha Neal Memorial Fund. This fund will be for AIDS babies, battered women and children who want to go to college. I am hoping through my poetry to raise money for this fund. I will not let her death be for nothing. I will fight to keep her name and her dream alive

NEEB, ANNE
[a.] Metairie, LA [title] "A Pen" [pers.] I write poetry because, the English language has beautiful words, and their use should not be limited to ordinary and necessary speech. Writing poetry captures feelings and observations with words, just as film records beauty in pictures. It's a way to "freeze frame" a thought, event or question. It also allows quiet reflections to become a permanent part of your life, and truly defines the human species

NELSON, AINSLEY DREW
[a.] Bronxville, NY [title] "Pretending Enormous" [pers.] Ainsley Drew Nelson is currently a student at Sarah Lawrence College. She has stalked words from Portland in New York City

NEOH, ENG KIM
[a.] Manchester, UK [title] "The Gift of Time" [pers.] I'm a Malaysian student studying engineering in England. "The Gift of Time" is a reflection on the use of time. Sometimes we hear people say they don't have time for this or should have done that. We are all given 24 hours each day. It's up to us how we use it. We can use it productively to our advantage or idle it away. We always have time. We just have to use it to our advantage

NEWBERRY, LARRY
[a.] Brownsboro, TX [title] "Home" [pers.] I retired with a Major Freight Co. (Roadway Express) after 30 years of service, at age 50 years old. I was born in 1945 at Dallas, Texas. I have a 10th grade education. I wrote this poem in 1958 for an assignment in school. Never thought a truck driver would become a poet. Thanks for this opportunity

NEWCOMB, AMANDA
[a.] Langley AFB, VA [title] "Supermodel" [pers.] This poem came to me as I was watching television. I was thinking about how modern society sometimes bases a person's capabilities on looks and charm. I wanted to stress the fact that neither of those would last forever. I am certainly not a beauty queen, but that doesn't affect who I am in any way. I just wanted people to know that beauty isn't just looks, it's the individual as a whole; mind, body and soul

NEWCOMB, MARY-LISA
[a.] Reseda, CA [title] "Car Driving in Love" [pers.] My poem is simple but realistic. It would be easy for anyone to identify with either the oblivious lover in the front car, or the impatient driver in the rear one. Love often blinds us to anything but the object of our affection. But empathic observers would have the capacity to temper their impatience with understanding. I hope I will always be able to use the power of words to foster a greater level of compassion between people. Perhaps, with the encouragement of my loving husband and my three little boys, it will not be a difficult task to accomplish

NICELY, SCOTT
[a.] Elkhart, IN [title] "Empty Space" [pers.] Poetry is simply the easiest way for me to express myself to others. It helps me to escape the everyday problems in life. Sometimes dark and sometimes bright but nonetheless it gives people who look at my life some insight

NICHOLS, DONNA
[a.] Sophia, NC [title] "A Friend So Dear As You" [pers.] Poems from the hearts the poems I have written to date express the true feelings I have in my heart for those who have played a significant part in my life. It helps to ease the burdens I carry by putting down on paper the feelings I have. My poems portray moments of joy, anticipation, desires, frustration and sadness in my life. My poetry is how I choose to relax and spend some of my free time bringing pleasure to those I care about. My family consists of Michael, My Husband of 19 years and my two sons Aaron (14) and Corey (9)

NICHOLS, KENDRA
[a.] Star, NC [title] "Have You Ever?" [pers.] This poem holds a special place in my heart. I will never forget the people who gave me the strength to write poems that can really go out and touch someone else's heart as well as mine. Thank you mom and dad for believing in me. Your love and your out look on life will never be forgotten. I love you!

NICHTER, DEBORAH
[a.] Lebanon Jct., KY [title] "In a Mind of Darkness" [pers.] I was born on August 7, 1954 and studied at Shepherdsville High School and worked for State of Kentucky for 11 years. Worked five years in Retail. I am a money depressive Bi-Polar and I am now on Social Security Disability. Poem mimics my life

NIGRO, JULIE
[a.] North Andover, MA [title] "What Has Become of Us" [pers.] This poem was inspired by all my life trials and the people who I've met throughout the years. I hope this poem inspires everyone who reads it to look deep inside for the true meaning of life. And realize that life is a journey and that every obstacle can be overcome

NISHIDA, LYNN
[a.] Longmont, CO [title] "Forever Still" [pers.] This poem like others that I have written come from the heart. Writing has always been a release for me. I need to feel a poem before putting pen to paper or fingers to ivory keys. My wish is for just one person who reads one of my poems to not only read it but experience it. Perhaps, grace it with a smile of their own

NISTOR, RONALD
[a.] Milpitas, CA [title] "The Feelings of Leaving Home" [pers.] This poem means alot to me. It was about the feelings of leaving my mom and 13 brothers and sisters. My 13 brother's and sister's name are (From oldest to youngest) Victor, Randy, Mike, Traino, Valentine, Lucy, Ligi, Adrian, Emanuel, Ester, Tabitha, Diana, and the Youngest one is Jennifer. I am between Tabitha and Diana. So in my family there are a total of 14 kids! I like

poetry, just not a lot. That's sort of weird because I always seem to catch rhyming things that people say but I don't like poetry that much!

NIX, WILLIAM
[a.] Chattanooga, TN [title] "Forever" [pers.] My is name William Boyd Nix. I am a religion/ philosophy major with a minor in History. I follow the Shamanistic path. Shamanism is the native American belief system. I write poems about nature and religion I live in an area rich with History and spirituality for the native people. I'm a native American priest and ordained minister

NJOKU, ALLEN
[a.] Woodhaven, NY [title] "Extend Your Arm" [pers.] I was inspired to write this poem from my observations. Having travelled to many countries including my country of birth, Nigeria, I have seen people languishing in poverty while many live Lavishly in endless wealth. The countless millions who die of wants and use the massive wealth thrown away by the very rich. Extend your arm is an appeal to the very rich who have a lot to waste or to a throw away. These things thrown away could go a long to heal lives. After all, a candle loses nothing of its light by lighting another candle. I am a 6th, 7th and eight grade teacher and also an adjust teacher in a junior college for 14 years. I have a masters degree in Public Administration. I am married to a lovely lady; Nwadinma and blessed with four beautiful children: Nwanne, Onyedika, Nyechukwu and Amara. We all live in Woodhaven section of Queens, New York

NOBLE, STEPHANIE
[a.] Granger, IN [title] "Heavenly Dance" [pers.] Before I could read or write, my cousin Alex and I would scribble on paper and show it to our Granny. She'd look at it with enthusiasm, while we stood, wide eyed, and ask "What does it say?" We'd merely scribbled on paper but Granny had the creativity to indulge us with an elaborate story, claiming that's what we'd written. Happily my cousin and I would scamper off, scribble something else, and come back to have Granny tell us again what we'd written. That was my first recollection of gratification achieved from writing, because of that I haven't stopped scribbling

NOEL, KAREN
[a.] Euless, TX [title] "Cliches" [pers.] I enjoy poetry because it allow me to illuminate my feelings artistically. Daily news of shootings, road rage, domestic abuse, and other violence inspired me to write this poem questioning where our basic appreciation of life and being alive, has gone. I also wonder why we can't break the cycle of history repeating itself. Hopefully my poem motivates others to examine and take responsibility for their own attitudes and actions, as well as how they fit into their families, their communities, their nation, and the world as a whole. Apathy is the bane of a strong society

NORDSTROM, HEATHER
[a.] San Diego, CA [title] "Declaration of the Self" [pers.] I wrote this poem while taking a women's self-defense class in College. The instructor, Darlene Baumgartener was an especially inspiring woman. I felt so empowered and limitless that at the end of the course, I went home and drew a poster (of a woman climbing on rocks), with the poem as her declaration to live as she should. It also symbolized, myself and the emotionally freeing experience I gained in that class; something valuable I will carry with me throughout my life

NORMAN, AUTUMN
[a.] Newark, OH [title] "The Grave" [pers.] I was born on May 24, 1982, and I haven't had a hard life; however, I have experienced some rough times. I haven't had a lot of tragedies in my life; the feelings I've had my point to a tragic past life. As for my poetry, it is a door to a world where I can be myself and feel free. I've had these feelings all my life, but have only expressed them with poems for a few years. Poems are mysteries. They can mean one thing and be interpreted differently; therefore, may people can be inspired by one poem

NORRIS, CHRISTINE
[a.] Succasunna, NJ [title] "Angels Wings" [pers.] I have enjoyed writing stories and poetry since 12 years of age. It has always been one of my greatest passions. I have a very creative and artistic background. With a B.A. in Art. Much I have kept to myself for my own reflection and now want to share my works in hopes to inspire others to laugh, love and dream. Currently I am working on a more challenging forum of writing, fantasy and romance, to be published in the near future. Expression of oneself is a wonderful talent that can best be expressed in writing. Any comments or expression are more than welcome.

NORWOOD, DEBBIE
[a.] Camden, TN [title] "Shall" [pers.] Poetry is the window to my soul. It vents the thoughts of my innermost feelings. This poem was written for someone who has touched my soul and inspired my heart

NOWAK, PAULA
[a.] Chicago, IL [title] "In Memory of My Dad, Dr. Frank J. Nowak" [pers.] This poem is special to me because it is about my father, Dr. Frank J. Nowak. He went to be with the Lord on January 31, 2000. My father was well liked by all who knew him and was one of the best physicians on the south side of Chicago. My father's story is permanently located at legacy.com on the World Wide Web. He was an amazing person and will not be forgotten. As for myself, I love poetry and will continue to be inspired to write. This is because I have been blessed with a zest for life and unique outgoing personality

OBERDING, MARK
[a.] Toronto, ON [title] "This I Shall Behold" [pers.] This poem is dedicated to my family and friends for the support they have given me in times of illness. It is for them I wrote "This I Shall Behold." I hope others can take comfort in these words. And to my glowing inspiration I say thank you

OKEHIE, JENNIFER
[a.] Columbia, MD [title] "Hiroshima" [pers.] This poem is very special to me because it's the first poem that I ever wrote and it completely changed a part of my life. I never thought that I could write poems because it seemed so hard to find words that expressed my feelings. But after reading the book "Hiroshima," I just wrote down my feelings about it and then conformed it into a poem. This is how I found interest in poetry and started to write more poems

OKEREKE, NKECHINYERE
[a.] London, England [title] "End of the World" [pers.] This poem means a lot to me. It was my first attempt at writing poetry and was written at a time in my life when I had a lot of questions about my own mortality and that of the people around me. I hope that people who read my poem will come to understand and appreciate the fragility of life

OLESCH, CHRISTOPHER
[a.] Schaumburg, IL [title] "Tears of Joy" [pers.] This poem is one of a collection of poems dealing with the cycles of deep depression and memories of elated feelings, after having been divorced. It has special meaning, because it applied to me as well. Both of us opened ourselves to each without fear

OLKO, DOROTHY
[a.] Lanett, AL [title] "Silent Words" [pers.] Poetry was always been very important to me. It is the way that I express my thoughts my fears my happiness. I am very happy and honored to have been chosen in this. And I also want to say thank you, I have been writing for as long as I can remember and I've always hoped that my writing would touch someone in a special way. And reading this letter from poetry.com showed me that it did. Thank all of you so much

OLSEN, ANGELA
[a.] Mulkilteo, WA [title] "Tornado" [pers.] I grew up in Monroe, WA. I spent three years in the army and I have an AA in criminal justice. I have been writing poetry since I was a child. I love to write poetry because it is an essay way to release what's on my mind

OLSON, JOANNE
[a.] Chalfont, PA [title] "Angels" [pers.] As a Registered for twenty years, death and dying have become a real part of my life's work. Just as I help to bring a life into this world, I also must help a life pass out of this world and into Heaven. Through Scriptures, I realize that death is not an ending, but a beginning of a new and everlasting life. Morgan Lee Pena, and all of God's Children are resting comfortably in the arms of our Dear Lord Jesus. God Bless Rob and Patty—Morgan's Mom and Dad

OLSON, TAMI
[a.] Kingsford, MI [title] "Are You Ready" [pers.] This poem has enabled to me to share God's Word with my family and friends. I hope that others are able to share this poem with their loved ones and that the Holy Spirit is able to touch the hearts of those who read it

OPPENHEIM, LISA
[a.] Marietta, GA [title] "I Am a Falling Leaf" [pers.] When I wrote my poem, I had to think about how I'd feel if I were a leaf falling off a tree. I always loved to write so it was not hard to imagine how I'd feel when my first grade teacher gave us this assignment. I'm in 2nd grade now and I'm seven years old, but by the time this poem is published, I will be 8. I love art and reading, I also enjoy gymnastics, dancing, tennis, bike-riding and jumping rope. I'm happy that my poem is being published. I like to write poems about feelings

ORTIZ, GALENE
[a.] Yakima, WA [title] "Grandpa" [pers.] I was born in Yakima, Washington in May 1971, the youngest of four children. Poetry has always been a great emotional release for me. "Grandpa" was written in 1998 for my grandpa when he died. I was blessed with a wonderful grandpa. I am very happily married to the most amazing man in the world. I have two daughter's lone surviving. I would like to thank my husband for his support and encouragement. Also, my Mom for always being there for me. I love you S.J.D.

ORTIZ, ROBERTO
[a.] San Juan, PR [title] "Heart of Darkness, Heart of Sun" [pers.] I always tended to be a somber person, and this was reflected in my short stories and poems. This changed the day I married my best friend. She showed me a world I had never really noticed before and gave me a whole new outlook on life. This poem was written for her, for her support, her love and the beautiful son she gave me. She's my inspiration and my strength—my wife, Myriam.

OSAKPA, ATYATHOABE
[a.] Brooklyn, NY [title] "Virginia at Meson Ole" [pers.] This poem was inspired by love. I have never written a poem before. One day, I was on a date with the subject of the poem—Virginia, at a restaurant; Meson Ole, in Long Island, New York. Behind the restaurant was a pond that provided the background against where she was sitting. Under inspiration, I told her that I was going write a poem for her, and for the first time in my life, I wrote Oh! Virginia. The poem has two other verses, which were not included for the contest due to space. I enclose them with this profile

OSWALD, MICHELE
[a.] Three Springs, PA [title] "I Don't Understand" [pers.] I live in Central, PA. I'm in 6th grade with alot of friends. Poetry, to me is a great gift from God. I discovered it when I was in 5th grade. I came up with the poem by thinking of people who are abused by their boyfriend/girlfriend or husband/ wife. My goal in life is to become a singer/ songwriter or actress. My hobbies are singing, dancing and of course writing poems. Many of my friends and relatives support my talent of writing poems. I'm also in co-ed basketball. At church, I'm in youth group. Like I said, I love poetry. It's just a great gift. Thank You

OTTEN, JOCELYN
[a.] Wilton, CA [title] "Good-bye Millennium" [pers.] I believe that poetry is an art. An art in which your mind is your paintbrush; that requires no specific use, just to express your thoughts and compile them into beautifully painted pictures of artistic meanings and qualities. So with the curiosity that this new century has put before us I have also put before you a memoir. A memoir of all the past memories, experiences, and challenges that our nation has endured in the previous century. This poem was written to say something that was meant to be heard. "Good-bye Millennium!"

OTTO, WALLY MAX
[a.] Johnston, RI [title] "Pool Day" [pers.] I never figured a triangle fashion for submission, why bell with bother kept in song lays written intension fun, for everyone a phrase of thanks, an Hanks, feelings are true-dis-eve. Lifted from out a dark doom into an excepted room. A seed from us all meet the public who like to perform and be entertain. We is dramatic person, in these ever similar lives, we need each other, to move each other, to just love each an every other

OYLER, DEANN
[a.] Tremonton, UT [title] "Your Heart and Mine" [pers.] This poem is special to me, because it commemorates someone who is very important in my life: My very special husband of seven months inspired me to write this poem when we were just dating. About a week after I wrote the poem he asked me to marry him. My husband Jed Abbott has helped inspire me a lot. This is my favorite poem out of the many different poems that I have written, because it was the first poem that I ever wrote for my husband

PADDOCK, VICKY
[a.] Ontario, CA [title] "Heaven's Lyrics" [pers.] I live in a cabin without modern conveniences, located in a remote area north of Fairbanks, Alaska. One arctic night, while in deep sleep, God came to me in a dream. Angels were playing beautiful music and singing the words of this sonnet. I believe it is a gift meant to be shared

PAGANELLI, SAMANTHA
[a.] Palmdale, CA [title] "Artist's Thoughts of the Sunrise" [pers.] My history teacher, Mrs. Skomsvold, said this poem was "like a hope or promise." And now that I think about it, she's right. My writing is mostly inspired by my friends and family, whom have supported my writing ever since I started. I'd like to thank all of them for their positive input. Including Martin Mann, Beth Lamb, Justin Klocman, Mike Underwood, my dad, Heidi King, Jeff Hutchinson, Grant Robinson, Stephanie Kimbrell, and everyone else. Thank you

PAHL, ANTHONY
[a.] Hoppers Crossing, Australia [title] "None for Your Money" [pers.] As a Vietnam suffering from war related post traumatic stress disorder, I started writing as a therapeutic means of venting the causes and symptoms of my illness. No other than my immediate family, friends and caregivers had read my writings until I joined "Western Union

Writers in July 1999, and "Poetic Justice," an internet writing group. These groups befriended, encouraged and ultimately instilled in me, the confidence to present my works in a more public forum. For this I am truly grateful. More particularly, I thank my wife and family for their continued love and support, despite my chronic illness

PAPPAJION, DIMITRIOS
[a.] Spetses Island, Greece [title] "Aware" [pers.] I am an American Greek residing on a Greek Island. I write and am a sculptor. I was admitted into the L.A. County Fine Arts Academy because of my works—love and the humble art of understanding to make the warmest formula in producing fuel for firing the mind's eye in a natural way.

PARK, LEE
[a.] Tustin Ranch, CA [title] "I Feel So Far Behind" [pers.] This piece is not about loving another. I've all should love each other this way. I wrote this poem for my wife Jeanne, whom I sent to Heaven. She was an angel from Heaven that Jesus sent me, for a while

PARK, SUNG
[a.] Providence, RI [title] "The One" [pers.] This poem is dedicated to my wife, Elizabeth, who has reestablish my belief in true love. In happiness or despair, I will always have her by my side. In today's busy world, it takes patience and courage to keep the faith to finding "The One." I hope that others will have the strength to search for that special person in their lives

PARKER, KAREN
[a.] Acworth, GA [title] "The Divorced Daddy" [pers.] This poem is dedicated to my loving husband. My life with him has inspired me to try and make people aware of the sadness for fathers after a divorce. Writer poetry is one way I express my own feelings

PARKER, LINDA
[a.] Millbrook, AL [title] "A Student's Prayer" [pers.] This poem was written for my husband's niece, who decided to further her education and become a teacher (in her forties). She was thrilled and it is framed and banging in his classroom. Poetry has always come naturally to me and has allowed me to give to friends and family on many occasions. The biggest blessing is that the words come from my mind and heart. God gives each of us a gift to share and we should put to use and strive to improve it. It is a small way to brighter someone's day and possibly their life

PARKS, CHERYL
[a.] Chicago, IL [title] "Funny Love" [pers.] Poetry is a way to capture moments in life. Writing helps me to express my emotions and opens me up to others so they understand what is going on in my mind. I share this talent with my brother and mother while my father tells anecdotes. "Funny Love" was written while I was falling put of love. Without a dear friend. The hard part was letting go when I realized the love was gone. Love is not fun when you are in it alone, it can be that way

PARKS, EDDIE
[a.] Norwich, KS [title] "The Storm Within" [pers.] This poem was written during a time of great pain, but it is very dear to me. It symbolizes the blacks and whites," Yins and Yangs," for life. It describes both the pain, and joy of relationships

PARKS, WILLIE
[a.] College Park, GA [title] "Therapy" [pers.] To me writing poetry is a gift God wanted me to have. I've used it as a tool to communicate with people I was vocally challenged to speak to. My poem "Therapy" started as something I wanted my best friend to check out. I heard about poetry.com from my fiancee so I decided to enter it into one of their contests. He knew I might struggle with telling loved ones my feelings, so to help me show it; God Almighty brought me into this world a poet

PARRILL, SHARON
[a.] Cheyenne, WY [title] "Life" [pers.] I believe we are all a part of life's great experience. How and where we end up at the end of it all depends solely on how we make our journey through life's path. How we act and react from each experience will make us who we are. Growing spiritually, emotionally and physically will be determined by our own actions. The gift of life is a treasure to behold. We must nurture it and love it and all of those who share it with us. I believe in a good day's work. Whatever work you choose in life should be done to the best of your ability, or it is not worth doing at all. I have been married and lost two husbands and a six year old child. I have three daughters, Darla Pepper, Shelli Olson and Summer Parrill. I have one son, John Velvick who has three children. Darla has one daughter. My mother is 89 years old and has to be in a life caring center. My brother is retired and lives in California. My education is two years, business. I have some education in arts; Creative writing, drawing and oil painting. My passion is for arts, and would like to try sculpting. I have developed two businesses; a successful night club that I have operated for 25 years and a Deli, gift shop and Colorado Lottery outlet for three and one half years. We have the highest lottery sales outlet in the State of Colorado

PARRISH, CYNTHIA
[a.] Thompson, PA [title] "Echoes in the Mind" [pers.] Dedicated to my mother, Lynne and my step-father, Stanley. Who taught me that love does conquer all. To my four beautiful children, Jennifer, Marissa, Briar, and Shirlynne, who will all come to know how much I love them. To grams, who planted the seed of imagination for life. And last, but certainly not least, to Rick who always held his hand out for me when I fell in the water

PASMANIK, WOLF
[a.] New York, NY [title] "To Be Reborn" [pers.] Wolf Pasmanik is a Poet-Laureate and a former distinguished professor of Yiddish and Eastern European Literature at Rutgers University. He has been a guest on several television and radio programs, including Johnny Carson, Joe Franklin, Jerry Lewis, and Dick Rufman. He is also the founder of the American Holocaust Committee to erect a monument in memory of the six million Jews who perished during the holocaust

PATERSON, TANYA
[a.] Tunica, LA [title] "Interior" [pers.] I want to thank my Heavenly Father, without whom I would not have written this or possess my talent. He has blessed me. This was written at a time when God was calling and drawing me to him. Special thanks to my sisters in Christ—Cindy, Barbara, and Linda; whose unconditional love, quiet honesty, and ceaseless encouragement are a living testimony to me. I pray this poem will show others, even at the blackest periods of life God gives us hope and strength. Only his love picks up and gives us courage to continue when we think we can't

PATIBANDLA, MURALI
[a.] Fredericksberg C, Denmark [title] "I Am a Child" [pers.] I dedicate this poem to my mother, Indira Devi. I was born in a small village in the south of India three months after my father died. My mother brought my elder brother and up through hardships. This poem is an expression of my love for her. At present, I am associate professor of economics at the Copenhagen Business School. I am married to Aruna with two lovely daughters, Pratyesha (eight) and Nikhita (five).

PATRICK, WILLIAM
[a.] Shepherdsville, KY [title] "And Then I See the Truth" [pers.] Poetry to me is the reflection of my emotions. This poem shows how I truly feel about life and people in general. The world we live in

today, where people try so hard to fit in. They will think, talk and act like the populous just to be accepted. This poem holds special meaning for me because it reflects all the people in my life. Not all of them were liars, but to those who get humor out of others pain and suffering the joke is on you

PATRIDGE, DREW
[a.] Toledo, OH [title] "The Fantasist Dream" [pers.] "The Fantasist Dream" is a poem that describes a hobby. It describes my second, favorite hobby, Epic Fantasy. Epic Fantasy is at the core of my being. I read it, I write it, and I dream it. Eventually I would like to take this part of myself and add the part of myself that enjoys computers to it. Using that combination I would like to develop RPG's. My ultimate goal is to become a rival to Squaresoft, Sony, and Nintendo. I would also like to extend out to other kinds of software in order to rival Microsoft itself

PAUL, PATSY
[a.] Winston-Salem, NC [title] "Shadows" [pers.] In this poem, each new day is like a seed planted yesterday that flowers according to the nurture we give it. For me, poetry is my soul singing a picture with words. It is my hope that others who read my words can find a lost memory, dream a new dream, feel the essence of life, and taste the newness of each tomorrow

PAUL, RODNEY
[a.] Statesboro, GA [title] "Life is Wonderful (How Wonderful is Life" [pers.] I must simply thank my parents for everything that I am. I would also like to thank all of my family members for encouragement. I would also like to say that I am very proud to be Jamaican recognizing that my eleven years on my island shaped who I am becoming. I must let if be known that I am deeply in love with writing if did not translate my thoughts into words on paper, my soul would shatter and the pieces in the pieces of falling would destroy my insides

PAULIN, CHRISTOPHER
[a.] Massapequa, NY [title] "Enchanted Horizon" [pers.] The poetry that I write consists of my life's past experiences, and future endeavors that I plan to explore some day. "Enchanted Horizon" was inspired by my strong belief that a person should have self pride and love who they are, and who they have become throughout their life. This poem is one of hope and new beginnings. I love you Anna Leigh, Jen, mom, dad, Barbara, Mark and all my friends. Most important I thank God for this precious gift of life, you have so generously given to me. A life filled with love, my life divine. Thank you

PAYNE, MARINA
[a.] Myrtle Creek, OR [title] "Haiku 4" [pers.] In this poem, I reflect on myself, my heritage, and who I am to others. Poetry is very important to me, aside my Japanese Liniage in this Medium. I can combine these aspects. As an artist, I try to identify with my media. Very little do I write when I am not stressed. This is one of the few poems where I was calm. Other than my poetry, I work in pencil, many paints, clay, and charcoal. Art has always been important to me, and since I was young, I have known who I was: an artist with a soft spot for animals, especially cats. I am steadily working at improving, realistic portraits of animals and a wildlife

PAYNE, SHELOHAM
[a.] Framingham, MA [title] "America" [pers.] I thank God for all that he has blessed me with, including the gift of writing poetry. I also thank my family for all of their support and for giving me such a good, strong foundation. I enjoy writing poems and short stories that hopefully inspire people

PEARSON, SARAH
[a.] Paducah, KY [title] "Love Is" [pers.] Everyone in some point of their life has experienced love and affection. My poem expresses some of the many "little" things that people do to express how much they care. Throughout my childhood I was surrounded with love. My parents, and grandparents (Mammy and Pop) show their love to me in every waking moment of my life. (I love you all!) I enjoy writing about love because it is something that anyone can relate too. It is a part of everyone's life whether it be through family or a special someone, and that to me is truly inspiring

PECK, ROBERT
[a.] Auckland, New Zealand [title] "Mr" [pers.] I left USA as a child to live in New Zealand and have used poetry, throughout my life to express my beliefs, emotions and observations. This poem is one of regret, written after the loss of my mother, dealing with my perception of a much loved brother

PELOTE, ARTELELIA
[a.] Honolulu, HI [title] "Life" [pers.] This poem was written during a very trying time in my life in 1992. The turmoil I experienced at that time inspired this poem, though untitled at the time, and it helped me get back on track and to see the "Big Picture." "Life" means a lot to me. It is uplifting and positive and it gives you a new perspective on your life. My prayer for anyone reading this poem is that they too can find the courage and strength to rise up from their abyss and into a world full of love and life

PEMBERTON, SHAWN
[a.] Cape Girardeau, MO [title] "A Song for You" [pers.] I, as many before me, have seen a dream become reality by having my words recognized in publication. I believe that what I write is an expression of my heart, my soul, and my spirit. I believe that writing songs and poetry allows me to preserve the emotion of a moment and I have found wisdom through reflection. For my beautiful wife, Angie, you helped me find the words and your love gave me the freedom of expression. When I found you, I found myself

PENDLETON, LORI
[a.] Astoria, NY [title] "Codependence" [pers.] I've kept everything I've ever written most of it embarrassingly bad so I can mark my progress, not just as a writer, but a human being. My outlook and my work have become more realistic, skeptical, but still somewhat hopeful. Where I once wrote happy endings, lovelorn odes, and not so subtle symbolism, I now prefer to write harsh ambiguous pieces whose weight comes from experiences real or imagined. I try to keep intact all the complex emotions that go with these experiences and hope that it resonates with readers much as life does uncertain, with no simple answers

PERCIVAL, JANIS
[a.] Miami, FL [title] "Thinking of You" [pers.] I wrote his poem at the age of 16 for my first love. Now, three year later even though we are no longer together, I still repeat the actions day after day. I have written over 400 poems in the last four years and this one touches me the most

PEREZ, ALBERT
[a.] Corpus Christi, TX [title] "The Loss of an Angel" [pers.] This poem was written about a girl who means the world to me: my ex-girlfriend. I'm 16 years old and attend W.B. Ray High School in Corpus Christi, TX. I would like to mention my parents: Albert and Rosie Perez. My grandparents Elena Perez and Victoria Castellanos and the rest of my family. My Pastor: Msgr. Lawrence White and my life teen director Gilbert Juarez. I would also like to mention the people of Sts. Cyril and methodius Catholic Church. The main person I want to thank is God for blessing me with all these people that are in my life

PEREZ, DAVID
[a.] Springfield, OR [title] "Salvation" [pers.] I was born in 1975, at Mercy Hospital in San Diego, CA. My interest include hackey-sack, scuba diving, and reading. It wasn't until the age of 17 that I discovered my yearning for writing poetry. I found it to be a wonderfully freeing form of self-expression. Encouraged by family and friends I plan to attend College and pursue writing. I give dedication of this poem to my sister, Marie, who, believing in me, made my first publication possible. I would also like to give my thanks and appreciation to my family who has supported me over many exhausting years

PEREZ, RACHEL A.
[a.] Fremont, CA [title] "Blooming" [pers.] Poetry comes within the soul. Feelings immerse and poetry is written. A teacher has guided me on the right path, for she was "the teacher." Blooming is a poem I wrote for the great empathy I have for others that surround me. I feel everything. Life is not easy for me or even the soul next to me, but I have a story, stories that are meaningful. Influences in my life have shaped me to be who I am. I am strong and I am weak. My mom and dad are number one, and they would understand

PEREZ, RITA
[a.] Keene, TX [title] "I Love You Mom" [pers.] I chose to write a poem about my mom because she is a strong figure head in my life. She has always been there to support me. I hate to see her go through pain and that is why I can't wait to go to Heaven where there will be no pain

PERLA, JENNIFER
[a.] Newark, NJ [title] "Give Me Light" [pers.] I would like to thank my mom and dad, my grandmother and my cousins Cindy, Hilda, Tristan, Milton, Ivan, Lisette, Juan, Jerry, David, Annayansi, Oscar, my aunts Yesenia, Patricia, Vicky, Annayansi, my uncles Milton, Gian Carlo, my brother and sister for everything they have done for me. I would also like to dedicate this poem to the Class of 2001 my friends Julyana, Stephanie, Alexis, James, Richard, Simon, Jonathan, Anthony, Frank, Miguel, Bonn, my principal Mr. Clare, my teachers Ms. Pagano, Mrs. Stefhanelli, Mrs. De Stefbano, Ms. Leconte, Mr. Luke, and Mr. Romano. To my school Saint Francis Xavier, and Kitty

PESSOA, ISHMAEL
[a.] Gruver, TX [title] "A Love That Cannot be Known" [pers.] I have God to thank for this poem, because although I was inspired by a few actions that took place in my life at the time, it was He who put the words in my mind. I was extremely glad of being able to put the words in my mind. I was extremely glad of being able to put my feelings down on a piece of paper to remember the reason for its existence. A poem is an excellent way to tell everyone and no one of your thoughts and feelings; I hope that someone may be able to relate to "A love that cannot be known."

PETEL, RYAN
[a.] Cantonment, FL [title] "The Mistake of Psyche" [pers.] Classical Mythology has captivated me since childhood. I was fascinated by the stories and poems, recounting feats of great heroism and grim tragedy. I would like to thank Dr. Charles Schuler for rekindling my passion for mythology, and for introducing me to "Cupid and Psyche," the story that inspired this piece. This poem is dedicated to my family, friends, those at the museum, and to my loved ones that are no longer with me. They are my inspiration and the true authors of my poetry. All I do is put it on paper

PETERS, BENJAMIN
[a.] Andover, MN [title] "A Cloud or a Dream" [pers.] My poem was inspired by a trip I took to Florida with my parents, Jeraldine and Donald. I attribute this poem to my parents, because my parents have given

me everything. They gave me life, love, happiness, and now success. Thanks mom and dad, I love you

PETERSON, FELICIA
[a.] Naples, FL [title] "Life Without A Father" [pers.] This poem means a lot to me because it's not only true. But it comes straight from my heart. It tells a little of about my past and a little about what's happening now. "It is also jammed pack with my feelings. I am thirteen now. I like people to understand what has happened to me. I have better poetry about more that has happened to me. Thank you for letting me reach this goal. The Backstreet Boys inspired me to write poetry. I thank every one in having faith in me

PETRILLO, NICOLE
[a.] Farmington Hills, MI [title] "Helpless" [pers.] Poetry, this art is not just created by our hands or our thoughts, but with our hearts. It is formed by honest souls. We are the pieces, the pieces of a puzzle this book and many others of its kind. The pen is to us as a sword is to a noble knight. To some this creation is easy, but to others it is most difficult both the struggle with words and the fight with running emotions. Let us write 17 lines have been omitted to meet the requirements for the contest. If the omitted lines could be added to the published work it would be appreciated. Begin after "when you stand before me."

PETROSKI, SUSAN
[a.] Humble, TX [title] "The Miracle" [pers.] The inspiration for my love of writing poetry comes from my love for Jesus and his teachings. It is my desire to convey the love and compassion that he has bestowed on my life to others. I have also realized that my poetry reflects the direction in which my life is being guided. My hope for the reader is to see themselves in my writing as they come to know Jesus more and more

PETTIBONE, JESSICA
[a.] Mansfield, MO [title] "Christmas" [pers.] This is a wonderful opportunity for me to have one of my poems published in a book. I have written only a few poems within a years time. Now that I am about to turn fourteen, I decided to write about the special things that has happened in my life. My family has always encouraged me to try my best at whatever I choose to do. My sisters, April, Vicki, and Sarah, has always loved to read and it is a dream come true to have them read something from a book that was written by me

PEYATT, JAMIE
[a.] Asheville, NC [title] "Together" [pers.] This poem was written for my husband. He was sentenced to prison for four 1/2 years on an armed robbery case. He is 18 and was in the wrong place at the wrong time. This was written to reassure him that I plan to wait for him. I love you!

PFLEGER, JOHNATHON
[a.] Oceanport, NJ [title] "Not Even Alive" [pers.] This poem is my best one yet. I feel that in a world of politicians. It is very hard for a 16 year old the express his or her views on issues like abortion. That's why poetry means so much to me, I know that through poetry I tell the world exactly now I feel

PHARR, LEESA
[a.] Dothan, AL [title] "The River Wind Butterfly" [pers.] This poem is special to me because it is the only one I have ever written about myself. Life is about understanding yourself every day. I believe that we are all individuals that can teach and learn from each others strengths. May you find peace in each moment, passion in your relationships and positivity in every day of your life

PHONGSAVAN, VITHAYA
[a.] Springfield, VA [title] "Silhouette of My Desire" [pers.] I am a dreamer. My hope is that

through writing I may encourage, inspire, and comfort people. This poem seeks to identify with a person's longing in finding true love. It's important to know what's essential in looking for a mate and to develop yourself to be the right person. In due time, your desire will be filled, as you wait in God's perfect timing. Providence is moving. May you learn to love yourself and use your singleness to grow and serve people. Be content and trust that love will find a way to you. Believe it

PICKETT, SARA
[a.] Indianapolis, IN [title] "Guardian Angel" [pers.] My poem holds special meaning for me. I hope that others who have lost a loving and wonderful mother can also relate to my heartfelt emotion in the creation of this poem. For it was my guardian angel that helped to shape and mold me into all that I am today and all that I will be in the future. I am daughter, wife, mother, friend, songwriter and poet. Now my guardian angel watches over me till the end of my days

PIERCE, MARGARET W.
[a.] Greenville, AL [title] "Innocence" [pers.] My mission in life is to "live, love, learn and leave a legacy." My poetry covers the gamut of my mission and is part of the legacy I hope to leave to my children an grandchildren. Writing poetry gives me wide latitude for expressing my thoughts on the many facets of "Living, loving and learning" and provides an avenue for uniquely sharing the experiences of my life. It also brings great relief from the stress of my work in the corporate/political arena. My love of nature and the rich experiences of my life provide inspiration for my writing

PIGG, ADAM
[a.] Wasilla, AK [title] "Life" [pers.] If it's dark and gloomy, or it feels that way inside, then poetry can make you feel so much better. I am currently in high school, and when I am bored (in school) I like to write. Poetry, and writing allow for escape, which is why both mean so much to me. One day I hope to live the "American Dream" and write a novel. I have no idea what it should be about, or where it should go; inspiration, is everywhere, however, and I will find my way

PINA, JOSE G.
[a.] Greenfield, CA [title] "Roses Are Red" [pers.] This poem is dedicated to Diane Garcia, the woman, responsible for these thoughts, and specially dedicated to my father Agapito Garnica, who was hospitalized shortly after writing this poem. "I dedicate this poem and all of my successes to you dad. I pray to the good Lord that you get well enough to come home soon, so that we can spend some quality time together. Of all the mistakes I have made in my life, not spending time with you is the one that I regret the most." "I Love You Dad."

PINE, THOMAS
[a.] Colonia, NJ [title] "Night Flight" [pers.] "For me, poetry is by far the purest distillation of speech and the written word. A poem's economy of words elicits thoughts that spring from our emotional core, unencumbered by the weight of prose. The profundity of ideas, distilled to a mere few lines of verse, never fails to blow me away. No writer should shirk the discipline of creating poetry, for it improves any writing style. I'm honored to have my humble work chosen for publication. Though I consider myself a writer or prose, I know I am, and will be, a better writer for having written poetry."

PINEL, RICHARD
[a.] Fall River, MA [title] "Through this Rain" [pers.] Writing for me is an outlet for my emotions. Words I would have trouble saying flow freely with a pen in my hand. A very special person had reopened my eyes to this wonderful world that I had lost for awhile. For this I am truly grateful. She holds a special place in my heart, always

PITCHER, EDWARD
[a.] San Bruno, CA [title] "Awareness" [pers.] It seemed to me the wealthy had become so greedy and selfish. They like power! But, fear losing it! I thought maybe some have already lost it. I sometimes think the poor are richer than the wealthy

PITTS, BRANDON
[a.] Portsmouth, VA [title] "Passionate Kisses" [pers.] I would first like to thank God for blessing me with a talent to express my inner most feelings. Secondly, I would like to thank my mother, Joycelyn Pitts, for being a strong inspiration and back bone for my emotional and spiritual growth. Last butnot least, I would like to dedicate all my poetry to my little brother, Drew Pitts, for being there for me when all others weren't. Don't always look for the prize, focus on the lives you've helped along the way!"

PLACKY, JESSE
[a.] Crested Butte, CO [title] "Looking In" [pers.] This poem was written in one of those "Lost" times for me. The world we live in has a lot of illusions and the truth can be very hidden. It is easy to get "caught up" in the illusions, but as a writer/poet, I try to persevere and find the truth. It's not an as easy road, but it's the only one I know. If you've ever felt as I hang when I wrote this poem, I hope you realize you're not alone. I only wish my poem helped you see that space we all can reach, we just need to look within

PLAUTZ, BRIAN
[a.] Waterford, MI [title] "Mine Heart" [pers.] This poem was written for Canay. Someone so special, she brought these words out of "Mine Heart." To her, I say thank you. For her, my eternal love

PLEASANTS, PAMELA
[a.] Charleston, WV [title] "The Messenger" [pers.] Death of a loved one is devastating. God will send messages that help us through the hard times, and to let us know after the dark there is a light. I thank God for the 16 years he gave me with my daughter, Jennifer, and for her accomplishments in life. She truly left a mark in this world and I believe she will be standing in the light to greet me. This poem is dedicated in the memory of my daughter Jennifer Pleasants (1979–1995)

PLETICHA, ANDREA
[a.] Mesa, AZ [title] "The Promise" [pers.] This poem was conceived shortly after my boyfriend and best friend of six 1/2 years proposed to me. "The Promise" is my feeble attempt to communicate the way I feel about him and our future together. I believe the poem begins to capture the essence of our relationship, but words alone cannot express the nature of our bond. I must thank my fiance for the inspirations to write this testimony, and I would also like to recognize my family members for their support in this and all other endeavors

PONCEK, KATRINA
[a.] Chelsea, WI [title] "Depression and Disappointment" [pers.] Although I am only seventeen, poems have become important to me. They allow me to express myself and share my feelings. This poem is especially important to me because it explains in a unique way how I feel empty inside

POND, JUDITH
[a.] Mt. Vernon, NY [title] "Peace" [pers.] Writing has always been very important in my life. One of my childhood dreams was to become a published author. I remember the stories that I wrote in second grade and how much pleasure I got from writing those stories and being able to express myself in such a special way. I also remember the first poem I wrote at age nine. It was about life and opportunities. At the time, though, I never dreamed that five years later, I'd be a published poet! I only hope this is just the first step towards becoming a prolific writer!

POOLE, SIRINA
[a.] El Paso, TX [title] "Today" [pers.] This poem "Today" was written about my life. After spending the last year trying to understand trials, illness, and death I do not have all the answers, but I do have peace. There are things in life that can not always be explained or controlled. Instead of turning and facing fear we seek people, places and things only to find they are not the answer. After finding that these things or people were not the answer I turned to Jesus. I listened to the voice of my heart and found peace, I wish the same for you

POPE, JOHN
[a.] Odenton, MD [title] "A Rose I Found" [pers.] This poem is for my very special girl, India. I love you!

POPE, SARAH
[a.] Westminster, MA [title] "Fallen Angels" [pers.] Poetry has had a large impact on my life. Without it I wouldn't have made it through alot of life's obstacles. To me, poetry is a healer of all souls. I started writing poetry last year, when I was only twelve years old. But this very well may be the most meaningful poem I have ever written

PORT, JAKE
[a.] Brier, WA [title] "Think" [pers.] When I wrote "Think," I was in a state, of realization, I found that people give up on their dreams very early in life when we all they need is a little help. Patience is a great virtue. Most dreams will fulfill themselves in time, but some need a push or greater support. Either way, with patience, your dreams will come alive

PORTER, JENNIFER
[a.] Kalamazoo, MI [title] "Red" [pers.] Hatred and Racism are very much like a private. They are slowly out a nation, handing out nothing got death and grief. Nobody wins! The sad thing is it's many times handed down from one generation to the next, something learned not chosen. Everyone experience its affects but when will we learn from it. It physically hurts for me to see it. I don't want to become numb to death. I don't want to persecute what is right and tolerate what's wrong. Life is a gift all deserve to live

POWERS, PATRICK
[a.] Webster City, IA [title] "It's 2000" [pers.] The year 2000 to me is an exciting time. It means hope, change and a positive attitude for everyone. For me I was fortunate to kick off 2000 by being in Times Square in New York City to watch the arrival of this new century, this poem is dedicated to my family, my co-workers at KQWC radio and friends

PRENDERGAST, LAUREN
[a.] Phoenix, AZ [title] "Cupid's Arrow" [pers.] This poem just shot into my mind one day and I wrote it down. I would like to thank my mom and dad for being supportive of my poetry writing as well as my language arts teacher, Debbie Dubin. This poem has to do with loving yourself . . . a very important aspect of life

PRESCOTT, MARION
[a.] Fairfield, CT [title] "For My Daughter" [pers.] My poem was written to express my pride in my daughter when the agency she directs dealing with victims of domestic violence received an award recognizing their achievements. I am eighty-five years old; have been writing poetry only since last summer for family members and others who have touched my life. I find it a unique way to express my deepest feelings. My family consists of a son and daughter, both married, five grandchildren and two great grandchildren, aged three years and seven months. Writing poetry has added a new dimension to my life

PRESNELL, COLEMAN
[a.] Jayess, MS [title] "Winter Solstice" [pers.] My poetry is not so true as it is clever, not so new as

it is reborn, my paper absorbs all emotion true or false with equal zeal, so you can read of this loneliness even if I never felt it. I hope that this glimpse into my loneliness can help you overpower your own. I wrote this poem because loneliness is best when viewed objectively I believe that God doesn't want us to be lonely. God doesn't ever leave me all alone; in the fourth line of "Winter Solstice," I plainly state that I am never alone. If loneliness is your life's recurring theme, you should look to the God of Heaven and Earth for the eternal cure

PREVOST, TYLER
[a.] Northbay, ON [title] "Nightshade's Promise" [pers.] Tyler Prevost was born on April 20, 1986 in North Bay, ON. While in elementary school he placed second in a provincial speaking contest. Attending Windfield High School in 2000. Tyler has been asked to compose a poem for his cousins wedding this summer which will be titled "Empress" Tyler's favorite hobbies are reading, writing and the outdoors. His dream is to become a world reknowned chef. Tyler's favorite author is Stephen King

PREWITT, MARLYN
[a.] Indianapolis, IN [title] "A Love Lost" [pers.] "A Love Lost" is but one of many beautiful poems that I have written, yet it ranks highest to me personally, as it pertains to the death of my only biological child, Stephen Eugene Prewitt, June 10, 1991. Writing has been an emotional outlet for me since childhood, and at times, overwhelms me right out of the blue. Scribbling on toilet paper or whatever is nearest. Feeling like a pressure cooker, with a need to release trapped steam. Read it with heart and I know that you will enjoy it as much as I do! "God is my pilot!"

PRICHARD, ROBERT
[a.] Taylorsville, UT [title] "The Mist" [pers.] Being a writer and an artist, I felt compelled to share a thought of calm reflection. For nothing moves me more than the serenity and peacefulness of a small slice of God's quieter moments. I hope "The Mist" takes you to a place like this

PRYOR, BRENDA
[a.] Grandview, MO [title] "Love Longer" [pers.] I have been writing poetry since I was a little girl. My family and friends have been huge inspirations in my life. With their love and encouragement I have been able to achieve so many of my goals. I thank them all and God for all the love and blessings I have in my life every day. They are my strength, and have helped me become the person I am today. If everyone in the love that has been given to me, everyone would be truly blessed. I hope someday that will happen

PUTZ, LINDA
[a.] Cambridge, MN [title] "The Man I Feel Within" [pers.] The person who inspired me to write my poem is my best friend in life (my husband) He was there for support and strength when I was not so strong. I hope someone else will get the enjoyment out of reading my poem as I have when writing it

PYMN, JULIE
[a.] Lyndhurst, OH [title] "Leaving a Legacy" [pers.] This poem was written for my dad. It has been posted on a big yellow presentation board, which will, one day, be shown at his funeral service. He is alive and well today. I want to share with the world the legacy he left to his children, and what more could a father give than to teach his children how to live. He knows all about this poem that I wrote to commemorate him, but he chooses not to read it. He said to surprise Him with it, and that's exactly what I'm going to do

QIN, XIAOMING
[a.] Flushing, NY [title] "Someday You Will Tell Your Children About a Woman" [pers.] I wrote this poem as an English class assignment in high school. My teacher, Theresa Young. Gave me

the title and I developed it from there. Miss Young brought out my talent in poetry writing. She suggested I pursue a degree in English, and although I am going to complete my degree in Accounting this June. I have not forgotten her suggestion. I would like to use this opportunity to thank Miss Young for her encouragement. She was the best teacher I ever hade. I would also like to thank my mother for inspiration and unconditional support all these years

QUINN, RACHEL
[a.] Woodstock, IL [title] "The Earth Talked To Me" [pers.] I feet that Artistic expression is such a powerful tool to communicate with. It reaches people on all levels. Poetry is so beautiful and this honor of publication has meant to me that one unique moment of my time has been immortalized for all to share. I hope the inner voice I listened to while writing "The Earth Talked to Me" will inspire people to feel and live their own truth. There is so much beauty in words. Poetry is a trail of wisdom, history, and a timeless expression for all to take part in

RADER, NANCY
[a.] Niles, MI [title] "Funny Little Poem" [pers.] Poetry has always been a love of mine, but I had never tried to write poetry until now. I have just recently lost my Dad, Kenneth V. Eager Sr. to Huntington's Chorea, and I was also feeling lonely and blue over losing some very special friends, I cared a lot about, to other women. Even though at the time I wrote this poem, I wasn't crying, my heart inside of me was hurting and crying, over the loss of my Dad and the painful hurt of being rejected. Yes, I was feeling very empty, lonely, and blue. Even though this poem is very short, it helped me to feel a little better, as I was able to express my feelings in writing. It was my way of saying to the ones I have loved, but lost, that I miss them and that I love them!

RAGAN, KAREN
[a.] Pell City, AL [title] "Work of Grace" [pers.] My faith in God and his son, Jesus Christ, is the center of my life. Poetry is pure inspiration flowing from the author's heart. The grace and mercy of God working in my life sparks my inspiration and colors my verse. The art of writing beautiful poetry, that makes the reader dream is a gift. I thank God for my gift inspired by that Eternal Book, The Bible, which is filled with some of the greatest poetic praise ever written. "Work of Grace" seeks to paint a word picture of God's beautiful love and bring Heavenly places into Earthly hearts

RAGEN, BEN
[a.] Upper Saddle River, NJ [title] "The Sky, My Family" [pers.] Since I've only lived a little while, 14 years, I haven't experienced much, but with my two older siblings my interests have developed quickly. My older sister was the real one who interested me in poetry, she has won several awards for her poetry and she somewhat passed her talent down to me this poem is about my family. My mother has named each of her children after the three bright objects in sky. My sister named after the moon, my brother after the sun, and me after the star. Child really reflects the celestial body they are named after

RAHIER, BRENDA
[a.] Kelso, WA [title] "Will You" [pers.] Poetry, songwriting, and singing has been a deep passion of mine, since I was a little girl. I am so excited to have the chance to share my poetry with the world. Poem "Will You" was written from my heart, as all my poems are, it was written for my husband, Timmy Joe to show him how much I love and care for him. I would like to say thanks to all my family and friend for their

support and interest in my writing, but above all, I thank God for the talent He has given me

RAIA, JOHN
[a.] Richmond, VA [title] "The Days Will Pass" [pers.] The days will pass . . . this I know

RALSTON, BRENDA
[a.] Welland, ON [title] "Shapes of Feelings" [pers.] This poem was written while contemplating life as a memory landscape, tomorrow is but an illusion today's realities are tomorrows memories. In the evening of each day I love to sit and listen to the of each day I love to sit and listen to the quietness time is so fleeting, so precious and fragile. Poetry is a way to paint a mental portrait. With words. I've learned that life itself very precious time is often lost fretting about tomorrow, yet this moment is all we have, and it is a gift to be savored and experienced, whatever the joy or sorrow it brings. Poetry allows me to embrace my emotions, my thought, my very self, it is a release and it is medicine it will be here when I am gone

RAMIREZ, MAURICIO
[a.] Camp Pendleton, CA [title] "For the First Time" [pers.] This poem was inspired by the longing of a loved one in my life. Poetry is a means for me to speak indirectly to the people in my life. I thank God for the talent he has given me with my artistry and my poems and many other things. I'm originally from Soledad, CA. I'm currently in the marine corps and my best works is yet to come. I invite you to discover my poetry and my artwork, for it will mesmerize the mind and soul

RAMIREZ, PAMELA
[a.] Los Angeles, CA [title] "Childlren of Darkness" [pers.] I'm a senior at Franklin High and a volunteer. T.A. at Yorkdale Elementary. I believe poetry is the ability to express intense underlying feelings in a lyrical way. I consider this to be my best work. The darkness symbolizes the fear of death and the vampires symbolize the desire for immortality. I would like to thank my friends (especially Nancy Frausto, Marisol Castillo, Jennifer Duenas, Stephanie Ladner, and Vanessa Valle), my mother Martha Cardenas, my mentors, and my loving boyfriend Carlos Rangel for their undying support. In closing, my advice is: don't sweat the minor details; think, do, act, conquer

RAMOS, GLADYS
[a.] Bronx, NY [title] "Thinking" [pers.] This poem represents the veritable essence of my innermost sensitivities. I appreciate the love, support and encouragement of my fiancee Levi and my children Maegan, Lizette, Brandon, Linette, Sara and Alex, as well as, my sister Sarah for always believing in me. Having my poem in print will further encourage me to continue my writing and believe in myself. They say that writing is a "Gift" so I thank my parents Sara and Rafael for giving me that gift. Growing up in the Bronx, with its medley of culture and diversity, has also enriched my passion for writing

RANDALL, MARIE
[a.] Bethel, AK [title] "Drumbeat of Love" [pers.] As an Alaskan Native, Traditionally and culturally my way of life surrounds the drum. Listening to the drum, learning to native dance by my mother Theresa Demientieff and grandma Miska Savage. My parents are Alfred and Theresa Demientieff of Holy Cross. Mom died in March, 1992, Dad died in September, 1995. Their spirit of love, Tradition and culture continues to guide me through the Drum. I had seven brothers and, three sisters. Robert, Freda, Phillip, Floyd, David, Alvin, Margie, Peter, Alfred and Mary Ann, died April 1, 1999. Their spirit of love, unity and fellowship lives on through the Drum. Now I have six brothers, two sisters and thank God for their love daily. My husband, James Randall, is from Minnesota. We lived in the village of Holy Cross and have five wonderful children: Regina, James (Jr.), Rebecca, Joshua and Rachel. The Drum is the heart beat of my family. It beats of a treasured time, of precious memories, of the true native spirit

RANDOLPH, DEB
[a.] Nashville, TN [title] "Silent Compassion" [pers.] Since childhood, I have found poetry to be a most natural and meaningful method of expression. Poetry can express the deepest emotion, provoke thought, bring serenity, and help others know they're not alone. A single poem can bring a different message to each reader. This is the beauty of this form of writing. To have the opportunity to share a piece of myself with others through my poetry is a dream come true

RANNEY, NATE
[a.] Whitewater, WI [title] "Lonely Sorrow" [pers.] I feel poetry is a beautiful art form. It can express many variety of emotions and tapestry. I try to enthrall my audiences with vivid paintings of inspiration, I usually put all of my emotions into my poetry. I do it for enjoyment and also to express my innermost feelings. Poetry is one way for me to immortalize my past

RANVILLE, JESSICA
[a.] Quebec, QC [title] "One of Many Muses" [pers.] I am thirteen years old and attend Quebec High School. I have always enjoyed writing and am thrilled at my first opportunity to be published. The poem I wrote talks about how the world is turning out and how there's no choice but to pass it on to the next generation. I'm pleased that this thought can be shared through this anthology. Here's hoping that this is the starting point for a writing career

RATHBURN, VICKTORIA
[a.] Columbus, OH [title] "My Baby Girl" [pers.] Eleven years ago I was overwhelmed with grief when my daughter died from anencephaly. Unable to hear even the slightest whimper or breath when she was born, I found solace in writing my emotions. With the help of my husband Michael and our new unborn baby I was prompted to share this sad yet wonderful experience with the world. "Taylor, may you soar with the Angels, my baby girl."

RE, ANNE
[a.] Westfield, NJ [title] "My Pride" [pers.] I was born July, 18 1990. Year 2000 in 3rd grade. Daughter of Chris and Rick, with two children Fran and Kate. My poem means (music) everything has a rhythm; (art) designing is a big part of life; (pride of world) it's my home, I believe in it; (love is beauty) love is rare and delicate, which makes it precious and beautiful. That's what my poem means

RECORD, MICHELLE
[a.] Dallas, TX [title] "Who Are We to Judge?" [pers.] This particular poem to me is just a statement to others in life. Meaning that no one can truly judge anyone in life and to just basically consider other's feelings, and try not to be so judgmental, because when you spare one's feelings or emotions, you spare yet another broken heart

REED, CINDY
[a.] Verona, WI [title] "Compassion" [pers.] I have been a child and teen, student, wife, mom and mom of teens, in all of this life has been full of moments. We live them and hopefully they do not pass us by. I want my readers to feel moments in life are amazing, and feel the emotions! "Compassion" is a heart's cry to others to see people they meet with openness, in a desire to inspire hope. One question always remain for me: when, can I write some more?

REED, GLENDA
[a.] Versailles, KY [title] "My Daddy" [pers.] He called me Glenda Bear when I was born. My daddy was the bright light in my life, and everyone he knew. When he went to Heaven he left me behind and I began to wonder where my path would lead without him. I have survived but it was hard. I wrote this in his precious memory. His light will never go out in my life, his love was so dear to me. His loving daughter

REED, LARRY
[a.] Houston, TX [title] "Russian Romance" [pers.] Poetry, the gift of expression, is the means for the hopeless romantic to share his heart with beauty that lifts his spirit, and his hope for tomorrow. Russian Romance is one of a larger collection of unpublished poems of romance inspired by beautiful women from around the world. The shrinking world of the new millennium brings romance without barriers, and new truthfulness to the age old cliche, "I've searched the world over for you."

REESE, SARAH
[a.] Pace, FL [title] "Poverty" [pers.] To me, an 8th grade student at Sims Middle School in Pace, FL, poetry defines ones personality. The story behind my poem "Poverty" is nothing more than sadness witnessing two children live like animal. This is what inspired me. It was rather sad to see the environment the young children lived in. Poetry is a way of showing my feeling towards someone or something. I enjoy reading and writing poetry. I hope that you all enjoy reading my poem

REEVES, KIMBERLY
[a.] Minden, LA [title] "Wanting You" [pers.] I live in Minden, LA with my husband, Jimmy and our three children, Mary, J.J. and Catie. My passions have always been writing and painting. They all have come from what is in my heart, and my thoughts of the realities in life. You have to find ways to express yourself. Not only does it help you, but it can touch the hearts of others who might be feeling the way you are. It shows that you're not alone

RENALL, BROWYN
[a.] Auckland, New Zealand [title] "A Lonely Shell" [pers.] I wrote this poem when I was going through a particularly rough period in my teens. Poetry was the only medium through which I could tell my family what I was feeling and it managed to bring us close together. Everyone has an angel in their own hearts. Yes it has some of our deepest fears, but it also holds all our dreams and hopes

RENEAU, REBECCA
[a.] Dandridge, TN [title] "You Are the Greatest" [pers.] This poem is very special to me. I gave it to my mother for Valentine's Day a couple of years ago and she loved it. I got my talent for poetry from her and I am lucky to have it. I just hope everyone that has a wonderful mother like mine can relate to it

REQUENA, JUAN, JR.
[a.] Lemoyne, PA [title] "Should it Really Matter" [pers.] I dedicate my first time ever poetry publication, to my family and friends. Those who had a profound impact in my life, and have given me the inspiration to write and the encouragement to submit my works for publication. A special thanks to the two most inspirational people in my life, my love Lorie and my God, Jesus

REYNOLDS, DANA
[a.] Columbus, GA [title] "Mother, I Thank You For:" [pers.] I watched my mother suffer physical and emotional abuse to finally find the courage to divorce and raise five children alone, without us ever realizing we were poor. When I was eighteen, my four month old daughter, Brittany was murdered while in the care of a sister. Throughout my life, my mother has always told me that "God takes the strong ones" and with those words I'm able to swallow the knot in my throat and move forward. Thanks Mom for a life time of kind words and kisses

REYNOLDS, MICHAEL, JR.
[a.] Spokane, WA [title] "My Little World" [pers.] I wrote this poem on the day my daughter was born. I was so inspired by the 1st moments of her life that "My Little World" was the result. My wife and my children have been the inspiration for almost all of my poetry since they came into my life. My fathers mother was a published poet, a fact which I was unaware of until my 20's. I've been a poet since my teen years, always hoping to be published. I hope everyone enjoys this gift of poetry that I've given to my sweet little girl Mikayla

RICE, ARMANDA
[a.] Gary, IN [title] "Love Is" [pers.] Since the age of twelve I have been expressing myself through poetry. At age twenty-one, I have more experience to add to the poetic delirium that burns inside me. This fire is fueled by my beliefs and aspirations. For me, writing is a way to "Scream" at the world and not have it scream back. I have God and my family to thank for this positive form of communicating. Hopefully I can give others the motivation to vent when necessary. My poetry is life without the sugar coating. It's beautiful, raw, and honest

RICHARDS, BRIDGET
[a.] Columbia, MD [title] "What Hurts" [pers.] This poem was something I wrote during a time where I felt alone, but my friends and family helped me realize that I'm not. I've learned a lot from writing poetry, it gives me the chance to express myself in a good manner

RICHARDSON, KEITH
[a.] Saskatoon, SK [title] "Idle Thoughts" [pers.] Poetry for me has always been a way to release negative thoughts. I'm Bipolar so it seems like I am always suffering one pain or another, so I just write it all down and try to look at it in a different light, so to speak. It's probably one of the only things preventing me from losing my mind. Sadly enough I never feel moved to write unless I'm in pain. Some people call my state of mind a creative gift, I prefer to call it a burden. This particular poem is about a rebirth through death, and that no matter who or what you become, you will always know your core self

RICHLIN, JASON
[a.] Milwaukee, WI [title] "My Dreams" [pers.] I often write just for the joy of writing on line. This however has been one of my favorites because it touched everyone who has read it. Poetry has been the doorway to the book I am writing

RICHMOND, CATHERINE
[a.] Austin, TX [title] "Friends" [pers.] I wrote this poem after boyfriend broke up with me. His famous words "I want to be friends" inspired this poem. Someday I hope to have a book published with all my work. I am honored this first chance to be published. I am currently preparing for a degree in Equine Science. I hope to be able to help God's horses for the rest of my life, and maybe someday write a book about them

RIEDL, ELBERTA
[a.] Phoenix, AZ [title] "Mother" [pers.] This poem was written to my Mother back in 1970. I was 11 years old. I wrote the poem for I loved and missed her deeply. Over the years I have found that writing poetry is very relaxing and soothing to the soul. Poetry can say a lot about a person. Where life has taken them. When it hurts inside the words just come out so natural and real. I have written about fifty different poems over the years. I plan to continue writing, hoping to have my own book published one day

RIES, AMANDA
[a.] San Antonio, TX [title] "She's Not Ready Yet" [pers.] I believe that poetry is a gift to the world. Through poetry you can share your deepest thoughts and emotions. This poem describes the pain of lost first love, but also the hope for the distant future. I would like to dedicate this poem to my family, mom and dad, and kipper, who encourage me to do whatever I choose because anything's possible. To my teachers, especially Coach Kloewer, who push me to do my best thank you for everything you've done for me. To my friends you mean the world to me, I love you all!

RIGGINS, JOSHUA
[a.] West Jordan, UT [title] "I Drift Away" [pers.] I believe that poetry is the most unique way of expressing your love for someone or something. This poem was written for someone who is very special to me. Someone whom I loved and lost, but learned true love through lose. She was my inspiration, my muse. I will cherish you, always and forever

RILEY, GLORIA
[a.] Chicago, IL [title] "What You Need" [pers.] My poetry is an expression of the gratitude I feel for having come as far as I have, and for being given another chance to live life to the fullest by being the best person I can be. I write because it gives me joy to share how faith and believing in myself have helped we accomplish certain goals. Poetry is my way of saying "Thank You!

RIZZO, JOANN
[a.] Landing, NJ [title] "A Single Rose" [pers.] My poem was written for a person in my life, whom I was physically, emotionally and spiritually low. Tricia touched my life with enthusiasm and encouragement. She is truly blessed with long and compassion. She gives encouragement in my everyday life. She is like a sister to me. Always there to hear my troubles and share in my accomplishments. No matter how bad I feel she makes me smile. I thank the Lord for bringing it on into my life

ROBBINS, MICHELLE
[a.] Queens Village, NY [title] "An Existing Concept" [pers.] The following poem was written because I have a very stressful occupation as an emergency medical technician for the city of New York. While working with the sick and injured one's emotional state varies hour to hour. I wrote the poem because it helps me release. Both occupationally and personally. I would like to thank my mother God rest her soul for showing me the proper way to love. To my son who gives me joy every day when I see him. My best friend, who's family has treated me like their own daughter and encouraged me to share my feelings with others. Especially my lover, who through good and bad times brings out the emotional side of me to bring out the creativity to write poetry. A special thanks to all, who are close to me. It has been a great honor to have my poem published by the International Library of Poetry. Thank you, so much

ROBERTS, LINDA
[a.] Yakima, WA [title] "Ash" [pers.] Writing poetry lets me share what I experience and how it affects my life. "Ash" was written May 2, 1980, after the second pyroclastic eruption to Mt. Saint Helens, and is dedicated to my daughter Rebecca. It reflects my concerns for the affects the ash may have on nature and our health

ROBERTS, SHELLY
[a.] Texarkana, AR [title] "A New Day" [pers.] This poem is special to me because it was written shortly after the birth of my beautiful daughter Shelby Dawn. Before Shelby came into my life I found myself complaining about so many things that I did not have or could not afford. One day as I looked into her innocent little eyes those complaints seemed so obsolete. At that moment I knew that God had given me the greatest gift of my life and that I should embrace this wonderful gift and be thankful for her each and every day

ROBERTSON, BARBARA
[a.] Montgomery, TX [title] "The Doll" [pers.] When my mother read this poem, she said "I am sorry you had that experience." I replied, "If enough of us write about those experiences, then maybe someday they won't happen anymore." I am so thankful poetry exists to be a safe haven for us to release the pain so many of us hold inside and also to be a voice for those who cannot or are afraid to speak for themselves

ROBERTSON, MONICA
[a.] Richmond, VA [title] "I Hold to Me So Dear" [pers.] I thank God for filling my soul with words and music, also, for making all things possible. God, my family, my friends and the arts helped me survive a broken home, abusive relationships, losses, addiction and depression. Through writing I have been able to express my greatest joys, deepest sorrows and the longings of my heart. It is my dream to share my testimony of hope and love with others. I believe one can survive anything as long as they have faith, hope, love, family, friends, a place to call home and the freedom of expression

ROBIDAS, RAYMOND
[a.] Northwood, NH [title] "Spirit Song" [pers.] I hope others can venture deep into these words, and benefit by them as I have. When I wrote this poem I cried for awhile, you see my eyes had been shut without just cause. I would like to dedicate this poem to my entire family. Whose put up with me through the years. I love you. How often I sit in solitude on the mountaintop, and think tenderly of you all. And for my loved ones who have departed, I still hear there singing

ROBINSON, NATALIE
[a.] Pleasant Grove, UT [title] "I Miss My Love" [pers.] This poem was long ago dedicated to a man I once loved. I wrote it from my heart. Even though I didn't know him well, I meant every word of it when I said how much I missed him. Some say it wasn't love, maybe it was more of wanting to love and to be loved. They say it wasn't how much I missed him, but how much I missed love itself. Today I love a new man, he gives me the love I missed most. I still dedicate this poem to David; for the chance he gave me to open my heart and express how much I missed something I truly missed in my life

ROBOTHAM, CURT
[a.] Fayetteville, NC [title] "A Riddle" [pers.] Poetry has been an outlet for me for most of my twenty eight years. It has allowed me to express anger, happiness, sadness, and love which I might otherwise be reluctant or unable to demonstrate fully. Although I have written plays, short stories and novels, poetry supersedes all as my vehicle of self-expression. I enjoy performing at local readings and experience tremendous fulfillment when an audience seems to share a moment of clarity or new perspective. I expect to continue writing as long as words exist

ROCHE', TROY
[a.] Springfield, VA [title] "Words Spoken!" [pers.] The inspiration for this poem, came from a comment that I wish I had never made. But as we all know, we can't change the things that we say, however, we can reflect on them and try to understand why we said what we did. Maybe this poem will be useful by giving an insight into some of the reasons we should "bite" our tongues!

ROCKWELL, JESSICA
[a.] Little Valley, NY [title] "Jessica Rockwell" [pers.] Writing is as natural and necessary as eating and sleeping, to me. I use my writing to help me view myself and others and also as a release of emotions I cannot verbalize. The feelings of my heart and mind flow from my pen and collect in a reflecting pool. Many times when I return to this

"pool" I am amazed at my interpretations of life within and that which surrounds me. When I share my writings, others are surprised and moved by or even when share my inner most thoughts. My goal is a literary career

RODENROTH, DEAN
[a.] Plano, TX [title] "The Journey Through Me" [pers.] I wrote this poem when I was eighteen years for reasons why I was depressed. I found the answers three years later when I became a Christian. I needed Jesus Christ. I am now twenty-nine years old with a beautiful wife, Shilene is her name. I hope to write many more poems and songs. Thanks so much for the blessing of publishing this poem! It feels wonderful!

RODGERS, WILLIAM
[a.] Burton, MI [title] "Bride to Be" [pers.] In this life there's so many wonderful dreams to be made, and if it wasn't for friends we'd be lost and fade away. I love you Avis, Mom and Dad, Brandy, Ben, Baily, Bethany, Myke, Grampa Stallard, Aunt Nancy You to, uncle Norm Grampa and Grandma Webster I thank all of you. Larry and Stacey who's always there. Anthony Brian. Bob, Brenda, I know you care. The little ones Veronica, Tyler, Devon, Nickki, Larry and Andrew. The listeners Michelle, Melonie, Carrie, Amy, Andrea and You. My school friends since childhood start and the memory of my grandma within my heart

RODRIGUEZ, ROGER
[a.] Miami, FL [title] "Love" [pers.] The poems that I write are short and sweet. I write of the heart. The poem love mean to me that you should love everyone for who they are. Your heart should be fill with love, not hate, I hope my poem will touch someone heart

ROMANELLI, STACEY
[a.] Philadelphia, PA [title] "Has Anyone Seen My Dad?" [pers.] This poem is an expression of the day that my dad didn't show up to take me to the father/daughter dance. That day my stepdad took me to the dance. My family is very close, even though we have a large family. I think because of my close family ties on the one side of my family, helped me cope with and expressed the broken relationships on the other side of my family, by writing poetry. My family encourages me a lot. They are always there for me, in the times, I need them the most

ROMANO, CHRIS
[a.] Manalapan, NJ [title] "Hold On" [pers.] I am a tenth grader in Manalapan High School. To me, poetry is a way that I can express all my inner-most thoughts and feelings. This poem has great meaning to me because it was written while my dad was in the hospital. I used this poem to let my dad know how much I cared about him, and how I needed him to get better. This is only one of many poems that I have written and one-day hope to have all these poems published in my own book

ROSE, GINGER
[a.] Kenai, AK [title] "Eternity" [pers.] Although this poem seems somewhat depressing at first, there is a certain comfort in things staying the same. Consistency is something that has been hard for me to find but is endlessly important. May these words inspire you to seek more butterflies

ROSE, JAMES
[a.] Wellington, FL [title] "Friend" [pers.] Poetry is a wonderful gift that I have been blessed with. Since friends and friendship are things that I hold dearly, I cannot think of a more appropriate poem to share with the world. "Friend" holds a special place in my heart and succinctly expresses my belief of how we should live as friends. A friend once told me that she could see Jesus and his love in my eyes. I can only hope that others will be encouraged by my poem. A little window into my soul

ROSE, DOUGLAS, JR.
[a.] Flint, MI [title] "Daughter" [pers.] I have dedicated this poem to my daughter Keeley my first born. I wanted to give her something she could hold and keep to know how much I love her, and to my wife, for loving me so much

ROSETE, ROLANDO
[a.] Westminster, CA [title] "The Feeling Inside" [pers.] "My feelings inside is a priceless treasure of mine I give to you in dedication of my precious time." This poem was originally written based on the fact that I have never truly witnessed a beautiful sunrise before. After revising this poem, I realized how much more I felt about this special someone in my life. I hope the feelings I express can relate to many others. Sharing your feelings with a special someone is a priceless treasure of anytime. The person you share them with . . . is a very special someone

ROSS, BRANDI
[a.] Topsham, ME [title] "Utopia" [pers.] As you all know our existence in life is to enhance our surrounding Tranquility. I breath air enticement and grasp what appears to bring solitude. My poetry arouses from with in put together by my experiences, decisions and what makes my inner most emotions speak out. Empowered by myself, society and life. Always remember when you travel bring good vibes. Peace love unity and respect

ROTH, ROBERT
[a.] Aberdeen, NJ [title] "Agony" [pers.] My wife brutally murdered in May 1991. No arrests, no indictments. Totally inept investigation. I've tried everything: rewards, media interviews, private investigators, airplane displays, all major crime agencies, TV shows, psychics, and more. Nothing. But, if this poem is worthy of setting to music (a soulful ballad?) and gets extensive exposure, then—just maybe some caring person could provide information to help balance the ledger

ROUSE, CATHERINE
[a.] Mesa, AZ [title] "Silent Pain, Silent Shame" [pers.] I am the oldest of three children, born and raised in the Phoenix Metropolitan area, to a Deputy Sheriff and his Real Estate Broker wife. A mother of four, I have been in medicine since 1976 and experienced Domestic Violence, along with its effect on people first hand. I am currently pursuing my dream of opening my own Domestic Violence Shelter

ROVANG, DANA
[a.] Chicago, IL [title] "Alembic" [pers.] Life is measured in singular moments that deeply move us. I have been very blessed to have beautiful people give such moments to me

ROY, MOUMITA
[a.] Simcoe, ON [title] "A Drop of Our Descent" [pers.] A drop of our descent is a poem inspired by mankind's emotions. Even the strongest people on this Earth has shed tears and felt the pain it causes within us. We also feel the power that forms as we realize the truth which acts as an obstacle. To overcome this, it must be opened with a unique key, a true soul that will determine our fate in the future. A dear friend, Nyrice is a woman who had this soul, and with her departure, another soul came back to Earth and the truth of life was released

ROY, SAURABH
[a.] Flushing, NY [title] "One" [pers.] To me, poetry is a fusion of love, feelings and relationships expressed in words. Every word that a poet writes, always, has a deep and soulful relation with his past, present, future or the moments that happened in his/her life. My poem is from a special moment like that, from the pass. I sincerely hope all the readers will look beyond the words, into the heart

RUDDERHAM, BONNIE
[a.] Lunenburg County, NS [title] "Golden Tears" [pers.] Writing poetry is a true gift many of us are fortunately given. As a child I found a beauty in words that rhymed. As an adult writing became a way of taking daily life experiences happy or painful and finding lessons or morals through them within words. Golden tears was inspired by my three daughters, and is dedicated to all moms and dads. The lesson in this poem is not only within the words, it lies upon your hearts

RUEFF, WALTER
[a.] Jackson, MS [title] "As the Leopard Stalks His Prey" [pers.] Poetry, to me has always been a way of confronting my most pent-up feelings. And along with art I feel that poetry is one of the most constructive and beneficial ways of dealing with these feelings. My poem "As The Leopard Stalks His Prey" deals with everyday life, how it is expressed outwardly, as well as internally. To me this poem symbolizes all of the dirtiness and deceptiveness in everyday life and tries to open up the world through expression of the subconscious. This poem also exemplifies all of life's predators, from the seemingly most benign, to the most blatantly malicious

RUIZ, RAYMOND
[a.] Bronx, NY [title] "You and Me" [pers.] In all modesty I never imagined any of my poems being published. If someone finds talent in my words it is only through the will of God and the devotion of my loving wife. May you enjoy this poem in reading as I did in writing it

RULE, AMANDA
[a.] Susnaville, CA [title] "Inside" [pers.] This poem is very special, it shows feelings; I am honored to have many dead it. Mom, dad, Travis, thanks for loving me, I love you too. Kira Haydes and Katana Brown, thanks for being my best friends . . . me loves! There have been many people who've pushed me down but my friends and family have always been there, Crystal Doane, Sonny Branum, Jessica Baird, Sandy Baily, Amber Murphy, Mrs. Dudkowski; you're all never last with me. Thanks for the love. I hope everyone has as great as people as these. Mom, dad's love you again and Sarah white. Thanks

RUMPLER, DEREK
[a.] Somerville, OH [title] "The Echo of A Child's Laughter" [pers.] My name is Derek Rumpler and I am a creator of words. Perhaps my biggest dream is to attend Digi Pen in Seattle, Washington to earn a bachelor's degree in video-game development. As a creator, I have the capacity to avail worlds unimaginable. Human conflict is perhaps my biggest inspiration . . . especially conflict within oneself. Special thanks goes to my family, friends, and the God who gave me the ability to create

RUSSELL, GERRY
[a.] Rotonda West, FL [title] "I Wasn't Looking" [pers.] "I Wasn't Looking," was written for Harvey E. Russell, my husband of 43 years, who went with the angels on March 5, 1999. His love for me, Ken, Marc, Bobby and Diana (our children) and his grandchildren was endless. Our loss was devastating, but find comfort in the knowledge that he will be waiting for me when I leave this world. He will always be in the hearts of the family he loved

RUSSOM, STEVEN
[a.] Yuma, AZ [title] "Butterfly" [pers.] This poem describes the struggles we all go through in life. Feelings all wrapped up and held down at times. And even though that butterfly was such a tiny thing, it was still beautiful on a grand scale. In the eyes of God, we are so wonderful and ground that He gives each of us His total and undivided attention and love. This is what this poem is all about. The beauty that God sees when He looks at each of

us; no matter what we think of ourselves. When He looks at us, He sees us individually with love in His eyes, forgiveness in His heart, and no memory of anything that we have asked Him to forgive and forget. All that He sees is a beautiful and grand creation; created by His own loving hands. Formed in His image and set free to display the very beauty He has placed within each one of us

RYAN, PATRICIA
[a.] Decatur, GA [title] "A Poem About A Man Who Becomes God" [pers.] This is my first time being published, and I am delighted that mine was among the poems chosen. Being published will certainly open doors for me, and I hope to have more of my works published in the future! In the sample of my poem, on line 17, there should be a space between the words "out" and "in" thank you!

RYAN, VANESSA
[a.] Arabi, LA [title] "River of Stress" [pers.] Many times I try to explain to people how I feel but they don't "Get the Picture." Because I enjoy painting and drawing pictures to express my feelings, I try to pain a picture through words with my poetry. This poem was written out of a fit of rage during a very stressful and discouraging day. When people are feeling angry, I wish they could channel their energies toward things less violent and more creative such as writing

S., LINDSEY
[a.] Marble Falls, TX [title] "Smile" [pers.] "Smile" is self explanatory. To understand the world today you must always look past the problem and look for the solution. Well I am not quite sure about my inspiration but I would say if you want an inspiration try experiencing a smile

SACHDEVA, G.
[a.] Miami, FL [title] "Forever" [pers.] This poem is a special tribute to my wife Ipsi who has stood by me forever and should serve as a reminder to all happily married couples, never underestimate your spouse beneath the weathered shell, lives a heart so profound and sensitive it is so easy to hurt one another. Respect togetherness and rise beyond pettiness. You only have one life so make the most of it. Life is love and love is God. With love you live forever. This is the message and my true feelings I have tried to convey with my first to be published poem

SADANANDAN, SUBHADRA
[a.] Sydney, Australia [title] "The Grub" [pers.] My career as a port developed from my career as a teacher of English to the philosophy of life expressed by many of the authors who have written on nature. "The Grub" was induced by mother's love evinced by all created things. The grub is dedicated to all children of the universe. I'm grateful to the publishers for choosing my poem. "Creative Pang" by my brother Karunakaran Vettanatte is also appearing in your book. "The Grub" was written by my mother, Subhadra. I was moved to tears when I read the poem. She has suffered a lot while raising me and my sisters. Her body is getting weak day by day from diabetes but her soul gets stronger every day. She sent me to study here in Sydney very reluctantly and misses me a lot. I received for publishing on her birthday. No other present could have brought her greatest happiness that day. I thank ILP from the bottom of my heart

SAFRONOFF, GREG
[a.] Traverse City, MI [title] "Vision of Love and Hope" [pers.] This poem flowed into my mind as turned away from the darkness of night to the morning light. A new year, a new millennium, searching deep inside for a ray of hope. A moments flash the day is dawned. Even so my thoughts are flooded with the quickening silver of the mirror of eternal love. I stand in awe recording the wonder of it all. I am a humble scribe, a translator of the grandeur, that awaits all those who turn to the light

SALAZAR, LOUIE
[a.] Las Vegas, NV [title] "Beaten" [pers.] I am exceedingly filled with a mixture of pride and joy to see a work of mine published at the youthful age of 15. My poem was of a serious nature because of my experiences here in Las Vegas. My poem was an expression of personal unfairness. I felt cheated to see others with more than I have, though, I had to admit only I put myself in most of those situations. Through my poem and caption, I want others to know that one should be content with what has been dealt, rather than dwelling on what has not

SALMON, CRYSTAL
[a.] Dubois, IN [title] "Life" [pers.] I myself love poetry—this poem explains the way I feel about life. I think life is a game and it has a lot of rules in it. Some of these rules make no sense to me. About the friends part, well in my life I have had a lot of friends and some of them have hurt me really bad before they left out of my life. In life if you love someone they might not love you back so love can be blind. In life I feel that you are either rich or poor. And in life you can play the game, but if you can't play or get tired of playing then you die

SALYERS, WILLIAM
[a.] Blaine, KY [title] "Thoughts at Sixty" [pers.] A life long student of mysticism, I try to express mystical principles and concepts in my poetry by being as brief and simple as possible

SAMUELSSON, KAJ
[a.] Goteborg, Sweden [title] "The Accidental Hero" [pers.] I wrote this poem while on the "Life Orientation Course" at the Church of Scientology Advanced Organization in Copenhagen, Denmark. This course revitalized my purpose of writing and improved it, and I would not be in this book if I had not met Scientology. I am a Scientologist, working in the church of Scientology in Gothenburg, Sweden. It is the works of L. Ron Hubbard that made me a writer and a poet, and by studying his works I will ensure that I continue writing. Life is fun, and becomes even more fun when writing, so write!

SANABRIA, LETITIHIA
[a.] Schofield Barracks, HI [title] "He Will Always Be Watching" [pers.] This poem was written for a dear friend of mind. Poetry is my salvation, it is my escape. I hope that others who have the talent will share with the rest of the world. Thanks to my mother and husband!

SANDERS, CHARLES
[a.] Lompoc, CA [title] "Double Image" [pers.] I have written poetry for decades, sharing it only with my wife, until other family members began requesting copies. Double image was written for my daughter-in-law. She was given an heirloom double mirror by her parents. One evening, she happened to glance at it at such an angel that an image of a child in 1800's dress appeared. She telephoned her parents and explained the phenomenon. They hadn't noticed it during the twenty years it graced their living room. This surprise discovery became the inspiration for my poem. I reside in Lompoc, CA with my wife, Ruth

SANDERS, JUDY
[a.] Morden, MB [title] "When You're Grown!" [pers.] When I wrote this poem, my first attempt, it didn't occur to me that someday it would be published. I am honored and surprised! It brings to mind one literature teacher who would have been very proud and others who would have been very surprised. I now know what inspiration is. This poem was inspired by our son who arrived ten years after the birth of our youngest of three daughters. It is an expression of slight trepidation, which dissolved into absolute joy at this little person. This was a test but the Lord provides, seventeen years later David remains an inspiration and joy!

SANDOZ, EDEN
[a.] Slidell, LA [title] "If I Had A Thousand Years" [pers.] This poem, "If I Had A Thousand Years," was written for a college English assignment. It is actually a response to Andrew Marvell's poem, "To His Coy Mistress." I entered my poem as an after thought and never expected it to make it this far. I am pleased to be a part of this book

SANSOM, DAWN
[a.] Tigard, OR [title] "The Giving" [pers.] This passage was written for a true friend, who helped me to believe in myself, especially in my writing talent. It takes a very special kind of person to put their own needs aside and think of someone else's. That kind of friend means more than all the riches in the world

SANTANA, AUDERY
[a.] Great Lake, IL [title] "You Left One Day" [pers.] This poem honors a great father, husband and especially a great friend to all who knew him, my father. He was a man who helped you turn personal difficulties into life's lessons A and S assisting you to grow, heal and love. You left one day signifies my father's decision to decline life support secondary to a very poor quality of life. Strong and dignified he felt it better to leave this world and the ones he loved to enter a world that was anesthetized to pain and suffering. We love you dad!

SATTERFIELD, KIMBERLY
[a.] Oakland, CA [title] "Believe" [pers.] For me, poetry is the language of love that leaps from the depth of my heart to the page and changes the way I view the world by giving me the experience of God's grace. It is my fervent wish and prayer to express my gratitude in the form of my poetry and to share the gift of the richness and joy of the inner life with my brothers and sisters. "Believe" is spirit, a voice that unifies race, religion, creed and is based on the universal and fundamental principle of love

SAUM, KANDICE
[a.] Russia, OH [title] "Good-bye" [pers.] My name is Kandice Saum and I'm 12 years old. I attend a very good country school and am on the honor roll. I'm carrying a 3.9–4.0 grade average. I enjoy writing poetry, both happy and sad. My motivation for this particular poem was that I recently lost my grandfather. My grandfather was more like my father. My parents are divorced and I live with my mother, my grandmother, my aunt Tanya and previously with my grandfather. I dedicate this poem to the memory of my grandfather, because he taught me about things like fishing and playing softball

SAUNDERS, HOLLY
[a.] Bloomington, IN [title] "Earth Comforts" [pers.] Poetry is my vent for my emotions when there more than I can handle or if I can't tell what they are. It is also my souls speech that when the ink is flowing tells me its secrets. Poetry is also my friend, lover and teacher

SAURIOL, MARGARET
[a.] Bronx, NY [title] "Conflict" [pers.] Many people are confronted at one time or another with conflict between what they want to do and what is the right thing to do morally or otherwise. "Conflict" was written by me because of a state of mind I had at one point in my life. A point we can derive from "Conflict" is that when a person finally decides on a matter, he should stick to that decision and not retract. Indecisiveness can produce more friction or conflict within us

SAURIOL, MARGARET
[a.] Bronx, NY [title] "Conflict" [pers.] Many people are confronted at one time or another with conflict between what they want to do and what is the right thing to do morally or otherwise. "Conflict" was written by me because of a state of mind

I had at one squint in my life. A point we can derive from "Conflict" is that when a person finally decides on a matter. He should stick to that decision and not retract. Indecisiveness can produce more friction or conflict with us

SAVAGE, AMANDA
[a.] Lafayette, IN [title] "Follow" [pers.] "Follow" represents the manipulation of words and thoughts that takes place when expressing myself through poetry. Poetry allows others to experience life through my eyes. It gives me a feeling of control over my thoughts. Expression is a very big part of my soul and it is revealed through my words. Poetry is my #1 love in life and I hope to share more of it in time

SCALF, SUZANNE
[a.] Livermore, CO [title] "The River" [pers.] My poem is a reflection on how the world around us tells us a lot about ourselves. It is there for all of us to see if we only take the time to do so. It is my sincere desire that those who read my poem will take a moment and ponder over just one of the wondrous aspects of our world "Love."

SCARROW, RODNEY
[a.] Hazlet, SK [title] "Introduction" [pers.] I grew up on the family farm in the beautiful Moose Mountains in the Southeast corner of Saskatchewan Canada. I started writing poetry as a way of "dealing" with my life and how society influence it. This particular poem was written as an Introduction to my book of poems. I consider myself to be a prose style poetry. Unfortunately for me most of my poem will go unread, especially in cases like this, due to their length. Nonetheless, I will continue to write and collect them until I feel they deserve public attention

SCHEETZ, BRIAN P.
[a.] Marietta, GA [title] "Dear Father" [pers.] The cards that life deals can make you feel cheated. I've discovered hidden memories that were buried in the ashes of time through my poetry. A day never passes that I don't entirely miss my father. Poetry has become my way of expressing my loves and losses. My mother instilled in me a love for poetry as my grandmother did the same for her. Thank you mom for this gift, and my sister for being a wonderful friend. I love you both. To my friends and family, I am truly blessed to have all of you in my life

SCHERCK, VICKY
[a.] Waupaca, WI [title] "Millennium Thoughts" [pers.] I have, from the time I was 13, used poetry to express the contents of my heart and soul. In fact, my first poem took shape out of my grief over the assassination of President Kennedy. The gift of writing verse was handed down to me and my three siblings from both of our parents. I am pleased to have this opportunity to share one of my poems with you

SCHLICHTER, TODD
[a.] Los Angeles, CA [title] "A Poem for Julia" [pers.] Writing is magic, and love is its source. Therefore this poem and all of my written work is dedicated to Julia Hankel. She is my center, my inspiration, my perfect compliment, my true soul mate. Happy Birthday my love, may we share a hundred more

SCHMIDT, ANNE
[a.] West Bend, IA [title] "To Our Angel: Mason Nicholaus Schmidt" [pers.] This poem is in memory of a very special baby who never made it to birth, yet certainly made it into our hearts. Mason, only eighteen weeks along, died after a serious car accident involving my sister-in-law and two years old nephew. Along with the other tragedies the accident brought, it was devastating and heartbreaking for all of us to lose Mason. This baby boy

will always be held in our hearts, kept in our thoughts, and remembered throughout our lives

SCHNEIDER, JASON
[a.] Pearl City, HI [title] "The Robe" [pers.] The reverse came to me while trying to decide what to write in a birthday card. It didn't make it into the card, but found fertile ground elsewhere and thus a life of its own. I hope others will enjoy the nuances that I have enjoyed in these words

SCHNEIDER, MARGE
[a.] San Jose, CA [title] "Pandora" [pers.] I wrote the line "A Candle Burns in Darkness" on a camping trip. When I returned home I started doodling and come up with "A Candle Burns in Darkness Pandora is a watchful soul." I've written over four hundred fifty poems

SCHNEIDER, ROGER
[a.] Airdrie, AB [title] "Bluebird" [pers.] In a sense, I packed my whole life into those seven lines. It stems from repressed feelings resulting from living with a permanent physical disability, which I hadn't really learned to deal with. Also the realization that people will never see me as I want to be seen if I never show myself. The battle continues, but now I have the man with the plan in my corner. To that end, I dedicate Bluebird to Christ my savior, for His most precious gift. And to Geri, who taught me to receive it, and encouraged me to write

SCHOENECKER, ROBERT
[a.] Milwaukee, WI [title] "Night Shakes" [pers.] I was inspired by experiences as a US Marine. This poem describes the loneliness and isolation soldiers often feel, along with the deep appreciation for being alive and not taking for granted the beautiful things in this world

SCHRAGER-BOZDAG, TAMMI
[a.] Mount Prospect, IL [title] "The Beach" [pers.] Not too long ago, I had an eight years old describe how he was beaten. As he told me his story it was all I could do to keep from crying. I looked into his eyes knowing no one should ever have to go through this. I never forgot his words. This poem is dedicated to the children and families in Chaos that I've worked with. I can only hope I have made some difference. To my family and friends, never forget where you come from much love! Always believe in yourselves! Atahan, incredible man, I love you

SCHROEDER, CHERYL
[a.] Fridley, MN [title] "Old Lace" [pers.] I quit high school in my freshman year to marry. 19 years later it ended. Poetry has been my method of expressing the feelings I sometimes cannot. My thanks to an english teacher who in a short amount of time taught me to love words!

SCHULTZ, MARSHA
[a.] Cleves, OH [title] "The Peace Poem" [pers.] This poem was written in response to our world in crisis, our children at risk. I have featured the peace poem in my "Spirit Collection, for women" I thank God for the gift to write poetry and the ability to use my hands, eyes, mind and heart to relate to. And reach out to others

SCHWANEBECK, NEIL
[a.] Millersville, PA [title] "Weak" [pers.] Pain, Love, Violence, Lust. All simple words. It's the individual's perception of these words that makes us who we are. From time to time we can catch a fraction of another's thoughts. But never can anyone fully understand what goes on in someone else's mind

SCOTT, JEFF
[a.] Parma, OH [title] "Her Love" [pers.] This poem represents my new life in Christ. It is the

turning point from which my life went from pain and hardship to the utmost joy. The reason I have titled it "Her Love" is to honor a dear friend of mine. Her love towards Jesus Christ really was an eye opener for me. She helped change my world through her own innocent love for Christ. This poem symbolizes the birth of the "New Me." My friends, trust God, His grace truly is amazing. Thank you Corey for your perfect inspiration and love. This poem is forever dedicated to you

SCOTT, MARY
[a.] Mt. Holly, NC [title] "Faces" [pers.] I was given away when I was a child and always felt like somebody's throw-away. I had a hard time adjusting to life and getting close to people so I learned how to get my feelings out and go on in a poem. When I write my feelings down on paper in a poem the confusion ends and the solution to a problem becomes clear. I have helped a lot of people by sharing my story. I have a family and a good life, with lots of people to share it with. Writing helped me survive and be happy!

SEATON, NICHELLE
[a.] Dolton, IL [title] "R.B. My Man" [pers.] I began writing in high school. When I gave my life to Christ, my poetry blossomed. My poetry encompasses earthly and spiritual experiences. I am richly rewarded when my poetry heals others, because it heals me. Poetry can raise one's spirit and conscious, for "as a man thinketh, so he is." R.B. is conceived from the alarming dependence and addiction to gambling in our society. It conveys the emotional euphoria and torment experienced while engaging in such a deceiving courtship. It is my desire that R.B. will go forth and break the chains that have bound so many.

SEEMAN, JUDY
[a.] Cedar Rapids, IA [title] "A Tribute to My Elders" [pers.] "A Tribute to My Elders" is the result of an assignment given to me in a reading and writing class at Kirkwood Community College. My talent for writing poems was discovered at the young age of 11 years old, when my uncle passed away. I wrote and recited a poem for his funeral. I have written several since then

SEGO, JENNY
[a.] Pembroke Pines, FL [title] "Love's Definition" [pers.] This poem is dedicated to the love of a lifetime, my precious Steven. He is the inspiration of my life. His love has been an encouragement to awaken, renew my spirit and my soul and urge me to draw out the best in me. Steven gave me back the belief in myself and in the goodness and boundless potential that a life can offer. Having given up on fairytales and dreams coming true, he is all that and so much more. This is to you, my wondrous Lancelot, my soulmate, my Steven, a love eternal. I love you

SEIPP, KYLE
[a.] Burnet, TX [title] "Time Forgotten" [pers.] My poem reflects on the nostalgia of time that has passed and the reflection of the quality of that time. We take life one day at a time and should live each individual day to its fullest capacity. My writing just allows me that chance to escape the toils of everyday life and enjoy every aspect of life that comes before me

SHAHID, AFSHEEN
[a.] "Watford, UK [title] "My Little Candle" [pers.] I am a student of literature (Bahons) at the (University of Hertfordshire. This is my first poem ever brought in public. My poetry is about waiting for, that something, everyone awaits. It also expresses the uncertainty of life in general. Although I use first person, it does not necessarily convey my personal feelings. Poetry has always been my companion. It is my only companion when I am all alone.

I hope orders of "From the Mountaintop" enjoy reading my poem "My Little Candle"

SHAKYA, SHEETU
[a.] Mountain View, CA [title] "Restoration" [pers.] This poem reflects the very human tragedy of not giving enough effort to find peace. The subcontinent that is the birth region of two enlightened figures Siddhartha Gautam Buddha and Mahatma Gandhi is today, ironically submerged in turmoil of advocating and promoting nuclear proliferation. It is a call to leaders of great nations to help and restore peace in this region where the poorest people on Earth struggle for daily existence. Most of my poems are a result of my father's faith in my poetry. "Restoration" is inspired by my husband's love for me. I was born in Kathmandy, Nepal

SHANABARGER, STEVE SHANABARGER
[a.] Niles, OH [title] "The King I Am" [pers.] The King I Am, is one of many poems I've written to try to show God's love and concern for us all. In this day and age, when we see the violence on the news and drugs and obscenities everywhere it's comforting to know that we don't have to live this way. It's our choice. I'm forty nine years old, and I've been writing poetry most of my life. I write about the things I know, and love, family, children, my beautiful wife Tammie. Something as simple as a feeling, or as complex as life itself

SHANNON, MEAGAN
[a.] Colorado Springs, CO [title] "By Myself" [pers.] In fifth grade a professional poet spoke to our class. This motivated me to write "By Myself." Two years later I am still writing. I also enjoy animals, especially horses, where I volunteer with Therapeutic riding for the disabled. I participated in acting with Forensics competitions, yet still like to be "By Myself" and dream of those magical places

SHAW, JOHN
[a.] Canoga Park, CA [title] "Prince of Darkness" [pers.] One of the things that's impressed me most about myself is the way I have with written words. This poem is no exception. Since I'm in a band, the other guys wanted songs with different themes to them, so I wrote some guitar parts and later wrote lyrics for them. These are part of them I was restricted to twenty lines. I'm very happy with this because the song is about the tale of Lucifer, the archangel and how he tried to kill God and take his place. I believe these lyrics best capture that story

SHEA, VALERIE
[a.] Stoughton, MA [title] "Her Eyes" [pers.] This poem is very special to me, it was written for my mother. Her courage and strength before she passed away helped me to write this. She will be missed and remembered forever. My name is Valerie Shea. I am married to my best friend and soulmate Kelly James Shea. We live in Stoughton, Massachusetts with our seven children Dan, Tim, Stephen, David, Tanya, Stephanie, and Tommy. I enjoy doing crafts but writing and drawing are my passion. I hope to someday be able to publish the many poems I have written and have my own book out for all the world to see

SHEDA, ALBERT
[a.] Lexington, KY [title] "Across the Bridge" [pers.] I wrote this poem while sitting in the computer room of the Lexington Public Library, all of it within 15 minutes from the time and date it was e-mailed to you. The significance in the poem, is, it is a parable to my own life of trials and errors. I had quit school, I had been in treatment for alcohol and drug abuse, and I had been through numerous employable defeats; all of these things because I crossed a bridge of uncertain boundaries. In 1991 I committed myself to sobriety, hence, "Where My Nature Forever Blossoms"

SHELTON, LANE
[a.] Austin, TX [title] "There Beats in Thing a Secret Heart" [pers.] Poetry can turn mundane into mystery, common place into celestial. It gives us New eyes to see a world that is too often hidden in plain sight. I have written a poem about poetry to express the sense of wonder it can bring to even the most ordinary of things

SHEPPARD, AARON
[a.] Gt. Barrington, MA [title] "The Value of Togetherness" [pers.] "The Value of Togetherness" The selection which, appears in this book is devoted to the endless search for someone to share my life with. At the time this poem was written, I thought that my search was over. I felt that I had someone who would never fade away. The feeling faded and now the search is on once again. Poetry allows me to express feeling when it seems those feeling will never get out. I have many poems that deal with topics such as: love, life, and belonging. My hope is that this poem will touch or inspire someone to never give up their search for that feeling to togetherness

SHEPHERD, SALLY
[a.] Earl, NC [title] "Just Richard" [pers.] This is a very special poem for a very special young man, my youngest son Richard. Richard left to join the Lord on August 20th, 1995, victim of an auto accident. It was an accident without rhyme or reason, the Lord just called him home. The poem is on Richard's gravestone. He was very close to his three sisters and five brothers. He would rather golf, bowl, or play games with them than anything. He loved camping and fishing and friends. He was a wonderful young man and we, his family and friends will hold him in our hearts forever, he was marvelous, no one can ever replace just Richard

SHEPPARD, DAVID
[a.] Auburn, IL [title] "Angels! God's Open Doorway" [pers.] I am David Wayne Sheppard from Auburn IL. I was born in Springfield IL on May 21, 1959. Doris and Wayne Sheppard (retired) are my parents. I have two sons Matthew Jay 11 and Jason two also my loving wife Rhonda. One of my hobbies is composing poetry. I have many more poems such as some of the beauty from my heart, I wrote this one from. When I was five years old, I got into an auto wreck with my mom while in a coma for three days, the angels, white gates, and being able to return to live my life. Poetry is like a flower which has to open up from the inside of one's heart, bringing out wisdom, love, beauty, life holds

SHEPPARD, ELIZABETH
[a.] Port Hope, ON [title] "Confusions End" [pers.] This poem is symbolic of how I, and I believe many others, feel. In our busy lives we never have the time to decipher exactly where we are or if we're where we want to be! We're always waiting for tomorrow but are too afraid to take the next step to get there!

SHERFIELD, K.
[a.] Anchorage, AK [title] "Setting Out to Sea" [pers.] As a child I was given a book of poetry, and the poem "At The Seaside" by Robert Louis Stevenson had a huge impact on me which I have remembered all of my life. Many of my writings have something to do with the sea; its energy, power, force, and mystique in our lives. This poem reflects the power of the sea to transport you, in your mind, away from the things that "land" can bind you to

SHIPLEY, LENORE
[a.] Vernon, FL [title] "Nor" [pers.] The hill behind my childhood home in Kentucky was often a challenge to my two younger sisters and me. This poem speaks of the love my sisters and I had, and still have, for each other. Sisterly love does not

need to be nurtured. It thrives on its own. It makes no demands. It is love in its purest form

SHUPTAR, CASSANDRA
[a.] League City, TX [title] "Friends" [pers.] This poem is very special to me. It represents the meaning of friendship in my eyes. Friendship is a very special thing to me. If you don't have friendship, you have nothing. Friendship is a special gift to have if you have friends, you are very lucky. I am very lucky to have friends that love me. I am lucky to have found such a great group of people who like me for who I am. Just to name a few: Stacy, Laura, Stasha, Celia, Ryan and Chris. These are my best friends and I am lucky to have found them

SICKLER, RON
[a.] Centreville, VA [title] "True Love Found" [pers.] I love to express love through poetry. In my poems, I attempt to capture the goodness that this life has to offer and the many blessings that God has so graciously bestowed upon His creatures here on Earth. Writing poetry for over thirty years, I have become very fond of structure meter, cadence, and rhyming verse. This particular poem, written as a birthday present for the love of my life, Nancy, celebrates the conclusion of a somewhat arduous journey during which I've looked for, but never found, love that is true . . . until that is, I met her

SILVERMAN, JASON
[a.] Harleysville, PA [title] "Never Have I Asked" [pers.] This poem was written several years ago. It speaks of the awkwardness of falling in love with a very close fried, especially when her sister is a close friend as well. True love is complicated—it thinks of the rights of others. "Love is patient, love is kind and is not jealous . . . bears all things, believes all things, hopes all things, endures all things." I Corinthians 13:4, 7

SILVERMAN, RACHEL
[a.] Columbus, OH [title] "Not All Gone, A Tribute to My Heritage" [pers.] I wrote this poem the day after I visited Dachau, a World War II concentration camp in Germany. I have been educated on the Holocaust ever since I can remember, but nothing prepares even the strongest hearts for an experience like Dachau. I needed to reflect on the visit, so I wrote this poem—the recognition of the anguish of the Jewish people, throughout history. I am truly grateful for the chance to express my thoughts on the sufferings and hopes of my people; for the opportunity to share my poetry with all who will read and remember

SIMMONS, REGINA
[a.] Maple Valley, WA [title] "Remembrance" [pers.] This poem reflects the appreciation I have for my brother's love and support. I know I will see him in Heaven but it is a great consolation that God brings clear remembrance of his love to my mind in times of sorrow

SINGLETON, FRANCES
[a.] Gladys, VA [title] "Afterlife—A Mothers and Daughters Love" [pers.] My mother and I shared a very special bond. I was born on her birthday, even in the same house and room. One night while thinking of her, the words of this poem just started coming to me. I feel like they were sent from her above, comforting me that we will be together once again, "when on Earth ends." Thanks my dear mother, I love you

SKIDMORE, BRYAN
[a.] Wilmington, DE [title] "Feelings of Love" [pers.] Hopefully to be a well established Artist soon. I was born in Altoona, PA. Raised here and there, but learned everywhere. Still searching for my purpose in life, at the age 21. Also continuing to seek for Mrs. Right. Bearing, a compassionate soul I serve the Lord, every day that I pray

SKINNER, MICHAEL
[a.] Fullerton, CA [title] "In Sanity?" [pers.] Most of my poetry is a kind of deep blend of both a dark life and the strange workings of my own mind. This poem in particular was, and I feel, could only be written as a question. Who's to say what is sane and what is insane? Furthermore on that, who's to say what point of view this poem takes place in? Sanity or insanity; for me they are two completely different things that are exactly the same

SLAGLE, CONNIE
[a.] Liberty Center, OH [title] "For Mervin R. Eiche" [pers.] I wrote this poem in memory of my father. I also wanted to promote a website that donates money to help fight cancer. I spoke directly from my heart. I feel it's an important issue and what a wonderful way to say it

SLATTERY, JOHN
[a.] New Lenox, IL [title] "Grandma" [pers.] This poem was very special to me because it gave me a way to express my feelings about my grandmother. She did a lot for me and this poem is a little way to give something back. She died on February 19, 1999, this day inspired me to write this poem. My relationship with my Grandma was a very close and loving one. But the thing that hurt me most about her death was that I never got to say good-bye, and this poem was my way to say good-bye. So good-bye grandma, I love you!

SLAUGHTER, RICHARD
[a.] Quinlan, TX [title] "Soldiers Letter" [pers.] Poetry is a gift that everyone has but only a few choose to express it. I am from a long line of military men who have served and honored their country in peace time and in war. I was taught by my grandfathers to be loyal, to each for my dreams and to honor the nation in which I live. I wrote this poem so, that message will continue on. Though I have not served as of yet, I hope to follow in the footsteps of those who inspired me. In honor of those who fought and fell

SLEDGE, ERIKA
[a.] Tuscaloosa, AL [title] "Until I Found You" [pers.] Although this poem was not originally written for her. I dedicate it to my daughter, Leah Briana. Leah was born in May of 99 three months premature. She weighed only one pounds, seven ounce and was twelve inches long. Through God's grace and mercy she is doing great. This poem is about not knowing love until you find that special someone. Well, I can truly say that you never know love until you have a child. She is the light of my life and the joy in my heart. I thank God for her each day

SLUSHER, KRISTI
[a.] Sunnyvale, CA [title] "Lonely Wake" [pers.] This poem is very close to my heart. I have written poetry for many years now; it has been a way to express my emotions. "Lonely Wake" was written to bring to light my feelings on lost love and hope for the future. I want to thank my family and friends for their love and support. I can only hope the poem touched your heart, as it did mine

SMITH, BLAKELEY
[a.] Los Angeles, CA [title] "Some Other Parade" [pers.] Sometimes in our lives we don't get what we want, and that's a good thing. We must check those areas we don't always see. Examine them, study them, and search through our holes. When we don't confront the real issues in our lives, we march to different beats than we should, we begin to march with strangers. As those strangers become closer and closer, our friends and loved ones are distanced. Blakeley Smith was born in Hartford, Connecticut c.1977 Mr. Smith is the founder and front man of his modern rock band Envy, he is also an actor and filmmaker.

SMITH, CARIE
[a.] Nellis AFB, NV [title] "Creamy Vanilla/Rocky Road" [pers.] I Never thought that my poem would be published, and here it is in black and white. This poem helped me make a decision between two guys that I wanted date. Well I chose creamy vanilla. I hope that this poems helps others as much as it helped me. May you also enjoy it as much as I do

SMITH, JEFFREY
[a.] Santa Monica, CA [title] "Pumpkin Tears" [pers.] Writing poems, for me, is a form of self therapy and a striving for pure self expression. It is rewarding to me to shape words, rhythms, sounds and even the layout of the poem to fit what I am feeling and trying to express

SMITH, JEREMY
[a.] Charleston, SC [title] "My Monster" [pers.] What can you say of poetry? Poetry in all its forms is an extension of ones soul. There is no greater way for me to express my true emotions. Poetry though is not just for the author but for the reader for they may read my work and take something from it other than the meaning and emotion it has for me. I live in beautiful Charleston, South Carolina and while the politics of the state annoy me the beauty keeps me here.

SMITH, KARISSA
[a.] Severn, MD [title] "Christmas Miracles" [pers.] Poetry is a way to show how you feel. People can tell how a person lives his or her life by reading their poetry. Poems like "Christmas Miracles" tells true meaning of something. Being a Christian, Christmas means a lot to me. Out of thirty 5th graders very few captured the true meaning of Christmas. Most focused on presents and Santa Claus. I wanted to bring out the Christ in Christmas. Since I was saved, I've been thinking of guiding others to salvation. With other missionaries and I, people will think more when "writing their poem"

SMITH, LAUREN
[a.] Murfreesboro, TN [title] "If Only" [pers.] When you're a teenager you worry a lot about your future and I'm 14. Sometimes when I look back on my childhood, I wonder if I have lived it to the fullest. I wonder if I have if only I could keep just one person from falling, if only I had just one achievement to show for my life. If only I could stop just one dream from fading or one soul from falling. If only I had just one moment to look back on and know that I made a difference. If only I had done just one thing right, so that long after I'm gone people would remember for it instead of. If only

SMITH, MARY
[a.] Mullins, SC [title] "Autumn" [pers.] During the fall of the year, I become inspired as I drive along super highways, city streets and through wooded areas and see God's handiwork, then I say to myself, "Only God can change tree leaves from green to the many miraculous shades of color before they shed, leaving a touch of evergreen year round." I thank my mother, Mrs. Mildred Smith, for the writing talent I inherited from her and hope that I have passed it to my children, Gregory and Shirlian. This is my first published poem and I thank the International Library of Poetry for the opportunity

SMITH, RALPH
[a.] Las Vegas, NV [title] "Struggle for the Secret Place" [pers.] The art of poetry is a gift that should be encouraged. It's in the beauty of a mountain lake and in the pain of every day life. The ability to put one's most passionate thoughts on paper is truly an intimate experience. Thanks to God for a gift that not everyone has but provides so much inspiration in a dark world. Thanks to my wife Penny and my children Ashley and Breanne for your support

SMITH, TERRY
[a.] Emmaus, PA [title] "Winter" [pers.] "Winter" was written during a very dark, confusing period in my life. It speaks to the pain and regret of a lost love. A love never to be reclaimed. A love that should have never happened. A love I would never trade. The kind of love that lasts lifetimes. The kind of love you would die for. The kind of love that kills you anyway. In sharing this poem, I felt there may be more than one other person who identifies with this sorrow, and hoped my words were not only cathartic for me, but allowed another to know they're not alone. Always loved Su Su best

SMITH, WILBUR
[a.] Palmyra, PA [title] "In Memory of an Ordinary Boy" [pers.] I became interested in poetry in 4th grade when the teacher posted on the classroom bulletin board, "The Pelican," a limerick. My poem is about the death of the little boy of a very special friend. It is my hope that this poem honors him and all young children that lost the chance to be "extraordinary" adults

SNYDER, STEVE
[a.] Phoenix, AZ [title] "The Wall" [pers.] I believe that "The Wall" will be recognized by many people ones who have built theirs, or, are now in the process of building one. It would be my wish that this poem opens those people up to their own wall, so like myself, they could escape it. I would like to dedicate this poem to my wife and my grandmother, both of whom have shown such courage when faced with the impossibilities of life

SOLEY, CAROLINE
[a.] Waldorf, MD [title] "Thank God" [pers.] First and foremost, I "Thank God" because only through him all things are possible. I also give thanks to my family for the support and encouragement provided throughout the years. Poetry gives me the opportunity to express myself when a given situation does not allow me to. I hope and pray that other find as much enjoyment reading my poetry as I found fulfillment writing it

SOUTHERN, THELMA
[a.] Marbury, MD [title] "Life Struggles" [pers.] Many times throughout my life I felt very sorry for myself and desired an end. Through God's graciousness, I received a way of expressing myself through poetry. "Life Struggles" is a far cry from the negative writing I once did. We do choose the outcome of our life are we losers or winners? I chose the latter. I pray this poem reaches the heart of these who wish for release from negativity. We can all choose to win, no one wishes to lose, God bless us all

SOWELL, SHAUN
[a.] Fairbanks, AK [title] "Joe" [pers.] This poem is written from my heart, dedicated to my brother, Joe, after a car accident in 1996 has left him with Traumatic Brain Damage. So with love this is to Joe (22 years old) from your little sister Shaun (17 years old) junior at West Valley High School, Fairbanks, Alaska

SPEARS, SHEREE
[a.] Eastover, SC [title] "A Visit to the Farm" [pers.] Poetry is an expression of ones inner being—their wishes, their dreams, their desires of things past, of things present, of things to come. Poetry should always be from the heart so that all who read it, live the feelings of the one who penned the words. Poetry is meant to snared. This poem here is of my childhood memories of visiting my grandparents at their farm. Those visits always produced meaningful memories

SPENCE, JOHN
[a.] San Luis Obispo, CA [title] "Fall" [pers.] This poem was inspired by a terrible, painful period in my life. Trough despair, adversity, and heartache, a flood of words was inevitable. Betrayal is at the center of this work, although each can take it and make it their own. The darkness has passed, and a new light has come forth in my life. I hope and pray that others can read this work and come away with a deeper realization of how, so often, our actions hurt others so deeply. God Bless

SPENCE, SYE
[a.] Riverhead, NY [title] "Haiku" [pers.] There's no long story behind "Haiku," in this poem, I could be serious. Poetry helps me to let out all my suppressed emotions. Everyone believes I'm a jolly 13 year old, but my smile covers a lot of feelings I wish to pour out, that's what "Haiku" is about. I live with my mom, Marguerite in New York. In June, I will be graduating Junior High School. I hope to be an endocrinologist someday. Other than writing poems, I write lyrics, short stories and essays. In my spare time, I listen and play music. I'm very proud that "Haiku" is receiving this great recognition

SPIERS, PHOEBE
[a.] Amelia, VA [title] "I Have the Light of God in Me" [pers.] I am 28 years old and I live in Amelia County, VA. I was born with Cerebral Palsy. I have had a lot of disappointments because of my disability, there have been things I wanted to do that I couldn't. However I have always been a happy person. My church, my friends and family have helped me deal with my disability. I have always enjoyed poetry. Paula Echols, who was my first grade teacher and is my best friend inspired me to write poems. Linda Crawford, who is another dear friend has also given me a lot of encouragement

SPRADLEY, DUSTY
[a.] San Jose, CA [title] "Whisper" [pers.] This poem is very special to me I hope others enjoy it as much as I do

SPURGEON, SALLY
[a.] Mesa, AZ [title] "Life Ever After" [pers.] I've always believed I would break into print as a novelist. I'd never thought about writing poetry. Last year I went to Bisbee. It was like coming home after being away for many years. The memories and emotions that came to the surface during my stay there inspired me to write "Life Ever After." I grew up in Oregon, the youngest of five children. My parents; two of the most wonderful people in the world, gave me the guidance that every child needs, and the freedom to be myself

STAHL, JASON
[a.] Gibsonburg, OH [title] "Change" [pers.] One thing special about most of my poems is that they stand for important events in my life. My poem "Change" is about my grandma. She was recently lost to cancer. Being a sixteen year old in America is tough sometimes, and poetry helped me through some hard times. In a way, I owe it all to my English teacher, Mrs. Rapsawich. It was she who opened my eyes to poetry

STAINBROOK, DENISE
[a.] Nashville, TN [title] "I Met Myself Today" [pers.] I grew up abused, as died most people. Only through very supportive friends, great inner strength and the will of God did I survive. This cycle must stop generation to generation. It stops with the annihilation of denial. Through verse, stories and autobiographies, I have a voice

STARNES, JOLEE
[a.] Iron Mountain, MI [title] "Eternity" [pers.] My poem is dedicated to others who shall one day find love within their hearts. I feel that this world deserves love, not hatred. So if others may see another's love, it shall go on as inspirations. Peace could be held and endured at last. Let the world use love as a single weapon against hatred an evil. I wish that someday we may all live in peace together, and cherish each other. Let this be a lesson to all, love is the eternal key to great wisdom and fortune. I have found love in family and friends as well as others. Let everyone cherish love and friendship. We may inspire others through poetry. True emotions allow to be released through the art of poetry. Writing is a gift to be cherished and recognized, for the world to see and read

STAUSS, TINA
[a.] Magna, UT [title] "In the Midnight Hour" [pers.] This poem came to me one night after a dream. Every time I look at the moon and see her glory I am reminded of all those who have lived here before us. I wish that this little poem can help bring us all closer. To those we have lost or have moved on. Just know they are all still with us, still inside us enjoy

STEARNS, JOSHUA
[a.] Peoria, IL [title] "Someone Else" [pers.] Poetry is something I've always loved to read but I always hated being forced to write any in school. I've been out of school for two years and have written four poems, each of which was written within a two week period this year. This poem is about a period of my life that happened just as recently as my new found joy in writing poetry

STEELE, COURTNEY
[a.] Enfield, CT [title] "Living"

STEELE, LENORA LYNN
[a.] Kansas City, KS [title] "Sonnet to Sunrise in Micronesia" [pers.] I have been writing poetry since I was six years old, although I am not very prolific since I have always been my own worst critic. This poem was a lived experience on the island of Pohnpei in Micronesia. When the rain filled the catchment on the roof, we had running water for showers and shampoos. I dove from a dock that was built by the Japanese after WWI. Visiting the Pacific Islands was the most inspiring experience of my life. I have written several poems about the trip

STEELE, ROB
[a.] Pierrefonds, QC [title] "Love of My Life" [pers.] I wrote this poem when I had feelings for someone, who was special to me. Now that love has shifted me towards a brighter light, I feel love again, but instead of the bird who can almost fly, I soar high over the clouds, feeling free with not a worry on my mind

STEIMLE, ALICE E.
[a.] Barnegat, NJ [title] "An Angel in My Pocket" [pers.] This poem was written after losing both my parents in 1996. Later it was dedicated to a very special person in my life. I've written many poems through the years for friends and family. Although they were written from my heart, I never thought they'd come to mean so much to others. Thank you for this great honor, and may God bless you all always. I pray this poem will heal others as it healed me. This talent came from God and my dear Papa

STEPANEK, CYNTHIA
[a.] Rolling Meadows, IL [title] "Beauty in Which We Walk" [pers.] As an artist, I like to explore through my thoughts. Sometimes for example, "Beauty in Which We Walk," which came to me by standing in a particular place on the family farm. The poem always makes me feel free with nature in all of its distinguished blessings. For me, writing is self-fulfilling in that my imagination is so stirred, and I discover so much. What inspires me to write, or what comes to me to write clown, at times seems explainable and unexplainable. My songs are similar, well inspired!

STEPHEN-MAPP, DEBORAH
[a.] Richmond, VA [title] "What is Man" [pers.] I wrote this poem to honor my husband, who is my best friend. Too often men are not told how special they are, and I want the good ones to know that we think so and want to let them know. I hope that all of you women who have a good husband will dedicate my poem to him

STEVENS, REBECCA
[a.] Terre Haute, IN [title] "Mistress Becca"

STEVENS, ROBIN
[a.] Cincinnati, OH [title] "Special Friend" [pers.] This poem is special to me because I have someone there to help me through hard times. I want to thank my parents Rosemary and Charles for encouraging me to follow my dreams and to my grandpa Harvey King Stevens Sr. For helping me put my feelings into words. To all my family thanks for being my pot of gold at the end of the rainbow. Thanks Angel, Buffy and Mandy for giving me your love

STEVENS-KITTNER, NORAH
[a.] Arlington, VA [title] "My Life" [pers.] I am 12 years old and live in Arlington, Virginia with my mom, dad, brother, and our many pets. I am in 7th grade at Williamsburg Middle School. I wrote this poem because it really explained how I feel sometimes. I write poetry to explain how I feel when I can't explain it by talking to someone. For fun, I play soccer, basketball, and I want to start my own girls football team. I believe strongly in animal rights and hope to help protect them in the future

STEWART, JOANNE
[a.] Reading, PA [title] "Just Remember" [pers.] I wrote "Just Remember" for my sister Pat, with my devoted love for reasons her and I will only share. And to the fond memories of my brother-in-law George, for he too gave my sister his devoted love

STEWART, LYLE
[a.] Chattanooga, TN [title] "True Love" [pers.] I wrote this poem one night very late, and had in mind what I would tell people about love. If you could not hear, see, feel, taste, smell or even thing; Then you would notice the love inside of you. As if you could turn your brain off with a switch. The first step to true love, is realizing that there is a power inside of you. I am not a poet, but poetry is a way to release feelings for me.

STEWART, SCOTT
[a.] Aberdeen, UK [title] "What About Personality" [pers.] This is my view of the world we live in. It represents a view that we all believe but few give thought or need to act upon. If it makes people pause and think, even for a moment then I have achieved what I set out to do. Thank you

STINE, JAMIE
[a.] Lewisville, TX [title] "Twilight" [pers.] Poetry allows the soul to take flight, and passion to be expressed in ways most have never thought possible. I have always loved the freedom eroticism of poetry, and the feeling of unbridled liberty that writing allows me

STINGILY, MILAN
[a.] Pittsburg, CA [title] "What is Love?" [pers.] My poetry is an extension of self and my interbeing. It is my special ex-cape and motivation. This poem is special to me and inspiration came from a special person, who I can always confide in, and to be able to share my poetry is a true blessing

STOCKDALE, MIKE
[a.] Clovis, NM [title] "The Ones That God Away" [pers.] Some of my favorite memories are when I was fishing with my dad. When I was nine, he bought a fly rod for me, and taught me how to use it. We went fishing every chance we got, but some always got away. Somewhere in the bottom of Kerr Lake is a big catfish with stringer in his mouth. But fish aren't all that got away, time got away from us too. Good luck fishing, dad

STOLFI, LYDIA
[a.] New Fairfield, CT [title] "Only Him" [pers.] I wrote this poem as an assignment about someone very special to me, that wasn't as close to me as he is now. He has inspired me to do such wonderful things, like writing my poetry (which so far has only been about him). When I submitted my poem

"Only Him" I didn't think anything was going to happen, but it did and it has made me realize that I do have some talent. This all happened because of him and I would like to thank him for everything he has ever done for me

STONE, AMMIE
[a.] Gowrie Mountain, QL, Australia [title] "The Bad Luck Bushman" [pers.] My poem, "The Bad Luck Bushman" was rushed for a year eight English assignment on Australian bush ballads. I never expected my poem to do so well. I have always enjoyed writing poetry in my spare time, as I believe it is a very exciting genre, which enables expression to be shown through words. My favorite poems are those including humour, a story or poems about nothing in particular, I enjoy ballads, limericks and acrostic poems most of all. Coincidentally, as the anthology is titled, "From the Mountain Top" I have lived on the top of a mountain all my life!

STONE, ANNETTE
[a.] Shawnee, OK [title] "Trick or Treat" [pers.] From the moment I began to read, my father, Charles Armstrong, put his beloved poetry book, "101 Famous Poems," in my hands to read to him. I was six. When I was 12 he died, but what better tribute could I have given him than my love for poetry. As a child, and as an adult I love holidays! Such wonder and expectation to experience! Children today miss out on the door to door adventure of "Trick or Treat"! I hoped to capture that feeling for whomever has never participated, while refreshing the memory for those who have

STONE, BONNIE
[a.] Center, CO [title] "Mighty Giant" [pers.] I love trees, I inherited that from my dad who is a carpenter. I also love poetry, theatre and the arts which I inherited from my mom. Combining these, I sat at the computer and wrote "Mighty Gian" in two minutes. It all just came out of my brain and into my finger, and onto the screen. I hope my poem helps those who read it to see trees and life differently. Coming from a hunting family in Colorado has made me see the world from a different perspective than everyone else, and for me poetry is a way to help other people see it different too

STONE, MISHALYN
[a.] Clarksville, TN [title] "Little Ones" [pers.] I am honored to share my poem, "Little Ones" with others, as well as with parents, who believe that their children light up their lives. My two children, Kristin and Logan, are the inspiration behind this poem, as well as so many others I write. I hope that other people who have children in their lives, can relate to these words, and maybe slow down in their hectic lives, of today's world, and let their little ones know just how special they are. I would be delighted, if they took just a little more time, to share this with them

STONE-ANDERSON, MELISSA
[a.] Marion, IL [title] "Your Guardian Angel" [pers.] This poem was written for my sister, Kimberly. We recently lost our father. Charles Stone in a trucking accident. She has told me several times to think optimistically that it inspired me to write "Your Guardian Angel." Knowing our father is in Heaven, we must have several angels watching over us. I wanted her to know that he is still with us only in a different way. Without the positive support from my family, mom Rose, sister Kimberly, husband David, and step-son Jonathan, I wouldn't be able to write the poetry the way I do

STONER, ASHLEY
[a.] Harrisburg, PA [title] "Wondering" [pers.] I would like to dedicate this poem to my English teacher. She inspired our whole class to get involved with poetry. So thank you Mrs. Long for all you've done. Now for a little about me. I am

14 years old. I live in Harrisburg, PA. I am in 8th grade and I love to play sports. I also play the piano. I would like to thank my friends and family for all they have done too. And don't forget "Live life to its fullest you never know when it could end."

STORENG, ERIC
[a.] Ann Arbor, MI [title] "Dragon of January" [pers.] I am not of extraordinary brilliance nor am I gifted in a prophetic nature, I simply put life into words. This is my calling and my passion. I seek the perfect words to portray, an imperfect world, my source of satisfaction and my unique love of humankind all spelled out neatly so that the world may learn of itself one poem at a time. One beautiful word after another

STORK, MATTHEW
[a.] St. Louis, MO [title] "Free to Decide" [pers.] I believe the force behind this poem to me was created by society. Every single person I had the honor to meet in my lifetime gave me a part of his or her personality and thinking to create the poem I wrote. With every growing knowledge found out in people's lives, the more inspiration will be given to me in the hopes of writing more wonderful poems for the people I know and love

STOVER-TAYLOR, KAREN
[a.] Troy, OH [title] "Protectors of Our Land" [pers.] This poem was written in November 1983, while I was in high school. It was a time that I wanted to join the military, but was unable to enlist because of their physical requirements. Since I was unable to serve in that way, I wrote this poem to let all military persons know they have not been forgotten. Later in my life, I married a man that served us for nearly 17 years. So here's to you Michael, with all my love. Thank you for protecting us, and loving us with so many years of your life. I love you!

STRICKLAND, VICKIE
[a.] Roebuck, SC [title] "Empty Cocoon" [pers.] While I was grieving the death of my father, Leland Page Hodge, a friend, Tami Cribb, mailed me a little note that profoundly changed my focus. Her note described caterpillars grieving over a friend's empty cocoon. If only they could see the beautiful butterfly and the freedom it now expressed. I know that Jesus died and rose again because He raised me out of grief. Changing our focus from our loss to our loved one's freedom and peace forces grief to take flight. It's then our hearts can once again soar. Grief is focus caught "Between Darkness and Light"

STROM, ROSWITHA
[a.] Crawford Bay, BC [title] "Black Tide" [pers.] I love the beauty and flow of poetic rhythms shared by the immortal poets throughout the ages, finding within their well chosen words, comfort, peace, joy, inspiration and insight. Reading poetry throughout my life has given me a deep appreciation and admiration for the power of the written word. This beauty and power enables me to share with others my love of my magnificent surroundings, to give comfort and peace as needed and to impart my innermost emotions and insights

STYKEMAIN, JAMES
[a.] Virginia Beach, VA [title] "A Friend of the Net" [pers.] As an Analyst in the computer industry, most of my time is spent in computers both at home and at work. I read a lot of my daughter's poetry and enjoy her creativity. Over the years I have made a few friends on the net as a way to relax and converse ideas and thoughts. Never realizing that a long term friendship would emerge with someone I have never met. It is that one special friend on the net I dedicate this poem to, Maja 628. Other influences in my life are my wife Karen, Alan and Sarah

SUBEDI, HOM
[a.] Woodbridge, VA [title] "To Love" [pers.] Hom Nath Subedi was born in Takam, Myagdi, Nepal, on October 5th, 1947. He studied in Nepal,

India, and USA. He holds a B.Ed. and an M.A. In his early years, he published several short stories, poems, articles and research papers about Nepali language and literature in the magazines such as Madhu Parka, Jhankar, and Ruprekha. He founded Dhawalagiri Jana Club in Kathmandu and Annapurna Library in Myagdi. He edited Dhawalagiri Magazine while running other activities of the Dhawalagiri Jana Club as the president. He has written and published six novels: *Nyauli, Ratna, Najar*; one folk story collection called *Nepali Lok Katha-Chhantyal ko chheuchhaubat Pravasi Swor* (collection of poems, *Takam Darpan* (joint writing). In addition, He has written *Chhantyal Lok Katha*, another folk story collection and "Yo Samaj" epic, that are in the process of being published. He has published articles in several US-based magazines such as *Diyalo, Anterdristi*, ANS Newsletter, and ANA Newsletter. He was the founding president of INLS and Editor of *Insight* trimonthly magazine of INLS in USA. He achieved Ratna Shrestha Puraskar for his novel *Ankur* in 1997. He has been living at Virginia since 1981 with his wife Nanda Devi. He has two sons and grandchildren—Medha, Priya and Kavita Subedi.

SULLIVAN, DOUGLAS
[a.] Shrewsbury, MA [title] "The Clown Speaks" [pers.] This poem has no specific meaning other than it is for all those people who feel they are looked at, but never seen. Perhaps that is why I write: I want the world to feel my thoughts and sweat my emotions. Life for me is not about the money I may earn, the clothes that may drape my skin or even the people that may hold my hand; to me the good life is one that's worth the days I put into it

SULLIVAN, WILS
[a.] Louisville, KY [title] "Rain Songs" [pers.] The connection I feel the words I write comes from many aspects of my life. My love of people, Mother Earth, the beauty of life, the wonders of love. After having a near death experience, I became more in touch with my inner voice, the muse that speaks softly to all of us if we will just stop to listen

SUMNER, RANDAL
[a.] Cincinnati, OH [title] "Death Shard" [pers.] At the best, my poetry is a reflection of me. This was owe of many poems I wrote to show my confusion over someone I loved. To me it show a theme of love, with and eerie sense of coldness too. I write for fun, but many have told me I was I good enough to be published to which I humbly declined until. Now, I feel others should have the right to share it too

SUPITUX, LEAH
[a.] Miami, FL [title] "Boredom" [pers.] Poems express my somewhat pessimistic outlook upon life. I'm not personally suicidal, but most of my friends are. I've been subjected to ridicule from most of my peers. Today's society for teenagers has three kinds of classes, the outcasts, the somewhat popular, and the popular. I used to be an outcast, but have gradually brought my way up to the somewhat popular, but even with my small group of friends, I am still somewhat different. This poem is for, Bianca, Tiffany, Ismet and Charline, and especially Sara who is one of the few people that I trust, also Rosa too

SURJO, DAISY
[a.] Honolulu, HI [title] "Only Love Can Breaks Your Heart" [pers.] This poem means a lot to me in away of remembering my two special friends who inspired me to write this poem. They were my closest friends and I regretted that I had to leave them to study abroad. It was hard and it broke my heart when I saw them cried when they said goodbye. I enjoy writing poems, especially when I have a lot of things on my mind and I like to share them with people who I care about

SVENSSON, HEIDI
[a.] Alexandria, VA [title] "Passing Reflection" [pers.] In her single days, born in 1971 has been writing poetry since she was twelve years of age. Poetry has been an artistic outlet for Heidi and she feels free in expressing herself in many forms of art from writing to sculpting and painting. "I feel poetry is in all things surrounding us and I have been inspired by the love my husband and I share for one another to write the poem published in this Anthology." "It is a symbol of timeless love, the soul meaning of our existence."

SWAGGERTY, DANIEL
[a.] Mesquite, TX [title] "One's Passing Grade" [pers.] I have been writing poems since the fourth grade. Thank you Mrs. Shepherd and Mrs. Pyles, however I never took it serious until professor Kay Pulley brought to my attention by example. That when I look inside someone or a situation. Just write what I see without disturbing anything. I believe poetry is the expression of what the soul sees, feels and hears. The ability to translate it from eye to hand is a gift of God. Thanks Mom, Kathy M., Carla, Dori C., Stick Stickly, and Ron and Joet, the cattle prods of my motivation.

SWIMM, JAMIE
[a.] Chicopee, MA [title] "Giving In" [pers.] Well, to make this long story short, I literally went to sleep one night, woke in the morning a wrote a poem. I had no prior interest and never even thought twice about it. It's very weird. I love it and I can feel the burning passion in my body unleashing my creative mind with endless ideas that never stop popping into my head. I currently have a book that I wrote with a friend, that we produced/published ourselves. "Giving In" is a poem about, the temptations that we are exposed to every day, and not acting out on our impulses. For more of my writings, people can check out my website. My dream is to have my book that I wrote to be discovered and published, so people can buy it in bookstores. I will not stop, even on making my creative writing dreams come true

SYDOW, ELIZABETH
[a.] San Francisco, CA [title] "Juvy Bird" [pers.] "Juvy Bird" is dedicated to my good friend, slim. It was written when he was in Juvenile Hall serving his sentence. Once written, "Juvy Bird" quickly became one of my favorite as well as a hit with friends and family

SYKES, MONIQUE
[a.] Jesup, GA [title] "A Friend Like No Other" [pers.] First I would like to thank the Lord up above, and you guys at poetry.com for making this all happen. And the two people who encouraged me the Mos Hoc "Jay" Manuel and Aquana Kincy. With out their inspiration to let my poems be noticed by others I wouldn't be giving my thanks today regarding this poem, which is about my dog name diamond. Which was just like having a child of my own. Who is no longer here with me physically. But will always be apart of my heart

TALBOTT, HEATHER
[a.] Portland, OR [title] "On the Edge" [pers.] I always have kept a journal of poetry as an outlet. It was private and personal until a friend encouraged of the dark times we experience at one time or another. I like to read something like this and really grab onto the feeling of the poem. I think the goal is to visualize how a poem may relate to your own life and take wisdom and joy from that

TALBOTT, LINDSAY
[a.] San Marcos, CA [title] "It All Comes Down to You" [pers.] I am a fifteen-year-old high school sophomore. I feel fortunate to have been given this honor. I began writing poetry and one act plays several years ago I also began acting at an early age. My family expresses themselves artistically and I am proud to be no exception. I am so grateful to be able to share this with you

TALKINGTON, KAREN
[a.] Redding, CA [title] "Precious Gift" [pers.] Friendships are treasures along life's road to brighten our way. My poetry is usually a word picture about life experiences. Poetry is a creative Don in Redding, California and I have two grown children, Corina and Mark. I have an AA degree in Clothing Design. I am at home and enjoy several hobbies: Creating cards, drawing, acrylic and watercolor painting, decorative tole painting, flower arranging, bicycling, and gardening. Writing, singing, and learning guitar are special too, in life's everyday school

TAM, SHUSHAWNA
[a.] Corona, NY [title] "Student" [pers.] I feel very proud to have written this poem. This poem will help others to stay out of trouble. This poem was written for my little brother. It was written for my little brother. It was written to help him stay on the right track. By reading this poem every night and every morning my brother has improved a lot in his behaviour. Therefore, I believe that by writing this poem, children with similar problems will learn not to be followers and be leaders. It's all up to me!

TANIS, RAY
[a.] Blaine, MN [title] "My Answer" [pers.] "My Answer" responded to a real question posed while studying writing in 1996 with Jennifer Martin, a poet at the University of Indiana. In talking to friends about my love of writing one day, I was asked: "Who do you write like?" I answered with this poem. The importance of these words emphasizes my belief that we be known and respected for who we are; not for whom we are alike or a part of, nor for what we do; all too frequent. I am a farmer, masquerading as an engineer, with a passion for writing

TAPP, JACQUELINE
[a.] Lacey, WA [title] "Sunsets" [pers.] I wrote "Sunsets" because I love sitting on the beach at sunset and watching the waves gently crash against the sand. It give me a sense of joy and happiness. My family and I always gone camping and hiking in the woods. I love being out in nature and the beach is my favorite

TAYLOR, FRANCENE
[a.] Muskegon, MI [title] "Missing You" [pers.] Poetry for me is a part of my soul. A gift given to me. This poem is very dear to me and it was written for a special person in my life. He touched my soul for a moment in time. In my poetry that moment will last forever

TAYLOR, JEANE
[a.] Shelbyville, TX [title] "Lilies for Mama" [pers.] My greatest joy in life has been that of being a mother. For this reason I am happy to share my poem. "Lilies for Mama." The poem is dedicated to my only son, Michael. From the time he could walk he loved to pick flowers and share them with me. Tiny hands extending stubby flora offerings touch a mother's heart like no other gift does. The older one gets the more beautiful long ago tributes and memories become. Mother's know the apprehension and heartache of having her "little birds" leave the nest. Expressing motherly sentiments in poetry is a privilege.

TAYLOR, SCOTT
[a.] Dublin, GA [title] "The Hour-Glass" [pers.] Poetry has long been a mystery to me. However, after falling in love with the most inspiring and beautiful woman, I began to experiment with poetry. Shortly after we started dating, my wife began to suffer from the eating disorders, Anorexia and Bulimia. This poem, "The Hour-Glass" was written to help me to try and explain to myself as well as to others the struggle that a person suffering from these deadly diseases must endure. I hope that by reading this poem one can understand how difficult a battle that Anorexia and Bulimia are. Just remember, love always conquers

TEMPLE, JUDY
[a.] Warren, MI [title] "Lord Jesus" [pers.] My poem gave me great comfort in my life when I was going through some very hard times. Divorce and raising three small children alone were what I was trying to overcome. By writing this poem and having faith in the Lord, it gave me the strength I needed to go on with my life. My children, who are the great treasures in my life still recite this poem weekly, just to keep it alive. I am the luckiest mother in the world for having Tina, Mike and Chris in my life. My children make my life complete

TEO, SIEW FONG
[a.] Singapore, Singapore [title] "Wings in Despair" [pers.] An expression of incredible evidence of a far-fetched inner beauty. Poetry is a perfect way of recording that true evidence of something beyond the belief of the human race. A world of words caught between the spoken and the unspoken, "Pride and prejudice." Our creator, God almighty, Heaven's angels, the joys and cries present a great inspiration. Michael Jordan's perfect flight, intriguing, must be his imagination of a pair of wings. A point life be it happy or sad, a time to "take leave." Poetry is a persuasion to endorse to the living, truth beyond eyes

TEPANA, KATHLEEN
[a.] Sydney, Australia [title] "Rollercoaster Man" [pers.] Poetry is my friend, it's how I leave the world and play. When I write I feel like a little girl with toys. I play with the words for a while and then I think "wow" I like that—and I have a poem. People and how they impact our life fascinate me. Rollercoaster man is about seeing a reflection of me that I didn't like. "Rollercoaster Man" is a friend and we had a mutual and we had a mutual attraction, then followed confused chaos about is meaning. The poem shows my being set free from chaos and the misconceptions I had about myself

TERRENZI, SANDRA
[a.] Bradenton, FL [title] Personal Discovery [pers.] This poem came to me in an intuitive "flash" one morning when I was thinking about making unique Christmas presents for my husband and friends. Initially, I was going to find a poem I liked and put it in a handmade decorative frame. My husband Tom said, "Why don't you write your own poem." Immediately created, "Personal Discovery." My goal in life has been to truly love and accept myself and see the "God part" in all others. This poem, though simple, describes how I feel about myself and every other human spirit in this Universe. Look for my book "Grandmas: Twenty-First Century" that will be out soon

TESSIER, JUSTIN
[a.] Wingham, ON [title] "Our Dentist's Secret Work" [pers.] Justine Wayne Zbigniew resides in London, Canada, where he is in attendance at the University of Western Ontario. He was introduced to writing at a young age by his parents who encouraged exploration into short stories and poetry. Justin continues to chronicle the lives and situations of everyday people, capturing the images of human existence through the written word. At twenty-three years of age, Justin shows great promise for a future in Canadian literature

THANI, GIRESH
[a.] Waterloo, ON [title] "Through Everything" [pers.] "Through Everything" wholly touched the awareness of true love beyond our realm of understanding. The experience of skeptic we endure within our findings of this wonderful thing we know as love. And the endless nature of truth and loyalty between two whole-heartedly intertwined souls. Composed for the one whom I believe to be. Through everything, the endless love of my life, "Through Everything" and its

award of publishing has blessed me with yet another billion opportunity to express to her my love. I'll always love you Twalitha

THOMAS, GARY
[a.] Des Moines, IA [title] "What Jesus Might Say" [pers.] I grew up in Cleveland, OH, I am 31 years old. I was inspired to write this poem, not by a person or the world we live in, but by the holy spirit who guides me through life. Everything changes in life except for the love that Jesus has for us and the words he left for us to try and live by

THOMAS, LEROY, JR.
[a.] Syracuse, NY [title] "A Falling Leaf" [pers.] I hold a B.A. in International Relations and Diplomacy from Schiller International University-London, England. I am currently a paralegal student attending Bryant and Stratton College in North Syracuse, NY. I have lived and studied in the following countries: Germany, The Netherlands, The United Kingdom, and Spain. Poetry has been a very important creative outlet for the many experiences I have had. I am honored to have the opportunity to share my poetry with all of you. I live with my wife Dina, my mother Won, and my two dogs Lucy and Captain in Syracuse, NY

THOMPSON, JENNIFER
[a.] Punta Gorda, FL [title] "The One" [pers.] Poetry is a way of saying what's really going on inside of your head. My poetry stems from personal experience. This particular one was inspired by an ex-boyfriend of mine. The experience was definitely a good one. But, as all things, it came to an end. I believe poetry is a healthy way of letting out feelings; whether they be good or bad. Poetry is a gift, and I am pleased to share it with all who choose to read it

THOMPSON, LAURA
[a.] Houston, TX [title] "Broken" [pers.] For me, poetry is a way of expressing emotions. Within the words of my poems, I can offer companionship and courage to those that mean so much to me, and perhaps remind them that I am always with the mind spirit. I own a world of thanks to those who have supported me in my artistic endeavors. May their Muses always be kind, and may their angels always be watchful, as my own angel has so carefully guarded me. My heart will always be her for his kindness and encouragement

THOMSON, FELICIA
[a.] St. Charles, MO [title] "You, Me and Time" [pers.] I am fourteen years old. And I truly enjoy writing poems. This is the most exciting thing that's ever happen to me. Thank you for publishing my poem

THOMSON, RONALD, JR.
[a.] Amityville, L.I. NY [title] "Birth, Life, And Purpose" [pers.] My background is in the visual arts. For years I illustrated books, reading stories, poems historical and scientific texts. All this gave me great insight and knowledge on many subjects. As I matured as an artist I found poetry somewhere along the way, or should I say it found me. I am compelled as an artist to create. So, what I saw visually I began to express in poetry as well. Sometimes I combine the two. My problem is most of my poetry is of great length. This poem means a great deal to me as it is one of my first. Inspired by the births of my sons, after experiencing the life and death struggles I saw in Vietnam. Being a veteran and survivor of that war, I am constantly looking for a purpose in life

THORPE, KAREN
[a.] San Antonio, TX [title] "Why" [pers.] This poem is very special to me, because it is about the way I felt when I lost my mother. My mother was and is very important in my life. And even though

she is not here with me physically. Spiritually, she will be with me always. Thanks to my husband James, and my two daughters, Alesha and Ashlee. Who helped me through the pain, and encouraged me to write this poem. And special thanks to my mother. I love you

THORPE, TREASURE
[a.] Connellsville, PA [title] "Dreams and Puzzles" [pers.] Well I am 51 years old. Mother and grandmother. My hobbies are I love old cars and car shows my favorite car is 1966 Chevelle. Right now I am going back to school to get my GED. I live in Connellsville, PA. I have a black chow and a cat the things most important in my life is my Lord savior Jesus Christ my friend Marty enthused me to write poetry. I dedicate my poems to my Lord Savior, Jesus, children, grandchildren

TILGHMAN, WADE
[a.] Ellsworth, ME [title] "Hunter's Trip" [pers.] This poem is special to me, because it takes me back to the wonderful times I spent with my dad hunting in Jackman, Maine. This poem is for my dad, John Tilghman. Thanks dad

TITLAND, ROBERT
[a.] Vaughn, MT [title] "Be Unlike" [pers.] Writing poems is like having a place holder for my thoughts. I try to communicate the feelings I have and at the same time make it so someone can relate it to their experiences. This poem in itself is very vague, but it clarifies if you can apply it to your life. Be your own, be unlike

TOM, CHRISTOPHER
[a.] Vista, CA [title] "Software Engineer" [pers.] This poem is dedicated to my partner who helped me open my eyes, touch and feel the world around me, give me a life that I thought I could never have and specially handle the distress that we have shared . . . Tuan (Shnuggle Bunny) Nguyen

TORTORICI, JOANNE
[a.] Staten Island, NY [title] "An Innocent Child" [pers.] This poem was written about and for a very special boy—Vincent Mannino. He has touched the hearts of all his teachers. Vincent has recently undergone brain surgery. Now he has to go through extensive follow-up treatments. This poem was written with every intention of winning a monetary prize that would help his family with the cost of his treatment. We all pray it will win!

TOTH, JULIA
[a.] Washington, PA [title] "My Heart" [pers.] Poetry is the best way I know to express my feelings. No matter which direction my life is headed poetry always seems to bring encouragement. In this poem my life was turned upside down from a relationship that was lost. Having no way from a relationship that was lost. Having no way to express my emotions I turned to my haven, poetry. It has become my favorite pastime and my passion

TRACY, LILLIAN
[a.] Moreno Valley, CA [title] "Country Girl" [pers.] Agnes wanted her family to know the extent of her capabilities. My dearest mother—congratulations your poem "Country Girl" is your fifteen minutes of fame!

TRAITLER ESPIRITU, ALEXANDER
[a.] Zurich, Switzerland [title] "What Should My Shipwreck Be?" [pers.] Despite the pervasive injustices that govern our world, I find that there is a measure of redemption in solidarity and compassion in the act of seeing yourself in another person. "What Should My Shipwreck Be?" can thus also be read as a song, or a prayer—both of them cradles of poetry for a world desperately in need of redemption. A prayer in the hope is restaking claim in the age-old Earth, resorbed into itself a thousand times. A prayer also with a look to the

future as a birthplace and heath, as that relentless trombone and oracle of life

TRAKTMAN, STACY
[a.] Freehold, NJ [title] "In a Lifetime" [pers.] Poetry to me is the way I release my thoughts and feelings and to have that connection of people feeling the same way I felt while writing this. My mother has been a big support in my life, as well a both my brothers. My hobby is spending time with my two dogs and my soon to be husband, Brian Schimpf. My voice is within my words

TRAN, LEO
[a.] Calgary, AB [title] "At Then" [pers.] This poem is very crude in that it is probably my first real poem. I wrote it because for most of my life, I had experienced loss; especially a loss of myself. It might be difficult for most to understand this but the main expression of this poem is loss, and I am sure everyone can relate to that because, well, haven't we all lost something or someone dear to us?

TRIMBLE, LARRY
[a.] Tulsa, OK [title] "Our Greatest Treasure" [pers.] While visiting Aspen, Colorado, I took a spectacular picture of these mountains. Thoughts of my sons and the times we spent in the mountains were heavy on my mind. My sons are the reason I have enjoyed so much in life. They were the reason I came to this place. They are the reason I return. My love of my sons inspired this poem, which I gave them for Christmas. No greater treasures has been given to me than Brian and Mark. I hope they bring their children to this place and feel what I feel . . . and remember

TRIVELLIN, TIMOTHY
[a.] Philadelphia, PA [title] "In My Ship" [pers.] I knew what awaited me if I gave up pride, selfish desire, and fear, but I could not do it myself. The Lord's love is vast, endless, and eternal, but I was not embracing it; just floating on top of it. The Lord loved us so much He died to pay for my sins because I could not. My desire is to return that love by living every moment faithfully. Yet, the only way to do that is to die to ourselves. My cry was to drown in His love; to let every breath be filled by Him, Jesus Christ

TRUJILLO, JENNIFER
[a.] San Jose, CA [title] "Sticky" [pers.] Everyone likes to believe he or she is a poet, right? I am no exception. I have always loved and loathed words. They are simple and elegant, and yet sometimes they fail us and loathed words. Language is a medium for emotion, and depth gets lost in the translation, but I find myself attempting to reflect the patterns I detect in life with these tools. Desperately exposed in the hopes that someone will notice. Writing for me is like loving, and the only rule I apply to both is this: Trust no one, but love/ write without fear

TUHACEK, ANGELA
[a.] Midway, AR [title] "Wish Upon A Star" [pers.] Poetry to me should be elegant, meaningful, passionate and emotional. It is the true window to the soul of those who read it and write it. I dedicate this poem and my heart to Karl Tuhacek, my one and only soulmate, to forever love

TUNICH, ELIZABETH
[a.] Clinton Twp, MI [title] "Love Is" [pers.] God gives everyone special gifts and talents to share. I believe poetry is a gift is a gift the at can be understood and appreciated by anyone. I use poetry to express things to others that I may not otherwise be able to. Poetry is my way of expressing my thoughts, feelings and emotions. It is also a way of sharing love, joy and encouragement when it seems that the world around us is losing touch with those most important things

TURNER, ANDY
[a.] Duluth, MN [title] "Tarnished Bonds" [pers.] This poem is very special to me, for it commemorates someone who has been a very important part of my life: Ms. Anita White, my soul mate. Although our actual contact has been far less, each time we're together my "Tarnished Bonds" are released, and pure joy becomes a part of my life. I can only hope that each of you has found such happiness. Thank you for being a part of me Anita

TURNER, BEVERLY
[a.] Harrington, DE [title] "My Life" [pers.] I feel that life has taken many turns. There have been times of great hardships, and times of wonderful joy. Some things I would have changed, if I could have (such as being diagnosed with breast cancer in 1991 and the days of seemingly endless pain, medication and treatment.) But each juncture of my life has produced another characteristic element that has made up the whole person. And when I look back I find I have no regrets. I can thank God for the person I am, and for His gift of poetry that I may express it

TURNER, CINDY
[a.] Cynthiana, KY [title] "The Spiders Web" [pers.] When I try to say how I feel the words in my mind become scrambled, but through poetry they flow. After several hard wrote. Four years I wrote nothing and my life was lost. Then God sent me a special friend who brought back the breath of life to my soul. My first poem published I dedicate to him, for with his friendship I found poetry again but most of all I found life. Hugs and kisses Kelly Joe, "I love You" my special friend

TURNER, GARY
[a.] Mesquite, TX [title] "The Unforgiven Wrong" [pers.] Born and raised south of Detroit, I began writing elementary school. Much of my poetry centers around confusion as life is never as straight forward as we presume. I would like to thank my parents Richard and Gayle Turner, for always encouraging me to follow my dreams, no matter how far south they take me! I hope to always make them proud in everything I do. And also thanks to my best friend, Brando whom I love dearly and could not have grown up without. At least not grown up the same way. Love you too Kimmie-Pie!

TURNER, KANDI
[a.] Gurley, AL [title] "Friends to the End" [pers.] This poem was wrote for my best friend Mandy Graves. She died two years ago. She was the best friend anybody in the world could have. She left three wonderful babies behind and her loving family. We will always remember you in our lives. You brought joy to everyone around. I have two kids Kyle which is six and Brianna which is three. I write poetry for fun or when I have nothing else to do

TURNEY, DESSYLYN
[a.] Gettysburg, PA [title] "The World Is a Coffin" [pers.] I am a freshman in High School. I am exploring the world and every turn of it. I enjoy expressing myself through poetry. My friends, family, over dramatic love life and the world around me inspired this poem. It was a homework assignment. I got angry and let the words flow. It is about being lied to about love

TWOMEY, NATHAN
[a.] Loch Arbour, NJ [title] "Falling Down" [pers.] This poem was written for all the people we meet along our journey through this life that disappear all too soon. Like a flame of beauty cast out by the wind. It was brief, but beautiful. Those days will never end as long as we keep our memories close. This poem is for them. If life ever seems to drag you down just put a little faith in this poem and everything will be okay

UHDE, SUZAN
[a.] Evansville, IN [title] "There's Always You" [pers.] Since writing poetry as a child, it has been a dream of mine to be published. I am humbled by the recognition. Writing, to me is an emotional expression that my voice cannot master

ULLMAN, KARL
[a.] Hoganas, Sweden [title] "The Tombstone" [pers.] My parents' gave me love and strength. I got the best prospects. Now it depends on me what my future will be. I am studying environmental accounting in Sweden and hope to take care of our world

UYENO, SUMMER
[a.] Commerce City, CO [title] "I Love You" [pers.] My name is Summer Uyeno. I am currently a freshman at a public high school in Colorado. Poetry has always been a big part of my life. It is a way of expressing my feelings. This poem, in particular, has a special meaning. It is about my first love and how he makes me feel. Most people know what it feels like to have emotions that sometimes can overwhelm you. It's amazing how you can be floating one minute and fuming the next, but still, no matter what, you still love that person. In closing I want to say thank you to the one who gave me the inspiration for writing this poem. Without him, this poem might not have existed. I hope those who read "I Love You" will remember, or still feel, what it is like to love someone

VADALA, DAVID
[a.] Universal City, TX [title] "Life's Inspiration" [pers.] Life, nature and poetry and gifts bestowed upon us by God. Noticing my love for nature since I was a child, my grandfather taught me that nature is an unfailing source of inspiration. I hope that others would inculcate the eternal values of life after reading my poem `Life's Inspiration

VAGHINI, ROBERT
[a.] Enfield, CT [title] "?" [pers.] "?" is a poem that represents our constant search for the "perfect life." We search for so long trying to reach the goal of our society's image of the ideal life. Why do so many of us waste our lives searching for something that doesn't exist? Too many of us worry about tomorrow so much we forget about today. The only advice I can offer to anybody is remember today; don't worry about tomorrow, and follow your heart to your own happiness

VAN AUKEN, BRANDON
[a.] Campbell, CA [title] "Forsaken Dreamer" [pers.] Forsake Dreamer is the first verse in a song I created named "The Witching Hour." It deals with World Issues as well as the condition of humanity. Here's the chorus: "The Sleeper must awaken before the dreamer is forsaken and taken past the point of no return, no way out, no where to run, nowhere to hide and seek your fortune." Poetry is one of cleanest way to filler feelings, through the soul. It is a direct translation, along with any other forms of art

VAN DER KLEY, THOM
[a.] Noordwijk, Netherlands [title] "Powerplay" [pers.] I am kind of proud to be in this book. First of all because English is not my native language. Second I always felt that my English poems weren't up to standard. The publication in this book proved me wrong

VAN DER VELDE, SVEN
[a.] Muntendam GR, Netherlands [title] "A Woman Walking By" [pers.] It is such a great privilege to enjoy a moment like it was a painting and on top of that finding the right words to describe it well enough to enjoy it again

VAN HAUEN, KATHERINE
[a.] Cedar Falls, IA [title] "Untitled" [pers.] I got inspired for this poem from an ex-boyfriend Nick. It means a lot to me. It is really nice to be a published at the age of 17. It inspires me to write even more. My poem talks about how different feelings come about and how it feels when someone you love come in and out of your life. Being in love is a very special thing. I won't ever forget those I love. I live in Iowa and go to Cedar Falls High. I graduate in January of 2001. I want to continue my writing career

VAN HORN, JENNIFER
[a.] New Paltz, NY [title] "Untitled" [pers.] For me, poetry is the best, and sometimes only, way to express my feelings. When the words don't want to come in speech, they tend to come on paper. I've been writing since I was fourteen, and I hope I never feel the need to stop. Poetry is my escape, and my release

VAN HOUTEN, SUE
[a.] Thomaston, GA [title] "Moment in Time" [pers.] Writing poetry is an achievement many people share. It is a great personal honor for me that goes well beyond all my expectations. I enjoy writing poetry for many reasons. Some, I give as gifts to loved ones, and others are a release of emotions from deep within myself. Whether it be funny, serious or deeply filled with love, putting pen and paper together to create a poem is something I will always treasure

VANDEBEEK, WIM
[a.] Meeuwen-Gruitrode, Belgium [title] "Left" [pers.] After working as a social worker for about four years, I more and more came to realize death and sorrow are an essential part of life. By writing my feelings I try to give them a place and I hope other people will be able to recognize themselves in these few lines and know they are not alone

VANGATES, DESS
[a.] Monticello, FL [title] "'Cause and Effect of Clone Upon Christmas" [pers.] Dess Vangates information available to the public is a twenty year conclusion of a part I play in a secret government germ study entitled, 'cause and effect Epstein-Barr virus germ mutant clone has upon Earth, 'Cause and effect Epstein-Barr virus germ mutant clone has upon human, 'cause and effect of Epstein-Barr virus germ mutant clone upon bovine. The reason, the one reason, the only one reason I write conclusion in poetry is so I, Dess Vangates can deny, and deny to I, Dess Vangates mean 'not knowing and or not having any credible knowledge of what I am writing about

VANGILDER, TESS
[a.] Vienna, OH [title] "Ponderance" [pers.] Excepting Christ in my life at age sixteen has been the most blessed relationship I've ever had. Knowing Christ has saved my life and those I love, brought new meaning to the words adventure, and shows true colors to the word love. If he reaches out to you, take his lead and follow. God Bless. I've been inspired since I can remember to write poems and stories. Currently I am indulging in writing a book. Its story will surely enlighten your mind and open some eyes

VANHOOSER, TODD
[a.] Springfield, MO [title] "Little Stones" [pers.] I have been telling stories in one form or another since my childhood, and have only found in recent years the satisfaction of conveying a thought in the form of poetry. "Little Stones" was written as an expression of the lasting impression a loved one leaves even in death. A year after losing my grandmother, I was moved by the resonating impact of her life, and wanted to capture that feeling in verse. Poetry in itself has a ripple effect on people, passing along a thought or emotion and lending insight to both the simplistic and the profound. In sharing this poem with others, I hope those ripples continue to expand

VAUGHN, BECKY
[a.] Groveland, FL [title] "My Luxuries" [pers.]

This poem was written for my family and friends. My parents Ray and Bertha Shepherd, who taught me the importance of family values. My husband, JW who has always been by my side. Our children, Ricky, Jason, Kisha, Jamie, Travis and Tony, you are my life's treasures. Our, grandchildren Payton and Julia and those to come, may you always know how special you are. My friends Pam, Carolyn and Dawn who have always been there for me. My family and friends are so special to me and I love them dearly

VAUGHT, STEPHANIE
[a.] Grand Prairie, TX [title] "Our Little Tyler" [pers.] This poem was written as a memorial to my son who died of SIDS at age four months. It reflects the eternal love our family will have for him and he touched our lives with his smile

VAYSBERG, KONSTANTIN
[a.] Wheeling, IL [title] "Believe . . . " [pers.] Life is a journey. It teaches us, comfort us, and tests us to help us find our way. The paths are different but one things is true in all. And that is our belief in the light. Never stop believing! Never!

VAZQUEZTELL, NELSON
[a.] Brooklyn, NY [title] "Thank You Dear Lord" [pers.] This piece was my fifth in a series of romantic poems which lead me to creating my first book and beginning on my second. Although the rest of my poetry also has comic and "non-romance" work, I find that poetry expressing one's innermost feelings can be the most gratifying and appreciated work. That is why my first (not yet published) book is almost entirely devoted to romance as well as to the beautiful girl that I fell in love with for the very first time. Truth, Comedy and poetry for all is dedicated to Toni, my first true love and this poem is only one of the many that showed my deepest feelings for her. The manuscript I am currently working on, *The V-Files*, will reveal many more heart-felt verses and lines. What more can I say, I'm a hopeless romantic

VELASQUEZ, KRISTOFER
[a.] Hoffman Estates, IL [title] "Sleep" [pers.] Each passing moment in our lives can be infinitely described in words. The connection that one makes to him or her self in the process in essential to their growth as individual. The connection made through the sharing of these words with others is equally as rewarding. Poetry, music, and all other forms of expression are the emotional bindings of human connection. To communicate, feel, and share on a purely abstract level is the most fulfilling thing to me. I am forever thankful for the gift of words and speech

VENKATESWARAN, MARGARET
[a.] White Plains, NY [title] "Your Eyes (A Poem About Adopting from India)" [pers.] My daughter has the most beautiful eyes. I cannot describe the feelings of love I experienced upon seeing her for the first time in Bombay when we were adopting her. I wish for all children of the world to have a happy home and that their eyes mystify their mothers with the joys of the physical souls they are

VERMETTE, CHRISTOPHER
[a.] Longmont, CO [title] "A Soliloquy to the World" [pers.] This poem reflects my feelings and emotions toward hatred, prejudice, and discrimination. I wanted to address it in Shakespeare's powerful tool, the soliloquy, as if I were the one addressing the audience, the people of the world. Only through a paradum shift will such emotions be eliminated, and only when this happens can we find true peace. I hope to one day complete a Doctoral Program in Philosophy and continue to write poems, essays and books (Fiction Novels and Research Material) that continue to examine the world around us. My driving force is the search for truth

VICK, TRISTAN
[a.] Bozeman, To [title] "Blank Light, At My Computer" [pers.] Blank Light (at my computer) is the creation of my own personal procrastination. One evening as I sat in front of my computer contemplating an essay for one of my most tedious college courses, I set forth on a journey of procrastination. This poem is the very special final product of my straying mind. Looking back, I chuckle about how through the practice of procrastination. I conceived the final product of such a charming poem

VILLELLA, HEATER
[a.] Greenville, NC [title] "The Hattras Light" [pers.] I was inspired to write poetry from a poetry class I took at East Carolina University. The poem "The Hattras Light" is about one of the oldest brick lighthouse on the eastern coast. This lighthouse was recently moved closer to land because it was endangered by the Altantic ocean. The moving of the lighthouse was a major concern to the people in North Carolina. I wrote this poem to share the excitement and thrill that this lighthouse has brought to everyone, and that the Hattras lighthouse's light still lives on

VINCENT, HAZEL
[a.] Port Neches, TX [title] "Life" [pers.] Poetry has a very special meaning to me. I use my poems to express my feelings and emotions which I sometime have a problem showing. This poem was written at a low point in my life. I thought my patience, will, strength, and everything were running out. I looked inside my heart and found love. My family, friends and especially God helped to lift me from my downfall. Just remember, when you think things are bad and couldn't get any worse, look in your heart for those who you love and love you. Life is what you make it

VINDIS, MIHA
[a.] Slovenia, Europe [title] "Morning Crime"

VOGAL, ADAM
a.] McMinnville, OR [title] "I Am" [pers.] If when you look forward, you see nothing, back up and look at the steps you have taken. Adam Vogal there are many thing of which I am proud of in my life, but one more so than my son Austyn Zay Vogal. I love you Buddy! I also wish to take this opportunity to thank my mom for her inspiration and love, Ed Cliff, who knows the meaning of friendship and Dolly for showing me things that I had forgotten!

VORE, KERRY
[a.] Eglin AFB, FL [title] "Teachers" [pers.] I wrote this poem for my daughter's 1st grade teacher Ms. Pelfree. We used as a bulletin board display. I hope that all the teachers out there enjoy this poem as this is for them. For a long time I wanted to send a poem in for a book. Thanks to this poem and Ms. Pelfree I finally can see my dream come true

VRABEL, RITA
[a.] Russelville, AR [title] "Missing You" [pers.] Life is filled with high and low moments and during the darkest times and at the peaks of joy, words flow from my heart. Poems are my way of cleansing hurt and pain and expressing feeling of joy. This poem is memory of a dear step-father whose love made a broken family whole again. In the last years of his life, his love, appreciation and humor made caring for him a joy. No matter how bad he felt, he could brighten your day and make you laugh. One day he left my home in an ambulance and never returned

WAGNER, JENNIFER
[a.] Blackwood, NJ [title] "Sullen and Somber" [pers.] I am currently a senior at Paul VI High School. Next year I will be attending the college of New Jersey. I would like to use this space to thank my parents, Mark and Mary, and my sister, Tiffany, for always giving me support and guidance in everything. I am so grateful for my parents' devotion and sister's friendship. My hope is that I've made them proud over the past 17 years. My grandmother, Mary, has also been an inspiration to me. I will never be able to truly express my gratitude to my family for my words alone could never be enough

WALDROP, JOE
[a.] Fairhope, AL [title] "A Life Well Spent" [pers.] My poem is about a person's salvation combined with the physical and mental anguish I've faced in my life. It's my way of trying to put into words, in an emblematic scenario, God saving me physically and spiritually. I hope that someone other than me finds meaning in it

WALKER, RICHARD J.
[a.] Humble, TX [title] "Father in My Eyes" [pers.] My Passion has always been writing but when I wrote this it was more about closure. All my life I believed I had it rough but I was wrong. Sure my father wasn't the Dad I wanted and time could only tell when he would become that man. When lance entered my life I was amazed and angry why could a man not of my blood love we unconditionally yet my own Dad denied me that which I wanted. Soon Lance became my father not only in name but also in action he taught me what it meant to be a man, to be a father. Now I have two daughters Raeven and Megan my true passions are watching them grow one day I wish to publish all my poetry for them to tell all I have even felt since I was young

WALKER, SHUJEN
[a.] San Diego, CA [title] "Are You My Other Hall?" [pers.] Loneliness comes in many colors, shapes, and sizes. As a spiritual being, a soul, a person, you must venture through this world alone. The need and desire to find your other half, someone who will fulfill the gap, the hole, the emptiness felt deep down inside becomes stronger and stronger as the days go by. I'd like to thank my father, Howard Charles Walker, who recently passed away, for 23 years of raising a respectable young lady. He is the source of my knowledge

WALKIN, DEBORAH
[a.] Baltimore, MD [title] "Someone's Deeper Than Flesh" [pers.] This poem represents a turning point in my life, in embracing love. It is allegorical, as it speaks through the `seasons' of the Sea. I wished to portray that true, unconditional love is found and given, only, when God is its foundation, hence the title "Someone Deeper Than Flesh." Being a Native of the Bahamas and having a familiar and enduring relationship with the Sea, made it a natural choice for me to use it, to express my view of love. I hope that this poem touches everyone where it touched me

WALLACE, JANICE
[a.] Richmond, VA [title] "Summertime My Slumbertime" [pers.] Born on Grandmother's Farm, in the North Carolina Mountains, there were lush, sweet cherry trees to climb and cold, rocky mountain streams with crawfish running wild. The poor in wealth I was blessed with the beauty of nature and the love of great paintings, music and books through my poetry and my paintings, I pass this legacy to my son and to my grandson

WALLER, JOHN
[a.] Bronx, NY [title] "Here I Stand" [pers.] I feel that poetry is a blessing, from the creator, without whom nothing is possible. This poem was inspired from various stories on police brutality. I hope that others can relate to what it feels like to daily live as a black man. Special thanks to Inger for bringing out the inner voice, by getting me to express myself and putting the words on paper. Waller, John New York, NY

WALLEY, NATHAN
[a.] Memphis, TN [title] "My Mark in Time" [pers.] As a former practicing dentist of many years, I naturally am conscious of time and how it is spent. And as a Christian I am naturally concerned about today and the future. It's always been important to me to encourage everyone to never waste a single moment and as my wife Donna has said "we should make our mark of love while we are here on Earth." We do this by what we say, by how we live and the example we get

WALTON, NANCY
[a.] Dover, PA [title] "Oh Father of Mine" [pers.] My poem is dedicated to my father, James Gembe who passed away July 1999. He had a liver disease, went through a liver transplant. He never recovered enough after the transplant to come home. His courage and caring attitude for others during his illness was an inspiration to me. Even when he was in the hospital he displayed a sense of humor. I enjoyed my father's ability to make others laugh. He was a great man and father. "Oh Father of Mine"

WARD, FAYELLE
[a.] Jacksonville, AL [title] "Mystery" [pers.] I feel this accurately describes my thoughts about a mysterious creation by God—stars. So far away, yet possessing of so many qualities, they provide delight for some and wonder for others. Of everything in our physical world that has been touched by the creator's hands, celestial beings are by far the least understood. A large part of me hopes they will remain a mystery forever

WARD, JAMILYN
[a.] Phoenix, AZ [title] "Adieu" [pers.] This poem, Adieu, is not highly unusual among my poetry, in that I like to write poetry from an unfamiliar perspective. I wrote this poem to represent the peace of mind that I would like to have when I am ready to die, which hopefully, is still many years in the future. I am sixteen years old, and I started writing poetry a little over a year and a half ago for a summer English assignment. I have been unable to stop writing poetry ever since that day in August, 1998, when I wrote my first poem

WARE, ADRIENE
[a.] Conway, AR [title] "There Be Freedom when Jesus Comes" [pers.] I was born in hope, Arkansas twenty-three years ago to Alma and Richard Phillips. I received an associate of arts in General Studies from the University of Central Arkansas. I presently work for the central office of child support enforcement in little Rock. My husband, Eric, and I have no children. I have been writing poems and short stories since I was in elementary school. I began to write "There Be Freedom . . ." when I was in the seventh grade. I put the poem away in a folder and forgot about it. Two years later, while going through some of my writings, I discovered that I hadn't finished the poem. That is when I wrote the second half of the poem. "There Be Freedom" . . . tells the story of a slave who has much misery and has lost everything, but he or she finds hope in the thought of freedom during the second coming of Christ. The poem can also symbolize being bound not only physically, but mentally, emotionally, or any worldly slavery that causes grief for oneself and one's family. Even though things may seem bad now, we must remember there is freedom in Jesus Christ!

WARGO, CATHERINE
[a.] Brooklyn Center, MN [title] "Dear Soldier" [pers.] This poem is very special to me, as it was written for my husband when he was overseas during the Persian Gulf War. We were married just seven hours before he left for eight months. We have been married now for ten years. I have always expressed my thoughts in verse and this poem was no exception. I hope you will enjoy reading it as much as I did writing it

WARNER, DANIEL
[a.] Readlyn, IA [title] "Silent Sadness" [pers.] The first poem I wrote was for a girl when I was in eighth grade. In the years since then I have been writing for myself. It seems to me that the most inspiring thoughts are those which one struggles to remember as the busy day runs to its end. Poetry is my way of holding on to these small eternities which may otherwise become invisible for all other than my subconscious. This poem embodies my thoughts as I was driving home from school. It tells of the frustration brought on by my choices for a new relationship

WARNOCK, J. MATTHEW
[a.] Columbia, MD [title] "Look to Find" [pers.] One week in early February 2000, I got fed up with the rat race, negativity, misunderstanding and pessimism. I thought to myself, "There has to be more out there." So I started driving. With only a sleeping bag, a couple to-shirts and old blue jeans along with my ever confidential field, journal I set off on one of the most eye-opening journey's of my life. I found my way to Key West and met some of the most wonderful, carefree, people I have ever met. I observed, and wrote. I experienced new things and wrote. I talked to complete strangers and wrote more. Finally, while having a beer in Margaritaville, "Look to Find" came to me and I wrote it in no more than five minutes everything came together and it flowed out of me. I'll always remember the big smile I had on my face and the feeling of contentment that came with drinking up life!

WARREN, LINDA
[a.] Belton, MO [title] "Memories" [pers.] While going through a difficult time in my life, I wrote this poem and for others relating to child sexual abuse and myself, I began my healing and recovery journey three years ago at the age of forty-nine. Through poetry, my inner child was able to express her pain and the hurt of a lifetime. My children and their families are my rock and I have been truly blessed with their encouragement and support. There are two special people, Drs. Wenner and Stewart who I will be eternally grateful to for giving my life back to me

WARRINER, DONNIE
[a.] Russell Springs, KY [title] "Broken Heart" [pers.] Poetry to me is beauty of thought or expression written in verse. The way a person expresses him or herself with life's experiences. Whether real or imaginary. Most of my poems are invented from imagination are based on affairs of the heart. Mainly the human emotion of love. The strongest emotion of all

WATKINS, MARY
[a.] Loganville, GA [title] "My True Love" [pers.] My ability to write poetry is a God given talent. I use it to praise Him and to tell people about the Gospel of Jesus Christ. My life has been forever changed since I invited Jesus into my heart. I have peace, hope, joy and I am able to love . . . genuinely love. Matthew 6:33 says "Seek first his kingdom and His righteousness, and all these things will be given to you as well." I just want to say that no matter who you are or what you've done Jesus loves you!

WEAVER, DAVID
[a.] New Holland, PA [title] "To the Women I Have Known" [pers.] The poem was written to the remembrance of all the women that I have met and are about to meet. It's content has been a long journey, many miles of distant thought, and beautiful memories. I thank them

WEBER, LIZZIE
[a.] Brentwood, NH [title] "Floating Clouds" [pers.] I started writing poetry in fourth grade with first poem. "Yesterday," and have been adding to my collection. Floating clouds actually came to me on a clear cloud-free day. I guess I was just longing for, the clouds

WEBER, LIZZIE
[a.] Brentwood, NH [title] "The Rain" [pers.] I live in a small town in New Hampshire and will be 13 years old as of October 11, 2000. Writing is one of my favorite hobbies. The Rain is one of my personal favorites of my 20 poems. I am involved in theater productions at school, as well as softball, basketball and track. I am an honor student

WECH, DAVID
[a.] Kingston, PA [title] "How Can I Be Free?" [pers.] This poem reflects the feelings of rejection we all face from time to time. Dam a twenty years old gay male. My poem "How Can I Be Free" is a collection of thoughts that ran through my head in high school, a place where I was subjected to a great deal of rejection. However, I realize now, that you have to live for yourself and to not let other people take that from you. I hope that people reading this poem will understand just how much words and actions can hurt

WEILAND, DODY
[a.] Beresford, SD [title] "The Basketball Coach" [pers.] I love and respect my husband Darrell, and this poem is truly him. It flowed out of my mouth one day so easy and that's how the poem came to be. I wish the world could have him as their coach, children truly benefited from him. We have had so much fun in our lives going to games, as he brought out the talent they had even more in his young boys I love to write. I have three beautiful children, son Joe and wife Terri, daughters Jo-Lee and husband Larry Jill and husband Brian, eleven grandchildren

WEINHOLD, DANIELLE
[a.] Valparaiso, IN [title] "Suburbs" [pers.] I am a seventeen year old artist of many genres. I have been playing guitar for five years writing for seven, and drawing since I was big enough to hold a pencil. I draw inspiration from everything to hold me which has gained me much criticism for focusing too much on the negative. But, not only is there an abundance of it, I feel it is equally important to express the darker side of creation as it is the light. It seems the only way to overcome our destructive impulses is to acknowledge and appreciate them

WELLS, B. F.
[a.] Grayson, GA [title] "The Guest" [pers.] It has been said of B. F. Wells that he is a true southern gentleman having spent his life in Texas, Alabama and Georgia haunting bookstores, fishing and having a very occasional cigar. A 1983 graduate of Auburn University, he has been interested in writing and poetry since childhood and as an adult, had to buy a house just for his book collection. Certain folks say he is influenced by Erskine Caldwell and Flannery O'Connor but he is a reclusive man and will neither claim or deny these statements

WELLSWORTH, EMILY
[a.] Geinfelden-Musberg, Germany [title] "Eyes of Man" [pers.] I think of us as wordsmiths—and, like its iron-orientated counter part, the job is difficult, capable of causing agonizing pains the morning after, and sometimes not all its cracked up to be. I discovered this winning a national award for poetry at the tender age of fourteen—a more two years ago. But like a drug, you get addicted. So I write. For others, for everybody, but mostly for myself, because I'm a normal (i.e., selfish) person . . . But I thank everyone who reads poetry, and also C.M. Doan, because he is a wordsmith, too

WERKHEISER, LYNN
[a.] Effort, PA [title] "Volcano" [pers.] I am a freshman in high school and a member of the National Junior Honor Society. I enjoy reading, writing, listening to music, singing, in the school chorus, playing on the school's junior varsity girl's softball team, and watching television and movies. I also love camping, hiking, fishing, and studying

science and history. I want to become a volcanologist and an author. I would like to thank my three closest friends, my family, and my teachers for helping me believe in myself, my singing, my sports, and my writings. I hope that someday I will be able to return the favor

WESHO, CYNTHIA
[a.] Bellflower, CA [title] "Sun Idealized in You" [pers.] This poem was written for my love, Leoncio Barbosa III. We met at the darkest point in our lives. I had no direction and one month out of a relationship. He was getting over the loss of his, Anastasia of nine years. The night we met was one year to the day of her passing. We picked each other up from ourselves. He saw in me a light I thought could never shine again. His talents and intelligence astounds me. This poem is the proof that true love exists. After three years together, we still are purely in love

WEST, ANNA
[a.] San Francisco, CA [title] "Budapest in Black and White" [pers.] This particular poem was written as an introduction to an exquisite collection of black and white photographs show cased on the CD-ROM, "Images of Budapest" When asked to define my poetry, I cannot, except to say it is a voice that comes from an uncensored part of my being an essential place that demands expression. My poems are lucid moments, psalms, a celebration of life in all its nuances. The dark, the light, the joy and confusion . . . all of it. I consider this gift a great privilege

WEST, SALLY
[a.] Las Vegas, NV [title] "You and Me" [pers.] When I was in seventh grade an English teacher, singled out a short story I had written and read it to the class. The same thing happened again in college. I started to write poetry, when my daughter was born. This poem "You and Me" was written about my daughter, and how I feel about her. I have written many beautiful poems, and I am honored to have my first published in "From A Mountaintop." I also write short children stories, searching for ways to get them published. While living in Las Vegas, with dreams of becoming an author of children's literature

WESTCOTT, KAREN
[a.] Castalia, OH [title] "The Roses' Timid Beauty" [pers.] I am a freshman at Margaretta High School, and I plan to attend College at Firelands Branch of Bowling Green State University in the fall of 2000. I live in the country with my two older sisters, Kim and Kelly, along with my terrific parents, Dan and Deb. All of the poems I write are about what I am feeling at the time. I think that I can express my emotions best through poetry. I have always enjoyed writing poetry, and will continue to do so

WHEELER, JODI
[a.] Tiffin, OH [title] "It Hurts" [pers.] This poem reflects my inner-feelings. I lost my cherished father to pancreatic cancer about two 1/2 years ago. I still miss him and his love for me terribly. "It Hurts" come out to paper very naturally. Writing poems to me is great therapy, as it totally reflects my inner-self, joyful or sad. Thanks to my family (Mom, Shane, Craig, Nichole, Katie, Sherri, Emily and Michael) for helping me to be strong and to believe in myself

WHITE, CHANCY
[a.] Roseburg, OR [title] "Marshindas" [pers.] My poems have come from my heart for the sorrow of the lose of a close a friend that was struck by a car. We were very good friends and my family knew him well. God has touched my heart and inspired me to write feelings from my pure heart. I am 13 and go to a small school of about 100 students 7th to 12th grade. I hope to write a whole book of poems in the future

WHITE, CHERYL
[a.] Carney's Point, NJ [title] "Ode to Garth" [pers.] The music of this man is the inspiration for this poem. In my darkest hour, he embraced my soul and gave me the belief that dreams can come true. We could all do without the pain and sorrow that comes with life but the love and friendship we find along the way, make life worth living. The love and friendship I have acquired through garth is something I will eternally be grateful for. While I will never be able to fully thank him, I will die trying

WHITE, LYNN
[a.] Winterville, NC [title] "Empathy" [pers.] My name is Lynn White, I am 24 and I live in Eastern North Carolina. I have recently graduated from East Carolina University. My passions in life are creating beautiful music and expressive writing. I feel that empathy is a very special quality to possess. Within my lifetime, I have found that very few people genuinely empathize with their fellowman. If a trait is exemplified, it is usually sympathy which is completely different. Those who have the capacity for empathy are truly blessed individuals and should be cherished. This poem is meant to highlight these uniquely loving people

WHITE, THOMAS, III
[a.] Middleburg, FL [title] "Just the Other Day" [pers.] Poetry for me is the gift of expression in a life full of questions. "Just the Other Day" was born of them questions, God speaks to us all, but on this morning I listened with my pen not really aware of what I was writing, just letting him guild my hand so I know my gift of writing poetry comes from God, because no one, least of all me knew that I would find my passion in writing!

WHITFIELD, FELISA
[a.] Pittsfield, MA [title] "Why Do I Love You?" [pers.] This poem was a healing factor me. I wrote it in February regarding my ex-husband. Since grammar school I have written poetry. It is a true passion of mine. I love poetry and writing it as well. I only hope that my poem will inspire and help those in the world who have had marriage turn sour on them. May poetry forever live in the world. I am 33 years old and have three teenage daughters. I live in Pittsfield, Massachusetts. I moved up here from NYC the Bronx five years ago. I have worked as a NYC school volunteer which I won two awards. Worked as an executive secretary with word processing for six years after I received my business certificate from Manhattan Career Institute. I have a grandmother 86 years old who has always told me to keep up my writing and I am proud to say she was right. This is for you grandma Bruno.

WHITTEN, KEVIN
[a.] Lexington, KY [title] "Escape" [pers.] Until now my poetry has been for my enjoyment alone, but I am grateful for the chance to share it through this publication. I am 23 years old, I am from Princeton, Indiana but I now like in Lexington, Kentucky. Most of my poems are written from a songwriting perspective, but "No Escape" is one that I never put to music. It is basically the story of loves "ups and downs" and the ability to try again. A poem is a bird with wings of words that flies in the clouds of my mind

WICKETT, APRIL
[a.] Omaha, NE [title] "I Will Survive" [pers.] April M. Wickett currently resides in Omaha, NE at the age of twenty four. Graphic Design is her occupation with a B.F.A. from Concordia College in Seward, NE. She occupies her personal time painting in acrylics, multi-media, and composing personal writings.

WIGG, ANDREW
[a.] Sydney, NSW [title] "Dreams" [pers.] I guess it's a simple, but often overlooked piece of advice to follow your dreams. It is the only true way for you to live life, to know and experience what it's all about, to have "lived." That is what "Dreams" is about, with more important piece of advice follow your dreams for you but make sure that you don't lose touch with the important people in your life like family and friends. Don't take it for granted that they will always be there or else you'll regret it. This poem is dedicated to mom and dad, I know where home is and I also know that you will always be there

WILCOX, ANNE
[a.] Bowie, MD [title] "Misty and Joe" [pers.] This poem is of encouragement. When my 20 year old daughter committed suicide. I believe I'd never pull through. Then two years later when my 59 year old father died from alcohol, I was sure I'd be in the Abyss forever. My blessings are my children. Alex and Chris, my husband DeVitt, my mother, Harlene, and my faith in God! God doesn't let you, walk alone, sometimes he even carries you

WILCOX, MELANIE
[a.] Worcester, MA [title] "The Unknown" [pers.] Writing is an artist's soul poured out like dreams onto paper! Feel words are immortal and the best heirlooms passed down from generation to generation. One should never hesitate. I have been writing ever since I was very young and plan to keep writing for a long time

WILDER, JACINDA
[a.] Jacksonville, FL [title] "Little Girl" [pers.] Poetry, songwriting is the main way I release my negative feelings. Soul searching helps come to terms with my emotions. This particular poem describes how my mind attacks itself, hurling me into extreme depression. It's how I see the vicious cycle taking over and not being able to stop it. I dedicate this piece to my husband, Danny, for all he does for me and to Chris Cornell (Sound garden) for showing me the way to writing again. I thank Jesus for my gift

WILDS, JUSTIN
[a.] Forth Worth, TX [title] "What's Left?" [pers.] This poem has a two-fold meaning for me. It was initially to inform someone that I would no longer write, at least not for her. I've always loved writing, and will continue to write, but I will write for me. The second thing this poem reminds me of, is what my parents have always told me. My parents tell me every day, "you can achieve anything you want to, as long as you put your mind to it." This poem prove that to be true

WILEY, DREMA
[a.] Mammoth, WV [title] "A Reason to Live" [pers.] My talent for writing poetry is definitely a gift from God. I hope it will be an encouragement or a help to others. There have been many times in my life when I could not find the words to fall someone how I felt. Then later, when I was alone I could write it all down on paper very easily. My poetry is a blessing from God. I would like to share it in the hope that others will be blest, too!

WILEY, JOAN V.
[a.] Goshen, NY [title] "We Are a World Within Worlds" [pers.] For my family, for my friends, for the world, for the universe, for all denizens, for space, for time, for . . . I give. Family, friends, world universe, denizens, space, time, forgive!

WILHITE, BRETT
[a.] Lompoc, CA [title] "Worthwhile" [pers.] Poetry is my tool that I use to express a feeling or an emotion. Worthwhile is a poem about the most beautiful woman I know. She could inspire me to do anything. I will always be stunned by her beauty, and her kindness is something I'll never forget. She is a true goddess. A woman like her is definitely worth waiting for. Poems are great for expressing emotions like this

WILLEMSEN, CHARLES
[a.] Miami, FL [title] "My Soul Has Gone Off Somewhere" [pers.] I have been writing since I was 14, as a way to express my feelings when I'm reluctant to talk about them. Writing has seen me through from heartache and depression to peacefulness and bliss. This particular poem was written while sadness was with me, and it takes about obtaining inner peace. Although sometimes we all feel low, I have learned that it is in our power to lift our hearts up to God and feel replenished by His love. With Him, we will triumph come what may

WILLIAMS, ANDREW J.
[a.] La Habra, CA]title] "Promise" [pers.] I write about that which I love and delight in; the people, events and things that I am passionate about. It is special to share these in poetry

WILLIAMS, DANIEL
[a.] Conway, AR [title] "Without Her I Am Empty" [pers.] So many times people overlook what is wonderful and beautiful in their lives. I feel a need to write down the things I feel. Through my writings I hope that some will stop long enough to think on the positive things in life. Even if it is only for the short period of time that it takes them to read something that God has given me the insight to put on paper

WILLIAMS, DONNA
[a.] Bristol, PA [title] "Searching Yet" [pers.] In the time since this poem was written I have found my heart content. It is wonderful to leave something that was so important to me, to my grandchildren. Torrin, this one's for you!

WILLIAMS, FRANKLIN
[a.] Lumberport, WV [title] "Appalachian Meditation" [pers.] "Appalachian Meditation" is actually a song that I wrote back in 1984 while working in a coal-fired power station in West Virginia. I wrote the lyric first and then strummed out the tune on my acoustic guitar. The song was originally written with twenty-one lines. I axed the second line of the refrain after the third verse in order to enter it as a twenty line poem, however, the full ending is implied at least in the imagination! The scenic Appalachian Mountains are a tribute to the handiwork of our gracious creator whom I live to serve

WILLIAMS, REGINA
[a.] Durham, NC [title] "For Those of You Who Still Have Mom" [pers.] I was inspired to write this poem because of an e-mail I received entitled, "Do You Love Your Mom?" I began to contemplate on what would be the need to ask such a question? As I reminisced on twenty-two blessed years of my life with mom who died at the youthful age of forty-five of breast cancer, I thought that many times I felt I needed such a moment of peace. In knowing that there remain, many people that think as I once did, I felt a strong desire to express the permanent impact of a temporary notion

WILLIAMS, TRISH
[a.] Roscoe, TX [title] "My Angel" [pers.] I believe that poetry is one of many ways to express your mind, such as your thoughts, feelings, and emotions. My name is Trish Williams and I am 12 years old. I write poetry because it helps me relieve stress, or express what I'm feeling at the moment. The poem I wrote, "My Angel," was written for my sister, Traci, and her boyfriend. She was trying to express yourself

WILLS, RYAN
[a.] McKinney, TX [title] "Watcher of Night" [pers.] I am a sophomore at Texas A and M and serve as Guidon Bearer in my squadron, Gator 2, in the Corps of Cadets Home in McKinney, Texas. Future plan is to be a commercial pilot

WILSON, SHERRI
[a.] Hawthorne, NY [title] "Living Today" [pers.] I wrote this poem as I sat and pondered on my surroundings and the current events taking shape in our world. I am blessed by being brought up in a family where closeness and kindness rules. There are so many who are less fortunate than I and I am grateful for all that I have. As my sister, Lyn says . . . this is just me giving back. Truly an unselfish act, I am hopeful that one can learn from my words and be happy to have life

WILSON, TERRY
[a.] Montgomery, AL [title] "Soul" [pers.] This poem is a greater tribute to the struggle of living, and in that, that there is a kind and gentle world out there. Regardless of what struggle we each must walk through. In particular to this poem, inspiration come through the pain of accepting my brother's death. Steven's passing brought me around to see how important it is to be forgiven and to forgive others. Lest I be judged for my actions over judging others

WILSON, DAVID, JR.
[a.] N. Biloxi, MS [title] "Mother's Prayer" [pers.] I'm currently a student at the University of Southern Mississippi. I'm a junior I was born and reared in Mississippi. I've always had a strong interest in writing. I'm also very interested in chemistry (my major) more because of the manipulation of the world than any practical use. As a child, I was and still am mystified by the idea of being a wizard or sorcerer, and this is as close to the real thing as I can get. On paper you can be anything

WIMBERLY, AMBER
[a.] Yuma, AZ [title] "Happy Girl" [pers.] This poem is about how life takes its down fall for various reasons, yet you shouldn't let it bring you down and take away your pride. I wrote this poem, because I hit a really stressful point in my life, where I felt miserable, but after I sat down and wrote "Happy Girl," I felt almost 100% better. Poetry has a very positive effect on my life and I plan on writing it for the rest of my life

WINGFIELD, JONATHAN
[a.] New Port Richey, FL [title] "The False Realm" [pers.] I write poetry that reflects my mood and state of mind. This particular poem was written after a long separation from the woman I love. Through the long nights and hard days I knew that I would see her again if I had the will power to make it happen

WINKLER, SARAH
[a.] Duluth, MN [title] "A Single Tear" [pers.] I have always believed poetry a skill that all possess within themselves, maybe it's the way some cry or think, but overall, it's a feeling. My family has always supported me, from the first poem I wrote in fifth grade and they continue to support me now tat I'm fourteen

WINTERTON, CANDIDA
[a.] Tacoma, WA [title] "Pain's Passing" [pers.] My loves are sci-fi and fantasy. Poetry is a sideline, but one I am found of when I do it. I am married and first child is due July 29, 2000. I am a certifiable bookworm and have training as a health unit coordinator. My favorite animals are cats. This poem grew out of my experiences with painful events and my realization that pain will pass if you have faith. My faith is in the Lord Jesus; my faith is Christian, Christianity, with no additional added-on qualifiers. Have faith in what you will, but have faith

WISEBAKER, MICHAEL
[a.] Tiffin, OH [title] "Apology (To A Mouse)" [pers.] The funny thing is, I used to the hate poetry. I used to think it was pointless. I don't know how the change occurred, but I clearly remember when it happened: near the end of my junior year of high

school. Since then, I have come to appreciate the subtle yet powerful complexities of verse. To me (with a nod to Shakespeare's claim in "Hamlet"), poetry is both a reflection and a mirror. It speaks both of the poet and of the world at large. More of my poetry can be found on my personal homepage.

WITTE, NANCY
[a.] Las Vegas, NV [title] "My Crystal Jar" [pers.] Poetry has always been the outlet for my overwhelming emotions. "My Crystal Jar" was born when my husband, my love was quite ill and I realized what a true wish should be. He is my light and inspiration I am blessed and thankful if others are touched by my words. May they comfort and inspire for all time

WITTMAN, BOB
[a.] Tulare, CA [title] "Melissa" [pers.] A special note of dedication to my wife Retha, for her inspiration and support of my writing. She has encouraged me to continue to writing and express myself. Retha has been my partner, friend and companion for the last 30 years. We have endured many things together while raising our children, Michelle, Bobby 11 and Sean. We both love the art of poetry writing styles. This poem will always hold a special place in my heart. A true story about an accident involving my niece that occurred a couple of weeks before Christmas 1999. My wife suggested writing about this incident as an enlightenment for others to share

WITTMAN, RETHA
[a.] Tulare, CA [title] "Rosie, Cappuccino and Me" [pers.] This poem, although simple in appearance was written with great insight. Poetry, a gift of art and freedom of expression, a message in a bottle, a legacy left in time. The message is, she's on TV and I'm on the sofa. I watched Rosie on TV, grow through the years into an accomplished woman. This inspired me to follow my dream and write. Here I am as you read. Women everywhere, follow your heart and dreams, be true to yourself. If someone is your inspiration, share that gift in someway. Dedicate to Rosie, the Rose in my heart

WOLF, JULIE
[a.] Moodus, CT [title] "To My Davie" [pers.] This poem has a deep meaning for me. I wrote it for someone who I could never get through TV. I guess you can't just knock on some people's brains

WOLPERT, SABRINA
[a.] Fort Worth, TX [title] "The Child Garrett" [pers.] I was born January 16, 1959, Salina KS. My parents are Henry Baltine, Doris Baltine and my husband name is Charles Wolpert, December 15, 1999. My children are Justin and Garrett, I finish high school at Wichita Falls, Tarrant County College, and my occupation is Clayton Childcare. I belong to the Catholic Church, I write several poems my address Indiatlantic, Florida and Fort Worth, Texas. My inspiration came from my husband, Charlie and son, Garrett, They both love living, so it touched me deeply

WOLSKI, KORDIAN
[a.] Mississauga, ON [title] "Awakening"

WONG, ALAN
[a.] Montreal, PQ [title] "All Maple" [pers.] I passionately believe we possess the imagination to spread our wings and fly. Poetry and music are my tools of communicating with the world. My words capture the purity of a hopeless romantic. My sound defines the depth of my emotions. The drums can be tuned to its melodic pitch. Piano and guitar chords can be created to sound harmonious and melodic. However, the missing ingredient that must never be forgotten or taken for granted, is the special someone who must always glow. Love is a

beautiful thing and ultimately poetry becomes second nature. From me to you, I selflessly share my gift to help you soar above the rest

WOOD, GEORGE
[a.] Charleston, SC [title] "Margueritte" [pers.] G.J. Wood is originally, from Columbia, MD and is now living in Charleston, SC. He is currently, working on his first novel *The Memories of Johnny No Parts* which he hopes to have completed by the beginning of 2001.

WOOD, KINDRA
[a.] Topeka, KS [title] "Why I Don't Like the 'Nice Guys'" [pers.] This poem is collection of some of the humorous thoughts that run through my head every time I meet the nice guy. I have always had big dreams and enormous aspirations. Yet, I have this innate fear that I am going to settle with the nice guy. For some strange reason I equate the nice guys with boredom. As a psychology student at Washburn University, I am continually analyzing everything and everyone. In short, this poem is just me making fun of my fear of commitment in an attempt to explain myself.

WOODS, RODGER
[a.] Balch Springs, TX [title] "Tear Trails" [pers.] Raised in the Texas Hill Country with a few years spent in the Wind River Range of the Rocky Mountains of Wyoming, I have spent numerous days enjoying the views "From the Mountaintop." I am a career Police Officer and Rescue Specialist, but my joy comes from writing cowboy poetry. Growing up and living a large part of my life on horseback has provided me the opportunity to see and appreciate some of the most beautiful moments and places in life. These are the experiences that I share with my writing

WORDEN, DE
[a.] Wamego, KS [title] "Emotions" [pers.] I am an unpublished writer of short stories about myth and legends. I write spell poetry and poetry from my soul; to keep myself grounded, the power of the written word is so dynamic, it gains power close to nature's own. I will write till the end of time. When I die my printed word will live on; my laments forever on the wind

WORRELL, ANTOINETTE
[a.] Bronx, NY [title] "Loving Only You" [pers.] I am a native New Yorker, born and raised in Brooklyn, but now currently resides in the Borough of the Bronx. This poem was written out of love for my soon to be husband. Darrell little, who has shown me that love is better the second time around

WORTHEY, ROBIN
[a.] Forth Worth, TX [title] "Sailorman and Me" [pers.] A very special person in my life was the inspiration for this poem. As the years go by I will remember him warmly and smile. When this sailorman reaches his home I wish for him the love and kindness he deserves

WRAY, DAWN
[a.] Brantford, ON [title] "Memories" [pers.] This poem is very special to me. Life is a mystery filled with memories. They are a gift that you can look back on. Hold all your memories close to your heart and maybe you to will see what made you fly

WRIGHT, KAYLA
[a.] Everett, PA [title] "Why Do People Go?" [pers.] My name is Kayla Denee Wright. I am 12 years old and a 7th grader all the heritage Christian Academy in Bedford, PA. This poem was created by me as an assistant I was asked to write about something or someone. My grandfather passed away on January 3rd 2000 and I wrote this poem for him I wish to thank you my mom and dad for there love and support, my teacher Mrs. Myrna Focht, my aunt Hope for believing in me and I

dedicate this poem in loving memory of my grandfather William James Moore

WYNN, BRIDGETTE
[a.] Hesperia, CA [title] "When She Cries" [pers.] Poetry and music have been my favorite means of self-expression since I was a little girl. In those days, however, I wrote and played piano solely for my own enjoyment. Coming from a musical family, performing was encouraged, thereby giving me the confidence to share my talents. And now, my hobby has become a blessing to me and I grateful that others appreciate my work. "When She Cries" was born of a conglomeration of vignettes from my own life, melded into one moment. I wish to thank my family, loved ones, and friends for their continued encouragement and support

YACOVONE, ELISE
[a.] Pittsburgh, PA [title] "Blue Mountain" [pers.] Poetry is one of the most beautiful expression of human life. This poem recreates a moment of pure spirituality and peace. It is dedicated to my grandmother and grandfather in gratitude for all they have done for me and for inviting me to experience the glorious blue mountains of Virginia

YANG, FANG
[a.] Ramsey, MN [title] "The One" [pers.] I have been given many things in life by many people, and it is time that I return the a sweet favor. This one is for you Stephanie Vang

YATES, NICK
[a.] New Carlisle, OH [title] "Oblivious Jackal" [pers.] First things first, I am 15 years old and a freshman in high school. Now you're probably wondering what my poem is about. It is basically about me. Call it my Native American name or what have you. As you can guess I am a very depressed person, but I like my depression. If it wasn't for my depression, I might not have deep poetic thoughts. My hobbies are listening to music, role playing poetry and video games. I like listening to techno, blues, jazz, acid jazz, and classic rock. Well I will stop talking about myself because it feels like I'm bragging, and possibly it will be one less tree cut down.

YON, MARK
[a.] Mechanicsburg, PA [title] "The Twins" [pers.] Children of all ages need to smile. My motivation to write has been born of my desire to know that I can take common experiences in life and create a reason to feel good about them. My own writing often amuses me and I imagine that there are some children who might find some answers or at least identify with my curiosity about life while finding humor in it all. What you read comes from my heart of joy and joy comes back to you when you give it away

YOUNG, ASHLEY
[a.] Marion, IN [title] "Fatigue" [pers.] This is one of the first poems that I have ever written. Being as young as I am it was very exciting to find out that it was appreciated and liked. I have always wanted to write and I hope that this publication will mark the beginning of a career

YOUNG, SANDRA
[a.] Manchester, CT [title] "Your Kiss to Me" [pers.] Poetry has always been very special to me. It is the way I best express myself. At age 11, I had my first poem published in "The Hartford Times." I attended Roger Williams College in Bristol, R.I. This particular poem, "Your Kiss To Me," is especially tear to me and was inspired by two very special people that like most of America, only knew from a distance. It is written for and about Carolyn Bessette Kennedy and John Jr. After their tragic death, there were pictures of them displayed in many papers, and one of the pictures was Carolyn sitting on John's lap. She had his black

tuxedo jacket across her shoulders and he was kissing her cheek. Carolyn looked so beautiful and happy. I remember crying as I looked at that picture that night, "Your Kiss To Me" was conceived

YUAN, HAI
[a.] North York, ON [title] "Love" [pers.] Life is a journey, enriched to the core of an individual/person by the problems they confront, relationships that they engage in and any other experience that arise. This poem is very special to me, as it celebrates my fiance who is very important in my life. As she said: "I just want you to know that I will always be here or there or wherever I am. I am for you, through emotional support and any other kind of support that you will be needing. I'm here for you darling." I hope everyone in the world can find their true love. And perhaps share my poem with their loved ones

YUSUF, MEHRUNNISA
[a.] Islamabad Pakistan [title] "Chaotic Reflection" [pers.] Writing has always been a passion for me. I feel that poetry is an extension of my thoughts and feelings. My poem "Chaotic Reflections" is an impulse poem. It is almost like an answer to the emotions that are .brewing inside me

ZABINSKI, DIANE
[a.] Chicago, IL [title] "A Game of Hunting in the 1700's" [pers.] I wrote this poem seven years ago in College for a creative writing course. I was going through a box of old writing sample. And I stumbled upon the poem. I rewrote parts of it, and felt the message is still strong today. I wrote this poem after seeing a commercial for roots. When roots came out, I was a child, and I remember the movie scaring me

ZABODYN, DONNA
[a.] Elon College, NC [title] "My Mother's Hands" [pers.] I am forty years old. I have an eighteen year old son, Jeffrey, and a wonderful husband of twenty years, Jeff. We live on a small farm in Caswell County, N.C. My mother Georgia Johnson, was the inspiration behind "My Mother's Hands." The poem was a tribute to her for care she gave me through a six month hospitalization. She is the most wonderful, crafty person. She and my father Vernon Johnson have been married fifty years. I've never considered myself a poet. I've always just let the feelings flow from my heart to the paper

ZAIDI, ATIF
[a.] Cos Cob, CT [title] "Decadence" [pers.] This poem talks about my generation of kids who are not at peace with themselves. Kids who are trying to escape reality because it is so horrible. We are tired of living in a world where the dollar comes before the people. So long have tried to unveil the truth of how horrible a world we live in and we have no more strength to fight. We just want to drop out of society

ZAINABU, OLANIYI AYO
[a.] Cincinnati, OH [title] "Waves Over Pachan" [pers.] I have always possessed a deep loved and appreciation for the written word. Books of all kinds have been a great part of my life since I started reading before the age of four. My sole purpose for writing was initially an avenue to express my unique creativity. I give a large portion of myself each time I write, and it is a way of sharing my deepest innermost thoughts and feelings. This particular poem was written during a time of meditation, and introspection, in appreciation of nature, just for itself

ZIEGELBAUER, VICKI
[a.] Germantown, WI [title] "Let Go" [pers.] When sadness and confusion come over me, I turn to two things; writing and music I don't think I need to explain my piece "Let Go," for I believe it speaks for itself. It was written for a very special

friend in my life who has always been there for me whenever I couldn't help myself. Although we are miles apart, remember you are always in my heart. For all others, may you be happy and joyful! Always remember to smile and hold your chin up with confidence. It is more than an honor to see my writing in this book. I am so proud of all I do, but this completely tops it off!

ZIEGLER, ROSEMARY
[a.] Blasdell, NY [title] "Your Flowers" [pers.] Rosemary received the International Library of Poetry Achievement Award for the Years 1999 and 2000 writing this poem was a labor of joy. I so loved my family. Each member of my family was so very special to me. One day I hope to honor each one of them with a writing that will capture the renders heart it is only when family life once again takes priority over materialistic things that this world will become what almighty God intended it to be "A world Rich in love and Peace for One Another" Rosemary's recent writing appears in SPF 2000 "Voices of the New Century"

ZIMMERMAN, NICOLE
[a.] Mount Prospect, IL [title] "Remember When: Our Memories" [pers.] I'm fourteen years old and have always been told that I have a natural talent for writing poetry. This is a very special gift, which I'm honored to be blessed with. My poem "Remember When: Our Memories" describes my relationship with my very first dog, Zak, and the special bond of life we shared while growing up together since birth. His death inspired me to write this poem as a tribute to him. This was my way of saying good-bye to my best friend. My poem expressed my love for Zak, further illustrating that a dog really is "Man's Best Friend."

ZIPFEL, BUCHELE
[a.] Perris, CA [title] "My Fall" [pers.] Every person we meet, everything we do, and all that we learn brings meaning to our lives. I thank fate for helping me realize that like a single drop of rain amongst a storm, all of us have our purpose. I dedicate this publication to those common day heroes who are overlooked as they do the right thing without reward. May life reward you all with peace, love, and the respect you deserve. With that in mind, I give thanks to Kathie, Heather, and my family. You have all done more than you can ever know

ZUBRZYCKI, LEAH
[a.] Blackwood, NJ [title] "My Greatest Fear" [pers.] I have always been close with my dad, so when he went away on a business trip for two days it felt like he would never return. On his first night away, I wrote this poem. I was so scared something would happen to him, and someone would call to say he was never coming home. I first started writing poetry when I was 13 years old. I wrote "My Greatest Fear" when I was 16. Writing poetry is something I enjoy very much and find relaxing, especially at the end of the day

ZUCKERMAN, ROSIE
[a.] Los Angeles, CA [title] "The Song" [pers.] This poem was written two years ago, when I was twelve years old. I never believed it would go anywhere past my torn-up notebook. I'm shocked and honored and I would just like to say thank you to my writing inspiration, my friend, and my brother, Alex

ZUNIGA, DIANA
[a.] Covina, CA [title] "Why I Love You" [pers.] I have always used poetry to express myself. Words always seem easier to say when they are written down. My favorite poems to write are love poems. This poem I wrote about a year ago, when a friend of mine left to the navy. I then realized that from this friendship an unrecognizable love was growing."

Index
of
Poets

Index

A

Abdelwahed, Mohammed 103
Abel, Daniel 5
Abernethy, Sarah 30
Abrams, Peter M. 23
Acosta, Leticia 195
Adamiak, Sarah 69
Adams, David 162
Adams, Irene 67
Adams, J. Hunter 78
Adams, John 131
Adams, Lance 188
Adams, Meg 246
Adams-Evans, Gwendolyn 233
Adamson, Sam 173
Adcock, Elizabeth 50
Adkin, Cathleen 72
Advani, Ameet 71
Agarwal, Neha 28
Agel, Charles 205
Ageret, Prince 36
Aguila, Caroline 148
Al-Ghafri, Abdullah 220
Alastra, Tommy 110
Albelo, Betsy 198
Albrecht, Sylvia 198
Albright, Nathan 204
Albumblatt, Eidelweiss 83
Alcorn, Pamela 93
Alicea, Lori 108
Allen, John 106
Allen, Shaun R. 149
Alston, Jackie 44
Alvarado, Elsie 133
Alvarez, Krystal 176
Ament, Elizabeth 15
Ammons, Victoria 184
Anastasoff, Steve 86
Anderson, Anita 174
Anderson, Barbara 107
Anderson, Breanna 187
Anderson, Dave 95
Anderson, Jason 102
Anderson, Jennifer 168
Anderson, Joan 166
Anderson, Jonathan 80
Anderson, Susan 140
Anderson, Tracy D. 202
Anderson, Uriah 12
Andrews, Stephen 153
Anfiteatro, Anthony 236
Angel, Angie 12
Angus, Elaine M. 18
Annis, Joshua 104
Antley, Mark 218
Anumakonda, Ravi 200
Archibald, Wayne 20
Arjumand, Firdous 42
Armentrout, Aliza 77
Armitstead, Janet 140
Armstrong, Hart 23
Armstrong, Joanne 146
Arthur, David 50
Ashley, Benjamin 244
Ashworth, George T. 94

Asselta, Nicole 64
Au, Deborah 123
Auriemma, Anthony 178
Austin, Arvetta 116
Austin, Nathan 198
Avery, Mike 34
Avison, Ian 192
Ayers, Angela 33
Ayers, Josh 174
Azlee, Zan 161

B

Babij, Daniel 104
Baczkowski, Anthony 104
Badger, Casey 152
Badri, Mohammad 214
Bafia, Randa 27
Bagshaw, Jeannine 155
Bagwell, Nicholas 118
Bailey, Carol 100
Bailey, Jeanie 139
Baird, Brooke 74
Baird-Remba, Rebecca 25
Baker, Angela 72
Baker, Daniel 135
Baker, James 202
Baker, Susan 236
Baku, Ylli 192
Balash, Anna T. 13
Baldridge, Willis 244
Balek, Pamela 173
Balitz, Greg 147
Ball, Celeste 44
Ball, Jennifer 59
Ball, Lance C. 154
Ballou, John 129
Bankhead, Alisa 155
Bankston, Madison 54
Bantug, Chito 235
Baraceros, Nina 113
Barber, Heather 70
Barber, Sandra 140
Barbosa, Archie Maure 42
Barker, Brian Paul 156
Barker, Stephanie 195
Barkley, Jenna 42
Barnes, Bibbie 147
Barnes, Dixie 77
Barnes, Michael 218
Barnes, Terrance 39
Barrett, Adam 160
Barrett, Barbara 208
Barrett, Charles 85
Barrett, Kevin 179
Barringer, Whitney 85
Bartlett, Echo 5
Bartlett, Tonja 32
Barto, Stephanie 97
Bates, David 5
Baumann, Rita 121
Bavaro, Angie 50
Baxley, Michelle 53
Bays, O. 78
Beannan, Dennis 67
Beasley, Jessica 49
Beasley, Marianne 9
Beaudry, Amanda 151
Beaulieu, Jessica 123
Becker, Lauren 124
Bednard, Samantha 172
Beers, Lenora Lynn 170
Behrends, Jason 126

Bekkers, Bel 126
Belashuk, Veronica 138
Belin, Don 91
Bell, Rose 171
Bell, Sarah 246
Bengtson, Kris 94
Benson, Billy Jack 158
Bentsen, Patrick 121
Berger, Kevin Michael 56
Berlia, Aditya 110
Bernier, Farah 205
Berry, Lisha 72
Berryhill, Susan 159
Beugre, Remy 104
Bharucha, Manoj A. 30
Bhat, Aditya 82
Bhattacharya, Sudipto 122
Bialek, Jeff 143
Bickler, Brittany 167
Biggs, Duffy 217
Bilbrey, Julie 184
Billing, Steven 22
Birch, Hope 59
Bird, Carol 174
Bisaha, Tracey 135
Bivens, Marreo 200
Black, Bill 164
Black, Jessica 210
Black, Michael 127
Black, Ruby 127
Blackwell, Sarah 220
Blair, Karol 85
Blakeney, Bonnie Jean 168
Blanchard, Jennifer 116
Blazy, Doris 18
Blessing, Falon 69
Blessing, Karen A. 53
Blische, Cory 138
Blomqvist, Tomas 55
Blume, Leslie 225
Blumert, Jessica 50
Bock, Rachel 73
Bocklage, Laurene 221
Boehle, Jill 29
Bogdanovich, Anya 101
Bohn, Diane 199
Boivin, Tallie 200
Bolejack, Christopher 117
Bondi, Salvatore 17
Bonitz, Bette 20
Booker, Shavona 118
Boresi, Beverly 160
Bose, Tricia 73
Bottomley, Susan 235
Bottone, Edward 185
Boudreau, Francis 151
Bovee, C. 83
Bowden, Carla "Celeste" 53
Bowe, David 48
Boyd, Charleston 243
Boykin, Anastasia 101
Boyles, Lena 38
Bradley, Ian 62
Bradtke, Debra 56
Braegger, Nichole 204
Brandon, Kerry 184
Braswell, Dwight 229
Bratby, Will 205
Brauer, Leigh 202
Braun, Alysha 173
Braxton, Robert 49
Brazier, Erica 63
Brenner, Lori 138

Brewer, James, II 29
Brickner, C J 129
Brickner, Cynthia 61
Brimm, Mark 11
Briner, Gayle 143
Brinkhoff, Kelly 172
Brister, Michael 214
Bristow, Charles 190
Britton, Francis 20
Britz, Marisa 33
Brodersen, Jared 139
Brombach, Nataly 214
Broo, Karen 114
Brooks, Brendan 163
Brooks, Christina 80
Brown, Christopher 218
Brown, Curtis 102
Brown, Fitzroy 102
Brown, Florence 18
Brown, Lloyd 244
Brown, Mary 230
Browning, James 95
Browning, Teresa Langley 28
Brubaker, James 12
Bruce, Jonathan 48
Bruce, Judith 246
Brunnberg, Fredrik 59
Bruno, Meg 200
Bryant, Vanessa 124
Buchanan, Joy 210
Buck, Karen 206
Bucksot, Patrick 177
Budimilic, Manuela 26
Bufano, Teresa 111
Bulger, Jadin 199
Burden, Angela 112
Burgett, Ashley 233
Burke, Diane 28
Burke, Kevin 216
Burke, Terry 142
Burlak, Eduard, Jr. 71
Burque, Michelle 106
Burr, Marlowe C. 67
Burroughs, Patrice G. 68
Burton, Charlean 118
Burton, James 243
Burton, Jonathon 112
Burton, Joyce 208
Buss, Patrick N. 204
Butler, Amanda 146
Butler, Andrea 11
Butler, Rosanna 172
Butler-Jones, Evan 69

C

Cabrera, Lucas IV 243
Cacho, Redentor 191
Cady, Tasha 156
Cagney, Caitilin 14
Caldwell, Fushsia 213
Caldwell, Michelle 15
Calle, Jevon 137
Cameron, Mark 194
Campbell, Collin 241
Campbell, Elaina 88
Campbell, Heather 166
Campbell, Stephanie 143
Canavos, George D. 163
Candelaria, Felipe 62
Candler, Jason 167
Caouette, Brian 73
Cardenuto, Anthony 128

Cardwell, Shawn 192
Carino, Marcus 164
Carlsson, Kent 108
Carlstedt, Linsey 238
Carman, Terra 191
Carnrike, Jason 92
Caron, Neysa 238
Carpenter, Justine 7
Carreon, Joshua 89
Carrera, Teresa 169
Carroll, Christopher 45
Carroll, Kevin 17
Carroll, Steffan 103
Carson, Edith 19
Carson, KC 126
Carter, Courtney 192
Carter, Donice Peavy 241
Carter, Dwan 110
Cass, James R., IV 101
Castaldo, Richie Michael 81
Caster, Beth 196
Castillo, Emir Jose, Jr. 29
Castleberry, Gerald 39
Caudell, Nicole 22
Cerda, Jessica 164
Chalkley, Irene 24
Cham, Jun 144
Chamberlain, Patrick 118
Chamney, Hali 86
Champ, Amy 10
Chan, Rosalynne 71
Chang, Peter K. Y. 150
Charger, K. 145
Charuckyj, Liana 136
Chase, Greg 126
Chattman, Jacob 26
Chavez, Victor 226
Chesbro, Eldon 144
Chevere, Vickiey 203
Chickering, Jessica 131
Chinigo, Steven 134
Chira, Adrian 200
Chiu, Susan M. 112
Chong, Shing-Yan 175
Chow, Sonya 103
Christ, Darlene F. 56
Christensen, Robert 63
Christian, Kymberli 210
Christianson, Brent 8
Christie, Sean 137
Christopher, Patricia Gael 61
Chu, Margaret 215
Chung, Erica 152
Cipowski, Scott 218
Cipres, Lisa 107
Clark, Jeffery 96
Clark, Lieza 240
Clark, Lisa 27
Clark, Nicole 64
Clark, Paula 106
Clarkson, Edward 67
Clay, Ceneth 174
Cleghorn, Peggy 28
Clifford, Toni 181
Clymer, Jennifer 137
Coard, Donald 88
Coburn, Angela 125
Cofer, Ashlee 220
Cogburn, Angela 24
Cognasso-Waters, Lori 237
Cohen, Josh 219
Colbenson, Laura 232
Coleman, Kriss 28

Coleman, Lindsay 64
Coleman, Toya A. 247
Coleman, Tracey 201
Collier, Egan 210
Collinge, Jason 213
Collins, Natalie 5
Collins, Shonn 159
Comaniuk, Len S. 181
Comentale, Carolyn 85
Commisso, Marlena 36
Concepcion, Ebenezer 40
Conley, Daniel 153
Conner, Danielle 38
Connor, Si 140
Conrad, Jacob 219
Coo, Patrick 29
Cook, Beverly 223
Cooper, Donald, Jr. 36
Cooper, Peta 122
Cooper, Robert 85
Coover, Cole 243
Copeland, Chad 85
Copeland, Clay 82
Corbett, James 33
Cordell, David 143
Cordoba, Lorena 133
Cossens, Lori 11
Costello, Alejandra 91
Courtis, Edward 80
Cowdrick, David 186
Cowie, Mason 195
Cox, Jennifer 114
Cox, Linda 177
Cox, Sheila Denise 202
Coyle, Matt 167
Craddock, Dawn 194
Craft, Chris 41
Crandley, Melissa 51
Craver, Deborah 110
Crawford, James 193
Crawford, Marnee 115
Cregier, Grace Evelyn 141
Crisafulli, Kim 186
Crispin, Chelsea 205
Cristi, Marilyn 9
Cromer, Wendy 165
Cross, Danielle 219
Cross, Melina 186
Cross, Michael 217
Crowder, Rebecca 241
Cuadro, Daniel 52
Culbertson, Frances 184
Culbertson, John 183
Cullum, Clive 135
Culp, Robert D. 96
Cunningham, Alana 234
Cunningham, Alice 94
Cupper, N. 17
Curry, Erica J. 147
Cvengros, Steve 198

D

D., Sappho 82
Daehn, Marta 98
Dahle, Nancy 90
Dahn, Deneen 7
Daines, Michael 100
Daly, Evan 172
Dandron, Jeremy 115
Daniels, Vickie 38
Datey, Smita 32
Daub, Roger 61

Davenport, Roy 114
Davenport-Weston, Nathelia 123
Davidson, Jennifer 11
Davis, Cesanne 10
Davis, Darrel 139
Davis, Gloria 83
Davis, Leah 131
Davis, Stephen 231
Day, Cari 111
De Freitas, Jacqueline 3
De La Cruz, Annabel 47
Dean, Jamie 183
Deaton, Sue 197
Debacker, Carolyn 146
Debrouse, Christina 179
DeChristoforo, Julia 146
Deck, Olivia 46
Decker, Glenna 54
Decker, Terra 60
Dejewski, Stephanie L. 247
Dejumo, Lanilyn 83
Delarm, John 80
Delgado, Elizabeth M. 178
DellaGrotta, William Jr. 105
Dellamora, Loretta 236
DeMeo, Julieann 229
Denes, Csilla 141
Denkins, Kelly 232
Dennehy, Tanya 45
Dennison, Elaine 77
Dent, Cherryl 128
Derry, Maxie 73
DeSimone, Christine 3
Dheer, Sachin 61
Diaz, Dawn 33
Dibble, Melissa 8
DiBonaventura, Cristina 95
Dierickx, Jennifer 79
Diggs, Franceno A. 102
Dinsmore, Emilee 231
Dismuke, Terri 134
Dixon, Kathy 100
Doehring, Erika 128
Doran, Lyn 63
Doroslovac, Bob 168
Dover, Cliff 109
Dover, Courtney C. 240
Doyle, Jeannette 224
Dricker, Jessie 201
Driggers, Joyce 42
Drinan, Mike 76
Driver, Jackie 203
Drollette, Loretta 143
Dropmann, Damian 23
Droske, Kathryn 31
Drum, Wayne 40
Dryden, Ashley 232
Ducharme, Normandie 230
Duchesneau, Carol 79
Dugre', Mark 89
Dunbar, Samantha 165
Dunlop, Ryan 242
Dunn, Jason 213
Dunn, Thomas 141
Durbin, Dannielle 216
Durden, Carla 232
Dyke, Crystal 105
Dymarsky, Irina 38
Dyson, Christina 223

E

Ealy, M. 126

Easom, Deborah 21
Echebarria, Daniel 81
Ecker, Tracey 236
Edison, Brittany 52
Edvartsen, Stig 161
Edward, Monteiro 231
Edwards, Amy 201
Edwards, Dewell, Jr. 36
Edwards, Inga 76
Edwards, Labarron 185
Effman, Jesse 149
Ehrmann, Jay 3
Eldridge, Doran 137
Elliott, Ammie 244
Elmlinger, Robbin 76
Emanuel, Edward 124
Emm, Nick 70
Encarnacion, Tabitha 164
Engel, Jessica 46
Engle, Justin 142
Engley, Dennis 237
Engman, Amy 88
Eppler, Teri 131
Erickson, Chad 235
Escareno, Suvi 249
Escriche, Manuel 74
Espinola, Naomi 66
Espiritu, Alexander Traitler 39
Esque, Rickey, Jr. 57
Estrada, Jessica 150
Evans, Elaine 123
Evans, Sally 163
Eyster, William 144

F

Faciana, Paul J. 168
Facorro, Lorenzo A. 69
Fair, Dawn 196
Fan, Yu 144
Farazmand, Saman 51
Farmer, Donna 46
Farmer, Lynda 194
Farren, Deborah A. 170
Fattorini, Stefano 92
Faulkner, Rebecca 212
Favatas, Dionisios 141
Fawley, Alyson 227
Fay, Jana DeLaune 149
Fedie, Amanda 234
Feirer, Denise L. 60
Fennel, Shelia 47
Fernandes, Josephine 158
Fernandez, Donna 243
Fielding, M. 109
Files, Carolyn 18
Fineday, Rebekah 80
Finestead, Bethalene 179
Finley, Mark 188
First, Lisa L. 245
Fischer, Erin 139
Fischer, Jim 156
Fischer, Korynthia 75
Fisher, Ann 203
Fisher, Erica 239
Fisher, Laura 73
Fiske, Jacqueline 245
Fitzgerald, Bonnie 145
Fitzpatrick, Suzanne 147
Fives, Marilyn 65
Flanders, Neil 119
Fleming, Danae 239
Fletcher, Vinsin 124

Floberg, Sara 76
Flores, Lindsey 245
Ford, Joseph 154
Formeister, Marc 117
Foster, Daniel 134
Foster, Lakicia 45
Foster, Victor 242
Fouty, Leonard 189
Fox, Carroll 25
Fox, Gail 141
Francis, David 58
Francis, Debra 154
Franco, Danielle 129
Frank, Christiana 13
Frank, Daniel L. 222
Franklin, Mia 48
Franks, Timothy 218
Frazier, Kellye 247
Fredrick, Roy 65
Freeman, Donald 175
Freeman, Heather 184
Freeman, Nicole 208
Friedman, Howard 17
Friedman, Rachel 115
Fu, Edmund 240
Fugina, Dawn 85
Fuglestad, Linda 71
Fuller, Lisa 135
Fulton, Dara 130

G

Gajadhar, Steven 124
Galaway, Richard 143
Galgano, Mary 77
Gallagher, Michael 80
Galvin, Emily 6
Gan, Steven 197
Gangadharan, Nicholas 96
Garay, Sarah 90
Garber, Daniel 232
Garcia, Tadeo 237
Garcia, Yvonne 237
Garey, Jo 185
Garmaize, Jeanne 185
Garner, Jeffrey 213
Garrett, Timothy 35
Garrison, Roberta 97
Gassmann, Virginia 35
Gavrilchuk, Katy 49
Geha, Janice 112
Gehrke, Stevw 5
Gelinas, Sarah 174
Gendreau, Kelly 19
George, Frank 67
Gerard, Michael 71
Gerlach, Taylor 28
Ghouleh, Sammer 66
Giangrande, Phil 33
Gibbens, Laura 40
Giese, Stacie 126
Giesen, Hildegard 21
Gifford, Donna 14
Gilbert, Hannagh 127
Giles, Linda Shows 121
Gilmore, Michael 76
Giuntini, Wanda 191
Glenn, Mendy 18
Godfrey, David 216
Godfrey, Terrilyn 49
Goldapp, Carol 189
Gomes, Antonio 234
Gonzalez, Margarett 127

Gonzalez, Pascual 107
Gooch, Tommy, III 68
Good, William 103
Goodman, Laura 108
Goodrich, Jess 77
Goodrich, Rodney 191
Goodwin, Elaine 68
Goodyear, Evelyn 107
Gordon, Kristopher 41
Gorschek, Tony 190
Gosi, Lance 104
Gotschall, Benjamin 78
Gottfried, Michael H. 115
Graber, Gardner 175
Graham, Iana 70
Graham, Kenneth 119
Graham, Matthew 145
Grant, Shar F. 167
Gray, Aleta 41
Gray, E. Russell 8
Gray, Nicole 117
Gray, Stephanie 72
Green, Alvin-Dale 89
Green, Brant 55
Green, Cynthia 96
Green, Kristal 136
Green, Larry, Jr. 143
Green, Nicholas 149
Green, Nick 188
Greenberg, Jason 192
Greene, Kerri 226
Grenfell, Chelsea 199
Gretter, Robert 189
Griffin, Liz 87
Griffin, Michelle 173
Griffith, Rebecca 71
Grison, Deborah 84
Groff, Matthew 74
Gross, Francine 48
Gross, Samuel, Jr. 130
Gudgel, Jack 181
Gudmundsson, Kristjan 181
Guilfoyle, Mark 221
Gundelach, Carrie 78
Gunter, Rennise 40
Gurul, Jeffrey, Jr. 126
Guthrie, Krista 167
Gutierrez, Cynthia 152
Guzman, Olivia 53

H

Hackett, April 141
Haddigan, Luceal 180
Hagberg, Christopher 196
Hager, Tammy 145
Haggis, Lauren K. 64
Hagler, Angela 84
Haktorson, Jarle 124
Hall, J. Carlton 123
Hall, Kristalynn 143
Hall, Michael 211
Hamaker, Jesse 99
Hamler, Schiquitta 241
Han, Jason 24
Hancock, Rondell 78
Handsaker, Michelle 132
Haney, Andrew 180
Hanna, Renea 157
Hanner, Ronald 127
Hannington, Karen 66
Hansen, Joseph 220
Hansen, Regina 172

Hanson, William 69
Hardrick, Joi 181
Hardy, Ian 194
Hare, March 41
Hargrave, James 61
Harmon, Stephanie 114
Harper, Kenneth 24
Harris, Dorothy 148
Harris, Stephanie 160
Harris-Minor, Sheila 212
Harrison, Judy 134
Harrison, Lora 162
Harth, Rebecca 8
Hartz, Lesley 62
Hartzell, Kathryn 156
Hashim, Lamyaa 128
Hauge, Daniel 138
Hauser, Joshua 15
Hawkins, Doris (Dee) 175
Hawkins, Sam 194
Hawkins, Winifred L. 164
Hawks, Richard 106
Hawkshead, John 152
Haworth, Irene Myrtle 67
Hawthorne, Jeffrey 135
Hawthorne, Michele 121
Hay, Deborah 198
Hayes, Rejji 151
Hayner, Tina 186
Hazelton, Natalie 242
Hazen, Joseph 138
He, Bihuai 209
Headen, Christopher 238
Healzer, Cassidy 4
Heath, Jennifer 35
Heath, Tammy 182
Heck, Elisabeth 137
Heckman, Robert 80
Heffernan, Beth 145
Heffner, Kathryn 59
Heidebur, Amanda 205
Heiskell-Simmons, Deborah 108
Heisner, Marion 245
Held, Daniel J. 241
Heller, Kaonohi 93
Helmkamp, Emily 82
Henderson, James 114
Henderson, Kelly Ann 58
Henderson, Shari 241
Heneghan, Sueanne 177
Henniger, Martha 101
Henry, Margo 55
Henry, Shirley 147
Hepp, Rachel 146
Hernandez, Jesus 195
Hernandez, Manuela 152
Hernandez, Mario 83
Hershberger, Linda 176
Hess, Joshua 196
Hester, Christine 173
Hetrick, Clyde 240
Heuer, Jeanne 201
Hibbard, Justin 228
Hibbert, Lenka 26
Hicks, Christopher 1
Hieronymus, Nancy 89
Hight, Akili 132
Higinbotham, Heather 206
Higuera, Jose 117
Hill, Donna 99
Hill, Jennifer 187
Hill, Martha 206
Hill, Niki 244

Hines, Susan 248
Ho, Jody 235
Hobbs, Diane 78
Hodges, Helen Milburn 7
Hodges, Kellie Vaughn 103
Hodgson, Carmen 74
Hofer, Benjamin 82
Hofstetter, Chrisitna 139
Hogan, Randy 221
Hohenberger, Mary 6
Holder, Wendy 197
Holiday, Rachel 203
Hollerman, Justin 114
Holley, Asher 149
Hollin, Hanna 31
Hollis, Madelyn 37
Holmes, Anne 229
Honea, Eric 65
Hooser, Bess 75
Hopkins, Dennis 32
Hopkins, John 47
Hopkins, Rosalyn 70
Horn, Casandra 73
Horsley, James 198
Hosein-House, Charleen 58
Hoskin, Bernis S. 230
Hotov, Andrei 92
Howard, Addi 27
Howard, Alex 118
Howard, Robert 174
Howard-Briggs, Ruth 77
Howell, Tia 105
Howk, Andrew 19
Howlingwolf, Edward 80
Huang, Benjamin 196
Huber, Leticia 52
Huckaby, Benjamin 162
Huckins, Bradie 43
Huddleston, Marilyn 219
Hudson, Joshua 127
Hudson, Latisha 93
Huebner, Kristen 187
Huggins, Clayon 238
Humbert, Erica 155
Humble, Neely 176
Humen, Jackie 229
Humphrey, Anna 199
Humphries, Jack 72
Hunt, Brandi DeAnne 132
Hunter, Daryl 161
Husted, Christina 13
Hutchens, Karla 15
Hutchison, Rosella 145
Hutton, Montie 138
Hwang, Juliette 10

I

Iannone, Michael 34
Ide, Rich 81
Igic, Rajko 207
Imhoff, M. Rebecca 245
Ingram, Christina 235
Ingram, Edna L. 246
Ingram, James 95
Ingram, Michelle 125
Isley, Ken 243

J

Jackson, Charles 102
Jackson, Edith 233
Jackson, Jeffery, Jr. 186

Jackson, Patricia 19
Jacob, Emil 8
Jacoba, Christie 182
James, Don, Jr 117
James, Trisha 75
Janes, Leonard 232
Janosik, Daniel 100
Jarrett, Mary 145
Jebb, Kimberly 225
Jefferson, Gary 92
Jenkins, Clane 100
Jenkins, Marc 240
Jessup, Veronica 94
Jimenez, Jolene 142
Joe, Kathleen 226
Johannes, Edda 57
Johnson, Ashley 157
Johnson, Brenda 71
Johnson, Cassia 54
Johnson, Christopher Lee 249
Johnson, Elizabeth 217
Johnson, Evelyn 193
Johnson, Jane 65
Johnson, Margaret 191
Johnson, Mark Shannon 246
Johnson, Nicholas 217
Johnson, Reche' 42
Johnson, Wanda 141
Johnson, Willie 56
Jones, Ben C. 191
Jones, Catherine 220
Jones, Crystal 44
Jones, Eddie 98
Jones, Gordon 53
Jones, Lisa Marie 162
Jones, Mandy 77
Jones, Sherry 6
Jonte, Maribel 63
Joshi, Pankaj 21
Juarez, Amanda 216
Jump, Briana 153

K

Kaestner, Elizabeth 202
Kamarah, Sheikh 126
Kanno, Hiro 60
Karacic, Azra 156
Karidis, Maria 21
Karim, Rahman 144
Kasen, Valerie 157
Kasner, Jason 236
Kasthuri, Raj 228
Kava, Mike 114
Keating, Michelle 82
Keller, Melissa 226
Kelly, Kristen 83
Kelly, Sean 171
Kemp, D. Renee 32
Kennedy, Latisha 79
Kennedy, Natalie 180
Kent, Mary Victoria 84
Kern, Russell C. 145
Kerr, Robert 193
Kessler, Bonnie 111
Khachatryan, George 11
khader, shabeer 158
Khairina, Nani 170
Khambhampati, Shivaji 142
Khuansathavoranit, Mallika 214
Khurana, Anshika K. 112
Kidd, Cheryl 201
Kieran, Kathryn 5

Kiesinger, Sonya 203
Kile, Chris 141
Kimberly, Katie 223
Kindle, Charlotte 115
King, Christopher 110
King, Heather 237
King, Jason 133
King, Jennifer 45
Kinney, Michael 143
Kinsey, Robert 121
Kinter, Megan 207
Kirkwood, Pete 109
Kittel, Claudia 145
Klakamp, Christopher 107
Klebba, Sharon 9
Kleine, Lisa 45
Kline, Rose 190
Knight, Robin 32
Knoblauch, Jennie 87
Knox, Jean A. 225
Kobus, David 206
Kohler, Jeremy 238
Koller, Margo 13
Kolombatovich, Katherine 200
Kolynych, Glenna 86
Koontz, Jessica R. 168
Kopilchack, June 146
Korschot, Marie 229
Kossiski, Ellyn 224
Kostick, Tara 87
Krajeski, Ken 180
Krall, Mark J. 168
Kravchak, Deborah 124
Kremer, Barbara 92
Krishnan, Vethamalar 43
Krueger, Jaymie 131
Kryder, Carrie 41
Krys, Jaime 70
Kuca, Elizabeth 230
Kuebler, Kathrine 52
Kulothungan, Sheba 235
Kurtz, Andrea Jo 229
Kutuso, Edwin 40
Kyle, D. Ward 12

L

Labadie, Sandra 60
Labay, David 86
Lafferty, Ashley 191
Lafollette, Lydia 230
Lagace, Lauraine 69
Lamb, Debbi 25
Lambert, Sandra 69
Lamon, Colleen 81
Lamoureaux, Sarah 11
Lampkins, John 212
Landers, Buck 188
Landesco, Jean 143
Lane, Autumn 179
Lane, Michael 43
Lane, Monica 34
Langlois, Alan 232
Lanning, Linda 233
LaPointe, Christopher 142
Lara, Sandra 83
Large, Gailor 4
Larkin, Melanie 203
Larrabee, Angel 34
Larson, Kris 15
Larson, Sarina 197
Lasco, Haydee 223
Lasky, Helaine 190

Lasley, Carlynn 89
Laughhunn, Courtney 147
Laughlin, Hugh 148
Lauver, Ned 53
Lawson, Sheri 230
Lay, Kathryn 159
Layne, Crystal 226
Layton, Elizabeth 93
Layton, Helen 204
Le, Thom 194
Leake, Randy 81
Leblanc, Chantal 179
LeClaire, Jolene 140
Lee, Jennifer 49
Lee, Patricia A. Brown 49
Lee, Tess A. 100
Leftwich, Hillary 106
Legere, James 51
Legg, Pamela 69
Lemon, Michael 204
Lenard, L. 168
Lepe, Joseph 105
Lester, James 32
Letourneau, Peter 47
Leucuta, Tracie 177
Leveen, Aimee 85
Levy, Deedra 76
Lewis, Willemien 101
Li, Jill S. 81
Liebow, Joanne E. 182
Lightburn, Arifah 187
Likness, Sonja 3
Lindenbaum, Michael 57
Lindgren, Theodore 79
Lipscomb, Heather 72
Liss, Andrea 137
Liszanckie, Richard 62
Livingstone, Barry 209
Lloyd, Kasey 136
Lockie, Ellaraine 1
Loftis, Lori 55
Logan, Christopher 110
Lombino, MaryEllen 141
Long, Jennifer A. 12
Longueira, Joshua 178
Lopez, Aquilah 27
Lopez, Shaina 148
Lott, Tina 206
Lounsbury, Courtney 74
Love, Genevieve 84
Lowe, William 9
Lower, Elizabeth 62
Lowin, Elisa 222
Lu, Andy 162
Lucas, Andres 82
Lucas, E. Richard 3
Luciani, Alicia 103
Luga, Melissa 25
Lujan, Maya 184
Lumia, Santo 46
Lundberg, Ashleigh 94
Lundberg, Eric 218
Lundgren, Thomas Wade 112
Lupinacci, Fran 65
Lutsenko, Boris 170
Lutz, Jean 182
Lyonnais, Lillian 189

M

McCarty, Joshua 129
MacDonald, Catherine 190
Machado, Sierra 68

Mackin, Joan Marie 215
MacLaren, Ashley 148
MacMillan, Jan 37
Madison, Hannah 138
Magalong, Choya 80
Mahelona, Keoni 224
Mahnert, Kai 136
Maiello, Bonnie 41
Maijala, Justin 226
Makoski, Calie 91
Maldonado, Curtis 146
Maness, Barbara 183
Manganaro, Chelsea 97
Mann, Michele 137
Marara, Emmanuel 69
Marchani, Mandy 228
Mardirosian, Susan 5
Marquez, Maria Corinna 69
Marshall, Robert 81
Martin, Anna Marie 140
Martin, Brenda 139
Martin, Jason L. 240
Martin, Michael J. 55
Martin, Michael E. 161
Martinez, Alyna 90
Martinez, Anthony 4
Martocci, Christina 185
Mason, Charles 90
Massaro, Michelle 243
Masters, Melissa 166
Masters, Sean 142
Mata, Virginia 159
Matheny, Emily 99
Mathis, Jaime 230
Matias, Ramon 125
Matos, Michael 238
Matras, Christopher 137
Mattka, Jennifer L. 210
Mau, Dhani 45
Maxwell, Jason J. 102
May, Laura 7
Maynard, Carol Estep 19
Maynard, Phillip 211
Maynard, Trent 157
Mazeikis, Jeanette 52
Mazerolle, Marc 97
Mbanefo, Jideofo 78
Mbobi, Emmanuel 214
McAuliffe, Chad 228
McAuliffe, Treasa 82
McCartin, Dianne 58
Mcclain, Zelda 248
McCormack, Michael P. 245
McCormick, Dennis 150
McCoy, Cynthia 146
McCoy, Tim 211
Mcdade, Melody 158
McDevitt, Amanda 20
McDevitt, Elizabeth 146
McDonald, Bethany 24
Mcdonald, Georgina 49
Mcdonald, Jason 60
Mcelwee, Lincoln 77
Mcenery, Katie 135
McGhie, Diane 147
McGinn, Kelly 71
Mcgoff, Theresa 4
McHorse, Deana 59
Mchugh, Sarah 49
McIntosh, Charlie 171
Mcintosh, Josephine 130
McIntosh, Patrice 178
McKellar, Ashley Jean 91

McKinney, Catherine 148
Mckinstry, Alese 223
McKlosky, Dawn 120
McLaurin, Darren 245
McLean, Katherine 247
McLean, Sharon D. 171
Mcleod, Michelle 75
Mcnab, Alex 106
McNally, Jessie 151
Mcneal, Joel 47
McNeill, Donna 192
Mcpherson, Scott 37
Medig, Brad 189
Meizler, Marcy 99
Melcher, Don 50
Mellon, Vivian 234
Meloche, Brian 211
Menard, Frantz 57
Menig, Donald 207
Meno, Julia 156
Mercer, Michael 31
Merrington, Jason 166
Mersing, Kristin 75
Messina, Lisa 139
Meyecic, Stephanie 160
Micchelli, Nicholas 192
Michela, Michael 25
Mickel, Sara 35
Mihalcea, Ana Maria 221
Miles, Edgar 80
Miller, Carole 109
Miller, Jamie 193
Miller, Lynn 215
Miller, Randy 22
Mingo, John 70
Minkewicz, Laura 217
Mirchandani, Cheryelona 140
Mirchandani-Sanchez, Joshua 143
Misiak, Shanna 197
Misner, Kelly 231
Mitchell, Angela Carol 208
Mitchell, Helen 248
Mitchell, Sara 79
Mitti, Caryl 175
Mojomick, Jimmy 246
Molczyk, Kelly 135
Mollan, Vivian Gloff 249
Monk, March 145
Monos, Michele 241
Montano, Anthony 215
Moodley, Justin 246
Moody, Vanessa 190
Moore, Melissa 108
Moore, Sarayah 119
Moore, Tina M. 122
Morales, Debbie 187
Morales, Erasmo 26
Morales, Mario 113
Mordoh, Michael 173
Morgan, Brittany 196
Morris, David 78
Morris, Mary 221
Morris, Ted 140
Morrison, Kyle W. 33
Morton, Veronica 185
Moser, Jason 227
Moss, Glenn 193
Moyer, Lynne 122
Mucha, Greg 12
Mucha, Gregory 113
Mudget, James 25
Mullikin, Kevin 137
Mullin, Sean Patrick 72

Mullins, Paul 105
Mullins, Traci 6
Munch, Lia 9
Mungo, Nichelle 154
Munves, Jonathan 207
Murdick, Laura 151
Murphy, Krystal 37
Murphy, Megan 246
Murphy, Michael 32
Murphy, Ryan 179
Murray, Meghan 36
Myers, Gerald J. 17
Myers, James Lewis, Jr. 65
Myers, Lindsay 131
Myers, Pat C. 85

N

Nail, TaRena 155
Naiman, Jill Palmer 4
Nard, Steve 57
Narkiewicz, Paul 149
Nason, Julianne 1
Neal, Bobby 48
Neal, Mary 76
Neal, Valerie 187
Neeb, Anne 75
Nelson, Ainsley Drew 186
Neoh, Eng Kim 177
Newberry, Larry 158
Newby, Kristyn 30
Newcomb, Amanda 56
Newcomb, Mary-Lisa 84
Nicely, Scott 176
Nichelle, Nikki 118
Nichols, Donna Jo 82
Nichols, Kendra C. 165
Nichter, Deborah 198
Niemann, Kandice 120
Nigro, Julie 233
Nishida, Lynn 30
Nix, William 155
Njoku, Allen 113
Noble, Stephanie 96
Noel, Karen 65
Nordstrom, Heather 79
Norman, Autumn 213
Norris, Christine 225
Northey, Angela 149
Norwood, Debbie 46
Nowak, Paula 118
Nunez, Anne-Jeanette 68
Nwatu, Ijeoma 64

O

Oberding, Mark 189
Oh, Han 152
O'Keefe, Kenneth A. 148
Okehie, Jennifer 22
Okereke, Nkechinyere 227
Olesch, Christoph G. 136
Olesen, Danielle 120
Olko, Dorothy 94
Olmeda, Nina 41
Olsen, Angela 207
Olson, Joanne 98
Olson, Tami Rice 227
Olwagen, Mariette 71
Omvig, James, Jr. 69
Oppenheim, Lisa 84
Orr, Jason 122
Orta, Ana Milagros 148

Ortiz, Galene 76
Ortiz, Roberto 129
Orton, William 217
Osakpa, Atyathoabe 219
O'Sullivan, Sharon 13
Oswald, Michele 125
Otten, Jocelyn 247
Otto, Johanna 35
Oyler, Deann 52

P

Paddock, Vicky L. 131
Paganelli, Samantha 46
Page, Jenny N. 83
Pahl, Anthony 189
Paige-Wright, Laura 127
Panarello, Lisa 122
Parish, Christine 227
Park, Lee 150
Park, Sung 66
Parker, Karen 161
Parker, Linda 47
Parks, Cheryl 92
Parks, Eddie 54
Parks, Willie 249
Parrill, Sharon 211
Parrish, Cynthia 116
Parsons, Cathyjo 115
Pasmanik, Wolf 211
Paterson, Tanya 142
Paterson, Therese 208
Patibandla, Murali 233
Patrick, Lucas 16
Patrick, William IV 44
Patridge, Drew 62
Patterson, Julie 59
Patterson, Larry 9
Patterson, Marsha 233
Paul, Connie 148
Paul, Patsy 144
Paul, Rodney 43
Paulin, Christopher 154
Payne, Marina 65
Payne, Sheloham 178
Pearce, Jared 7
Pearson, Sarah 106
Peck, Robert 203
Pedersen, Christine 123
Peeva, Iva 6
Pelote, Artelelia 156
Pemberton, Shawn 25
Pender, John 169
Pendleton, Lori 227
Percival, J. Nerissa 103
Perez, Albert, Jr. 193
Perez, David 88
Perez, Rachel A. 231
Perez, Rita 222
Perla, Jennifer 238
Peronto, Joan 13
Pessina, Holly 83
Pessoa, Ishmael 224
Petel, Ryan 187
Peters, Benjamin 44
Peters, Erin 120
Peterson, Felicia 39
Peterson, Shelby 60
Petrauski, Lori 19
Petrillo, Nicole 144
Petroski, Susan 144
Pettibone, Jessica 208
Peyatt, Jamie 130

Pfleger, Johnathon 39
Pharr, Leesa 199
Phillips, Sonja 29
Phongsavan, Vithaya 151
Pickard, Thaddeus 16
Pickett, Sara 102
Pierce, Margaret W. 159
Pietz, Sarah M. 239
Pigg, Adam 81
Pikowski, Stacey 188
Pina, Joe 175
Pine, T. H. 21
Pinel, Richard 228
Pitcher, Edward 195
Pitts, Brandon 54
Placker, Regina 20
Placky, Jesse 234
Plautz, Brian 84
Pleasants, Pamela 27
Podhradsky, Rebecca 75
Pointer, Mark 38
Poncek, Katrina 26
Pond, Judith 81
Poole, Sirina 104
Pope, John 119
Pope, Sarah 70
Pope, Trisha 91
Port, Jake 90
Porter, Jennifer 26
Posey, Kristi 154
Powe, Randolph 67
Powell, Lisa Christina 13
Prendergast, Lauren 73
Prescott, Marion 170
Presnell, Coleman 163
Prevost, Tyler 91
Prewitt, Marlyn 209
Price, Chris 65
Price, Melanie 176
Prichard, Robert 141
Pridmore, Chris 64
Prisza, Michael 79
Proudman, Arlene 43
Pryor, Brenda 80
Pucci, Kathy Leong 149
Putz, Linda K. 50

Q

Qin, Xiaoming 242
Quandt, Melanie 58
Quinn, Rachel 104
Quist Christopher, Alexandra 38

R

Rabito, Jessica 14
Rader, Nancy 43
Ragan, Karen 204
Ragen, Ben 133
Rahier, Brenda 178
Raia, John 54
Railey, Megan 74
Ralston, Brenda 144
Rambo, Jori-Michelle 8
Ramirez, Mauricio 162
Ramirez, Pamela I. 147
Ramos, Bernadette 189
Ramos, Cindy 4
Ramos, Gladys 141
Ramsay, Susan 136
Randall, Marie 75
Randolph, Deb 225

Ranney, Nate 99
Ranville, Jessica 158
Rassner, S. Anders E. 198
Rathburn, Vicktoria 179
Raubolt-Hurst, Kim 155
Ray, Agnes Kanaby 147
Re, Anne 68
Rebelez, Carlie 6
Record, Michelle 88
Redlawsk, Sandra 64
Reed, Cindy 74
Reed, Glenda 163
Reed, Larry 221
Reed, Sharon 83
Reese, Sarah 142
Reeves, Kimberly 201
Renall, Bronwyn 22
Reneau, Rebecca 160
Rensel, Manda 212
Renwick, Cyra Grace 7
Requena, Juan, Jr. 225
Reynolds, Dana 195
Reynolds, Harvard 14
Reynolds, Michael S., Jr. 182
Rice, Armanda 95
Rich, Gary 35
Richards, Barbara 38
Richards, Bridget 33
Richards, Chandar 156
Richards, Jeanne 205
Richardson, Alan 174
Richardson, Keith 158
Richlin, Jason 209
Richmond, Catherine 98
Riedl, Elberta 160
Ries, Amanda 61
Riggins, Joshua 202
Riley, Gloria 97
Rivera, Alicia 119
Rizzi, Kathleen 163
Rizzo, Joann 234
Rizzocascio, Valerie 222
Robbins, Matthew 146
Robbins, Michelle 31
Roberts, Joseph 155
Roberts, Linda 157
Roberts, Shelly 72
Robertson, Barbara R. 34
Robertson, Monica M. 239
Robidas, Raymond 153
Robinson, Justin 226
Robinson, Natalie 216
Robinson, W. Brad 129
Robotham, Curt 129
Roche', Troy 75
Rockwell, Jessica 130
Rodenroth, Dean 132
Rodgers, William 184
Rodriguez, Roger 41
Romanelli, Stacey 26
Romano, Chris 113
Rosado, Maria 45
Rose, Douglas, Jr. 121
Rose, Ginger 81
Rose, James 136
Rosete, Rolando N. 92
Ross, Brandi 30
Ross, Marc 166
Ross, Ruby 18
Roth, Robert W. 244
Rouse, Catherine 29
Rousell, John 117
Rovang, Dana 248

Roy, Moumita 159
Roy, Saurabh 75
Rudderham, Bonnie 212
Rueff, Walter 111
Ruhlman, Leisha 16
Ruiz, Raymond 74
Rule, Amanda 34
Rumpler, Derek 107
Rumpler, Starlene 20
Runkle, Cory 188
Rusin, Dawn 67
Russell, Gerry 236
Russom, Steven 66
Ryan, Patricia 27, 103
Ryan, Vanessa 216

S

S., Lindsey 68
Sachdeva, G 183
Sadanandan, Subhadra 153
Safronoff, Greg 121
Salazar, Louie 203
Salmon, Crystal 197
Salyers, William 31
Samet, Aaron 18
Sampson, Jamie 169
Samuelsson, Kaj 72
San Nicolas, Elizabeth M. 199
Sanabria, Letitihia 70
Sanders, Charles 31
Sanders, Judy 24
Sandoz, Eden 46
Sansom, Dawn 248
Santana, Audery 214
Santiago, Theresa 27
Santos, Nelson 159
Sapienza, Beverly 44
Sargent, Kirsten 126
Satterfield, Kimberly 237
Saum, Kandice 179
Saunders, Holly 30
Sauriol, Margaret 66
Savage, Amanda R. 54
Scalf, Suzanne 101
Scarrow, Rodney 29
Schaal, Jason 74
Scheetz, Brian P. 165
Scherck, Vicky 119
Schlichter, Todd 230
Schmidt, Anne 35
Schneider, Dustin 202
Schneider, Jason 62
Schneider, Marge 70
Schneider, Roger Neil 138
Schoenecker, Robert 162
Schrager-Bozdag, Tammi 91
Schroeder, Cheryl 129
Schultz, Marsha 71
Schumacher, Brooke 194
Schwanebeck, Neil 139
Scott, Donald 193
Scott, J. L. 230
Scott, Kathy Haggins 249
Scott, Melissa 65
Seal, Christine 65
Sebree, Matthew 154
Sedia, Adam 93
Seelen, Margaret 90
Seeman, Judy 220
Sego, Jenny 237
Segurado, Paulo 19
Seim, David Michael 195

Seipp, Kyle 93
Serignese, Alyssa 88
Severaid, P-R 10
Shahid, Afsheen 169
Shakya, Sheetu 138
Shanabarger, Steve 31
Shannon, Meagan 109
Sharpe, Caren 72
Sharpe, Justine 185
Shattock, Rob 59
Shaw, John W., II 142
Shea, Valarie 110
Sheda, Albert 23
Shelton, Lane 22
Shepard, Aaron 222
Shepherd, Sally 242
Sheppard, David 99
Sheppard, Elizabeth 218
Sherfield, K. 148
Sherrill, Tallulah 95
Shinnaoui, Imad 142
Shipley, Lenore 209
Shoemate, Erin 4
Shonk, Ray 98
Shuptar, Cassandra 180
Sickler, Ron Butch 132
Siek, Debra 201
Silverman, Jason 181
Silverman, Rachel 190
Silvestre, Mike 145
Simmons, Regina 63
Simpson, Jessica 68
Singleton, Frances 216
Sirianni, Christopher 240
Skidmore, Bryan 207
Skiest, Christopher 109
Skinner, Michael 125
Slagle, Connie 177
Slattery, John 57
Slaughter, Richard 169
Sledge, Erika 58
Sloane, Sharon 5
Slone, Jerry 130
Slovek, Hannah 4
Slusher, Kristi 219
Smallman, Rick 136
Smith, Alexander 106
Smith, Ashley 242
Smith, Blakeley 95
Smith, Carie 84
Smith, Eric 79
Smith, Jeffrey Judson 231
Smith, Jeremy 150
Smith, Joanne 58
Smith, Karissa 74
Smith, Lauren 245
Smith, Mary 96
Smith, Ralph 152
Smith, Terry 99
Smith, Tiffany M. 83
Smith, Wilbur 54
Smoyer, Terri 115
Smyth, Alan 17
Snyder, Ian 9
Snyder, Steve 82
Snyder, Veronica 12
Soley, Caroline 169
Somerville, Darlene C. 171
Southern, Thelma 31
Sowell, Shaun 61
Spears, Sheree 24
Spence, John 116
Spence, Robert J. 165

Spence, Sye 66
Spencer, Leo 127
Spiers, Phoebe 180
Spily, Carolyn C. 68
Spradley, Dusty 63
Spratt, David W. 29
Spurgeon, Sally 98
Stacho, Crystal 141
Stahl, Jason 44
Stainbrook, Denise 88
Starick, Neville 14
Starnes, Jolee 101
Starnes, Olivia 124
Stauss, Tina 90
Stead, Kayrl 15
Stearns, Joshua 99
Steele, Courtney 66
Steele, Rob 207
Steimle, Alice E. 133
Stepanek, Cynthia 80
Stephen-Mapp, Deborah 116
Stern, Susan R. 7
Stevens, Robin 170
Stevens-Kittner, Norah 231
Stewart, Joanne 70
Stewart, Lyle 193
Stewart, Scott 42
Stine, Jamie 63
Stingily, Milan 223
Stockdale, Mike 89
Stolfi, Lydia 225
Stone, Ammie 157
Stone, Annette L. 165
Stone, Bonnie 150
Stone, Mishalyn S. 167
Stone-Anderson, Melissa 146
Stoner, Ashley 40
Stork, Matthew 134
Stover-Taylor, Karen 81
Strain, Scott 227
Streit, Katie 10
Strickland, Vickie 46
Strickland, Yvonne 152
Strobino, Rachel 132
Strock, Adrienne 6
Stykemain, James 87
Subedi, Hom Nath 215
Sullivan, Douglas 224
Sullivan, Wils 79
Summers, Linda 225
Sumner, Randal 114
Supitux, Leah 74
Surjo, Daisy 166
Svensson, Heidi T. 192
Swaggerty, Daniel B. 93
Swain-Giboney, Rhian 20
Swanson, Amanda 111
Sweet, Jodie 123
Swimm, Jamie 188
Sydow, Elizabeth 134
Sykes, Monique 235

T

Talbott, Heather 234
Talbott, Lindsey 186
Talkington, Karen 120
Talley, Catherine 68
Tam, Shushawna P. 223
Tandon, Rajat 134
Tanis, Ray 143
Tann, Justin 242
Tapp, Jacqueline 110

Tasker, Becky 126
Taylor, Francene 138
Taylor, Hans 6
Taylor, Jeane 116
Taylor, Scott 105
Teaderman, Douglas 78
Teo, Siew Fong 44
Tepana, Kathleen 33
Terrenzi, Sandra 186
Tessier, Justin W. Z. 104
Thani, Giresh 217
Thelen, Lindsay 94
Thoi, Jenny 215
Thomas, Gary D. 87
Thomas, Leroy, Jr. 40
Thomas, Robert 238
Thompson, Jennifer A. 239
Thompson, Laura 189
Thompson, Stephanie 136
Thomson, Felicia 201
Thomson, Ronald, Jr. 37
Thorpe, Karen 37
Thorpe, Treasure 60
Thrasher, Glenn 70
Tilghman, Wade 167
Titland, Robert 163
Tobin, Heather 76
Tolley, Carlene 182
Tom, Christopher 144
Toomey, Mardell G. 16
Tortorici, Joanne 119
Toth, Julia 204
Traktman, Stacy 128
Tran, Leo 150
Tran-Lam, Van 17
Trimble, Larry 87
Trivellin, Timothy 159
Trujillo, Jennifer 113
Tufts, Meredith J. 170
Tuhacek, Angela 215
Tunich, Elizabeth 188
Turner, Andy 77
Turner, Beverly 43
Turner, Cindy 111
Turner, Gary 153
Turner, Kandi 40
Turney, Dessylyn 211
Twomey, Nathan 39

U

Uhde, Suzan 36
Ullman, Karl 194
Uyeno, Summer 116

V

Vadala, David 37
Vaghini, Robert 66
Van Auken, Brandon 56
Van Der Kley, Thom 178
van der Velde, Sven 187
Van Hauen, Katherine 212
Van Horn, Jennifer 108
Van Houten, Sue 51
Van Schaick, Paul 228
Vandebeek, Wim 137
Vanest, Cara 181
Vangates, Dess 247
Vangilder, Tess 55
VanHooser, Todd 197
Varni, Mary Lovee 172
Vasiltsova, Mary 3

Vaughn, Becky 162
Vaught, Stephanie 164
Vaysberg, Konstantin 74
Vazqueztell, Nelson Onit 42
Velasquez, Kristofer 138
Vellani, Marie 136
Venkateswaran, Margaret 175
Vennari, Eva 96
Verkler, Maria 249
Vermette, Christopher 28
Vick, Tristan 213
Vigoren, Alena 10
Villella, Heather 128
Vincent, Hazel 184
Vindis, Miha 177
Vogal, Adam 231
Vore, Kerry 237
Vrabel, Rita 164

W

Wagner, Edward 68
Wagner, Jennifer 209
Waldrop, Joe 133
Walker, Richard 32
Walker, Shu Jen 161
Walkin, Deborah 109
Wallace, Janice D. 147
Wallace, Lorenco 241
Waller, John 176
Walley, Nathan 248
Walsh, Holly 224
Walton, Nancy 213
Ward, Fayelle 55
Ward, Jamilyn 77
Ware, Adrienne 23
Wargo, Catherine 73
Warner, Daniel 69
Warner, Madelyn 3
Warnock, J. Matthew 21
Warren, Linda 219
Warriner, Donnie 170
Watkins, Mary 102
Watson, Amy Lane 144
Weaver, David 96
Webb, Sandra 18
Weber, Julianne 136
Weber, Lizzie 55
Webster, Sharon Hay 142
Wech, David Jay, Jr. 244
Weiland, Dody 139
Weinhold, Danielle 86
Weinstein, Roslyn 14
Welch, Pam 195
Wells, B. F. 121
Wellsworth, Emily 243
Werkheiser, Lynn 51
Wesho, Cynthia 214
West, Anna 71
West, Sally J. 130
Westcott, Karen 68
Wetteland, John 3
Weyhrich, Andy 140
Wheeler, Jodi 51
White, Chancy 115
White, Cheryl 212
White, Lynn 138
White, Mark 10
White, Thomas, III 98
White, Whitney 233
Whiteman, Lesli-Jones Tokar 210
Whitfield, Felisa 112
Whitlock, Suzanne 121

Whitlow, Alice 16
Whitney, Christine 16
Wickett, April 184
Wigg, Andrew 22
Wiggins, Wes 140
Wilbon-Parks, Diane 23
Wilcox, Anne 180
Wilcox, Melanie 128
Wilder, Cynthia 120
Wilder, Jacinda 78
Wilds, Justin 217
Wiley, Drema 171
Wiley, Joan 199
Wilhite, Brett 206
Willard, Courtney 140
Willemsen, Charles 160
Williams, Andrew J. 73
Williams, Daniel 182
Williams, Donna 79
Williams, Franklin 161
Williams, Lawrence, II 239
Williams, Regina 19, 132
Williams, Trish 236
Wills, Ryan 205
Wilson, Barbara 222
Wilson, Bryan W. 136
Wilson, David, Jr. 234
Wilson, Sherri Diane 25
Wilson, Terry L. 108
Wimberly, Amber 57
Wingfield, Jonathan 139
Winkler, Sarah 21
Winterton, Candida 236
Winyschel, Dorothy 182
Wisebaker, Michael 248
Wiseman, Deborah 166
Witte, Nancy 154
Wittman, Bob 94
Wittman, Retha Mary 176
Wojtylko, Bryan 120
Wolf, Julie 23
Wolpert, Sabrina 22
Wolski, Kordian 118
Wong, Alan 172
Wong, Samantha 36
Wood, G. J. 133
Wood, Kindra 125
Woods, Rodger 78
Worden, De 213
Wormington, Robert N. 122
Worrell, Antoinette Theresa 56
Worthey, Robin 89
Wray, Dawn 153
Wright, C. 8
Wright, Kayla 228
Wrightsman, Ginny 140
Wycoff, Joseph 12
Wyllie, Keri 72
Wynn, Bridgette 51

Y

Yacovone, Elise 183
Yancey, Kimberly 67
Yang, Fang 51
Yasuge, Miki 73
Yates, Nick 125
Yocom, Sarah 180
Yon, Mark 72
Young, Ashley 86
Young, Sandra 66
Yuan, Hai 174
Yusuf, Mehrunnisa 196

Z

Zabinski, Diane 48
Zabodyn, Donna 229
Zaidi, Atif 171
Zainabu, Olaniyi 34
Zardecki, Lauren 107
Ziegelbauer, Vicki 199
Ziegler, Rosemary M. 249
Zimmerman, Nicole 219
Zipfel, Buchele 222
Zubrzycki, Leah 165
Zuckerman, Rosie 208
Zundel, Jeffrey 220
Zuniga, Diana 31
Zwicke, Phillip 144